KU-522-072

THE REVOLUTION AND THE CIVIL WAR IN SPAIN

THE REVOLUTION AND THE CIVIL WAR IN SPAIN

by Pierre Broué and Emile Témime

Translated by Tony White

FABER AND FABER
3 Queen Square London

Originally published in France by Les Editions de Minuit under the title La Révolution et la guerre d'Espagne

First published 1972 by Faber & Faber Ltd.
3 Queen Square, London, WC1
Set in Baskerville, 11 pt. on 13 pt. body
Printed in Great Britain
by Ebenezer Baylis and Son Ltd.
The Trinity Press, Worcester, and London
Bound in Great Britain

ISBN 0 571 09773 1

INTRODUCTION

We were ten years old in 1936. To us, the Spanish Civil War was, first of all, a shock, the sight of thousands of emaciated men, women, and children, hungry and often ragged, the Spanish refugees. Disturbing words, charged with anguish, fell from grown-ups' lips: Hitler, air raids, the fifth column, the war. So the war itself did not come as a surprise to us: we had, if not understood, at least sensed, quite simply, that these crowds of Spaniards had been through it before ourselves. Later on, Spanish comrades, for whom the struggle had never ceased, informed us of the end of their hopes; Franco had survived the collapse of the dictatorships.

It was the vagaries of academic life that led to our meeting at the Lycée Condorcet, both of us having been attracted for some years by the Spanish Civil War, which one of us saw as the neglected, distorted preface to the Second World War, the other as a workers' and peasants' revolution, disfigured, betrayed, and stifled. We were in agreement only on the need to work, and it was for this very reason that we undertook, while there was still time, to listen to the survivors, both observers and protagonists, and to write a history of the Revolution and the Spanish Civil War from 1936 to 1939. We intended, in the face of ignorance, neglect, and falsification, to recreate this struggle in the most truthful possible way and to rid it of the legend that had prematurely buried it. Today we realize that this objective, once attained, is but a first step in the compilation of a more complete history, which would require thousands of eye witness accounts and, even, documents from archives that are still inaccessible, whether in Spain herself, France, Great Britain, the USSR, or the Vatican.

It would be wrong to expect more from our work than we intended, more than we could include in it. Those readers to whom, we hope, we have conveyed the feeling of Spain will have to look elsewhere, to experts on Spain, for answers to the questions that will arise when they start reading us. We suggest that they go and look in geographical works for a detailed description of this country that is a world apart, as African as it is European. 'Spain,' wrote Joan Maragall, is 'as far from the world as a lone planet. And its people, who are in the world, seem forgotten.' They will then learn that Spain is a 'homespun cloak fringed with lace,' that she covers 506,000 square kilometers, that her population consists of almost 30 million inhabitants, that she 'survives with difficulty', that 'her production is inadequate for a very frugal people', and that she lacks capital and means of transport.[1] If they pursue their investigations into history books, they will learn that the ancients placed the Elysian Fields in Spain, that Strabo, the first geographer, called Andalusia the 'dwelling of the Elect,' and that Muslim Spain, because of her agricultural and craft techniques and her scientific and philosophical knowledge, was in the vanguard of civilization in the Middle Ages. They will also learn that the ravages of the *Reconquista*, the first trial of strength between a prosperous if exhausted Muslim world and a barbaric Christian West teeming with life, did not prevent Spain from becoming mistress of the Old and the New Worlds: in all the books, the age of Louis XIV follows that of 'Spanish dominance.' But they will also be reminded that the Golden Age of Spain, as Gaston Roupnel called it, was both a 'fount of pride and vale of tears, according to whether one considers its potentates or its masses, its Court or its vast, wretched territories stretching from frontier to frontier.'

Perhaps then our readers will find their way more easily into the Spain that 'shrinks back as you approach her,' as Dominique Aubier and Manuel Tuñon de Lara tell us.[2] With them, they will be able to negotiate the difficult journey toward 'the subterranean unity that forms the bone structure of a Spaniard, whether he be loquacious and Andalusian, severe and Castilian, crafty as a *gallego*, self-interested as a Catalan, or industrious as a Basque.' They will learn the words 'that make up the Spanish reality': *tierra*, the earth, 'which gives life but does not maintain it,' *hambre*, which we translate as 'hunger,' but 'which is to our hunger what rage is to anger,' *castizo*, inadequately translated as 'of good race,' whereas it daily affirms the craving for dignity that emanates from the whole history of the Spanish peoples. Perhaps they will also grasp what, more than anything, defies description and explanation, the place occupied by death in the life of the Spaniard, whose passion for *toros* will have already hinted at its importance. They will pursue their inquiry still further, in order to fathom the profound spirituality that goes hand in hand with the most fanatical faith and virulent anticlericalism. They should learn about the land of the Inquisition, of auto-da-fé, in which the act of burning a man—whether ill-converted Moor, baptized Jew, secret Protestant or enlightened spirit—was termed 'an act of faith.' They should pause for a long while in front of Goya and the *Dos de Mayo* drawings, to ponder the violence and the death of these bare-handed men facing the guns of the firing squad or the sabers of the Mamelukes. They will not easily forget the uprising against Napoleon by this people whom he called 'beggars' and will note that, while the great fawned on the conqueror, the peasants, in their village assemblies, declared war on the Grand Army and coined the word *guerrilla*. They should spare a few moments for the siege of Saragossa, captured by the French in fifty-two days, house by house and floor by floor, and for its 60,000 victims, including women and children, because they too were combatants. They should listen to Marshal Lannes: 'What a war! Having to kill such brave people, even if they are mad!' Because these madmen fought with their fists and their teeth. They will stumble on this violence again in the Carlist wars, in all the nineteenth-century civil conflicts, in the Royalist repression that sickened even the French *Ultras* who had come in the name of the Holy Alliance to crush the Spanish Revolution (the first one) in peasant uprisings, in strikes and repressions, and in the tortures and the 'exploits' of the Civil Guard immortalized by Federico García Lorca's *Romancero*.

In discovering this Spain, they will discover thousands. They will learn that the same Castilian word, *pueblo*, stands for both people and village and that the village is a small homeland, Brenan's *patria chica*, living its own almost autonomous life. Then they will be prepared to follow, in Rama's works for instance, the laborious construction of a state on top of an incomplete nation, the vanity and artificiality of this 'liberal' enterprise in a country where *caciques* and *señoritos* still hold sway. Because the *caciques*, those local tyrants, are not merely the traditional bailiffs of the large estates, using their delegated authority to slake their lust for power and to crush at will and contemptuously those whom they employ and control. 'Caciquism' has permeated the whole of social and political life: the administration, the parties, and to some extent the unions, the fact being that this vice of medieval society can still be spontaneously secreted by twentieth-century Spain.

No doubt our readers will then have a better understanding of certain distinctively Spanish features of the Revolution and the Civil War, the arrogance of the nobility, confident of embodying a superior race, the contempt for death and the ferocity in battle of all the combatants, their particularism and their attachment to their towns, their villages, and their soil—what is known as 'individualism,' 'lack of discipline,' and 'anarchist tendencies'—the violent fanaticisms, the hatred, and the mistrust that binds social hierarchies, but also the constant affirmation of dignity, the part played in the lottery of war by each contestant's idea of man—*hombre*, an interjection and an affirmation—whom they wish to exalt and 'liberate' or attack and destroy by systematic humiliation.

Preliminary researches into our subject suggested many routes that a Hispanist might take. A Spanish woman friend, once deported to Germany, proposed that we should describe, after a scientific study, what she had witnessed in her own life and in the files of the dead, the long journeys by peasant groups from their *pueblo* to the front and then, still together, to the death camps. No doubt this would be a perfectly Spanish way of writing the history of the Revolution and the Spanish Civil War, and it would have brought us closer to the secret reality, the collective soul of the people during those terrible years, and nearer to an understanding of what this drama meant to the millions of individuals who comprise the 'masses.'

However, we did not chose to approach Spain by this path. First, because we are not genuine Hispanists. Second, because the preoccupations that bound us to this work extended far beyond the context of Spain alone. We have not tried to understand everything, still less to explain everything, neither Boabdil nor Avicenna nor Don Quixote nor Torquemada nor even Ignatius Loyola. Our intention was to confine ourselves to facts that were perhaps simpler, but above all universal. Spain is Spain, of course, but she is also one of those countries that were once known as 'backward' and that today have been hypocritically rechristened 'underdeveloped' countries. All the tests that the modern economist applies to countries to reveal the characteristics of 'underdevelopment' place the Spain of 1960, like the Spain of 1930, among the most populous and poorest nations, those of which it cannot be seriously maintained that their poverty bears any relation to the opulence of the rest. In spite of the unreliability of Spanish statistics, it is clear that it is only with great difficulty that Spain attains an average of 2500 calories a day per inhabitant, the minimum below which undernourishment occurs. Infant mortality remains high. Life expectancy at the age of one is fifty-five, more than in India, of course, but far less than in the West. The birthrate remains healthy. The number of illiterates is still considerable. The proportion of the 'active population' does not exceed 37 percent, mainly agricultural workers. The inferior position of women is underlined by the fact that only 9.4 percent of them can be classed among the active population. Child labor is still widely practiced. The middle classes are numerically small. The average national income is half that of the French, and there are far greater divergences in the social scale. According to Professor Birot, Madrid includes 300,000 servants among its 1,800,000 inhabitants.

As in the other backward countries of the world, mineral wealth and industrial development in Spain are in the hands of foreign capitalists, except in some subsidiary sectors. Big proprietors and middle-class businessmen form a small oligarchy, wholly preoccupied with defending its privileges. The Church's only mission seems to be the one attributed to it by the hardly religious Napoleon I, to acknowledge 'inequality of wealth' and to accept the fact that 'one man dies of hunger alongside another who is gorging himself.' The teaching of history, in the Spain of 1960, just as a hundred, thirty, or twenty years ago, devotes a hundred pages to counterreform and one—and what a one!—to the French Revolution. In short, the Revolution and Civil War in Spain were merely a bloody and violent interim period. They simply inspired great fear and made the regime of the ruling class harsher. Primo de Rivera's dictatorship, which held sway (under the aegis of the Spanish monarchy) until 1931, to the proclamation of the Republic, was replaced by a more absolute dictatorship. The Republican experiment did not convince anyone, and the weak state, which did not succeed in reforming Spain or even in really becoming organized, was the first victim of the events of 1936. The soldiers' victory robbed it of all hope of revival in the near future. In an authoritarian state, the army dictates its own laws, and it will never be adequately stressed what weight is carried in such unessentially stable countries by armies, which are good only for civil war and for the preservation of an appointed order.

It is not, in the twentieth century, a feature peculiar to Spain to contain a mass of landless and impoverished peasants, on the border of survival, who fling themselves all the more willingly into the struggle because they have all to gain and nothing to lose; nor is the existence of a working class, still closely linked with the peasantry and made up chiefly of laborers and non-specialist workers, in which there is practically no 'working-class aristocracy' apt to temper the aggressive impulses of the masses, rough but capable of sacrifice. It is not only in Spain that such workers and peasants have set themselves up as the shock troops of the revolution that the bourgeoisie refused to fight through fear of the future: the twentieth-century third estate, even though it was dubbed 'popular front,' everywhere cracked very quickly under the impact of the 'fourth estate' of workers and poor peasants, fighting on their own behalf. Nor is Spain the only country to have provided a striking demonstration of the popular trend towards direct democracy. The same determination to wield power through people in arms already existed among the Paris sans-culottes in 1794.[3]

Those who cry 'Eternal Spain' at the sight of the militias of the Republic with their elected workers' leaders and their high-flown titles should remember the Paris Commune and its Federates, its elected officer-militants, its 'Commune Turcos,' its 'Avengers of Flourens,' and its 'Lascars.' For it is not only in Spain and in Cuba that revolution is romantic. Need one recall that it was in Russia in 1905 that the first 'councils' emerged—where, as in Spain, parties and unions, sitting by virtue of their qualifications, had equal representation—and that the word, in Russian, is translated as *soviet*? Need one, nearer to our own time, invoke the role played in 1956 by the 'Revolutionary Committees,' the 'Workers' Councils,' and the 'Central Workers' Council' during the Hungarian Revolution?

Moreover, the Revolution and Civil War in Spain were far from being an exclusively Spanish affair. From near or far, all governments had a hand in them, intervention and non-intervention being founded on immediate interests, and strategic and diplomatic preoccupations, but also on general interests, those known as 'historic.' The affairs of Spain could no more be settled within her own frontiers than could those of Korea and the Congo yesterday, and those of Cuba, and Vietnam today. Such civil strife ultimately involves all powers and all peoples, because it is merely a particular aspect, in a precise geographical context, of the crisis that is rocking humanity in the century of world wars.

Jean Jaurès, who was also a historian, admitted that he would gladly have sat alongside Robespierre during the Revolution. We shall be equally frank. There has never been such a thing as a perfectly objective historian, and anyone who thinks he is one is lying to himself just as he lies to others. All the precautions with which scientific research and criticism are surrounded do not in the long run suppress either our feelings or our personal reflexes. Why hide it? The choice of subject itself reveals our deepest sympathies. We, too, having 'lived' our subject, were inclined to take sides: though in spirit we were on the same side of the fence, we willingly parted company, one of us more in sympathy with the progressive Republicans and the moderate Socialists in his concern with organization and efficiency and the world balance of power, and the other with the dissident Communists and revolutionary Socialists, because he felt, like St. Just, that 'those who fight revolutions halfheartedly are merely digging their own graves.' Our division of labor is proof of it. The Revolution is the subject of Part 1, edited by Pierre Broué, whereas Emile Témime dealt with the international aspects of the war, as well as with the birth of the National-Syndicalist state. However, it should not be thought that our book is the result of a juxtaposition of two accounts on related themes. We intended these two parts to be distinct in order to emphasize two points of view—in our mind the most important—from which the study of our subject can be approached. The main disadvantage of this method is to produce unavoidable repetitions, which we have however limited as far as possible.[4] Its advantage is that this dual clarification may shed a more revealing light on events, illumine their complexity yet not overload the exposition with comment and flashback. During the three years of our collaboration, we have made daily comparisons of our points of view, exchanged our notes and index cards, criticized our documents and interpretations, forcing each other into fresh researches and, in the final stage, successively fruitful editing. May we be forgiven if, being our own first readers, we feel it our right to maintain that this collaboration, our sometimes lively though always friendly mutual criticism, is proof of the conviction and the seriousness we brought to our common task. We think that we have made our point, at least to the extent that this is possible with the only printed sources, already vast, that could be placed at our disposal. Whatever their origin, we have tried to judge them as historians and to eliminate all prejudice, to set out the facts honestly while passing only a minimum of judgments; we hope thereby to have given everyone the opportunity to stress one or another aspect of primary concern to him. This is why we shall be glad to listen to objections, criticisms, and fresh evidence, all of which, in and through our work, may contribute toward the truth, which in our view can only be the fruit of constant research.

All that remains for us—and it is not the least of our duties—is to thank all those without whom this work would not have seen the light of day: Jérôme Lindon, Director of the Editions de Minuit, our friends on *Arguments*, Edgar Morin and Kostas Axelos, who introduced us to him, and, above all, our co-authors, all the witnesses, Spanish and non-Spanish, politicians, writers, and workers, in Europe and America, too numerous to be mentioned, who have responded to us, ransacked their memories and their records, devoted hours to our questionnaires, and searched for unpublished documents and missing witnesses. Their sole concern, in spite of the diversity of their political outlooks, has been to help us in our search for the truth. We are especially grateful to Jordi Arquer, who placed his library and document collection, unique on this subject, at our disposal and helped us with his advice. Finally, Jean-Jacques Marie translated Russian material for us.

Pierre Broué Emile Témime

Notes

[1] *Géographie de 4ème*. Cours Varon (A. Colin).

[2] *Espagne*, in the Petite Planète Collection.

[3] See Albert Soboul, 'Les sansculottes parisiens en l'an II,' an academic study confirming Daniel Guérin's pioneer work, *La lutte des classes sous la IIème République*: *Bourgeois et bras nus*. Guérin developed his ideas still further in '*Jeunesse du socialisme libertaire*.'

[4] To see each event in its chronological order, the reader is referred to the table at the end of the work.

LIST OF INITIALS, GROUPS, AND POLITICAL PARTIES

Acciòn Popular: Conservative Catholic party.

Alliance of Antifascist Youth: Alliance, in early 1937, of the majority of the JSU and 'Republican' Youth.

Asaltos: Republic Assault Guards.

AVER: Association of Volunteers for Republican Spain.

Camisas Viejas ('Old Shirts'): Veterans of the Falange.

CEDA (*Confederación Española de Derechas Autónomas*): Spanish Confederation for Autonomous Rights.

CNT (*Confederación Nacional del Trabajo*): National Labor Confederation (Anarcho-syndicalist Union).

CTV (*Corpo Truppe Volontarie*): Italian Expeditionary Corps.

Esquerra: Catalan Autonomist party.

Euzkadi,Nationalist party of: Basque Antonomist party.

FAI (*Federación Anarquista Ibérica*): Iberian Anarchist Federation.

Falange: Spanish Fascist organization.

Flechas: Falange Youth.

GEPCI (*Federación Catalana de Gremios y Entidades de Pequeños Comerciantes y Industriales*): 'Syndical' organization of small tradesmen and manufacturers, belonging to the UGT.

HISMA (Compañía Hispano-Marroquí de Transportes): German company in charge of relations with Nationalist Spain.

IC: Communist Youth.

JC: Communist International (Comintern).

JCI (*Juventud Comunista Ibérica*): Iberian Communist Youth (POUM Youth).

JL: Libertarian Youth.

JONS (*Juntas de Ofensiva Nacional-Sindicalista*): National-Syndicalist Offensive Juntas, which merged with the Falange in 1934.

JS: Socialist Youth.

JSU: Unified Socialist Youth (after the merger in 1936 of the JS and the JC).

Lliga: Catalan bourgeois party.

NKVD (People's Commissariat for International Affairs): Russian secret police (OGPU).

PCE: Spanish Communist party.

POUM (*Partido Obrero de Unificación Marxista*): Workers' Marxist Unification party.

PSOE: Spanish Workers' Socialist party.

PSUC: (*Partido Socialista Unificado de Cataluña*): Unified Socialist party of Catalonia (from 1936).

Requetés: Carlist military organization.

Revolutionary Youth Front: Alliance, in 1937, of the JCI and the JL.

SEU (*Sindicato Español Universitario*): Spanish University Union (founded in 1937).

SIM (*Servicio de Investigación Militar*): Republican secret police.

Single party: The only Nationalist party after April 1937.

Tercio: Spanish foreign legion.

Traditionalist Community: Carlist Monarchist party.

UGT (*Unión General de Trabajadores*): General Workers' Union, of Socialist origin.

CONTENTS

PLATES

LIST OF MAPS

Part 1

CHAPTER I

OLIGARCHS AND REPUBLICANS

Spain, at the beginning of the twentieth century, was the anachronism of the West: she was an oasis of tradition in an increasingly uniform world, and her masters were proud of having preserved her *Hispanidad* in spite of modern political and economic trends. Yet it was in this country, deeply entrenched in her past, that in 1936 the last interwar revolution broke out. Like Russia in 1917, Spain was at the time the weakest link in the capitalist world; here, however, the similarity ends. Unlike the October Revolution, the Spanish Revolution was not the first spark in a growing conflagration but the last flicker of a fire already extinct throughout Europe. The Russian Revolution had heralded the end of the First World War. The Spanish Revolution merely provided a rich testing ground for the powers then preparing for the Second. The revolution that turned into a civil war was in the end merely a dress rehearsal for World War II.

A Country Weighed Down by its Past

Czarist Russia owed her extremely backward character to the slowness of her general economic development. Spain, by a curious paradox, owed hers to the direct consequences of her lead over the other European powers at the beginning of modern times.

During the period when her hegemony over Europe coincided with her dominance of world trade, her Monarchy was becoming centralized and her regional characteristics were growing blurred: feudal Spain was on the wane and a modern state was emerging. But the very precocity of this expansion recoiled upon her. The discovery of America and the creation of a vast empire in the New World contained the seeds of decadence. While precious metals brought home by the King's galleys infused Western Europe with fresh blood, it was as if the home country were paralyzed, becoming 'the vale of tears' as well as the 'fount of glory' described by sixteenth-century historians. In the nineteenth century, Spain lost her remaining world outposts and was in the end barely touched by the industrial and liberal revolution that succeeded in transforming the old Europe.

The classes in the old regime continued to disintegrate, without however completing the formation of the emergent bourgeois society. The slowness of capitalist development and the withering of economic relations acted as a brake on the formation of the nation and strengthened centrifugal trends and the separatism of the provinces: businessmen in the Basque provinces and Catalonia, who had benefited from restricted industrial development in the nineteenth century, bore the yoke of Castilian oligarchy with impatience but had no means of shaking it off. The mass of proletarianized peasants sometimes gave vent to their anger in violent outbursts, actual peasant uprisings in the midst of the machine age. Still linked in a thousand ways to the peasant world, a proletariat, stimulated by the same aggressiveness, began to organize itself. Thus, the seeds of destruction of a past so alive and so burdensome that at the beginning of the twentieth century it seemed eternal were building up in every pore of a complex society.

A Semicolonial Country

At the turn of the century, Spain was a basically agricultural country. More than 70 percent of her active population was engaged in agriculture. The Spanish peasant used the same implements as his forebears in the Middle Ages: throughout most of the country the hand plow was preferred to the horse plow. The yield per acre was one of the lowest in Europe, and more than 30 percent of the arable land lay fallow.

Industry, where it did exist, had barely emerged from the manufacturing age. There was very slow progress in industrial concentration: only the iron and steel works in the Basque provinces bore any resemblance to the heavy industry of capitalism. In Catalonia the textile industry, the most important in terms of total output, was still split up into a mass of tiny business firms.

Spain had nothing to offer on the world market except the products of her soil and subsoil, in return for manufactured goods from foreign industry. But she was also—an inevitable corollary—fertile ground for foreign capital invested several decades earlier in the most substantial and profitable sectors: Belgian capital ($1 million) in railways and streetcars; French capital ($6 million) in mines, textiles, and chemicals; Canadian capital in the hydroelectric works in Catalonia and the Levante; British capital ($10 million) controlling the entire metal industry in the Basque provinces, the naval shipyards, and the copper mines, including Rio Tinto;[1] American capital, recently arrived but already substantial, controlling the telephone companies;[2] and finally German capital which was already invested in the Levante power companies and was trying, in 1936, to infiltrate the metal industry.

The First World War brought Spain relative prosperity by providing her with trade outlets. She became at one and the same time a supplier of foodstuffs and even, to some extent, of manufactured goods. But the return of peace drove her out of the world market, where she was unable to compete with the industrial powers. The 1929 world crisis hit her hard: customs tariffs imposed by the great powers meant that she could not export her agricultural produce and brought about the collapse of her domestic market, already barely able to absorb the products of her national industry. Countries like Spain, with a semicolonial structure, were probably even more affected by the crises of the thirties and their social repercussions than were the more advanced countries.[3]

The Structure of Spanish Society

Extremes in social differences aggravated the slightest economic setback and hardened an organism whose chances of adaptation were already limited. As Henri Rabasseire[4] estimated, of the eleven million Spaniards making up the country's active population, there were eight million poor, whose work provided no more than subsistence: a million small craftsmen, two to three million agricultural workers, two to three million industrial workers and miners, and two million tenant farmers or small rural proprietors. Between this mass and the million members of the privileged class, whom Rabasseire called 'parasites'—officials, priests, military, intellectuals, big landowners, and the upper bourgeoisie—were sandwiched fewer than two million members of the 'middle class,' half of them well-to-do peasants, the other half members of the petty bourgeoisie concentrated in the more advanced centers, such as Barcelona, Valencia, Bilbao, and Santander.

No expansion was possible while these eight million poor workers had no alternative except to try and survive painfully in unvarying living conditions, with expenditures reduced to a strict minimum and a budget devoted mainly to food. The development of means of production within the framework of capitalism was sealed off from outside by customs barriers, or the competition of the great powers, who denied Spain a market. At home, the creation of a solid and prosperous peasantry would have permitted the formation of a domestic market. But this presupposed the solution of Spain's chief problem, that of land. It was in the rural areas that the fiercest social antagonism existed and that secular hatreds were fostered.

The Agrarian Question

In 1931, two million agricultural workers owned no land at all, whereas 50,000 members of the gentry owned half of Spain's acreage. While 1½ million small proprietors whose land did not exceed 2½ acres were forced to work on the estates of the big proprietors in order to live, 10,000 landowners owned more than 250 acres each. In certain provinces, the big landowners were in complete control: 5 percent of the landowners in the province of Seville owned 72 percent of the total; in the province of Badajoz, 2.75 percent of the landowners owned 60 percent. It was common knowledge that the Duke of Medinaceli owned 200,000 acres and the Duke of Peñaranda more than 125,000.

Yet the overall picture of the condition of the land and the peasants was infinitely more complex than these crude figures might suggest. The agrarian systems varied according to natural conditions, especially the degree of drought. These different forms of tenure were also the result of centuries-old battles among the peasants for land. Between the seasonal worker and the small independent proprietor was a whole spectrum of farmers and tenant farmers, with leases of varying length, and of small proprietors compelled to pay dues that derived straight from the medieval feudal regime. Thus, as Gerald Brenan[5] pointed out, there were two basic agrarian problems: the smallholdings in the North and the Center, often too small for subsistence, and the large estates in the South, developed through the work of laborers who were kept at starvation wages through the plentiful supply of manpower.

The small proprietor in Asturias, who benefited from the addition of vast stretches of commonage, and the tenant farmer from the Basque provinces, Navarre, or the Maestrazgo only very occasionally experienced poverty, though they enjoyed little comfort. But the Galician peasant, on his tiny patch of land, was crushed by the weight of the *foro*, a survival from the seignorial taxes, and his counterpart from León, Old Castile, and the Aragon plain was too often struggling in the clutches of moneylenders. Although the peasant from the Levante sometimes managed to buy back the hereditary holding, subject to the payment of the *censo*, the farmer on the well-irrigated plains of Granada and Murcia had to pay enormous rents. The small Catalan proprietor enjoyed relative ease, but the condition of his neighbor, the *rabassaire*,[6] had deteriorated in recent years.

On the plains of New Castile, the estates of the aristocracy were nearly always rented out. The trouble here was the shortness and precariousness of leases, the absence of any obligation on the part of the landowner, who could raise his rents at will and often allowed his agents to abuse the peasants. According to the 1929 tax records, 850,000 heads of families out of a total of 1 million had a daily wage of less than one peseta.

In La Mancha and Estremadura, estates were larger and small cultivators less common. In the plains the typical peasant was the *yuntero*, a landless peasant with a mule team who cultivated the land of an absentee estate owner whenever he could.

Andalusia was the traditional domain of the *latifundia*. Here the average annual income of a big landowner was about 18,000 pesetas and a small one about 161 pesetas. But the majority of peasants did not own any land: they were *braceros*, day laborers who seldom worked more than one day in two and had to survive all year on starvation wages by working on the large estates in the worst of conditions,[7] under the supervision of the *labrador*, the predatory bailiff, who was always ready to line his pockets through arbitrary fines or blackmail over jobs. Much arable land remained fallow, its owner either preserving it for shooting or because he was able in this way to make the *braceros* pay through the nose for their demands. For this region, which probably included some of the wretchedest people in Europe, was also the land of class hatred, of the slave ever ready to revolt against his master: the rebellious peasants were hungry for land.

In short, a handful of big landowners held sway in Spain.[8] The 'oligarchs,' as they were known to their enemies, had for centuries managed to preserve the majority of their privileges and their wealth at the expense of the peasant masses. Their regime had been the Monarchy, the only one in keeping with their interests and aspirations. It was to save it that they agreed in 1923 to the *pronunciamiento* that heralded General Primo Rivera's dictatorship. In 1930, it was the general agreement between the King and the oligarchs that led to Primo's dismissal and the summoning of General Berenguer. In 1931, the Republic was proclaimed without any violence: it was the 'glorious exception' of a 'peaceful revolution,' as the landowner Alcalá Zamora, the new president, described it over the air. The Monarchy made way for the Republic without seriously damaging the social and economic system. Alfonso XIII left Spain but did not abdicate. The vast majority of the oligarchs remained loyal to him. Under the new political system they preserved the solid pillars that had supported their dominance over the years: the Church and the Army.

The Church

The Spanish Church, which seemed to come straight from the Middle Ages with its 80,000 priests, monks, and nuns, was also an anachronism. Its spiritual and temporal power was considerable. However, it is difficult to assess its wealth accurately. It was almost certainly not the largest owner of land in the country, as has often been stated, but it was not far from it. The inquiry made shortly after the proclamation of the Republic attributed to it 11,000 estates, valued at some 130 million pesetas. Its urban properties were no less great, and it was a force in the business world, in banking as well as in industry, controlling directly or through puppets firms as important as the Urquijo Bank, the Riff copper mines, the railways of the North, the Madrid streetcars, and the Transmediterranean Company.

Under the Monarchy and to a large degree under the Republic, the Church still controlled education:[9] in a country with twelve million illiterate—half the population—its schools taught and educated five million adults. But this control over education was far from being matched by equal influence. The anticatholic disturbances and the burning of convents and churches that occurred in May 1931 revealed a deep-rooted phenomenon: the popular masses were freeing themselves from the Church's sway and were turning against it.[10] Here it is also interesting to note that the Church was still heeded by the rural masses only in the regions where social inequality was less pronounced, either because everyone there was poor, as in Galicia, or because the general level of existence was acceptable, as in the Basque provinces, Navarre, the Levante, Catalonia, and, to some extent, Old Castile. Elsewhere, in the Spain of the *latifundia*, the Church was regarded as an instrument of propaganda and the province of the rich, as the defender of property and an iniquitous social order, and as the determined foe of all social betterment, the enemy of the workers. Cardinal Segura, the Archbishop of Toledo, whose annual income was 600,000 pesetas, was a perfect example of the integrative, reactionary side of the Spanish Church. This prelate, primate of Spain, 'a thirteenth-century churchman' who 'thought that a bath was the invention of heathens if not of the devil himself and who wore a hair shirt like an early monk,'[11] was the champion of unyielding opposition to the Republic, the resolute opponent not only of all 'subversion' but of all liberalism.

The Spanish Army

Unique in its structure and in its place in society, the Spanish Army had no equivalent in Europe. Although it was defeated regularly for a century while defending its remaining colonial possessions, it established itself as an autonomous political body. In short, it was a *pronunciamiento* army—it is no accident that this is a Spanish word. Repeatedly beaten and humiliated, the officers blamed their reverses on successive governments. The Riff war against the Moroccan leader Abd-el-Krim dragged on from 1921 to 1926: it cost Spain the lives of 15,000 soldiers in 1924 alone and was successfully concluded only by the intervention of Lyautey's French troops. In spite of such disasters, the military leaders regarded themselves as the champions of colonial reconquest in the face of negligent governments, and it was in this role that Lieutenant-Colonel Francisco Franco, one of the commanders of the Spanish foreign legion, first appeared in the political arena. After the victory, Morocco remained the fief of the Army: the generals there behaved like veritable proconsuls.

An honorable outlet for rich men's sons—the *señoritos*—the officer caste, jealous of its privileges, the most important of which was to 'pronounce,' was, in the view of traditionalists, the incarnation of every Spanish virtue. In the general morass, it was the only real weapon of the ruling classes, their final recourse and their supreme hope. The Republic had been proclaimed with the consent of the Army leaders. But the failure of the highly respected General Sanjurjo's *pronunciamiento* on 12 August 1932 showed that this consent could be withdrawn at any time if the Republic decided not to fall in with the injunctions of the oligarchs.[12]

It is a remarkable fact that this army, whose artillery consisted of old 75-mm field guns, whose infantrymen were armed with 1909 Lebels, and whose planes could not have taken on any foreign air force, was plentifully supplied with machine guns. It would not have lasted a week against a modern army; it was still able to drown a revolutionary upsurge in a sea of blood. Ill-fed, ill-clothed, and ill-equipped, its recruits were also very poorly trained. Its officers were very mediocre technically, the most experienced being the colonial officers who had served in Moroccan units. Yet it had its élite, a genuine professional army, in the *Tercio* of the foreign legion, organized during the Riff war by General Millán Astray, its Moroccan regiments recruited from the most backward and most warlike mountain tribes. These mercenaries, legionaries and Moors, were the shock troops of the Civil War army. When the miners of Asturias rose up in October 1934 to prevent the Right's accession to power, it was these élite units, unsympathetic to *Hispanidad* but efficient, that crushed the workers' uprising in twelve days. In the front ranks were some of the officers sentenced for serving in the insurrection against the Republic that was led by Sanjurjo two years earlier.

However, this army was not short of officers. Under the Monarchy there were 15,000 of them, including 800 generals, that is, one officer to six men and one general to just under a hundred men. Under the Republic there were fewer and fewer Republican officers. The Azaña government, in order to free the cadres, offered full pay to anyone who applied for early retirement: many left-wing officers seized the chance of leaving the Army and its stifling atmosphere. The overwhelming majority of the cadres and all of the senior officers were resolutely Monarchist, supporters of the oligarchy, opponents of change, and deadly foes of the Revolution.[13]

The Bourgeoisie

The weight of the past lay even on the theoretically new forces of the young Spanish bourgeoisie. The industrialization of Spain had, as we saw, progressed very slowly during the nineteenth century and then only in geographically limited areas. This slow progress and localization explain the peculiar characteristics of the resultant middle class. It was only in Biscay and Asturias that a genuine financial oligarchy existed, as exemplified by the Banks of Biscay and Bilbao. The majority of historians have made a point of stressing the political circumstances of the emergence of this financial capitalism, which flourished after the defeat of the liberal movement by the agrarian oligarchy of the Restoration. Bourgeois liberalism not only suffered from the ineffectual implantation of the middle class in the country, it also labored under the handicap of always having been denounced by its opponents as a foreign product. At the height of the twentieth century, the liberal bourgeois had first to avoid being an *afrancesado*.[14] Suspected of being nothing but a mouthpiece for foreign ideas or a front for foreign capital, the Spanish bourgeois, in his concern to be accepted by the leading circles, was driven to further concessions, denials, and capitulations.

The millionaires of Bilbao and Asturias were anxious to join the landed oligarchy and to share with it the directorship of the Bank of Spain.[15] The new financial oligarchy was, from the outset, linked by a thousand ties, personal as well as economic, with the aristocracy. The Count of Romanones, one of the most prominent statesmen in the Monarchy, was a large landowner in the province of Guadalajara, the biggest apartment owner in Madrid, and a substantial shareholder in the Penarroya mines as well as several important banks. The bourgeoisie was therefore quite unable to provide the Spanish economy with the impetus necessary for a radical change, since this would imply an attack on the landed interests, which were ultimately only one section of a vast oligarchy of men of property.

This oligarchy found its most vigorous exponent, on the eve of the Revolution, in Juan March. A former smuggler, then director of the tobacco monopoly under Alfonso XIII, this powerful financier and industrialist, accused of treason and fraud by the first Republican government, was at one and the same time the owner of vast country estates, the confidential agent of British capitalist circles, president of the Central Office of Spanish Industry, where he sat alongside Romanones, Sir Auckland Geddes of the Rio Tinto mines, and representatives of Italian, French, and German capitalist interests. He put money into anything that was opposed to the Republic and played a decisive role in the events, both at home and abroad, that led up to the Civil War.

The Spanish Aristocracy and the Conservative Parties

The Spanish aristocrat was very different from his English counterpart, who had succeeded in joining the tide of capitalist expansion. He was not particularly concerned with making his estate prosper as a business but was mainly occupied with preserving his seignorial authority over the cheap manpower that he believed was his right by birth. His only *raison d'être* was his caste, and he would have openly admitted that he was the very incarnation of Spain. Behind him were his ancestors, who had bequeathed him the inseparables of name, fortune, and authority.

The majority of the aristocrats were supporters of Alfonso XIII and of the Monarchy as a principle of social preservation. Under the Republic they supplied cadres for *Renovación Española*, which was, according to Ansaldo, a 'legal cover for insurrection,' led by Goicoechea and José Calvo Sotelo. The latter, on his return from exile, became the figurehead of a much more avowedly conservative party, 'corporatist and authoritarian' rather than Monarchist. Still young—he was born in 1893—he already had a brilliant political career behind him. A deputy at twenty-five, he became governor of Valencia the following year, and then minister of finance under Primo de Rivera's dictatorship. Through Balbo he was in constant touch with the Fascist government in Rome. Linked with all of the oligarchy's influential circles, especially with Cardinal Segura, a self-confessed admirer of National Socialism and

Fascism, he was a remarkable orator and a good journalist with a reputation as an economist. In the 1936 Cortes, he became the spokesman of the Extreme Right and one of the leaders of the Generals' plot.

The Traditionalist Communion, the other Monarchist movement, unquestionably had a popular base among the small peasants of Navarre, led by a fanatical priesthood. The Carlist movement, born after the Napoleonic wars, had for more than a century been attracting the most fanatical Catholic Conservatives under the motto 'God, King, and Country' and plotted tirelessly to restore the 'legitimate' authority of its successive pretenders, the last of whom was the ageing Alfonso Carlos. Its true leader, Manuel Fal Conde, had for several years been systematically preparing it for an armed uprising against the Republic.

On 31 March 1934, Antonio Goicoechea for *Renovación Española*, Antonio Lizarza for the Carlists, and Lieutenant-General Barrera signed a pact in Rome with Mussolini, by which the Duce undertook to support their movement for the overthrow of the Republic by supplying it with arms and money. Between 1934 and 1936, many young men from the Carlist military organization of the *Requetés* underwent periods of military training in Italy. Stocks of arms were built up in Navarre, thanks to Italian funds.[16]

In fact, both Carlists and Alfonsists refused to bow to universal suffrage, the very conception of which was an insult to *Hispanidad*, and believed themselves to be entrusted with the providential mission of saving Spain and Christianity from the threat of subversion by liberals and revolutionaries.

Acción Popular

The Church in Spain did not immediately respond to those of its members who wished it to follow in the tracks of the Monarchist conspirators. Apparently it was on the advice of the more politic Vatican that the subtler line of the Jesuits and their confidential agent, Angel Herrera, director of *El Debate*, prevailed under the Republic. The idea was to create, staff, and inspire a mass Catholic party, rejecting both the Monarchist and Republican labels, agreeing to participate within the framework of the parliamentary system but openly proclaiming its intention to abolish all reference to the secular state in the constitution.[17] Thus formed, *Acción Popular* was merely the entry into the electoral arena, in the guise of a reactionary and authoritarian party, of Catholic Action (*Acción Católica*), with its hierarchical leadership. Its head was José María Gil Robles, son of a Catholic barrister, brilliant pupil of the Salesian priests in Salamanca, and a journalist on *El Debate*. Chosen by Herrera to lead the party of the Church and the propertied class and married to the daughter of an extremely rich count, he had the qualities his role required: a good organizer, a capable orator, and not without a flair for action, he took for a model not Hitler, whom he disliked for his anticatholic attitude while admiring him for his efficiency, but the Austrian Chancellor Dollfuss and his corporative state.

In 1933 he merged his organization with other right-wing groups to create the CEDA (*Confederación Española de Derechas Autónomas*); this electoral alliance with the Monarchist groups won him enormous success. From 1934 to 1936 the CEDA was the heart of the coalition with the right-wing Republicans, who systematically destroyed every achievement of the first Republican government. These two years, christened the *bienio negro* (the two black years) by the Republicans and Socialists, led to the shelving of agrarian reform, the systematic reduction of wages, and the restoration of Monarchist officers, momentarily on the sidelines, to positions of authority. Ferocious in its repression of the Asturian miners, the CEDA left the coalition government when the president of the Republic refused to order the execution of González Peña, the Socialist leader who directed the uprising. It opposed even the modest reforms in favor of the *yunteros* proposed by one of its members, Jiménez Fernández, the minister of agriculture.[18] In 1935 it vied for the power that from then on it meant to wield alone.

The Military Plot

The military conspiracy, on which the extremist elements were relying, burgeoned under the benevolent eye of Gil Robles, minister of war from 1934 to 1935. One of the first acts of the government formed after the 1934 elections was the proclamation of an amnesty for the troops implicated in General Sanjurjo's 1932 *pronunciamiento*. Convicted and dismissed officers were rehabilitated. In 1934, on Sanjurjo's initiative, the *Unión Militar Española* was formed; it very soon became the nucleus of a conspiracy in which most of the top leaders participated: General Franco, chief of staff, General Fanjul, undersecretary of state, and General Rodríguez del Barrio, Inspector-General of the Army, all Monarchists and Conservatives with positions of authority in the Republican Army. One of them, Lieutenant-General Barrera, in company with the Monarchists Lizarza and Goicoechea, signed the pact with Mussolini.

Under the *nom de guerre* Don Pepe, Colonel Varela—soon to be promoted to general—cemented relations with the Carlist leaders and supervised the military training of the *Requetés* in Navarre. In summer 1935, during the annual maneuvers in Asturias, Franco, Fanjul, and Goded, according to one of the movement's official historians, laid 'the groundwork for the preparation of a national uprising.' The leaders of the Army were ready to move if Gil Robles's party proved unable to seize power by means of elections.

The Falange

The German and Italian examples led certain sections of the oligarchy to contemplate the use of political instruments more modern than the traditionalist parties.

Long before 1936, Juan March, the millionaire, had financed[19] a movement that was to play a leading role during the Civil War. In 1932 José Antonio Primo de Rivera, the dictator's son, founded the *Falange Española,* which became the *Falange Española Tradicionalista* in 1934 when it merged with the *Juntas de Ofensiva Nacional-Sindicalista* (JONS), and which remained a tiny group without real influence until after the February 1936 elections.

The Falange's twenty-six-point program was typically Fascist: it reproached the Republicans for their timidity toward the oligarchy, advocated nationalization of the banks and railways and radical agrarian reform, but at the same time denounced the corrupt and disruptive Marxist doctrine of class struggle and countered it with the ideal of 'harmony between classes and professions in a unique destiny,' that of the Fatherland and Europe. Only in its attitude toward the Church was the Falange different from Mussolini's *Fascio*: a Falangist, even an atheist, respected in the Catholic Church the historical ideal of Spain.[20] The successes of Hitler and Mussolini seemed to José Antonio's supporters to guarantee rapid victory, and their dreams of an empire turned them toward French Morocco and the restoration of sovereignty over South America, that other product of *Hispanidad* and the 'common destiny.'

The founder and leader of the Falange, José Antonio, as he was known, was a young Andalusian of great charm, with all the qualities of youth in his favor, undeniably elegant in appearance, and even quite generous, which meant that many of his fiercest opponents found it hard to resist a natural liking for him. Nevertheless, his movement was not yet taken seriously. Like Fascism and National Socialism, Falangism had only been placed in a 'social' context in order to combat the Marxist organizations and oppose them with the weapons of terror and violence. Until 1936 the Spanish oligarchy remained cool toward this apparently plebeian movement and preferred to look to Gil Robles for a victory to be won within the legal framework of elections: it was not yet ready to accept the disadvantages of being saved by a party with Fascist methods and doctrines, often as harsh with its allies and supporters as with its opponents. In February 1936 the Falange had only a few thousand members, a thousand of them in Madrid. It entered the elections alone and was resoundingly defeated. It remained a reserve force, ready for use if the working classes threatened to take to the streets again. José Antonio, who had met Mussolini too, was at any rate in close touch with the military and political leaders of the plot.

The Autonomist Republicans

The forces that could have countered such threats were weak and, more important, divided.

It was one of the tragedies of the Spanish Liberals and Republicans that, in spite of the existence of a Basque and a Catalan bourgeoisie, the incompleteness of the Spanish nation and the persistence of autonomist leanings had hindered the formation of a genuine Spanish bourgeoisie. The bankers in the Basque provinces and the biggest Catalan businessmen were hand in glove with the oligarchy. All the petty-bourgeois elements, which in the Western countries served as the base for the parties most strongly drawn to the parliamentary system, had turned toward Autonomist movements.

Included in them were barristers like Manuel de Irujo and Leizaola and industrialists like José Antonio Aguirre y Lecube, who in 1936 led the Euzkadi Nationalist party,[21] founded in 1906 on a racial, political, and religious basis that its motto expressed perfectly: *Todo para Euzkadi y Euzkadi para Dios*. The country priests gave solid support to the determinedly conservative Basques. The capitalists were glad to subsidize an antisocialist party that had managed to rally strike-breaking Catholic trade unions and 'Solidarities of Basque Workers' against the UGT and the trade unions adhering to the ideology of class struggle, a party that acted as a solid rampart protecting both the Church and the propertied classes. In the early days of the century, the industrial development of Biscay, though continually a prey to the incompetence and corruption of the oligarchical state, increased the attraction of the nationalist ideal, firmly rooted in the ancient traditions of a people that was indisputably unique and proud of it.

Under the Republic, the Basque Nationalists, naturally enough, made common cause with the Right and the conservative and reactionary parties. But in November 1933, the majority of the Right having rejected the autonomous status provided for the Basque provinces, the party was forced into opposition and into a *de facto* alliance with the left-wing Republicans and Socialists.

A similar phenomenon occurred in Catalonia. Here too autonomism was fostered by the industrial revolution and conflict with the retrogressive agrarian oligarchy. The upper bourgeoisie of course remained cautious: it needed the Spanish market and the support of the central government against a restless proletariat. Its leaders, Cambó and his friends in the *Lliga*, were more oligarchical than Catalan. But the petty bourgeoisie did not have the same reasons for caution once it was clear that Catalanism could only succeed if it enjoyed the support of the workers and peasants. Moreover, its party, the Esquerra, was a party of the masses; it was started in April 1931 by an alliance between different Republican parties and groups in Catalonia, and it leaned on the powerful peasant trade union, the Rabassaires. Its prime mover and inspiration, Luis Companys, once linked with Salvador Seguí, was for a long time the legal representative of the CNT, with which he remained in close touch. The Republic was proclaimed in Barcelona before it was in Madrid, and the status of autonomy for the province of Catalonia was voted on 15 September of the same year. But in 1934 autonomy was revoked, because the Autonomists, disquieted, had launched and bungled an uprising against the Right. The Catalan Autonomists found themselves in prison alongside the militant workers.

The Bourgeois Republicans

Apart from a few towns and the rich, irrigated plains of the Levante, nowhere in the rest of Spain was there a genuine base for the bourgeois Republican parties. Alejandro Lerroux's Radical party stood for the aspirations of the petty bourgeoisie hostile to the Army and the Church and typified its desire to see the creation of a new Spain, freed from the shackles of the feudal era, opening the way to creative capitalist expansion. But, terrified by worker and peasant unrest, the Radicals very soon drew back and, in 1933, through fear of revolution, opted for an alliance with the CEDA, with which they shared governmental responsibilities. Lerroux's party was totally discredited as the result of a financial scandal in 1935.[22] Part of his staff, behind Martínez Barrio, a worker's son and a leading freemason, then joined Manuel Azaña's left-wing Republicans, who differed very little from them.

Premier from October 1931 until the victory of the Right in the 1933 elections and president in 1936, Azaña was, for the record, a typical Spanish Republican. Born in 1880 in Alcalá de Henares into a well-to-do family, a brilliant pupil at the Augustinian college at El Escorial, which did not in the least prevent him from being fiercely anticlerical, he was for a long while attracted more by literature than by politics. President of the Madrid *Ateneo*, he played an important part in the Republican opposition at the end of the Monarchy and very quickly made his mark in the Cortes at the head of a group of deputies in *Acción Republicana*. An admirer of bourgeois France, he dreamed of an orderly and well-balanced republic, led by eminent men and firmly based on a middle class of peasant proprietors. Worker-peasant unrest did not drive him into the arms of the Conservatives. It persuaded him, on the contrary, of the need for the Republicans to give priority to a program of reforms capable of winning over enough workers to check the revolutionary movement.

His first government was a profound disappointment to those who had expected nothing from the Monarchy but who were in a mood to expect everything from the Republic. The agrarian law attacked only the problem of the *latifundia*, neglecting the urgent question of the precarious lives of the small peasants. In two years, only 12,000 peasants out of the millions hungry for land received a plot, which they had to pay for as well, since the big proprietors were given compensation.

The reform of the Army merely led to the departure of the Republican officers, only too glad to leave the cadres on full pay; the Monarchist leaders remained in their jobs. Efforts by the Azaña government in the field of social reform were completely frustrated by the effects of the world crisis on the Spanish economy. Its anticatholic legislation antagonized a large section of the middle classes without making a serious breach in the citadels of clericalism. Above all, order was more firmly maintained in the face of worker and peasant unrest than against the Monarchists. The Law for the Defense of the Republic permitted a repression that was no less severe than the Monarchy's. The Civil Guard, inherited from the Monarchy, remained intact. It was duplicated by another police force, recruited from among Republicans, the *Guardia de Asalto* (Assault Guard), no less energetic in its handling of the workers and peasants.

In January 1933, prompted by Anarchist militants, the peasants of Casas Viejas in Andalusia rose up and proclaimed 'Libertarian Communism.' Azaña and Casares Quiroga, his Galician minister of the interior, carried a large part of the responsibility for the repression that followed: the Civil Guard killed twenty-five *braceros* and burned their houses. When Azaña relinquished power, the tally of his struggle against worker and peasant agitation was a heavy one. The prisons were full of militant revolutionaries: 9000, mostly Anarchists, according to official documents. It was this aspect of his government that enabled another Republican, even one as moderate as Martínez Barrio, to say that the regime drawing to a close was one of 'mud, blood, and tears.'

Discredited after his stay in power, Azaña gained back some of his popularity as a result of persecution by the Right. Although he had had no hand in the October 1934 uprising, he was pursued and imprisoned: thus he recovered in opposition the prestige he had lost when in power. Leader of the Republican Left, this 'small, squat' man, with a greenish, bilious complexion and 'fixed, expressionless eyes,'[23] whom his opponents liked to compare to a toad, was a good parliamentary speaker but a poor democratic leader. Yet 40,000 persons flocked to a meeting at Comillas near Madrid after his release, at which he spoke in support of the political prisoners. This was because once again he symbolized union between Republicans and Socialists, the parliamentary Republic that appealed to the workers to support it for the sake of a restored and modernized Spain, freed from the oligarchy.

Spain and the Labor Movement

It was over this question that a split occurred in the ranks of the bourgeois Republicans. Lerroux opted for an alliance with the CEDA for fear of working-class revolution. Azaña and Martínez Barrio chose to join with the workers' parties and spare Spain a revolution. They felt that the constitutional framework provided every chance for deep-rooted structural reforms. The Cortes, the only chamber elected by universal, secret, and direct suffrage by citizens of both sexes, was able to provide safe majorities, thanks to the electoral law that gave 80 percent of the seats to majority lists in regional divisions. The president's sweeping powers—the right to choose and to dismiss the premier and to veto laws—and the existence of the Tribunal of Constitutional Guarantees looked at the same time like a guarantee against intrigue. Within this context they hoped to complete the work, barely adumbrated in 1931, of constructing a genuinely liberal, secular, democratic state and of regenerating society by an agrarian reform that would grant estates to millions of landless peasants.

They could not hope to fulfil such a task without the support of the labor movement, with its trade unions and parties. In the course of the century this movement had become a decisive force whose influence had been deeply felt in the very heart of Spain, in the peasant world. Of course, the peasants of Euzkadi remained attached to their traditions and to the Nationalist party, the Navarrese and the people of the Maestrazgo formed the popular basis for Carlism, and the small peasants in Catalonia and the Levante readily voted for the Republicans, both Right and Left. But the influence of the Socialists in the Asturian countryside, among the agricultural workers of Old Castile, and among the well-organized farmers in the *huertas*[24] of Granada and Murcia was appreciable. It was the Anarchists who organized and inspired the struggles of the *subforados*[25] in Galicia, the revolts of the Andalusian *braceros*, and the battles of the landless peasants in Aragon. The labor movement was busy winning over the peasant class. It became both an enemy and the stake of the game. Even its most moderate claims posed a direct threat to the vital interests of the oligarchy.

Because it was a tremendously explosive force, the Republican petty bourgeoisie sought its friendship and its support for its own ends. In the face of formidable enemies, it was indispensable to have the labor movement as an ally, in order to achieve in rural Spain the revolution that the country was yet to experience and without which no serious social and economic progress seemed possible. But the Spanish labor movement had its demands and its objectives too. By the end of 1935 it seemed ready to challenge the oligarchs, who wished to destroy it, as well as the Republicans, who were planning to use it.

Notes

[1] On the eve of the Revolution, the Rio Tinto copper-mining company was making annual profits in the order of a $4.5 million, while its capital was $18 million. The Duchess of Atholl (*Searchlight on Spain* [Harmondsworth: Penguin Books, 1938]) accused it of having financed the military rebellion by supplying its leaders with pounds sterling at 40 pesetas, whereas the normal exchange rate was from 80 to 100 pesetas. It is also worth noting the presence in Spain of the large British armaments firm, Vickers-Armstrong, closely linked with the Zubira and Urquijo banks.

[2] Traction, Light & Electric Power was in control of nine-tenths of the production of electrical power in Catalonia.

[3] It was at this point that the American millionaire Deterding withdrew his support from the peseta, by way of reprisal against the establishment of the oil monopoly by General Primo de Rivera's dictatorial government.

[4] *Espagne, creuset politique* (Paris: Fustier, 1938), p. 60.

[5] *The Spanish Labyrinth* (Cambridge: University Press, 1943), pp. 87–131.

[6] *Rabassaire*: tenant farmer of a special kind (*rabassa morta*: dead root) whose lease expired when three-quarters of the shoots were dead. Comparatively favorable in the nineteenth century, these conditions became disastrous through the ravages of phylloxera and the introduction of new shoots that required more care and did not last so long. Under the influence of Cambó and the Right, the Tribunal for Constitutional Guarantees abrogated the law that was voted in favor of the *rabassaires* by the Catalan Parliament shortly before the 1934 uprising.

[7] The work lasted from sunrise to sunset. At the beginning of 1936, the majority of the agricultural workers' salaries varied between 0.60 and 3 pesetas, but work was both intermittent and seasonal.

[8] Rabasseire estimated the number of landless peasants at 2 million. The Conservative Mateo Azpeitia stated that, in addition, 84 percent of the small landowners needed a wage in order to live (*La reforma agraria en España* [Madrid: Editorial Reus, 1932]).

[9] The *Ley de Congregaciones*, voted by the Republicans, which was to have removed control over teaching from the congregations, was never applied. Among the secular achievements of the early days of the Republic, there remained by 1936 only the separation of church and state, the institution of divorce, and the ban on the Jesuits.

[10] The events of May 1936 are significant in this respect. Since a rumor had circulated that priests and Catholic women were handing out poisoned sweets to the children in working-class districts, there were attacks more or less everywhere in Madrid on churches, on priests, and on persons known for their religious zeal. All the parties had, of course, cast the blame for the

origin of the rumors on *provocateurs*. But anticatholic feeling must have gone very deep for them to have found a hearing.

[11] Ramos Oliveira, *Politics, Economics and Men of Modern Spain 1808–1946* (London: Gollancz, 1946), p. 438.

[12] The *pronunciamiento* failed because of the general strike launched by the unions in Seville. The police, who had not intervened against the troops, fired on the workers who were asking for them to be punished. Sanjurjo and some other officers were sentenced to death. The general stated before the court that he had been in favor of obtaining the return of the Jesuits and preventing the application of agrarian reform and Catalonia's autonomous status (see below).

[13] Colonel Doval, guardian of public order in Asturias, went so far as to state that he was 'determined to exterminate the seeds of revolution, even in the bellies of mothers.' Summary executions and wide-scale torture were features of the 1934 repression, which working-class opinion attributed entirely to the Regular Army.

[14] Reminder of the Napoleonic era, in which only a few bourgeois dared to 'collaborate' with the French occupiers.

[15] According to Victor Alba (*Histoire des républiques espagnoles* [Vincennes: Nord-Sud, 1947] p. 307), 16,000 persons held all the shares in the Bank of Spain whose profits, over some five years, redeemed the capital. The dividend paid out was never less than 16 percent. During the year of repression in Asturias, it reached 130 percent.

[16] Antonio Lizarza, in his *Memorias de la conspiración en Navarra* (Pamplona: Gómez, 1953), pointed out (p. 50) that Italian money allowed the purchase from Belgium of 6000 rifles, 150 heavy machine guns, 300 light ones, 10,000 grenades, and 5 million bullets. The first military unit, the Pamplona *Tercio*, was formed on 10 January 1936 (p. 73).

[17] Thus it was that the party's moving spirit, Gil Robles, could write: 'Democracy for us is not an end but a means to go to the conquest of a new state. When the moment comes either the Cortes will submit or we shall make it disappear.' (*El Debate*, quoted by Brenan, *The Spanish Labyrinth*, p. 280). Gil Robles criticized the 'disastrous tactics' of the Monarchists, who by reacting against the dictatorship, risked provoking a 'social revolution, the communist republic.'

[18] Jiménez Fernández, a kind of Spanish Christian Democrat, was for several months the *bête noire* of the oligarchs, who dubbed him 'the White Bolshevik'. When he ventured, in support of his plans, to quote an encyclical by Pope Leo XIII, a Monarchist deputy replied: 'If you try to take our land from us, encyclicals in hand, we shall end up schismatic.'

[19] Among the Falange's financial backers it is interesting to note the name of De Lequerica, later ambassador in Vichy, and then foreign minister. (Emmet John Hughes, *Report from Spain* [New York: Henry Holt, 1947].)

[20] In contrast to José Antonio Primo de Rivera, a genuine *señorito*, the plebeian quality of Falangist Fascism was more clearly revealed in Ramiro Ledesma Ramos, founder of the JONS. An admirer of Hitler and an enemy of Catholicism, he directed the propaganda of the JONS, whose flag was also red and black, against the CNT. Member of the Falange (in

company with José Antonio and Ruiz de Alda), he left it at the end of 1935. He was shot at the beginning of the Civil War by the militias.

[21] Euzkadi: Basque provinces.

[22] Prieto went so far as to say that Lerroux and his friends stripped the ministries down to the bare boards.

[23] Ramos Oliveira, *Men of Modern Spain*, pp. 301 ff.

[24] Watered gardens.

[25] Peasants compelled to pay the *foro*.

CHAPTER 2

THE LABOR MOVEMENT

The Spanish labor movement had a unique character too. In the other European countries the struggle between Marx's supporters and Bakunin's that began during the First International ended in the victory of the former, then known as the 'authoritarians'; they formed the social-democratic parties affiliated with the Second International and the reformist trade unions. In Spain, on the other hand, the victory of the Libertarians, Bakunin's friends grouped in the secret society of the 'Alliance of Socialist Democracy,' had lasting consequences, branding the Spanish labor movement for a long while with the revolutionary stamp of Anarchist and Anarcho-Syndicalist traditions.

THE ANARCHISTS

Bakunin's Ideas

There was nothing surprising about this victory; in an agricultural country where so many ties linked the industrial worker with the landless peasant and the day laborer, where peasant riots, short, violent revolts, and banditry by outlaws were the time-honored form taken by popular explosions of anger and revenge, Bakunin's ideas fell on fertile ground.

In his view, in fact, only the spontaneous unleashing of the forces of the oppressed could overthrow capitalism, with energetic action by an organized minority intervening only in order to coordinate the efforts of the masses in their uprising against the forces of repression. To political action by parties, which appealed to more advanced countries, Bakunin and his friends preferred insurrection and the glamor of revolutionary example, more in line with Spanish traditions of class struggle. Thus it was that, in their work of emancipation, they attributed a decisive role to the 'much-loved bandits,' to the 'avenging angels of the poor,' whom the Spanish peasant both loved and feared.[1]

Fierce opponents of the state as the ancient form of oppression, Bakunin's disciples, rejecting 'any organization of a so-called provisional or revolutionary political power,[2] saw the germ of the just and brotherly society of the future in the 'free commune,' so akin to the medieval peasant communities in which every revolutionary in Spain recognized his ideal.

Anarcho-Syndicalism

The influence of Anarchist theoreticians, such as the famous teacher Francisco Ferrer and especially Anselmo Lorenzo, and of the influence of the Syndicalists of the French CGT combined in 1910 to produce, from a basis of Catalan Libertarian cells, the *Confederación Nacional del Trabajo* (CNT), a Syndicalist organization that the repression could not prevent from leading the great wave of strikes in Catalonia in 1917.

Briefly tempted to join the Communist International, as had been proposed by two of its leaders, the schoolteachers Andrés Nin and Joaquín Maurin,[3] who had been sent by it to Moscow and converted to Communism, the CNT held aloof after the events of Kronstadt. In its bastion in Catalonia, it had to carry on, in the years to follow, a bloody struggle against the governor, Martínez Anido: hundreds of militants fell to the bullets of the *pistoleros*, among them the general secretary of the CNT, Salvador Seguí.[4]

It was under Primo de Rivera's dictatorship, at the height of the repression, that the FAI, the mysterious and powerful *Federación Anarquista Ibérica*, came into being in 1927. Very soon, it dominated the CNT completely. A clandestine organization along the lines of the *Alianza*, made up of kindred groups similar to Masonic lodges under the authority of a secret Mainland Committee, the FAI very quickly became the heart and soul of the Anarcho-Syndicalist union.

It was not merely an active, anonymous group but a typically Spanish state of mind. This was what the French trade unionist, Robert Louzon, friend of and sympathizer with Spanish Anarcho-Syndicalism, wrote: ' "FAIism" is peasant rebellion raised to the level of working-class struggle by the peasant masses, joined, of course, in Spain as elsewhere, by the workers, and which is to some extent systematized and "theorized".'[5] The FAI adopted the revolutionary methods preached by the Italian Anarchist Malatesta: 'Seize a town or a village, render the representatives of the state harmless, and invite the population to organize itself freely.'

It was at the instigation of the FAI that brief revolts broke out, violent local and regional flare-ups establishing a short-lived Libertarian Communism: at Llobregat in January 1932, at Casas Viejas in January 1933, and in Aragon in December 1933. It was the FAI that dissuaded the CNT from any *entente* with the Republicans or Socialists and that kept up, in the union's propaganda, the fierce hostility of the Anarchists to electoral and parliamentary 'trickery.'

The CNT–FAI

Not all Syndicalists were prepared to accept FAI domination. In 1931, many of the leaders rose up against the adventurist and 'putschist' policy that it imposed on their union. Well-known leaders, such as the former secretary-general, Angel Pestaña, chief editor of *Solidaridad Obrera*, Juan Peiró, and Juan López called for a return to more genuine Syndicalist action, involving less indifference to immediate claims and more long-term prospects of action. When their group, known as the *treintistas*, was expelled from the CNT, it formed 'opposition unions' that had some influence in Asturias, in Levante, and in a few towns in Catalonia. The supporters of the FAI accused them of having gone over to reformism: in 1934 they took part in the insurrection in Asturias and Catalonia, while the CNT and the FAI held aloof.

On the eve of the Civil War, the FAI seemed to be completely incorporated into the confederal organization, as witnessed by the ever-linked initials CNT–FAI and the red and black colors of the flag. Yet, led by Peiró and López,[6] who always spoke up for the independence of the unions in regard to any political group whatsoever—including the FAI—the opposition unions reinstated the CNT. The Saragossa Congress in March 1936 solemnly reaffirmed its aim, which was the establishment of Libertarian Communism. However, the FAI ideology had taken a step backward: the CNT in February had not given the cue to boycott the elections, and the restored *treintistas* won acceptance for their point of view more than once in the weeks that followed.

Whatever the CNT's indisputable difficulties, the fact remained that, through its loyalty to the principles of class struggle and direct action,[7] it had maintained a militant and combative working-class base, with some very tough strikes to its credit: the Felguera metalworkers held out for nine months, and in 1934 the Saragossa workers sustained a general strike for six weeks. More important, the Anarcho-Syndicalist tradition made the unions in Spain far more than a defensive weapon in the daily struggle; they became a living cell in the social organism, often monopolizing the worker's entire leisure. Furthermore they monopolized what was the revolutionary means par excellence, the instrument of social change: class solidarity, infinitely more influential in this respect than the political parties.

Yet this highly active organization had obvious weaknesses. Faced with the complexities of a modern economy and the interdependence of its different sectors, the CNT's political and economic theories seemed highly ingenuous. Everything was simplified to an extreme by the pens of propagandists describing the idyllic 'commune' whose budding and later flowering would be made possible by militants willing to sacrifice their lives for it. It would seem that for some people nothing had changed since Malatesta, and that in their view it was no more difficult to establish Libertarian Communism on a permanent basis in the whole country than it had been to establish it for a few hours in Llobregat or in Figols.

The Anarchist Leaders: Durruti

However, it was not the theoreticians who emerged as leaders among the Anarchists. It would be hard to define the roles of personalities as different as Federica Montseny, a tireless woman speaker and propagandist, the formidable journalist Diego Abad de Santillán, an exotic pseudonym that was said to conceal an Argentinian militant,[8] or the invalid Manolo Escorza del Val, physically weak but morally implacable, who prompted the FAI's Mainland Committee and the CNT's Defense Groups from the sidelines. They were all equally representative of the diversity of the Spanish Liberation movement. However, not one of them achieved the notoriety of Buenaventura Durruti.

Durruti was born in León on 14 July 1896, into a family of eight children. His father worked on the railroad. At fourteen he was a mechanic in a railroad workshop. After taking an active part in the 1917 strike, he was forced to leave for France, where he worked for three years. He then returned to Spain, joined the CNT, and became an Anarchist. It was at this point that he went to Barcelona, the heart of the movement. There he joined the *Los Solidarios* group and those who were to be his companions in a life of struggle. Durruti, Jover, Francisco Ascaso, 'a little dark man of insignificant appearance,'[9] and José García Oliver, the most 'political' of the four, became the 'Three Musketeers,' legendary heroes of Spanish Anarchism. Terrorists and marauders, they seized a Bank of Spain bullion van in order to finance the organization and helped to prepare the attempt on the life of Dato, the premier. Durruti's involvement, confirmed by most of the biographical notes written about him after his death, seems to have been only ancillary. Federica Montseny informed us after our first edition was in print that the preparation of the attack on Dato was in fact the work of Ramón Archs, who died under torture. One of the instigators of the attack is still alive. One of the participants, Ramón Casanellas, had to seek asylum in Russia and was converted to Communism there before dying in a motorcycle accident. It was Ascaso and Durruti who killed Cardinal Soldevila in Saragossa to avenge the death of

Seguí. After seeking refuge in Argentina, they were accused of terrorism and theft and once again had to flee. They crossed South America before going underground in France, where they were arrested just as they were putting the finishing touches to plans for an attack on Alfonso XIII. They spent a year in jail, threatened with extradition. Freed as the result of a left-wing press campaign, they resumed their nomadic life, refusing the political asylum offered them by the USSR. Returning to Spain after the fall of the Monarchy, they were again arrested in 1932. Before his deportation to Africa, the imprisoned Durruti managed to arrange for the judges to be burglarized and the evidence for a trial in which other Syndicalist militants were involved to be destroyed. Back in Barcelona after his release, he was playing an active part in the textile union when the Civil War broke out.

To some an indomitable hero, to others a killer, what was the truth about this man with the Herculean build, with the terribly expressive face, 'a fine, imperious head eclipsing all others'?[10] According to his friends, he 'laughed like a child and wept before the human tragedy.'[11] No doubt that was why so much love and hatred were lavished on this symbol of Spanish Anarchism who exclaimed at the height of the Civil War: 'We are not in the least afraid of ruins. . . . We are going to inherit the earth. . . . We carry a new world in our hearts, a world that is growing at this very moment.'[12]

THE SOCIALISTS

The opponent of this undeniably unique Anarchist movement was a Socialist movement of a far more classic type. Spanish Socialism was in fact only one of the branches of European Socialism, its particular features deriving mainly from its comparatively late development and its prolonged minority position within the labor movement.

The Beginnings of the Socialist Party

The small group of authoritarians expelled in 1872 by Bakunin's friends from the Spanish branch of the International became the nucleus of the *Partido Democrático Socialista Obrero*, founded in a café in 1879 by five friends. Through José Mesa and Paul Lafargue this small group, dominated by the remarkable personality of Pablo Iglesias, was strongly influenced by Jules Guesde and his rigid Marxist orthodoxy. Legalized in 1881, the young party had barely more than a thousand members and had to wait until 1886 before bringing out its first organ, the weekly *El Socialista.* This was because the conditions in which elections were held in Monarchist Spain and the total absence of social reform were not very favorable to the development of Socialist organizations linked with parliamentary and municipal activity and the struggle for reform; whereas the Anarchists, already in the majority in the working class, derived additional arguments for their cause from them. However, its minority position, together with the need for tirelessly explaining and convincing new members one by one, gave the Socialist organization a remarkable discipline and cohesion, as well as a lofty sense of mission and a determination to preserve the purity of its doctrine, perfectly embodied in the severe, handsome, forbidding figure of Pablo Iglesias. In 1888, two Socialist leaders, Mora and García Quejido, had founded the *Unión General de Trabajadores* (UGT). Centralized, moderate, and overtly reformist, the new union, founded with just over 3000 members, took more than eleven years to double its numbers.

Yet since the beginning of the century, the Socialist party and the UGT had been losing their original sectarian nature and had gradually become mass organizations. In Madrid, the original nucleus of printers rapidly spread to all the guilds. The success of the strikes by the Bilbao metalworkers, due to Socialist leadership in the UGT, established its influence there and formed a solid bastion in the region. The widespread establishment at that time of the *casas del pueblo* (Socialist clubhouses) made the Socialists the educators of thousands of militant workers. Also, before World War I, the UGT made gains at the expense of the Anarchists almost everywhere except in Catalonia. It played a prominent part in leading the 1917 strikes, and in 1918 already had more than 200,000 members.

The problem of whether or not to support the Third International dealt a harsh blow to the Socialist party. The events of 1917 in Spain had seemed to justify those Socialists who denounced the parliamentary path as a snare and an illusion. The Russian Revolution fascinated the militants. Finally, after two contradictory decisions taken by two extraordinary congresses and the dispatch of two envoys with differing views to Moscow, a third extraordinary congress decided, by 8880 votes to 6025, to reject the twenty-one conditions for adherence to the Third International. Mora and García Quejido, the founders of the UGT, and Daniel Anguiano, back from Moscow, then broke with the organization, taking with them nearly half the militants, and together with Andrés Nin, Maurin, and the other CNT members who had been converted to Communism they formed the Spanish Communist party.

From Reformism to Revolution?

Under Primo de Rivera's dictatorship a fresh crisis rocked the Socialist party. The general, who was looking for support from the labor movement, asked the Socialists to collaborate with him. This was the cue for the first major clash between the leaders of the new Socialist generation. Largo Caballero, secretary-general of the UGT, a Madrileño by nature and an authoritarian by training, had the better of the liberal Prieto, Socialist leader in Bilbao, who was linked more closely with Republican circles. The 'collaboration' was agreed upon: Largo Caballero became a state councillor and attempted, by means of paritary commissions of arbitration, to increase the influence and enlarge the base of the UGT at the expense of the harshly persecuted CNT.

During the first two years of the Republic, following the example of the Western Socialist parties, the Spanish Socialists collaborated with the Republicans in the government. Largo

Caballero was minister of labor in an Azaña government that made no bones about harrying CNT militants. Yet, taking advantage of the extreme freedom for trade-union propaganda and organization and benefiting from the awakening to political life of new strata of workers, the UGT during this period gained considerably in numbers. In 1934, it had just over 1,250,000 members, including 300,000 factory, mine, and railroad workers.

After the victory of the Right in the 1933 elections, the Socialists seemed to turn their backs on the traditional reformist attitude of the Social Democrats: the October 1934 uprising confirmed this radical switch to clear-cut revolutionary positions.

Largo Caballero and the Labor Alliance

By an odd reversal, the inspiration of the leftist trend of the Socialist party, one of those responsible for its development, was Largo Caballero, until then a pillar of reformism.

Born into a poverty-stricken working-class family in Madrid in 1869, Francisco Largo Caballero had to earn his living from the age of eight; he did not learn to read until he was more than twenty-two. A plasterer, he joined the UGT in 1890, the Socialist party in 1894, and soon took on important responsibilities in both organizations. Sentenced to death, a sentence that was commuted to life imprisonment after the 1917 strike, he was pardoned in 1918 after his election as deputy to the Cortes. A resolute opponent of adherence to the Third International and bitterly hostile to Communism, he brought the support of the Spanish Socialist party to the reconstituted Second International. A state councillor under Primo de Rivera, minister of labor in Azaña's Republican government, he was the champion of Syndicalist and Socialist collaboration with the state, the leader of the most overt reformism. Yet in February 1934 he openly asserted that 'the only hope of the masses today is a social revolution.'

This was because his experience as a minister disillusioned him profoundly. He was the first among the Socialists to clash with Azaña; the staff of the ministry and its senior officials overtly sabotaged his orders, deriding his plans for reform. From this he concluded that reformism was leading the labor movement into an impasse. 'It is impossible,' he said, 'to achieve a scrap of socialism within the framework of bourgeois democracy.' From then on he was forced to seek a new route.[13]

The first practical result of this new orientation was the organization in 1934 of the *Alianza Obrera*, a single front of working-class unions and parties with which the Communist party and the CNT refused to associate themselves except in Asturias. After the 1934 general strike against the entry of the CEDA into the government, it was the *Alianza Obrera*, joined at the last moment by the Communist party, that led the revolutionary rising in Asturias. For more than a week, with makeshift weapons, led by militants from different organizations, the miners fought the Army and the shock troops, consisting of Moors and *Tercio* and commanded by General Lopez de Ochoa. The movement in the rest of Spain collapsed: in Catalonia it was because of betrayal by certain Catalanists, the wavering of the Esquerra, and, above all, the abstention of the CNT; in Madrid, for lack of serious preparation. The repression that followed—more than 3000 workers killed, most of them dispatched on the spot, 7000 wounded, and more than 40,000 imprisoned—did not succeed in destroying the revolutionary consciousness that had inspired the movement. The Asturian uprising became, in the minds of the Spanish workers, Anarchists as well as Socialists, an epic example, the first attempt by the workers to seize power through class organizations (the revolutionary Committees) and to range their troops, the armed workers; in short, to set their own state against the state of the oligarchy. Its rallying cry, UHP (*¡Uníos, Hermanos Proletarios!*) was taken up by the entire class.

In prison, Largo Caballero, an old man, the 'practician' and administrator of the labor movement, began to read for the first time. At the age of sixty-seven, he discovered the classics of Marxism: Marx, Engels, Trotsky, Bukharin, and above all Lenin. He became enthusiastic over *State and*

Revolution and the Russian Revolution that he had so vigorously contested. These readings and the influence of the brilliant staff of intellectuals surrounding him, Araquistáin, Álvarez del Vayo, and Carlos de Baráibar, added strength to the conclusions drawn from his own experience. In his view, 'the reformist and parliamentary democratic socialism of the Second International' was as dead as 'the Moscow-inspired revolutionary socialism of the Third.' He dreamed of a Fourth International that would adopt from its precursors what was best in them, the autonomy of national parties from the Second and revolutionary tactics from the Third. He stepped up approaches to the CNT and welcomed those made to him by the Communists, who were in reality attracted more by his favorable attitude toward 'unity' than by the revolutionary outlook he had so lately discovered.

His development was the same as that of the broad masses of workers and peasants, like him disillusioned by the Republic and reformism and like him won over to the Revolution all the more after the setback of October 1934. Largo Caballero became their man. No working-class leader enjoyed comparable prestige, which the Communists tried to exploit by dubbing him the Spanish Lenin. Jean-Richard Bloch drew an engaging portrait of him: 'A robust sixty-seven . . . square, bald head . . . massive face, stubborn forehead, bitter mouth, the lines of his body slim and handsome in its strength, bright eyes . . . terribly weary.'[14]

A mediocre writer and a rather dull speaker, he owed his popularity to the fact that he was of working-class origins and indisputably honest and austere in his habits. Thousands of workers recognized themselves in him: by turning his back on reformism, he had taken the same step as they had. He was one of them. 'He won't betray us,' his followers never stopped saying. He was the man of the *casas del pueblo*, the idol of the Madrid workers, who listened passionately to him, the 'old man,' as they affectionately called him. A man of the masses, his authority over them made him one of the key figures of the Spanish political scene at decisive moments.

Indalecio Prieto

From 1919 onward, Indalecio Prieto was Caballero's rival in the Socialist party. He was the only Socialist leader with comparable authority, if not among the masses, at least within the party apparatus and in political circles. They had been at odds with each other for a long while, not only by virtue of their contrasting temperaments and personalities, but also because they represented two distinct forces, two aspects of Spain and Spanish Socialism, whose antagonism was one of of the chief features of the political scene.

Also born into a very humble family, in 1883, Prieto began work at the age of eleven by selling newspapers and pins in the streets of Bilbao. His brilliant mind brought him to the notice of Horacio Echevarrieta, the banker and industrialist, who made him his right-hand man. He soon became owner of the large newspaper *El Liberal*, a Socialist leader and political figure respected by the entire Left.

Claude Bowers, the American ambassador, described him making a speech in the Cortes as 'small, fleshy, almost bald, except above the nape of the neck . . . His dynamic eloquence makes an immediate impression.' He referred in turn to 'his voice, resonant and subtly inflected,' but also to 'the complete armory of his eloquence: wit, irony, sarcasm, humor, invective, and mimicry.'[15]

Koltsov depicted him in his armchair as a 'great mass of flesh with a wan, ironic look . . . the most searching look in Spain.'[16] His subtle and brilliant intelligence, his social triumphs—he had become a remarkable businessman—his exceptional gifts as a parliamentary speaker, and his talent as a polemicist made him the Socialist of Republican circles, just as Caballero's patient work as an organizer and his unremitting toil made him the Socialist of the *casas del pueblo* and the workers. Prieto offset the intransigence and Castilian sectarianism of Caballero, the Madrid plasterer, with the liberalism of business circles, the success of the self-made man, and the conciliatory reformism of the Bilbao trade unionists, infinitely more in tune with the spirit of the Western Social Democrats and, in any case, the Spanish Republicans.

Thus it was a deeply divided Socialist party that faced the difficulties of 1936. Prieto had been in control of the party executive since 1935; he had the confidence of the cadres and the élite, especially the prestigious leaders of the Asturian miners, González Peña and Belarmino Tomás. He was the 'man of the apparatus,' whereas Largo Caballero was the 'man of the masses.' He controlled the UGT and enjoyed great sympathy outside the party, and it is notable that he was favored within the CNT, in spite of old resentments. The party wavered under their contradictory influence, and each new problem seemed to provide an opportunity for a reckoning between these antagonistic brothers pursuing opposed policies within the same organization.

CNT and UGT

The political realignment that took place in the ranks of the working-class parties and unions during the final months of the Republic makes it difficult to give a precise analysis of the forces involved. It is however indisputable that it was the unions, rather than the actual political organizations, that set the lead: the worker's life gravitated around the *casas del pueblo* and the labor exchanges, centers of collective life that were veritable class strongholds.

During this last period, there was a modification in the balance of power between the UGT and the CNT, with rifts between the two unions forming in an entirely new way. Naturally each of them preserved what had until then been its bastion. It was the CNT that organized the industrial workers in Catalonia, while the UGT's influence there was limited. It was also the CNT that organized the *braceros* in Andalusia. But the UGT was still dominant among the Asturian and Rio Tinto miners, the Bilbao metalworkers, and in the region of Madrid. In areas where the other was dominant, each union still contrived to organize strong minorities, whose influence was far from negligible. The UGT had strong organizations in Cordoba, Seville, and Málaga, and in all the Andalusian towns. It also organized the day laborers in the provinces of Badajoz, Cáceres, and Seville. The CNT managed to win a foothold in Madrid, where it controlled the majority of the building workers, one of the most militant guilds. And in Asturias, the CNT metalworkers in La Felguera and Gijón were competing seriously for influence over the miners of Mieres and Sama de Langreo.

In the Basque provinces, although the UGT was predominant in Bilbao, it was up against very serious competition from the Nationalist 'Solidarities,' while the CNT only drew recruits from the strata of foreign labor in the country. In Valencia, the Anarchists controlled the dock workers, but the UGT was powerful in the factories. The Federation of Land-workers in the UGT controlled the workers in the central region, while those in the poorer, outlying regions belonged to the CNT. Yet the radical direction of the UGT in the years immediately preceding had tended to narrow the traditional division that won it the adherence of the more privileged and relatively more conservative strata of the proletariat, whereas the CNT's indecisiveness was not always calculated to win the support of the more determined elements.

Yet on the whole the forces of the UGT, which was more efficiently staffed and organized, seemed more stable than those of its confederal rival, which was subject to violent fluctuations and varied considerably according to the success or failure of activities undertaken locally. Though the two trade-union organizations had roughly the same numbers in 1935, a million each, the last months of the Republic saw rapid strides by the UGT, which very quickly reached 1½ million members, while the CNT seemed to lag behind.

In any case, the attraction these trade-union organizations had for millions of workers made it possible for new ideological currents to grow up within them, deriving from traditional currents but developing outside and counter to them. In effect, orthodox Stalinist Communists and Communist dissidents from the POUM put themselves forward as candidates and were ready to fight the Anarchist and Socialist currents for control of important sectors of the UGT and the CNT.

THE COMMUNISTS

The preceding pages have described the birth of the Spanish Communist party. For several months, the lure of the Russian Revolution had seemed to give substance to Victor Serge's old dream, the union within Communism, around Lenin and the Third International, of the two currents that had diverged after Marx and Bakunin, the Authoritarians and the Libertarians, the Socialist current and the Anarchist current. The immediate results were mediocre. A few years later they were derisory.

Three currents had emerged to found the Communist movement in Spain: the Socialist Youth movement, with Andrade and Portela; then the Socialist minority with Pérez Solis, García Quejido, Anguiano, Lamoneda, and Andrés Nin; and shortly afterward the *La Batalla* group, inspired by Joaquín Maurin, Pedro Bonet, and David Rey and made up of POUM militants. Two years later, García Quejido, Lamoneda, and Anguiano left the Communist party and went back to their old Socialist home. Under Primo de Rivera's dictatorship, the Party was severely hit by the repression and weakened by internal struggles and conflicts provoked by directives from the International. Although toward the end of the dictatorship it received the support of militants from the Andalusian CNT led by José Diaz and Mije, it lost 3000 militants from the Federation of Catalonia and the Balearic Islands led by Maurin and Bonet. The Communist Federation of Catalonia and the Balearics joined the Catalan Communist party led by Jordi Arquer and Joan Farré Gasso and formed the *Bloque Obrero y Campesino*, which contained militants such as Portela and Gorkin, a former official in the Communist International in Moscow, with Maurin as secretary-general. Andrés Nin, secretary of the Red Trade-Union International, then joined the Left opposition and defended Trotsky's political position against Stalin. Returning to Spain in 1931, he and Andrade founded the Communist Left. Meanwhile, Oscar Pérez Solis, the Party's first secretary-general, began moving in a direction that eventually took him into the ranks of the Falange. From 1923 to 1930 the Party never had more than a few hundred members and could not even manage to hold a congress. At the congress in 1932 the 'conquerors' of Nin and Maurin, Bullejos, the secretary-general, Trilla, and Adame were in turn expelled, accused of mistakenly launching the opportunist slogan 'Defense of the Republic' against General Sanjurjo's *pronunciamiento*. In the 1933 elections the Communist party only managed to elect one deputy, Doctor Bolivar, in Málaga, less for his program than for his reputation as 'the doctor of the poor.'

The Stalinist Communists: The Spanish Communist party, the PSUC, and the JSU

Thus the Communist party had barely developed: on the eve of the Civil War it had no more than 30,000 members. Its leaders were practically unknown, sometimes recent acquisitions, such as the secretary-general José Diaz, who had only joined in 1929. Jesús Hernández, the leadership's 'strong man,' was twenty-six: he had joined the Party at fourteen, the political bureau at twenty-two. Neither he nor his comrades, Antonio Mije, Martínez Carton, and Uribe, played a genuine role in the labor movement. At no time were they leaders of mass organizations, but rose exclusively within the party apparatus that had trained them and rewarded them with promotion for their flexibility in resorting to one device after another. The only personality in the Communist party leadership who enjoyed real prestige outside the Party was a woman, Dolores Ibárruri Gómez, known as *La Pasionaria*, a mass orator and veteran militant; she was sentenced to fifteen years' imprisonment after the Asturias uprising.

Apart from certain sectors—Asturias, where they had a substantial minority among the miners, Málaga, Cádiz, and especially Seville, where they took over certain unions—the orthodox Communists were very isolated in the Spanish labor movement, and all their efforts were directed to breaking out of this isolation.

The advent of the Spanish Republic actually coincided with

the third stage of extremist sectarianism on the part of the Communist International: the Communist parties of the entire world reserved all their animus for the Socialists, styled 'Social Fascists,' and refused to form a single front with them. Until 11 September 1934, the Spanish Communist party dubbed the *Alianza Obrera* 'the rallying point of reactionary forces' and 'the holy alliance of the counterrevolution.' It was only at the last minute that, suddenly taking a new tack, it joined the October uprising. But it was just then that the Communist International changed its direction. Stating that it was necessary to 'transcend' and 'broaden' the *Alianza Obrera*, the Communist party produced a formula in practice quite different from the Popular Front put forward by Dimitrov at the seventeenth congress of the Communist International, one of alliance with the liberal Republicans in a program of democratic reform. At the same time, it fostered an active campaign in favor of trade-union and political unity for the working class. It dissolved the few unions that it controlled, until then grouped in a CGTU affiliated with the Red Trade-Union International, and invited their members to join the UGT individually. In the political field, the theme of unity permitted it considerable progress. In Catalonia, the remnants of its official organization arranged an alliance with other Catalan Socialist groups, including Juan Comorera's Socialist Federation, which materialized on 24 July 1936 as the Unified Socialist party of Catalonia.[17] Under the influence of Álvarez del Vayo, Largo Caballero's lieutenant, an alliance was also effected between the Socialist Youth and the Communist Youth within the ranks of the JSU (United Socialist Youth). This alliance, which Largo Caballero apparently had not intended but which his policy made possible, deprived the old UGT leader and the Socialist party of 200,000 young militants, the élite of the young working-class generation. In effect, a few months later, as the result of a visit to the USSR, the entire JSU leadership joined the Communist party. Its twenty-year-old secretary-general, Santiago Carrillo, son of the parliamentary deputy and Caballerist Syndicalist Wenceslao Carrillo, was formerly secretary of the Socialist Youth and after 1934 a Trotskyist sympathizer; he soon became one of the Communist party's new leaders, proffering the achieved unity of the young as an example to the adults in the Socialist party.

This was an important victory for the orthodox Communists, all the more because at the same time that it guaranteed them a mass basis and a lever for activities within the Socialist party, it gave them a decisive advantage over their sworn enemies, the dissident Communists, some of whom had at one point thought that they could become the intellectual masters of the Socialist Youth.

The Dissident Communists: the POUM

The groups that claimed links with Communism but were divorced from its official organization had various origins. Maurin and his friends in the *Bloque Obrero y Campesino* refused to apply the tactics imposed by the International and create CGTU Red unions in opposition to the UGT and the CNT. Moreover, they had shown Catalanist sympathies that on occasion brought them closer to the Esquerra. Like all the dissident movements that emerged during this period from a split to the Right, as against the Communist International's Extreme Left line, the *Bloque* however refused to take a line on exclusively Russian questions, and its newspaper, *La Batalla*, often defended positions very close to those of the Stalinist press.

On the other hand, the Communist Left of Andrés Nin and Andrade, other pioneers of Spanish Communism, took the position of the Trotskyist Left opposition, which stemmed from divergences within the Russian Communist party. Until 1934, this small group of valuable cadres was mainly devoted to theoretical work, publishing the magazine *Comunismo*. But at this point they broke with Trotsky, who wanted them to join the Socialist party and form its revolutionary wing,[18] and decided to merge with the *Bloque Obrera y Campesino* to form a new party, the *Partido Obrero de Unificación Marxista* (POUM).

Dubbed Trotskyist by its opponents,[19] disowned and vigorously criticized by Leon Trotsky and his friends, the POUM, whose only real forces were in Catalonia, had barely more than 3000 militants in July 1936. But the weakness of the Spanish Communist party and the Catalan Socialists, the prestige and valor of leaders like Nin and Maurin, and the presence at its head of genuine cadres of the Communist movement like Gorkin, Portela, Andrade, and Arquer seemed to justify its hopes. It was at all events a source of concern as much to the orthodox Communists as to the leaders of the CNT, who systematically eliminated its militants from their unions.

It was the POUM, which considered itself the representative of true Communism and proclaimed its loyalty to Lenin's ideas, that was the real danger to both sides in a revolutionary era. It claimed to provide an answer to the dilemma that had arisen in the Spanish labor movement in the form of a choice between alliance with the Republicans and violent struggle outside the parliamentary framework: political struggle for the Socialist revolution and the dictatorship of the proletariat. A supporter of the *Alianza Obrera*, it criticized the Popular Front policy advocated by the Stalinist Communists, which it denounced as a policy of collaboration between classes, and tried to convince the Spanish workers that the only alternative to the victory of Fascism was that of the Revolution. No one can dispute that its chances of succeeding were real, to the extent that it could convince and attract the 'instinctively revolutionary but politically confused masses'[20] who followed the CNT–FAI.[21]

Notes

[1] See below on the figure of Durruti. Here was the root of what may be called the El Cid-*guerrillero*-brigand tradition.

[2] Congress of St. Imier, 1872.

[3] Victor Serge, referring to his first meetings with them in Moscow, wrote: 'One could tell at a glance the qualities of Maurin, the Lérida schoolteacher, and Nin, the Barcelona schoolteacher. Maurin looked like a young knight as drawn by the Pre-Raphaelites; Nin, behind his gold-rimmed spectacles, had a look of concentration relieved by zest' (*Mémoires d'un révolutionnaire* [Paris: Club des Editeurs, 1957], p. 140). (English

translation: *Memoirs of a Revolutionary, 1901–1941* [Oxford: Oxford University Press, 1967].)

[4] Salvator Seguí, nicknamed *El Noy de Sucre* ('The sugar child'), was, like José Negre, first secretary of the CNT, a militant Anarchist, trained by Anselmo Lorenzo. Like the metalworker Pestaña who succeeded him at the head of the CNT, he had belonged to the *Els Fils de Puto* group at the beginning of his life as a militant.

[5] *La Révolution prolétarienne*, 25 January 1936.

[6] Pestaña, for his part, founded the Syndicalist party. He was elected a deputy in February 1936.

[7] The CNT Defense Committees were genuine paramilitary organizations.

[8] According to José Peirats, Santillan's real name was Sinesio García Hernández. Born in León, he had emigrated to Argentina when young, which would explain this point in his story.

[9] Brenan, *Spanish Labyrinth*, p. 250.

[10] Mikhail Koltsov, *Ispanskii dnevnik* [Spanish diary] (Moscow: Sovietskii pisatel, 1957), p. 43. (Spanish translation: *Diario de la guerra de España* [Madrid: Ediciones Ruedo Inerico, 1963].)

[11] *Buenaventura Durruti* (Barcelona: Services Officiels de Propagande de la CNT–FAI, 1937). CNT–FAI pamphlet.

[12] Statement to Pierre van Paasen, correspondent of the *Toronto Star*, reprinted by Felix Morrow in *Revolution and Counter-Revolution in Spain* (New York: Pioneer Publishers, 1938), p. 189.

[13] See the pamphlet *Discursos a los trabajadores* (Madrid: Ediciones El Socialista, 1934).

[14] Jean-Richard Bloch, *Espagne, Espagne!* (Paris: Editions Sociales Internationales, 1936), pp. 79–80.

[15] Claude Bowers, *Ma mission en Espagne (1933–1939)* (Paris: Flammarion, 1956), p. 43. (Translation of *My Mission to Spain* [New York: Simon and Schuster, 1954].)

[16] Koltsov, *Ispanskii dnevnik*, p. 73.

[17] Negotiations for the alliance, entered on at the beginning of the year, had led to an agreement on 25 June.

[18] Only a very small group remained loyal to Trotsky and tried to apply his line by joining the Socialist Youth. Among them was G. Munis (see later).

[19] Koltsov described the POUM as 'a Trotskyist-Bukharinian bloc.' *Ispanskii dnevnik*, p. 24.

[20] Juan Andrade, 'Marxists, revolutionaries, and Anarchists in the Spanish Revolution,' *La Révolution espagnole*, 15 April 1937.

[21] See Leon Trotsky (*Leçon d'Espagne*; *dernier avertissement*, 2nd ed. [Paris: Editions Pioniers, 1946], p. 40): 'The CNT unquestionably attracts the most aggressive elements in the proletariat. The selection was made during the course of many years. To consolidate this confederation and change it into a genuine mass organization is the pressing duty of every progressive worker and especially the Communist workers.'

CHAPTER 3

THE PROLOGUE TO THE REVOLUTION

It was the president of the Republic, Alcalá Zamora, a Catholic and a Conservative, who brought an end to the *bienio negro* by dissolving the Cortes. In 1935 the coalition government of the Radicals and the CEDA had received a severe jolt. Two scandals had besmirched the politicians in the Radical party. The discredit that fell on the Center-Right party was so great that the CEDA could no longer think of pursuing the alliance. Gil Robles, who had been clamoring for power for his party ever since the beginning of the legislature, seized his opportunity. The CEDA ministers turned down the budget, which provided for an increase of 1 to 3 percent in the death duties on landed estates as well as a reduction of 10 to 15 percent in civil servants' salaries. The government resigned. Gil Robles solicited the post of premier. Alcalá Zamora refused: he did not care for Gil Robles, and he had no wish to offer power to a professed enemy of the parliamentary system. He called on a politician from the Center, Portela Valladares, to form a government whose essential mission was to prepare for new elections. He did not succeed: the Cortes had become unmanageable. After only a few weeks, Portela Valladares gave up serious preparations for elections that would strengthen the Center and resigned: he agreed to the president's signature on the decree dissolving the Cortes and fixing the elections for 16 February 1936.

The Electoral Campaign: Right against Left

The stakes at the elections were considerable. Naturally the events of the previous few years, the 1934 uprising and the ensuing repression, the reaction of the *bienio negro*, and labor radicalization had hardened many positions and created an atmosphere lending itself to the creation of uncompromisingly hostile voting blocs. But in this case it was the demands of the electoral law that weighed on the strategies of both sides, at any rate among those who wanted to see the parliamentary game through to the end. The electoral areas provided for were immense and campaigning required vast sums, which only huge organizations had at their disposal. The inflexible majority ballot tended to create mammoth coalitions: in 1933 the Right, united in an electoral front, had fewer votes than the left-wing parties, but twice as many deputies. It had good reason to remember this, since the Monarchists naturally made difficulties about renewing the 1933 alliance with the CEDA, and in certain constituencies the *Renovación Española* entered the election against a list from the CEDA. The Falange of course went to the polls under its own banner. Yet on the whole the Right presented the voters with a united front, even broadened, in several districts, by some right-wing Liberals who had held aloof in 1933. It ran a massive propaganda campaign: immense posters, on which Gil Robles's picture accompanied the 'Leader's' slogans, covered the country's walls. Robles himself waged a campaign of extraordinary verbal violence, insulting and threatening the enemy and making it perfectly clear that his victory would mean the end of the Republic and the coming of an authoritarian regime.

A left-wing electoral coalition emerged in response to the alliance of the Rightists. On 15 January 1936, the left-wing Republican parties, Martínez Barrio's Republican Union and Azaña's Republican Left, signed the Popular Front pact fixing the coalition's program with the Socialist party (and consequently the UGT), Angel Pestaña's Syndicalist party, the Communist party, and the POUM. However, this eight-point pact-cum-program was not so much the result of a common accord as an acceptance of the Republican program by the workers' parties. Along with some old Republican demands for agrarian reform and educational schemes, it came out in favor of reforms for the control of the Cortes, reforms for municipalities, the establishment of schemes for financial reorganization, the protection of light industry, and the development of public works. It was a liberal program set in a bourgeois framework and deliberately excluded Socialist demands for the nationalization of land and banks and working-class control over industry. 'The republic that the Republicans have in mind,' it stated, 'is not a republic inspired by social and economic class considerations but a system of democratic freedom prompted by motives of public interest and social progress.'

This indisputably moderate program, in which, as Ramos Oliveira wrote, 'each point was like an evasion,'[1] did however include a demand that met with very broad approval and permitted real popular mobilization: an unconditional amnesty for the 1934 insurgents and the reemployment, with compensation, of all workers forced out of their jobs. It was out of anxiety to obtain the release of the 30,000 workers still imprisoned and at the same time to receive the seal of approval for their revolutionary gesture that the friends of Caballero and the POUM—champions of the *Alianza Obrera*—justified their membership in the Popular Front: they regarded it as an electoral alliance without a future. At any rate, this anxiety explains the workers' massive vote for a program otherwise unlikely to have mobilized them. It also explains the Anarchists' change of attitude. The CNT and the FAI were of course always hostile to electoral struggles and like the opposition unions held aloof from the Popular Front and the so-called electoral campaign; for the first time, however, they abstained from launching their usual slogan of *No Votad* and did not boycott the elections.[2] Observers estimated at 1½ million the number of votes that were usually lost as a result of Anarchist campaigns, votes that in February 1936 went to the Popular Front lists in order to obtain the release of the 1934 prisoners.

Result of the Elections

These votes undoubtedly swung the balance. On 16 February the Popular Front triumphed with 4,206,156 votes against 3,783,601 for the right-wing coalition and 681,447 for the Center, figures that, after auditing procedures that were promptly dispatched in Parliament, became respectively 4,838,449, 3,996,931, and 449,320, out of 11 million registered and 9½ million ballots cast.

Thus the Popular Front obtained a rather slender majority, which nevertheless took the form, in the Cortes, of an overwhelming numerical superiority of deputies elected under its aegis: 277, as against 132 from the Right and 32 from the Center. The electoral law that benefited the majority operated here in favor of the Left: the Right, though it won more votes than in 1933, won fewer than the parties joined in the Popular Front and lost more than half its seats. In such close competition, it was inevitable that bitter disputes should arise about pressures and false returns. None of the parties held back: it is of course undeniable that many of the bourgeoisie must have hesitated to vote in certain proletarian districts, but it is a fact that many villages voted for the Right only under direct threats from the police or blackmail from the big landowners over unemployment. The historian has no further conclusions to draw from such quarrels.

Whatever one's view of the validity of these elections, the important thing is that they profoundly altered the face of the Cortes and the political atmosphere of the country even more profoundly.

Contrary to the president's hopes, the elections came as a resounding defeat for the Center and the Center Right. Politicians like Lerroux and Cambó were not reelected: there were only 6 of Lerroux's Radicals, and the most important Center group, the one led by Portela Valladares, the outgoing premier, consisted of only 14 deputies. The CEDA still formed a solid bloc with 86 seats, nearly always joined by the 13 Agrarians. Goicoechea was defeated, and it was Calvo Sotelo who became the spokesman of the Extreme Right, in which *Renovación Española* had only 11 deputies.

There is no way of telling how many votes fell to each party out of the total recorded for the Popular Front. The number elected on their lists in fact depended not on the votes recorded for the coalition, but simply on agreements reached between organizations unconnected with the compilation of the lists. Azaña's Republican Left had 84 deputies, Martínez Barrio's Republican Union 37, and Luis Companys's Catalan Esquerra 38. The Socialists won 90 seats, the Communists 16, the POUM 1, its secretary-general Maurin, and the Syndicalist party 1, the ageing Pestaña.

The Aftermath of the Elections: The Government

The aftermath of the elections gave rise to various emotions: enthusiasm but also fear among the victors, panic and revolt among the defeated. Rumors of all kinds were rife: on the Right, there was talk of an armed uprising by the 'Marxists' or the Anarchists; on the Left, there were denunciations of preparations for a military coup d'état. None of this was groundless: popular unrest seemed to confirm the statements of the Right, and Portela Valladares later revealed that General Franco had offered him the Army's support in order to annul the elections.

Portela Valladares at any rate considered the situation sufficiently delicate to hand in his resignation without delay and to advise the president to call on one of the leaders of the Popular Front to take his place. Azaña immediately formed the new government, made up of bourgeois Republicans, which the working-class parties backed, though without taking part themselves. The Socialist refusal to participate—surprising at first glance after the precedent of 1931—can be explained by the party's internal crisis and the struggle that was going on between the supporters of Caballero and Prieto. In December 1935 Caballero and his friends had been powerless to prevent the Socialist party from following Prieto in his policy of alliance with the bourgeoisie within the framework of the Popular Front. But they had made him reject a priori any lasting alliance, restricting the pact to a simple electoral coalition that did not commit them any further. After 16

February Prieto once again came out for a government resembling the Popular Front, made up of Republicans and Socialists. Caballero, who had sworn never again to repeat the experience of 1931 and never again to take part in a coalition government with the Republicans, retorted that since the Popular Front program was a bourgeois one, it was up to the bourgeois Republicans themselves to carry it out, and that the Socialists had no right to carry out a program other than their own: at the very most they might give loyal support to Azaña's new government with their votes. With that, Largo Caballero carried the day.

The Socialist party adopted the same attitude in May toward the new Casares Quiroga government. One of the first important acts by the legislature was in effect to depose the president, Alcalá Zamora, and to replace him with Azaña. The president's mandate did not expire until the end of the year, but the majority of the Popular Front, anxious to guard itself against any risk of premature dissolution or any future backing the president might give to a military coup d'état, charged him with having dissolved the Cortes without cause, the only accusation that enabled them to depose him constitutionally. The Right, which had good reason to dislike Alcalá Zamora, abstained. The president was deposed. Many observers were astonished that Azaña agreed to let himself be put forward as a candidate. The role played by Prieto in the affair suggests that it was probably a question of realizing a plan designed to force the Socialists' hand: Azaña, as president, could sooner or later have been replaced at the head of the government by Prieto.[3] He obtained at any rate a comfortable majority with only six votes against him, the CEDA abstaining. His presence at the head of the state seemed to provide a dual guarantee, against reaction as well as against revolution. He was too committed to become the future accomplice of a coup d'état, too attached to economic and political liberalism ever to become the harbinger of the Revolution. In short, he could act as a rallying point and symbol for all Spaniards who still hoped to avert civil war.

In his first speech after the elections, he called for unity, for the 'defense of the Republic,' from 'Republicans and non-republicans, and all who put love of country, discipline, and respect for constitutional authority first.' But this appeal to the supporters of law and order was accompanied by unequivocal measures designed as a sop to popular unrest. He promised the 'redress of atrocities committed by public officials' and, without waiting for the official meeting of the new Cortes, made the Standing Committee approve the restoration of the municipal councils revoked during the *bienio negro*, the appointment of new civil governors throughout the country, and, most important, the amnesty decree. Catalan autonomous status was reestablished, and Companys made a triumphal return journey from Madrid to Barcelona. As the Asturian workers left the prisons, General López de Ochoa, the man who had carried out the repression against them, was arrested. Agrarian reform was put in hand; Basque autonomous status was investigated.

In the Cortes, where henceforth each session turned into a brawl, the Republican government tried to pass the social reforms that it felt were appropriate and to appease the popular demands that grew daily both in scope and depth.

A Revolutionary Situation

After the elections, impressive mass demonstrations had opened the prisons and released the workers detained since 1934, without waiting for the amnesty decree to be signed. On 17 February the opening of the prison in Valencia by CNT demonstrators and the release of those sentenced in 1934 was reported, along with several hundred released in Oviedo alone and several thousand throughout Spain. The following day strikes began throughout the country for the immediate reinstatement of those sentenced or out on bail, the payment of wages to all workers detained during the *bienio negro*, increases in wages, the dismissal of various employers' agents, and improvements in working conditions. In addition to these union strikes there were also some strikes of a more political nature, solidarity strikes and general, regional, and local strikes. Some of the conflicts dragged on and brought others in their wake. The employers replied with lockouts, and the struggle grew in bitterness.

In the countryside the situation was truly revolutionary. The Popular Front had talked of agrarian reform to peasants hungry for land: as the American ambassador, Claude Bowers, wrote, 'the peasants, simple and rough creatures, had believed that their victory at the elections was enough to make it a *fait accompli*.'[4] By the end of February, in the provinces of Badajoz and Cáceres, then, during the ensuing months, in Estremadura, Andalusia, Castile, and even Navarre, *asentamientos* were increased. Alcalá Zamora's lands were occupied in April; so were the Duke of Albuquerque's. The peasants settled on the big landowners' estates and began to cultivate them on their own account. Bloody incidents soon occurred between peasants and Civil Guards. The most serious was at Yeste, near Alicante, where the Civil Guard intervened and arrested six peasants who had begun to cut down the trees on the seignorial estates. Exasperated, the peasants of Yeste, armed with pitchforks, cudgels, and stones, attacked the Civil Guards who were taking away their comrades. In the shooting that ensued, eighteen peasants were killed.

Town and countryside were thus plunged into an atmosphere of violence: there were reports from more or less everywhere of churches and convents being burned, following street demonstrations or because of rumors about a monks' plot. One thing was certain: property and the established order were threatened.

Caballero's Role

Largo Caballero was gradually emerging as the man of the coming revolution. Since 6 April, his evening newspaper, *Claridad*, had been brilliantly edited by an excellent team of young intellectuals. He had his shock troops, the Socialist Youth. On 1 May, during the great workers' procession, in what *Claridad* called 'the great army of workers on the march toward the approaching pinnacle of power,' the uniformed Socialist Youth, fists raised, chanted slogans for a 'workers' government' and a 'Red army.' Caballero stepped up his approaches to the CNT and took the floor at a large meeting in Saragossa on the occasion of its congress. *Claridad* sustained the revolutionary fervor of its supporters and predicted the inevitable and imminent triumph of socialism. In every speech and every article, Largo Caballero drove home the same message: 'The revolution that we want can only be achieved through violence. To establish Socialism in Spain, we must triumph over the capitalist class and establish our authority.' He came out in favor of the 'dictatorship of the proletariat,'[5] which he intended to be exercised not by means of soviets—whatever name they were given—but by and through the Socialist party. Before seizing power, he and his supporters were waiting for the Republicans to produce evidence of their inability to solve Spain's problems. But how were they to seize it? This was not very clear. On 14 June in Oviedo he invited the Republicans to withdraw and 'leave things to the working classes,' but it seemed unthinkable that President Azaña could ever entrust him with the leadership of the government. He meant to establish the dictatorship of the proletariat through the Socialist party, but it was Prieto who controlled the party executive: how could Largo Caballero hope to seize power by means of a party whose apparatus he did not control? Many historians were hard on him—Brenan said that he was a 'social democrat playing at revolution.'[6] Salvador de Madariaga thought that it was the fear prompted by the violence of his supporters that made the birth of Fascism possible. By stating so often that the workers did not have to modify their revolutionary activities for fear of a military coup d'état, he was credited by many people with the foresight that only such a coup d'état, by forcing the government to arm the workers, would offer him the road to power.

At any rate, in June, faced with the imminence of the military *pronunciamiento*, he went to ask Azaña to arm the workers: undoubted evidence of his good faith, but also of a degree of naïveté. Lenin, the Russian Lenin, would certainly not have taken the same step as the Spanish Lenin, at least not in the same form.

Prieto's Efforts

It was Largo Caballero's Socialist rival, Prieto, who made the most serious accusations against him. In his view, strikes, demonstrations, disorders, and excessive demands stemmed from a 'childish revolutionism' that played into the hands of Fascism by scaring the middle classes. Predictions by intellectuals in *Claridad*, demonstrations by the uniformed Socialist Youth, fiery resolutions in favor of a workers' government and a Red army merely succeeded in increasing the fears of the right-minded men of property, whose imagination, as soon as there was talk of revolution, fed on emotional images evoked by eighteen years of anticommunist propaganda about the terror of the *checas*, the Bolsheviks with knives between their teeth, and the massacres and famine that were Russia's lot in 1917. As Prieto saw it, this fear would drive them to despair, and they would fling themselves into the arms of the Generals.

On 1 May, while Largo Caballero was playing at leader of the Revolution in Madrid, Prieto made a far-reaching speech in Cuenca. Instead of the Fascism-breeding anarchy that, according to him, his rival was preparing, he was offering what he called 'constructive revolution.' In his view, the first reasonable and possible task was the formation of a coalition government: in company with the Republicans, it would be the Socialists' mission to 'make the power of the working classes indestructible.' This would mean a thorough and efficient agrarian reform, accompanied by a plan for irrigation of the countryside and industrialization, possible only within a capitalist framework, to absorb the excess rural population. This was why the workers must not make demands that could destroy a capitalist economy incapable of satisfying them. At best, even if they managed to defeat the inevitable armed reaction by the oligarchy, they would eventually succeed only in 'socializing poverty.' However, this was, in Prieto's view, a less probable hypothesis than the other: a preventive military coup d'état, which had at all costs to be avoided. The Socialist leader pointed out how Franco's qualities would make him the obvious leader of such a movement[7] and called on the workers to abstain from anything that might provoke it.

The Cuenca speech was without doubt a government program. *El Sol,* the bourgeois Republican newspaper, hailed it as the work of a true statesman and compared Prieto with Aristide Briand, another Socialist who had become a 'realist.' But this program of discreet and progressive reforms within the framework of capitalism met with little response from the masses other than the revolutionary fervor daily inciting them to fresh activities.[8]

On the contrary, Largo Caballero's friends regarded the program as an open betrayal, denouncing Prieto's words as an apology for Franco. Passions rose: already threatened in Cuenca, Prieto and his friends, González Peña and Belarmino Tomás, were greeted in Ecija with shots from the Socialist Youth and barely escaped death.

It was in these circumstances that the Socialist party executive deferred the national congress originally scheduled for 29 June until October. On 1 July, the press released the result of the elections for the Executive Committee of the Socialist party—boycotted, challenged, and denounced in advance by the Largo Caballero faction. Prieto's friends triumphed; González Peña was elected chairman, Jiménez Asua vice-chairman, and Ramón Lamoneda secretary. Henceforth a split seemed inevitable.

Counterrevolutionary Terrorism by the Falange

In a speech at the Cortes on 16 June, Gil Robles gave a list of official figures indicative of the country's atmosphere since the elections: 269 killed and 1287 wounded in street brawls, 381 buildings attacked or damaged, 43 newspaper offices attacked or ransacked, and 146 bomb attempts. These incontestable figures could not, as Robles would have liked, be laid at the feet of the revolutionaries alone. In fact, since February, systematic counterrevolutionary activity prompted by the Falange had increased. It was in the streets, as in Germany and Italy, that the Falange emerged most clearly in its Fascist guise: its aim was to crush the revolutionary and labor movement with terror and violence, to attack party offices and newspaper vendors, meetings and processions, and to kill when it became necessary to eliminate an enemy or to set a salutary example. After the elections the Falangists had taken to armed struggle. In Madrid, carloads of *escuadristas* armed with automatic weapons sowed terror in the working-class districts. In Andalusia, *pistoleros* in their pay slaughtered fresh victims daily. Their aim was twofold: at one and the same time to eliminate the class enemy, 'Marxist' and Anarchist militants and journalists and the judges and policemen who helped them, and to create an atmosphere such that the friends of law and order would ultimately see no solution but to place the fate of the country in the hands of a dictatorship. Disillusion born of electoral defeat impelled many Conservatives to renounce 'legal' prospects and espouse direct action. In February the Falange's progress was staggering: the flow of right-wing malcontents swelled its ranks. Among those who turned to it were the young men from Gil Robles's party, the *Juventudes Acción Popular*, then led by Ramón Serrano Suñer.

Although it is impossible for the historian to attribute responsibility for rarely avowed crimes with any certainty, it is more than likely that some of the most famous attacks were the work of the Falange and its *pistoleros*: the abortive bomb attempt against Largo Caballero, another against the Republican Ortega y Gasset, and the one that cost the life of the inspector entrusted with protecting the Socialist vice-president, Jiménez de Asua; the exploding of a bomb under the presidential stand during the 14 April procession; the bomb that destroyed the Socialist newspaper offices in Oviedo; the many political murders, such as that of the journalist Casaus in San Sebastián, the Socialist Malumbres in Santander, the judge Pedregal, guilty of sentencing a Falangist killer to thirty years' imprisonment, Faraudo, a captain in the *Guardia de Asalto*, killed in the streets in his wife's arms, and finally, on 12 July, José del Castillo, a lieutenant in the *Guardia de Asalto*, who had become a marked man in the eyes of the Falangists after the street battles that had followed the 14 April attempt.[9]

Preparations for the Military Uprising

In spite of its growing influence in the months after the elections and during the drift toward civil war, the Falange cannot be regarded as the decisive factor. The oligarchy, the traditionalists, the Monarchists, and the Conservatives were awaiting salvation from the Army. Republicans and revolutionaries lived in daily fear of its activities. Practically everyone could see that it was preparing to intervene and seal the fate of the revolutionary movement once and for all. To the Army leaders, it was quite clear that the victory of the Popular Front had caused a revolutionary crisis that the moderate left-wing Republican politicians were helpless to end.

On 17 February, Calvo Sotelo and, just as we have said, Franco himself beseeched the president to take the initiative with a *coup de force* and annul the elections. After Portela Valladares's refusal on 20 February, meetings instigated by the leaders of the *Unión Militar* were held throughout Spain between the political and military leaders of the right-wing parties. Their conclusion was that the time for action had not come, because the troops, carried away by popular enthusiasm, were not wholly reliable.

With this information, the government acted. Franco, the Army chief of staff, was dismissed and transferred to the military command of the Canaries. Goded, Inspector-General of the Army of the North, was transferred to the Balearic Islands, and General Mola, former chief of the security police under the Monarchy, who lost the African army command, was transferred to Navarre. Franco, Mola, and Generals Villegas and Varela met in Madrid, in the Monarchist deputy Delgado's apartment, for necessary last-minute arrangements before each took up his new post.

The conspiracy went on unhindered in these new circumstances: Colonel Galarza took charge of communications between Madrid and the Canaries. It was the Inspector-General of the Army, General Rodríguez del Barrio, who was General Sanjurjo's personal representative in the ruling Junta. In agreement with the pact signed with Goicoechea, Lizarza, and General Barrera in 1934, Italy was to supply the movement with material aid, arms, and money. Juan March was in London and had the job of winning sympathy for the military movement in international banking circles. General Sanjurjo left his home in exile in Estoril to go to Germany in March and April, where he established official contacts. The political objective still remained just as vague: the Junta's first written instructions in April 1936 merely recalled that the aim of the movement was to set up a military dictatorship and fixed the rewards to be offered to the officers and NCOs who were to be won over. The plan for an uprising was modified in accordance with the new circumstances: Franco was to leave the Canaries for Morocco and there take charge of the Army of Africa, Mola was to alert Navarre, González de Lara Burgos, and Rodríguez Carrasco Catalonia, while Varela and Orgaz were to lead the uprising in Madrid. Everything seemed to be ready, and the date of the uprising was fixed for 20 April. But on the eighteenth, General Rodríguez del Barrio informed the Junta that the government was in the know: it had decided to transfer Varela to Cádiz and Orgaz to the Canaries. The plan had to be altered, all the more so because two generals, Queipo de Llano and Cabanellas, supposed to be Republicans—this was an important trump—had just joined the conspiracy. The men in Madrid were being too carefully watched. The central organization for the rebellion was established in Navarre, where Mola had complete freedom of action and where the officers enjoyed the active sympathy of a large section of the population. Madrid remained a worry to the Generals, who finally decided to entrust the leadership of the uprising there to Generals Fanjul and Villegas. Four columns, setting off from Navarre, Burgos, and Valencia, where rapid success was anticipated, were to converge at once on the capital to support the insurgents. But there were other difficulties: General Villegas took fright and ran away, and the government, which seemed to be keeping daily track of the conspiracy, began to shuffle the pack and replaced General González de Lara in Burgos with a thoroughly trustworthy Republican general, Batet. Each time a new start had to be made.

Meanwhile, the conspiracy was taking shape: in the Canaries,

Franco had long talks on the *Jaime I* with Admiral Salas, who was bringing him the support of the naval officers; the nucleus of conspirators had grown considerably larger with the arrival of many junior officers, who were to play a decisive role. It was a question in fact of identifying the cadres in the Army who would come out against the uprising, officers who were either Republican or simply disciplined and determined to remain loyal to the government no matter what it might be. They had to be watched, rendered harmless, and if possible eliminated when the time came. Close contact was established with right-wing leaders. It seems clear that Calvo Sotelo was one of the leaders of the plot. But the soldiers had not given up hope of winning over Gil Robles and his friends, who were holding back. The Carlists gave Mola their support and the valuable contribution of their 7000 *Requetés* 'on a war footing, with arms, equipment and organized regular formations.' Mola accepted only 4000, which he intended to split up among the regiments of *Regulares*. But a note written by Mola on 5 June provoked a crisis with the Carlists. Mola prescribed a directorate of five military leaders for Spain, which would suspend the constitution and govern by orders in council, but which would undertake to preserve the Republic during its tenure of office. The separation of church and state had to be preserved. The movement's objective was, according to Mola, the founding of a 'Republican dictatorship.' This program did not suit the Carlists, who wanted, as an absolute minimum, the adoption of the twin-colored Monarchist flag and the rejection of the Republican emblem, the immediate dissolution of all parties, and a corporative organization for Spain. Mola refused, and the Carlists informed him that they were no longer on his side; the plan with which the Navarrese should have launched the movement on 12 July was dropped. The leader of the *Requetés*, Lizarza, went to see Sanjurjo, whose decision was accepted by everyone: there was to be no flag for the military units in which *Requetés* were required to serve. The government would be an 'apolitical' military government, whose first move would be to abolish all legislation in social and religious matters, and whose objective would be to destroy the liberal parliamentary system and to adopt, in Sanjurjo's own words, 'the norms that many are now observing, modern for them, but ancient for our country.'[10] The final difficulty was removed in June: during the army of Morocco's summer maneuvers, the conspirators swore the famous 'vow of Llano Amarillo.'

After many false starts, the date of the uprising seems to have been settled once again, because Mola told the conspirators to stand by on 15 July. Franco was to alert Morocco from the Canaries, Goded to alert Catalonia from the Balearic Islands, and Queipo de Llano Seville. Elsewhere things were left to the officers on the spot: Cabanellas in Saragossa, Saliquet in Vallalodid, Fanjul in Madrid, and González Carrasco in Valencia. On the sixteenth, Mola warned José Antonio Primo de Rivera that the uprising was fixed for 18, 19, and 20 July. These dates were not to be postponed.

The Government's Attitude

The government's attitude during these decisive months has been the object of much criticism. It was undeniably aware of what was being hatched by the military leaders. It had only taken a few measures, and these were particularly clumsy ones. What was the point of dispatching General Franco to the Canaries, when such an exile took him nearer to the army of Morocco, with which he was very popular, and when the conspirators could still count on the Inspector-General of the Army, who remained at his post in Madrid? Mola's appointment to Navarre, far from weakening the uprising, placed a dangerous leader in one of the most active centers of the conspiracy. And Goded led the uprising in Barcelona from the Balearic Islands without any difficulty. Furthermore, the government in a note on 18 March shielded the soldiers who were conspiring by protesting against rumors of a coup d'état, which it considered harmful. It referred to its 'concern' at the 'unfair attacks' made against the officer corps, 'loyal servants of the constituted power and firm in their obedience to the popular will,' and denounced 'the stubborn, criminal intent to undermine the Army' in Socialist, Communist, and Anarchist press campaigns. The feebleness of the steps taken against the conspirators and the government's avowed intention to close its eyes to them undoubtedly succeeded in rallying many hesitant officers to the *coup de force*. Azaña's successor, Casares Quiroga, deserves to go down in history for the blind optimism that he showed in refusing to believe the information and rumors about the Generals' plot, which culminated in his final refusal to believe in the news of the uprising, even when it had actually taken place.[11] Even then Casares persisted in counting General Queipo de Llano among the loyal officers he was relying on to crush the uprising, while at the same moment this leader was in command of the rebels in Seville.

However, it would be somewhat unfair to level such harsh strictures against the Republican leaders for their indulgence toward the Generals' plot. Like the political groups they represented and the social forces they embodied, Casares Quiroga, and Azaña vacillated because they were caught between two fires. President Azaña had exclaimed in 1933 that he preferred to lose power after honest struggle than to win it by some trick. But the struggle that began in Spain in 1936 was not the honest struggle he hoped for or the parliamentary joust that was familiar to him. It was a bitter struggle between antagonistic social classes, a confrontation he tried in vain to avoid. The parliamentary framework was particularly unsuited to this task: a few months after their election, the Cortes were no longer a true reflection of the nation that had elected them. The right-wing deputies, mainly from the CEDA, were representing voters who—at least the most active of them—had now joined the extremists, and whose spokesman was Calvo Soleto rather than Gil Robles. Meanwhile, the majority of the electors of the Popular Front now constituted an explosive force over which their leaders no longer had any control. The victory of the Popular Front had been their victory, they wanted to wield it, perfect it, cement it, and complete it, by methods that were spontaneously their own, direct action and revolutionary violence.

The workers' and peasants' revolution threatened the

parliamentary Republic in the same way as the military and Fascist reaction. Armed struggle between them, civil war, would signal the end, the bankruptcy of the policies of Azaña and Casares Quiroga. This was why they sought to avoid it, by hitting out at each of their enemies in turn, taking care not to weaken any one too much, in order not to play into the hands of the other.

The government changed tack in the country at large just as it had in Parliament, arresting Falangists and Anarchists in turn and closing down the offices of both sides. In any case, it refused to hit hard at the Generals because it could not then avoid arming the workers, and it refused no less vigorously to deal severely with the strike movement and worker and peasant unrest in order not to fall into the hands of the Generals. Trapped between hostile forces, it could only play a dangerous double game: Primo de Rivera's arrest was a concession to the Left, but the Falangist leader had all the visits that he wanted, and official military circles explained to any who cared to listen that it was the only way of ensuring his safety.[12] Many revolutionary militants hinted that the government was not wholly displeased with the threat of a military plot, which alone could contribute to checking the revolutionary movement, as Prieto wished, by confining it to 'reasonable' claims.

All the reproaches cast up to the government boil down to its one and only defect: its weakness. Its only *raison d'être* was to endure, to play for time in order to avoid the clash that would annihilate it.

Notes

[1] *Men of Modern Spain*, p. 535.

[2] Diego Abad de Santillán (*Por qué perdimos la guerra* [Buenos Aires: Ediciones Imán, 1940], pp. 36–37) said that he agreed with García Oliver on this point against Durruti.

[3] Prieto, in a note to the press, quoted by Carlos Rama (*La crisis española del siglo XX* [Mexico City: Findo de Cultura Económica, 1960], p. 238), stated that he refused president Azaña's offer to form a government mainly because of the hostility shown him by a 'certain sector of his

party,' since it might cause a weakening of the Popular Front, whose 'integrity had to be preserved at all costs.'

[4] *Ma mission en Espagne*, p. 220.

[5] See the resolution of the Madrid Socialist group (*Claridad*, April 1936): 'The proletariat must not confine itself to defending bourgeois democracy but must use every means to assure the conquest of political power in order to achieve its own social revolution. In the transition period from capitalist society to Socialist society, the form of government will be the dictatorship of the proletariat.'

[6] *Spanish Labyrinth*, p. 305.

[7] 'General Franco, because of his youth, his talents, and the range of his friendships in the Army, is the man whose personal prestige gives him the greatest chance of taking charge of a movement against the Republican regime.'

[8] Note that the Communist party was defending positions infinitely closer to Prieto's than to those of Largo Caballero. See the speech by its secretary-general José Díaz in Saragossa on 1 June: a strike—according to Díaz—was the 'powerful weapon that it [the proletariat] has for obtaining higher wages or better living conditions.' But one had to think hard, before embarking on a strike, 'about means of settling disputes without having recourse to one.' 'Because,' he added, 'we are today in a period when employers provoke and foster strikes for political sabotage and when Fascist elements infiltrate some organizations as *agents provocateurs* in order to serve the purposes of reaction.' This attitude contrasts with that of the POUM: 'For bourgeois democracy, the Revolution is over. For the working class, on the contrary, this is merely a stage in its development. . . . Each reactionary retreat, each revolutionary advance, is the direct result of the proletariat's initiative and extra-legal action.' (Article by Andrés Nin in *Nueva Era*, July 1936, reprinted in *Les problèmes de la révolution espagnole* [Paris: Fleury, 1939].)

[9] Clara Campoamor said that Faraudo and Castillo were shot because they had been the instructors of the Socialist militias. The Falangist Bravo Martínez claimed the honor of having carried out these executions for the Falange's 'front line.'

[10] Lizarza, *Memorias de la Conspiración*, p. 106.

[11] He was nicknamed 'Civilón,' the name of a famous bull that had fled the arena.

[12] Bowers, *Ma mission en Espagne*, p. 213.

CHAPTER 4

PRONUNCIAMIENTO AND REVOLUTION

In July, when the military uprising actually broke out, in both camps violence seemed to prevail in the face of government impotence. Not a day went by without a brawl, an exchange of shots, a murder, or a demonstration that resembled a riot. In the Cortes, the deputies were searched: watch was kept to see that no firearms were brought into Parliament. Violence reigned in the countryside, in the words of the premier himself. In the towns, terrorism and reprisals kept the troops of both camps under pressure. In Valencia, on 11 July, the Falangists seized the radio transmitter and announced: 'This is Radio Valencia! The Spanish Falange has seized this transmitter by force of arms. Tomorrow the same will happen to all transmitters in Spain.' A huge counterdemonstration by unions and parties in the Popular Front ended in violent assaults on the CEDA headquarters and an attack on the newspaper *Diario de Valencia*. Yet it was unquestionably in Madrid that daily incidents most clearly announced the approaching Civil War.

The Building Strike

Since February, Madrid had been affected by many strikes, which had spread even to the most conservative sectors, such as elevator-operators and waiters. Yet, as the months went by, the character of these strikes altered. Many workers were apparently less concerned with satisfying one claim or another than with actually taking over their companies. The workers on the Madrid streetcars decided to seize the company and to run it on their own: they were immediately backed by huge offers of money. In the capital, stronghold of the UGT, the CNT had made substantial progress in the preceding months. It was now, if not the numerically strongest organization, at least the most aggressive. It was the young Anarcho-Syndicalists who now emerged as the leaders of the vanguard of the Madrid working class, David Antona, Cipriano Mera, and Teódoro Mora, moving spirits of the CNT builders' union.

On 1 June the 70,000 Madrid building workers began their indefinite strike after a general meeting jointly organized by the two unions, which had undertaken to return to work only by a common decision taken at a new meeting. But the employers resisted. The strike hardened. There was hunger in the working-class districts. The strikers, weapons in hand, forced the shopkeepers to serve them, seized restaurants, and ate without paying. The shopkeepers and petty bourgeoisie took fright. The police were powerless against the masses, in spite of daily brawls with the strike pickets. The building workers seemed to provide a good opportunity for the Falangists to try out their methods of counterrevolutionary violence. They attacked isolated workers, then groups in front of the occupied work sites. At that point, the CNT Center Defense Committee took over control of the strike and the organization of armed defense by the workers. The government did its utmost to resolve the conflict. On 4 July the minister of labor made a decision that essentially satisfied the strikers.[1] The UGT consulted its members and gave the order for a return to work: the strike had to be ended because the basic objective had been achieved, and secondary claims could be settled through negotiation. As Domínguez, secretary of the Madrid UGT builders' union, pointed out in *Claridad*, the conflict could 'degenerate into a serious danger for the regime.' But this may have been the very consideration that prompted the CNT to carry on. The building strike had now exceeded the scope of a simple struggle for an increase in wages and the reduction of working hours: the employers had conceded as much as they could, but the Madrid CNT, under the influence of the most aggressive workers, wanted to continue what was in fact a trial of strength with the bourgeoisie and the state, a veritable strike of insurrection. The CNT immediately denounced the UGT leadership and the Socialists and Communists who supported them as scabs and strikebreakers: hadn't they decided to return to work on their own, in breach of the decision taken by the joint meeting? On 9 July, the Monarchist newspaper *ABC* announced that workers in UGT unions had not returned to work because they feared violence on the part of CNT members. Fights broke out between strikers and non-strikers, CNT and UGT, all armed with some kind of weapon. The same day, five dead were counted at the entrances to the work sites, three UGT and two CNT. It looked as if there would be a repeat in Madrid of the battles in Málaga from 11 to 15 June between the Anarcho-Syndicalists and the Socialists and Communists.[2] The Falangists, once again under the control of one of their most capable leaders, Fernández Cuesta, who was released from prison on 4 July, stepped up their attacks in the hope of crushing the strike. The CNT retaliated by machinegunning a café that was being used as a Falange office: three Falangists in José Antonio's bodyguard were killed. The government took advantage of the conflict between the UGT and the CNT to try to decapitate the CNT, which had become isolated and which it judged the more dangerous of the two. The police closed down their offices and arrested the building workers' leaders, with Antona and Mera at their head. The strikers, led by Eduardo Val of the CNT Center Defense Committee continued to fight the UGT workers, the police, and the Falangists for control of the streets and access to the work sites. It is understandable that in such special circumstances, even when faced with the growing danger of a military uprising, the government should have refused to distribute arms, as Largo Caballero had demanded. In the view of its leaders, 'arming the people' meant first of all the building workers of the Madrid CNT; it meant arming the revolutionary vanguard, the force which they feared even more than the reactionary Generals.

The Murder of Calvo Sotelo

The murder on 12 July of the *Asalto* lieutenant, José del Castillo, was, as we said, an important milestone on the road leading to Civil War. He was, after Captain Faraudo, the second officer in this Corps shot in similar circumstances, and probably at the instigation of the same men. His comrades reacted promptly: the *Asaltos* in fact became a target for Falangist *pistoleros*, whereas the murderers, in such an atmosphere, were almost guaranteed impunity. Moreover, the *Asaltos* in Castillo's company decided to do what they had neglected to do after Faraudo's murder, to avenge themselves, since the state that employed them to maintain law and order was incapable of protecting them by punishing those who struck them down right in the streets. In order to wreak full-blooded vengeance for Castillo's death, they decided to punish a prominent figure whom they considered the instigator of the plot and the leader of the murderers, Calvo Sotelo, who a few days earlier had denounced Castillo in the Cortes as the organizer of an attack on the Falangists.

At dawn on the following day, a truck drove a group of *Asaltos* to Calvo Sotelo's house, led by Lieutenant Moreno and accompanied by a major from the Civil Guard, Fernando Condes. They told the Monarchist leader that they had come to arrest him. Anxious, Calvo Sotelo asked to phone the police for confirmation of the warrant. But the *Asaltos* had cut the telephone wires: he decided to follow them. A few hours later his corpse, riddled with bullets, was found at the East Cemetery and identified at the morgue.

The funerals of José del Castillo and Calvo Sotelo were like the final parade before the battle. The antagonists hurled defiance at each other in broad daylight. Antonio Goicoechea declared over Sotelo's tomb: 'We swear to avenge your death.' Gil Robles, in a speech of extraordinary violence at the Cortes, said: 'Sotelo's blood will drown the government.' And Suárez de Tangis read a document in the name of the Carlists and *Renovación Española* that amounted to a declaration of civil war: 'Ever since 16 February, we have been living in a state of total anarchy, in the grip of a monstrous subversion of all moral values that has ended in yielding authority and justice up to violence. Those who wish to save Spain and her moral heritage as a civilized people will find us first on the road of duty and sacrifice.'

In the atmosphere of the previous months, there had been such a torrent of insults and threats that it was not hard for the murdered leader's friends to pick out denunciations and attacks from their enemies' speeches that could be regarded as provocations to murder. They did not stint themselves. Sotelo's murderers and Castillo's avengers were known: they were the fifteen guards from the lieutenant's patrol. It was clear that they had acted on their own initiative, without official orders. But right-wing propaganda went to great lengths to pin direct responsibility for the murder on the Republican government against which it was preparing to revolt. Sotelo's death provided the perfect excuse for an uprising long under preparation. All over Spain, the workers dug up arms hidden since 1934 and tried to procure fresh ones. The government transferred a few generals, speeded up the demobilization of recruits and arrested Falangists, including those whom it had just released. Prieto, in *El Liberal*, did not mince his words: 'If the reaction dreams of a bloodless coup d'état, it is mistaken.'

In this atmosphere of alarm and uncertainty, the premier remained imperturbable. On 14 July, a group of Basque deputies, among them the future president, Aguirre, who reported the incident, asked him if it was true that he had had Mola, known leader of the conspirators, arrested. He took offense at these rumors and declared: 'Mola is a general loyal to the Republic.'[3] In the same way, he rudely rebuffed the governor of Huelva, who had proof of Queipo de Llano's subversive activities and asked for authorization to arrest him. Several witnesses, Prieto among them, finally reported that when he was informed of the uprising by the troops in Morocco, he merely replied: 'They're rising? Very well, I shall go to bed.'

The Insurrection in Morocco

In Morocco, the Army felt secure, as it always had. In February the troops there were already reliable, whereas on the mainland they were vacillating. The Moroccan troops, the Moors, were recruited from the mountain people of the Riff. They were fearsome warriors, savages unaffected by propaganda who were concerned only with fighting and pillage, as they had shown after the repression of the Asturias uprising. The Spanish foreign legion was a body of élite mercenaries, volunteers from all countries, desperadoes and often fugitives from justice; they too were all ready to fight, since that was why they were being paid and that was what they had chosen to do. The labor movement of course existed, and there were strong union organizations in the towns. However, they had little influence over a well-organized native population and, above all, had no contacts with the professional soldiers, the Moroccans and foreigners of the élite troops of the army of Morocco.

Nearly all the cadres were in the conspiracy. The officers greeted each other cheerfully in the streets with shouts of *¡Café!*, abbreviation of their rallying cry, *¡Camaradas, arriba Falange española!* They were preparing openly—or almost so—for the conquest of the decaying mother country, which was to be regenerated by the military virtues that were the appanage of every colonial army. After Llano Amarillo's intrigues, as we saw, the leaders had taken their bearings. Everything was ready for the Army, which the state had been unwise enough to send to guard Morocco, to hurl itself on the Republic. The authorities there were so weak in the face of the military leaders that the conspiracy was hidden only so that information received on the mainland should not be too precise. In early July the police had found stocks of arms, uniforms, and proclamations in the Tetuán Casino. Nothing was done about it, although the names of the conspirators' leaders were on everyone's lips.

The movement began on 17 July in Melilla. At the head of his officers, the appointed leader, Lieutenant-Colonel Seguí, won over the *Guardia de Asalto* and dismissed the commander of the garrison. The foreign legion attacked the *casa del pueblo* where the building workers had assembled. Here and there, troops and workers attempted to resist. They were shot down. Master of the town in a few hours, Seguí telegraphed the order to revolt to the other garrisons. Communications with the mainland were cut off. The heads of the foreign legion, Yagüe and Tella, and the heads of the Moorish troops, Colonels Bautista y Sánchez in the Riff, Sáenz de Buruaga in Tetuán, and Múgica in Larache, went into action about 11 P.M., seized strategic points, controlled traffic, and began manhunts in the working-class districts. The airmen in Tetuán resisted: brought to heel by artillery, they were shot 'in accordance with martial law.' The Caliph and the Grand Vizier were asked to approve the action by the rebels, who were occupying the High Commission. They agreed. The strike launched by the unions became general on 18 July, but the Army supplied native 'volunteers' to crush it and it was short lived, after a few arrests and executions. In Ceuta, where the uprising was announced by the tocsin, Yagüe took control of the town within two hours. The heroic resistance by the workers in Larache did not last more than twenty-four hours. By 18 July the Army had crushed all resistance. Its nominal leader, General Morato, learned the news of the uprising by telephone from Madrid. Now it awaited its true leader: Franco.

The Republican Government and the Uprising

Franco left Las Palmas in a plane piloted by an Englishman.[4] Wisely, he did not arrive in Tetuán until 19 July, after touching down in French Morocco to find out how things had gone. But a proclamation was made in his name in Tetuán: 'The Army has decided to restore order in Spain. . . . General Franco has been placed at the head of the movement and is appealing to the Republican sentiments of all Spaniards.' During the night of 17–18 July, a government plane dropped six bombs on the Tetuán Headquarters. There was an ominous reply: 'Reprisals will be in proportion to resistance encountered.'

On the morning of 18 July, the government had to admit

in a note that 'part of the Army has revolted in Morocco.' It went on: 'The government states that the movement is confined to certain areas in the Protectorate and that no one, absolutely no one, on the mainland has joined such an absurd venture.' However, the same day, the 'absurd venture' spread throughout the country: the troops in Málaga and Seville were revolting. But the government contradicted the report and broadcast a second communiqué at 3 P.M. in reply to the parties and unions:

'The government has noted the offers of aid it has received and, while offering its gratitude, states that the best way to help is to carry on normally with everyday life, in order to set an example of calm and of trust in the military powers of the state. . . . Thanks to preventive measures taken by the government, it may be said that a vast antirepublican movement has been wiped out. It has received no help on the mainland and has merely succeeded in rallying a few supporters from one portion of the Army.' After hailing the forces that were busy mastering the uprising in Morocco, the broadcast concluded: 'The government's action will suffice to restore order.' The government radio even went so far as to state that the uprising in Seville had been crushed.

The same evening, the Cabinet, including Prieto, again turned down the request made by Largo Caballero in the name of the UGT to distribute arms to the workers' organizations. A joint communiqué from the Socialist and Communist parties stated: 'It is a difficult, not a desperate time. The government is sure that it has adequate means to crush this criminal move. Should its means prove inadequate, the Republic has the Popular Front's solemn promise. It is ready to intervene in the struggle as soon as it is asked for help. The government commands and the Popular Front obeys.'

That evening, the CNT and the UGT gave orders for a general strike. At 4 A.M. on 19 July, just as Spain was preparing to fight, Casares Quiroga handed President Azaña his government's resignation.

The Martínez Barrio Government

Azaña immediately appealed to Martínez Barrio, president of the Cortes, who at once formed a government made up exclusively of Republicans, but broadened on the Right with groups of Sánchez Román's National Republicans, till then outside the Popular Front. He appointed a soldier, General Miaja, to the ministry of war.

Historians and commentators are generally agreed in regarding this ministry as a last attempt to avert civil war by reaching agreement with at least one section of the rebel Generals. They agree less about the course of events and even the content of the attempts at compromise. Salvador de Madariaga said that Martínez Barrio had kept posts open for the rebel Generals. Caballero claimed that Martínez Barrio had told him of a telephone conversation with Mola in person; other witnesses, mentioned by Clara Campoamor, also heard Martínez Barrio refer to it. Bertran Güell, the French historian, stated that Mola had peremptorily refused to become minister of war: 'If you and I should reach agreement, both of us will have betrayed our ideals and our men.'[5] Martínez Barrio—today president of the Republic in exile—protested against these versions and stated in a letter to Madariaga: 'At no time did we seek the cooperation of the rebels. We believed that, faced with this change of policy, they too would change their attitude.'[6]

Whether or not the rebel Generals were warned—and it seems clear that they were—the attitudes of some of them seemed to confirm Martínez Barrio's theory and his hopes. Mola himself, Aranda in Oviedo, and Paxtot in Málaga temporized and seemed to waver before burning their bridges, in case Martínez Barrio succeeded and the Republicans specified their concessions. But the announcement of the formation of a new government came as a bombshell even in Madrid. Hundreds of thousands of demonstrators gathered without waiting for the order from any organization and demanded arms to fight the troops. Salvador de Madariaga and Borkenau, who claimed that Caballero was threatening the government with an armed Socialist uprising, agree on this point with Martínez Barrio, in whose view the government 'had perished at the hands of Caballero's Socialists and the Communists.'[7] In his memoirs, Caballero merely suggested that the UGT made the arming of the workers a condition of support for the new government. But Martínez Barrio, like Casares Quiroga, rejected what in his view would mean the beginning of the workers' revolution and the end of the parliamentary Republic. He too resigned.[8]

Among the Republican figures sounded out, only Doctor José Giral, an eminent university professor and friend of Azaña, agreed to take the decisive step: his government would decree the dissolution of the Army and the distribution of arms to the workers' militias formed by the parties and unions. At the same time he signed what seemed to be a reprieve for 'Republican legality' but which was at that date merely the recognition of a *fait accompli*: henceforth it was force, the Generals and their troops against the armed workers, that would control the destiny of Spain. 'Legality,' faced with a clash between social forces, vanished into thin air.

The Movimiento: *Success and Failure*

The rebel leaders had not anticipated long-term resistance to their move. Their plan undoubtedly took into account the special difficulties to be overcome in certain areas, but the map of Spain, as it emerged after several days of fighting, revealed some very unexpected features. Navarre, traditional stronghold of the Carlists, welcomed the movement with enthusiasm. The streets of Burgos and Pamplona were full of volunteers from Carlist paramilitary units, *Requetés* in red berets and green armbands with a cross on them. They came down from the mountains, their rolled blankets over their shoulders, to ensure the victory of 'Christ the King,' as the inscriptions proclaimed. Delaprée observed them 'spitting with disgust when the words "republic" or "union" were mentioned.' He added: 'I would not have been a bit surprised to see an auto-da-fé take place in a Burgos square.'[9] The mass of the people there were for the Generals, and volunteers poured in to strengthen Mola's army in its march on the capital. It was perhaps only the ill-disguised hostility between the 'Red Berets' and the Falange 'Blueshirts' that destroyed the enthusiastic unanimity of this launching of a crusade.

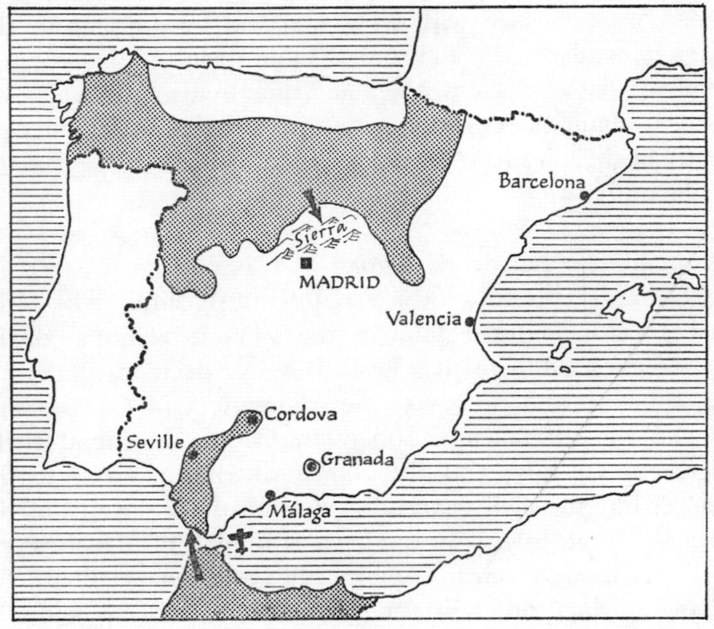

July 1936

But elsewhere success and failure depended on many often unforeseeable factors: the attitude of the police forces, the Civil Guards, and the *Asaltos*, whose adherence to one or the other camp often decided victory, the resolution or vacillation of the civil governors, the boldness or hesitancy of the military commanders, and the vigilance or naïveté of the working-class leaders. In fact, each time that the insurgents made a quick seizure of their enemies' organization, the *Movimiento* very quickly prevailed; it also prevailed, though with some slight delay, each time that the workers' leaders let themselves be duped by protests of loyalty from officers. To this extent, it may reasonably be claimed that the key to the outcome of the early fighting lay less in the actions of the rebels than in the reactions of the workers, parties, and unions and their capacity to organize themselves militarily; in short, in their political outlook. In effect, each time that the workers' organizations allowed themselves to be paralyzed by their anxiety to respect Republican legality and each time that their leaders were satisfied with what was said by the officers, the latter prevailed. On the other hand, the *Movimiento* was repulsed whenever the workers had time to arm and whenever they set about the destruction of the Army as such, independently of their leaders' positions or the attitude of 'legitimate' public authorities.

A Movimiento *Victory: Andalusia*

The insurgents took over rapidly in Algeciras, where the civil governor refused to arm the workers so long as the soldiers declared themselves loyal. When he decided, on the evidence before him, to arrest the commander of the garrison, he was himself taken prisoner. In Cádiz, a general strike began on 19 July, and the *Asaltos* distributed arms to the unions, but the civil governor guaranteed the loyalty of the officers. On 20 July, with the news of the fall of Algeciras and the arrival of a rebel warship, the garrison revolted: the following day, all resistance had been crushed and the military commander banned strikes and union meetings. In Cordova, the civil governor refused to give arms to the striking workers. The Civil Guard and the garrison, on the orders of an allegedly Republican officer, Colonel Cascajó, revolted at the same time and crushed all resistance. In Granada, the *Asaltos* revolted along with the Civil Guard and the garrison: they rapidly put an end to armed resistance in the suburbs. In Huelva, the Governor had assembled the Civil Guard: the Rio Tinto miners, mobilized by their unions, were marching on insurgent Seville. Their Civil Guard escort ambushed and massacred them. Then they went on to acquire the mines.

But the rebels' great victory was the capture of Seville, stronghold of workers' organizations. General Queipo de Llano, whom the government had refused to arrest, arrived incognito in the Andalusian capital, where the commander of the Civil Guard was the only person won over to the plot. In the Civil

Guard barracks, Falangists and volunteer *señoritos* were armed and drafted into units to take part in the uprising. The commando groups thus formed made a surprise attack on the barracks of the *Asaltos*, who held out there and in the telephone exchange until the last round. Meanwhile, a small detachment had seized the Radio Seville transmitter without firing a shot. Queipo had the Republican anthem played over the air and then suddenly announced that he was master of the town. The workers' organizations did not react, whereas the general, master of the art of bluff, occupied strategic points and had the same army trucks driven through the streets again and again to give an impression of overwhelming numerical superiority in the troops under his command. When at last the CNT and the UGT began to assemble their militants for armed struggle, it was too late: the *Asaltos* had been wiped out to the last man, and the first reinforcements of Moroccan soldiers were landing at the airport, which the rebels had seized at the start. Their arrival was evidently a considerable trump card from the military point of view, because the Moors were fearsome, warlike, and disciplined troops. But the clever general also had to be credited with a psychological victory—another one—because the Moors' reputation for cruelty was well known and the rumors of their arrival spread terror. Resistance by the workers began too late and in the worst of circumstances. In Seville, there was not a struggle but a massacre. An account by the College of Lawyers stated that more than 9000 workers were slaughtered.[10] Bertrand de Jouvenel, correspondent of *Paris-Soir*, has described the Moors' attack on a working-class suburb: 'With a fierce war cry, the men charged into the streets of the district. Then came a relentless mopping-up operation with grenades and knives. There was no mercy. When I managed to steal into the ruins the following day, I saw men clutching each other, both of them transfixed by bayonets and long switch knives.' However, the suburb of Triana held out for more than a week. Once Seville had been 'mopped up,' the troops set off to capture other towns and villages. Everywhere the same methods triumphed over fierce and desperate resistance: Morón held out for a week and many rebel soldiers fell at Carmona. But the *Movimiento* was victorious throughout the region. Mass executions of workers and militants sometimes led the hesitant and half-hearted to submit in advance. Often the authorities and the leaders of the Civil Guard took the initiative and, as a sign of adherence to the Army's cause, executed workers' leaders even before the arrival of Queipo's troops. Andalusia was conquered in a few days: by his decisiveness, by a clever use of modern propaganda methods and mass terror, and by means of the radio transmitter and the airport, Queipo de Llano managed to gain an advantage that the workers could not match. Caught napping and bewildered, the militants could only reply, most of the time, with a courage as indomitable as it was futile.

A Movimiento *Victory: Saragossa*

The Army brought off a similar type of victory in Saragossa, another working-class bastion. The commander of the garrison there, General San Miguel Cabanellas, was also the leader of the plot. He was a Freemason, supposedly a Republican, and, like Queipo de Llano, only joined in at the last minute. On 17 July, at the news of the uprising in Morocco, he professed his loyalty to the Republic and proclaimed a state of siege in defiance of 'Fascist moves.' He had to give in to the threat of a general strike brandished by the CNT, but he hastily included Falangists and *señoritos* among his troops. The government begged the workers' leaders not to cause disturbances, refused to arm the workers, and preached calm. At its request, the CNT leaders invited the workers to return home. On the morning of 19 July, a purged Army, strengthened by right-wing militants and the Civil Guard, occupied the capital of Aragon and set up field guns and machine-gun posts. The radio declared: 'We shall not march against the Republic. . . . Workers, your demands will be respected.' The rumor that Cabanellas was marching against the Fascists was skilfully kept in circulation.

Here too the workers' leaders only grasped what was happening to them when the police began to arrest their followers. On 19 July, the CNT and UGT gave orders for a general strike and tried to organize armed resistance in the suburbs, where the troops had not dared to venture. Civil Guards attacked a force organized by the Libertarian Youth and inflicted heavy losses on it. Yet it took more than a week to end the general strike, which the workers' leaders, even under torture, refused to call off. One of the leaders of the Saragossa CNT, Chueca, later recognized the naïveté of the union leaders who had wasted their time on talks and had even believed the governor's promises, and who had been unable to provide for 'anything more effective than the thirty thousand workers organized in the Saragossa unions.'[11] In the course of a few days, nearly the whole of Aragon had fallen into rebel hands.

An Unexpected Success: Oviedo

Mola's plans had not anticipated success in Oviedo, in the heart of working-class Asturias where the Socialist and Anarcho-Syndicalist militants had a strong tradition of combat, experience of armed struggle, trained cadres, and a few weapons. A special, uncensored edition of the Caballerist newspaper *Avance* announced the uprising on the afternoon of 18 July. The miners immediately collected in their union buildings, improvised units, and dug up arms hidden since October 1934. At their prompting, parties and unions set up a Provincial Committee with the task of supporting and controlling the actions of the governor, Liarte Lausin, whose loyalty some suspected.

Colonel Aranda, commander of the garrison, was quick to reassure the working-class and Republican leaders: he proclaimed his loyalty to the Republic and solemnly repudiated the dissidents. However, the previous evening he had arranged for all available arms to be moved to the barracks and had given secret orders to the Civil Guard in the province to march on Oviedo. But this was not known, and he was trusted. Furthermore, when demands for reinforcements came from beleaguered Madrid, the Socialist leaders agreed, on his suggestion, to form three columns of miners and send them to the capital by train. Sixteen hundred young men from Sama de Langreo and several hundred from Mieres joined the crew of *dinamiteros* from Oviedo. Of these 3000 men, commanded by *Asalto* officers, barely 400 had firearms, guns, or rifles. In León, General Gómez Caminero supplied them with 300 guns. The reinforcements meant much to Madrid, but Oviedo had lost its workers' defense.

In spite of the optimism of the Socialist leaders, anxiety increased. Indeed, Aranda had confined the soldiers to barracks, the approaches to which were guarded by sentries. They were known to be armed, whereas the few weapons in the miners' hands were on their way to Madrid. The Provincial Committee split up, with the right-wing Republicans and the Socialists continuing to trust the colonel. But the CNT leaders knew that he had had arms moved to the barracks; with the Communists and left-wing Socialists grouped around Javier Bueno, director of *Avance*, they refused to persist in what they regarded as a dangerous game. They demanded proof of Aranda's loyalty: the distribution of stockpiled weapons to the workers' militias, the opening of the barracks, and the amalgamation of soldiers and armed workers. Aranda equivocated. González Peña begged him to give some guarantee to the extremists and invoked Prieto's authority in order to obtain a distribution of arms. Aranda retorted that he was waiting for orders from the minister of war. All this time the Civil Guards were on the march toward Oviedo. Aranda found an excuse and managed to leave the room in the governor's palace where the Committee was sitting. He then joined his troops, seized Mount Narranco, and trained two field guns on the palace. The Committee dispersed as the soldiers seized strategic points. The colonel's ruse had paid off: the armed miners were far away, and he had occupied the capital without firing a shot. However, the suburbs were alerted and barricades were erected. In the mining villages, groups of Civil Guards were arrested, attacked, and disarmed. The garrison in Gijón revolted too, after proclaiming its loyalty, but it was immediately surrounded by the La Felguera metalworkers, whom the Defense Committee, improvised at the *casa del pueblo* near Segundo Blanco, had summoned to the rescue. Finally, one of the two columns of miners heading for Madrid, informed about the uprising in its rear, turned tail, seized the arsenal in Trubia, and completed the encirclement of the Asturian capital. The capture of Oviedo by the rebels did not lead to the fall of Asturias, but it immobilized tens of thousands of workers, who were in any case almost without arms. Aranda's astuteness and the naïveté of certain leaders detained fighting men whose absence was cruelly felt elsewhere.

A Setback for the Soldiers: The Fleet

Along with these successes, both expected and unexpected, the Generals also experienced some reverses. First there was an accident that deprived them of one of their leaders. Sanjurjo was supposed to be arriving from Estoril, where a plane went to fetch him on 20 July. The propeller broke on landing, the plane caught fire, and Sanjurjo was killed.

But the reverses met with in the rest of Spain were not the result of chance. The mass disembarkation of the Moroccan troops, scheduled in the plan for the hours immediately after the uprising, did not take place, because the fleet had not rallied. Yet its role had been meticulously prepared and thoroughly worked out to the last detail at the time of its maneuvers off the Canaries, during meetings between the Admirals and Franco. The vast majority of the officers supported the *Movimiento*. But it was the crews who made the plan fail: probably better trained politically because of their mainly working-class origins, the sailors knew, at least better than the soldiers, how to organize themselves to oppose the preparations of their leaders. On nearly all the ships small clandestine cells were formed, made up of some eight to ten NCOs and Socialist or Anarchist sailors, maintaining links with their organizations in ports of call. There was a Central Council of sailors on the cruiser *Libertad*. Alerted by it, delegates from Councils on the *Cervantes*, the *Almirante Cervera*, the *España*, and the *Velasco* were able to meet it in Ferrol on 13 July to decide on what steps to take against the Admirals' uprising. On the fourteenth they managed to establish contact with the Sailors' Council on the *Jaime I.* In Madrid, Balbao, an NCO attached to the Naval Broadcasting Center, arrested the head of the center, one of the mainsprings of the conspiracy. Through him and through the radio transmitters on each ship, the crews were given minute-by-minute information as to how the plot was taking shape and stood by to hit back at their commanders.

The crew of the destroyer *Churruca*, which had taken a *tabor* of Moroccans to Cádiz on the nineteenth, revolted on the twentieth and shot its officers. Then the crews of the *Almirante Valdés* and the *Sánchez Barcáiztegui* followed suit and left Melilla for Cartagena. In San Fernando, the crews of two gunboats and a cruiser were eventually crippled by coastal batteries, and the *Almirante Cervera*, immobilized by repairs, and the *España*, out of ammunition, were recaptured from the sailors by the rebels in Ferrol. But the crew of the *Jaime I*, informed by radio that their ship was making for Ceuta, mutinied at sea, winning control of the cruiser after a bloody struggle. Then they rejoined the main part of the fleet, whose history those few days had been identical with their own, in the Bay of Tangier. Everywhere Sailors' Committees were in control; after executing the majority of their officers, they forced those who remained to serve under their orders. Instead of ensuring communications and the arrival of reinforcements from Morocco, the warships prevented them from landing. The action of the sailors, by giving a serious jolt to the Generals' plan, thus emerged as one of the most important events in the early days of the uprising.[12]

A Movimiento *Defeat: Barcelona*

In Barcelona the soldiers suffered their greatest defeat, inflicted by the Catalan workers, who were helped, it is true, by support from the Civil Guard and the *Guardia de Asaltos* at the crucial moment. Thus it was the workers who emerged victorious from the days of fighting, even though the Republican bourgeoisie, because of its autonomism, had adopted a more determinedly hostile attitude to the soldiers here than in the rest of Spain.

In the preceding days, the CNT leaders had in fact maintained almost permanent contact with the Generalidad and the leaders of the Esquerra: the Anarchist leader Diego Abad de Santillán later recalled 'nights spent at the ministry of the interior.' However, they had not received the arms they had requested. Santillán, who had asked for a mere thousand rifles to be issued to the men of the CNT, wrote: 'The thousand guns were not given to us: on the contrary, some of the ones our men had seized were taken away from us.'[13] During the afternoon of the eighteenth, the militants seized everything that they could find, from shotguns in shops to dynamite from the dockyards. On the night of 18–19 July, groups of Anarchist dock workers made off with all the arms from the ships in the harbor. Their leaders, Durruti and García Oliver, were quick to intervene personally at the risk of being lynched by their own supporters, in order to avoid any incident between the police and the workers, even agreeing to hand back some of the arms seized by the dock workers.

However, some *Asaltos* distributed arms taken from the racks in their barracks to groups of workers. Day and night the workers mounted guard on their offices and headquarters.

The insurgents' plan, to be supervised by Goded, who had arrived by plane from Majorca and who immediately had the Republican officers arrested, was carried out to the last detail. For several weeks young volunteers, *señoritos* and Falangists, had flocked to the *Asaltos*. On an agreed signal, the 12,000 men from the barracks were to converge on the Plaza de Cataluña in the town center. At dawn on the nineteenth, the troops from the Pedralbes barracks set off. All over the town, after another night of vigil, the workers, armed with makeshift weapons, lay in wait for them. The units from the Atarazanas barracks who were occupying the military government and the *Capitanía General* remained in their buildings for the time being.

But for the Barcelona workers, who were in the majority, this was the moment of reckoning, long dreaded yet finally eagerly anticipated. They hurried from Barceloneta and the harbor areas to bar the way to the insurgents. Ill-armed, even empty-handed, without any central control, they had only one tactic, which was to surge forward, suffering heavy losses. But the dead and wounded were at once replaced and the soldiers overwhelmed by the crowd. The workers' militants were in the front ranks and fell by the dozen. The secretary of the Catalan JSU, Francisco Graells, the secretary of the POUM Youth, Germinal Vidal, and the secretary of the Anarchist groups in Barcelona fell in the Plaza de Cataluña, where the insurgents occupied the most important buildings, the Hotel Colón, the Telefónica, and the Eldorado. There they were subjected to a genuine siege: courage was as contagious as fear, and the calculations of regular soldiers melted before a crowd that was not afraid of death and in the face of masses who exposed themselves to the fire of machine guns and made off with them, leaving hundreds of corpses in the squares and streets.

In the early afternoon, Colonel Escobar of the Civil Guard—Colonel Ximenes in André Malraux's *L'Espoir*—reinforced the workers with 4000 regular soldiers. The Hotel Colón was stormed and the Ritz fell immediately afterwards. It was at this point that news came of the rallying of several units to 'the people's cause' and of the Loyalist victory at the Prat airport, led by a Republican officer, Lieutenant-Colonel Díaz Sandino. The men of the CNT recaptured the Telefónica. The fighting continued, but the uprising had taken a fearsome hammering, and here and there the soldiers were mutinying more and more frequently.

On the morning of Monday 20 July, field guns produced from nowhere, taken by storm or yielded up by the soldiers, were trained on the *Capitanía General*. A temporary officer and former gunner, the dock worker Lecha, was in command of the bombardment. Resistance seemed futile: General Goded hoisted the white flag just as the assailants, commanded by a former officer, Pérez Farras, entered the building. Most of the besieged officers were massacred on the spot; Goded, rescued with some difficulty from popular anger,[14] was led to the Generalidad where, at the president's request, he agreed to make a statement over the radio: 'I wish to inform the Spanish people that fate has been against me. I am a prisoner.

I say this for all those who do not wish to continue the struggle. From now on they are relieved of any commitment to me.'[15]

The game was now up. In many barracks the soldiers mutinied. In Fort Montjuich, they shot their officers and then distributed arms to the workers. Elsewhere the officers preferred to take their own lives. The Atarazanas barracks was the last to fall. It was bombed by the few planes at Díaz Sandino's disposal, but it was finally taken in an onslaught in which Francisco Ascaso met his death. For a long time afterward, fighters, before leaving for the front, filed past the place where the Anarchist militant had fallen, symbol of all those who had given their lives during these three days.

A Setback for the Movimiento*: Madrid*

On the eighteenth, the CNT in Madrid, on a war footing ever since the building strike, decided to use force to reopen its offices closed by the police and began to requisition cars and search for arms. David Antona, secretary of its National Committee, was freed on the morning of 19 July; he went to the ministry of the interior and threatened to send his men to attack the prisons and release the militants who were still imprisoned there. The two big unions gave orders for a general strike. In the UGT offices, Carlos de Baráibar very hurriedly set up an information center with the help of post-office workers and railroad workers from all over the country, which would enable Madrid to know, minute by minute, the precise situation in the provinces. The Socialists had unearthed and distributed arms kept hidden since 1934. In the streets the first barricades were erected. The first shots were exchanged with strangers who fired from a convent in the Rua de Torrijos. The first workers' militias were already on patrol, even though nothing had stirred in the barracks.

In fact, the soldiers were losing precious time.

No attack came during the day of the nineteenth from regiments still entirely controlled by the conspirators. Pardo's regiment had revolted and had immediately left the capital for the North, presumably to meet Mola. In Getafe, there was fighting between rebels and Loyalists in the artillery barracks. In all the units, the rebels first attacked the officers hostile to the *Movimiento*: in this way Lieutenant-Colonel Carratala, Prieto's personal friend, was murdered. The rebels' stronghold was in the Montaña barracks; this contained the military leader of the conspiracy, General Fanjul, around whom were collected officers from other units, *señoritos*, and Falangists. But either because he was wavering or because he was waiting for reinforcements, Fanjul wasted time: he harangued his supporters and proclaimed a state of siege. By the end of the day, relinquishing the idea of a sally, he gave orders to fire on the crowd massed on the approaches to the Montaña, an open provocation, which aroused popular anger. Meanwhile, a loyal officer, Lieutenant-Colonel Gil, was distributing 5000 rifles in the Artillery Park: many of them had no bolts, because the rebels had wisely stripped them and removed them to the Montaña.

It was only on the twentieth that the decisive fighting began. Loudspeakers broadcast the news of the Barcelona victories and Goded's surrender throughout the streets. The insurgents were ultimately forced onto the defensive. Two 75-mm field guns and then a 155-mm began to shell the barracks. Reinforcements of planes soon arrived from the airport at Cuatro Vientos, where the rebellion had been crushed. About 10 A.M., the besieged men hoisted the white flag. The crowd surged forward and was mowed down by machine-gun fire. Anger mounted at what seemed to be a betrayal. Yet the same scene was repeated twice, in reality reflecting the struggle that was going on inside the barracks. In spite of the loyal officers present, who thought that the Air Force and the artillery were enough to force Fanjul's men to surrender, the assailants launched a mass attack and stormed the barracks, at the cost of heavy casualties. Fanjul and some officers, protected by a detachment of *Asaltos*, were locked into an armored car and taken away, but almost all the besieged were killed on the spot, while the workers shared out the arms of the defeated.

The following day, the people put the finishing touches to their victory. While small detachments were mopping up the streets of Madrid, chasing the *pacos*, isolated snipers who were still hanging on in churches, convents, and on rooftops, improvised columns set off all around the capital for Guadalajara, where the garrison had revolted. They captured it, shot General Barrera, and marched on Toledo, which they also seized, while the insurgents took refuge in the ancient fortress, the Alcázar. Then they marched on Cuenca, which Cipriano Mera, the building worker released from prison two days earlier, recaptured with 800 men and a machine gun, and finally on Alcalá with Antonio and Mora. These columns and others, hastily formed, marched on the sierra to meet Mola, toward Aragon in the direction of Sigüenza, and toward Valencia and Málaga. The war had begun.

A Setback for the Movimiento: *Málaga*

The vacillations of the Madrid insurgents had given the workers time to get organized. A mistake that was perhaps more serious, breaking off an engagement already begun, brought them a grave setback in Málaga, an important place for communications with Morocco. The forces of the military seemed overwhelming. Only the *Asaltos* were hostile to the uprising. The workers had no arms. The move began on 17 July: at the head of a company, Captain Huelin marched on the military government and ran into the *Asaltos*. The colonel in command of the Civil Guard was arrested by his men just as he was trying to get them to revolt. At 8 P.M., on General Paxtot's orders, the troops left the barracks and seized the center of the town. But the next day the general gave the order to retreat, and the troops returned to their barracks. Was he short of information about the uprising in the rest of the country and afraid of advancing too far and becoming isolated? Or was it, as Martínez Barrio himself suggested, and as Foss and Gerahty claimed, the formation of Martínez Barrio's government and the hope of an agreement that made him draw back? In any case, the workers' organizations seized the proffered opportunity. The workers, who had no arms, set fire to the houses surrounding the barracks and then sprayed them with dynamite. Smoked out, encircled, and faced with the prospect of being burned to death, the soldiers surrendered to the *Asaltos*: Captain Huelin was lynched by the crowd.

A Setback for the Movimiento: *The Basque Provinces*

The hesitancy of the rebels also explains their defeat in the Basque provinces. The garrison in Bilbao did not make a move. The one in Santander was surrounded on the spot. The general supposed to be in command of the uprising in Guipúzcoa slipped away at the last moment. Moreover, the Basque Nationalists, in a radio appeal by Manuel de Irujo on 18 July and then in an official party communiqué on the following day, threw their authority in the balance and called on their supporters to fight for the defense of the Republic.

In San Sebastián, Colonel Carrasco assured the Popular Front Committee of his loyalty, and the Basque Nationalist deputies came and interrogated him. But the Loyola barracks revolted on the orders of Lieutenant-Colonel Vallespín. Carrasco promised to bring the garrison to heel and sent his aide-de-camp, who did not return. He therefore decided to go to the barracks in person. The deputies agreed. He did not return either. The Civil Guards, who had, until then, declared themselves Loyalists, also revolted on the twenty-first with the officers they had arrested and attacked the CNT offices. But the workers had mobilized. The town was protected with barricades. The Civil Guards cracked in front of the CNT and fell back on the María Cristina Hotel, which was taken by the workers on the twenty-third. The Loyola barracks, shelled by an armored train, also surrendered on the twenty-eighth, after negotiations between the officers and the Basque Nationalist deputies, who did not however succeed in having the promises they had made respected: the majority of the leaders of the *Movimiento* were shot on the spot. Colonel Carraso, taken prisoner, was kidnapped two days later and shot without a trial.

In Valencia: The Garrison Does Not Revolt

Valencia was a law unto itself: the soldiers in its garrison did not revolt. Nor, for all that, did they join the Revolution.

The first rumors of the uprising reached the capital of the Levante in the afternoon of 18 July. The governor refused to distribute arms to the unions and gave assurances that the leaders of the garrison were above suspicion. During the night of 18–19 July, the workers' organizations and the Republican parties mobilized their supporters. The CNT and the UGT gave orders for a general strike from midnight on the nineteenth. The first incident took place in the evening: some building workers attacked a convent of Dominicans suspected of sheltering an arms depot.

On the morning of the twentieth, the CNT Strike Committee gave its militants orders to block the approaches to the barracks. The Popular Front parties set up a Revolutionary Committee to which they invited delegates from the CNT Strike Committee. The governor was still wavering. A Civil Guard officer, Captain Uríbarri, a Socialist, took command of those who wanted to force his hand and prevent the barracks from rebelling. The CNT delegates put conditions to the Popular Front in return for their support: they wanted the mobilization of the workers' forces around the barracks, an immediate 'amalgamation' of Loyalist troops and workers through the formation of 'intervention groups' on the basis of one *Asalto* to two militants, the occupation of all strategic points (post office, telephone exchange, Radio Valencia) by these units, the dispatch of an ultimatum to the garrison, and an immediate assault on the barracks should the Generals refuse to hand over their arms. The Committee accepted the CNT's proposals and turned itself into a 'People's Executive Committee.' But General Martínez Monje refused to distribute arms, demanded the end of the general strike, which in his view had no justification, since he and his men remained loyal to the government, and made this public knowledge in a communiqué broadcast by Radio Valencia. Yet the troops remained on standby. The general impression was that the Army was wavering: the conspirators knew that the insurgents had been defeated in Barcelona and in Madrid and in any case were now concerned with playing for time. In the towns, skirmishes between workers and Falangists and attacks on convents and churches increased. Sailors from warships anchored in the harbor rose up against their officers and fraternized with the dock workers. It was at this point that Martínez Barrio and three other Republican leaders, Ruiz Funes, Esplá, and Echevarría, armed with a delegation of authority from the Giral government, arrived in Valencia. Three distinct powers confronted each other in a revolutionary atmosphere for another two weeks: the Army, Martínez Barrio's Provincial Junta, and the Popular Executive Committee. The assault on the barracks, which in most of Spain occurred between 18 and 21 July, did not take place in Valencia until the beginning of August.

The Situation on the Evening of 20 July

By the evening of 20 July, except in Valencia, attitudes had hardened. Fighting naturally continued on the barricades and in the streets of Corunna, where the workers battled with cobblestones; in the suburbs of Saragossa and Seville; around the various barracks; in San Sebastián, Gijón, and Santander; near Algeciras, where rebel detachments had just landed; and wherever isolated snipers from either camp were pursuing a desperate struggle. However, these were on the whole only mopping-up operations. Each camp now had its own territory and was completing the work of pacification.

Franco wired an actual victory bulletin to Queipo: 'Spain is saved: the provinces of Andalusia, Valencia, Valladolid, Burgos, Aragon, the Canaries, and the Balearics have joined us.' The general was very optimistic. In fact the *pronunciamiento* as such had failed. Not only had the rebels suffered terrible reverses, but they had kindled the workers' revolution that their action had been intended to prevent. One by one, they had lost some of their most highly regarded and ablest leaders, Calvo Sotelo, Sanjurjo, Goded, and José Antonio Primo de Rivera,[16] killed by militiamen in Alicante Prison. Above all, their defeats, by destroying the legend of the Army's invincibility in civil clashes, had deprived them of their major trump card, fear. Now they were no longer pitted against a weak Popular Front government, but against a revolution. The *pronunciamiento* had failed. The Civil War had begun.

Notes

[1] Wages were increased 5 percent for those below twelve pesetas and 10 percent for the rest, and a forty-hour week was granted. The CNT was demanding, besides a larger raise, a thirty-six-hour week, a one-month paid vacation, and the recognition of work-related illnesses, including rheumatism.

[2] In Málaga, the conflict had pitted CNT militants from the striking fish salters against the UGT fishermen. On 10 June, the former had assassinated Andrés Rodríguez, a UGT leader. An attack on the CNT leader, Ortíz Acevedo, cost the life of one of his children. On the eleventh, before Rodríguez's funeral, a Socialist, Ramón Reina, was shot. The governor had the offices of both unions closed. It was only on the fifteenth that violence ceased, with both the CNT and the UGT condemning the attacks.

[3] A. de Lizarra, *Los vascos y la República española* (Buenos Aires: Vasca Ekin, 1944), p. 31.

[4] Captain Bebb, hired by the well-known engineer Juan de la Cierva.

[5] Bertran Güell, *Journal d'un expatrié catalan* (Monaco: Editions du Rocher, 1946), p. 76.

[6] Preface to Salvador de Madariaga's *España*, 4th ed. (Buenos Aires: Sudamericana, 1950). (English translation: *Spain* [London: Ernest Benn, 1930].)

[7] Ibid.

[8] In a radio speech on the first anniversary of the *Movimiento*, Franco stated that Martínez Barrio wanted to 'form a ministry that would back the Army, reestablish law and order, and obtain the withdrawal of troops.' According to him, this ministry 'was betrayed by the criminal hordes that its predecessors had armed.' *Franco ha dicho . . .* (Madrid: n.p., 1947).

[9] Louis Delaprée, *Mort en Espagne* (Paris: Pierre Tisné, 1937), p. 22.

[10] Account reprinted by José Peirats in *La CNT en la Revolución española*, 3 vols. (Toulouse: Ediciones CNT, 1951–1953), 1:182–186.

[11] 'Le 19 juillet en Aragon,' in *Dans la tourmente* (Paris: Bureau d'Information et de Presse, 1938), p. 71. (Translation of *De julio a julio* [Barcelona: Tierra y Libertad, 1937].)

[12] See the report by the German chargé d'affaires, Voelckers, dated 23 September 1936: 'The defection of the Navy was the first thing that upset Franco's plans. This was a very serious failure of organization. It threatened the entire scheme with collapse, and it made a futile sacrifice of the garrisons in the big towns, who were vainly waiting for orders, arms at the ready. Above all, it wasted valuable time.' *Documents on German Foreign Policy, 1918–1945*, Series D (1937–1945), vol. 3, *Germany and the Spanish Civil War, 1936–1939* (Washington, D.C.: Government Printing Office, 1950).

[13] Santillán, *Por qué perdimos la guerra* (Buenos Aires: Imán, 1940).

[14] Through an irony of history, it was—according to *La Dépêche de Toulouse*, 26 July 1936—the Communist militant Caridad Mercader who had saved General Goded's life in these circumstances. It is generally accepted today that this woman was involved in the murder of Trotsky by the NKVD agent Jacson-Mornard, who was in fact her son, Ramón Mercader.

[15] Companys, after his defeat in 1934, had made a similar statement over the radio.

[16] José Antonio Primo de Rivera was judged by a popular tribunal before which he defended himself unhesitatingly, even with brio. He was sentenced to death and executed on 18 November 1936. Beforehand, the Republican Cabinet had examined a proposal brought by the Exchange Red Cross from the Falangist leader to Largo Caballero's son, Paco Largo Calvo. Largo Caballero opted to refuse the Nationalist proposal.

CHAPTER 5

DUAL POWER IN REPUBLICAN SPAIN

In places where the uprising had been crushed, it was not alone in suffering defeat. The state, caught between its insurgent Army and the armed masses of the people, had shattered to pieces. Authority had literally crumbled away, and wherever the soldiers had been overwhelmed, it had passed into the streets, where armed groups dealt summarily with the most urgent tasks: the fight against the remaining pockets of resistance, the purging of the rear, and survival. The Republican government was of course still in existence, and no revolutionary authority had come forward as an avowed rival to it in the zone that left-wing correspondents were very soon calling the Loyalist zone. But the authority of Giral's Cabinet did not extend far beyond the outskirts of Madrid, and it survived there less because of its own activities and prestige than because of the workers' organizations: the UGT, whose information and communication system alone maintained the government's links with the remaining Loyalist areas; and the Socialist party, whose executive was in permanent session at the ministry of the Navy, where Prieto, minister without portfolio, was installed.

However, in between the streets and the government there gradually emerged new organs of power that enjoyed real authority, often claiming kinship with the former as much as with the latter. These were the countless local Committees, virtual governments on a regional and provincial scale. In them was invested the new power, the revolutionary power that was being organized at full speed to deal with the enormous tasks, one immediate and the other long-term, of pursuing the war and resuming production at the height of a social revolution.

To the foreign journalists and militants who crossed the frontier, lured by the crisis, Spain provided an unusual sight, both confused and confusing, but always colorful. She was the scene of a revolution that the Generals had meant to forestall but had in the end provoked. At first defensive, it had become offensive and aggressive. A spontaneous reaction, deriving from thousands of local initiatives, it also wore a thousand forms, in which superficial and hostile observers saw nothing but anarchy and chaos and failed to grasp its deeper meaning: the workers' adoption of responsibility for their own defense and consequently for their own fate, the birth of a new power.

Barcelona symbolized this revolutionary situation. To Franz Borkenau, an expert observer, it was the 'bastion of soviet Spain'—in the original sense of the word—the Spain of Councils and Workers' Committees. It was in fact not only a city exclusively inhabited by workers, but also one where the workers had power: they were everywhere to be seen, in the streets, in front of the buildings, and on the *Ramblas*, rifles slung across their backs and revolvers stuck in their belts, wearing their working clothes.[1] No sign of the Civil Guard's two-cornered hats, very few uniforms, no bourgeoisie and no *señoritos*: the Generalidad had, it was said, 'discouraged' the wearing of hats. No more nightclubs, restaurants, or luxury hotels: requisitioned by workers' organizations, they were used as popular eating places. The usual beggars had disappeared, taken care of by the unions' welfare system. All cars bore the flags, emblems, and initials of workers' organizations. Everywhere, on buildings, cafés, shops, factories, streetcars, and trucks, were notices saying that the business had been 'collectivized by the people' or that it 'belonged to the CNT.' Parties and unions were established in large modern buildings, hotels or headquarters of right-wing organizations. Each organization had its daily newspaper and its radio transmitter. Apart from the cathedral, which was closed, all the churches had been fired. The Civil War continued, claiming fresh victims nightly. 'The Ramblas,' wrote Bloch, 'have gone on living at a twofold rhythm. The Ramblas by day are full of flowers, birds, strollers, cafés, automobiles, and streetcars. By dusk, the flower stalls have vanished, the bird sellers are far away, the cafés are shut. The Ramblas by night means the reign of silence and fear and a few furtive shadows stealing along walls.'[2]

Madrid, a few days later, presented a different scene to visitors from France. Here too, of course, unions and parties were established in fine buildings and had organized their own militias, but there were few armed workers in the streets and nearly all were in the new uniform, the *mono*, a blue coverall. The old uniforms had not disappeared; on 27 July the official police resumed their normal duties. All the churches were closed, but by no means all of them had been fired. There were fewer Committees, few signs of expropriation. The usual beggars held out their hands at street corners. Smart restaurants and nightclubs were operating as before. The war, close at hand, had halted the course of the Revolution.

Between these two extremes, Republican Spain provided a whole range of variations, differing from one town and from one province to the next. A detailed analysis will make these clearer.

The Power of the Armed Groups

There was at any rate one feature that was common to the whole of Republican Spain and that especially attracted the notice of foreign observers at this point. This was what the influential foreign press of the time called 'Anarchist terror' or 'Red terror.' On the actual day of victory the armed workers launched a bloody purge.

Moreover, everything was ripe for such an explosion, prepared for by six months of daily excitement and violence. The struggle, feared and desired, released and unleashed accumulated hatred and terror. Every man was fighting in the knowledge that there was no other outcome than victory or death and that the road to victory led first of all past the graves of his enemies.

In Republican Spain, there were no longer practically any

forces for the preservation of law and order, no police force. Their members had gone over to the ranks of the insurgents or had merged with those of the combatants. Everywhere, beginning on the eighteenth or nineteenth, there was a general strike, which lasted for at least another week: the workers were out in the streets from morning to night, weapons in hand. In the early days, only the militants had been armed. But after the barracks had been captured and arms distributed, anyone who wished to had a weapon: some tens of thousands of rifles had been distributed everywhere, in Madrid, in Barcelona, in San Sebastián, and in Málaga. The doors of the prisons had been opened for political prisoners, but often for common criminals too. When there are no police about, when anyone can carry arms without attracting attention, the riffraff has a field day.

Thus the terror that every observer described was a complex phenomenon, several of whose factors they confused, often by design. Initially there was without question a spontaneous movement, a veritable mass terrorism, given the number of killers and victims alike. A reflex born of fear, a defensive reaction to danger like the one that led to the September massacres in the French Revolution, it answered the demands as well as the inevitabilities of the revolutionary war.

Officers, Civil Guards, Falangists and *señoritos* were killed on the spot whenever there was no authoritative militant well-known enough or police unit loyal enough to stop the chase and protect the victims.

Alarmist rumors and collective anxieties gave rise to other massacres: at the news of massacres in Badajoz by rebel troops, and believing that the prisoners had mutinied, the Madrid mob seized the Model Prison. Exasperated by the bombing raids on 27 July, in the atmosphere of unhealthy suspicion created by Queipo de Llano's speeches on Radio Seville, the mob seized the prison in Málaga and executed the rebel prisoners inside. In the same way, terror became both a means of prevention and a spur to revolutionary action. The columns of militiamen that arrived in villages recaptured from the rebels, anxious to push on, knew no other means of securing their rear than systematic mopping-up operations and the immediate liquidation, without trial, of class enemies conveniently dubbed 'Fascists.' On its arrival in Fraga, the Durruti column executed thirty-eight such Fascists: the priest and the big landowner, the lawyer and his son, and all the rich peasants. In the view of some people, the conditions for a genuine revolution were created by the disappearance of members of the ruling classes from the old regime. Here too terror was inseparable from civil war and revolution.

Similar reactions, though more organized, threatened the towns with *paseos* in the weeks after the uprising. *Paseos* always took place along the same sinister lines: the victim, singled out by a Defense or Watch committee, was arrested at night in his home by armed men, driven outside the town, and killed in some remote spot. In this way victims of actual political reckonings perished along with priests, large and small employers, politicians, members of the bourgeoisie, and reactionaries: all those who at one time or another had fallen out with a workers' organization—judges, policemen, prison warders, informers, torturers, *pistoleros*, or simply anyone whose political reputation or social position singled him out in advance as a victim. Moreover, the 'class frontier' did not always mean adequate protection: thus, in Barcelona, workers' militants were killed, such as the general secretary of the UGT dock workers, the Communist Desiderio Trillas, denounced by the CNT as the 'cacique of the docks,' and the head of the UGT union in the Hispano-Suiza factory.

Such an atmosphere naturally lent itself to personal vendettas as well as acts of pure and simple banditry, pillage, and common murder. It was probably because of their increase that parties and unions, having organized *paseos*, turned against them and began to 'organize' the repression. Since tradition lays responsibility for the majority of the crimes at the feet of the Anarchists, it must in fairness be pointed out that it was one of them, the not unimportant Juan Peiró, who in *Libertad* was always denouncing crimes committed 'by taking refuge behind the revolutionary movement . . . by sheltering behind the impunity created by the atmosphere,' and who stressed the need, 'in the name of revolutionary honor,' to 'have done with that regular nightly *danse macabre*, that procession of the dead,' and 'those who kill for the sake of killing.'[3] The Barcelona CNT set the example by having one of its militants, Fernández, general secretary of the catering union, who was guilty of settling a personal vendetta during this period, executed on the spot.[4]

Terror Against the Catholic Church

The burning and sacking of convents and churches and the arrests and executions of priests and clergy that characterized the early days must be seen in a different light. It has been said—and it is largely true—that this was often a question of reprisals: in Barcelona many insurgents barricaded themselves in the churches, in Figueras the priests fired on workers from the cathedral, and everywhere *pacos*, isolated snipers, benefited from complicity with religious institutions.

But the movement against the Catholic Church went deeper than a simple reaction during the confusion. There were of course a few churches pillaged by common thieves. But most of the time it was these treasures that financed the early revolutionary activities: in this way the militiamen in Gerona seized 16 million pesetas' worth of jewels from the bishop's palace in Vich and handed them over to the Central Committee.

In actual fact, frequent spectacular demonstrations, such as gruesome exhumations of corpses and skeletons, showed that such actions—which went far beyond simple reprisals—derived from an urge to reach back into the past to attack a force regarded by the revolutionaries as their worst enemy. By shooting priests and firing churches, the Spanish workers and peasants were not merely seeking to destroy their enemies and the symbol of their power but to rid Spain once and for all of everything that, in their view, stood for obscurantism and oppression. A fervent Catholic, the Basque minister Manuel de Irujo, confirmed such an interpretation when he stated: 'Those who burn churches are not thereby exhibiting anti-religious feelings; it is just a question of a demonstration against the state, and, if I may say so, the smoke rising to the sky is merely a sort of appeal to God in the face of human injustice.'[5]

The Power of the Committees

The French trade unionist Robert Louzon gave this description[6] of the sight that greeted visitors from France in early August:

'As soon as you cross the frontier, you are halted by armed men. Who are these men? Workers. They are militiamen—that is, workers wearing their normal clothes—but armed with rifles or revolvers and with signs on their arms indicating their functions or the power they represent. . . . They are the ones who . . . will decide . . . not to let you in, or to refer it to the "Committee."

'The Committee is the group of men who are in charge over in the next village and who exercise complete power there. It is the Committee who see to the normal municipal functions, who formed the local militia, armed it, and supplied it with food and lodging from funds raised by a levy imposed on all the inhabitants. They are the ones who give you permission to enter or leave the town, who closed down the Fascist shops and who carry out essential requisitions. They had the interiors of the churches demolished so that, according to the notices displayed on all of them, the churches, now the "Generalidad's property," could be used for popular establishments.'

In all the towns and most of the villages in Spain, similar Committees were operating under various names: Popular Committees, War and Defense Committees, Executive, Revolutionary, or Antifascist Committees, Workers' Committees, and Committees of Public Safety. All had been set up in the heat of action to direct the popular response to the military coup d'état. They had been appointed in an infinite number of ways. In the villages, the factories, and on the work sites, time had sometimes been taken to elect them, at least summarily, at a general meeting. At all events, care had been taken to see that all parties and unions were represented on them, even if they did not exist before the Revolution, because the Committee represented at one and the same time as the workers a whole and the sum total of their organizations: in more than one place those elected 'came to an understanding' as to who was to represent one or another union, who would be the 'Republican' and who the 'Socialist.' Very often, in the towns, the most active elements appointed themselves. It was sometimes the electors as a whole who chose the men to sit on the Committee of each organization, but more often the members of the Committee were elected either by a vote within their own organization or were quite simply appointed by the local governing committees of the parties and unions. It was rare for the Committees to have their composition endorsed by a broader vote once they had been appointed: however, the Revolutionary Committee in Lérida ratified itself by means of a 'constituent assembly' made up of representatives of the town's party and union organizations, to which it was accountable. But the 'base' had real control only over the Village or Business Committees. On the higher levels, the will of the organizations prevailed.

Representation of parties and unions on the Committees varied from one place to the next. Often the Popular Front Committee was simply broadened with representatives from the various unions. Sometimes—where the municipalities were Socialist ones—the municipal council, expanded by co-opting CNT leaders, became the Committee. In Catalonia, and soon afterward in recaptured Aragon, many Committees were made up exclusively of militants from the CNT–FAI or the Libertarian Youth: however, those from the towns included representatives from the UGT, the Esquerra, the PSUC, and the POUM, along with those from the CNT and the FAI. However, in Lérida, the POUM saw to it that the Republicans, who had supported the commissioner of the Generalidad against the unions, were expelled from the Committee, which was thus confined to the workers' organizations alone. The representation of the different groups was sometimes equal and sometimes proportional. But it more often corresponded to the balance of real power within industry. The Socialists were in the ascendancy in Santander, Mieres, and Sama de Langreo, but each mining locality had its own political complexion. The Basque Nationalists shared the Bilbao Junta with the Socialists but were in control of all the other Juntas in the North. The Anarchists were masters of Gijón and Cuenca. In Málaga, Socialists and Communists, represented through the UGT, were gradually winning ascendancy over the CNT. In Valencia, the unions had two delegates, whereas the parties had only one. In Castellón, the CNT had fourteen representatives and the UGT seven, the Socialists and Communists had no actual representation, but the Republicans and the POUM had seven delegates each. In Catalonia the CNT–FAI controlled the Committees in the big towns except for Sabadell and Lérida.[7]

All the Committees, whatever their differences in name, origin, and composition, had one basic feature in common. All of them, in the days after the uprising, had seized all local power, taking over legislative as well as executive functions, making categorical decisions in their areas, not only about immediate problems, such as the maintenance of law and order and the control of prices, but also about the revolutionary tasks of the moment, the socialization or unionization of industry, the expropriation of the property of the clergy, the 'factionists,' or simply the big landowners, the distribution of land to the metalworkers or its collective development, the confiscation of bank accounts, the municipalization of lodgings, the organization of information, written or spoken, education, and welfare. To take up G. Munis's striking term, everywhere 'Government Committees' were set up, whose authority was based on the force of armed workers and which the rest of the specialist bodies in the old state—Civil Guards here and there, *Asaltos*, and various officials—obeyed, whether they liked it or not. No greater homage was paid to the authority of the Committees in this respect than the testimony of one of their most resolute opponents of the time, Jesús Hernández, leader of the Spanish Communist party: 'The Committee was a disturbing, shadowy, intangible kind of power, without distinct functions or express authority, but which, in an unrelenting dictatorship, wielded indisputable power, like a real government.'[8]

However, what was true on a local level was not entirely so on a regional level, where authorities of various origins were either at variance or coexisted with each other.

The Antifascist Militias Committee in Catalonia

ORIGINS

On 21 July, after the fighting in Barcelona, the revolutionaries, in control of the streets, were summoned to the palace of the Generalidad. Santillán, the Anarchist leader, described the incident: 'We went to the seat of the Catalan government, clutching our weapons, not having slept for several days, unshaven, confirming by our appearance the legend that had formed about us. Some members of the autonomous regional government were trembling, white-faced, at this interview from which Ascaso was missing. The government palace was invaded by the escort of combatants who had accompanied us.'[9] President Companys congratulated them on their victory: 'You are masters of the town and of Catalonia, because you defeated the Fascist soldiers on your own. . . . You have won and everything is in your power. If you do not need me, if you do not want me as president, say so now, and I shall become just another soldier in the antifascist struggle. If, on the other hand, you believe me when I say that I shall yield this post to victorious Fascism only when I am dead, then perhaps with my party comrades, my name, and my prestige, I can be of use to you. . . .'[10]

The president undoubtedly had little choice. As his deputy Miravittles wrote, a few weeks later: 'The Antifascist Militias Committee came into existence two or three days after the movement, in the absence of any regular public force and because there was no army in Barcelona. Another reason was that there was no Civil Guard and no *Guardia de Asaltos*, because they had all fought so ardently, united with the forces of the people, that they now formed part of the same mass and remained closely linked with them.'[11]

The real power was held by the armed workers and the organization Committees in the streets of Barcelona and by the Government Committees in the towns and villages. The Socialists and Communists, according to Comorera, suggested to the president the formation of 'Generalidad militias,' which would vie for the streets against the men of the CNT and the

POUM.[12] Companys did not heed them: to him the fight seemed too unequal, and at that stage his person, his 'name and prestige,' as he said, were in fact all that survived of the Republican state in Catalonia. The fate of the state and its hopes of restoration in the ensuing months depended on the acceptance or refusal of his services. As it turned out, the leaders of the CNT agreed to go on with the collaboration. The previous day, after a lively discussion, the Regional Committee had stated: *No hay comunismo libertario, primero aplastamos a la facción.* (There is no Libertarian Communism; let us first destroy the faction.) They agreed to Companys's offer. This is how Santillán commented on their decision:[13]

> 'We could have remained alone, imposed our absolute will, declared the Generalidad null and void, and imposed the true power of the people in its place, but we did not believe in dictatorship when it was being exercised against us, and we did not want it when we could exercise it ourselves only at the expense of others. The Generalidad would remain in force with President Companys at its head, and the popular forces would organize themselves into militias to carry on the struggle for the liberation of Spain. Thus was born the Catalonia Antifascist Militias Committee, and we had all the political, liberal, and workers' sectors represented on it.'

COMPOSITION AND ROLE

In the room next to the presidential office, the delegates from the organizations met and instantly set up a Central Committee, which included delegates from the moderates, three from the Esquerra, one from the Rabassaires, one from *Acción Catalana*. The PSUC, in process of being officially established, had one representative, and so did the POUM. The FAI was represented by Santillán and Aurelio Fernández, the CNT by García Oliver, Asens, and Durruti, whom Marcos Alcon replaced a few days later. The UGT, ten times its size, had three representatives too.

This was a somewhat paradoxical initial result. The powerful

CNT, whose total victory Companys had just recognized, agreed to equal representation with the meager Catalan UGT. Was this pure generosity, as García Oliver suggested?[14] Was it a political gesture, the desire of CNT to receive similar treatment in the regions where it was in a minority, as Santillán claimed?[15] Both factors may have operated. In addition, it is probable, given the context of rivalry that emerged during the early days of the Revolution between the POUM and CNT, that the Libertarian leaders were quite glad to have a margin for serious maneuver with the four delegates from the Catalan Republicans, the three from the UGT, and the one from the PSUC. On the Central Committee, the POUM was in a far more obvious minority than in the other important centers of Catalonia. And as Santillán pointed out, this mode of representation on the Central Committee was adopted through the wish of the CNT–FAI.

Fruit of a compromise, born of negotiations between leaders of parties and unions, officially sanctioned by a government decree, the Central Committee was thus, because of the circumstances of its birth, a hybrid organization. In permanent session in the presence of four delegates from the government and acting in its name, it had the appearance, in certain respects, of an annex to the government, a committee of mutual understanding enjoying a delegation of power. In actual fact, except in Barcelona, where it was in contact with the leadership of the parties and unions, its base in the country was made up of Government Committees, the local revolutionary authorities of which it was at the same time the supreme expression. This was what Santillán made very clear when he wrote:[16]

'The Antifascist Militias Committee was recognized as the only effective power in Catalonia. The government of the Generalidad continued to exist and to deserve our respect, but now the people only obeyed the power created by the force of victory and revolution, because the people's victory was the economic and social revolution.'

In effect, nothing escaped the competence and authority of the Central Committee, as Santillán explained: 'An establishment for revolutionary order at the rear, an organization of forces more or less on a war footing, with schools for communications and signals, food and clothing, economic organization, and legislative and judiciary action, the Antifascist Militias Committee was everything, supervised everything, the transformation of peacetime industries into war industries, propaganda, relations with the government in Madrid, help for all the fighting centers, relations with Morocco, the cultivation of available land, health, the supervision of coasts and frontiers, and a thousand and one problems of every kind. We had to pay the militiamen, their families, the widows of combatants; in a word, with a few dozen people, we faced tasks for which a government would have required an expensive bureaucracy. The Antifascist Militias Committee was simultaneously a ministry of war, a ministry of the interior, and a ministry of foreign affairs, inspiring similar bodies in the economic and cultural fields.'[17]

A political body, both with legislative and with executive power, the Committee was organized by the formation of labor commissions and specialized executive committees that soon did the work of actual ministries. The administrative secretariat-general, in charge of propaganda, was run by a young Esquerra leader and former extreme left-wing militant, Jaime Miravittles. Around this center functioned the Committee for the organization of the militias, under Santillán, the War Committee, under García Oliver, charged with the task of carrying out military operations, the Transport Committee, under Durán Rosell of the UGT and Alcon of the CNT, the Food Committee, directed by the Rabassaire José Torrents, the Commission of Investigation under the Anarchist Aurelio Fernández, a veritable ministry of the interior, the War Industries Commission under the Catalan Tarradellas. Around them other departments were set up, the Commission for Standard Education, whose secretary was the trade unionist Harvas of the POUM, and various technical services: statistics, munitions, censorship, press and radio, cartography, and specialist schools. A workers' government born of the workers' Revolution, the Central Committee adopted the structure it needed.

Conflict of Power in Valencia

The situation at that time in Valencia was nothing like so clear. While the garrison and the workers on strike were still eyeing each other, the Provincial Junta, under Martínez Barrio, challenged the rebels' authority with the legal authority of the Republican government, which was anxious for an end to the sieges of barracks and a return to work and legality. On 21 July, it tried to convince the delegates from the Executive Committee that the strike ought to end because the garrison was loyal. But this move caused deep mistrust: it was known that Martínez Barrio and Mola were, like General Monje, commander of the garrison, Freemasons. The government delegate was under suspicion of trying to reach the compromise with the Army that he had been unable to achieve during the few hours of his ministry on 19 July. There were lively discussions in insurgent Valencia, where officers and priests no longer ventured into the streets and where the Executive Committee was running a workers' police force in conjunction with the regular police force. On 23 July, Esplá, in the name of the Provincial Junta, proclaimed the dissolution of the Popular Executive Committee and announced that he was assuming the functions of civil governor, aided by a consultative council made up of one representative from each party and union. The Committee split up: the CNT, the Socialist party, the UGT, and the POUM wanted to reject the government ultimatum. The Republican Left and the Communist party felt that the Committee ought to set an example of discipline and submit to the government's legal authority, as embodied in Valencia by the Provincial Junta.

In the end, the Popular Executive Committee refused to dissolve itself. The CNT–UGT strike committee, its leading wing, decided on the publication of a daily newspaper called *CNT–UGT*, on a return to work in sectors dealing with food, and on the organization of a union committee to ensure food supplies, but the Provincial Junta handed over control of food supplies to the municipality. It continued its negotiations with the garrison, against which there were daily demonstrations for the departure of the rebel troops.

In Madrid, the minister of the interior assured Antona, general secretary of the CNT, that he could rely at least on the neutrality of the Valencia garrison. But the arms that he promised did not turn up. The Madrid CNT then sent machine guns and rifles to Valencia; arms also arrived from Barcelona to equip the newly formed militias. The garrison was still shut up in its various barracks, access to which was forbidden. The Executive Committee threatened to storm them but kept putting off a decision. A new bone of contention arose when it was decided to send forces to Teruel, where a threat from the rebel army was developing. The Executive Committee suggested a merger on the basis of three militiamen to one Civil Guard. The Junta insisted on the inverse ratio of three Civil Guards to one militiaman. The column left, but at Puebla de Valverde, on the way to Teruel, the Civil Guards massacred the militiamen and went over to the enemy.

Events now began to follow hard on each other's heels. There was unrest in the barracks: as the second week of the strike opened, the regiment of engineers in Paterna, led by an NCO, Sergeant Fabra, mutinied against its officers. The mutineers now swelled the ranks of the militias, which were also daily winning over soldiers fleeing from their barracks with their arms. However, the CNT–UGT strike committee finally gave the order for a return to work, except in the transport sections, on 27 July. The workers' reaction showed that it had miscalculated: the workers refused to obey and went on with the strike. The CNT and the UGT took their stands. The Executive Committee appointed a board of three members, López of the CNT, Tejón of the UGT, and a young officer, Lieutenant Benedito, to prepare an attack on the barracks, arranged for 1 August. On 31 July, Radio Seville announced that the garrison had risen up and that Valencia had fallen into rebel hands. In fact, three regiments had risen up, but the soldiers were mutinying against the officers while the militiamen were on the attack. The garrison was disarmed, the suspected officers arrested and tried, and the soldiers demobilized; the militiamen took over their arms. The government then capitulated: the Provincial Junta was dissolved and the authority of the Popular Executive Committee recognized, the appointment of its president, Colonel Arín, as civil governor, being merely the recognition of a *de facto* situation.

From now on, the Popular Executive Committee, which was rapidly extending its authority to the whole of the province, was playing a part similar in all respects to that of the Central Committee in Catalonia. Andrés Nin, at a meeting in Valencia, saw fit to hail it as the 'government of the proletarian revolution in the Levante.' It set up an Economic Council with full powers and organized columns of militiamen for several fronts. Its Commissions for Public Order, Justice, Agriculture, and Finance were known as 'ministries.' General Miaja, Martínez Barrio's former minister of war, sent by Giral to command the military region, confessed to Major Martín Blázquez his impotence in the face of the authority of a 'young puppy of a lieutenant,' Benedito, assigned to the defense side of the Executive Committee: the general embodied an illusory Republican authority, whereas the lieutenant represented the new 'soviet' authority.[18]

Other Revolutionary Governments

Other bodies took power in the other regions of Spain. In Asturias, in the mining towns and villages, it was in the hands of Workers' and Peasants' Committees. On the provincial level, two rival authorities emerged, the Gijón War Committee, led by Segundo Blanco of the CNT, and the Sama de Langreo Popular Front Committee, led in turn by the Socialists González Peña and Amador Fernández. Each set up its Commissions for War, Transport, Food Supplies, and Health: the Sama de Langreo Committee was, according to Aznar, able to mobilize 20,000 men in six days in September. During the course of the same month, the two Committees merged into a War Committee, based on Gijón but headed this time by a Socialist, Belarmino Tomás.

In Santander, the Socialists dominated a War Committee where the commissions functioned like actual ministries, with full sovereignty. On several occasions, however, the Anarchists there disputed the authority of the president, Juan Ruiz.

The Málaga Committee of Public Safety gradually took control of the whole region from 20 July. A Watch Committee led the repression, while Workers' Committees dealt with health and food supplies and Women's Committees with refugee problems. Its armed patrols gradually eliminated the loyal units of Civil Guards. It had sufficient authority on its own to halt the massacres of inmates in the prisons. On 18 August, Delaprée wrote: 'The Workers' and Militiamen's Councils hold all the power here. The civil governor is a mere rubber stamp. He is a pale Girondin, trembling before Jacobins beside whom ours were but small children.'[19] In September, the Committee of Public Safety was officially formed, like an actual ministry, with ministries of war, the interior, justice, and confiscations. Its chairman, the Socialist schoolteacher Francisco Rodríguez, was appointed civil governor: legality ratified *de facto* power.

The most original regional revolutionary power was eventually established in Aragon. As we saw, the whole of the Republican cadres there had joined the military uprising. The recovery of a large part of the Aragon countryside by the Catalan militias was accompanied by radical revolutionary measures in every village. While the authorities and Civil Guards had either fled or been massacred, the village's general assembly tried the 'Fascist' prisoners and elected the Committee which was to run the village, supported by the armed militias. Most of the Committees thus elected were mainly or wholly Anarchist: there could be no kind of collaboration between them and the Republican authorities, which were completely eliminated. In early October, near Durruti's headquarters in Bujaraloz, a conference of Town and Village Committees was held. It elected a Defense Council, made up exclusively of CNT militants and led by Joaquín Ascaso, who based himself in Fraga. The Defense Council, in agreement with the leaders of the Anarchist columns, exercised undivided authority over Aragon: a Supreme Committee, representing the Committees as a whole, it was thus the only regional body in Spain that resulted from the federation of local Committees and derived its authority from them. Vigorously attacked, soon after its formation, by the Communists, who dubbed it a factionist and 'cantonalist' body, it was many months before it was recognized by the government. It was also the body of revolutionary power that remained in existence the longest.

A Special Case: The Basque Provinces

In the Basque provinces, the situation was very different from that in the rest of Spain. The Basque Nationalist party, which was unquestionably in the majority, took its stand against the military uprising on 19 July and joined the Popular Front a few days later.

However, its objectives created a huge gap between it and the workers' parties and unions, whose militants were waging a revolution throughout the whole of Spain. The Basque Nationalists were ardent champions of the Church and property and found themselves from very early on in direct conflict with the majority of the troops of their allies in the Popular Front and the unions. The Defense Juntas that were set up in all the Basque provinces were organized to combat the military uprising and at the same time were bastions against the Revolution. In the Buenos Aires *La Nación* on 7 September 1936, the Basque leader, Manuel de Irujo, put his finger on his party's difficulties at that time perfectly when he wrote: 'The extremist parties of the capitalist dictatorship and the proletariat were organized as *Requetés* and militias and had outstripped us from the start.' Moreover, in all the Juntas where they were in the majority, the Basque Nationalists demanded posts as 'Commissioners of Public Order,' to 'impose discipline and respect on the rear.'[20] Thus the Commissioner for Public Order in the Guipúzcoa Junta made it his first task to stop the *paseos* and to protect property by placing a guard on the banks. To guarantee the maintenance of law and order and the defense of property, the Nationalists organized their own units, the Basque militias, led by Major Saseta: recruited from Nationalist militants and with a strong leavening of chaplains, they flew the Basque flag and spoke the Basque language. In the space of a few weeks, they managed to recover almost all the arms acquired by the workers in San Sebastián after the capture of the Loyola barracks.

The collapse of the Republican state in the Basque provinces permitted the creation not of a revolutionary authority, but of a new state, specifically Basque, a bourgeois state for the defense of property and the Church that, while organizing the country's defense against the military adversaries of Basque freedom, led the victorious struggle against the internal revolutionary movement.[21] In the middle of September, the Basque Nationalist party leadership decided to take the decisive step, establishing, under its control, a Basque provincial government.[22]

Outline for a New State Apparatus

In the early days, the majority of Committees operated without specialization or delegation of responsibility. It was the Committee or even the village assembly that was at one and the same time the deliberative body, tribunal, and council of war. Armed workers and peasants mounted guard, patrolled, supervised, requisitioned, and carried out arrests and executions. However, specialist bodies very soon appeared, at least in the large towns.

At first these were units with police duties: it was a question of maintaining revolutionary law and order, as much against the enemies of the Revolution as against those benefiting from it, the instruments of blind terror. Units of loyal Civil Guards and *Asaltos* were severely purged; however, they inspired only limited confidence, and in the majority of the large centers the Committees gave special commissions the task of controlling the old police forces and organizing the new ones. In Barcelona, the Commission of Investigation under Aurelio Fernández was empowered to hear denunciations, make inquiries, conduct searches, and arrest suspects. It gradually imposed its authority on the private police force of the unions and parties. In Málaga it was the Watch Committee and elsewhere Commissions of Public Order and Security Councils that all, under various names, had the job of organizing terror in the rear.

In the same way, units of militiamen, soon to be known as 'rear militias,' performed the specialized duties of actual police.

In Barcelona there were the famous Control Patrols, under the Anarchist Asens. These were made up of 700 and later of 1000 worker militants, half of them appointed by the CNT–FAI and the other half by other organizations, and provided, after their formation by the Central Committee, with up-to-date means of transport and communication. The Gijón Control Patrol, the Lérida Social Workers' Brigade, and the Castellón Antifascist Popular Guard were similar bodies.

In spite of the Anarchists' repugnance at dividing up what Santillán referred to as 'total revolutionary power,' the same development took place in the field of justice. The Palaces of Justice were closed, the magistrates killed or in flight, there were swarms of 'judges,' and the Committees were overburdened with work. In Barcelona, some militiamen from the CNT, led by the lawyer Samblancat, sacked the Palace of Justice and threw files and crucifixes out of the windows. They established a Committee of Justice made up of professional lawyers, mostly left-wing lawyers, whose first act was to dismiss all the officials in the department and whose second was to set itself up as a revolutionary tribunal. Revolutionary tribunals of a different kind appeared in Valencia, Castellón, and Lérida in early August: judges, prosecutors, and president were militants appointed by the parties and unions.[23] Their decisions were harsh and their procedure summary, but the rights of the defense were generally respected. They even made acquittals and in any case were, in this respect, a distinct advance over the practice of *paseos*.

The Militias

However, given the context of the war, the construction of a new army emerged as the most important task. At any rate, it was this need that produced new organs of power.

The militias were born as the result of efforts by parties and unions and were at first armed versions of these organizations. Each one's name proclaimed its origin, whether it was the name of a guild (*Artes Graficas, Madera*), or a political emblem (the UGT *Caballero* and *Claridad*, the PSUC *Carlos Marx*, the POUM *Lenin* and *Maurin*, and the Esquerra *Maciá* and *Companys*).

In Barcelona, on 24 July, the Central Committee organized the first column, 3000 strong, under Durruti, assisted by Major Pérez Farras. Its only organized force was made up of a few soldiers armed with mortars and machine guns. Later on, the other columns formed under the aegis of the Central Committee were in fact under the influence of political and union organizations. Santillán, who was acting in the name of the Central Committee, seems to have fought a losing battle against the party spirit in the militias and its often regrettable consequences, rivalry for arms and for men and occasional bloody clashes. In Valencia, it was the Executive Committee that took the lead: the 'Iron Column,' the '*Desperada*,' the 'Steel Column,' and the 'Ghost Column' were set up under its aegis, but political influences also played a decisive role. The Ghost Column was led by Socialists and the Iron Column was the most notorious of the Anarchist columns. In Madrid, each organization had its own troops, whose only link with each other was the government, which merely fed them as best it could, supplied them with arms, and paid them. It was the National Committees of each party or union, the CNT Center Defense Committee, that assumed the task of organizing them. The Republican Left made a name for itself by forming a 'Steel Regiment' and the Communist party the 'Fifth Regiment,' which became the famous Quinto, but which was for the time being only a unit of militiamen, barely differing from the rest.

It is difficult to give an exact figure for the militias. Rabasseire estimated the total number in the combat militias at 100,000: 50,000 CNT, 30,000 UGT, 10,000 Communist party, and 5000 POUM, to which must be added 12,000 *Asaltos*, a few hundred Civil Guards, a few thousand soldiers, and only 200 officers. In early September the *Boletín CNT-FAI* listed 22,000 militiamen in Catalonia and Aragon, including 4000 former Civil Guards, 2000 PSUC and UGT, 3000 POUM, and 13,000 CNT. Meanwhile Valencia had sent 9000 militiamen to different fronts, including 4000 to Teruel. In Madrid, armed men soon took the road to the front, but Santillán estimated the number of rifles still in the hands of the rear militias in Catalonia at 6000 and admitted the Central

Committee's inability to reinforce the strength of the combat militias: Durruti had to march on Sabadell to acquire the ten machine guns that the PSUC was holding there, and the men of the CNT–FAI kept even longer in Barcelona the forty machine guns and the few tanks that were so badly needed on the Aragon Front.

The leaders of the first columns were political and union militants. Very few of them had any military training. In Barcelona they were workers, the Anarchists Durruti, Jover, and Ortíz, the POUM militants Rovira, Arquer, and Grossi,[24] and the PSUC militants Trueba and Del Barrio. A few regular soldiers rubbed shoulders with them: Major Pérez Farras, Major Pérez Salas, who commanded the Esquerra column, Major Martínez and Captain Escobar, Santillán's technical advisers, leaders of the Antifascist Republican Military Union in Barcelona.

Captain Bayo of the Air Force was in command of the Majorca expedition, and it was a Navarrese colonel, Jiménez de la Beraza, who organized the artillery. The NCOs played a more important part in organizing the militias: after Pérez Farras, it was the former sergeant Manzana who was the military brain of the Durruti Column. Naturally the rare foreign antifascists who arrived as technicians were welcomed with open arms. In Valencia, it was the junior officers, Captain Uríbarri, Civil Guard and Socialist, and Lieutenant Benedito, who commanded the first columns that Sergeant Fabra, hero of the uprising by the soldiers in Paterna, was organizing in conjunction with them. In León, General Gómez Caminero took charge of the miners, but he was made prisoner. In Asturias, there were very few officers around González Peña, and the columns were commanded by worker militants: the Socialist miner Otero from Mieres and the CNT metalworker Carrocerra. In Madrid, the first Socialist columns were led by retired officers: Lieutenant-Colonel Mangada was the most popular, but his star waned quickly after the first few defeats. At first the Fifth Regiment consisted only of a few officers and NCOs.[25] The CNT recruited several regular officers, Lieutenant-Colonel Del Rosal and Major Palacios of the Medical Corps, who led its first two columns. But here too new leaders took over: the building workers, Mora and Cipriano Mera, who at that time had only a few weeks' military experience. Málaga, which boasted a good officer, Lieutenant-Colonel Asensio Torrado, was the favorite place for militias with high-sounding names: according to the war communiqués, the 'Pancho Villa' detachment disputed the honors with the 'Scrap Iron' detachment.

The mass of the militiamen had no idea how to handle weapons and were ignorant of the most rudimentary rules of self-defense. It was of course owing to lack of arms, but also to lack of leaders, that the mobilization of the workers had to be dropped: recruits could be neither equipped, instructed, nor officered. Moreover, the militias differed in character according to the ideologies of those who had formed them. The Anarchist columns were commanded by 'political delegates' flanked by 'military technicians.' The Socialist columns, the UGT, POUM, and PSUC columns and the Fifth Regiment, were led by officers flanked by 'political commissars.' In Catalonia, the Central Committee attempted to unify the organization. Ten militiamen made up a 'hand' under an elected delegate. Ten hands made up a *centuria* whose 'delegate-general' took direct orders from the 'head of the column.' The CNT militias in Madrid were organized on the basis of hands of twenty men, *centurias*, and battalions, and the battalions' delegates, along with the representative of the Defense Committee and the delegate-general, formed the column's leadership. In the Fifth Regiment, officers and commissars were in theory appointed by the leadership, but Lister said that he was 'elected.' In all columns, NCOs and other ranks drew ten pesetas a day. No outward sign of respect was required from any man, and there were no badges of rank. But the Fifth Regiment was proud of having revived the military salute and made it a point of honor, like the POUM columns elsewhere, to march along in faultless ranks, whereas the CNT militia made it theirs to march along in total—and deliberate—disarray.

In Madrid, the Fifth Regiment at first made every effort to

form cadres: the original NCOs were recruited from the leaders of 'Red Aid.' In Barcelona, the Central Committee gave García Oliver the task of organizing a 'Popular School of Warfare,'[26] and batches of 2000 volunteers received a crash military-training course at the Bakunin barracks.

Thus an armed force whose efficiency in street fighting and enthusiasm could not be denied was gradually being built up. It was the true realization of the old slogan of 'people in arms' and, for the time being, seemed to be completely independent of government authority.

The Power of the State

The government was in fact surviving. President Giral, resigned to arming the workers, was struggling, wherever he still preserved a vestige of authority, to maintain respect for forms and legality and to preserve, if not a state apparatus—it was too badly damaged—at least the principle of his own legitimacy. It would seem that he had played his last card in the eastern provinces with the Provincial Junta of Martínez Barrio, Ruiz Funes, and Carlo Esplá. The latter had undoubtedly contributed to the feeding of Madrid and helped in the Levante with the formation of militias that had recovered Albacete and marched on Andalusia, but it had lost the political battle with revolutionary power, in Valencia as well as in Murcia, Alicante, and Cartagena. After its dissolution, it seemed to be little more, in Borkenau's phrase, than a 'monument of inactivity,' owing its survival only to the docility that it had shown in the face of demands by parties, unions, militias, and Committees.

Yet the government was still in existence, and first of all where foreigners were concerned, in whose eyes it strove to embody legality. In August, yielding to pressure from foreign powers, it gave orders to the fleet to leave the coast of Tangier only forty-eight hours after Dr. Giral had assured the people of Valencia that the rebels would not receive any help from Africa, because the Republican Navy, he said, would prevent it from coming. The government thus gave proof of its existence at sea, and it seemed to be persisting curiously in its dream of conciliation with a group of rebel generals. On 29 July, in the name of the Republic, Martínez also made this solemn appeal: 'Let those who should never have taken up arms hand them back, thus reestablishing normal life in the country.' The next day, Prieto, as official spokesman, was quick to state that the government had not given up all hope of conciliation: 'The government forces,' he said, 'have not so far been deployed as they would have been in order to repel a foreign adversary.'

In Madrid, a few days after the Revolution, the government managed to recover control of the streets from the workers' militias and hand them back to the police: government passes replaced union cards and committee passes. The police force had been decimated but attempts were made to re-form it. The Security Service, under Manuel Muñoz, recruited trusted Socialist militants: *Asaltos*, who formed the 'Dawn Squad,' and the 'Lynxes of the Republic,' made up of *Asaltos* and Socialist militants, played an important part in the repression. The Socialist typographer García Attadell was made head of the 'Brigade for Criminal Investigation,' which was soon to become famous and which was fashionably rechristened 'Popular Militia for Investigation.' Sayagües, a Republican from Azaña's party, organized 'special services' at the Ministry of War. Naturally all these police authorities coexisted with the Provincial Committee of Investigation, formed in early August from representatives of all parties, and with what were beginning to be called the parties' *checas*, yet they represented a considerable weapon in the government's armory.

The situation in the military field was more difficult. The government had no army. It managed to acquire a few thousand rifles in Madrid by exchanging them for revolvers with the militiamen. The 31 July decree, which provided for the payment of militiamen by the state on presentation of a party or union certificate, clearly endorsed its weakness but also represented a first sign of recovery. It was the parties and unions that organized the militias, as well as the food supplies, but they did so in the name of the state and to some extent through delegation. At the ministry of war, which General Castello left on 7 August, hospitalized for mental illness, a handful of

Republican officers, members of the Presidential Guard, military attachés to Ministers, Lieutenant-Colonel Sarabia, Majors Menéndez, Hidalgo de Cisneros, Martín Blázquez, Díaz Tendero, and Captains Cordón and Ciutat, set up a militia supply corps, recruited officers, and distributed ammunition: at the same time they were an embryo general staff, to which leaders of columns more and more often had recourse. On 4 August, 'Battalions of Volunteers' were created. On 20 August, it was Martínez Barrio, once again, along with Ruiz Funes, who was given the task of recruiting them. Thus the state hoped eventually to rebuild an armed force and to assert its authority more boldly.

The armed forces were of course pinned down a few miles from Madrid, and there was nothing on the outskirts of the capital to protect a working minister from the dangers of arrest. However, some continuity had been maintained: the government recognized the Councils and Revolutionary Committees because it had no alternative, but it always tried, at least on paper, to draw them into its own framework, the Republican state. When it appointed Arín Governor of Valencia or Rodríguez Governor of Málaga, it added nothing to the authority that they enjoyed, and it added nothing to its own, but it maintained a principle. And although the wretched General Miaja, appointed through its efforts, was forced to click his heels before the 'recruit' Benedito, who represented the Executive Committee in Valencia, his presence as Military Governor in a *Capitania General* that did not even possess a car was at least a sign of the Republican state's intention to endure, in anticipation of better days. In Catalonia, in spite of the strong popular basis that President Companys's party enjoyed, the Generalidad government undoubtedly enjoyed still less effective authority in respect to the Central Committee. However, it continued to 'decree' the formation of militias to mount guard in front of its offices and the formation of the Central Committee, which it wanted to make into a mere 'liaison' committee, and it 'appointed' the Committee's choice as commissar to the ministry of defense. Were these pointless formalities, since all these decrees merely confirmed decisions already taken by the bodies of revolutionary power? No, because they acted as a safeguard for the very principle of Republican legality. The government did not govern, but it was still in existence.

It was the Generalidad government which was the first to try and resume its activities. On 2 August, Casanovas, of the Esquerra, formed a cabinet that included three representatives from the PSUC; Comorera, minister of economic affairs, Ruiz, minister of food, and Vidiella, minister of communications. However, the move was so obviously aimed at the Central Committee that the CNT and the POUM reacted vigorously: fearing discredit and the isolation of their party in the working class, the PSUC ministers deferred their resignation until the eighth.

About the same time, the Madrid government tried, by mobilizing three classes that it hoped to stiffen with loyal officers and NCOs, to acquire the armed force that, alone in the area, it did not possess. Militiamen and workers' organizations, excluding the Communist party, reacted violently. The Caballero Column threatened to march on Madrid to prevent this reconstitution of the Regular Army. On 20 August, *Claridad* unequivocally stated: 'To think that another type of army ought to be substituted for the ones that are actually fighting and that, to some extent, control their own revolutionary action, is to think in counterrevolutionary terms.' In Barcelona, 10,000 conscripts convened by a summons from the CNT voted for a resolution that stated: 'We wish to be militiamen of freedom, not soldiers in uniform. The Army has proved itself a danger to the country, and only the popular militias are protecting public liberties: militiamen, yes! soldiers, never!'

In the barracks, the soldiers burned rosters and mobilization orders. In Catalonia, the Generalidad allowed new recruits to be incorporated into the militias. Elsewhere, parties and unions pressed for the election of 'Workers' and Soldiers' Councils' in barracks and new units; a fresh obstacle stood in the way of the reconstitution of a regular army.

The outcome of this first open conflict between the two powers revealed the Giral government's weakness to the full. As Juan López said, six weeks after the uprising, 'All the joints of the state were broken, none of its political organs were working any more'; neither Giral nor Companys had the strength to 'glue the broken pieces together, make the state's organs function again, or recreate a new centralized state.'[27]

Notes

[1] All observers were struck by the attachment of the workers, both men and women, to their arms. Delaprée (*Mort en Espagne*, p. 21) described a woman returning from market, her child, her shopping basket and her gun in her arms. Koltsov (*Ispanskii dnevnik*, p. 17) said that weapons were never laid down in restaurants or in places of entertainment, in spite of notices that recommended leaving them in the cloakrooms. On 8 August, he remarked: 'The workers have seized arms, they will not let them go as easily as that.'

[2] Bloch, *Espagne, Espagne!*, p. 45.

[3] Quoted by Brenan, *Spanish Labyrinth*, p. 323.

[4] Fernández had shot a man and a woman who had once denounced him to the police.

[5] Reported by Hubertus Friedrich von Loewenstein, *A Catholic in Republican Spain* (London: Victor Gollancz, 1937), p. 98.

[6] 'Notes sur Barcelone,' in *La Révolution prolétarienne*, 10 August 1936.

[7] In Sabadell, the Committee's chairman was the former *treintista*, José Moix, member of the PSUC and the UGT. In Lérida, it was José Rodés of the POUM, who held both the chairmanship and the office of Commissar for Public Order.

[8] *Negro y Rojo* (Mexico City: España Contemporánea, 1946), p. 233.

[9] Santillán, *Por qué perdimos la guerra*, p. 168.

[10] Juan García Oliver, 'Le Comité Central des milices antifascistes', in *Dans la tourmente*, p. 251.

[11] *Heraldo de Madrid*, 4 September 1936.

[12] Manuel Benavides, *Guerra y Revolución en Cataluña*, Colección 'Luz sobra España,' 3 (Mexico City: Ediciones Tenochtitlán, 1946), p. 190.

[13] Santillán, *Por qué perdimos la guerra*, p. 169.

[14] Ibid., p. 255. He said that the Anarchists refused 'to imitate the big fish whose desire to gobble up the small ones gives them no peace.'

[15] 'In this way,' he wrote, 'we are demonstrating that we want to collaborate like brothers and that, in the rest of Spain and the areas where we shall eventually be in a minority, we should wish to be treated with the same consideration and the same respect with which we ourselves treated those who had more or less collaborated for victory' (ibid.).

[16] Ibid., p. 170 ff.

[17] Ibid.

[18] José Martín Blázquez, *Guerre civile totale* (Paris: Les Editions Denoël, 1938), p. 201.

[19] Delaprée, *Mort en Espagne*, p. 70.

[20] In San Sebastián, after the capture of the barracks, the men of the CNT were in control of the streets. Manuel de Irujo wrote: 'We had virtually become prisoners of those who held the booty of Loyola . . . subject to the control of the CNT.' (Quoted by Lizarra, *Los Vascos y la República española*, p. 53).

[21] The expression 'war on two fronts' originated with Irujo himself (ibid., p. 95) who referred not only to 'insurgent militants,' but also to 'extremist elements brought into the house.'

[22] See Manuel de Irujo's remark on the offer of a portfolio in the Caballero government made him by Álvarez del Vayo: 'The reader can imagine my surprise at being asked to join the government at the very moment when preparations were being made to establish, in revolutionary fashion, the autonomous government of Euzkadi.' (Ibid., p. 81.)

[23] The Lérida revolutionary tribunal was wholly made up of workers, a third nominated by the POUM, a third by the UGT–PSUC, and a third by the CNT–FAI. The President, Larrocca, from the CNT, and the Prosecutor, Pelegrin, from the POUM, were both railway workers.

[24] Delaprée drew an engaging portrait of Grossi, the Asturian miner and war leader, 'bravest of the brave' (*Mort en Espagne*, p. 55).

[25] Enrique Castro Delgado, Communist party leader, was the first commander of the Fifth Regiment. Alongside him were a militant, a former NCO, Barbado, a Portuguese political refugee officer, and only one regular officer, Márquez (see Enrique Castro Delgado, *Hombres made in Moscú* [Barcelona: Luis de Caralt, 1965], pp. 281–293). In October, Castro was replaced by Lister, a stonecutter: from now on, the workers' leaders stole the limelight. Among them, the carpenter Modesto had been a corporal in the Spanish Foreign Legion (Louis Fischer, *Men and Politics* [New York: Duell, Sloan and Pearce, 1941], p. 543). Enrique Lister, a Communist militant who had sought refuge in the USSR before the Civil War, as a result of strike activities, had worked on the Moscow subway and then attended military training classes (Ludwig Renn, *Der spanische Krieg* [Berlin: Aufbau Verlag, 1956], p. 192).

[26] Conditions of acceptance: ability to read and write, an elementary knowledge of arithmetic, and being proposed by a militia unit; with the second batch, proof of two months at the front. The course of study took two months, including a fortnight of theory at the beginning, followed by a period of training and then one of specialization. Two-thirds of the officers from the first recruitment were killed at the front.

[27] Quoted in *Catalogne 36–37*, pp. 59–60.

CHAPTER 6

THE REVOLUTIONARY GAINS

The Spanish Revolution was born of a profound social crisis. In mounting a spontaneous attack on the workings of a Republican state for which they had substituted their own, the Spanish workers had aimed beyond a mere political revolution. Their activities in the weeks following the uprising constituted a social revolution in every field. In their own way, without doubt summary and rather brutal, they had attacked Spain's major problems: the oligarchical structure of the state, the Army, and the Church and the economic bases of the oligarchy, industrial property and landed property.[1]

The Problem of the Church

Throughout Republican Spain, the problem of the Church was 'solved' at least as radically as that of the Army, except in the Basque provinces. As was pointed out in a memorandum from Manuel de Irujo to Caballero[2] a few months later, all the churches had been closed to worship, and many had been burned, especially in Catalonia. Altars, pictures, and sacred objects had very often been destroyed; bells, chalices, monstrances, and candelabra had been seized by the revolutionary authorities, melted down, and used for industrial or military purposes. Former churches were now serving as garages, markets, stables, and shelters. To this end the buildings had been permanently altered by the installation of running water, tiled floors, counters, scales, rails, doors, windows, and partitions. All convents had been emptied, and the buildings similarly used. Priests and monks had been arrested in droves and imprisoned or shot: only two had escaped the inexorable repression in Lérida, because it was known that they had voted and canvassed votes for the Popular Front. Those who refused to flee went to ground, risking arrest and execution at any moment. Rare were those who were given a chance at 'civilian life': however, there were odd cases of a former nun who married or a former monk who joined the militias.[3] In practice, the ban on worship had been extended to the private ownership of holy pictures and sacred objects, such as crucifixes, missals, etc. The revolutionary rear militias tracked down their owners, carried out searches, and made arrests.

All denominational schools had been closed, the buildings and teaching taken over locally by Committees or unions. In Catalonia, the buildings belonging to religious schools had been handed over to representatives of the New Standard Education Committee, based on 'the rationalist principles of human labor and brotherhood,' the 'feeling of universal solidarity,' and the determination to 'suppress all kinds of privilege.' In many places old and new schools were installed in new buildings, in the luxurious villas of big proprietors, in convents, in Civil Guard stations. Here the experiment was too short lived for anyone to assess its results. In Barcelona, however, the number of children attending school rose by 10 percent between July and October 1936.

Industrial Property

The economic bases of the power of the Church had been destroyed in a few days of revolution: in the majority of cases the same was true for the bourgeoisie. To the triumphant revolutionaries both looked as if they were the allies of the rebel Generals: the 'revolutionary gains' were as much the result of ideological demands as of practical necessities.

Already, in the weeks before the uprising, many heads of business firms had taken flight and had placed their assets in safekeeping, thus helping to increase economic stagnation.[4] The success of the Revolution and the terror that struck both heads and staffs of banking and industrial firms paralyzed the working of an economic apparatus already considerably worsened by the early fighting. Last and most important, the Revolution of July 1936 had had its social objectives: the workers had taken the factories and the peasants the fields, because in their view this was the final object of their revolutionary activity, its crowning glory.[5]

It would take an entire book to describe the extraordinary variety of solutions adopted by the Spanish workers to put an end to 'the exploitation of man by man':[6] the whole thing might seem incoherent and somewhat utopian. However, a detailed study only creates the desire to deepen one's knowledge of this blossoming of initiatives, not always happy but almost always generous in their inspiration.

The simplest case was the seizure of a business firm by the workers, known as *incautación*: this was the general rule in Catalonia, whether or not the employer had fled. But when there was no seizure, it very quickly became necessary to establish control, known as *intervención*, in which workers' delegates and official representatives participated jointly. These two legal forms, which seemed for the moment to be the concrete realization of the slogan, 'workers' factory,' gave rise during the next stage to the two distinct forms of collectivized or syndicalized firms and nationalized firms. For the time being, the scope of each varied according to the respective influences of the workers' organizations. According to Borkenau, in the Madrid region, where the UGT was most influential, 30 percent of the business firms were *intervenidas*, under dual government and union control: they were the most important. In Catalonia, under the influence of the CNT, 70 percent of the firms had been *incautadas*, and 50 percent in the Levante. In Asturias, industry and trade were almost wholly controlled, whereas the factories in the Basque provinces escaped any *incautación* or *intervención*. However, generalizations and schematization should be avoided: as a correspondent for *Le Temps* pointed out on 3 October 1936, the Workers' Committees were no less powerful in controlled firms than in the ones that had been seized, because their stamp was compulsory on every check issued by the management. When, in early August, a decree endorsed the *fait accompli* by authorizing the *incautación* of firms belonging to the factionists by the workers' assembly and their management by elected Committees sitting with government representatives, Robert Louzon wrote that this would 'tend to bring about the same situation in the factories as now exists in the state: a government delegate acting as a screen, while the Workers' Committee—itself inspired and controlled by the union—will be the real power.'[7] During this period of multiplicity and 'atomization' of authority, the government was nowhere strong enough to counterbalance the influence of the Committees.

Within this general context there were infinite variations; we shall confine ourselves to a few examples. In Barcelona, the stronghold of collectivization, the workers very early took over local transport (streetcars, buses, subway), the railroads, which were soon controlled throughout the area by a CNT–UGT Committee, gas and electricity, the telephone system, newspapers, entertainment, hotels and restaurants, and the majority of the large machinery and industrial firms and the transport companies: the Ford Iberia Motor Company, Hispano-Suiza, the Oil Company, Asland Cement, the Transatlantic and the Maritima. Each party and union took over an office or printing firm. Each newspaper was run by a Workers' Committee, elected with a representative of each wage-earning category, editorial, administrative, and shop.

The public services were taken over by joint CNT–UGT Committees. Two days after the uprising, they were working again: streetcars, buses, and subway trains were running normally, and gas and electricity were supplied without any cuts. After a longer delay, the trains began to function normally as well.[8]

Before the Revolution, the Ford Iberia Motor Company, an assembly plant, had 336 permanent employees, 142 temporary workers, and 87 clerical staff. At first the director agreed to stay on as a technician at a salary of 1500 pesetas a month; then he took flight. The factory was run by an elected Committee of twelve workers and six clerical staff, of whom half were from the CNT and the other half from the UGT. Leunois studied the working conditions and salaries there and reported on them in

La Révolution prolétarienne on 25 September. There was no piece-work, no bonuses, and no family allowance. Victims of industrial accidents drew their full salary for seven days, instead of the five of before the Revolution. It was mass production, but at a slow tempo. The Workers' Committee fixed a ceiling for wages: 1500 pesetas a month, received by the director and assistant director. The workers earned 22.4 to 36 pesetas for each full day's work, and the clerical staff 500 to 1200 pesetas a month. All were liable to a 13 percent deduction for the unemployed and for thirty of the factory's workers who were militiamen at the front. The old scale of wages under 1500 pesetas was maintained by the Workers' Committee because 'the categories that would have been affected by a standardization of wages protested: they regarded it as unacceptable to have waged a revolution only to end with a reduction in wages.'

The *Fomento de Obras y Construcciones*, a public works firm with a capital of 75 million pesetas, had employed 600 workers before the Revolution. It was run by a temporary Workers' Committee of CNT and UGT militants, in proportion to the number of members in each union. There were more than 300 workers in the militias. Those who remained worked forty hours and received wages for forty-eight hours with a 15 percent bonus. *Libertad* on 23 October reported that the account books had been opened and that it was the elimination of 'vermin' that had permitted the increase in wages. There were no foremen, only leaders elected on the work sites, and, on the most important ones, 'manual technicians' without any rights in regard to output.

The *Unión Naval de Levante* shipyards in Valencia, which had 1400 workers, with equal numbers from the UGT and CNT, were run by a Workers' Committee of seven members elected for six months, who made all decisions along with the director, the technical director, and the head foreman. After the Revolution, the firm gave up building and specialized in repairs.

The fishing industry had been collectivized in Gijón under the management of a Committee of Syndical Control, which supplied fish to the Workers' Food Supply Committees. Neither the workers nor the fishermen received any wages: the Food Supply Committees gave them foodstuffs on presentation of a ration card. In Laredo, all shipments had been seized and put under the control of an Economic Committee of twelve members, six from the CNT and six from the UGT. All fish caught passed through it. After expenses and 45 percent for improving equipment had been deducted, the rest of the proceeds from sales was shared equally among all the 'workers on the sea.' A Laredo fisherman earned 64 pesetas a week, far more than he had had with the shipowners and wholesalers.

The collectivization of the Barcelona cinemas had been proposed as an example by the CNT and immediately ridiculed by its opponents. All the theaters in the capital were grouped in a single firm run by a Committee of seventeen, two of whom were elected by the general assembly and fifteen others by workers from different professional categories. Those chosen, released from their jobs, received the same wages as their comrades with the same qualifications. Wages varied with the weekly receipts, which were shared according to a different percentage for each category (1 for the lavatory attendant, 1.5 for a projectionist). The weekly ceiling was set at 175 pesetas, and the eventual profits went into the union funds. Each employee was independently responsible for his job: a majority of three-quarters of the general assembly was needed to apply a sanction. A month and a half of annual holiday, including a fortnight in winter, was provided. In the event of sickness or unemployment, the employee drew his full normal salary, and in the event of disablement, a wage in proportion to his responsibilities, never falling below 75 percent of a normal wage. The profits had to be used, with priority going to the building of a clinic or a school.

In Puigcerdá, according to Louzon, the retail trade had been collectivized in the form of a cooperative of 170 members receiving a uniform salary of 50 pesetas a week for men and 35 for women.[9]

The variety of solutions adopted in the cases mentioned by way of example underlines the difficulty of the problem of wages. It is interesting to note that solutions fluctuated between two extremes, the Anarchist-inspired uniform wage in force at Puigcerdá and the wholesale preservation of the existing hierarchy. The Barcelona streetcar workers sought a compromise, reducing the number of wage categories from eleven to four and introducing a single pension scale. But the wage scale sometimes remained very flexible: in the Hotel España in Valencia, the cook earned nearly four times as much as the chambermaid, and a specialist weaver in a Barcelona factory received 90 pesetas, whereas an assistant received 50 and an apprentice 32.

We must also draw attention to the continuing retention of women's wages at a lower rate, even where Anarchist principles of equality applied, and the constant preoccupation of the Spanish workers with what may be called the application of social-security measures: pensions, retirement pay, holidays, and unemployment benefits.

Collectivization in the Countryside

The Anarchists in Puigcerdá who had collectivized the shops had not touched the farms of La Cerdaña. This was an early example of the immense variety of solutions brought to bear in this field.

In actual fact there was, during and after the Revolution, a widespread move toward rural collectivization which remained one of the points most passionately debated by protagonists and spectators alike. For some, mainly Anarchists, collectivization was the result of a powerful voluntary association movement inspired by propaganda and the collectivist example of their groups. For others, Communists and Republicans, agrarian collectivization was, in most cases, imposed by force, under terror, by militias and Anarchist action groups. 'Neutral' observers were equally divided: the Socialist Prats, the Independent Labour party MP Fenner Brockway, and the Italian Socialist Carlo Rosselli sang the praises of the Aragon collectives, in their view undoubtedly the result of peasant wishes. On the other hand, Borkenau, though he could hardly be accused of sympathy for the themes of Communist propaganda, thought that, apart from the La Mancha provinces, collectivization had been imposed on the peasants through terror.

It must be recognized that there are strong arguments in support of both theories. First of all, the form of collective exploitation was not a new one. The seizures of land that had taken place before the Civil War had always been followed by an attempt at collective farming. The two peasant union organizations, in the CNT and the UGT, had come out in favor of collectivization—voluntary, it is true. The most determined opponents of collectivization, the Communists, created a new peasant organization in the Levante out of nothing in order to fight the movement.[10] Finally, the collectives that came into being during the summer of 1936 sometimes lasted until the end of the Civil War, and were in certain cases reconstituted after their dissolution.[11]

Elsewhere, Andalusia, which could have been fertile ground for collectives, fell into the hands of the Generals very early on, and neither the Levante, Catalonia, nor Aragon provided particularly favorable conditions for such experiments. We know that they were often the scene of violent clashes between 'collectivists' and 'individuals,' which recurred frequently in 1937.

Here too there were many aspects to the situation. The massacre of big proprietors with which the collectivization of land frequently began—especially with Durruti and his column—did not mean that it was not voluntary. The massacres created the material conditions for collectivization, because land thus became available, as well as the psychological conditions, because they provided an opportunity that had until then been sealed off. Terror was one of the levers of the Revolution, and discussion as to whether collectivization was voluntary or compulsory is almost meaningless. Finally, every collectivization was both 'voluntary' and 'compulsory' each time that it was decided by a majority. It must be added that collectivization had without doubt fewer opponents in the early weeks of the Revolution than it had after several months of operation in the somewhat unfavorable circumstances of the war and under constant threats of requisition.

In Catalonia the movement ran into hostility from the

Rabassaires. The CNT there adopted a cautious attitude perfectly illustrated by the resolution adopted on 5 September by its Agrarian Union: 'It is our view that if we claimed to be committed to the immediate collectivization of all land, including that acquired by so much work and self-denial, we would run into a series of obstacles that would prevent us from achieving our final aim in a normal manner.' The peasant conference held by the CNT in Barcelona called on its militants to respect small private estates and to seek above all to convince the peasants by the example of successful sample experiments in rural collectivization.

Moreover, the Catalan collectives varied considerably: there were collectives involving all inhabitants, such as the one at Hospitalet de Llobregat with 1500 families on 15,000 square kilometres and the one at Amposta with 1200 collectivists, both of them exclusively CNT; there were also CNT–UGT collectives, or merely CNT ones, coexisting with individual estates and based exclusively on lands confiscated from big landowners (Vilaboa, 200 collectivists; Serós, 300 collectivists), or on the collectivization of small individual plots of land, or else on both (Lérida, with 400 collectivists; Orrios with 22 families of metalworkers; Granadella, near Lérida, with 160 collectivists out of 2000 inhabitants; Montblanch, nesr Tarragona, with 200 collectivists out of 16,000 inhabitants). At all events, oases in the middle of small estates, they were the exception rather than the rule.

The most frequent case in the Levante was of collectives founded jointly by the CNT and the UGT: such as Villajoyosa, in Alicante province, where not only the lands, which supported slightly fewer than 4000 persons, were collectivized but also the weaving industry, which employed 400 workers, and the fishing industry, which provided a living for 4000; and Ademúz and Utiel in Valencia province, which held 500 and 600 families respectively. In Castellón province, the village of San Mateo was unusual in that it had two communities, one CNT and the other UGT. The Sueca collective in Valencia province formed the *Cooperativa Popular Naranjera* for the sale of its oranges in an attempt to do away with middlemen, which later expanded.[12] Finally there was the much-quoted case of Segorbe, a large town of 10,000 inhabitants in the *huertas* region where a 'collective of agricultural producers and their like' was set up. Membership and resignation were voluntary, with each one contributing or withdrawing his share. But the lives of those who joined were strictly controlled by the elected administrative commission that managed the collective, shared out the work, and paid the wages on a 'household' basis (single man, 5 pesetas; single woman, 4 pesetas; head of family, 5 pesetas; his wife, 2 pesetas, etc.). How did people live in Segorbe? Brockway, an admittedly partial observer, stated: 'More than anything, I enjoyed my visit to the Segorbe collective farm. I shall not describe it in detail, but the spirit of the peasants, their enthusiasm, the way in which they contributed towards the common effort, the pride which they felt in it, all was admirable.'

A visit to the Aragon collectives led Rosselli, who took the same view, to write: 'The obvious advantages of the new social system confirm the spirit of solidarity among the peasants, spurring them to greater efforts and greater activity.'[13]

In fact, under the control of the Anarchists, the collectivization movement embraced more than three-quarters of the land, almost exclusively in communities affiliated to the CNT: there were more than 450 of them, comprising about 430,000 peasants. The collectivists were by far the majority: everyone in Peñalba, Alcañiz, Calanda, and Oliete, 2000 out of 2300 in Mas de las Matas, and 3700 out of 4000 in Alcorisa. The small proprietors could in theory survive as long as they cultivated their lands themselves and did not use wage-earning labor. Livestock for domestic consumption remained private property. The Peasant Federation made huge efforts to organize experimental farms, nurseries, and rural technical colleges. The defenders of collectivist theories claimed that output increased from 30 percent to 50 percent between 1936 and 1937, but it is impossible to check these figures, which were not based on careful statistics.

The most curious, although without doubt the least significant, of the Libertarian experiments in Aragon was the systematic application of Anarchist principles and theories on money and wages. There too wages were standardized on a household basis: 25 pesetas a week for a producer on his own, 35 pesetas for a couple with only one member working, 4 pesetas extra for each dependent child. But there was no money, only vouchers, known as *vales*, exchangeable for goods in the collective's shops. The system worked. However, the experiment was inconclusive, because the collectives, in order to obtain supplies from the rest of Spain, were obliged, whether they liked it or not, to use money, which had in theory been abolished. This was how the Anarchist Souchy described life in the village of Calanda in *Aragon libertaire*:

'On the village square, in front of the church, is a brand-new granite fountain. On its plinth are engraved the initials CNT–FAI. What was the church is now a food store. Not all the departments are yet complete.

'The butcher's is in an annex to the church, a bright, hygienic place, such as the village has never known. Nothing can be bought there with money: the women are given meat in return for vouchers . . . because they belong to the collectives, and that is enough to obtain meat and other foodstuffs.

'The village has 4500 inhabitants. The CNT is in the majority. Seven hundred heads of families belong to it. The collective comprises 3500 persons; the others are on their own. . . . The village, clean and pleasant, is rich. There are 23,000 pesetas in its coffers. It produces oil (4700 barrels a year), corn, potatoes, and fruit. . . . Once there were a few big proprietors. On 19 July, they were expropriated.

'Collectivists and individuals live peacefully side by side. There are two cafés in the village: one for the individuals, the other for the collectivists. . . . There is no shortage of cloth and clothes, because oil has been traded with a Barcelona textile factory.

'The work is strenuous, and there is a shortage of labor, because many young men, all CNT members, are at the front. . . . Everything here is collectivized, except for the small shopkeepers, who wished to remain independent. The chemist's shop belongs to the collective and so does the doctor. The latter is not paid. He is supported like the other members of the collective.

'The finest building in the village, a former convent, is the school, which works according to Ferrer's system. Before there were only eight teachers. The collective has appointed ten more.

'The individuals have also benefited from collectivization: they do not pay rent, nor do they pay for electricity. The village has its own power supply, fed by a waterfall.

'The collectivists are happy. Before, the peasants suffered from hunger in April, May, and June. Now things are better.

'Before, there was a branch bank. Today it is closed. Seventy thousand pesetas have been confiscated and transferred to the municipality for the purchase of goods.

'The peasants work in groups of ten. The land is parceled out into areas. Each group, with a delegate at its head, works its own area. The groups are formed on the basis of common sympathy. The collective is like a big family watching over everyone.'[14]

In contrast to this optimistic, if not idyllic, picture, here is one that was drawn later on by the Communist newspaper *Frente Rojo*:

'Under the reign of fire of the Aragon Council, neither people nor property could rely on any guarantee whatsoever. There were no peasants who had not been forced to join the collectives. Those who resisted were the object of terror, directed against them physically and against their small estates. Thousands of peasants emigrated, preferring to leave their land rather than endure the Council's thousand methods of torture.... The land was confiscated, rings, medals, and even saucepans were confiscated, along with grain and cooked foods and wine for home consumption.... Known Fascists and Falangist leaders were established in municipal councils. With their union cards, they functioned as mayors and municipal councillors, as agents of public order, these men who had come from banditry and had made it a profession and a system of government.'[15]

The truth must obviously lie somewhere between Souchy's

rose-tinted Libertarian paradise and the black Anarchist hell depicted by *Frente Rojo*.

Collectivization and the Problem of Power

Differences as to the scope and significance of collectivization actually concealed differences of a political order. The supporters of the Popular Front, Republicans, Socialists, and Communists, thought, like José Díaz, that in the early days it had 'its justification in the fact that the big industrialists and landowners had neglected the factories and the fields, and that it was up to them to make them productive.'[16] All those who felt that Spain in 1936 did not undergo a social revolution but was forced to remain a parliamentary and democratic republic condemned 'collectivization' and 'syndicalization,' which they saw as a danger to the united front between the working class and its allies from the peasantry and the petty bourgeoisie. The Communist party stressed the need to defend the small industrialist and the small tradesman. 'To embark on such projects,' said José Díaz, 'is absurd and is equivalent to playing the enemy's game.'[17]

In spite of active participation by the UGT in the Levante, it was basically the mass of CNT militants who assumed responsibility for collectivization and syndicalization. In control of local power overnight, after the collapse of the Republican state and its forces of repression, they immediately embarked on the destruction of the system of bourgeois property, in accordance with Malatesta's scheme, and in spite of their leaders' caution—*no hay comunismo libertario*—settled down to constructing the new Libertarian society.

This was an infinitely complex task, for which they had not been prepared and which they had had to tackle armed only with simplistic notions and general principles, employed until then in their propaganda and their criticism of the capitalist system. Lacking precise instructions in the face of an unforeseen situation, unions and militants took the lead without any criteria other than what Andrade so rightly termed the 'Anarchist egalitarian fantasy.' However, it was not enough to turn factories into collective enterprises, or 'social possessions' as they were often described, to set a new economy on its feet and make it work. The problem of credit remained obstinate. There was a need for money, currency for purchases abroad and working capital for collectivized firms. The Madrid government, which held the gold, refused any credit, even when Catalonia offered the billion pesetas deposited in its savings banks as security. Most of the collectivized firms thus survived on liquid assets seized after the Revolution. The Government Committees tried to support them from day to day by makeshift methods: by seizing the bank accounts of the factionists and by seizing and selling jewels and valuables belonging to rebels, churches, and convents. But the problem kept recurring.[18]

Since the banks, credit, and external trade had, thanks to the government, evaded collectivization, there was a growing trend toward what might be called 'syndical capitalism.' On 17 May 1937, a commission from the Barcelona CNT described it succinctly: 'The immoderate concern to collectivize everything, especially firms with monetary reserves, has revealed a utilitarian and petty bourgeois spirit among the masses. . . . By regarding each collective as private property, and not merely as its usufruct, the interests of the rest of the collective have been disregarded. . . . The collectivized firms are solely concerned with their liabilities, leading to an imbalance in the finances of other firms.' In an interesting study, Juan Andrade[19] highlighted some of the graver consequences of a *de facto* situation that was also perfectly in line with the CNT's traditional conceptions: 'Spontaneous, obeying no overall plan, the application of these measures—syndicalization as well as collectivization—resulted in putting the workers in very different material circumstances.'[20]

In a factory that on the eve of the Revolution held a considerable inventory and monetary reserves, work went on normally, with increased wages. The profits went to the upkeep of the factory, to the improvement of the workers' living conditions, and to the firm's social work. But a factory with a deficit or reduction in inventory at the time of the uprising could neither operate normally nor guarantee payment of wages. Certain firms simply survived by gradually spending their financial reserves. There were rich firms and poor ones: wages varied considerably from one branch of industry and even from one factory to another. Collectivization led to the same inequalities and even to the same absurdities that its supporters had criticized in the capitalist system. However, it did not lead to Socialism or to Libertarian Communism.

Nor did the collectivization of land lead to a satisfactory and coherent system of production. Of course it solved many problems, and undeniably it often enabled the peasants to live better, to work more rationally, and to increase production. But for this improvement to be appreciable and lasting and for the example it provided to have a stimulating effect, it would have had to bring these peasants, the poorest in the West, a support that industry was not capable of giving. Such radical measures as the sale of expropriated jewelry by the Aragon Council for the benefit of the collectives covered only a very small part of their needs. Agricultural machinery, fertilizer, and agricultural experts were needed for the collectivization of land not to seem, within a short space of time, the collectivization of poverty. As Borkenau pointed out, the Spanish Revolution 'was trapped in the impasse of discussing whether the land of the peasants themselves should be owned individually or collectively.'

The problem of land in Spain at that time, with the *de facto* abolition of feudal rents, boiled down to the confiscation of the estates of the big landowners, whether factionist or not. In this respect, the Spanish Revolution lacked what the Land Decree was to the Russian Revolution: a fortnight after the Durruti Column shot twenty-eight 'Fascists' from their village, the peasants of Fraga had not yet decided to touch their land, which they had neither shared nor agreed to cultivate collectively. They waited. After the confederal militias, Communist or Republican militias might come and claim that the land had not been seized legally, or—why not?—Civil Guards, who might demand that they be restored to the heirs of the executed Fascists. This was because it was still clear, even to an Aragon peasant, that not everyone saw the agrarian problem through Durruti's eyes. In early August, a decree by the Giral government granted farmers and tenant farmers who had cultivated a piece of land for over six years the right to buy it outright or by redeemable rent payments. Even though this decree had no force at the time, because no one any longer paid rents or tithes, it nevertheless meant that private property still existed and that the government recognized its rights, even though all the deeds had been burned in a great celebration bonfire on the village square. The passage of time soon made this evident: the peasants had taken the land, but after the first surge of enthusiasm, they were confident neither of really owning it nor of having profited by their action. They were quick to turn their hatred on the militiamen who requisitioned, imposed, and pilfered, and they were not wholly convinced that the new 'masters' really wanted to improve their lot.

The Revolution, at first so vigorous in the countryside, seemed to be bogging down there for lack of real leadership.

Efforts at Economic Control

The uprising had destroyed the whole economic and social structure: the industrial regions were cut off from their suppliers of raw materials, the productive regions from their markets. Short of raw materials, the textile factories in Catalonia were soon functioning only three days a week, and the Levante peasants were wondering how they were going to dispose of an excellent crop. The towns were not receiving supplies, and famine threatened. When the strike ended, things were slow to start up again, employers and their staffs were in flight, imprisoned, or dead, some of the workers were at the front and others in the rear. It was a daunting task: food supplies had to be maintained, productive forces redistributed, and markets reorganized. Above all, the militias had to be equipped and armed.

The legal authority of the unions and the Committees meant that immediate difficulties could be solved. The Bilbao Junta issued promissory notes for provisions. Barcelona lived for a fortnight without money, on the basis of requisitions and vouchers. The unions took over the 4000 taxi drivers, unemployed since the requisition of their vehicles, and managed to reclassify them. A decision by the Central Committee, backed by the authority of the CNT and applied by the Control Patrols, swept the Barcelona pavements clear of the horde of vendors and merchants that obstructed them after the revolutionary battles. After a few days the towns received food supplies. In Madrid, on 25 July, a Joint Committee of municipal councillors and market workers distributed 20,000 rations daily. In Barcelona, the Central Committee put the Rabassaire Torrents in charge of the Food Supply Committee: on 24 July, he banned individual requisitions, opened the shops, and took inventory.

Thanks to the Control Patrols and the Commission of Investigation and to reports from the Workers' Administrative and Control Committees, he was given reliable information and wielded effective control, punishing infringements with heavy penalties: essential food supplies for militiamen and for the inhabitants of the towns were guaranteed without an appreciable rise in prices. Moreover, the Food Supply Committee had a direct influence over commercial channels, guaranteeing Barcelona provisions for hospitals, charitable institutions, and popular restaurants: in August it fed up to 120,000 people a day in open restaurants on presentation of a union card and in September managed to reduce this figure to the more reasonable one of 30,000, excluding militiamen, of course. Committees of a similar kind, usually CNT–UGT ones, took care of the militiamen and the unemployed in Valencia, Málaga, and Asturias, and in most of the towns, establishing direct contact with the Village Committees. However, not all had the authority of the Barcelona Food Supply Committee, which was both commissariat and Economic Control Commission, and whose decisions had the force of law in the ports and markets of Catalonia.

Moreover, all this was achieved with genuine enthusiasm and much goodwill on both sides. Of course, the militiamen, who at the start lived completely off the peasants, were not always kindly regarded, and there were many incidents. The Durruti Column was forced to evacuate the village of Pina: proof, all the same, that it was tractable and that it was not a horde of looters. Many of the peasants sold much more willingly, without raising their prices, because they were now assured of not having to share the profits of their sales with the landowner.

Whatever else may have been said about it, the same goodwill and the same enthusiasm governed the improvisation of, or increase in, production in the war industries. In Asturias, the workers recaptured the arsenal in Trubia; work started there again on 25 July. It was the same in Toledo. In Catalonia, the situation was tragic, because there were no factories for war materials, and chemical and metallurgical firms had to be very hurriedly converted. Some machinery construction factories could not operate, because the engineers had destroyed the plans or carried them away, and no one was able to replace them. Colonel Jiménez de la Beraza, former director of the Oviedo arsenal, and two of his engineers, who had escaped from Navarre, applied themselves to the task with the contractor Tarradellas of the Esquerra and the CNT workers Vallejo, a metalworker, and Marti, a chemical worker. The Hispano-Suiza factory was converted. Naturally, after two months, there were only slender results, but at least factories for bullets, shells, rockets, bombs, and armor plating had been established. Moreover, the difficulties derived from the general political and economic situation: currency was needed for indispensable foreign steel and even for Basque steel and Asturian coal. 'Expropriated' fortunes financed the early efforts, but payments were merely deferred.

All these problems could be solved only by an overall policy for the control of the economy. The revolutionary organs of power were seeing to it: Economic Councils were set up in Málaga, in Valencia, and in Asturias. The Aragon Defense Council made a considerable effort to control the province's economy. In Catalonia, the Economic Council, set up on 11 August and ratified by a government decree as 'the ruling body of economic life,' drew up a program that amounted to a plan for the Socialist transformation of the country. It contained the following provisions:

1. Control of production according to the needs of consumption.
2. Monopoly of foreign trade.
3. Collectivization of large agrarian estates, which would be developed by peasant unions and through compulsory syndicalization of individual peasants.
4. Partial devaluation of urban property by the imposition of taxes and the reduction of leases.
5. Collectivization of major industries, public services, and local transport.
6. Seizure and collectivization of firms abandoned by their owners.
7. Extension of the cooperative system in the distribution of goods.
8. Workers' control of banking operations and even nationalization of banks.
9. Workers' syndical control over all firms that were still being privately developed.
10. Rapid reclassification of workers.
11. Rapid suppression of the various taxes in favor of a single tax.

The presence within the Economic Council of the labor movement's most eminent specialists in economic affairs, Andrés Nin and Santillán, was to many a sign that it would be the nerve center for the economic and social transformation of Catalonia, the body for economic centralization and planning. Thanks to the authority of the Central Committee and the workers' militias, for several weeks the Economic Council effectively maintained the governing and controlling role that was allotted to it. However, like the other revolutionary organs of power, it very soon ran into the political problem of currency and credit.

Economics, Politics, and War

In Catalonia, where it had reached the peak of its development, the Revolution was marking time. Economic problems could not be solved independently of political problems. The controlling bodies were restricted to parasitical functions. A whole bureaucracy was flourishing in the shape of new Committees and Councils. Santillán wrote: 'We were an anticapitalist, antiproperty movement. In private property we saw tools, factories, and means of transport, with the capitalist apparatus of distribution as the principal cause of poverty and injustice. We wanted the socialization of all wealth so that not even a single individual should be excluded from life's feast. We have done something, but we have not done it well. We have replaced the old proprietor with half a dozen who regard factories and the means of transport, which they control, as their own property, with the disadvantage that they are not always able to organize an administration and run a better management than the old one.'[21]

Six months after the Revolution, the Spanish economy ran into terrible difficulties. It became the fashion to attack the 'anarchy' of 'collectivization' and 'syndicalization' and the 'incompetence' of the new makeshift leaders. But if the revolutionary achievements are to be assessed fairly, the terrible burden of the war must not be disregarded. The revolutionary gains of the Spanish workers had appreciable and profoundly significant consequences in the early months. The new principles of administration and the abolition of dividends permitted an effective reduction of prices, which in the end was cancelled out only by the soaring increase in the price of raw materials; a capitalist economy, in similar circumstances, could not have avoided it either. Mechanization and rationalization, introduced into many firms and thereafter demanded by the workers themselves, increased productivity considerably. In their enthusiasm, the workers agreed to enormous sacrifices, because in most cases they shared the conviction that the factory belonged to them and that they were at last working for themselves and their class brothers. A genuinely fresh wind blew through the Spanish economy with the concentration of scattered firms, the simplification of commercial channels, and the whole fabric of social achievements benefiting elderly workers, children, the disabled, the sick, and employees generally.

The great weakness of the Spanish workers' revolutionary gains was, even more than their improvised character, their incompleteness. The Revolution, still in its infancy, had to be defended. It was the war that reduced the revolutionary gains to rubble before they had time to mature and prove themselves in a day-by-day experiment compounded of progress and retreat, of groping and discovery.

Notes

[1] Comparisons between the Russian Revolution of 1917 and the Spanish Revolution of 1936 lead to identical conclusions. See Andrés Nin: 'The launching of the rebellion of 19 July speeded up the revolutionary process by provoking a proletarian revolution more profound than the Russian Revolution itself.' (*Les problèmes de la Révolution espagnole*, p. 230.) And Trotsky: 'The Spanish proletariat displayed first-class military capacities. Because of its specific gravity in the economy of the country, because of its political and cultural level, from the first day of the Revolution it stood not lower but higher than the Russian proletariat at the beginning of 1917.' (*Leçon d'Espagne*, pp. 27–28.) One of the signs of the Revolution's depth was unquestionably the massive participation by women, present everywhere, on the Committees as well as in the militias: if revolution is, in effect, as Trotsky said, 'direct action by the deepest layers of the oppressed masses, those who are furthest divorced from theory,' it must be conceded that this was certainly the case in Spain in 1936.

[2] Quoted by Lizarra, *Los vascos y la República española*, pp. 201–202.

[3] An example from a headline in *ABC* on 4 September: 'Alicante: One priest weds, another joins the Communist party.'

[4] Santillán estimated the total amount of capital withdrawn from Catalan banks in the fortnight before the uprising at 90 million pesetas.

[5] In the view of the Anarchists, this was the ultimate stage after the destruction of the state, the one that settled everything.

[6] We quote, among the measures that had the greatest immediate psychological repercussions, the restoration without compensation of all vital possessions lodged with pawnbrokers. Malraux and Delaprée referred to the 'noise' made by the 3000 sewing machines thus 'restored' to the Catalans.

[7] *La Révolution prolétarienne*, 25 August 1936.

[8] This was one of the proud boasts of the Spanish revolutionaries who had been through the Russian Revolution: Andrés Nin liked to tell his companions that the return of public services to normal working order had been incomparably faster in Barcelona in 1936 than in Moscow in 1917.

[9] See his monograph on collectivization in Puigcerdá in *La Révolution prolétarienne*, 25 June 1937.

[10] The Levante UGT and the UGT Peasant Federation were both con-

trolled by Caballero militants. The Communists founded a peasant alliance inspired by Julio Mateu.

[11] Such as the Hospitalet de Llobregat, mentioned by Peirats.

[12] See Peirats' work, *La CNT en la Revolución española*, vol. 1, chap. 15.

[13] In *Giustizia e Libertà*, quoted by Morrow, *Revolution and Counter-Revolution in Spain*, p. 144.

[14] Extract from 'Chez les paysans d'Aragon,' quoted by Jean Bernier in *L'Anarchie*, special number of *Crapouillot*, p. 44.

[15] 14 August 1937.

[16] Speech to the Central Committee on 5 March 1937, *Tres años de lucha* (Barcelona: Ediciones del Partido Comunista de España, 1939), p. 297.

[17] Ibid., p. 298.

[18] The government, through the agency of the UGT, actually controlled the banks and handled credit, as well as gold. These two weapons enabled it to slow down and prevent at will the functioning of collectivized firms. Here, too, economic problems could not be solved, temporarily at least, except in the political field, the field of power. Durruti put his finger on it when he spoke of marching on the Bank of Spain, and so did Santillán when, faithful to the tradition of Anarchist 'expropriators,' he dreamed of a huge raid on its cellars.

[19] 'L'Intervention des syndicats dans la révolution espagnole,' *Confrontation internationale*, September–October 1949, pp. 43–48. It was he who reprinted the conclusions of the CNT. Commission in Barcelona. The expression 'syndicalist capitalism' was taken from *La Batalla*.

[20] Ibid., p. 46.

[21] *After the Revolution* (New York: Greenberg, 1937), p. 121.

CHAPTER 7

FROM REVOLUTION TO CIVIL WAR

According to several Nationalist historians, on the evening of 20 July General Mola felt that the rebels' cause was lost, and he only carried on the fight because he was no longer in control of the *Requetés* and Falangists whose advance he had led. In fact, there was an explanation for this pessimism: the *pronunciamiento* had been crushed in the most important regions, the industrial and commercial centers: in Madrid and the surrounding area, in the most active part of the North, in Asturias and the Basque provinces, and along the whole of the eastern coast. Moreover, the counteroffensive by workers' militias in the days after their victory in the urban centers seemed to be turning out to their advantage. The Catalan militias were engaged in the conquest of Aragon and were knocking at the gates of Saragossa and Huesca. The Madrid militias halted the advance by Mola's men at Somosierra and Guadarrama. Madrid was saved. A few days later, the recapture of Albacete by Loyalist troops and militia columns meant that communications could be restored between Valencia and Madrid. The recapture of Badajoz cut the insurgent forces in two and deprived Mola of any immediate aid from Franco or Queipo de Llano. The fall of the remaining barracks in Gijón gave the workers control over the largest naval port in the North. The fleet, off the coast of Tangier, commanded the straits and prevented reinforcements from the Army of Morocco from reaching the mainland.

The Balance of Military Power

The rebels, who were in a strategically disadvantageous position, had only slight superiority in terms of men and material. The Navy, as we saw, had come out against them. The Air Force, admittedly weak in numbers, had gone over to the popular camp. Mola had only a dozen old planes, captured by a surprise attack on the León airport, for the whole of the North. Naturally, the Generals had more men under their command. Rabasseire estimated them at 15,000 officers and NCOs, 38,000 legionaries and 'Moors' in Morocco, 30,000 Civil Guards, 30,000 *Requetés*, nearly all with Mola, and about 70,000 *Regulares*. But nowhere near all these troops could be used. The young recruits in the *Regulares* had often thrown in their lot with the workers, and there seemed to be doubt about committing them. It was necessary to keep substantial forces in the rear.[1] The struggle went on for several more weeks in Galicia and Andalusia. Moroccan troops were arriving only in dribs and drabs.

In early August, the rebel Generals were deploying only small columns with limited numbers: 3000 against Badajoz, 10,000 in Estremadura, and 20,000 for the first attack on Madrid. Throughout this period, German diplomats echoed the anxieties of Nationalist Spain: they were short of money, they were short of arms. Warlike and disciplined troops like the Moors and the *Tercio* were of course a substantial trump card; however, there was nothing to suggest that they were able to decide victory on their own.

On the other side, the workers' and peasants' militias very soon revealed their weaknesses and the limits of their efficiency. Their courage, enthusiasm, and spirit of sacrifice made them unbeatable in the streets of their towns and villages. But at war difficulties arose. Their military organization was, on the whole, total chaos. As Durruti said: 'Until now we have had a very large number of different units, each with its leader, its men—they vary incredibly from day to day—its arsenal, its baggage train, its provisions, its own particular policy toward the inhabitants, and very often its own special way of interpreting the war, too.'[2] Jean-Richard Bloch, describing what he called the 'picaresque stage' of the Civil War, wrote: 'The first scene provided by the Civil War was one of a large number of disparate columns, fighting on their own, carving out their own operational sectors, where they lived, got their food supplies, and sometimes developed along independent lines.'[3] Moreover, all kinds of surprises were possible on the 'front': wandering about, you could find yourself in the rear of the enemy lines, you could be ambushed in the rear of your own lines, and there was no way of telling to which camp the units whose passage was reported by the villagers belonged. It was not until 26 August that a War Committee of twelve people, officers and political militants, was set up. Even so, its authority remained quite illusory.

No overall plan was possible. The parties formed or reinforced a column for a particular raid, but once the sortie was over the men all went home. The militiamen protested against anyone who wanted not only to make them do guard duty but dig trenches too. Moreover, you went back home between two turns at guard duty, and you were regarded as a madman if you refused to sleep when you were on guard at night. A column that strayed from its base lost most of its militiamen: they liked to sleep at home at night. Durruti said that 'he was handed out all the old soldier's tales: the sick baby, the pregnant wife, and the dying mother.'[4] In the open countryside, the militias soon proved rather ineffective. Their initial successes were gained at the cost of very heavy casualties. Not only did the men not know how to protect themselves, they did not even want to know: the leader of an Anarchist column made it a point of honor to march exposed at the head of his men. This was how Ascaso had died, and this was how Mola was to die. There was contempt for the 'technique' of the professional soldiers, because the enthusiasm and spirit of the militants seemed to be the essential ingredient, as it had been during the street fighting. The militiamen did not know how to maintain their arms and often even how to handle them, and once they had them, they damaged them and wounded themselves through inexperience. Arms and ammunition were scarce. On the Aragon and Madrid fronts, units being relieved handed over their arms to new arrivals. In Oviedo, the military command put a ban on shooting at an enemy except during a general attack. Naturally, improvised weapons such as dynamite cartridges, skillfully handled by the miners, the *dinamiteros*, proved formidable. At Oviedo, in August, the militiamen managed to pierce the Nationalist defenses with trucks armored with cement, full of volunteers armed with flamethrowers. These were makeshift methods, capable of achieving surprise, but unable to swing the balance decisively.

Moreover, the militiamen were no better at dealing with their ammunition than with their lives: they wasted their cartridges on planes and even on ships. These men were not regular soldiers; they were not trained, nor did they have NCOs. Many temporary leaders proved helpless. Many of the 'Republican' officers turned traitor, rounded on their own men, and committed active or passive sabotage. Artillerymen knowingly shelled their own troops. Even the Loyalist officers were suspect: they were disobeyed precisely because they were officers and nobody trusted them.

In July and August, it was perhaps the unit of command that was most grievously at fault. The first successful strategic moves had been made just after the rebellion. Afterwards, everyone locked himself away in his own region. Anarchists and Nationalists eyed each other in the Basque provinces: Mola, in the early weeks, was able to turn his back on them in peace. The Catalans, who were hammering away at Saragossa without artillery, had little impact on the plans of an enemy aiming at Madrid.[5] Everyone seemed to be fighting his own war without caring what was going on in the next province.

Finally, the opposing forces seemed to cancel each other out in a precarious balance. Mola ran up against the sierra as the Catalans had at Saragossa. The miners were blocking Oviedo, but Aranda was preparing there for a siege that threatened to be a long one. The siege of the Alcázar in Toledo began. The Civil Guards who had revolted on 19 July had shut themselves in the old fortress with provisions, ammunition, and hostages. The militiamen who were laying siege to them, as they had laid siege to suspect garrisons in Valencia and elsewhere, were firing random shots at its thick walls. It was not until the thirty-fourth day of the siege that a field gun was brought up. It did not immediately shell the Alcázar but merely destroyed the surrounding houses in order to isolate it and to cut off altogether the besieged men's links with the outside. In Gijón the two barracks were captured by the end of the second week in August, literally dynamited by the miners. No one in Toledo dared take the initiative with such methods, because Colonel Moscardó, who was in command of the besieged, refused to release the six-hundred-odd hostages, women and children rounded up in the working-class districts after the retreat, who spent some terrible weeks in the darkness and stench of the cellars. The siege of the Alcázar was in fact a phony war: seeing it for the first time after thirty-four days on 24 August, Louis Delaprée wrote: 'In the town's little twisting alleys, as soon as you see one of its four towers between two roofs, you want to flatten yourself against a wall. . . . Here and there, piles of sandbags block the view. Militiamen in large straw hats, hiding behind the barricades, are watching the watchers across the way, at a distance of fifty, forty, and sometimes twenty yards. Now and again, fed up with exchanging bullets, they hurl insults at each other. In the end, you don't know if you are besieging or being besieged.'[6] 'The Reds,' wrote Henry Clérisse, 'only had to will it in order to crush the heroic garrison.'[7] The fact is that they did not wish to do so. It was 3 August before they brought up a heavy piece of artillery, a 420-mm field gun. Until then, the besiegers tried to spare the lives of the hostages by promising mercy to all the besieged in return, but they obstinately refused. Then Major Rojo, former professor at the Military Academy, Father Camarasa, canon of Madrid, and the Chilean chargé d'affaires tried to convince them, in the course of those colorful truces described in almost identical terms by Malraux and Koltsov: the militiamen insulted the Civil Guards by handing them cigarettes and razor blades.

For a few brief weeks, the Spanish conflict resembled what

1. Manuel Azaña, President of the Republic, at his desk in the cabinet headquarters

2. José Antonio Primo de Rivera addressing a mass meeting in Madrid

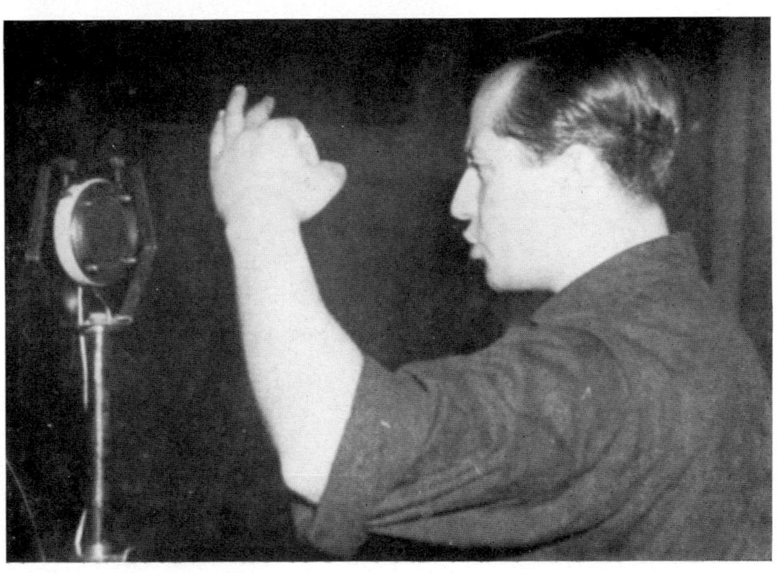

3. Largo Caballero, Prime Minister of the Republic 1936–7, on his way to a government outpost near Leguerinos

4. A view of the bombed city of Toledo

was taking place around the Alcázar. Neither of the two enemies seemed likely to carry the day.

The Balance Is Upset

Owing to foreign intervention, the balance was very soon upset. Portugal had long been one of the centers of the conspiracy: from the very first, it had been one of the bases for the uprising. The Hotel Aviz in Lisbon served as a relay station for telephone communications between Burgos and Seville. The rebels circulated freely between Spain and Portugal, and the first German planes were based on Portuguese territory at Caia, a mile from the frontier. In return, Salazar's government handed all 'left-wing' refugees over to the rebels. Italy, for her part, sent the first of the planes promised to the rebels at the end of the month. By early August, Germany was also supplying war material, landing it at Lisbon. The German and Italian fleets tried to protect the Moorish troops on their passage from Morocco to Spain by interposing themselves between the Republican fleet and the Nationalist troopships. Junkers and Caproni planes secured the first 'air bridge,'[8] which enabled Queipo to achieve victory.

The Republicans received no comparable aid. The first consignments of planes agreed to by the French air minister aroused public protest: the French Popular Front government yielded to British pressure and to the press campaign unleashed against it. On 17 July it banned arms deliveries to Spain and then initiated the idea of 'nonintervention,' to which Great Britain and the USSR subscribed.[9] From then on the rebels received continuous and substantial supplies of arms and ammunition, because Germany and Italy, while also belonging to the Nonintervention Committee, did not stop their deliveries.[10]

From this point on, the Spanish Republic was isolated, and the rebel Generals benefited from a *de facto* international alliance. Under pressure of threats from Franco and demands from Rome and Berlin for the 'status of Tangier' to be respected, the London and Paris governments persuaded Giral to remove the Republican fleet from the coast of Tangier in early August.[11] On 4 August, the first massive Moroccan contingents landed at Tarifa. From now on there was no hindrance to communications between Morocco and Spain: the Nationalists lacked neither men nor material.

The Nationalist Offensive

The Nationalists were able at that point to launch their first large-scale offensive and to try and link up their two zones. On 6 August, Franco's Moroccan troops attacked in a westerly direction: Portugal's complicity protected their left flank as they made a two-pronged advance toward the North to link up with Mola's troops. The columns moved forward without meeting real resistance, following the main roads, and first surrounding and then dismantling the flimsy barriers erected on the road through the efforts of Workers' and Peasants' Committees. On 11 August, the Tella Column seized Mérida, which, though completely mined, did not blow up. The Yagüe Column, 1500 motorized troops with a few batteries of light artillery, crossed the Sierra Morena on the seventh, reached Badajoz on the thirteenth, and took it on the fourteenth. By the twelfth the leader of the Badajoz *Asaltos*, Major Ávila, had crossed the Portuguese frontier, denouncing the domination of the town by 'the armed populace.' On the morning of the thirteenth, the mayor of Badajoz fled. Fifty militiamen shut in the cathedral resisted the assaults of the Moors for two days and killed themselves when their ammunition ran out: the heroism of the troops did not compensate for the military leaders' betrayal and the chaos resulting from the Revolution.

The Nationalists now brought their main efforts to bear on the northern front, where Mola, although he was well supplied with troops, red-bereted *Requetés* covered with holy medals and scapulars, was afraid of running short of ammunition. On 1 August the Marquis of Portago, his personal envoy, was in Berlin, asking for planes. On the eighteenth, the German ambassador in Paris passed on his request for 10 million cartridges. Material and munitions arrived by way of Portugal. The link with the South secured the rear. On 15 August the offensive began to take shape. On the nineteenth, San Sebastián was almost surrounded and the Beorlegui Column was at the gates of Irún. Franco's Moors now poured through Badajoz to reinforce Mola's troops.

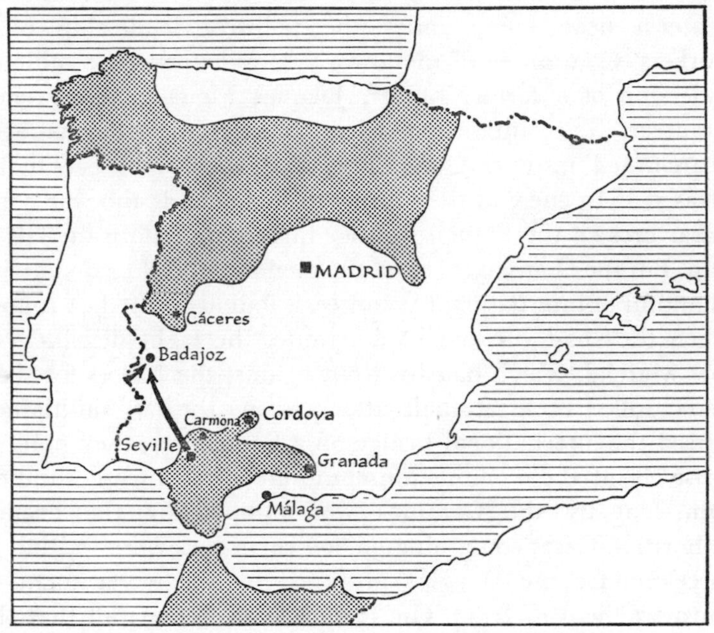

The March on Badajoz (July–August 1936)

This was the beginning of the Battle of the Fortresses.[12] Here the militiamen were fighting with their backs to the sea against a manifestly superior army. German planes were supporting Mola's offensive. Their sudden appearance and their strafing and bombing threw the ranks of militiamen in the open countryside into panic. But in the towns they were prepared to cling to any scrap of wall. It was not always so with their commanders. The same dissensions arose among the ranks of the defenders as in Badajoz. The men of the CNT, ready to defend to the last, threatened to shoot the hostages if the bombing continued and wanted to destroy the towns completely and leave the enemy only with ruins if they finally had to yield. On the other hand, the moderate elements in the

Popular Front, and especially the Basque Nationalists, wished to spare the towns and their inhabitants and refused to carry out reprisals against hostages. The Basque militias supervised the protection of property and the Church against the Anarchist militiamen to the end. There was fierce resistance at Rentería near Irún, under the political leadership of a Workers' Committee of metalworkers and under the military leadership of a former officer, Jacques Menachem, a French volunteer. The authorities tried to save the 180 hostages incarcerated in Fort Guadalupe, and they were eventually released.[13] In the end they threw in their hand: the war commissar crossed the French frontier three days before the fall of Irún. But the Communists and the men of the CNT, along with a handful of international volunteers, fought to the last round. When they had run out of dynamite, the eight defenders of Fort Marcial, which had held out against the Moors for sixty hours, rolled rocks at their attackers. As the last militiamen crossed the international bridge on 4 September, they pointed derisively at their empty ammunition belts. An ammunition train sent by the Catalans was stopped by the French authorities. Cases containing 30,000 cartridges were waiting in Barcelona for the Douglas promised by the government to transport them to Irún. The town was in flames: all that the Nationalists had gained was ruins.

The tragedy of Irún seemed to revive the differences in the Republican camp. On 8 September, San Sebastián was, according to the correspondent of *Havas*, the scene of 'actual street fighting.' The CNT militants had launched an attack on the pump room, where hostages had been incarcerated. The governor, a Socialist and officer in the *Carabineros*, Lieutenant-Colonel Ortega, tried to negotiate with Mola: his son went to France in order to enter Nationalist Spain. The rumor went around that he was offering the rebels a promise to respect hostages, houses, and monuments and to surrender San Sebastián if the Nationalists agreed to an amnesty for the troops beforehand. Nothing was officially published about these deals. But on the eleventh Nationalist planes dropped leaflets on the town: 'Respect law and order in your town. I am granting you forty-eight hours' respite. I am ready to listen to the voice of the Basque Nationalists.' The hostages, heavily guarded, were transferred to Bilbao. The situation in San Sebastián was confused. The Nationalist radio announced the murder of Leizaola and the arrest of Irujo by the Anarchists. On the eleventh, Maurice Leroy cabled *Paris-Soir* that Irujo was 'in control of the situation,' and on the thirteenth that the Anarchists were 'in control of the town.' In fact, the Basque Nationalists were in control. The revolutionaries were defeated in this civil war within the Civil War.[14] 'Looters' and 'incendiaries' were summarily shot by police and Basque militias. On the fourteenth the Republicans evacuated San Sebastián by the Bilbao road freed by the Carlists. The same day, immediately after their departure, Mola's troops entered the capital of Guipúzcoa, where fifty Civil Guards had remained to ensure that law and order were preserved.

Threat to Madrid

The balance of power, upset by massive aid from the Germans and Italians, was such that, in early September, most observers expected the imminent fall of Madrid: it seemed unlikely that the militiamen could hold out against the professional soldiers, tanks, and planes facing them. But the expected offensive was deferred. Franco cautiously postponed it because of the reinforcements that had to be sent to the North: he seemed to be willing to concentrate sufficient forces only in order to strike a decisive blow. But, more important, an emotional factor had intervened in the course of military operations. Since the beginning of August, the Nationalist press and the foreign newspapers who were in sympathy with the rebellion had been singing the praises of the cadets of the Toledo Military Academy. In fact, there were only a dozen officer-cadets among the defenders of the fortress.[15] But the heroic defense by the Civil Guards was put forward by this propaganda as the work of the cadets, who thus came to symbolize the resistance of Spanish youth to 'Red' domination: the 'cadets of the Alcázar' became legendary.[16] With the formation of the Caballero government, pressure by the besiegers increased: the building, shelled this time, was in ruins. The Civil Guards were still holding out in the vaults. But provisions began to run out, and stocks of water were diminishing.[17] Franco rejected the possibility of a march on Madrid and tried to liberate the Alcázar.[18] His army attacked in the South, along the Tagus Valley. On 4 September, Colonel Yagüe's Moroccan advance guard entered Talavera de la Reina.

Here and there the militiamen resisted, but elsewhere they were seized with panic and fled in a fearful stampede, of which Malraux gave a striking description. Two columns of motor-cyclists sent from Madrid to reinforce Toledo were encircled by surprise and wiped out. On 27 September, General Varela's Moroccan advance guard entered Toledo. At dusk, a section of Moors linked up with Moscardó's men. The Alcázar was liberated. The besiegers of the previous day, themselves besieged in the surrounding houses, fell one by one. From now on the capital was threatened. The whole world was waiting for its fall, and for terrible reprisals.

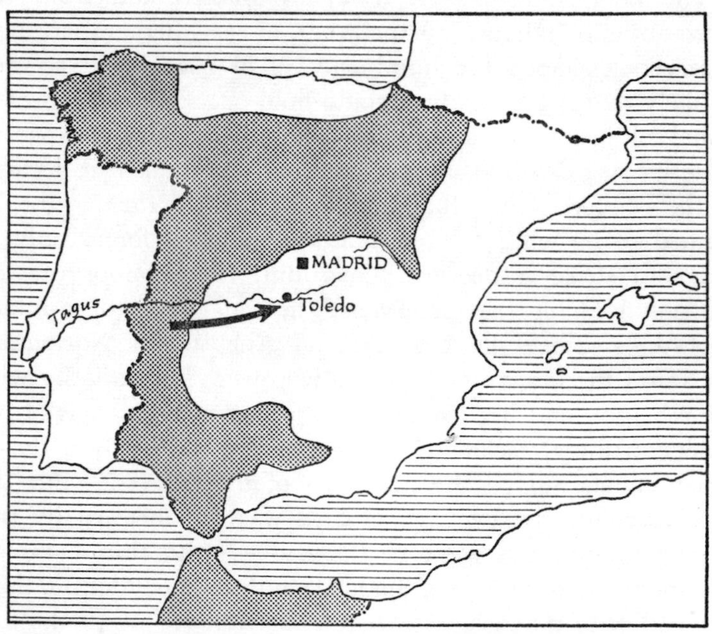

The March on Toledo (August–September 1936)

The Terror

The military uprising had begun everywhere with the arrest, murder, or execution after summary trial, of Republican officers and soldiers.[19] The purge thus initiated had been accompanied everywhere by the prompt elimination of anyone who could be regarded as a union, workers' party, or merely Republican leader.[20] The *paseo* was common here, too, with this difference only, that no one called for an end to it, because their organizers, *Requetés* and Falangists, were also in control of public order. Massacres of prisoners became a daily occurrence, the only means, it would seem, of making room in the ever-crowded prisons.[21] The urge to destroy the enemy was equally obvious on the other side. Among the Republicans it was massive, public, and spontaneous. Here it was organized, controlled, and justified by all, including the highest ecclesiastical authorities, such as the archbishop of Toledo, who proclaimed that it was 'the love of the God of our fathers that has armed half of Spain' against the 'modern monster, Marxism, or Communism, seven-headed hydra, symbol of all heresies.'[22] It was several months before precise indications were available as to the 'White terror' that was rife in the whole of Nationalist Spain.

Better known are the rebel Army's methods of handling its conquests: war correspondents were allowed to go to the front, while the prisons were evidently off limits for them. The Moorish soldiers, recruited from the most primitive tribes, were given their head. They raped women and castrated men, which was, in the view of Brasillach and Bardèche, a 'quasi-ritualistic type of operation.' But the other troops were not behindhand. Women were the preferred victims of general sadism; they were not only raped, but systematically humiliated, shaved, painted with red lead, and purged with castor oil. General Queipo de Llano was proud of it. On 23 July, he stated on Radio Seville: 'The Reds' women have also learned that our men are real men and not emasculated militiamen; kicking and screaming will not save them.'[23]

The international press was full of examples provided by correspondents whose sympathies, however, were often with the rebels. Bertrand De Jouvenel described in *Paris-Soir* on 23 July the execution of the railroad workers who had defended Alfera against the *Requetés* of the Escámez Column.[24] The entry of the Nationalists into Badajoz was accompanied by real carnage. The *Havas* special agent cabled that there were corpses in the cathedral, even at the foot of the altar, and that 'the bodies of government supporters executed en masse are laid out in rows in front of the cathedral on the main square.' The correspondents of the *New York Herald* and *Le Temps* described this butchery, which the Nationalist officers tried to justify by the impossibility of holding prisoners. A column of fugitives was driven back to the Portuguese frontier, led back into the town, and massacred on the spot. The correspondent of *Le Temps* referred to 1200 executions, of 'pavements covered in blood in which helmets are still weltering,' while the shooting continued in the main square. 'Rough methods,' Brasillach admitted, adding that 'every combatant was shot, because as long as there had been no general mobilization, he was considered a militant.'[25]

Terror was the means of putting an end to resistance by the masses. At least this was how the leaders of the rebellion saw it. On 30 July, Franco told a journalist on the *News Chronicle* that he was ready, if necessary, to 'shoot half of Spain.' On 18 August, Queipo de Llano stated: 'Eighty percent of Andalusian families are in mourning, and we shall not hesitate to have recourse to sterner measures.' And Colonel Barato stated to the correspondent of the *Toronto Star*: 'When we have executed two million Marxists, we shall have restored order.'

The massive flight of peasants before each Nationalist attack showed that, at any rate, the military leaders had achieved their aim and that their troops were inspiring profound terror. A dispatch from Delaprée described the 'vast exodus' of peasants from Estremadura, 'driving their pigs and goats in front of them, the women dragging along their brats.'[26] However, in this horror-stricken crowd, the men, 'peasants with tanned faces, short smocks, and large hats,' immediately demanded guns, from which they refused to be parted either to eat or sleep, and went back to fight. Terror is a double-edged weapon: tens of thousands were fleeing along the roads, but just as many workers, peasants, and intellectuals were seizing arms in order to fight, no matter how, so long as they fought. All earlier preoccupations and aspirations seemed to melt away at this desperate urge to resist, to bar the way, to win. Thousands were now ready to do anything to oppose what seemed to them a better trained and equipped war machine with another machine, no less efficient: the slogans 'discipline' and 'single command' found a ready echo. They had to fight and hold on at all costs. In order not to perish, they had first of all to end the chaos born of the multiplicity of authorities and the conflicts of power, establish discipline, build a command, and adapt the militias to their vital task: the war.

Notes

[1] However, it was the political militias, especially the Falangist ones, that seemed to devote themselves to the task of 'mopping up.'

[2] Quoted in A. and D. Prudhommeaux, *Catalogne, 1936–1937*, pp. 18–19.

[3] Bloch, *Espagne, Espagne!*, p. 127.

[4] Quoted by Peirats, *La CNT en la Revolución española*, 1: 221.

[5] According to Koltsov, Durruti told Trueba: 'Take the whole of Spain, but don't touch Saragossa: the Saragossa operation is mine' (*Ispanskii dnevnik*, p. 45). Every group more or less shared this outlook.

[6] Delaprée, *Mort en Espagne*, p. 77.

[7] *Espagne 36–37* (Paris: Georges Ventillard, 1937), p. 189.

[8] See Part 2, chapter 14.

[9] See Part 2, chapter 13.

[10] The Spanish government, however, did nothing to mobilize sympathetic opinion abroad against non-intervention. The Socialist de los Ríos, speaking in its name, insisted that Léon Blum not resign but remain in power, although he was taking the initiative in favor of nonintervention (see Part 2, chapter 1). On 9 August, Premier Giral stated: 'The Spanish government does not want any foreign intervention in the struggle that it is carrying on, whether it be overt or in secret, direct or indirect, and whether it favors one or the other camp.'

[11] See chapter 5.

[12] It was in fact a period of sieges. To Oviedo, Toledo, and La Cabeza were added Irún and then San Sebastián.

[13] On 25 August, Lieutenant Colonel Ortega released a certain number

of hostages 'on humanitarian grounds,' including the Count of Romanones, who sought refuge in France.

[14] It appears that the CNT leaders did not effectively seize the initiative in resisting the Basque authorities. Leroy, in *Paris-Soir* on 14 September, described a dramatic interview at which Governor Ortega, aided by the Communist Larrañaga, confronted the CNT leaders Gesgobu and Orthiano: the outcome was the decision to evacuate. Galo Díez, the CNT leader (*Dans la tourmente*, p. 30), wrote: 'We can declare that the evacuation of San Sebastián was, of all those carried out in so short a time, the calmest, the most orderly, and the most efficient.' This was to accept responsibility for it. However, he reproached the Basque Nationalists for leaving the rebels the 'wealth of the Church' and 'useful things in factories, workshops, and businesses.' He pointed out: 'When our comrades wanted to destroy them, they opposed it, weapons in hand, and we had to give in to avoid a fratricidal struggle.'

[15] Clérisse pointed out that the garrison included 650 Civil Guards, 150 *Asaltos* from the Fourteenth *Tercio* in Madrid, a dozen officers, and eight cadets.

[16] See on this subject the book by Henri Massis and Robert Brasillach, *Les cadets de l'Alcazar* (Paris: Librairie Plon, 1936; translated into English as *The Cadets of the Alcazar* [New York: Paulist Press, 1937]). For instance, the authors reported this particularly dramatic episode: on 26 July, militiamen telephoned Colonel Moscardó with threats to shoot his son if he did not yield up the fortress. Moscardó refused and his son was executed. Relying on Herbert L. Matthews' evidence and on comparative criticism of various descriptions of this affair, Pedro Isasi claimed in *El Socialista* (26 September 1957) that this episode had been a complete fabrication, Moscardó's son having, according to him, been killed in the assault on La Montaña and his family having remained free. He further asserted that the external telephone line from Alcázar had been cut since 22 July. Matthews, in the English edition of his book *The Yoke and the Arrows*, admitted that he had been wrong about the death of young Moscardó in the attack on La Montaña. After comparing theories and questioning various witnesses, Hugh Thomas confirmed the validity of the Nationalist version. (*The Spanish Civil War*, p. 203.)

[17] The fortress's meat reserves were made up of 98 horses and 12 mules, according to one of the besieged (*Paris-Soir*, 30 September).

[18] Of all the Nationalist historians, Aznar was the only one who approved Franco's move. All the rest held that the detour by way of the Alcázar had prevented the fall of Madrid.

[19] For instance, Lieutenant Colonel Carratala in Madrid and General Molero in Valladollid. Among well-known persons shot later were General Batet—the vanquisher of the 1934 uprising in Catalonia—Air Force General Núñez de Prada, and then, in Saragossa, Generals Salcedo, Carídad Pita, Romerales, and Campins, proof that not the whole of the Army was with the rebels.

[20] See on this subject the memoir by the Madrid College of Lawyers, reprinted by Peirats (*La CNT en la Revolución española*). Clérisse confirmed it.

[21] Bahamonde, Jean de Pierrefeu.

[22] Louis Martin-Chauffier, in *Catholicisme et Rébellion* (Paris: Comité Franco-Espagnol, n.d.), contributed many instances of persecution carried out by the Nationalists: churches burned, Protestant ministers shot.

[23] Quoted by Alba, *Histoire des républiques espagnoles*, p. 331.

[24] Cf., especially in *Le Journal* and *Paris-Soir*, the mass executions during the conquest of Andalusia. In each village, according to De Jouvenel and Leroy, the arenas were converted into cemeteries. Triana was mopped up 'by knife and grenade.' Executions of hostages followed, and their corpses lay in the open for days on end. See also Henry Danjou's account of the attack on Mérida by the legionaries and the execution of the worker militants who had defended it, such as Anita López, moving spirit of the Committee.

[25] The emotional effect of these press reports on international opinion was considerable. In the future, censorship was to be harsher in Nationalist Spain, out of which little information or documentation on the repression filtered from then on. Robert Bru, cameraman for *Pathé-Nathan*, was arrested in Seville and accused of having sent photos of Badajoz to France.

[26] Delaprée, *Mort en Espagne*, p. 89.

CHAPTER 8

THE LIQUIDATION OF REVOLUTIONARY POWER

Badajoz, Irún, Talavera, and Toledo were stages in a summer campaign that was a disaster for the revolutionaries and a condemnation of the duality of power that was largely responsible for these military reverses. In fighting a war a single authority is essential. The duality between the power of the Committees and the state was an obstacle to the conduct of the war. In autumn 1936, the only problem was to know which of the two powers, Republican or revolutionary, would prevail.

Committees and Soviets

When Spanish workers and peasants created, on every level, administrative organs of the council type, organs of struggle, and organs of power known as *consejos*, committees, and juntas, they were unknowingly and in their own way carrying on the tradition of the twentieth-century workers' and peasants' revolution, exemplified in the Workers', Peasants', and Soldiers' Councils of the Soviets in the 1905 and 1917 Russian Revolution and in the *Räte* of the 1918–1919 German Revolution.[1]

The traditional split in the Spanish working class easily explains how it was that the initial form of organization of revolutionary power, after 19 July, resulted from agreements between parties and unions. Such as they were, however, the Committees did represent at first far more than the sum total of the representatives of the various organizations, as we have seen. More than liaison committees, they were the expression of the revolutionary will of thousands of militants, independent of their political affiliations. The best proof of this was the hostility or indifference to their own parties' instructions on the part of many militants who, in the early weeks, had appeared far more tractable toward their Committees. But such a situation could not go on indefinitely. In order for the Committees to become real soviets, they would at some time or other have had to cease being made up of leaders of organizations, whether appointed or elected, and have become elected bodies subject to recall, acting democratically according to the law of the majority, not the rule of summit agreements. Now this did not occur anywhere in Spain. The workers and peasants appointed their Committees spontaneously. But, equally spontaneously, they placed them under the aegis of parties and unions, which for their part had not decided to yield up, in favor of a new body, the authority and power that they had managed to seize thanks to the collapse of the state.

No party or union championed the power of the Government Committees or their transformation into soviets. Santillán, referring to the Central Committee, wrote: 'It had to be strengthened and supported, so that it could complete its mission, because salvation lay in its strength, which was the strength of everyone,' and he conceded its failure: 'In this interpretation, we have remained isolated from our own friends and comrades.'[2] Andrés Nin, familiar with the Russian Revolution, declared that the Committees could never become soviets, because Spain did not need them.[3]

In this way, the Committees gradually ceased to be genuine revolutionary bodies, because of their failure to change themselves into a direct expression of the insurgent masses. They became 'nominal committees,' in which workers and peasants carried less and less weight as the revolutionary battles and the direct exercise of power in the streets by armed workers faded into the past, and in which, on the contrary, the influence of party and union apparatus came to play a dominant role.

It was also ultimately left to the latter to solve the problem of power, such as it appeared in autumn 1936, in the course of the Revolution and in order to counter the Civil War. Which authority was to supplant the other? Which was to have power? The Popular Front government, with its officials, its magistrates, its police, and its army—in short, a reconstituted state apparatus? Or a government of Councils and Committees, with its Regional and Local Committees, its Factory Councils, its combat militias, its Commissions of Investigation, its Control Patrols, and its revolutionary tribunals? A government based on respect for private property, deriving from the assembly elected in February on the Popular Front's liberal program? Or a government deriving from the Councils and Committees and setting itself the revolutionary task of achieving Socialism, with its Authoritarian or Libertarian undertones?

The International Context

It was the problem of the Revolution itself that now arose. Should it be pursued, or should it be halted? What were minor differences on such questions at the outset swiftly became immutable antagonisms. The pursuit of the Revolution at all costs included the risk of losing the war. The urge to halt the Revolution meant combatting it and thus completely altering the premises of the Civil War.

It is clear that in 1936 the world balance of power was by no means as favorable to the Spanish Revolution as it had been in 1917–1919 to the Russian Revolution. The USSR had ceased to be the inspiration of the world revolutionary movement. This was the time when Stalin was setting about the liquidation of the Bolshevik old guard and decapitating the international Communist movement by a series of trials and purges. Germany, where a workers' revolution had been threatening for more than a decade, was now seeing its labor movement, both parties and unions, crushed beneath the iron heel of Nazism. Mussolini's Fascist regime in Italy had not been challenged. There were no immediate prospects of revolution in Eastern Europe. England was perfectly stable. France, where the great June 1936 wave of strikes had just come to an end, was the sole exception. However, it seemed that the Socialist Léon Blum's Popular Front government had ruled it out once and for all. To the revolutionary Socialist Marceau Pivert, who had stated in June 1936 that 'all was possible' and who regarded the activities of the Spanish working class[4] as a revolutionary example to be followed in France, Maurice Thorez, secretary-general of the French Communist party, answered by saying that not everything was possible and that a strike ought to be ended when its aims had been achieved. The threat of Hitler weighed heavily against the arguments of those who were preaching moderation: it was clear that neither the SFIO Socialist party nor the Communist party would agree to go beyond the limits of the 'Radical-Socialist' program of the Popular Front, of which they formed the left wing. Moreover, it was fairly unlikely that they would be outflanked by their troops in the near future. There were no political or union formations in France equivalent to the CNT–FAI or the POUM, which played an essential role in the Spanish movement. The French working class manifested its sympathy for the Spanish Revolution in a thousand ways. But it knew it only through *Le Populaire*, *L'Humanité*, and *Paris-Soir*,[5] which pictured it in the same way. The French friends of the CNT and the POUM could counter the influential organs of the Popular Front and the national press only with propaganda put out by occasional newspapers and private magazines, stemming from tiny organizations violently at odds with each other. The Spanish revolutionaries felt isolated.

One could of course hold endless discussions about the opportunities that they had of compensating for this isolation with a bold revolutionary policy.[6] It might be thought, as Trotsky did, that the Spanish Revolution offered the possibility of a reversal of the world balance of power and that it was precisely its defeat that opened the way to the outbreak of the Second World War.[7] The fact is that their sense of isolation was one of the elements that determined the attitude of the Spanish revolutionaries, many of whom gave up the pursuit of the Revolution. This was because one of the motives, decidedly not unimportant, for the policy of nonintervention lay in the fears of French and English capitalists for their immediate interests in Spain and, over the long term, in their own countries.[8] London and Paris could envisage supporting, albeit very warily, a democratic and Republican Spain, but not a revolutionary one. Everyone in Spain, including the Anarchists, was perfectly aware of this. Whether reason or excuse, the argument carried weight: potential suppliers were not to be frightened off. Moreover, the USSR's policy was moving in the same direction: in Moscow's view, the Spanish affair must not, at any cost, provide an opportunity for isolating the USSR and cutting her off from the Western democracies. Add to this the fact that Stalin had not the slightest desire to support a revolutionary movement, some of whose moving spirits, dissident Anarchists and Communists from the POUM, he regarded as his worst enemies, because they were potential rivals of the Communist party's monopoly over the working class, and it is clear why the USSR saw no bar to joining the Nonintervention Committee from the outset.

Naturally, the international context does not explain everything. However, it alone accounts for the speed with which the weak Republican section of the Spanish petty bourgeoisie, caught between the insurgent Generals and the armed workers in July 1936, managed to reconstruct its state. For it was the international context that supplied the real architects of this reconstruction of the Republican state, Socialists, Communists, and, to a large extent, Anarchists, with their most effective arguments in favor of Spain's 'respectability,' of respect for property and parliamentary forms as opposed to the Revolution of the Committees and the collectivizations.

The Supporters of the Restoration of the Republican State

The Republican statesmen did not in fact seem capable of carrying on the fight that ought to have been theirs. It was the same men, former ministers under Casares Quiroga and Martínez Barrio, who made up the Giral government. We saw how they strove to endure, to ensure the survival of a semblance of legality. But they were incapable of imposing

5. Nationalists at the entrance to Oviedo

6. Republican troops marching to take up defence positions on the outskirts of Teruel

7. Juan Negrín, Prime Minister from 1937

8. General Franco in 1938

their authority, and the revolutionary troops completely eluded them.[9]

Only the workers' leaders, in so far as they tolerated the government at all, prevented its disappearance. Only they, through their prestige, could have restored some authority to a legal government. Prieto understood this perfectly. He remained firmly convinced, even more after the Revolution than before, that Spain faced a long period of normal capitalist development. The 'revolutionary excesses' were, in his view, compromising the country's future to an increasing extent. To him the only realistic task consisted of building a sound Republican regime, backed by a strong army: it alone could secure the aid of the London and Paris 'democracies' against the Generals and their allies. Thus he wrote in *El Socialista*: 'We hope that certain democracies' estimate of the Spanish Revolution will change, because it would be a pity, a real tragedy, to compromise these chances [of help] by stepping up the pace of the Revolution, which is not at present leading us to any positive solution.' His anxiety to preserve the sympathy of the West led him to say, in an interview to *Havas* on 2 September, that he was 'delighted that the French government had taken the initiative over proposals for nonintervention.'

Actually a minister without portfolio, Prieto was nevertheless the first to take in the gravity of the situation. In an interview with Koltsov on 26 August, he frankly recognized the government's impotence. As he had before the Revolution, he felt that the Socialists ought to take up governmental responsibilities. But the state of mind of the masses was such that he went so far as to advocate, without any hesitation, the formation of a ministry headed by his old enemy, Largo Caballero, the only person whose name and prestige could inspire the necessary popular confidence. 'My opinion of him is universally known. He is a fool who wants to be clever. He is a disrupter and a bungler who claims to be a methodical bureaucrat. He is a man capable of leading us all to ruin. And yet today he is the only man, or at least the only name, that it would be useful to put at the head of a new government.'

Indicating that he was ready to enter such a cabinet and work in it under Caballero's leadership, he stated: 'There is no other way out for the country. There is none for me either if I wish to be of use to the country.'[10] Ever clear-sighted and pessimistic, he declared a few days later to Álvarez del Vayo that a Largo Caballero government would be the regime's 'last card.'[11]

Prieto and his friends were not the only ones in the workers' camp to emerge as the champions of moderatism and loyalty to the Republican regime. The Spanish Communist party and its offshoot, the PSUC—freer in their movements because they did not have to contend, like the Socialist party, with internal strife—had often adopted, even before the Socialists, positions that were clearer still.[12] After 19 July, the majority of their militants had followed the revolutionary current, taking part in and backing the actions of the Government Committees. On the other hand, their leadership had backed all the Republican attempts to preserve the state. In Valencia, the Communist party had disapproved of the Popular Executive Committee's opposition to Martínez Barrio's Provincial Junta. In Barcelona, it was Comorera, leader of the PSUC, who had tried to incite Companys to resist the CNT and had then entered the Casanovas government, formed in order to abolish the Central Committee in early August. Moreover, the Communist party leadership made no secret of this policy. It had approved Giral's attempt to rebuild the Army and published a memorandum on the subject.

The international Communist press did not always understand this policy at first glance. The London *Daily Worker* stated on 22 August that 'things are moving toward a Spanish Soviet Republic,' through the triumph of the 'Red militia.' However, their aim was very soon adjusted. On 3 August, *L'Humanité*, at the request of the Spanish Communist party, stated that 'the Spanish people are not fighting for the establishment of a dictatorship of the proletariat' and that it 'knows only one aim: the defense of Republican law and order, through respect for property.'

On 8 August, Jesús Hernández declared: 'We cannot talk today of the proletarian revolution in Spain, because the historical circumstances do not permit it.... We want to defend our modest industry, which is in difficulties, on the same grounds as, and perhaps more than, the worker himself.' The aims of the Communist party were clearly stated by its secretary-general, José Díaz: 'We wish to fight only for a democratic republic with a broad social content. There can be no question at present of a dictatorship of the proletariat or of Socialism, but only of the struggle of democracy against Fascism.'[13]

However, this rigid attitude was still far from decisive. Neither the Communist party nor the PSUC was capable of really influencing the course of events during the summer months.

The Left-Wing Socialists at the Crossroads

Largo Caballero and his friends had rather less clear ideas about the problems of power than Prieto and the Communist party: the Madrid Socialist group's program, adopted in April at Araquistáin's instigation, in fact stated, as we saw, that the establishment of Socialism in Spain could only come about through a dictatorship of the proletariat. But they were hostile to the formation of soviets,[14] in their view a specifically Russian form of organization, and they explained no better in July and August than in April and May how they hoped to achieve the dictatorship of the proletariat by means of a Socialist party whose apparatus was still firmly in Prieto's hands.

The formal split had been avoided, but it was none the less real; through the UGT and *Claridad*, Largo Caballero carried out his own policy, different from that of the Socialist party. *Claridad* vigorously criticized Giral's mobilization decrees, countered them with Lenin's theses about 'people in arms,' denounced those who wished to separate the war from the Revolution, berated *El Mundo Obrero*, and accused the Communist party of sheltering reactionaries. However, this antagonism was short lived: on 23 July Largo Caballero told Carlo Reichmann that the formation of a 'purely Socialist government' would be the order of the day only after a victory over the uprising. In his daily visits to the militiamen at the front and in his activities at the UGT, he emerged rather as a willingly critical ally of the government. At a time when his troops were taking part in Government Committees throughout the country, his only ambition seemed to be to remain the all-powerful secretary-general of the UGT.

But the August defeats altered this attitude profoundly. The problems of efficiency and power seemed to confront him too. On 27 August, he explained his views to Koltsov. He could not speak harshly enough of the negligence of the Giral government, which he accused of not even having the will to defeat the rebels and of being made up of 'incompetent, stupid, and lazy men.' He stated: 'All the popular forces are united outside government cadres, around the Anarchist and Socialist unions. . . . The popular militia disobeys the government, and if things go on much longer, it will assume power itself.' Henceforth, he criticized in the same light what had been his own deficiency: 'The workers' parties must sweep away the bureaucrats, the officials, and the ministerial system of work as quickly as possible and move on to new forms of revolutionary control. The masses are extending their hands to us, they are demanding governmental leadership from us, and in our passivity we are shirking this responsibility and doing nothing.'[15]

Thus, through Largo Caballero's words to the Russian journalist, another conception of power took shape, in opposition to Prieto's, one of a 'workers' government' breaking with Republican legality and the Republican form of state.

The Anarchists Faced with Power

It was the first time in history that Anarchists were in a position to play so important a role: in fact, everything depended on them, at least in Catalonia. But the confrontation between their ideas and the social reality was a brutal one. Resolute opponents of the state, which they regarded as the form of oppression par excellence, the Anarchists had always refused to make a distinction between a bourgeois state and a workers' state like the Russian state that emerged from the Soviets in 1917. The collapse of the Republican state in July had created a vacuum that spontaneous action by CNT militants helped to fill through the formation of a new embryo state, that of the Government Committees. The dictates of war brooked no half-measures: an authority was needed, and no Anarchist could seriously advocate the Federation of Free Communes.

However, the Anarchist movement in Spain did not stop at a first revision of its principles. The massive participation by its militants in the February elections, a reaction against the vain and bloody attempts at an FAI uprising in the thirties, was contrary to its traditions and its doctrine, and was even an important concession to a new reformist current, close to the *treintistas*, which was springing up within its ranks. From FAI groups to the CNT unions, from one region and locality to another, Anarchist reactions varied during the decisive days. In Madrid, the CNT were in the vanguard of the struggle for the Revolution in the weeks before the uprising, whereas the Catalan CNT joined the Companys government against the threat of the *pronunciamiento*. After the revolutionary days, the Libertarian leaders held lively discussions: were they to seize power or not? This was the theory defended in the CNT Regional Committee by García Oliver, who won the day and rejected for the time being 'Libertarian Communism, which means Anarchist dictatorship,' and rallied to 'democracy, which implies collaboration.'[16]

The Catalan solution—the establishment of the Antifascist Militias Committee alongside the Generalidad—was, owing to the force of circumstances, a compromise between their principles and the needs of the hour. Yet, as we saw, the Central Committee very quickly became a second power. It was the Libertarians who ran it, instigated its major commissions, and took on the most important responsibilities. The same was true of the local Government Committees. This fact would seem to give the lie to the public statements of the CNT leaders. It was long believed in Barcelona that their hostility in principle to any form of state or power, revolutionary though they might be, would not stand up to the triumphal fervor that inspired them after the July days. It was believed that it was only caution that made them tolerate the survival of the

Generalidad, that they were working toward its 'silent extinction.' It was often said that they were only waiting for the fall of Saragossa before eliminating Republican power in Catalonia and Aragon.

In Madrid, the CNT had allotted itself a large share in the division of power: it had its police, its *checa*, its prisons, and above all its columns, a veritable independent army. Collaboration with the other parties and unions was reduced to a minimum. But this situation could not last either: the survival of the government and the danger that hung over the capital raised the question of power. The Madrid CNT proposed the establishment of a 'National Defense Junta,' made up of CNT and UGT representatives but excluding the Republican leaders. On the regional and local level, similar Juntas, 'the embodiment of revolutionary fervor,' were to provide the link, the *organismo aglutinante* that it seemed imperative to them to establish: in fact, the pyramid of Government Committees was to be crowned by a single power, in their image. While keeping up their hostility to 'democratic and bourgeois forms of government,' the Anarchists seemed ready, under the pressure of the needs of the hour, to set up a body that would, even if it did not carry the name, be a true 'workers' government.'

At any rate, this was how the POUM saw the development of the CNT. According to this party, which lay claim to Lenin's ideas about the dictatorship of the proletariat, there was no place in Spain in 1936 for a democratic republic. The conflict was one between Fascism and Socialism. To the CNT, there was no longer any question of forming a Popular Front government, but 'a workers' government resolved to carry through the struggle against Fascism and to give power to the working class, with its different parties and unions, and to it alone.' At a meeting in Barcelona on 6 September, Andrés Nin stated: 'The dictatorship of the proletariat means the exercise of power by the working class. In Catalonia, we can claim that the dictatorship of the proletariat already exists.' In his view it was therefore a question of establishing, for the whole of Spain, a 'workers' government' along the lines of the Central Committee and the Popular Executive Committee. This government should above all 'declare its intention to transform the fervor of the masses into revolutionary legality and to steer it in the direction of Socialist revolution.'

Moreover, the POUM was delighted that the CNT's 'revolutionary instinct' had prevailed over its traditional apoliticality and its hostility in principle to all government.[17] The slogan of the Juntas seemed to the POUM to answer the needs of the hour, those of the war and the Revolution: by launching it, the Anarchists, according to the POUM, took a step toward the Marxist conception of power. In this way, an identical conception, from Largo Caballero to Andrés Nin by way of the CNT, seemed to be emerging: that of a revolutionary government of workers' parties and unions.

The Formation of the Largo Caballero Government

On 4 September a short communiqué announced Giral's resignation and the formation of a new Popular Front government under Largo Caballero. Giral himself had asked Azaña to appoint the secretary-general of the UGT as his successor. That was the official version. But another version was going around by word of mouth in the political and trade-union circles of Madrid.[18]

At its origin was the emotion provoked by the fall of Badajoz, a Socialist bastion, lost early in the uprising and then recaptured by the militias. Caballero's views, as explained to Koltsov, matched those of the CNT. With the popular 'CNT–UGT National Junta' as a rallying cry, links were formed between militants from both unions in Madrid. Later on, Largo Caballero simply said: 'There was talk, in some circles, of seizing ministries and arresting ministers.' According to Rabasseire and Clara Campoamor, a joint assembly of UGT and CNT leaders was moving toward the formation of a Provisional Committee with the task of bringing about the coup d'état and setting up a Junta under Largo Caballero, with representatives from the Socialist and Communist parties, the FAI, and, of course, the CNT and the UGT: the Republicans were to be excluded from it.

Azaña, who according to Campoamor was warned by

Álvarez del Vayo, the Committee's spokesman, then refused to answer for what amounted to an end to legality and threatened to resign. It was the intervention of the Russian ambassador, Marcel Rosenberg, in Madrid since 24 August, that averted the crisis by restraining the Committee, which was determined to ignore Azaña's resignation.

During the course of impassioned discussions with the members of the Provisional Committee, the Russian ambassador stressed the incalculable consequences, on the international level, of a move that, by bringing about the president's resignation, would disarm Spanish diplomats, deprive Republican Spain's friends of the argument of legality, and appear to justify rebel propaganda by presenting to the world's view a government of 'Reds' that was not shielded by any parliamentary or Republican fiction. Instead of the workers' government planned by members of both unions, Rosenberg proposed to substitute a Popular Front government, also under Caballero, which would include some Republican ministers, and which Azaña could not refuse to support, because the forms would be respected. The arguments attributed to Rosenberg were strong ones: the conclusion of the nonintervention pact had put the 'old man's' back to the wall: until 24 August, it seems that he had calculated that Berlin's intransigence would frustrate Paris's plans and enable Spain to avoid a blockade. But after that date he had a choice of only two solutions. Either he would have to push the Revolution to its final consequences, establish the workers' government, denounce the 'betrayal' of the Spanish Revolution by the nonintervention policy of the French Popular Front government and the Russian government, and stir up such unrest in their countries that it would overwhelm them, while continually running the risk of not receiving any outside help until it was too late—or else he would have to unite all the political forces on a joint war program, which implied the maintenance of Republican forms and the halting of the Revolution, but which would open up possibilities of material aid from Paris and Moscow, the latter relatively short term.

Largo Caballero made his choice. On 1 September *Claridad*

wrote that France, 'ably seconded by England, had been more effective than some people imagined. In fact, an international war could only benefit Fascism, and this danger had, for the time being, diminished.' Ready to assume power at the head of a workers' government, Caballero accepted the offer that came to him from all sides: he was to be leader of a strong government—this was the whole point—enjoying the confidence of the masses and likely to receive support from outside, because it was still within the framework of the Republican state. He halted—temporarily in his view—the immediate pursuance of the Revolution in order first to win the war. He believed that his personality, his prestige, his influence, and the weight of his organization were guarantees that the halting of the revolutionary struggle could not at any rate mark the beginning of a move against it.

However, the Anarchists held aloof. 'The masses,' wrote *Solidaridad Obrera*, 'would feel disappointed if we continued to have a share in institutions with a bourgeois-type structure.' The CNT, according to Antona, could not forgo its insurrectional attitude toward all government. It could not therefore take part, though it promised its support and appointed a commissar to represent it in each ministerial department. Largo Caballero formed, without it, the Popular Front government that Prieto had been advocating for months, which seemed to him an acceptable compromise with his original position. Moreover, all his demands were satisfied in this framework, although, according to Koltsov, it had been 'extremely painful for everyone to agree to entrust him with the leadership of the government.'[19]

As he had demanded, Largo Caballero combined the functions of president with those of minister of war. Two of his UGT friends held key posts, Galarza as minister of the interior and Álvarez del Vayo as foreign minister. Prieto was Navy and Air minister, and his Socialist friends Juan Negrín and Anastasio de la Gracía were ministers of finance, and industry and commerce, respectively. The Communists, after refusing to take part, gave in to Caballero, who insisted on it: Uribe became minister of agriculture and Hernández minister of education. Five Republicans completed the government. José Giral was minister without portfolio, proof, he stated, 'that the new government is an enlargement of the old one.' The new premier stated, at any rate, that it was 'made up of men who have given up defending their principles and their personal views in order to unite around a single goal: the defense of Spain against Fascism.'

The participation of the UGT and the support of the CNT would in the normal way have given him the authority that Giral had lacked. But his program was the same, the 'union of forces fighting for Republican legality,' and 'the preservation of the democratic Republic.' Intended to do away with the duality of power, it reflected it: its Socialist leadership was a concession to the workers and its program a guarantee of 'respectability' for the major powers.

Its refusal to collaborate did not at first seem to have weakened the CNT, because the representatives of the regional revolutionary powers yielded. In Valencia, on 8 September, at a meeting organized by the UGT, the Socialist party, and the Communist party, it was Juan López, the distinguished leader of the CNT, who brought the adherence and support of the Popular Executive Committee to the new government and its program.

The Dissolution of the Antifascist Militias Committee

On 26 September it was the turn of the Catalan revolutionaries to yield. President Companys succeeded in the operation that he had attempted in vain with Casanovas in early August: the formation of a Generalidad government containing representatives of all the workers' parties and unions. The Republican Tarradellas was at its head. The Esquerra was given the ministries of finance, the interior, and culture, the Rabassaires the ministry of agriculture, and the PSUC the ministries of labor and public services. The revolutionary leaders had important posts too: the ministries of economy, supply, and health went to the Anarchists—secondary posts, it is true—and the ministry of justice to Andrés Nin.

Commenting on the event several years later, the moderate Ángel Ossorio y Gallardo wrote: 'Companys, who had recognized the workers' right to govern and had even offered to relinquish his post, handled things so skillfully that he gradually managed to reconstitute the legitimate organs of power, transfer influence to councillors, and reduce the workers' organizations to the role of assistants, helpers, and errand boys. . . . The normal situation was reestablished.'[20] Meanwhile, about the same time, Santillán wrote: 'After several months of struggle and unresolved difficulties with the central government and of reflecting on the pros and cons of independence for Catalonia, we were more than ever concerned with victory in this war that we began with such faith and order. Telling ourselves again and again that we should not be receiving so much help if the power of the Antifascist Militias Committee, the arm of the people's revolution, were so evident. . . . and having no choice except to yield or to worsen the conditions of the struggle . . ., we had to give in. We therefore decided to dissolve the Antifascist Militias Committee.' And he concluded: 'All to obtain arms and financial aid, to carry on our war successfully.'[21]

The formation of the new Generalidad Council in effect implied the abandonment of the organizations of revolutionary power. The Central Committee was merged with the Department of War under Colonel Díaz Sandino. The Economic Council and the Commission of Investigation were linked up with and subordinated to corresponding ministries. The Anarchists justified their 'participation in bourgeois-type institutions' by means of various arguments. They laid stress on the term 'Council,' applied to the new government at their insistence. In their view, the presence of CNT representatives was a guarantee, a legalization of the revolutionary gains.

On 27 September *Solidaridad Obrera* wrote: 'It was no longer possible, with the good of the Revolution and the future of the working class in mind, for duality of power to continue. It was necessary, in some simple way, for the organization controlling the vast majority of the working population to be promoted to the level of administrative and executive decisions.' And *La*

Révolution prolétarienne, though seldom guilty of sympathy for the CNT's 'reformist' line, concluded its analysis of the event by stating, through Antoine Richard: 'This penetration of old organizations by new ones born during the struggle and created for the Revolution represents a major step toward the conquest of power.'[22]

The POUM had insisted, as conditions for its participation, on a 'Socialist-oriented ministerial statement' and the 'active and direct intervention of the CNT.' It therefore accepted the new government coalition, declaring: 'We live in a transition stage in which force of circumstances has driven us into direct collaboration with the Generalidad Council and with other workers' groups.' The inadequacy of the program submitted and the importance of the participation of the Republicans, which it stressed, did not prevent it from concluding that Catalonia 'indisputably' possessed 'proletarian power.' And, in contradiction to its policy of the day, it made a new appeal: 'From the formation of Workers', Peasants', and Soldiers' Committees, for which we shall not cease to struggle, will spring direct representation of the new proletarian power.'

This optimism was swiftly contradicted by events. The formation of the Generalidad Council, with the support of the CNT and the POUM, was in fact the death sentence for the power of the Committees. On 1 October the Antifascist Militias Committee dissolved itself and embraced, through a manifesto, the new government's policy. On 9 October a decree in Council, with the approval of Nin and the CNT ministers, dissolved 'the Local Committees, whatever their name or title, and all the organizations that had been set up to destroy the subversive movement,' throughout Catalonia. President Tarradellas commented on the decree and announced the replacement of the Committees in their 'government functions' by municipal councils made up in the same proportions as the Generalidad Council. The workers' organizations as a whole approved of this dissolution: the POUM French-language newspaper even wrote: 'These Revolutionary Committees, whether Popular Executive Committees or Committees of Public Safety, represented only part of the workers' organizations, or else represented them in an incorrect proportion. . . . Obviously the suppression of their revolutionary initiative is to be regretted, but one must recognize the need to codify . . . the various municipal organizations, as much with the aim of replacing them uniformly as of setting them under the authority of the new Generalidad Council.'[23]

On 17 September Andrés Nin accompanied President Companys on a tour of Lérida: he combined his efforts with the latter's to convince his friends on the Revolutionary Committee that it was necessary to bow to the new organization of power by joining a municipal council in which they would be in a minority, and which the Republicans, till then kept in the background, would enter in force.

Aragon's Entry into Republican Order

In these circumstances, the position of the leading spirits in the Aragon Defense Council became difficult. Violently attacked by the Communists and Socialists, dubbed an illegal organization by the PSUC, and not recognized by the Republican authorities in Madrid and Barcelona, the Council could not defend the position of independent revolutionary power by itself. Even within the CNT, its chairman, Joaquín Ascaso, was the victim of harsh attacks by certain leaders: Mariano Vázquez, secretary of the National Committee, accused him of revolutionary infantilism and of quixotry. He was forced to back down: in late October, the CNT suggested extending the Council to the Popular Front parties. On 31 October, a delegation led by Ascaso went to see Caballero. It stressed, according to the account given by the CNT press, the exceptional circumstances of the Council's birth, in a chaotic situation created by the absence of public authorities and the occupation of its territory by columns of Catalan militias. It confirmed that the Popular Front unions and parties had recently agreed to a reorganization of the Council, from now on open to the representatives of all organizations, in proportion to their strength. Caballero meanwhile acknowledged the Aragon Council's right to appoint the civil governor and the provincial deputations and delegated to it, in view of the exceptional character of the situation, government powers in respect to the maintenance of law and order, economic reconstruction, and the organization of the military effort. It was agreed between the two parties that in the future a plebiscite would define the nature of the Aragon regime. On leaving the premier, Joaquín Ascaso stated: 'The object of our visit was to present our respects to the head of the government and to assure him of our adherence to the people's government. We are ready to accept all the laws it passes, and in return we shall ask the minister for all the help we need.'[24] The Generalidad Council was then able to award the Aragon Council the stamp of respectability: 'The talks with President Azaña, with President Companys, and with Largo Caballero,' it stated, 'have destroyed all the suspicions that could have lent credence to the idea that the constituted government [in Aragon] has an extremist character.'

Thus the last serious obstacle to the concentration of power was removed: all the other regional organizations gave in without difficulty. The Basques, at first determined to form their government without waiting for the Cortes to vote on autonomous status, agreed to take their place within the new legal framework. After the vote on the Basque status on 1 October, José Antonio de Aguirre was elected president of Euzkadi, on the seventh, and took his oath under the tree of Guernica. Manuel de Irujo joined the Largo Caballero government, whose program was identical with that of the government inspired by the Basque Nationalists.[25]

The Anarchists Join the Central Government

Meanwhile, the problem of the central government remained unresolved. Was a National Defense Junta to be set up, as the CNT newspapers continued to demand? The Republicans and Socialists were resolutely opposed to it. Ought the CNT to join the Caballero government? The UGT, the Socialist party, and the Communist party were insisting on it: in fact the CNT, like them, exercised a share of power without assuming its responsibilities. But fresh military reverses and the threat to Madrid accelerated events. During a meeting of the Popular Front in Valencia on 20 October, the leader of the CNT dock workers, Domingo Torres, came out in favor of Anarchist participation in an organization to direct the struggle, even if it called itself the government, because it was essential to win the war first. On 22 October, *Solidaridad Obrera* raised a corner of the veil over negotiations by stating that 'the government under Largo Caballero lacks the cooperation of the proletarian forces' of the CNT, and by denouncing the groups that 'reject participation by union forces that are simply demanding their rights in the proportion due to them.' According to Caballero, the Anarchists were asking for six posts, whereas he was only offering them four. It was not a question of the program: on 30 October, Caballero stated in an interview with the *Daily Express*: 'First let us win the war, and then we can talk about revolution.' On 23 October, Juan Peiró, in a talk on Radio CNT–FAI, had indicated the new Anarchist position, identical in every respect: 'From now on, those who talk of implanting a perfect economic and social system are friends who forget that the capitalist system has . . . international ramifications and that our triumph in the war depends greatly on the warmth, sympathy, and support that reaches us from outside. . . .' The discussion as to the number of posts lost all meaning: on 4 November, Largo Caballero reshuffled his ministry and brought in four CNT representatives, García Oliver as minister of justice, Federica Montseny as minister of health, Juan López as minister of commerce, and Juan Peiró as minister of industry. The task of justifying it from the theoretical point of view fell to Santillán, opponent of collaboration, on 13 September:

'The entry of the CNT into the central government is one of the most important events in the history of our country. The CNT has always been, by principle and conviction, antistate and the enemy of every form of government. . . . But circumstances . . . have changed the nature of the Spanish government and state. . . . The government has ceased to be a force of oppression against the working class, just as the state is no longer the entity that divides society into classes. Both will stop oppressing the people all the more with the inclusion of the

CNT among their organs.' Thus, in the ordeal of the struggle for power, the Anarchist leaders adopted the language of the most reformist Social Democrats. To justify himself later in the eyes of his friends, García Oliver, one of the 'Three Musketeers,' a former convict, now minister of justice, wrote: 'International bourgeoisie refused to supply us the arms that we needed. . . . We had to give the impression that it was not the Revolutionary Committees that were in control but the legal government, without which we would have nothing at all. We have had to bow to the inexorable circumstances of the moment, that is, to accept government collaboration.' And, Santillán, the first to justify this policy in 1936, was also, in 1940, the first to criticize it bitterly after defeat: 'We knew that it was not possible for the Revolution to triumph if we did not triumph in the war beforehand. We sacrificed the Revolution itself without understanding that this sacrifice also implied sacrificing the aims of the war.'[26]

A Decisive Political Factor: Russian Aid

Progress from the workers' government planned at the end of August to the Popular Front government established at the beginning of November with the participation of the Anarchists was rapid. This was largely because the left-wing Socialist leaders, like those in the CNT, had, when they referred to foreign aid, envisaged other aid than the problematical aid of the West. The great event of September, which coincided with the formation of the Caballero government and lent credence to the part played by Rosenberg in the 'crisis,' was the USSR's decision to supply material aid to the Spanish Republic.

It was in fact at the beginning of September that technical arrangements with a view to effecting this support were being made in Moscow. The first Russian officers were on the spot at the same time as Rosenberg. The first planes arrived in October. It was Russian aid that saved Madrid by allowing the militias and the young 'Popular Army' raised by the Largo Caballero government to be equipped with modern arms and ammunition. Henceforth, it was also Russian aid that to a large extent conditioned the policy of the government and the parties of the Popular Front, on the basis of advice and demands dictated as much by the official representatives of the USSR, Rosenberg and Antonov-Ovseyenko, the consul-general in Barcelona, as by its official spokesmen, Komintern delegates who were either Communist party or PSUC leaders and who derived their popularity and authority from it. A new period opened under the banner of 'antifascism.'

Notes

[1] See on these subjects, besides the classics, some recent works. On Russia: Oskar Anweiler, *Die Rätebewegung in Russland (1905–1921)* (Leiden, 1958). On Germany: W. Tormin, *Die Geschichte der Rätebewegung in der deutschen Revolution (1918–19)* (Düsseldorf, 1954).

[2] *Por qué perdimos la guerra*, p. 70.

[3] He stated: 'In Russia, there was no democratic tradition among the proletariat, no tradition of organized struggle. We have unions, parties, publications, and a system of working-class democracy. The importance that the Soviets enjoyed is understandable. The proletariat did not have organs of its own. The Soviets were a spontaneous creation that in 1905 and 1917 acquired a wholly political character. Our proletariat already had its unions, its parties, and its own organizations. This is why Soviets did not spring up among us.'

[4] See on this subject his articles, '*Révolution en Espagne! Et en France?*' (24 July) and '*Fascisme, guerre . . . ou révolution*' (14 August), in *Le Populaire*. On the other hand, on 13 August the leadership of the SFIO had, through Séverac, denied the existence of class war in Spain: 'The many survivals of privilege from the old regime have not yet permitted the world of labor to take full cognizance of its interests and of its mission.' Agreement with the French Communist party on this point was complete.

[5] Jean-Richard Bloch was the only Communist journalist who described the Central Committee such as it was and not as a vague liaison body. On 6 August *L'Humanité* highlighted Giral's statements: 'Communists are men of law and order.' On the sixteenth, Gabriel Péri, commenting on the entry of the PSUC into the government—an operation directed, as we saw, against the Central Committee—wrote: 'The CNT leadership has taken offense without any valid reason.' Readers of *L'Humanité* searched in vain for one of the 'reasons' invoked.

[6] See Trotsky (*Leçon d'Espagne*, pp. 24–25): 'Revolutions have by no means been victorious up to this time because of great foreign patrons who supplied them with arms. Usually the counterrevolution enjoyed foreign patronage. Must we recall the experience of the intervention of French, English, American, Japanese, and other armies against the Soviets? . . . Revolutions succeed in the first place with the help of a bold social program that gives

the masses the possibility of seizing weapons that are on their own territory and disorganizing the army of the enemy.'

[7] 'Franco's dictatorship would mean the unavoidable acceleration of European war. . . . The victory of the Spanish workers and peasants would undoubtedly shake the regimes of Mussolini and Hitler.' (Trotsky, in *The Case of Leon Trotsky*, p. 303.) Certain statements by CNT leaders echoed this view. Durruti, in particular, said: 'We are giving Hitler and Mussolini far more worry today than the whole Red Army of Russia. We are setting an example to the German and Italian working class of how to deal with Fascism. I do not expect any help for a libertarian revolution from any government in the world. Maybe the conflicting interests of the various imperialisms might have some effect on our struggle. . . . But we expect no help. . . .' (Quoted by Morrow, *Revolution and Counter-Revolution in Spain*, p. 189.)

[8] One of the most lucid and aware British politicians, Winston Churchill, expressed such misgivings clearly in his *Step by Step*: 'A revived Fascist Spain in closest sympathy with Italy and Germany is one kind of disaster. A Communist Spain spreading its snaky tentacles through Portugal and France is another, and many will think the worse.' 'All that is happening now increases the power of those evil forces which from both extremes menace the existence of Parliamentary democracy and individual liberty in Great Britain and France' 10 August (pp. 52–53). Noting that 'Soviet Russia has moved decidedly away from Communism,' which opens up the prospect of seeing her establish 'more points of contact with the West' (p. 61), he saw the presence of the Trotskyists in Spain 'their appearance as the POUM, as a sect achieving the quintessence of fetidity' (p. 72). Then in April 1937, he drew a grim picture of what 'the success of the Anarchist and Trotskyist forces' (p. 120) would be, pointing out on the other hand that Franco's victory could not interfere with French and British interests, and that it would ensure his independence of Berlin and Rome.

Irujo (Lizarra, *Los vascos y la República española*, pp. 58–59) pointed out that the setting up of Defense Juntas in the Basque provinces, whose conservative nature we have noted, was the result of 'pressing demands' from ambassadors and diplomats, in particular the French ambassador, Herbette.

[9] See Manuel Azaña: 'The revolutionary work began under a government . . . that would not and could not answer for it . . . a government that loathes and condemns events but can neither prevent them nor repress them' (*La velada en Benicarló* [Buenos Aires: Losada, 1939], p. 96). Casares Quiroga, in *mono* and sandals, left for the front, where many journalists were to meet him. An ordinary militiaman, 'he tried to redeem his sins,' according to Koltsov (*Ispanskii dnevnik*, p. 59).

[10] Koltsov, *Ispanskii dnevnik*, p. 74. There is no means of questioning the accuracy of Koltsov's report, though it was confirmed by Prieto's later attitude.

[11] Julio Álvarez del Vayo, *La guerra empezó en España* (Mexico City: Séneca, 1940), p. 216. Translated into English as *The Last Optimist* (New York: Viking Press, 1950).

[12] For a whole year, Communist orators had shown such moderation that during the electoral campaign in February the Socialists, to ridicule them,

had launched the ironic slogan: 'To save Spain from Marxism, vote Communist.'

[13] Within the ranks of the working class, they were in any case clearly on the defensive where CNT and POUM militants were concerned. They left the Casanovas government because the CNT protested. To the parties that on every occasion made references in their propaganda to the USSR, Moscow's adherence to the nonintervention pact presented a sizeable obstacle.

[14] See chapter 3.

[15] Koltsov, *Ispanskii dnevnik*, pp. 76–77.

[16] Quoted by Peirats, *La CNT en la Revolución española*, 1: 161. See also Agustín Souchy, *Nacht über Spanien* (Darmstadt: Verlag die Freie Gesellschaft, n.d.), pp. 95–96, and Burnett Bolloten, *The Grand Camouflage* (New York: Praeger, 1961), pp. 152 ff.

[17] In addition, the influence of the POUM was not to be discounted as a factor in the CNT's attitudes. In September Enrique Rodríguez, one of the POUM representatives in Madrid, was required to defend his party's views on power in *CNT*. These views seemed to coincide with those of the Madrid CNT organization.

[18] Rabasseire (*Espagne, creuset politique*, p. 98) repeated it. Clara Campoamor gave details of it in *La Révolution espagnole vue par une républicaine* (Paris: Librairie Plon, 1937), pp. 143–145. Koltsov (*Ispanskii dnevnik*, pp. 85–86) gave an account squaring with the official theory but did not even try to match it with Caballero's and Prieto's previous statements. According to him, it was Caballero who offered himself as a candidate to Azaña, while Prieto was hostile to his nomination. One likely claim in this account: it was Álvarez del Vayo who impelled Largo Caballero toward concessions.

[19] Koltsov, *Ispanskii dnevnik*, p. 86.

[20] *Vida y sacrificio de Lluys Companps* (Buenos Aires: Losada, 1943), p. 172.

[21] Santillán, *Por qué perdimos la guerra*, pp. 115–116.

[22] *La Révolution prolétarienne*, 10 October 1936.

[23] *La Révolution espagnole*, 14 October 1936. It is worth pointing out that Nin's efforts were not his personal responsibility but reflected the line of the POUM leadership.

[24] Peirats, *La CNT en la Revolución española*, 1 : 229.

[25] The first Republican government included, in addition to the Basque Nationalists, some Republicans, Socialists, and a Communist, Juan Astigarrabía. At that juncture there was no criticism of the latter within the ranks of the Communist party, whereas José Díaz later accused him (16 November 1937) of having been 'a prisoner of the government led by Basque Nationalists and representatives of the big industrialists, the big capitalists, and the banks.' The government program insisted on freedom of worship and respect for law and order and property. In the social field, it promised that 'workers will have access to capital through coadministration of business firms.'

[26] Santillán, *Por qué perdimos la guerra*, p. 116. Note the similar evaluation, based on two opposing points of view, of the Madrid revolutionary Socialists' and the Barcelona Anarchists' refusal to assume power. In Trotsky's view: 'To renounce the conquest of power means voluntarily to leave the power

with those who have it, that is, the exploiters. The essence of every revolution consisted and consists in the fact that it puts a new class in power and thus gives it the opportunity to realize its own program. . . .' 'The renunciation of the conquest of power throws every workers' organization into the mire of reformism and turns it into the plaything of the bourgeoisie.' (*Leçon d'Espagne*, pp. 20–21.) Whereas Azaña wrote: 'As a reaction to the military rebellion . . . a proletarian uprising occurred that was not aimed at the government. . . . A revolution must seize command, establish itself in the government, and run the country according to its views. But they did not do this. . . . The old order could have been replaced by another, a revolutionary one. It was not. All that remained was impotence and chaos. . . .' (*La velada en Benicarló*, p. 96.)

CHAPTER 9

THE CABALLERO GOVERNMENT AND THE RESTORATION OF THE STATE

It was remarkable that Largo Caballero, so harshly criticized in his own party, was able in a few weeks to become the man of destiny, the last card, in the words of Prieto himself.[1] The defection of the Socialist Youth had dealt a fairly severe blow to his personal position, and it was ultimately the impotence and disrepute of the Republicans and the refusal and inability of the Anarchists to seize power that made him the 'supreme savior.' He was disliked by most of the party leaders, but his popularity as an old warrior meant that he was the only leader capable of acting as a link between moderates and revolutionaries and of rallying the workers to a regular government, by imposing his authority on parties, unions, and committees.

He actually achieved what Giral and Prieto had failed to do before him: by rejuvenating state institutions through the legalization of certain revolutionary gains and the incorporation of entities and individuals who held revolutionary power, he managed to save them and to bring off a gamble: the regaining of control by the Republican state over all armed groups and the formation of an army and a police force; in a word, the founding of a single, strong power under the aegis of the Republic. To the majority of the revolutionary workers, however, this power was their power, the 'people's power.' His achievement was to have eliminated the 'second power' by giving the impression that he was endorsing their victory: the presence alongside him of García Oliver and Juan López, who had been the incarnation of revolutionary power in Catalonia and the Levante, appeared to guarantee the revolutionary character of his intentions. He did not destroy the regional authorities but seemed to wish to unite them by federating them. The Basques and Asturians kept responsibility for their front, the CNT for the Teruel and Aragon front, and the Madrid Junta soon became responsible for the Center front. But responsibility for military organization passed to a 'Junta of Militias,' in which all parties and unions were represented. The Supreme War Council, which linked every political and trade-union viewpoint with the handling of operations, met twice a week under Largo Caballero.[2]

It was in everyone's view the military reverses that had made the unification of power necessary, and he insisted from the start on unifying the military command:

'Our first task,' Caballero told Koltsov, 'is to establish unity of power and command. The leadership of the fighting troops in the whole of Spain, including Catalonia, is now concentrated in the hands of the minister of war.' This accent on the military command was even then a political choice. In an interview with the *Daily Express* on 30 October, he explained it thus: 'Civil war has, by definition, a social character, and naturally during the course of the war problems of a social and economic nature may arise.... Solving them will be subordinated to a single objective: winning the war.'[3]

The Government Versus the Committees

To achieve this program, the government first had to attack the Committees. Theoretically, its task might appear easy: the Committees were made up of representatives of parties and unions that took part in the government, supporting its program and backing up its actions. In fact, however, the militants were far more attached to the organizations that they had built themselves and, to defend them, balked at their own leaders' instructions. Also, the dissolution of the Committees never took a violent form. Parties and unions stepped up their arguments: it was a question of making the militants admit that the Committees, useful in the revolutionary period, were now obsolete. *Claridad*, for instance, wrote: 'We can claim that all these bodies have now accomplished the mission they were created for. Henceforth they can only be a hindrance to a task that devolves solely and exclusively on the Popular Front government, in which all the country's political and trade-union organizations play a fully responsible part.'

In Catalonia, Comorera, the PSUC leader, made the dissolution of the Committees the first task of the antifascist coalition: 'It must be possible,' he stated, 'to impose legitimate authority in the face of irresponsible dictatorship by the Committees.' Their disappearance, as we saw, was made possible through the goodwill of the CNT and the POUM after the dissolution of the Antifascist Militias Committee. In Valencia, the Popular Executive Committee held out much longer, backed by the POUM and a group from the CNT. Juan Peiró was barracked at the Apollo Theater on 27 November when he stated: 'In Valencia the government gives an order, and then instructions from the Committees thwart it. Either the government governs or the Committees govern!' In spite of interruptions, he insisted: 'It is not the Committees. What we need is that they should be subordinated to the government.'[4]

Caballero was skilled at avoiding clashes. He appointed the very leaders of Government Committees as governors and mayors and replaced revolutionary organizations with regular organizations, sometimes made up of the same men, barely differing in appearance but in fact less subject to influence from below and more easily controlled by him. He let certain organizations survive once he had 'duplicated' them and stripped them of their powers. In Valencia, after the departure of Colonel Arín and Juan López, the Popular Executive Committee was a mere facade once the popular Socialist deputy and UGT leader Ricardo Zabalza had been appointed governor. Juan Ruiz in Santander, Belarmino Tomás in Gijón, and Joaquín Ascaso in Aragon became 'government delegates.' To restrict the Málaga Committee of Public Safety, it was enough to transfer its former president, Governor Rodríguez, and to replace him with a new one, less involved with the revolutionary organizations.

On the local level, the Government Committees took a back seat in the face of the *Ayuntamientos*, municipal councils also made up of representatives of different parties and unions and established as the result of a 31 December decree on municipal reform. The difference, although apparently very slight, was in fact substantial. For one thing, the paritary system of representation benefited the official Communists represented through several organizations: the Spanish Communist party and the PSUC, the UGT, especially in Catalonia, and the JSU everywhere.[5] More significant, the initiative no longer came from below: even where they had a majority among the workers, the Anarchists, without the armed mass that had permitted them to use every form of pressure during the time of the Committees, found themselves in a minority in the municipal councils. Finally, the mayor, the *alcalde*, was chosen by the civil governor: in him the government possessed a direct agent, which it did not have in the Committees. Moreover, care in handling susceptibilities and a skillful admixture of appointments staved off many recriminations.[6] Valencia no longer had its Popular Executive Committee, but a left-wing Socialist governor and a CNT mayor. Few militants, either in the CNT or in the UGT, seemed to be alert to what a weapon against them such a municipal organization, in the hands of a government not led by Largo Caballero, would eventually provide. Equally rare were those who could see the paradox in promulgating a municipal reform abolishing all elections, within the framework of a regime that claimed to be democratic.[7]

Legal Reform

The same principles animated the legal reform carried out in Valencia under the leadership of the Anarchist García Oliver and in Barcelona under the POUM Communist Andrés Nin. The revolutionary victory in July was ratified by law. But the new institutions took their place within the context of the old legality and the obsolete bourgeois law. A general amnesty annulled all sentences passed before 19 July, some of which still hung over the heads of certain revolutionary leaders. Women received equal rights and, in particular, full legal competency, of which they had until then been deprived. Free unions of militiamen were legalized and marriage formalities simplified. The legal tax was abolished, justice became free, and all proceedings were speeded up. Every prisoner, at any tribunal, including the Supreme Court, was free to conduct his own defense or to enjoy the services of a lawyer, whether professional or not. García Oliver preserved the structure of the Popular Tribunals established on 23 July by the Giral government: they were made up of three judges, a president, and a prosecuting attorney who were professional magistrates, and fourteen jurymen appointed by the political and trade-union organizations. The Popular Tribunals in Catalonia, 'class tribunals' as they were called by their founder Andrés Nin, consisted of only two magistrates, the president, and the prosecuting attorney. Their jurymen were eight representatives appointed by the political and trade-union organizations. In both cases, the body of magistrates, severely tested by popular terror during the revolutionary days, was thoroughly purged, then reestablished: these judges from then on served the new legal system as 'technicians of justice,' ensuring the continuity of forms and the law.

A new legal apparatus was thus established, differing but little from the old one, merely rejuvenated, modernized, and open to all those whom the coalition parties and unions endorsed.

The Rebuilding of the Police Force

Dual power had in fact led to a proliferation of the organs of repression: rear militias, Control Patrols, Watch Committees, and Commissions of Investigation rubbed shoulders with the security police, the *Carabineros*, the *Asaltos*, and the Civil Guards, rechristened 'National Republican Guards,' whose scattered units the Giral government had gradually reassembled at the front and in the rear. On 20 September a decree united all these forces into a single body, the 'rear vigilance militias': the revolutionary police force was officially sanctioned and simultaneously placed under the direct authority of the minister of the interior; on 15 December the Superior Council for Security was organized,[8] consisting of political leaders. On 27 December the National Council was extended to a number of technicians: besides two representatives from the CNT, two from the UGT, and one from each party, it included a leader, a superintendent, and an agent elected by their peers, and the director-general, a leading official appointed by the minister, who acted as chairman. In each province, regional councils, with civil governors as chairmen, were established. These were transformed even more quickly than the municipal councils: their federal structure was a hindrance to the efficiency of police activities. Leading officials very soon dominated the scene. Largo Caballero must have realized this when he made his old friend Wenceslao Carrillo director-general of the security police.[9]

Simultaneously what was to be a real new police force came discreetly into being. At the very time when frontier smuggling was nonexistent, Juan Negrín, the minister of finance, considerably strengthened the *Carabineros*, weak in numbers before the war.[10] On 28 April 1937, the *New York Herald Tribune* correspondent cabled that a 'reliable police force is being formed': by that time more than 40,000 had been recruited, of whom half were armed and equipped.

In the early days, a guarantee from a party or a union was required from every new guard or policeman: this was a security measure to prevent the possible creation of cells by the Falangists. Fairly quickly, however, parties and unions seemed to leading officials to form a screen between the government and its forces of repression. A decisive step was taken with the split between the police forces and the workers' organizations, with *Carabineros* and guards being forbidden to belong to a party or union.[11] Thus the police once again became, in theory, the blind and willing instrument that every government needs.

The Militarization of the Militias

The military defeats of August and September had come as a severe blow to those who supported the preservation of the militias. Certain Anarchists, Durruti, García Oliver, and Mera, demanded a unified organization, a single command. It was clear to everyone that to avoid a catastrophe it was necessary to establish iron discipline into the service and during combat, to coordinate supplies, equipment, and communications, and to work out and apply an overall strategy. But this was where differences of opinion began. The Anarchists wanted to bring about these changes within the framework of the militias, by preserving the election of officers, a single pay scale, and the abolition of badges of rank. The POUM advocated the 1918–1920 Russian model, demanded control of officers by commissars and Soldiers' Councils, and published and distributed Trotsky's *Red Army Handbook*. No one dared advocate the reconstitution of an army of the old type, and the Communist slogan 'popular army' seemed to many capable of reconciling revolutionary aspirations with the requirements of discipline. The government went ahead step by step, avoiding a head-on clash with the unique spirit of the militias, which, however, it gradually transformed into an army.

The 29 September decree, which mobilized two contingents, heralded the beginning of militarization: the Junta and soon the *Comandancia* of the militias controlled, paid, fed, and armed all the militias in the organization. The government's initial decree had established a general staff, which began the task of coordination and centralization. Recruits were flanked by officers and NCOs mobilized and recruited from the columns. The corps thus formed were organized along the lines of regular units, with battalions, regiments, brigades, and divisions. Certain militia units refused to accept militarization. *Frente Libertario*, organ of the CNT militias, published a violent article on 27 October entitled 'Down with the Army.' The Iron Column revolted against the government, which clamped down on its credit. But such resistance was hopeless. If Giral had been unable to rebuild an army, it was because no one had faith in him and because he did not have the modern arms necessary.

The Caballero government enjoyed the confidence of the parties and unions that demanded unity of command, and it had arms, thanks to support from the USSR. Even the distribution of the arms worked in favor of militarization: only reorganized units received them. The successes achieved by the troops organized by the Communist party and the government also helped to dispose other columns toward militarization. The CNT ministers backed it, and the CNT and FAI National Committees sent delegations to the front to persuade the militiamen and their leaders. One by one, the most obdurate columns resigned themselves to being 'militarized,' in the hope of receiving arms. The Workers' and Soldiers' Councils were abolished, with the blessing of *Solidaridad Obrera*, which could no longer find any justification for them. In the first stage, the units lost their names. *Centurias* became companies or battalions, and columns became regiments or brigades, according to their strength. An early link with the workers' organizations disappeared when a number was substituted for the name of each column. On the Aragon front, the Durruti Column became the Twenty-sixth, the Carlos Marx the Twenty-seventh, the Francisco Ascaso the Twenty-eighth, the Lenin the Twenty-ninth, and the Maciá Companys the Thirtieth Division. Then ranks were reintroduced: the hand delegates became corporals or sergeants, the *centuria* delegates captains, and the column leaders majors. Badges of rank reappeared discreetly on jackets and *monos*. With militarization, the militias had to accept the reintroduction of the old military code of justice, put forward at the time as a temporary measure in anticipation of a new draft.

The problem of forming cadres remained difficult. There were, as we saw, very few regular officers in the militias: perhaps two hundred in the whole of Spain and only twelve in the entire North, according to President Aguirre. Also, they were not reliable, a large number of them, as Rabasseire said, being only 'geographically loyal.' General Walch, in *Le Temps* of 12 July 1938, referred to the token strike that some of them were staging. André Malraux mentioned the case of the gunner who fired on the militias, and Borkenau exposed some cases of sabotage. All, in spite of assurances given, were suspected by their fighting companions, if only because of their origin. Hernández Sarabia, Menéndez, and Martín Blázquez only just escaped the *paseo*. Riquelme and Miaja were threatened, and the government transferred them in order to protect them. Escobar and Martínez, Santillán's aides-de-camp, were murdered.[12] One of the first tasks, therefore, was to train officers. García Oliver had proved himself by organizing the Popular Officers' Academy in Barcelona for the Central Committee: Largo Caballero put him in charge of the Popular War Academies. Two months later, five academies had provided crash courses for 3000 officers, accepted on the basis of an introduction from a party, a union, or a column.[13] Thus an officer corps was created that the preservation of a single pay scale prevented from becoming a privileged body, in spite of the reestablishment, along with the old code, of discipline and external tokens of respect off duty. Moreover, the egalitarian spirit of the militias survived the more easily because the temporary workers' and militants' leaders of the early weeks nearly always had their ranks confirmed when the unit was militarized.

The leaders of the Popular Army themselves reflected the diverse origins of these cadres. Some of them had been junior or senior officers in the Army before the Revolution: Miaja and Pozas, who had been generals, Rojo who had been a major and became a general, Asensio, a lieutenant colonel, then a general in September, Hernández Sarabia and Menéndez, who had been Azaña's aides-de-camp, Majors Casado and Perea. Others rose swiftly in rank because they had held commands in the militias or had contributed to the organization of the general staff: Francisco Galán, Cordón, Barcelo, Ciutat, Lieutenant Commander Prados, who became chief of the Navy general staff, and Major Hidalgo de Cisneros, who became chief of the Air Force general staff. But there were already leaders of working-class origin by their sides, who had emerged from the ranks in the early weeks of the fighting, mainly Communists, such as the stonecutter Lister and the carpenter Modesto,[14] or the former Spanish foreign legion sergeant, Valentin González, *El Campesino*, and the typesetter Durán,[15] but also Anarchists, such as Jover, Vivancos, and Cipriano Mera, and even POUM militants, such as the metalworker Baldris or the clerk Rovira. For the time being none of them rose above the rank of major. But they held important commands: Lister was in charge of a brigade in 1936 and a division in January 1937, and Modesto, Durán, and Mera were soon in charge of divisions. These leaders were young men: Durán was twenty-nine, and Alberto Sánchez of the Fifth Regiment was in command of a brigade at the age of twenty-one.

However, along with the adoption of the red star as emblem on the flags of the Popular Army, it was without doubt the introduction of political commissars that contributed most, outside Spain, to the creation of the legend of a 'Communist revolution.' The phrase was still linked in everyone's minds with memories of the Russian Revolution and the organization of the Red Army by Trotsky.

Yet this institution did not date from 1917. The French Revolution, too, had found it necessary to create a regular army with politically unreliable cadres and had felt the need to control the regular officers and galvanize the men with political indoctrinators. The 'political delegate' of the militias was even then the equivalent, not only of the 1918–1920 'commissar,' but also of the 1794 'attached representative.' It was therefore an institution 'dreamed up by Carnot and perfected by Trotsky,' as Gorkin put it, which the Caballero government took up and developed in similar circumstances.

The October 1936 decree that created the Commissariat gave the commissar the task of 'representing the government's war policy in the Army and fulfilling its mission without interfering with the military command.' A vague and ill-defined mission: the commissar could, according to circumstances, be all or nothing. In fact, he was a good deal. The 5 November regulations stated that he was the 'first and foremost aide to the command, its right arm,' 'the sentinel, the *ojo avizor*,' as well as everyone's 'comrade and model.' He was political instructor to the soldiers and officers, liaison agent with the civilian population, and the man who organized work, rest, and leisure. 'The political commissar's first concern is the men,' stated the regulations issued by the Communist party.

'Red chaplains,' as their detractors termed them, the commissars were, according to the Communist party, to be 'the heart and soul of the Popular Army.' Beginning with the militias, it was they who, more than anyone else, helped to train the Army, of which they were very often the moving spirits and sometimes the actual leaders.[16]

The 'Legalization' of the Revolutionary Gains

In his account to the CNT militants of his conduct as minister, García Oliver stated: 'My administration has consisted of converting *de facto* gains into legal reality.' However, this was only one facet of the Largo Caballero government's policy, which was to stabilize and legalize the revolutionary gains while checking their expansion.

The outlawing of the Church and of religious worship and practices had not been sanctioned by any legislative measures. It had remained a concrete fact. According to Gabriel Péri,[17] in September Jesús Hernández had asked the government to authorize the reopening of the churches and to proclaim freedom of worship, which was to be one of the important points in the Communist party program.[18] At any rate, these were the proposals that were put forward to the Cabinet by Manuel de Irujo on 9 January 1937: they ran into García Oliver's intransigent opposition and Largo Caballero's veto. In the academic field, the task was enormous: the state tried to guarantee the continuance of denominational schools. Jesús Hernández, through a decree on 25 November, created a 'simplified baccalaureate' open to candidates put up by the Popular Front unions and parties. He organized specialist teams of instructor-militiamen who attacked the problem of illiteracy in the militias and the villages. Though the Generalidad recognized the 'New Unified School,' neither its academic principles nor its function under dual control by unions and instructors were extended to state teaching, whose structure was not altered.

The presence of a CNT representative at the Ministry of Industry could have lent hope to the pursuance of the collectivization that had begun spontaneously after the Revolution. A decree by the Giral government on 2 August provided for the seizure (*incautación*) of firms whose employers had been implicated in the military uprising. However, there was no legal control over the fate of those abandoned for other reasons, such as lack of capital or ill will. Juan Peiró stated that on his entry into the government he was met by a genuinely catastrophic situation: part of the industries were 'controlled,' the control actually being workers' management, other firms were collectivized, while others, finally, were controlled but directed by an employer whose sole concern was to rescue his capital. All these firms were on the brink of disaster: more than 11,000 requests for credit were piling up in the minister's office, none of which were to be satisfied. Peiró submitted to Caballero a decree for collectivization, which was not accepted because it would have meant a blow to industrial ownership and consequently the risk of Western reprisals and a tightening of the 'arms blockade.' Peiró's plans were eventually confined to a decree permitting government intervention in industries indispensable to the war effort.

In Catalonia, the Generalidad Cabinet went further, as a result of pressure from the CNT and the POUM, who made the 'legalization' of collectivization the condition for the liquidation of revolutionary power. The 24 October decree provided for the collectivization of firms employing more than two hundred staff and for control by Workers' Committees for the rest. Aware of the dictates of foreign policy, the CNT and POUM representatives agreed to compensation for foreign shareholders. But compensation for Spanish shareholders was also accepted, though the total sum was not fixed: thus, with a restoration of Republican legality, the prospect remained open that former shareholders could collect actual dividends from collectivized firms. The CNT and POUM had agitated loudly for the organization of a monopoly on foreign trade, in their view a corollary of collectivization and, above all, a condition for the planning without which collectivization could only lead to chaos. They were defeated on this point too, and foreign trade remained free.

The question of credit, the real bottleneck of collectivization, was not settled in accordance with the views of the revolutionaries either. It was this crisis, we saw, that threatened the functioning even of the collectivized firms. The Generalidad Cabinet in Catalonia rejected the creation of the bank for industry and credit demanded by the CNT and the POUM. The control of the banks by the UGT in Madrid prevented a flight of capital, but the banks were able to reserve their credits for private firms only and even to charge exorbitant commissions on transfers of funds ordered by the government. Juan Peiró suggested the creation of an industrial bank to finance the activities of collectivized factories. But the minister of finance, Negrín, was against it, just as he was against[19] the request for a credit of 30 million pesetas, which the minister of industry judged indispensable for handling the most pressing needs of collectivized industry. Thus the collectivization movement was checked and then halted, the government remaining in control of the firms through the banks. It gradually asserted its authority, both in the *incautadas* and in the *intervenidas* firms, through its choice of controllers and directors. Its concern for efficiency and its political preoccupations often led it to restore former owners or administrators under different titles.

A similar policy prevailed in the countryside. The government measures did not bridge the gulf that threatened to open between agrarian revolution and Republican defense. Uribe's decree of 7 October 1936 was far behind the times where the actual situation in the countryside was concerned. Silent on the decisive problem of leases and rents, which remained only under the *de facto* control of a wholly illegal suppression, it dealt with the 'expropriation without compensation and in favor of the state' of agricultural estates belonging to individuals linked with the rebellion, the peasants being free to decide whether their cultivation would be collective or individual. Thus it only legalized part of the expropriations: the names of the proprietors affected were to appear in the *Officiel*. Serious problems were left in abeyance. Proprietors who had not been implicated in the rebellion had had their lands expropriated. So had others, who had been regarded as factionists but who could have been cleared legally. Finally, certain heirs were enabled to enforce their rights. Henceforth thousands of peasants wondered if they would not be compelled to hand back the lands that they had seized during the summer of 1936.

Retreat by the Anarchists

The restoration of the state achieved by the Largo Caballero government had been possible only with the participation of the most popular CNT–FAI leaders and with the support of their governing bodies. But to the militants the switch had been all the more abrupt because explanations had been summary. Though, as we saw, certain leaders, such as Santillán, had resigned themselves to the liquidation of revolutionary power with a heavy heart, others very soon went much further and cheerfully trampled on what had until then been the Anarchist creed.[20] The CNT leaders put it about that Durruti was ready to give up everything except victory, and to many people this 'everything' meant the revolutionary gains.[21] The Anarchist ministers became true ministers,[22] and the minister for propaganda referred to '*el excelentísimo señor ministro de Justicia, camarada García Oliver.*' Anarchist officers and policemen now talked and acted more like officers and policemen than Anarchists: Eroles, commissioner of internal security, declared that his most 'fervent desire' had been accomplished by the creation of a single police force, and Mera, ignoring the comrades, declared that from now on he only wished to know captains and sergeants.

Many leaders felt profoundly uneasy: they remembered the time, not so long past, when judges, officers, and ministers had embodied the class enemy. They did not dispute the tactic of collaboration, but they freely criticized the zeal shown in its application. Thus Santillán, who found himself being divested of his responsibilities, finally stood aside, bitter and skeptical, powerless against his own organization's apparatus. In general, the militants had fewer qualms and scruples. More than ever, local and regional organizations and even individuals took the initiative without considering federal policy. Most of the opposition, the 'sectarians,' did not waste time arguing and elaborating theories. They acted, and their disagreement took the most diverse forms, from desertion to armed demonstration by way of assault. On 1 October, the Iron Column, trained in Valencia and officered by Anarchists, left the Teruel front to impose its conception of 'revolutionary order' on Valencia. It attacked and disarmed the Civil Guards, invaded the tribunal and destroyed its records, and moved on to the nightclubs and cabarets, relieving customers of their jewelry and their wallets. It took virtually a pitched battle to settle matters: among the dead was a Socialist leader, José Pardo Aracíl. On 30 October, again in Valencia, the funeral of one of the leaders of the Iron Column, Ariza González, possibly shot by way of reprisal, was transformed into an armed disturbance. Finally, surrounded in the Plaza de Tetuán by Communist units armed with machine guns, the demonstrators suffered heavy losses, leaving about fifty dead. Day after day, there were incidents of this kind, here and there, following a scheme that was almost always identical: a blind explosion of violence by the Anarchists, often unconvincing and certainly without any precise object, to which police forces and Communist units responded brutally, pressing home their advantage and eventually dismantling the Anarchist positions. This was what happened in Cuenca, where in August 1936 Borkenau had reported a real Anarchist fortress, but which he described in February as a bastion of the UGT.

A characteristic example of Anarchist disarray was demonstrated by the variety of reactions to the government's departure for Valencia in the early hours of the attack on Madrid. The Anarchist ministers who had fought this decision finally accepted it and followed Caballero. *Solidaridad Obrera* was quick to state that the government's moral authority would be reestablished and enhanced by the change of residence. At the same time, the Madrid CNT–FAI saluted the capital, now freed from ministers, and the Valencia CNT–FAI branded the members of the government as cowards and fugitives. In

Tarancón about a hundred Anarchist militiamen from the Sigüenza front halted the official train and molested and threatened the ministers and ambassadors, including Rosenberg, the Russian ambassador; it took all the powers of persuasion of Eduardo Val, the Madrid CNT leader, to obtain their release unscathed.[23]

These incidents discredited the Anarchist movement and gave ammunition to their enemies, who denounced the part played by 'unruly elements' in their ranks. Above all, they added to their isolation and allowed the forces that were hostile to them to assert themselves and emerge into the open.

The petty bourgeoisie in the towns had gone to ground during the early months. But while the Anarchists had inspired fear, they had not triumphed, they had not seized power, and, most importantly, they had not destroyed the enemy. Having been unable to see the Revolution through to the end, they now had to resign themselves to seeing it rear its head: the unfinished Revolution was turning on its originators.

Things developed similarly in the countryside. Even the peasants who had willingly accepted collectivization in the early weeks were anxious about their unstable position. Requisitions by the militias weighed heavily on them, and they did not regard collectivization as the paradise they had been promised. The enemies of collectivization had regained confidence, encouraged by official statements about order, legality, and property. They knew that they could rely on the new police force: in January 1937, in Fatarella, a village of 600 inhabitants in Tarragona province, the small proprietors took up arms against the Anarchists who wanted to collectivize them, and the result was several dead and wounded. More or less everywhere, the countryside was reacting against the Revolution.

The fact was that the Anarchists, who had been unable to break down the feeble Giral government at the peak of the revolutionary upsurge and with the cohesion of victory, were now, in broken ranks and without direction or policy, up against a strong government, recognized by all and supported by its own leaders. Above all, they were everywhere being challenged by the constantly increasing strength of the Communist party and PSUC organizations, which possessed disciplined cadres, material means, and a policy: on every level, they were the beneficiaries as well as the principal agents of the Anarchist decline.

The Communist Upsurge

After September 1936, as we saw, the Communist party and the PSUC became a dominant factor in the political life of Spain. From about 30,000 at the beginning of the Civil War, they increased in several months to some hundreds of thousands of militants, reaching a million in June 1937. But the Spanish leaders of the Communist party and the PSUC were no longer the only ones playing this important role, now that the Moscow government had committed itself to the war. By the end of July, delegates from the Communist International had taken over the leadership and organization of the Party. In Madrid, there was the Argentinian Codovilla, known under the pseudonym Medina, the Bulgarian Stepanov, and particularly the Italian Togliatti, known as Ercoli and Alfredo,[24] Moscow's éminence grise in Spain. In Barcelona, there was the Hungarian Gerö, known as Pedro. They were surrounded by technicians and advisers with valuable experience, who most of the time seemed to have been Russian secret agents. The Spanish Communist party's entire military policy was in the hands of the Italian Vittorio Vidali, one of the NKVD's most important foreign agents, a small man 'with the look of a comedian, a pink face with a tuft of blond hair,' as Simone Téry put it. He was known in Spain as Carlos Contreras, and more often as Major Carlos. All of them had access to substantial funds which enabled them to establish a large apparatus for action and propaganda.

While the reactionary press throughout the world did its best to describe the ravages of a 'Bolshevik revolution' in Spain, instigated by the Communists with their 'Moscow gold,' the Communist party had from very early on taken a clearly defined stand in favor of the preservation of Republican law and order, for the defense of property and legality. All its leaders' speeches reiterated the same theme: there was no question of a proletarian revolution in Spain; it was a national and popular struggle against semifeudal Spain and foreign Fascists, as well as an episode in the struggle that pitted the democrats of the world against Germany and Italy. The Communist party vigorously denounced everything that seemed likely to destroy the united front between the working class and the 'other strata of the people.' It seemed especially anxious to preserve good relations with the Republican leaders, and it tirelessly repeated its slogans of 'respect for the peasant, the small manufacturer, and the small tradesman.' 'We are fighting,' José Díaz proclaimed, 'for a democratic and parliamentary republic of a new type.' Such a regime implied the destruction of the material foundation of semifeudal Spain, the expropriation of the large proprietors, the destruction of the Church's economic and political power, the elimination of militarism, and the breakup of the large financial oligarchies. In Díaz's opinion, these results had already been achieved. Therefore, the only immediate task was to fight: 'defeat Franco first' was the Communists' main slogan. To succeed in this, it was necessary to consolidate the national and popular bloc and to strengthen the authority of the Popular Front government: the Communists were backing the Companys government against the Central Committee, Martínez Barrio's Junta against the Popular Executive Committee, and the legal authorities against the 'irresponsible Committees.' From the start they defended the need for the establishment of a regular army, supported Giral, and anticipated Largo Caballero on this tack. José Díaz stated on several occasions that 'plunging into attempts at socialization and collectivization . . . is absurd and amounts to playing the enemy's game.' In addition, the Communist party waged a fierce campaign against all who spoke of pursuing the Revolution. 'We cannot pursue the Revolution if we do not win the war first.' Accordingly, in the Republican camp, he aimed all his blows at the Left, against the revolutionaries. 'The enemies of the people are the Fascists, the Trotskyists, and the unruly elements,' José Díaz said in the same speech, and the Communist party's propagandists, leaning on the Moscow trials, tirelessly repeated the anti-Trotskyist theme: 'Trotskyism is not a political party, but a gang of counterrevolutionary elements. Fascism, Trotskyism, and the unruly elements are the three enemies of the people that must be eliminated from political life, not only in Spain, but in all civilized countries.' Franz Borkenau has demonstrated the consequences of a political line that, transcending the organization of the struggle against Franco, drew the Stalinist Communist organizations into a struggle overtly aimed at the Revolution itself, in the name of expediency: 'The Communists did not merely oppose the tide of socialization, they opposed almost every form of socialization. They did not merely oppose the collectivization of peasant plots, they successfully opposed every policy intended to achieve the distribution of the lands of the large proprietors. They did not merely oppose, and with good reason, childish ideas for the local abolition of money, they opposed state control of the markets. . . . They did not merely try to organize an active police force, they showed a deliberate preference for the old regime's police forces so execrated by the masses. They did not merely destroy the power of the Committees, they displayed their hostility to every form of spontaneous, unruly mass movement. They acted, in a word, not with the goal of transforming chaotic enthusiasm into disciplined enthusiasm, but with the aim of substituting disciplined administrative and military action for action by the masses, which they wanted to get rid of altogether.'[25]

This conservative policy ensured the growth of the Communist party and the PSUC and broadened their audience. In Catalonia, the decree on compulsory syndicalization had swelled the numbers of the weak UGT controlled by the PSUC. Under its aegis the GEPCI (*Federación Catalana de Gremios y Entidades de Pequeños Comerciantes y Industriales*) was formed into a trade union that, under the guise of professional protection for tradesmen, mechanics, and small manufacturers, was the tool used by the middle and petty bourgeoisie to combat the revolutionary gains. On the other hand, in the Levante, where the UGT had a mass basis among the small peasants, the

Communist party, under Mateu, organized an independent Peasant Federation, which all the enemies of collectivization, including the caciques, supported.

Generally speaking, the supporters of law and order and of property in Republican Spain turned toward the Communist party and the PSUC, the defenders of these very values. Magistrates, senior civil servants, army officers, and police regarded the Party as the instrument of the policy they favored, as well as a means of guaranteeing protection and safety, in case they were needed.[26] At the same time, the Communist party ceased to be a party made up of proletarians: in Madrid, in 1938, according to its own figures, it had only 10,160 trade unionists out of 63,426 militants, which suggests that no more than a small percentage were workers.[27] Moreover, the Communist party's propaganda made much of the well-known personalities recruited, some of whom were, however, far from being a hundred percent reliable where the sincerity of their devotion to a workers cause was concerned.[28]

Yet it would be a mistake to explain the growth of the Communist party only by its moderate policy and its Republican loyalism. In the chaos of the early months, in fact, the Communist party had proved itself a remarkable organizing force, a tremendously effective weapon. As a result of some of its achievements, its appeals for antifascist unity met a huge response from all those who, whether Republicans, Socialists, trade unionists, or unaffiliated, wanted more than anything to fight Franco. Hernández, La Pasionaria, and even Comorera were only taken seriously in their diatribes against the Committees and the unruly elements and in their appeals for discipline and respect for legality because their party had shown that it was able to fight well, because it knew how to build and set an example.

The story of the defense of Madrid also showed that in certain circumstances the Communist party was capable, not only of appealing to revolutionary traditions like those of the October Revolution and the Red Army, but also of using actual revolutionary methods—in a word, of appearing to the masses as an authentically revolutionary party. Many Spanish and international militants had experienced the defense of the capital as a revolutionary epic whose purely antifascist emblem was, in their eyes, only provisional. Against the German and Italian mercenaries, they had seen themselves as fighters in the international proletarian revolution. Many of them had opposed the Revolution for the moment in the conviction that it was a question of a temporary strategic withdrawal, that in the end the antifascist struggle would lead to world Communist revolution.

From this point of view, one of the most effective means of developing the Communist party's influence was the Fifth Regiment. On 19 July, Communist militants in Madrid seized a Salesian convent in Cuatro Caminos and organized a unit that numbered 8000 men by the end of the month. Even the choice of the title 'regiment' and its number, the Fifth, was significant: the Communist party leadership made the unit the Fifth Regiment because there had been four regiments in Madrid before the uprising. Enrique Castro Delgado, appointed by the Political Bureau and seconded by Major Carlos, was given the task of setting it up. In each battalion they formed 'Steel Companies,' largely made up of Communist militants, who made systematic appeals to officers and NCOs, both reserve and regular. With Russian aid, the Fifth Regiment grew with amazing rapidity. It was equipped, trained, and officered. The government smiled on it because it was a model of discipline: it reintroduced all the practices of the regular units, salutes, insignia, and ranks.

Regular officers serving in other columns asked to transfer to this unit, where they found service conditions that were to them normal. The Fifth Regiment had a band, a choir, and a daily newspaper, the *Milicia Popular*. It soon had its legends. By the end of September it consisted of 30,000 men. It later became the Fifth Corps, comprising more than 100,000 men, and eventually took in the vast majority of the Army of the Center.

It was in the Fifth Regiment that the title 'commissar' made its first appearance: in fact, its growth in the view of the Communist leaders, was not supposed to escape the Party apparatus. The commissars maintained the political discipline of a party in these regular units, controlled the technicians, and kept up the morale of the men. And the Communist party was able to use the experience of the Commissariat to spread its influence in the Army. It was the only organization that genuinely understood the possibilities that the corps of Commissars offered to an active party. With the protection of the commissar-general, Álvarez del Vayo, they literally managed to colonize the Commissariat during its first year of existence.[29] Thanks to it, they were able to spread their slogans and the principal themes of their propaganda among the troops: democracy, patriotism, and discipline. While the Red Army's political commissars had been the propagandists of revolution and socialism, these two words were banished from the vocabulary of the Spanish commissars, one of whose reasons for existing, through the wishes of the Party, was precisely to combat all those in the Army for whom instantaneous revolution was still as important a task as the war.

The Stalinist Communists, untouchable since the delivery of Russian arms, defenders, consequently, of the antifascist program for the restoration of the state as well as organizers of the Army, thus became the most dynamic element in the government coalition. Azaña, Companys, Prieto, and even Largo Caballero showed them the same trust and gave them the same support that they later reproached a Del Vayo for having granted. Their position gained in strength daily, not only in public opinion, but perhaps still more in the state apparatus. We have just shown the position they occupied in the Popular Army's political and military cadres. The Communists were also in control of the censorship and coding departments. Their men, Burillo in Madrid and Rodríguez Sala in Barcelona, held key posts in the new police force. Henceforth their cohesion and their discipline raised a problem: did they not already form a state within a state?

A few serious incidents showed that they had decided to use their posts for ends not justified by their concern, so often affirmed, for the general interest and a united front, and—what was even more serious—that they had adopted this course on the instructions of the Russian government. When the Madrid Defense Junta was formed, in spite of the decision to have all parties represented on it, the Communist party put an absolute veto on the presence of the POUM, which it dubbed 'Trotskyist' and 'enemy of the Soviet Union.'[30] *La Batalla* protested and forced the conflict into the open: 'What really concerns Stalin,' it wrote on 15 November, 'is not the fate of the Spanish and international proletariat, but the defense of the Soviet government in accordance with the policy of pacts made by certain states against others.' On 28 November, in a note to the press, the USSR's consul-general in Barcelona, Antonov-Ovseyenko, was quick to intervene in Republican Spain's internal policies, denouncing *La Batalla* as part of 'the press that has sold out to international Fascism.' It was this affair that led to a ministerial crisis in Catalonia and eventually to the exclusion of the POUM from the Generalidad Council. The commentary on this incident in *Pravda* on 17 December, coming after the first Moscow trials, contained an undisguised threat: 'In Catalonia, the elimination of Trotskyists and Anarcho-Syndicalists has already begun; it will be carried out with the same energy as in the USSR.'

Balance Sheet of the Restoration

There were also many other disturbing clouds on the horizon. Duality of power had certainly disappeared, but it had in many cases given way to a multiple administration whose organs counteracted or hampered each other. The case of Málaga was no exception. There the phantom powers of the governor, Arraiz, and the Committee, existed side by side, whereas the only true authority was held by military men unable to understand or to handle their worker and peasant troops. The disadvantages of having hundreds of village police bodies had disappeared with the reorganization of the police, but Borkenau was surely right when he stated that the villages' impassioned concern for the Civil War had disappeared with them. The Italian Libertarian Bertoni wrote from the Huesca front: 'The war in Spain, bereft of any new faith, of any idea of social change, and of any revolutionary grandeur . . .

remains a terrible question of life or death but is no longer a war in affirmation of a new regime and a new humanity.'[31]

Yet it was at this point that the battle of Madrid took place: a modern war in which two organized armies were face to face, in which planes, guns, and tanks were pitted against each other, as well as a revolutionary war in which the morale of the combatants achieved what was technically impossible, and in which people in arms stood up to two of the greatest military powers in Europe. The battles of Madrid and Guadalajara, the only major Republican victories in this war, came at the vital turning point: organization and discipline had not killed off enthusiasm and faith, and enthusiasm and faith were relying on discipline and organization—and also on arms, without which no cause can triumph, whatever sacrifices it may have been able to inspire.

Notes

[1] According to Álvarez del Vayo (*La guerra empezó en España*, p. 216).

[2] Besides Largo Caballero, the Supreme Council included Prieto (war production), Álvarez del Vayo (political staffing of troops), García Oliver (training of military cadres), and Uribe (food supplies and quartermaster staff).

[3] There was remarkable unanimity on this view within the antifascist organizations. Companys called for 'a strong government, a government with full powers,' since it was 'nothing less than the delegated authority of all the antifascist forces, both political and trade union, that are represented in it.' Azaña, in favor of a war policy, demanded 'a single discipline, responsible government for the Republic.' The Communist Mije stated: 'The watchword of the moment must be to gain everything through the government and for the government, to strengthen its authority and its power.' The Anarchist Peiró, now a minister, asserted: 'We say: first the war and then the Revolution. It is the government that is in command.'

[4] Reported in Peirats, *La CNT en la Revolución española*, 1: 253–254).

[5] The proportions were sometimes the other way around. Thus, in Castellón, the Committee consisted of 35 members, 14 from the CNT, 7 from the POUM, 7 from the UGT, and 7 Republicans. With municipal reform, the CNT, the UGT, the POUM, the Communist party, the JSU, the Socialists, and the Republican parties had equal representation.

[6] For many militants it was the beginning of an administrative career whose advantages perhaps explain why some were won over. David Antona, a building worker in 1936, was civil governor of Ciudad Libre (Ciudad

Real) in 1939. Only a few, like Juan López, returned to factories after having been ministers or senior officials.

[7] The Committees' capacity for resistance exceeded what might normally have been expected, given the unanimity of the organizations. On 8 February, José Díaz devoted more than half of a major speech at Valencia to the necessity of doing away with 'miniature governments' and of substituting municipal councils for Committees: the decree was a month old. On 27 April, *ABC*, seized by the Republicans in July 1936, reported that the Castellón government had been forced to intervene to replace a Committee by a municipal council.

More important, for want of documents, one great exception must simply be pointed out. The Committees were surviving in Asturias through the assent of organizations that elsewhere were militating for their dissolution. The Socialist deputy Amador Fernández, member of the Regional Council, stated to the press (*ABC*, 12 February 1937): 'It must be confessed that there is no phobia about the Committees here.' On 8 January the Asturian CNT and UGT had signed an agreement for the generalization of all ventures by the CNT–UGT Control Committees (with an equal number of militants from each union, under the chairmanship of a member of the majority organization in the venture). The Asturian UGT congress, on 13 April 1937, of which Javier Bueno pointed out in *Claridad* that it was the 'first congress of the Revolution,' confirmed this orientation. In the elections for the Executive Commission, the Communist list of the Committees' enemies, supposedly one of 'unity,' only obtained 12,000 votes, against 87,000 for the outgoing leadership. The Asturian JSU (see chap. 11) challenged the influence of the Communist party and formed a 'Revolutionary Front' with the Libertarian Youth.

Until its fall, Asturias remained a besieged commune. The resistance by armed groups of partisans for many months after Franco's victory gave proof of the depth of its revolutionary spirit, which the work of restoring the state, carried out more discreetly here, had been unable to subdue (see Part 2, chap. 16).

[8] It included Galarza (UGT), minister of the interior, Jesús Hernández, Esplá, and García Oliver.

[9] Carrillo replaced Manuel Muñoz, who had been director-general even before the Revolution. Negrín replaced him with the Communist Ortega.

[10] The *Carabineros* were the traditional customs officers. Their development at this stage earned them the nickname *hijos de Negrín.*

[11] This measure does not seem to have been respected, at least where certain parties were concerned. See, in chapter 11, fn. 15, the incidents provoked by Margarita Nelken's Communist 'proselytism' among the *Asaltos.*

[12] Escobar and Martínez were killed on 21 November. The official inquiry was inconclusive. Santillán said that their liquidation was carried out at the instigation of 'another antifascist group,' which wrongly accused its colleagues of playing a double game. Martín Blázquez accused some FAI militiamen of the attempted murder of himself and his friends.

[13] García Oliver modeled their organization on the one in Barcelona. But the progress achieved by modern war techniques explains the inadequacies of officers thus taught: no one could learn to lead a company in two months.

[14] See chapter 5, fn. 25.

[15] It seems that Durán served André Malraux as a basis for one of the main characters in *L'Espoir*, the Communist Manuel. What Manuel says about himself in the novel is not unlike what Durán confided to Simone Téry (*Front de la Liberté, Espagne 1937–1938* [Paris: Editions Sociales Internationales, 1938], p. 147). In the Fifth Regiment, Durán had commanded the Steel Company, a unit of motorized machine-gunners organized after an idea of Malraux's (ibid., p. 129).

[16] On 17 October, Álvarez del Vayo was appointed commissar-general. Under him were appointed, as deputy commissars-general, Mije of the Communist party, Crescenciano Bilbao, Socialist, Gil Roldán of the CNT, and Pestaña of the Syndicalist party. On 9 December Mije was appointed commissar-general. Throughout this period, Pretel of the UGT was secretary-general of the Commissariat.

[17] *L'Humanité*, 19 April 1937.

[18] A Catholic priest, Father Lobo, spoke to the *madrileños* over the Communist party radio, asking them to join the ranks of the people.

[19] According to Juan Peiró, the credit that was finally offered him, after a long discussion by the Cabinet, was one of 24 million pesetas, on which the Ministry of Industry still had to pay 6 percent interest.

[20] *Solidaridad Obrera* asked the French for their support against the 'Boches.' Federica Montseny said that the war was being fought against 'foreign invaders.'

[21] After his death, Durruti was used by all factions. We quote, in contrast to this oft-repeated phrase, his statement to Pierre van Paasen: 'Here in Spain we want the Revolution now and not perhaps after the next European war' (interview quoted by Felix Morrow).

[22] García Oliver told the officer cadets: 'Your soldiers . . . cease to be your comrades and must take their place as cogs in our Army's military machine.'

[23] Contrary to what the majority of writers claim, it seems that the Tarancón CNT militiamen did not belong to the Iron Column, and that it was elements from Madrid who were involved. See what Guzmán said about their leader, Villanueva, in *Madrid rojo y negro* (n.p.: Talleres Socializados del SUIPAG-CNT, 1938).

[24] Jesús Hernández stated that Togliatti was in Spain in the early days of the uprising, therefore during the summer of 1936, and that he was in permanent session with the Political Bureau of the Spanish Communist party. Togliatti's official biographers, the Ferraras, said that he had arrived in Spain in July 1937 (p. 280) and that he 'was to show himself as little as possible' (p. 288), and they confirmed that 'his work was entirely devoted to Spanish questions, to those of the Communist party and the Spanish popular movement.' Marcella and Maurizio Ferrara, *Palmiro Togliatti*, trans. Jean Noaro (Paris: Editions Sociales, 1954).

[25] Borkenau, *The Spanish Cockpit* (London, 1937), p. 292.

[26] Of course, members of the Right, anxious to provide themselves with a cover, had flocked to the CNT, to name one example. But only the Communist party offered, along with protection, the prospect of a struggle to achieve law and order.

[27] Borkenau said that the Communist party was first of all the party of the military and administrative staff. Then came the petty bourgeois and the well-to-do peasants, the clerks, and, only in last place, the industrial workers. Dolléans, quoting the case of Valencia, where the former members of the CEDA had joined the Communist party, said that it drew its recruits 'from among the most conservative elements in the Republican bloc.' The majority of regular officers, some of whom were only Republicans before the war, if they were not of the Right, belonged to the Communist party. Take, for instance, Miaja and Pozas, and younger men such as Hidalgo de Cisneros, Galán, Ciutat, Cordón, and Barcelo.

[28] On 1 January 1937, one of President Alcalá Zamora's sons, José Alcalá Castillo, a few days back from exile, joined the Communist party: on the sixth, the Communist party, with Balbontín taking part, addressed a special radio broadcast to the 'sons of the wealthy bourgeoisie who are fighting in the enemy camp,' who were asked 'to cross over en masse to the side of the Spanish people.' José Alcalá Castillo was chosen to take part in a delegation of 'workers' sent to the USSR for the May Day celebrations. The Spanish press reprinted an article by him which had appeared in *Izvestia* on the sixth, containing his thanks to 'great comrade Stalin.'

Another recruit, very typical of the new stratum of Communist party militants, was Constancia de la Mora. Daughter of one of the greatest families in the Spanish oligarchy, and granddaughter of Antonio Maura, the Conservative statesman, for whom she did not conceal her admiration, she took issue with her family and her circle as a result of a disastrous marriage with a *señorito* from Málaga (Bolín, mentioned in another connection by Koestler and Chalmers Mitchell). Divorced and married to Hidalgo de Cisneros, she ran the office of the censor in Madrid, not hesitating to criticize the government's decisions in accordance with Party orders. Her autobiography, *Doble esplendor* (Mexico City: Atlante, 1944; English translation, *In Place of Splendor* [New York: Harcourt, Brace, 1939]), is an interesting eyewitness account: this intelligent, energetic, and courageous woman still spoke the language of her class and manifested the same hostility to extreme revolutionaries as her grandfather had to Socialists.

[29] La Pasionaria, in *Mundo Obrero* on 19 March 1937, quoting a statement about casualties suffered by the Corps of Commissars, revealed, perhaps unintentionally, the Communist preponderance: of 32 commissars killed, 21 belonged to the Communist party and 7 to the JSU; of 55 wounded, 35 were from the Communist party and 1 from the JSU. Even allowing, as she did, that the Communists, more heroic by definition than the rest, were therefore more exposed, it is clear that their influence was preponderant. Caballero bluntly accused Del Vayo of having expedited their infiltration. Prieto blamed Antón, head of the commissars on the Madrid front and member of the Political Bureau of the Party. It cannot be denied that the Communist party understood better than the other organizations the importance of the commissars' role and that the Communist candidates were more numerous than the rest.

[30] Enrique Rodríguez, POUM leader in Madrid, was informed of this decision by the Socialist Albar, who told him: 'Ambassador Rosenberg

has vetoed your presence. It is unfair, of course, but try to understand us: the USSR is powerful; we have chosen between depriving ourselves of the POUM nominee and depriving ourselves of the help of the USSR. We prefer to give in and reject the POUM.' Andrade and Gorkin then went to Madrid, but they too failed. The POUM was not represented on the Junta.

[31] Quoted by Camillo Berneri, *Guerre de classes en Espagne* (Paris: Imprimerie Ouvrière, 1938), p. 40.

CHAPTER 10

MADRID: NO PASARÁN!

On 28 September 1936 the last flickers of resistance in Toledo died away with the extermination of the groups of CNT militiamen who were holding the hospital. A new chapter opened, that of the battle for the capital. In the view of the Nationalist leaders, it had to be the last: the fall of Madrid would be the signal for Republican collapse. None of them envisaged for a moment any serious resistance on the part of the militias. Most foreign observers shared this point of view: diplomatic circles were preparing for the fall of the capital, which in the eyes of Rome and Berlin was bound to change Spain's legal position and to permit the recognition of the Franco government.

The rebel Generals calculated that they would be able to enter Madrid for the Feast of the Race on 12 October.[1] General Varela was in command of the attacking army: 20,000 regular soldiers, Moors and legionaries, warlike, disciplined, and confident, convinced that they would not meet any resistance. At first the offensive went according to plan: the column that was moving up the Tagus Valley linked up, on 10 October, with Dávila's Army corps, coming from the sierra. The only resistance it had met had been some harassment by militias from the Levante, under Uribarri and Bayo, a guerrilla action incapable of halting the advance of a modern army that was not running into any opposition in its frontal attacks. In three days, the attackers advanced seventeen miles; the pincer movement that was to squeeze Madrid took shape between Chapinería, captured on the fifteenth, Navalcarnero, which fell on the eighteenth, and Illescas, which fell on the twenty-first.

A City to Capture

By late September, Voelckers's report to Berlin was highly optimistic. Madrid could not withstand a siege. It had no food stocks, no antiaircraft, no line of defense, and not even any trenches. The militiamen who were defending it were badly armed, inexperienced, and above all poorly led. It was true that the first modern arms had just arrived, the first concrete manifestation of Russian aid: the very astonishment that they caused

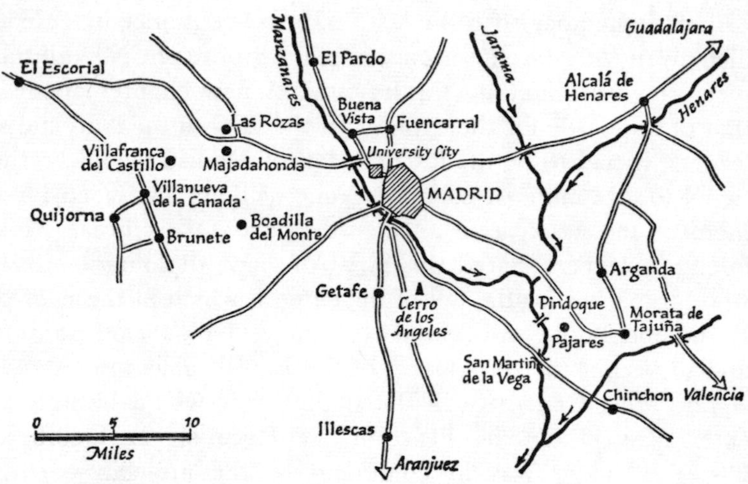

the militiamen proved their inexperience and seemed to invalidate the theory that they could really do anything to reverse the position. On 28 September, in a radio statement, Largo Caballero announced: 'We possess formidable mechnized armor. We have tanks and a powerful air force'; the same day forty Russian tanks, with air support, managed a breakthrough. However, the infantry did not follow it up, and the Republican Army's first counterattack ended in failure. Moreover, the military leaders in Madrid were conscious of the gravity of the situation and, it seems, were resigned to the inevitable fall of the capital. General Asensio, in command of the Army of the Center, made no secret of his pessimism, and General Pozas, who replaced him on 24 October, did not believe defense was possible either. Both advised the government to leave the capital while there was still time.

In early November General Mola, having reorganized the troops, took control of what bore all the signs of being the final assault; after discussions, the rebel general staff decided to enter Madrid through the Casa del Campo and the University City, thus avoiding street fighting in the working-class districts, which Varela, for one, feared. On learning of the aid Madrid was receiving from the Russians, the rebel Generals decided to strike before the defenders had time to collect themselves. On 4 November, the airport of Getafe fell into their hands; on the sixth, the Yagüe Column occupied Carabanchel and the stronghold of Cerro de Los Angeles. Mola summoned to his headquarters the future municipal council of Madrid, which was to enter the capital on his army's heels. On the fourth Radio Burgos had begun a program called 'The Last Hours of Madrid.' On the seventh Franco announced that he would be attending mass in Madrid the following day; on the eighth the Segovia and Toledo bridges over the Manzanares were reached.

The fall of Madrid was now only a question of hours: in the Cabinet, Largo Caballero literally forced the decision for the government to leave for Valencia on the recalcitrant Communists and Anarchists. In spite of the publicized unanimity, many of the combatants regarded this precautionary measure as a desertion.[2] The tragicomic incident of Tarancón[3] cannot be explained merely by the notorious lack of discipline of the Anarchists: the attitude of the CNT militiamen was in line with a spirit that was widespread in Madrid, where more than anywhere else the workers had trusted the government and had accepted its discipline. On 9 November they saw it in flight, its experts resigned to defeat, although no mass mobilization had been attempted for an all-out defense of the capital. In the early days of September, fewer than 2000 out of 20,000 volunteers had in fact been employed in fortification works. To the Socialist, Communist, and Anarchist militants, the battle was not yet lost. The temptation to shoot the ministers went hand in hand with the will to fight to the death. The cry of the Madrid CNT, '*¡Viva Madrid sin gobierno!*' ('Long live Madrid with no government'), clearly echoed a very widespread feeling.

The Defense of Madrid: General Miaja and the Junta

On leaving, the Largo Caballero government entrusted the defense of the capital to General Miaja. Writers and eye-witnesses have since frequently argued about the reasons for the appointment of a general until then on the retired list, but who was to become the hero of Madrid. A regular officer, 'a man about sixty, rather stout, but remarkably lively,' as Simone Téry described him, José Miaja had never been noted for his ardent Republicanism: he had even belonged to the *Unión Militar Española* before the war. Minister of war in Martínez Barrio's short-lived compromise government—a choice in itself significant—he had turned down the same post in the Giral government but had put himself at its disposal. He had led the expedition that had recaptured Albacete. Exiled to Valencia, he had been subjected to the insults of Lieutenant José Benedito. From Valencia he had been sent to command the front in Andalusia; he had been accused of 'sabotage' there by some of his men, and Largo Caballero had transferred him to Madrid on 24 October.[4] Whatever the true motives for this appointment, it is out of the question that he was, as some have claimed, 'prevailed upon' or 'prompted' by the Communist party, with which Miaja had no special ties at that time.

The decree that gave him the command[5] also empowered him to represent the government in the Defense Junta assigned the task of organizing and controlling the defense of the capital, which the Council of Ministers had also decided to set up at the meeting of 6 November. Created by government decree, presided over by a government delegate, and made up of representatives from all the parties and unions that supported it, the Madrid Defense Junta was nevertheless neither a simple consultative commission nor an appendage of the government. Placed at the head of the capital at a time when the government's departure in fact left the initiative to those who wanted to fight, the Junta became, as a result of its language and its methods, a genuinely revolutionary government.

It was revolutionary first of all in its composition. General Miaja had, it seems, at first considered appealing to some of the members of the Commissariat, since all parties were represented in it: but most of the well-known names had left Madrid with the government. He therefore appealed to unknowns. By temperament and outlook a professional soldier with a belief in organization, discipline, and efficiency, he naturally came to rely on the Fifth Regiment, which Mije immediately placed at his disposal, and with which Checa, secretary of the Communist party, established liaison. On the evening of 7 November, the Junta was formed: its members were so young—nearly all were under thirty—that they were nicknamed 'Miaja's kids.' The Communist party controlled it, through the UGT and Socialist Youth representatives as well as through its own, and through the importance of the posts it held.[6]

The defense of Madrid became the affair of the Communist party, the affair of the Communist International, and the affair of Soviet Russia. Their prestige and authority were committed to this battle. Never again, during the whole of the Spanish Civil War, did the Communists join the fight with such ferocity. Never again did the Russians repeat the efforts they made for Madrid in November 1936.

Consignments of material supplied by the Russians or bought by their agents in fact converged on Madrid during October, and again in November and December. The defenders of Madrid soon had rifles, grenades, machine guns, tanks, field guns, and ammunition. A modern army, set up during the actual fighting, was strung out in front of the capital. It had leaders, familiar with all the modern techniques, whose abilities far surpassed those of the few Loyalist officers. Rosenberg had even brought with him a group of officers who helped with the development of the Fifth Regiment. A second group of Russian soldiers, a more substantial one, arrived around 20 October; they were known only by their pseudonyms, but their role was indisputable and plainly more influential than that of Miaja and Rojo. Gorev was in charge of the general staff and became the actual organizer of the defense. 'Pavlov' was in command of the armored units, and 'Douglas' led an air force as powerful and effective as André Malraux's heroic squadron.[7] Finally, there was Mikhail Koltsov, whose military competence was beyond question, and who was at the same time a real political leader, his official function as *Pravda*'s special correspondent enabling him to maintain direct contact with Stalin and Voroshilov. Foreign Communists trained in Moscow also played a leading military role: apart from Carlos Contreras, already mentioned, a special place must be assigned to Miguel Martínez, who was in charge of the Madrid Army Commissariat.[8]

It was at the very moment of the decisive assault that the first International Brigades appeared at the front: according to Colodny, these consisted of 8500 men from the Eleventh and Twelfth Brigades, who took part in the fighting around the capital in November and December after the procession by 3500 soldiers of the Eleventh in perfect order along the Gran Vía, to enthusiastic shouts of *¡ Vivan los Rusos!* With them came able leaders, such as General Kléber, whose popularity eclipsed that of Miaja, Lukacz, and Hans. These were shock troops, and on the evening of 8 November their men were in position on the firing line in the Casa de Campo, one member of the International Brigade to five Spaniards: they were giving practical demonstrations of how to handle weapons and use cover. More important, these foreign volunteers were often men who had known years of harsh militant life, with strikes, street brawls, clandestine existence, prison and often torture, convict settlements, and the miseries of emigration. Colodny referred to the Germans in the Thaelmann and Edgar André Brigades as indestructible men.[9] At any rate, with their revolutionary fervour, their spirit of sacrifice, and their iron discipline, they made up an irreplaceable and prestigious shock force whose brilliant actions were as valuable in themselves as they were for their exemplary effect on their Spanish comrades.

The Junta's Methods

With the arrival of Russian military advisers and revolutionaries from every country in Europe, Madrid was in an epic atmosphere inspired by propaganda about the October Revolution. 'Madrid must be defended like Petrograd,' the huge Communist party posters proclaimed. The people of Madrid, who thronged to *The Sailors of Kronstadt*, *Chapaev*, and *Potemkin*, which had arrived with Rosenberg and which were being shown in all the cinemas in Madrid, were linked, through these films, with the tradition of the Russian Revolution, which they believed they were resurrecting. La Pasionaria, dressed in black and seeming to incarnate the workers' revolution, organized mass demonstrations of Madrid women who made a deep impression on every observer of the scene, and who chanted short, heroic slogans in Spanish: 'Better to die on your feet than live on your knees,' 'Better to be a hero's widow than a coward's wife.' To defend Madrid, its defenders had to be galvanized into action. The Junta realized this: hence there were no speeches about the legality of the government or respect for law and order and property. It did not hesitate to appeal to the workers of Madrid to glorify the proletarian revolution they were carrying out.[10]

In the defense of Madrid, the Junta employed methods that the men of the CNT and POUM had advocated elsewhere, in Irún and San Sebastián: arming the people, omnipotence of the Committees, action by the masses, and summary revolutionary justice. On 9 November columns of unarmed workers could be seen moving up to the front, detailed by the unions to go to the firing line and recover the weapons of dead and wounded soldiers. The *casas del pueblo* and Libertarian *Ateneos* became mobilization centers; barricades were erected in every street in the threatened districts. 'Women and children,' wrote Colodny, 'formed a human chain and passed the stones of Madrid to builders who erected symbolic walls, militarily useless but psychologically impregnable, which awaited the offensive . . . by Varela.' District Committees, House Committees, and Block Committees were set up and took on the immediate tasks of defense, antiaircraft observation, and surveillance of suspects. The Fifth Regiment itself called on the population to set up these Committees, which no one in the

Madrid Communist party dreamed of condemning as illegal organizations.[11] Spontaneously and at the instance of the Junta, specialized Committees were formed as well: Food Supply, Communications, and Ammunition Committees, and Women's Committees for preparing collective meals and doing laundry. There was no longer any question of denouncing searches and arrests made by other than the Republican police as being illegal or unauthorized. The *Asaltos* and the Civil Guards were promptly and brutally purged; more than a hundred Civil Guards were arrested in a few days. Most of the police units formed in the preceding months had been transferred to Valencia. García Attadell and his aides had fled abroad.[12] The security guards of the Fifth Regiment, under Pedro Checa, and the special services of the Ministry of War, run by one of Val's colleagues, the Anarchist Salgado, stepped up searches, arrests, and summary executions. According to Koltsov, Miguel Martínez gave the order on 6 November to evacuate the most important of the rebel prisoners from the Model Prison. The same day, the 600 inmates evacuated were shot on the Agranda road. According to Galíndez, 400 more met the same fate two days later. Executions without trial continued through November and December under the authority of Santiago Carrillo and his aide Cazorla. Scruples about the treatment of foreigners did not prevent the Junta authorities in Madrid from arresting refugees and agents of Franco even inside embassies.[13] Whatever may be thought of such methods, there is no doubt that they achieved their end: the Fifth Column[14] did not play the role that the rebel leaders had expected.

The November Fighting

The decisive fighting began with a stroke of luck for Miaja's army. On 9 November, some militiamen discovered, on the corpse of an officer killed in a rebel tank, papers that on examination proved to be a copy of 'Operational Order No. 15'—in other words, the attack projected by Varela for 7 November, the plan for the final assault. Lieutenant Colonel Rojo brought off a triumphant gamble. He assumed that the execution of the 7 November plan had been deferred and that the order he had in his hands concerned the operation that had just been launched by the Nationalist Army. In twenty-four hours, the Republican leaders reshuffled their forces to confront the main assault, which was to be launched against the Casa de Campo and in the University City, whereas they had been expecting it at Vallescas. On 8 November, two Moroccan *tabors* broke through the Republican lines and marched on the Model Prison. After fierce fighting, the lines were formed again. That evening, the Eleventh International Brigade took up position, with the Dabrowsky Battalion at Villaverde, the Edgar André Battalion in the University City, and the Commune de Paris Battalion in the Casa de Campo. General Kléber took command of the Casa de Campo–University City key area. Varela's advance was halted. That night Republicans, Anarchists, Socialists, and Communists held a joint meeting to commemorate the Russian Revolution: the crowd acclaimed the slogan popularized by La Pasionaria: *¡No pasarán!* During the night, reinforcements marched on Madrid. But on the morning of 9 November, only the Campesino Battalion from the sierra had arrived. Varela's troops redoubled their attacks on the Toledo and Princesa bridges. Russian planes destroyed an Italian armored column. The Edgar André Battalion, which had suffered terrible losses, was still holding out in the University City but was threatened from the north by the Moroccans' advance into the Casa de Campo. With a bold stroke, Kléber withdrew the whole of the Eleventh International Brigade dispersed along the front lines and hurled them, bayonets fixed, at Varela's Moors in a desperate counterattack on the Casa de Campo. After fierce fighting, which lasted all night, the Moors retreated. The International Brigades cleaned up the Casa de Campo but lost a third of their strength. The center of the fighting now switched to the lower part of Carabanchel, where the Moors attacked, house by house, a district whose defense was organized by El Campesino's *guerrilleros*. Miaja and Rojo made use of this respite to spread out their troops, about 40,000 men now reinforced by Catalan and Valencian columns, along an unbroken ten-mile front and to create an advance network of fortifications and trenches. On

12 November the Republican general staff launched a counter-attack against the Cerro de los Angeles. It failed but helped somewhat to ease the stranglehold.

On 14 November the 3500 men of the Durruti Column arrived from the Aragon front. The Madrid crowd gave them a triumphal welcome. Durruti asked for the most dangerous sector. He was given the Casa de Campo, opposite the University City. The general staff allocated him an officer, the Russian 'Santi,' as adviser. The Catalans, at first surprised because the war in Madrid bore no resemblance to the one they had experienced, fought bravely, yet not bravely enough for the tastes of their leader, who on several occasions reproached them for flinching.

It was in his sector that, on 15 November, the main attack actually began: the Yagüe Column, supported by field guns and mortars that pounded the Republican entrenchments on the edge of the Manzanares, launched assault after assault, while German bombers from the Condor Legion hammered the University City and West Park. By the end of the afternoon, the Asensio Column had managed to break through and gain a footing in the University City, which the Eleventh International Brigade immediately disputed. They fought house by house, floor by floor. As Louis Delaprée wrote: 'They fire at each other point blank, they slaughter each other from landing to landing.... In some houses, the attackers occupy the ground floor and the government troops the first floor.... In between, they hurl insults at each other up and down the chimneys.'[15]

In the Clinical Hospital, the militiamen sent the service elevator, crammed with grenades, up to the Moroccans from the ground floor. The Asturian *dinamiteros* were everywhere, tossing their lethal little cartridges, blowing things up, and wreaking havoc. Between 17 and 20 November the attackers made just a little more progress, at the cost of enormous losses. On 21 November Durruti was killed in the University City,[16] probably by one of the men in his column who resented the risks he made them run and the discipline he imposed on them during this hell. His funeral was the occasion for huge demonstrations of antifascist unity. But it was on the very day he died that the Eleventh International Brigade, under Kléber and Hans, made a triumphant counterattack on the University City, where the front remained from then on, scarcely budging an inch. The following day, the Twelfth Brigade, supported by *Carabineros*, counterattacked north of the racecourse, recapturing lost ground house by house. When this objective had been achieved, at the end of November, it was relieved: it had lost half its strength.

But the miracle had occurred. Madrid had not fallen. Now it was possible to believe what the fanatics and propagandists kept saying, that Madrid would be 'the graveyard of Fascism.'

Terror by Air Raid

Faced with Madrid's unexpected resistance, the Nationalist command lost patience. It wanted to snatch victory, whatever the cost. After announcing that he would never bomb the civilian population, Franco finally decided, in the words of his Air Force chief, to 'attempt a move to demoralize the population by means of air raids.'[17] He reckoned that Madrid's morale, subjected to harsh ordeals from the fighting and the shortages—there were long lines for any sort of foodstuff—would crack under the bombs. The first attacks took place on 23, 24, and 30 October. Yet it was only on 4 November that the first real raid occurred. There were 350 victims after the nights of 8 and 9 November. On 10, 11, and 12 November houses were set on fire; on 15 November the Cuatro Caminos Hospital was bombed. On 16 November the 'methodical slaughter of the civilian population'[18] began. The raid that night resulted in 5000 victims, according to Colodny. The entire city seemed to be on fire by the end of the alert: 'For twenty-four hours,' wrote Delaprée on 17 November, 'we have been treading blood and breathing sparks.'[19] The raids continued throughout November. Madrid seemed to be in a state of perpetual conflagration. The Nationalist planes, skimming the rooftops, completed their work of destruction by machine-gunning the firemen. Taking advantage of the chaos and panic, Fifth Column agents machine-gunned the militiamen and flung grenades, hoping that their actions would be attributed to the planes. In the ruins of Madrid, in the avenues full of gaping holes, 300,000 people were running the streets in search of shelter. Five hundred thousand refugees joined the million people normally living in Madrid. The destruction of hundreds of buildings threw the overflow of a tragic, haggard, desperate crowd into the streets, mothers looking for their children and exhausted old persons cluttering the sidewalks with their pathetic belongings. In the whole of the city, the shelters that provided a minimum of safety had room for no more than 100,000 people: there were fifteen times as many human beings in Madrid. The rumor went around that Franco had stated that he would not bomb the Salamanca district. It was already crammed although it could hardly take in more than 20,000 persons, and its sidewalks had become dormitories. Louis Delaprée, *Paris-Soir* correspondent, was the dispassionate observer who expressed twentieth-century man's revulsion at this sight, at that time unprecedented:

> Death has bread on the trencher.
> I have said I am only a bailiff;
> however, let me say what I think.
>
> Christ said: 'Forgive them, for they know not what they do.' It seems to me that after the massacre of the innocents in Madrid, we must say: 'Do not forgive them, for they know what they do.'[20]

The daily slaughter that shattered the nerves of the people of Madrid did not succeed in cracking their morale. The Basque Catholic Galíndez ended his account with a devastating judgment on the miscalculation of the Nationalist strategists, whose contempt for the masses had led them to commit an unspeakable crime: 'The enemy did not enter. He merely succeeded in arousing the hatred of those who were still indifferent, he merely succeeded in outdoing the massacres of the *checas* and in making them seem good by comparison.'[21]

The Turning Point

After the heroic chaos of late September, in October Delaprée had found a city 'sobered, almost silent, keyed up by its fierce determination.' The terrible month of November made Madrid, between air attacks, a nightmarish capital: completely dark after sunset, a gray mass enveloped in shadows, where cars drove through the pot-holed streets without headlights, their horns, mingled with the sounds of nearby shots or artillery fire, seeming the only signs of life. Death was in constant attendance on a population whose nerves were stretched to the limit, that was forever casting anxious looks at the sky, plunging into shelters at the first alarm, and burying its victims without mourning, that was ready at all times to stand guard at the request of the District or House Committee, to track down spies, or to set off for the front by subway. Yet gradually the flames of the heroic epic died away in the murk of an entrenched siege that threatened to linger on. Colodny, the American writer already quoted, made a remarkable analysis of the situation after December: 'Led by generals from the Red Army, the war in Madrid changed from a war by Revolutionary Committees into a war waged by the technicians of the general staff. The city switched from the exaltation of the early weeks to the dismal monotony of a siege, complicated by cold, hunger, and the familiar sight of desolation and death from the sky. The heroic period had passed into legend and history: with the enemy clawing at the fortifications, the mortal danger that had temporarily fused all energy into a single determination to resist seemed to have disappeared.'[22]

November had been a month of truce between the workers' parties. Representatives of parties and unions collaborated unreservedly on District and House Committees. The Anarchists hailed Communist soldiers from the International Brigades with the same enthusiasm that the Communists had shown toward the Durruti Column. The militias had all been equally employed in the common battle, the POUM Column receiving, like the rest, arms and ammunition to hold the sector it had been allotted. By the end of the month these good relations were deteriorating. The Junta withdrew by decree all grants made to the Popular Committees and the Committees of the organizations in that decisive period. The secretaries of the Communist party cells, groups, and districts were working for the dissolution of the Committees, which were to yield up their revolutionary initiative and make way for unilateral administration by the Junta. Again there were violent clashes between CNT troops and members of the Communist party. On 12 December,[23] the Junta decided on the immediate militarization of all militia units under the authority of Miaja and the Communist leaders in the Junta. On 24 December it decreed the transfer of all police, guard, and supervisory duties from the rear militias, which had looked after them since the beginning of the siege. There was a ban on the carrying of rifles in the capital. Police duties were reassigned to specialist departments of Security and the *Asaltos*, under the authority of the general staff and the heads of Security. On 26 December, the Junta's adviser on food supplies, Commissar Pablo Yagüe, was seriously wounded by CNT militiamen who claimed to be checking the identities of the occupants of his car. This attack provoked indignant statements from the Communist, Socialist, and Republican press. The newspaper *CNT*, which wanted to issue a reply, was censored, but the perpetrators, after being arrested, were acquitted by the Popular Tribunal. The CNT press accused Communist party members of shooting three of their men in a Madrid suburb by way of reprisal.

But it was mainly the POUM, comparatively weak in Madrid, that seemed fated to become the Junta's target. With militarization, its soldiers were deprived of pay, arms, and ammunition: Baldris and his men had no option but to join the confederal militias. An offensive was launched against its press; first the weekly *POUM* and then the daily *El Combatiente Rojo* were suspended. The Junta refused permission for the Madrid JCI (POUM Youth) weekly *La Antorcha* to appear; its secretary, Jesús Blanco, aged twenty-one, had just fallen at the front, leading his company. The POUM offices, its transmitter, and its headquarters, along with the headquarters of its Red Cross, were closed down, and the party and its youth practically banned. With the immediate danger over, the reckoning began once again: the warnings by *Pravda* seemed to be coming true. A turning point had been reached.

The military situation was also at turning point. It was true that the rebel leaders did not seem to have immediately realized the extent of their failure: Voelckers was still of the opinion on 24 November that military circles were underestimating the difficulties of capturing Madrid. Yet Franco continued to direct all his efforts toward this critical sector, which was probably the only one where the Republicans were at that stage in a position to resist effectively. The explanation doubtless lay in the fact that the defense of Madrid had become to the whole world the symbol of Republican resistance. The stakes were enormous: in Franco's own words, to end Madrid's resistance was to bring about the simultaneous capitulation of the whole of Spain.

However, both the methods and the numbers employed until then seemed inadequate. The November failure proved that it was almost impossible to succeed in breaking Madrid's resistance frontally. The Nationalists' material and strategic superiority lost all its effectiveness in street fighting, in the face of the morale and initiative of the workers' troops. The new objective was therefore to shift the fighting to favorable ground, in open country, where the Nationalist Army would recover its superiority, and on a sufficiently broad front to allow the deployment of tanks and broad strategic movements.

The Battles of Encirclement

The idea, from now on, was not to take Madrid by storm but, by mounting a flank attack, to surround it and thus force it to surrender. Italian and German material aid was adequate for carrying out the projected operation. The rebel Army on the Madrid front now comprised more than 60,000 well-equipped men.

The first attack took place in the northwest sector and was launched at Pozuelo on 29 November. Its objective was to reduce the northern salient, to cut off the defenders of Madrid from the sierra by severing the capital's water and electricity supply. The first day the Republican lines, held by Francisco Galán's Thirteenth Brigade, were breached, but the intervention of Russian tanks and then planes against the Stuka restored the situation. The Nationalist Army then recovered its breath, with Orgaz taking over general command and massing his reserves: the Twelfth International Brigade successfully resisted the assaults by the Moroccans in Pozuelo, but the counterattack led by Rojo against Mount Garabitas failed under the fire of skillfully camouflaged heavy artillery. The game was adjourned. It began again on 16 December, after a cold spell had slowed down communications: 17,000 men attacked Colonel Barceló's troops, who collapsed under the shock and had to evacuate Boadilla del Monte. There, too, Russian tanks and the Dabrowsky Battalion from the Eleventh International Brigade halted the offensive. After four days and nights of bitter fighting, in which the International Brigades suffered heavy losses, Orgaz called off an offensive which had become too costly for his troops.

The fighting in January took place in the same sector, in appalling weather conditions, which prompted Colodny to term it the battle in the mist. The attack launched on 3 January with reinforcements had been prepared by German generals: it was aimed in the direction of Villanueva del Pardillo, Las Rozas, and Majadahonda. There, too, the offensive initially met with great success. Villanueva del Pardillo fell; meanwhile, the International Brigades were posted at the trouble spots, the Commune de Paris Battalion in the Pozuelo sector opposite the attackers' right flank, and the Edgar André and Thaelmann Battalions to the east of Las Rozas. On 5 January the bulk of Orgaz's army broke through the front west of the Manzanares and, exploiting this success, made a deep thrust east, in a series of waves: planes, tanks, light artillery, and infantry followed by a second tank formation. The Republican general staff concentrated fresh troops at El Pardo under Major Lister and brought up the Thirteenth and Fourteenth International Brigades. For forty-eight hours the Republican troops retreated, foot by foot. On 10 January the Thirteenth and Fourteenth Brigades were launched against Majadahonda and Las Rozas. Miguel Martínez and Pavlov took over the sector: attacks and counterattacks followed on each other's heels for three days. In the end, Orgaz gave up: he had advanced twelve miles and had lost 15,000 men. Miaja had lost as many, and possibly a third of the International Brigades involved. Once again the offensive was halted, because of the exhaustion of the troops and the lack of reserves.

The battle of the Jarama went on throughout February. The immediate objective of the operation was to reach and cross the river, its long-term objective to open a broad front to the southwest of Madrid and to sever communications with Valencia. Heavy rain delayed it, and it was launched only on 6 February. The capture of the small fort of La Marañosa enabled the Nationalists to hold the line on the Valencia railroad within range of their field guns. The Republican defense seemed to waver. Torrential rains slowed down the Nationalists' advance, but they managed, on 10 February, to cross the Jarama in spite of desperate resistance by the André Marty Battalion, which was eventually almost completely wiped out between artillery fire from La Marañosa and charges by the Moroccan cavalry. On 11 February Nationalist troops reached the Valencia road at Arganda del Rey. The International Brigades suffered terrible losses while waiting for the promised Spanish reinforcements. But 14 February was to the rebels 'the sorrowful day of the Jarama': the Eleventh and Twelfth Brigades, the remains of the Fifteenth, the Fourteenth, which had just arrived, the Lister Division, and a battalion of tanks commanded by Pavlov counterattacked. On 15 February the troops were reorganized by Miaja and Rojo, who formed them into the Third Army Corps with the Walter and Gal Divisions, including the International Brigades, with Lister, Güenes, and Jubert; on 17 February they attacked but were forced to retreat in face of massive intervention by the Condor Legion.[24] On 27 February, with neither artillery nor armor, General Gal launched an insane attack on Pingarrón, and the Americans in the Lincoln Battalion and the Anarchists in Sanz's Seventh Brigade were decimated by machine-gun fire. The front became bogged down. Trenches were dug everywhere.

The Madrid–Valencia road had been freed, but the forces involved were exhausted: the battle had without doubt claimed more than 15,000 victims. The defenders of Madrid had avoided the worst but had been unable to reduce the hostile bridgehead over the Jarama, and the southern and southeastern fronts had become dangerously stretched. Franco could still hope that a supreme effort would enable him to achieve the encirclement of Madrid, in the only place that had till then remained calm: the northern sector. For this he could count on the Italian troops who had just taken Málaga and from whom the Duce was hoping for a resounding success.

The Italian troops, who arrived at the end of February, had so far played only a subordinate role. Apparently Mussolini had brought pressure to bear on Franco to commit them to a decisive battle. After February the Nationalist general staff concentrated a force of 50,000 men for an attack in the direction of Madrid and Guadalajara. The left wing, facing Guadalajara and commanded by General Roatta, consisted of four Italian divisions, each of 5200 men, two brigades of Italian-German light infantry, four companies of motorized machine gunners, 250 tanks, 180 field guns, and considerable equipment. On 3 March an order of the day from General Mancini announced to the legionaries the Fascist Grand Council's confidence in victory, which would mean 'the end of all Bolshevik plans in the West and the beginning of a new era of power and social justice for the Spanish people.'[25]

On the morning of 8 March, after three hours of artillery preparation, General Coppi's tanks went into the attack. On 9 March they took Almadrones, twenty-five miles from Guadalajara. The situation was critical. Colonel Rojo organized the defense and concentrated, facing Guadalajara, Lister's and Mera's divisions, Kahle's Eleventh International Brigade, and Lukacz's Twelfth, as well as the Garibaldi Battalion and El Campesino's *guerrilleros*. The battle took place along two lines, along the Madrid–Torija–Saragossa road and along the Torija–Brihuega road. On the evening of 9 March General Coppi captured Brihuega. He kept up his advance from 10 to 13 March, and all the Italian divisions were thrown into the battle. The Garibaldi Battalion marched on Brihuega to link up with Coppi's troops. At the Commissariat, Gallo, Nenni, Nicoletti, Major Vidali, and the political leaders of the Italian International Brigades had prepared a propaganda scheme aimed at their CTV (*Corpo Truppe Volontarie*) compatriots. Leaflets dropped by plane and loudspeakers across the lines attacked the morale of Mancini's soldiers: 'Brothers, why have you come to a foreign land to murder workers? Mussolini has promised you land, but you will only find a grave here. He has promised you glory; you will find only death.'[26] To these men, molded by Fascist propaganda and exacerbated by Nationalist slogans, who had come as arrogant conquerors, the Garibaldi revolutionaries talked of proletarian brotherhood and international solidarity. They asked them to desert, join the Republican ranks, and turn on their leaders, who were the enemies of the Italian and Spanish workers. Bad weather slowed down operations. Snow began to fall. The morale of the Italian troops began to sag: prisoners and deserters now harangued their comrades in the Italian legions, telling them how they had been welcomed and calling on their friends to join them. The Garibaldi patrols crawled through the woods and, instead of grenades, flung their compatriots leaflets weighted with stones. General Mancini grew anxious and relieved his frontline troops. At this juncture, Lister attacked and took Trijueque: the rearguard of legionaries surrendered en masse. The Garibaldians, led by Lukacz, encircled the fortress of Ibarra. Four tanks and some *dinamiteros* went into the attack while loudspeakers broadcast the Italian Communist anthem *Bandiera Rossa*, interspersed with calls for fraternization and surrender. The castle yielded, opening the road to Brihuega. From 14 to 16 March, Mancini managed to contain the attacks mounted by Pavlov's tanks and the Republican infantry. He was concerned for his men's morale and in an order of the day told the officers to remind the soldiers that their enemies were the same as those the *Fascio* had crushed on the roads of Italy. On the eighteenth, anniversary of the Paris Commune, the Fifth Corps attacked, led by Colonel Hildago de Cisneros and preceded by a massive bombing raid by 80 planes. Mancini asked for Moroccan reinforcements. Lister and Mera then launched an attack on both flanks: Mera to the west with the Twelfth International Brigade and Lister to the east behind the Edgar André and Thaelmann Battalions under Kahle pierced the Italian lines simultaneously. El Campesino entered Brihuega. This was the cue for a stampede by the 'Black Shirts,' who fled toward Sigüenza, abandoning their arms, ammunition, and equipment. The Republican troops pursued them as far as their inadequate reserves permitted. There were several thousand prisoners, whom the Garibaldians surrounded and catechized, and whom the political commissars harangued. On 18 March these thousands of young men, brought up under the Fascist regime, saw their dreams of grandeur fade and give place to new feelings as their astonished eyes beheld the 'Reds,' from whom they had feared the worst, sharing their meager rations with them and saying, 'Now we are going to talk to you, not in response to the aggression we have endured, but to show you our feelings of brotherhood toward the whole world.'[27]

The Implications of Guadalajara

Herbert Matthews, the American correspondent, wrote: 'In my opinion, nothing more important has happened in the world since the European war than the defeat of the Italians on the Guadalajara front. What Bailén was for Napoleonic imperialism, Brihuega was to Fascism, whatever may be the outcome of the Civil War.'[28]

The victory at Guadalajara, which the Popular Army won by fighting like a modern army and using the revolutionary method of spreading defeatism in the enemy ranks, over an army that was better trained and equipped, confirmed the wild predictions of those who, for some months, had been asserting that 'Madrid would be the graveyard of Fascism.' It was the first victory by the proletarians over the Fascist armies. In the eyes of the troops, both International Brigades and Spanish, the flight of the Black Shirts and the disintegration of the Italian legions had heralded the fate that lay in store for all Fascist regimes. It was, since the triumphs of Mussolini and Hitler in their countries, the international proletariat's first act of revenge.

It was a strategic victory but also a political victory, achieved by overcoming the troops of the class enemy. It seemed to be the triumph of international antifascism acclaimed by Koltsov in his dispatches. Yet this was its last victory. After the actual Revolution, the revolutionary war was to be engulfed by the war, raised up as an end in itself against the Revolution that had given it all its ardor.

Notes

[1] The Feast of the Race commemorates the discovery of America by Christopher Columbus.

[2] Caballero invoked the risk of surprise, the danger of the government's falling into the hands of the rebels, and the need for the ministers to devote themselves to the leadership of the whole country, an impossible task in the besieged capital.

[3] See chapter 9.

[4] The appointments introduced on 24 October were as follows: General Asensio became undersecretary of state for war, General Pozas was made leader of the Army of the Center, and General Miaja took command of the Army of Madrid. In *Mis recuerdos* (Mexico City: Ediciones Alianza, 1954), Largo Caballero stated that his concern was to shelter Miaja from threats of *paseo* without entrusting him with any but purely honorific functions. However, it is curious that he left control of the defense of Madrid to a staff officer in whom he had no faith.

[5] Miaja's biographer López Fernández, Koltsov, and after them Colodny, claimed that a mistake by General Asensio fortuitously avoided disaster: he had mixed up some envelopes containing top secret orders not to be opened until the last moment, intended for Generals Miaja and Pozas. Miaja, according to them, opened the envelope before the appointed hour and was thus able to discover the mistake in time and to forestall its fatal consequences.

[6] Frade, secretary of the Junta, officially a Socialist, was dubbed a Communist by Barea and Koltsov. In the 9 November Junta, there were three Communist militants: Mije for the Communist party, Carrillo for the JSU, and Yagüe for the UGT. Communist militants were placed alongside them in all key posts. The entire general staff of the Fifth Regiment surrounded Mije: Carlos Contreras was chief of staff, Castro Delgado in charge of operations, José Cazorla of organization, Daniel Ortega of the services, and Dr. Planelles of health. With Carrillo, the JSU executive moved into positions of command in interior matters: Caballero controlled the radio, Claudin the press, Serrano Poncela Security, and Federico Melchor the National Guards and the *Asaltos*. The Communists, Miguel Martínez (see fn 8) and Francisco Antón—La Pasionaria's lover, according to Hernández, Castro, and Campesino—ran the Commissariat. When the Junta was reorganized, on 4 December, a Communist, Diéguez, succeeded Mije, who had been promoted to commissar-general. Cazorla became Carrillo's deputy and replaced him on

1 January, after which he devoted himself wholeheartedly to the JSU. Yagüe, after being wounded, was replaced by a Communist from the JSU, Luis Nieto. The other members of the Junta were the Republican Carreño, Enrique Jiménez, González Marín, Amor Nuño of the CNT, Enrique García of the Libertarian Youth, Caminero of the Syndicalist party, and Maximo de Dios, Socialist, who replaced Frade on 4 December.

[7] On the Air Force and on the true identities of the Russian officers present in Spain, see Part 2, chapter 15.

[8] Robert Colodny (*The Struggle for Madrid* [New York: Paine-Whitman, 1958], p. 33) said that Miguel Martínez was a Soviet officer, indicating Koltsov as his source. Koltsov (*Ispanskii dnevnik*, p. 18) said that Miguel Martínez was a Mexican Communist. Was this Malraux's Enrique, who had fought 'six revolutions' and 'called himself a Mexican'? Finally, Castro Delgado (*J'ai perdu la foi à Moscou* [Paris: Gallimard, 1950], p. 33; translation of *Mi fe se perdío en Moscú* [Barcelona: Luis de Caralt, 1964]), referred to 'Miguel, a Bulgarian, who had been a commissar in Madrid and then became director of studies at the Leninist Academy.' At any rate, Miguel Martínez, who had an important role, remained in the shadows like the Russian technicians, at a time when the press did not hesitate to give the limelight to foreign Communists such as Vidali (Carlos Contreras).

[9] Hans Beimler, political commissar and force behind the German volunteers, was the perfect symbol of this type of man: born in 1895, a Socialist militant, he belonged to the Spartacus group, nucleus of the Communist party during the war, when he was called up into the Navy. He took part in the 1918 Revolution, became a member of the Sailors' Council in Cuxhaven, and joined the 1919 Bavarian Revolution, serving in the Red Guard of the Revolutionary Sailors. His part in the abortive 1921 uprising earned him two years in prison. Deputy at the Reichstag in 1930, he was arrested and interned in Dachau, from which he escaped a few weeks later. Having fled to Moscow, he published a pamphlet that was the first denunciation of Hitler's concentration camps (*Au camp des assassins de Dachau* [Moscow, 1933]). He arrived in Barcelona late in July 1936 and organized the Thaelmann Centuria. We shall refer again to his role and the circumstances of his death, in Part 2, Chapter 3. Note on this subject the work, sadly still unpublished, by Antonia Stern, *Das Leben eines revolutionären Kämpfers unserer Zeit: Hans Beimler, Dachau-Madrid.*

[10] On 13 November, Trifón Medrano, commander of the Fifth Regiment, secretary of organization in the JSU, and member of the Communist party Central Committee, broadcast an appeal: 'We must win freedom and the future, we must follow the wonderful example of the peoples of the USSR, whose solidarity so powerfully reinforces our faith in success, in order to make Spain a progressive country, a country that will ensure the well-being of its people and be a bastion of peace and progress in the world. Combatants of the Popular Army and the militias! Youth in arms! The future lies in our hands. Be worthy of those who have fallen! Let us give the stimulus of our victory to the oppressed of the entire world!' (*ABC*, transcribed from Quinto radio, 14 November.)

This text is, in our view, an excellent illustration (1) of the use of the USSR's revolutionary prestige and the legend of the October Revolution;

(2) of the evocation of proletarian internationalism at a time when an appeal to revolutionary sentiments was the best stimulus to working-class energy. This was a dangerous weapon, which the Communist party used only during a brief period.

[11] The general spread of House Commissions as well as elected Neighbors' Committees was in fact the second Madrid Revolution, the basis of a genuine commune. While backing this kind of organization—the only one capable of mobilizing all of the proletarian forces—the Junta, and through it the Communist party, tried to control it. Thus it was that the Junta only recognized (memorandum of 12 November) Neighbors' Committees containing at least three members of parties or unions represented on it and placed them under the authority of the Popular Front's Sector Committees. The Junta was opposed to all spontaneous moves by the Federation of Committees and Commissions and, in order to forestall them, provided for the organization of a Central Committee for House Commissions, which never existed except on paper. Finally, it also opposed (communiqué of 12 November) the 'many demands of members of Neighbors' Committees' for the representation of the Committees on the Junta, since 'the appointment of the Defense Junta was made by political and trade-union organizations, in agreement with the legitimate government.' Thus, at the very moment when it was stirring up this revolutionary movement by the Committees from which it drew its strength, the Junta was preoccupied with not being outstripped by them, and with retaining control of them by preserving, over their heads, a state authority that did not derive from them but from the government. Because of these precautions, the second Madrid Revolution did not become a commune.

[12] García Attadell and two of his aides had crossed the French frontier with jewels stolen during the course of police operations. Sailing for South America, they were unfortunate enough to drop anchor at Santa Cruz de la Palma. Arrested by the Nationalist authorities, they were transferred to Seville, where they were sentenced to death and executed.

[13] Thus the Junta and the government 'covered' the summary execution, by Salgado's special services, of Baron de Borchgrave, who was attached to the Belgian Embassy, and who was even thought by Galíndez to be working for Franco. Koltsov gave a vivid account of the attack by forces under Miguel Martínez and the young Communist Serrano Poncela, head of the Madrid security police, on the Finnish Embassy, where 1100 Spanish 'Fascists' had sought refuge. There was also the incident of the false Siamese Embassy, a trap set by the Anarchist Verardini on behalf of the Ministry of War's special services. Castro Delgado, in *Hombres made in Moscú*, referred on several occasions to a special group in the Madrid Communist party, the ITA and their leader, Tomás.

[14] The origin of the expression derives from the fact that the first rebel plan provided for four columns to converge on Madrid, supported by a friendly one within the capital. The phrase, whose fate is well known, was first coined by Mola, in a conversation with some journalists.

[15] Delaprée, *Mort en Espagne*, p. 171.

[16] The inquiry opened by the CNT did not achieve any official results. Durruti's comrades challenged this interpretation of his death (see Federica

Montseny's article, *CNT*, 15 July 1961), but Hugh Thomas (*The Spanish Civil War*, p. 328) also considers it the most likely. However, it should be pointed out that the bullet that killed Durruti struck him in front.

[17] Alfredo Kindelán, *Mis cuadernos de guerra* (Madrid: Plus Ultra, n.d.), p. 33.

[18] Delaprée, *Mort en Espagne*, p. 187.

[19] Ibid., p. 155.

[20] Ibid., p. 195.

[21] Jesús de Galíndez, *Los vascos en el Madrid sitiado* (Buenos Aires: Vasca Ekin, 1945), p. 70.

[22] Colodny, *The Struggle for Madrid*, p. 93.

[23] It was also on 12 December that by decision of the Junta, the street-cars ceased to be free. Rents were soon reintroduced. On this day began the abandonment of revolutionary defense methods.

[24] Castro Delgado, invoking Burillo's testimony, accused the Communist 'heroes,' Lister and Modesto, of incompetence.

[25] Quoted by Colodny, *The Struggle for Madrid*, p. 130.

[26] *¡Guadalajara!* (Madrid: Ediciones La Voz del Combatiente, 1937), p. 18 (pamphlet published by the government).

[27] Luigi Longo: *Le brigate internazionali in Spagna* (Rome: Editori Riuniti, 1956), p. 306. It was a speech given by Jesús Hernández, but Longo does not mention him.

[28] *Two Wars and More to Come* (New York: Carrick & Evans, 1938), p. 264.

CHAPTER II

THE BREAK UP OF THE ANTIFASCIST COALITION

To all those who in good faith think that the necessities of the war alone dictated the political evolution of Republican Spain, it is not easy to explain how the Largo Caballero government, under which such important military successes as the resistance of Madrid and the victory of Guadalajara had been achieved, could have fallen so soon afterward. This was because the strictly political problems eventually took priority over the rest, in accordance with Clausewitz's oft-quoted principle by which 'war is the continuation of diplomacy by other means.' The alteration in the military situation between September 1936 and April 1937 now became a secondary factor compared with the modifications in the political context, with the circumstances in which it took place, and with its consequences.

In taking over the leadership of the government, Largo Caballero had believed that his presence on its own would guarantee it against any risk of a swing to the Right and that, whatever happened, Spain would remain a 'workers' republic.'[1] But in so doing, he had restricted himself to a framework that was no longer revolutionary. The policies of France, England, and the USSR, which he had chosen not to offend for fear of isolating his country, had become primary factors in his domestic policies and controlled even the conception of his war policies.

Similarly, the restoration of the state had opened the way to the revival of forces that had seemed definitively crushed after the July days: expropriated shareholders and proprietors, old and new officials, and representatives of political parties whose authority in the new 'popular state' tended to grow at the expense of that of the unions. Carlos Rama wrote on this subject: 'These three linked forces, state officials, proprietors, and politicians, found the solution to their problems in the reconstruction of the state, in the restoration of the legal apparatus, and in its political, judicial and social prestige.'[2]

The reconstruction of the state, in Largo Caballero's view a means of winning the war, disrupted the *status quo* and the balance of power: for the broad strata, the petty bourgeoisie and the bureaucracy, it became an objective in itself. Caballero's authority over the workers had made it possible to achieve it under the guise of a compromise with the Revolution. But the restored state tended more and more to break with the Revolution and to combat it: the political forces that were at work in it linked up with those operating under pressure from the forces of the Western powers and the USSR. There was an urge to push on from halting the Revolution to struggling against it, and Largo Caballero was henceforth an obstacle on this path.

External Pressures: The Problem of Morocco

No example better illustrates the consequences for the war of its 'antifascist' policy than the position of Largo Caballero's government in relation to Morocco. Before the Revolution, the views of the 'old man,' as expressed in the program of the Madrid Socialist group, were unequivocally for the recognition of the rights of political self-determination, including independence. Participation by Moroccans in Franco's army during the Civil War made this problem still more acute. It is in fact easy to grasp that the proclamation of Morocco's independence by the Republican government would have had incalculable consequences on the morale of the native troops serving in the rebel army: all the Republican political groups, the Moroccan Nationalists, and Franco himself were alive to it.[3]

However, in 1936–1937, the question of an alliance between

the Spanish Republicans and the Moroccan Nationalists went far beyond the confines of Spain. France and England, from whom the Spanish Popular Front was expecting help, were colonial powers: revolutionary unrest in Morocco would constitute a direct threat to the French position[4] in Morocco and Algeria and would disquiet the English, who were grappling with Egyptian and Palestinian Arab agitation.

Certain revolutionary elements suggested 'triggering off revolt in the Arab world.'[5] The Caballero government chose the opposite policy: the delegations of Moroccan Nationalists who came to Valencia for money and material left empty-handed.[6] Nothing was to be done that might constitute a threat to English and French interests. Franco had an easy time authorizing newspapers and meetings banned in French Morocco by the Léon Blum government, potential ally of the Spanish Popular Front, in order to secure his rear in Spanish Morocco. The Caballero government went further and suggested territorial concessions in Morocco to London and Paris.[7] Its desire not to offend the Western powers now led it deliberately to renounce, not only the principle of self-determination for colonial peoples, but also a real chance to strike at the heart of Franco's power. The halting of the Revolution thus had a direct influence on the conduct of the war. The determination to respect international agreements after the Treaty of Algeciras, behind which Álvarez del Vayo, the foreign minister, took refuge, deprived the Popular Army of the revolutionary weapon of spreading defeatism in the enemy army, which would have provided it with an alliance between the Spanish Revolution and North African Nationalism, and which it had employed so successfully against Italian intervention.

Relations with the USSR

The isolation of the Republic and the material aid sent by the USSR lent a special flavor to the activities of the Russian diplomats in Spain. Rosenberg and Antonov-Ovseyenko immediately overstepped the role traditionally ascribed to ambassadors and consuls. They had daily contact and discussions with Spanish politicians and military leaders, intervened in the press, and made speeches at public meetings in order to defend their government's policy and to lend support to Spain's.[8] The government of the USSR regarded its alliance with Spain in an entirely new light, free of any formalist concern.

Luis Araquistáin had been the first to make public a letter from Stalin, Voroshilov, and Molotov handed to Largo Caballero by Rosenberg in December 1936.[9] The Russian leaders asked the head of the Spanish government if he was satisfied with the activities of the 'military adviser comrades,' were anxious to know whether they overstepped the mark as advisers, and asked him to give them his direct and unreserved opinion of Comrade Rosenberg. The interest of the document lies mainly in the 'friendly advice' given to the Spanish government by the Russian government, which said that it must pay attention to the peasants and gain their loyalty by a few decrees, dealing with agricultural question and taxes, obtain the support or at least the benevolent neutrality of the petty and middle bourgeoisie by protecting them against confiscation and 'by guaranteeing them, as far as possible, freedom of trade,' win over Azaña's friends 'to prevent Spain's enemies from regarding her as a Communist republic, which was exceedingly dangerous for Spain,' and finally make a solemn declaration that the government 'will not tolerate attacks on the property and legitimate interests of foreigners settled in Spain and citizens of countries that do not support the rebels.'

On 12 January Largo Caballero made a brief reply. Singling out a phrase in the Russian note about 'parliamentary action, action perhaps more effective in Spain than in Russia,' he stated bluntly that 'the parliamentary institution does not have enthusiastic supporters, even among ordinary Republicans.' He affirmed, moreover, that the Russian advisers 'were carrying out their mission with genuine enthusiasm and extraordinary courage.' As for Rosenberg, 'everyone likes him.' Largo Caballero thanked the Russian leaders for their advice and emphasized that the policy they were proposing to him was in fact his own. It is true that there was, at this stage, no basic divergence on general policy between Moscow and Valencia.

However, the tone of Largo Caballero's reply betrayed a certain displeasure: Stalin's 'advice' was perhaps fair, but the fact that it could be given indicated a certain lack of information on Stalin's part, as well as a condescension that ruffled the Spanish leader's susceptibilities.

Here, without doubt, was the root of a misunderstanding that was to increase. In a few months, the 'Spanish Lenin' was denounced by the Communists as a bureaucrat, a cacique, and a saboteur of unity. In fact, real disagreements sprang from this basic mistrust.

One of the initial factors in the worsening of relations seems to have been Caballero's resistance to the proposals made by the USSR for an alliance between the Socialists and Communists in Spain. According to Araquistáin, Caballero wanted to answer with a curt refusal to receive such a proposal, made in yet another letter from Stalin, brought this time by Pascua, the Spanish ambassador in Moscow. Yet the old UGT leader had always been the paladin of unity. But it must be admitted that the growth of the JSU and the adherence of the former Socialist Youth leadership to the Communist party did not in his view lend encouragement to such a policy. Above all, he seemed highly displeased with the attitude of the Madrid Junta, whose leading spirits were, as we saw, members of the Communist party and the JSU; he devoted several pages of *Mis recuerdos* to what he called the overt opposition of the Junta and Miaja and their determination to reduce the government to a subordinate role. The omnipotence of the Communist party in Madrid and the control that it exercised over the capital's army through the triple agency of the Fifth Regiment, the political commissars, and the body of Russian advisers gave him great cause for concern. He had the impression that Álvarez del Vayo, until then his faithful lieutenant, was under Russian orders, and he reproached him bitterly. In his view, the Russian advisers and the Communists were a hindrance to his authority. Finally, he complained of Rosenberg's 'meddling' in Spanish affairs and dismissed him, as he himself put it, 'in somewhat undiplomatic terms.' On 21 February 1937 Rosenberg was recalled to Moscow[10] and replaced by Leo Gaikins.

The crisis, until then latent, burst into the open. It had been fostered by many incidents and political developments concerning the whole of the groups in Republican Spain.

Right-Wing Opposition Makes Headway

Indispensable to the reconstruction of the state in 1936, Largo Caballero had by 1937 become an obstacle to those who did not want a social revolution and were anxious to remove all revolutionary traces of the popular state. The breaking off of the alliance between Largo Caballero and the Russians provided them with an opportunity. The French government's caution and the pursuance of nonintervention provided them with an argument.

There was a reshuffling of alliances within the Socialist party. As Largo Caballero's supporters veered away from the Communists, Prieto's drew closer. The executive, under González Peña and Lamoneda, became the champion of 'unity' and in February signed an agreement for the generalization of Liaison Committees on all levels, making the two workers' parties a single bloc within the Popular Front. Prieto at that period went still further and came out for an immediate alliance with the Communist party.[11] The very grounds that alienated Caballero from the Communist party merely served to reconcile Prieto with it. The right-wing Communists and Socialists were in fact agreed about the restoration of the state, they were for the organization of a regular army, against collectivization, for the defense of the middle classes, against intervention by unions, and for halting the Revolution. Neither regarded the conflict on the level of a class war but on an international scale, as a conflict between democracy and Fascism. The growth of the JSU, disturbing to Largo Caballero, reassured Prieto; at its congress in Valencia, in January 1937, Santiago Carrillo emerged as the champion of national unity and preached the relinquishment of all immediate Socialist objectives. The coalition he proposed against the three enemies, Franco, the Trotskyists, and the unruly elements, echoed the desire of the moderates to combat 'extremists' in the Republic.

The Republicans, too, were delighted at this development:

the 'Bolshevik Revolution' was now merely a bogey of the past, and the Communists had won their spurs as a 'respectable' organization. In Madrid, the Republican Youth formed a permanent 'alliance' with the JSU. The Republicans were hoping for mediation by the great powers with a return to normality. Carlos Esplá and other leaders were ready to make the journey to France, and Azaña was to send Besteiro to London.[12] Martínez Barrio's plan for reconciliation was re-adopted and brought up to date: there was talk of a military junta under General Miaja that would obtain support from London for a compromise peace.[13] None of this was very coherent or organized. The antifascist coalition was cracking on all sides, but many incidents would have to occur before there was any sign of a realignment of forces.

The Fall of Málaga: General Coalition against Largo Caballero

The first public battle was not fought against Largo Caballero, who was still too popular to be attacked head on. Since the battle of Madrid, the government's opponents had concentrated their attacks on his right-hand man, General José Asensio. 'Tall and strong, youthful-looking, intelligent, a good soldier, a demagogue . . . and a bit of an intriguer, bold, adventurous, and ambitious,'[14] this Republican regular officer, who had donned the militia *mono* and fought first at Málaga and then at Somosierra, had come to know Caballero in the summer of 1936, on the sierra front. He had become his under-secretary of state for war. In this capacity he had played a leading role after December 1936 in the organization of the Popular Army and the conduct of military operations and on several occasions had already clashed with the Communists, who had waged a systematic, discreet, but efficient smear campaign against him, in which they were joined by the CNT.[15]

The dramatic fall of Málaga, on 8 February, was the cue for a public attack on him. Under siege since the summer of 1936, the Andalusian city had never received the reinforcements nor, more important, the arms and material it had requested. Communists and Anarchists confronting each other there, weapons in hand. On the disembarkation of the Italian troops who later captured it, the Republican fleet, at anchor in Cartagena, did not move. When danger loomed, Valencia did nothing about it. Surely they had the means to save Málaga at that point without divesting Madrid? This was the most likely theory. In any case, in Málaga, neglected, divided, fiercely bombed and halfheartedly defended by officers with no control over their troops, morale sagged: the militiamen, seized with panic, fled along the refugee-encumbered roads, often in their leaders' footsteps.[16] The fall of the town, the last-minute rallying of units of Civil Guards and *Asaltos* to the enemy, and the fierce repression that followed the victors' entry left a deep impression. On the fourteenth, in Valencia, a huge joint CNT–UGT procession attracted hundreds of thousands of demonstrators, clamoring for general mobilization, the purging of the officer corps and the effective application of a unilateral command. Largo Caballero approved the slogans shouted and introduced mobilization. However, the Communist press denounced Asensio as responsible for the defeat. The Republicans, the right-wing Socialists, and the CNT joined the campaign: all the parties in the antifascist coalition called for the departure of the undersecretary of state. Largo Caballero, who believed in him implicitly, fought to the end to keep him by his side and 'wept tears of rage' when he was defeated: on 21 February Asensio handed in his resignation.[17] It was a personal defeat for the premier.

Caballero replaced his colleague with another of his disciples, Carlos de Baraíbar.[18] When the leftist Republican newspaper *Política* criticized this appointment, the premier answered personally and then, in a long article, attacked the foreign spies and agents who were swarming in political circles without mentioning any names and hinted that the Republicans were contemplating a compromise with Franco imposed by Western mediation. Carlos Esplá canceled his journey.

Largo Caballero's counterattack intimidated his opponents but succeeded in alienating what sympathy he still aroused. Republicans, right-wing Socialists, and Communists were looking for a successor to him. There was talk of Prieto, Martínez Barrio, and Negrín. On 23 March *Le Temps* wrote:

'A ministry under for instance M. Negrín, the present finance minister (with M. Prieto, moving spirit of this scheme, remaining discreetly in the background), could perhaps yield to mediation and offer Republican Spain a way out preferable to a hopeless struggle.'

The Conflict between the CNT and the Communist Party

The fall of Málaga also led to renewed hostility between the Communist party and the CNT. Having agreed to denounce the 'betrayal' and make Asensio scapegoat for the defeat, Anarchists and Communists accused each other in turn of having been the instruments of the betrayal. To the Communists, the Málaga Anarchists had 'played at revolution' and had produced too many Committees, leading to lack of discipline and irresponsibility. According to the Anarchists, the Communist party's proselytism had sown dissension in the antifascist front and had countenanced the release of disloyal officers. The arrest of Francisco Maroto, a known CNT militant and a column leader, on orders from the governor of Almería lit the fuse. At the same time, the Socialists, in a thunderous manifesto, denounced the activities of Anarchist *checas*, publishing an impressive list of Socialist militants murdered in the Center region. The CNT press retaliated by exposing the murders of several of its militants in Castile by Communist troops. The government tried to calm them down and suspended the CNT and FAI newspapers that had published these attacks, but released Maroto provisionally.[19]

However, the affair of the *checas* had only just begun. The newspaper *CNT* published detailed accusations by Melchor Rodríguez, delegate from the prisons, against José Cazorla, the Madrid Junta's commissar for public order. According to him, the Communist party still maintained private prisons in Madrid in which CNT militants, arrested without proper warrants by Communist police, were interrogated, tortured, and sometimes shot, not to mention former inmates of state prisons acquitted by the Popular Tribunals but immediately taken away by the police on Cazorla's orders.

The inquiry opened by the security police led to the

discovery, in Cazorla's entourage, of an actual gang making a fortune out of releasing regularly hounded prisoners. On 14 April the *CNT* headline stated that 'Cazorla is an *agent provocateur* in the pay of Fascism' and demanded his dismissal. The Junta, pressed on all sides, also announced an inquiry. There was a huge scandal; Caballero seized the opportunity to get rid of the Junta, which he dissolved on 23 April. From then on Madrid had a municipal council.[20]

Caballero versus the Communist Party

The dissolution of the Junta was a victory for the restored state and a revenge for Largo Caballero. It gave him back the initiative. The same day, the Madrid *El Socialista* and *Castilla Libre* denounced the 'Murcia scandal': Socialist militants were being detained and tortured in private prisons by the Communist party. The government dismissed the civil governor, accomplice of this clandestine activity, and had four Communist policemen involved arrested and tried. Then it turned on the Communist party's other bastion, the Army. Largo Caballero restricted the powers of its political commissars and retained the right to appoint them himself. Many commissars were forced to give up their jobs. It was a virtual declaration of war on the Communist party, and the Communists regarded it as such. They then opened a campaign against Caballero, no more than a distorted echo of which ever appeared in the press. They held him responsible for all the military failures. To them, he was acting like a 'boss' and a 'cacique,' wanting to run everything even though he was incompetent: in his criminal pride he distrusted the advice of the Russian specialists, intended to exercise sole command all by himself, and wanted to play at being a little Napoleon. Protector of the traitor Asensio, he had refused to purge the Army and in his jealousy would not make Miaja the chief of staff that the Popular Army needed.[21]

Largo Caballero did not have the best of it in this jockeying for power. After Guadalajara, he put forward a plan for an offensive that had been worked out by Asensio. The idea was to attack in the direction of Estremadura and Andalusia in such a way as to split Nationalist Spain along a line between Mérida and Badajoz. The numerical weakness of the Nationalists in this area, the sympathy and even the backing of the *guerrilleros* whom the Republican offensive would encounter were arguments put forward to support this plan, the first result of which would be to relieve the northern front. But it ran into opposition from Miaja, who refused to divest Madrid, and from the Russian advisers, who did not believe such an operation possible with the troops available on that front.

Premier and war minister though he was, Largo Caballero did not succeed in putting his offensive plan into action: the Russians only offered him ten planes, and Miaja refused to transfer the necessary troops from the Madrid front. It was clear that Largo Caballero no longer had sufficient authority over the restored state.[22]

The Rise of the Revolutionary Opposition

At this point the government had to face new economic and social difficulties, which heroic, flag-waving propaganda was no longer able to conceal. The factories were barely producing, or only very slowly. The supply system was poor. The position was catastrophic where food was concerned. The cost of living had doubled between July 1936 and March 1937, whereas wages had risen an average of 15 percent. The minimum promised by the ration cards was by no means always guaranteed. There were endless lines at bakers' shops. On the other hand, the black market was flourishing. Everywhere, even in Barcelona, restaurants and eating places were open again, but at prohibitive prices. The scores of offices that had replaced the Committees were often dens of corruption. The POUM and the CNT–FAI newspapers were full of letters from readers raising questions about the cost of living and calling for an end to privilege and inequality. On 14 April some women demonstrated in Barcelona against the price of food. Yet both the trade-union organizations and the parties never stopped asking the workers for ever-increasing sacrifices to contribute to military victory: they were greeted with skepticism and bitterness.

Thus in the early months of 1937 conditions existed that

favored the growth of revolutionary opposition in the heart of the very organizations that had, in the autumn, accepted collaboration.

It was the POUM, the first to be excluded from the antifascist coalition, that seemed to take this course from the beginning. For several weeks *La Batalla* waged a campaign for the reintegration of the POUM with the Generalidad government, and it denounced the 'counterrevolutionary orientation,' whose beginnings it saw in the exclusion of the POUM. However, resistance to this line was vigorous. It had taken Nin as well as Companys to obtain the submission of the POUM in Lérida. The Socialist Youth newspaper openly deplored the party's participation in the government. Later events seemed to confirm the supporters of the theory of 'nonparticipation': on 13 April 1937 Juan Andrade wrote in *La Batalla* that this participation had been 'negative and harmful.' Nin's theoretical plan for the POUM conference had nothing to say on this crucial point. The same uncertainty and the same contradictions were apparent in political strategy and tactics. In December the Central Committee called for the election of a constituent assembly on the basis of Workers', Peasants', and Soldiers' Committees. On 1 April Nin explained this as 'a conference of unions, peasants' organizations, and combatants' organizations.' On the fourth Andrade proposed, instead of unions, Committees elected at the grass-roots level and, in a series of articles in *La Batalla* during April adopted the slogan of Committees and Councils, which he regarded as the Spanish version of soviets. Moreover, the attacks on the POUM by the Communist party and the PSUC, its persecution by many local parties, and the effects of censorship did not leave it very much choice. It was definitively rejected by the coalition. It was moving, more and more clearly, toward a policy of revolutionary opposition, denouncing the results of an antifascist coalition that was being transformed into a Holy Alliance, the halting and the retreat of the Revolution, and the counterrevolutionary activities of the Communist party and the PSUC. The POUM, always concerned, above all else, not to isolate itself from the leadership like the CNT militants, tried to persuade them to join it in organizing, against the moderate bloc, a revolutionary united front for the defense of the labor movement and the gains of the Revolution.

The activities of its youth organization, the *Juventud Comunista Ibérica*, were free from such indecisions and equivocations. In a systematic campaign,[23] the JCI came out openly for the dissolution of Parliament and for a constituent assembly elected on the basis of Factory Committees and peasants' and soldiers' assemblies. Unlike Nin, it declared that the revolutionaries ought to devote themselves to the organization of Committees of the soviet variety. It proposed the organization of a revolutionary youth front for victory in the war and the Revolution.

A current of revolutionary opposition developed in the CNT, independently of the POUM. In Barcelona, a group of militants hostile to the militarization of the militias was organized under the label 'Friends of Durruti,' who issued the newspaper *El Amigo del Pueblo*. In a pamphlet distributed in March 1937, they drew up what they regarded as a balance sheet: 'Eight months of war and revolution have elapsed. We note with deep regret the deviations that have occurred in the trajectory of the Revolution. . . . An Antifascist Committee, Local Committees, and Control Patrols were set up, and eight months later nothing remains of them.' Their position on the war and the Revolution was similar to that of the POUM and the JCI: 'The war and the Revolution are two aspects which cannot be divorced. In any case, we cannot accept that the Revolution should be put off until the end of the military conflict.' In spring 1937 many local CNT and FAI organizations echoed these ideas, which appeared more or less everywhere in their newspapers, even in *La Noche*, the Barcelona CNT's evening paper, signed by Balius, moving spirit of the 'Friends of Durruti.'[24]

The great weakness of this opposition was in not having a prominent Spanish leader on its side. Santillán kept silent. A foreigner, the Italian Berneri,[25] emerged as the theoretician and inspiration of the revolutionary viewpoint. On 5 November 1936, in his Italian-language weekly newspaper, *Guerra di Classe*, he argued against the supporters of 'defeat Franco first': 'Winning the war is necessary; however, the war will not be won by confining the question to the purely military conditions of victory but by linking them with the political and social conditions of victory.' An old *émigré*, with a broader outlook and culture than his Spanish comrades, he had denounced the Moscow trials and established a relation between Stalin's general policy and the attitude of the Communist party, 'foreign legion of Spanish democracy and liberalism.'[26] Yet he asked his friends of the CNT–FAI, whose 'political naïveté' he reproached, to take care: 'The shadow of Noske[27] is looming.... Monarchist-Catholic-Traditionalist Fascism is only one branch of the counterrevolution.... The only dilemma is as follows: either victory over Franco through revolutionary war, or defeat.'

Yet this leaderless opposition attracted an increasing number of troops. In September the Catalan Libertarian Youth signed a pact for unity of action with the JSU. But in their newspaper, *Ruta*, they took up revolutionary positions. On 1 January a manifesto framed a positive indictment of the Caballero government.[28] The Catalan Libertarian Youth denounced the coalition between the Communists and the Republicans as a reflection in Spain of the USSR's alliance with France and England with the object of 'strangling the revolution.'

It is understandable that the JCI's slogans were favorably echoed in their ranks. On 14 February more than 14,000 young people attended a meeting in Barcelona for the formation of a revolutionary youth front in Catalonia. Speeches were made in turn by Fidel Miró, secretary of the Catalan Libertarian Youth, Solano, secretary-general of the JCI, and the young Libertarian Alfredo Martínez, secretary of the Catalan Front. The movement rapidly spread to other provinces: in Madrid[29] and in the Levante, Libertarian Youth and JCI organized joint meetings and campaigns.

The young workers were split into two camps. On one side, through an appeal by the JSU, the Alliance of Antifascist Youth was formed, which Santiago Carrillo meant to represent 'unity with young Republicans, with young Anarchists, and with young Catholics who are fighting for freedom..., for democracy and against Fascism and for the independence of the fatherland against foreign invasion,' but which boiled down to an alliance between the JSU and the youth of the Republican parties. On the other side, the revolutionaries of the JSI and the Libertarian Youth were grouped in the Revolutionary Youth Front. Young men had been in the vanguard of the revolutionary movement and the armed struggle, and they played an important role, if not in the parties and unions, at least in the armed forces. Outside Catalonia, it was the JSU that had collected and enlisted the bulk of the militant 'young guard' behind the Communist party. Many of its militants, especially veterans of the Socialist Youth, refused to take part in the Alliance, which they regarded as moderantist, and affirmed their revolutionary objectives. Immediately after the Valencia congress there were protests in the JSU against the 'new line,' the 'policy of absorption and confusionism,' and the 'neglect of Marxist principles.'[30] On 30 March the secretary of the Asturian Federation, Rafaël Fernández, resigned from the JSU National Committee. The federation rejected Carrillo's line, denounced the lack of democratic spirit in the organization, and signed a pact with the Asturian Libertarian Youth for the establishment of a revolutionary youth front.[31] A few days later, the secretary of the powerful Levante Federation, José Gregori, resigned from the National Committee, also with the backing of his group. Santiago Carrillo, in *Ahora*, accused his opponents of being inspired by the Trotskyists, Franco, and Hitler. Yet the movement went on, and even in Catalonia local groups joined the Revolutionary Front. The crisis thus revealed in the JSU threatened to challenge the influence gained by the Communist party over an important section of the youth.

An Explosive Situation

Thus, in spring 1937, the conditions for a revolutionary upsurge were joined once again. Theories of revolutionary opposition met, at least in Catalonia, with a growing response from the workers who followed the CNT and saw their gains threatened. In the UGT, the Army, and the administration Largo Caballero's supporters reacted against the Communists.

Economic difficulties and the *checas* scandals were fertile soil for unrest.

The government coalition's moderate wing grew anxious. To the external pressure for the halting of the Revolution, there had been added, in recent months, that of the petty bourgeoisie, which was recovering from the shock of the initial terror and wanted to see every vestige of the Revolution effaced altogether. In the Levante and in Catalonia, the peasants sometimes reacted violently against the supporters of collectivization and vented their wrath on the unions or workers' militias who had forced them into it. In Catalonia, the GEPCI, a branch of the UGT, was the mass organization that typified the antirevolutionary hostility of the urban petty bourgeoisie. The Basque government had firmly taken the offensive. Its police forces had occupied the printing office of the *CNT del Norte*, seized in Bilbao at the time of the July days, and the Communist newspaper *Euzkadi Roja* took over its premises. The CNT militants fought back, weapons in hand, and the Aguirre government had the federation's regional leadership arrested. A few days later, on 24 March, the Basque government announced huge celebrations, throughout Euzkadi, for Easter, and the closing of all theaters on Good Friday. The revolutionaries were furious and made plans to regroup. Republicans, Prieto Socialists, and Communists were alive to the danger of the threatened revolutionary regroupment and felt that it was necessary to dispense beforehand with the POUM, the CNT, and the FAI and to stabilize the Republic once and for all.

Largo Caballero was aware of his isolation. Around him there was increasing talk of a trade-union government,[32] CNT–UGT unity was praised to the skies, and there was a reversion to the plans of September 1936. On 1 May a joint CNT–UGT meeting was held in Valencia, at which Carlos de Baraíbar attacked, albeit in veiled terms, the Communist party and the USSR and praised the alliance between the CNT and the UGT, which together represented the whole of Spain. But what was possible shortly after the Revolution was no longer so. Neither the CNT nor the UGT were homogeneous forces any more: the ruling circles were divided, and the mass of supporters ranged itself more openly each day behind one of the two camps that were emerging. Largo Caballero remained in the center. He wished to be arbiter in the name of the state, taking issue on the Right with those who disputed his control and on the Left with those who denied his authority. He did not want to relaunch the Revolution for fear of losing the war, nor did he wish to deprive the workers of their reasons for winning the war by coming out openly against the Revolution. However, although he was the workers' representative at the head of the state, he had ceased to be master of either. Since the conflict would mean his resignation, he sought to avoid it but only succeeded temporarily, as Rabasseire put it, by 'sheltering behind the fossilized state' and in the long run by doing nothing. Rabasseire summed it up thus: 'He intrigued, he made arrangements with the forces that had come to the surface, and, while hoping to dominate them, he fabricated small private coteries; routine dominated the government more than ever, for the simple reason that he had intended to reconcile forces that could not be contained by any other means. He wanted neither the militia nor the regular army; he wanted neither the old bureaucracy nor the new revolutionary structure; he wanted neither guerrilla warfare nor trench warfare. He promised the Communists general mobilization and a fortification plan, and the Anarchists revolutionary war; in the event he did neither.'[33]

The Barcelona May Days

It was in Catalonia that the revolutionary gains and the arming of the workers essentially survived; it was the bastion of revolutionary opposition, too. It also had the organization most resolutely determined to put an end to the Revolution, the PSUC,[34] firmly supported by Companys's Republican state and the petty bourgeoisie, impatient to shake off the Anarchist yoke. Catalonia became the scene of the events that ignited the powder barrel.

First of all, there was the arrival, on 17 April, in Puigcerdá and then in Figueras and the whole frontier region, of Negrín's *Carabineros*, come to recover from the CNT militiamen control of customs, which they had held since July 1936. Faced with resistance by the militiamen, the Catalan CNT's Regional Committee hurried to the spot to negotiate a compromise. On 25 April Roldán Cortada, UGT leader and member of the PSUC, was murdered at Mollis de Llobregat. The PSUC reacted violently and denounced unruly elements and hidden Fascist agents. The CNT formally condemned the murder and called for an inquiry which would, in its own view, have vindicated its militants. But Roldán Cortada's murder re-awakened memories of the time of the *paseos* and the reckoning that followed the Revolution. The PSUC pressed home its advantage. The funeral of the UGT leader was the occasion for a powerful demonstration: armed police and soldiers, from troops under PSUC control, marched past for three and a half hours.[35] Delegates from the POUM and the CNT who had come to the funeral realized that the situation was graver than they had thought: it was a show of strength that the PSUC had organized against them. The following day, the Generalidad police made a punitive expedition to Mollis de Llobregat: it arrested the local Anarchist leaders, under suspicion of having taken part in the murder, and brought them, handcuffed, to Barcelona. In Puigcerdá, *Carabineros* and Anarchists exchanged shots: eight Anarchist militants were killed, among them the heart and soul of collectivization in the area, Antonio Martín.[36]

At this point a rumor was going around in Barcelona of the arrival of a memorandum from the minister of the interior calling for the disarming of all workers' groups not part of the state police. The workers reacted immediately: for several days, according to the balance of power, workers and police disarmed each other. Barcelona appeared to be on the verge of street fighting. The government banned all demonstrations and meetings for 1 May. *Solidaridad Obrera* denounced what it called 'the crusade against the CNT' and called on the workers to avoid all provocation. *La Batalla* called for vigilance 'with arms at the ready.'

On Monday 3 May the battle that had been threatening erupted, with the incident of the Telefónica. The building had been recaptured in July from the insurgents by members of the

CNT. Since then, the telephone exchange, which belonged to the American Telegraph and Telephone Company, had been taken over and was operating under a UGT–CNT committee and a government delegate. Guarded by CNT militiamen, it was an excellent example of what duality of power was and of what had survived of it, because the Catalan CNT was thus in a position to control or interrupt at will, not only the communications and orders of the Catalan government, but also communications between Valencia and its representatives abroad.[37] That day, Rodríguez Sala, commissar for public order and member of the PSUC, went to the Telefónica with three truckloads of guards and entered it. He disarmed the militiamen on the ground floor but was halted by the threat of a machine gun in position upstairs.[38] Immediately informed, the Anarchist leaders of the police, Asens and Eroles, hurried to the scene where, according to *Solidaridad Obrera* on 4 May, 'they intervened just in time for our comrades, who had resisted the operation by the guards in the building, to give up their correct attitude.' But, at the same time, the majority of the workers went on strike: Barcelona was bristling with barricades, though no organization had given the least word of command.

That evening, in the city, now on a war footing, there was a joint meeting of the Regional Committees of the CNT, the FAI, the Libertarian Youth, and the Executive Committee of the POUM. The POUM representatives stated that the movement was the Barcelona workers' spontaneous reply to provocation and that the decisive moment had come: 'Either we place ourselves at the head of the movement to destroy the enemy within or the movement fails, and that will be the end of us.' But the CNT and FAI leaders did not follow them and decided to work for appeasement.

The following day, 4 May, the workers, whose initiative had been approved by the POUM, the Libertarian Youth, and the Friends of Durruti, were in control of the Catalan capital, which they gradually surrounded. After an interview with the CNT leaders, Companys spoke over the radio, repudiated Rodríguez Sala's move on the Telefónica, and made an appeal for calm. The CNT Regional Committee supported him: 'Lay down your arms. It is Fascism we must destroy.' *Solidaridad Obrera* only mentioned the events of the previous day on page eight and did not say a word about the barricades that covered the city. At 5 P.M. Hernández Zancajo, a UGT leader and personal friend of Largo Caballero, arrived by plane from Valencia with two Anarchist ministers, García Oliver and Federica Montseny. They took turns on the air, adding their efforts to those of Companys and the CNT regional leaders: 'A wave of madness has passed through the town,' exclaimed García Oliver. 'We must put an immediate stop to this fratricidal struggle. Let each man stay where he is. . . . The government . . . will take the necessary steps.'[39]

On Wednesday 5 May the workers were still manning the barricades. The radio broadcast the text of the agreement made between the CNT and the Generalidad government: cease-fire and military *status quo*, simultaneous withdrawal by police and armed civilians. No mention was made of control over the Telefónica. However the movement was receding. CNT elements from the Twenty-third Division and POUM elements from the Twenty-ninth, which had concentrated at Barbastro to march on Barcelona at the news of the events, did not proceed beyond Binéfar: delegates from the CNT Regional Committee also managed to persuade the commander of the Twenty-sixth Division, Gregorio Jover, that any aggressive move should be avoided. After some hesitation, another CNT leader, Juan Manuel Molina, undersecretary for defense in the Generalidad, managed to persuade the Anarchist officer Máximo Franco to halt his men at Binéfar. Yet, on several occasions, everything threatened to rebound. PSUC elements attacked Federica Montseny's car, and Antonio Sesé, secretary of the Catalan UGT, whose entry into the government had just been announced over the radio, was killed, probably by CNT militiamen. The Friends of Durruti called for the struggle to continue: the CNT–FAI repudiated them with great vigor.

By Thursday 6 May order had nearly been restored. Companys announced that there were neither winners nor losers. The mass of workers in Barcelona had heard the appeals for calm, and the POUM backed down: 'The proletariat,' it announced, 'has won a partial victory over the counter-revolution. . . . Workers, return to work.' The new government, made up provisionally of a Republican, Valerio Mas, from the CNT, and Vidiella, from the UGT, no longer included either Comorera or Rodríguez Sala. Companys's interpretation would have seemed right but for intervention at this point from Valencia. Empowered with a government mission of appeasement, García Oliver and Montseny came to Barcelona with, if they are to be believed, an express promise that no military intervention would occur unless they themselves asked for it. Yet on 5 May warships had arrived off the coast, on Prieto's orders. A few hours later, at Companys's express request and on pressure from the ministers, Largo Caballero decided to take control of public order and defense in Catalonia. General Pozas, former head of the Civil Guard, now with the Communist party, was given command of the troops in Catalonia. To ensure law and order, the government sent a motorized column of 5000 guards from the Jarama front. Yet—and this is a good illustration of the ambiguity and uncertainty of the time—these police forces, who had just restored order in Catalonia and from whom it seemed, at first glance, that the Anarchists had everything to fear, were commanded by the former head of the Anarchist column Tierra y Libertad, Lieutenant Colonel Torres Iglesias: some of the guards entered Barcelona with shouts of *¡ Viva la FAI!*.

With their arrival, the fighting came to a complete stop. The official casualty list was 500 dead and 1000 wounded. Among the dead on the government side, apart from Antonio Sesé, was a Communist officer, Captain Alcade; on the revolutionary side, Domingo Ascaso, Francisco's brother, and 'Quico' Ferrer, grandson of the well-known professor, all killed in the streets. But other victims were soon discovered. On the evening of the sixth, the corpses of Camillo Berneri and his friend and collaborator Barbieri were found. The two men, taken from their homes in the daytime by UGT militiamen, had been shot at point-blank range. At the same time, it was noted that Alfredo Martínez, secretary of the Revolutionary Youth Front, had disappeared, and his corpse was found a few days later. Both had denounced the Moscow trials and had branded the attitude of the Communist party, the PSUC, and their allies as 'counterrevolutionary.' Both had emerged as leaders of the revolutionary opposition. Although an inquiry was not possible at this time of chaos (and what was more, its findings could scarcely have been published), there was no doubt in anyone's mind that Berneri and Martínez had perished as victims of a political reckoning. Many believed that it was as a result of the *Pravda* warning and the first brutal intervention by the Russian secret service.

Significance of the May Days

The origin of the May days has been the cause of many discussions and polemics. Was it provocation by Fascist agents at work in the ranks of the POUM, as the PSUC claimed?[40] Was it provocation by the Catalan bourgeoisie backed by the Western governments and designed to wipe out the revolutionary positions in Catalonia, as some Anarchists believed?[41] Or was it provocation by the PSUC, with the same aim, as others believed?

It would seem that such a discussion is a complete waste of time: provocation by one, two, or even ten agents is only effective if the situation lends itself to it. As we have seen, it did lend itself to it. We do not believe that the Communists in the PSUC, who were moreover not operating independently of the Republican forces and of the Catalan government, wanted the 3 May trial of strength. The attack on the Telefónica was one more stage in the restoration of the state. We even think that the reaction surprised them and that, if they had hoped to get rid of the Catalan Anarchists by force, they would not have waited until that day—which does not however preclude their having done their utmost, in the days that followed, to exploit the situation and to seize an advantage as the revolutionary movement proceeded to crumble. In the tension that prevailed at the beginning of May, the attack on the Telefónica was clearly felt by the Catalan workers as a provocation.

On the workers' side, in fact, the reaction was spontaneous, if by this it is understood that the CNT–FAI District Defense Committees played the leading part in the absence of any instructions. The discipline of the workers in laying down their arms on instructions from the CNT would prove this, were it necessary. George Orwell, who spent the May days in the ranks of the POUM, wrote: 'The workers went out into the streets in a spontaneous gesture of defense, and there were only two things which they were wholly conscious of wanting: the handing back of the Telefónica and the disarming of the *Asaltos* whom they hated.'[42]

Robert Louzon, in his study of the May days,[43] stated that he was struck by the overwhelming superiority of the armed workers, masters of nine-tenths of the city almost without a struggle. But he pointed out that this strength was used only for defensive purposes: throughout the whole of the disturbances, six tanks remained behind the CNT offices without joining the fight. The 75-mm guns were never aimed; Montjuich's, in the hands of CNT militiamen, never opened fire.[44] He stated: 'From the first shot to the last, the CNT and FAI Regional Committees gave but one order, which they issued continuously, over the radio, through the press, and by every means: the order to cease fire.' In his view, the CNT leaders were afraid above all of a power they could not handle and were prepared 'for every kind of abandonment, renunciation, and defeat.' In their private conversations, they invoked the threat of foreign warships in the harbor in order to justify their caution. For them, in fact, the matter had been settled ever since the previous autumn. They had chosen to collaborate, not to seize power. To Santillán, who was very quick to criticize an attitude that he had at first approved, García Oliver and Vázquez replied: 'All we can do is wait on events and adapt to them as best we can.'[45]

The POUM leaders had long feared, according to Victor Serge, that the indecision, feebleness, and political inability of the Anarchist leaders would result in a spontaneous uprising that, lacking leadership and launched, moreover, after provocation, would provide the counterrevolutionaries with the opportunity to inflict a bloody wound on the proletariat. Knowing themselves to be in a clear minority, they had to risk isolating themselves by trying to outflank the CNT: 'The orders . . . which came directly from the POUM leadership,' Orwell pointed out, 'enjoined us to support the CNT but not to fire unless we were fired on first or if our buildings were attacked.'

It is of course arguable[46] that the spontaneous reaction of the Barcelona workers could have opened the road to a new revolutionary impetus and that it was an opportunity to steam in reverse. Historians can merely state that the Anarchist leaders did not wish to do so and that those of the POUM did not believe that they could. The 'draw' announced by Companys was no such thing: in fact, the May days sounded the knell of the Revolution and heralded political defeat for all and death for some of the revolutionary leaders.

Immediate Consequences of the May Days

The first visible consequence was, at any rate, the end of Catalan autonomy, the seizure by the state and the Madrid government of the essential machinery of the country's political and economic life. But this did not seem to mean the launching of the pogrom feared by the CNT and the POUM. Of course, arms were confiscated and newspapers and radio stations placed under the control of the censorship, but the delegate for public order solemnly affirmed that his forces 'would not regard any union or antifascist organization as enemies.' This was the position dictated by Caballero and his minister of the interior, Galarza. On 4 May their official mouthpiece in Valencia, *Adelante*, wrote that the events in Barcelona were an 'inopportune and ill-prepared collusion between organizations with different orientations and contradictory trade-union and political interests, both of them within the general Catalan antifascist front.'

In this light and in this context must be seen the many appeals for calm by the CNT and the statement by the *Casa CNT* on the last day of the barricades: 'The CNT and the FAI are continuing to collaborate loyally as in the past with all political and syndicalist sections of the antifascist front. The best proof of this is that the CNT is continuing to collaborate with the central government, the Generalidad government, and all the municipalities.' The CNT leaders believed that, in order to contain the fire, it was enough not to mention it, and a communiqué on 6 May stated: 'As soon as we knew the scope of what had happened, we gave orders to all organizations to preserve calm and to avoid broadcasting facts that could have fatal consequences for everyone.' Unfortunately for the CNT, just as it was trying to conceal the magnitude of the events in Barcelona, the Communist press waged a vigorous campaign against the uprising 'planned by POUM Trotskyists,' in which it saw the hand of 'the German and Italian secret police.' The campaign was so well managed and the CNT so cautious that even *Frente Libertario*, mouthpiece of the confederal militias in Madrid, adopted the Communist party's thesis and wrote: 'Those who rebel . . . against the government elected by the people . . . are accomplices of Hitler, Mussolini, and Franco,' who 'must be dealt with mercilessly.' Apparently a draw for the time being, the May days were, in the weeks to come, to be won by those of the protagonists who had their own clear political line along with boldness and determination.

The Fall of Largo Caballero

The Communist party did its utmost to call for the punishment of the Trotskyists and of those disguised Fascists who talk of revolution in order to sow confusion. On 9 May, in a speech at Valencia, José Díaz called on the minister of the interior either to punish the unruly elements or to resign. 'The Fifth Column has been unmasked,' he exclaimed, 'what we need is to destroy it.' On the eleventh, *Adelante* replied: 'If the government were to apply the repressive measures to which the foreign section of the Comintern is inciting it, it would be acting like a Gil Robles or a Lerroux government; it would destroy working-class unity and expose us to the danger of losing the war and undermining the Revolution. . . . A government consisting mainly of representatives of the labor movement cannot use methods that are the prerogative of reactionary governments and Fascist tendencies.' From now on, the government's days were numbered.[47] On 14 May several Madrid daily newspapers announced a ministerial shuffle for the following day which would give satisfaction to the Communist party on questions of public order and the conduct of the war. On the fifteenth, Uribe, the Communist minister of agriculture, made a speech in the Cabinet calling for the dissolution and the outlawing of the POUM and the arrest of its leaders. Largo Caballero replied that, as a militant of worker's organizations long persecuted by reactionaries, he refused to dissolve any worker's organization whatsoever. The CNT ministers supported him: Federica Montseny, opening a file, undertook to show that the May days were a provocation in which the PSUC had played the leading role. Uribe and Hernández then got up and left the Cabinet room. 'The government will carry on,' declared Caballero. But the Republican ministers and Prieto's friends did not accept this.[48] Largo Caballero resigned.

Notes

[1] Statement by Largo Caballero to the Cortes on 1 October 1936. *Le Temps* for 3 October saw it as the announcement of the reorganization of the state in the direction of a profound proletarian and socialist revolution.

[2] *La crisis española del siglo XX*, p. 270.

[3] Santillán referred to negotiations held by the Central Committee with the Moroccan Nationalists. *La Batalla* waged a campaign for the independence of Morocco and the alliance of the Republicans with Abd-el-Krim. Koltsov was astonished by the passivity of the Republican rulers toward Morocco, whereas Franco stated: 'We Spanish Nationalists understand very well the nationalism of other peoples, and we respect it.'

[4] When the French Popular Front government pronounced the dissolution of the revolutionary Nationalist movement *L'Etoile Nord-africaine* (later reformed as the PPA, then as the MTLD), militants of this party, like Bastiani, were fighting in the ranks of the International brigades.

[5] See in particular Berneri's article in *Guerra di Classe*, 24 October 1936.

[6] G. Munis (*Jalones de derotta: promesa de victoria* [Mexico City: Lucha Obrera, 1948], p. 329), referred in particular to a delegation to Spain led by a French Trotskyist militant. (Was it David Rousset, as some of his former friends claimed?)

[7] It was *The Times* on 18 March that, in announcing its rejection by the Foreign Office, was first to mention this proposal—never denied—which

Morrow claimed was made in a note dated 9 February. 'The Spanish government,' said the Conservative newspaper, 'was in a mood to consider a modification of the situation in Spanish Morocco; . . . a territorial agreement.' Largo Caballero—silent on this point—claimed in *Mis recuerdos* that he was negotiating with the Moroccan Nationalists when he was overthrown. See on this subject Bolloten, *The Grand Camouflage*, pp. 135–138.

[8] Rosenberg spoke at the *Monumental* cinema in Madrid on 1 and 9 November. Antonov, at an open-air meeting, had Companys acclaimed by 400,000 persons.

[9] This text, which first appeared in the *Cincinnati Times-Star*, has been reprinted widely since.

[10] According to García Pradas, Largo Caballero had informed Moscow that he thought that Rosenberg, who was sick, needed 'a change of air.'

[11] Álvarez del Vayo (*The Last Optimist* [New York: Viking Press, 1950], p. 288) gave an account of this meeting of the executive. He had himself come out in favor of unity of action, considering organic unity inopportune. Pietro Nenni (*La Guerre d'Espagne* [Paris: François Maspéro], p. 67) described a conversation with Prieto who, on 3 March 1937, argued the need for an immediate merger.

[12] For Esplá's travel plans, see *Le Temps*, 23 March. Azaña stated to Fischer that he had sent Besteiro to the King's coronation in order to ask for British mediation, with a view to a cease-fire followed by a withdrawal of foreign troops and a conference of powers for a 'democratic settlement' (*Le velada en Benicarló*, p. 420). A note from the Largo Caballero government on 15 December had rejected the Anglo-French plan providing for an armistice followed by a plebiscite. In February, Cordell Hull, the American secretary of state made fresh proposals (statement to the *Washington Post*, 26 February).

[13] The CNT National Committee in particular took umbrage, in a note on 26 April, at information provided by the *Daily Express* on moves aimed at bringing a Miaja government to power for an 'honorable peace' between the military leaders.

[14] Julián Gorkin, *Caníbales políticos* (*Hitler y Stalin*) *in España* (Mexico City: Ediciones Quetzal, 1941), pp. 215–217. Gorkin had known Asensio in prison.

[15] According to Gorkin (ibid., p. 218), Asensio explained the Communists' hatred for him by two incidents: he had refused to endorse the Fifth Regiment's accounts, and he had threatened to have Margarita Nelken shot for her propaganda among the *Asaltos* on behalf of the Communist party.

[16] Lieutenant Colonel Villalba, military commander of Málaga, accused of having deserted his headquarters and of having abandoned his troops, was court-martialed. But the Cortes refused to waive the parliamentary immunity of Commissar Bolívar, a Communist deputy, who had remained by his side. It is difficult in affairs of this kind to distinguish treason, impotence, and incompetence from justified repression and political vengeance.

[17] Accused of high treason after the fall of Gijón under the Negrín government, Asensio was acquitted and received new commands. His

codefendant, his chief of staff, Martínez Cabrera, acquitted with him, was finally shot, but by Franco.

[18] Carlos de Baraíbar, seriously ill after the July Revolution, had been kept away from all activities for several months. According to his account (*La traición del stalinismo*, pp. 70–71), the Communists had offered him their support for the Ministry of War; his refusal to take part in this move directed against Largo Caballero won him, from then on, their enmity.

[19] Accused of high treason under Negrín, sentenced to death and then pardoned, Maroto too was ultimately shot by Franco.

[20] The municipal council was provided for by a decree on the eighteenth, published in the *Gaceta* on the twenty-first. On the twenty-fourth, during a press conference, Miaja announced the dissolution of the Junta, which the Communist party later approved publicly. In the Cazorla affair, the Communists and the JSU alone defended the young commissar for public order. In a 23 February editorial headed 'Public Order in Madrid,' with censored blanks, the Republican newspaper *ABC*, though often procommunist, advised Cazorla to respect the law. On 24 April, the Junta, already dissolved, stated in a note that it was calling off the inquiry into the affair. On the twenty-sixth, Cazorla protested in a note to the press, objecting to the accusatory silence and threatening to defend himself if the other members of the Junta took no interest in his fate. A few days later, in a report appearing in *ABC*, he merely insisted on the difficulties of the struggle against the Fifth Column, camouflaged in antifascist organizations. The affair remained inconclusive.

[21] We are here summarizing the indictment drawn up by Hernández after the fall of Largo Caballero, in his speech on 29 May.

[22] Men who were as wide apart in 1936 as Casado, Hernández, and Araquistain but who were drawn together after the war by a common hostility to the Communist party, confirmed Caballero's accusations on this point about the Estremadura offensive. But it is difficult to go as far as Hernández, who saw this affair as a decisive factor in the government's fall. Largo Caballero stated that the Communist ministers backed him in order to obey Miaja and that the offensive was ready for 16 May. If this is true, nothing had leaked out about it.

[23] See in particular the articles by W. Solano and Luis Roc in *Juventud Comunista*.

[24] Among the Anarchist newspapers won over to the revolutionary opposition was Bajo Llobregat's *Ideas*. Carlos Rama drew a clear-cut distinction between the pure Anarchist line it represented and that of the 'Friends of Durruti,' whose phraseology betrayed Marxist influences. Moreover, Balius had been part of the *Bloque Obrero y Campesino*. On the other hand, foreign Trotskyists, such as Moulin and Franz Heller, collaborated with his group.

[25] Born in 1897, militant in the Socialist Youth and then an Anarchist during the war, Camillo Berneri, professor of philosophy at the University of Florence, emigrated after Mussolini's victory. Enlisting in the CNT ranks as a volunteer in July 1936, he enjoyed great prestige in the international Liberation movement and a certain authority in that of Spain.

[26] *Guerre de classes en Espagne*, p. 17.

[27] Noske: German Socialist attached to the general staff, who defeated the German Revolution of the Councils in 1919, and whose officers murdered Karl Liebknecht and Rosa Luxemburg.

[28] 'The central government is boycotting the Catalan economy in order to make us renounce all revolutionary gains. Sacrifices are being asked of the people, and the workers and militiamen are giving up a large proportion of their pay, but the government is hanging on to its gold, guarantee of the new bourgeois and parliamentary Republic. The jewels and fortunes of the capitalists are respected . . ., and fantastic salaries are maintained and sometimes tripled. . . . While the people are suffering privations, businessmen are permitted shameful and criminal speculation. . . . Arms are denied the Aragon front because it is staunchly revolutionary, in order to sully the columns operating there. . . . The children of the people are sent to the front, but uniformed troops are kept in the rear for counterrevolutionary ends.'

[29] On 2 March, at the Congress of Libertarian Youth in Madrid, the speech by Enrique Rodríguez, secretary of the JCI and member of the POUM, was acclaimed. García Pradas, who was regarded as a revolutionary opposition leader in the capital, made a violent attack on the Communist party and the JSU. He stated that revolutionary youth should unite for a 'social revolution' and that it 'would never accept the democratic and parliamentary Republic's watchword.'

[30] Santiago Carrillo had stated in Valencia on 15 January 1937: 'We are not fighting for a social revolution. Our organization is neither Socialist nor Communist. The JSU is not a Marxist youth group.'

[31] It was probably as a result of the opposition by the Asturian JSU Federation that a journey to the North by a delegation from the JSU executive had been organized. Two of the JSU leaders, Rodríguez Cesta and Trifón Medrano, died after a bomb explosion in a Bilbao office where they were holding a meeting, on 18 February.

[32] The Communist party leaders were however those who talked most about this government, whose proposal they fought energetically. The idea of trade-union government seems to have been the readoption, in an even milder form, of the old slogan, 'worker's government,' abandoned by Caballero's friends in September.

[33] *Espagne, creuset politique*, p. 152.

[34] Benavides, spokesman for Comorera and the PSUC, wrote: 'The Communist party has been credited with this phrase: "Before taking Saragossa, we must take Barcelona." It accurately reflected the situation and faithfully expressed the aspirations of the country, which was calling for the devolution of the power held by the Anarchists to the Generalidad.' (*Guerra y revolución en Cataluña*, p. 426).

[35] *La Batalla* wrote on this matter: 'A counterrevolutionary demonstration, by those whose object it is to create, within the petty bourgeois masses and the backward strata of the working class, an atmosphere of pogrom against the avant-garde of the Catalan proletariat: the CNT, the FAI, and the POUM.'

[36] Antonio Martín, a former smuggler, was, after July 1936, an effective chief customs officer. According to Santillán, this was what earned

him such powerful antagonism. However, Republicans, Socialists, and Communists regarded him as the butcher of Puigcerdá and responsible for a long reign of terror. Benavides, in *Guerra y revolución en Cataluña*, drew up a long indictment against the man he called 'the Málaga cripple.'

[37] Arthur Koestler described how, for secret communications between Valencia and the embassy in Paris, the minister Del Vayo and the ambassador Araquistain used their wives, two sisters of Swiss-German origin whose conversations, in their native dialect, could not be monitored. According to Benavides, Azaña's conversations were often tapped by the CNT Control Committee (*La velada en Benicarló*, p. 424).

[38] Later measures taken by the government seem to prove that Rodríguez Sala had acted in agreement with the minister, the Republican Ayguadé. On the other hand, it is interesting to note the variety of motives invoked by the Communist press to justify Rodríguez Sala's move: to insure the functioning of the union (*Daily Worker*, 11 May); to relate the union from the POUM and the unruly elements, which had seized it the previous day (*Corr. Int.*, 29 May); or simply to install a government delegate (Rodríguez Sala to the press).

[39] After this speech, a rumor circulated among the workers on the barricades that García Oliver and his friends, prisoners of the Generalidad police, were forced under threats to launch such appeals for calm. On the PSUC side, it was claimed that García Oliver had warned his friends not to take notice of any message he sent unless it was preceded by a password.

[40] In a note on 11 May, the German ambassador stated that Franco had informed him in person that the May days had been the work of his agents; he pointed out that Barcelona contained thirteen Nationalist agents. But there was nothing to show that these agents were in the ranks of the POUM rather than the PSUC or in any other union or political organization.

[41] Santillán described how the Argentine writer González Pacheco, coming from Brussels, had heard Ambassador Ossorio y Gallardo say that it was known there what was afoot in Barcelona. This, and the presence of British and French warships off the coast, led him to think of a provocation of international origin, in which the Communists were on the receiving end, as was shown by the presence in Barcelona, on the day of the disturbances, of José del Barrio, commander of the twenty-seventh Division, and of his chief of staff.

[42] *Controversy*, August 1937. See also, in his work *Homage to Catalonia*, the chapter on the May days.

[43] 'Were the May Days a 15 May?' (parallels with the Revolution of 1848), *Le Révolution prolétarienne*, 10 June 1937.

[44] Santillán told how, before going to Companys, he had had the guns of the coastal batteries leveled at the building with orders to the commander to telephone him at regular intervals in Companys's office and to open fire if he did not answer in person.

[45] Santillán, *Por qué perdimos la guerra*, p. 164.

[46] As claimed by Felix Morrow, the Trotskyist, and, to some extent, Santillán, who very soon regretted the role he had played in the establishment of an unconditional cease fire.

[47] Jesús Hernández described the session of the Communist party Political Bureau at which, according to him, Caballero's fall was decided. According to his version, he and José Díaz had argued against a move that amounted to 'destroying the fighting front.' Against them, the Russian Embassy adviser, present at the meeting with Gerö, Codovilla, Stepanov, and Orlov, won acceptance for Moscow's point of view by asserting that 'Caballero has stopped heeding our advice,' and that 'he has vetoed the suspension of *La Batalla* and the proclamation of the illegality of the POUM.'

[48] Hernández having written that Prieto had followed the Communist ministers and had called for the resignation of the government after their departure, Prieto stated (*Entresijos de la Guerra de España* [Buenos Aires: Bases, 1954], p. 52) that he had merely warned Caballero, who wanted 'to continue, pointing out to him that he could not do so without giving an account of himself to President Azaña.' Prieto's concern, after his expulsion from the Negrín government, to disassociate himself from the Communists in the past, explains this interpretation, admittedly a pretty unconvincing one: the development of the ministerial crisis and its outcome gave proof in fact of the agreement, tacit at least, between Prieto and the Communist ministers on the need to overthrow Largo Caballero.

CHAPTER 12

THE NEGRÍN GOVERNMENT AND THE LIQUIDATION OF THE OPPOSITION

The crisis that broke after the Cabinet meeting on 15 May was the second ministerial crisis since July 1936. The very circumstances in which it was settled indicated how profoundly things had changed in the interim. In fact, it fell to President Azaña, consigned to the background since September, to solve it, by consultations in the purest parliamentary tradition.

The first solution envisaged, the reshuffling of the government by replacing the Communist ministers,[1] came to grief before the Socialist executive, which decided on the resignation of its ministers. The crisis officially in the open, Azaña entrusted Largo Caballero with the first lap. In fact, the CNT and the UGT on the one hand and the Socialists and Communist parties on the other declared themselves ready to support a government with the same constitution as the previous one, the CNT and the UGT stating further that they would not take part in a government that was not led by Largo Caballero. The latter immediately proposed a new distribution of ministries: the UGT would have three ministries, the Ministry of War along with the premiership, the Ministry of the Interior, and the Foreign Ministry, and all the other formations would have two, the Socialist party the Ministries of Finance and Agriculture, Industry and Commerce, the Communist party the Ministries of Education and Labor, the Republican Union the Ministries of Communications and the Merchant Marine, the Republican Left the Ministries of Public Works and Propaganda, and the CNT the Ministries of Justice and Health. Did Largo Caballero hope that his plan would be accepted by the parties? Naturally, the CNT representation was cut by half, but the UGT held the key posts. Moreover, Prieto and Álvarez del Vayo had disappeared from the combination. In any case, Largo Caballero was not proposing the 'trade-union government' that his friends were bandying about.

The highly diplomatic statements by the representatives of the parliamentary groups clearly indicated their reserves about the new government. For the Republican Left, Quemades insisted on the 'maintenance of public order' and 'economic reconstruction.' Irujo said that the Basques wanted 'a government of national concentration, led by a Socialist with the confidence of the Republicans,' in order 'to firmly suppress the causes of chaos and insurrection.' This was the same course adopted by the Socialist Lamoneda, who wanted 'a radical change in the policy of the minister of the interior.' Meanwhile, the Communist party did not name any specific appointment but called for handing over the Ministries of the Interior and War to 'persons enjoying the support of all parties and organizations composing the government.' But at that juncture Azaña already knew that the Socialists wanted Prieto at the Minstry of War and, through José Díaz, that the Communists were against Largo Caballero's still combining the War Ministry with the premiership.

During the night, Azaña called together Largo Caballero, Prieto, Lamoneda, José Díaz, Martínez Barrio, and Quemades. Largo Caballero refused to give up the War Ministry. The Communist party refused to take part under such conditions. The Socialist party and the Republican Left made Communist participation the condition of their own. The new Largo Caballero combination was therefore an impasse. Azaña begged José Díaz to make an attempt to alter his party's position and then called on Negrín, whom the Communists, Socialists, and Republicans were ready to support and whose candidature seemed to have been prepared months in advance.[2]

On the seventeenth, the formation of the Negrín government was announced. Three Prieto Socialists held key posts, Negrín taking the Ministry of Finance and the premiership, Prieto the War Ministry, and Zugazagoitia the Ministry of the Interior. Jesús Hernández and Uribe retained the Ministries of Education and Agriculture. The Catalan Ayguadé, from the Esquerra, whom the CNT denounced as one of those responsible for the May days, became minister of labor. Irujo was minister of justice and Dr. Giral foreign minister. The CNT and the UGT, true to their initial stand in support of Largo Caballero, did not take part.

Juan Negrín

The new premier was little known. He was a man of forty-six, in his prime (he was endowed with uncommon vitality), who, until the Civil War, had merely been a brilliant dilettante in politics. 'Child beloved of fortune,' as Ramos Oliveira, his admirer, said, born of a rich family in the Canaries, he had wandered the world at will and at Leipzig University had won the medical diplomas that had earned him the chair of physiology at the University of Madrid in 1931. Married to a Russian woman, he had many connections with the West. He had joined the Socialist party in 1929, had become a deputy in 1931, and had been constantly relected ever since. He did not regard himself either as a Marxist or as a representative of the working class: a 'Western-style' Socialist, he was a man of the upper bourgeoisie and a distinguished academic, far more of a Prieto than a Largo Caballero. But he had only taken part in the Socialist party's internal struggle from a distance and had no ambition or taste for political struggle, to which he seemed to prefer the good things of life. Also, he had been practically unknown when, on Prieto's suggestion, he had become minister of finance in the Largo Caballero government. He had only accepted, he said, out of duty, convinced that 'the international aspect of the war was crucial to its outcome and that, because of this, a Largo Caballero Cabinet with representatives of the Extreme Left of the Socialists and of Communism was a gross error, worse . . . than the entry of the Fascists into Getafe.'[3]

The same preoccupations had inspired him once in office at the Ministry of Finance; he had been the uncompromising defender of capitalist property, the determined enemy of collectivization, and a hindrance to the CNT ministers in all their proposals. He had reorganized the *Carabineros* on a sound footing. He had also supervised the dispatch of the Republic's gold reserves to the USSR. He enjoyed the confidence of the moderates and his name had been put forward during the crisis, first by Irujo. He was regarded as a Prieto man. He was on excellent terms with the Communists, who had guaranteed him their support in advance and who, through Jesús Hernández, had made him their candidate for the coalition government that they were advocating. With him, it was their policy, the policy of Prieto—for the time being they were one and the same—that prevailed.

While the FAI, in a secretly distributed manifesto, denounced 'the victory, not only of the bourgeois-Communist bloc, but also of France, England, and Russia,' Western reactions were favorable. *Le Temps*, on 17 May, called on the new government to choose between 'democracy and proletarian dictatorship, between law and order and anarchy.' The *New York Times* announced on the nineteenth that Negrín intended to 'use an iron hand at home' and pointed out: 'By acting thus, the government hopes to win the sympathies of the two democracies which mean most to Spain—Great Britain and France—and to retain the support of the nation which has helped it most—Russia. The government's chief problem today is pacifying or crushing the Anarchist opposition.' The semiofficial French review *Affaires Etrangères* pointed out the profound significance of the choice of the new premier and the new foreign minister, the departure of the extremists and the growing importance of the Basques, and the new government's 'reasonable' character and the hopes that it now permitted for a conciliatory solution.

At any rate, the coalition parties' press hailed the new government as the 'government of victory.'

The Suppression of the POUM

Before Caballero's fall, the Communist party and the PSUC press had launched a virtual witch-hunt against the

POUM. It was stepped up after what the Communists called 'the Fascist uprising in Barcelona.' Largo Caballero had vetoed the repression of the POUM. Negrín could only agree to it. On 28 May *La Batalla* was suppressed. Julián Gorkin was indicted for his 1 May editorial calling on the workers to be on guard, 'arms at the ready,' and proposing a 'revolutionary united front' to the CNT. During the night of 16 June, all the members of the POUM Executive Committee were arrested, Nin in his office, some at home, and others at the front. The police, unable to find Andrade or Gorkin for the time being, arrested their wives.

On 11 June an initial charge against the POUM appeared. It stated: 'The main trend in this party's propaganda was the suppression of the Republic and its democratic government through violence and the installation of a dictatorship of the proletariat.' There was nothing extraordinary about this accusation, normal enough against revolutionaries who invoked the ideas of Lenin. Yet what followed the charge implied another state of mind: the POUM was accused of having 'slandered a friendly country whose moral and material support had enabled the Spanish people to defend its independence,' of having—a reference to the Moscow trials—'attacked Soviet justice,' and of having been 'in touch with organizations known under the general heading of "Trotskyists" and whose activities within the borders of a friendly power show that they are in the pay of European Fascism.'

The content and even the tone of the charge recalled the threat by *Pravda*: the same hand that, in Moscow, had struck the old Bolsheviks was preparing to strike in Spain. The same services were fabricating the same 'evidence' against the accused, clumsy forgeries intended merely to back up 'confessions.' In the POUM affair, this was 'Map N,' a map of Madrid on graph paper discovered on the Falangist Golfín on which the police had deciphered a message in invisible ink referring to 'N' as a reliable agent. N was of course Nin. Jesús Hernández stated that the Communist party leaders were infuriated by the crudeness of this worthless forgery. Miravittles declared publicly that the document was so obviously false that no one would dare to use it. Yet this 'evidence' served to justify the arrest.

On 29 July a note from Irujo, the minister of justice, announced the appearance in the courts, for spying and high treason, of Gorkin, Andrade, Bonet, and seven other POUM leaders, as well as the Falangist Golfín: the technique of 'association,' tested in the Moscow trials, was still in favor. The note specified that 'numerous documents found on POUM premises are involved: keys, telegraphic codes, documents concerning arms traffic and the smuggling of money and valuables, different periodicals originating from various capitals, communications from foreign elements referring to interviews having taken place inside and outside loyal territory, and participation by foreign elements in the preliminaries of spying and in the subversive movement in May.' But, in response to questions from the Maxton Commission, Irujo stated that there was 'no evidence of spying against any POUM leader,' and that 'document N was worthless.'

In his view, the POUM would answer to the courts for 'its revolutionary action against the Republic.' Prieto agreed with the idea of a political trial: 'The Republic must defend itself against all those who want revolution at any cost, whereas the time for it is not ripe in Spain.' Only the Communist party, which could not accept recognizing that revolutionaries were beeing persecuted, went on referring to 'spies' and 'Fascists.' The examining magistrate was of the same mind, because his report stated: 'The accused, having thrown in their lot with members of the German Gestapo who, up to now, have not yet been presented [*sic*], carried out in Barcelona, in May, hostile acts of a secret nature, as well as a military-type uprising, with the aim of harassing the government.' On 13 November, before the Communist party Central Committee, José Díaz demanded, since the POUM treachery had been 'proved,' that 'the firing squad do its work and make an end of the traitors and terrorists.'[4]

However, at the trial, in October 1938, the charge of spying was dropped. Andrade, Gorkin, Bonet, and Gironella were sentenced to fifteen years' imprisonment for 'having tried to overthrow the established order.'[5] The POUM and the JCI were dissolved. In fact, even before this date, the arrest of the members of the Executive Committee in June and then of their successors, Rodes, Farré, Solano, and Pelegrin, in the autumn, had lopped off the head of the POUM, potential leader of the revolutionary opposition: in short, the objective aimed at had been attained.

The Murder of Andrés Nin

The POUM trial was not however a follow-up to the Moscow trials. The matter had been set up along the same lines, with a phony police officer, 'association' with a genuine Fascist, and an accusation of spying. But there was a vital piece missing from the works: confessions, an essential element for the success of operations of this kind. It would seem that it was Andrés Nin's resistance that caused the eventual failure of the venture meant to show that, in Spain as well as in Russia, the 'Trotskyists,' enemies of the Stalinist regime, were in the pay of Hitler, Mussolini, and Franco.

Andrés Nin had been arrested, as we said, on 16 June, at the same time as his comrades. But his name had not appeared on the list of POUM leaders sent to the court on 29 July. For some time already, the rumor had been going around that he had, after his arrest, been handed over to the Communist police, transferred to a detention center in the Madrid area, and there murdered. Federica Montseny was the first to ask the question, 'What have you done with Nin?' The government replied: 'Nin has been arrested, he is in detention.' But, by word of mouth, ministers let slip the truth and confessed their impotence: Zugazagoitia told Jordi Arquer, the POUM column leader, that Nin was in a private Communist prison. He advised him not to try and find him because, in that case, no official safe-conduct could protect him. There were violent incidents in the Cabinet: Negrín summoned the Communist minister and stated that he was ready to cover up what must be covered up but that he insisted on being kept informed. Soon, on 4 August, faced with a growing scandal,[6] part of the truth had to be recognized. On 4 August, the government published a note stating: 'From information received, it appears that Nin was arrested by the general security police at the same time as the other POUM leaders, that he was transferred to Madrid to a detention center converted for that purpose, and that he has disappeared from there.'

The Nin affair had immense repercussions. Former secretary of the CNT and former secretary of the Red Trade-Union International, the POUM leader was world famous in the working-class movement. Inside and outside Spain, committees, commissions of inquiry, letters, and telegrams appeared by the hundreds. On the walls of towns the same question was constantly repeated: 'Where is Nin?' The Communist party militants, who were good at rhymes, found the answer: 'In Salamanca or in Berlin.' Besieged with questions, the ministers contradicted each other: Irujo stated that Nin had never been detained in a government prison, whereas Zugazagoitia, minister of the interior, said that he had been but that he had left it, transferred 'elsewhere.' The minister of justice appointed an examining magistrate to inquire into Nin's disappearance. Several police officials, implicated and threatened with arrest, disappeared, and some took refuge in the Soviet Embassy. Finally, the examining magistrate only just escaped an attempt by government police in Valencia to kidnap him. Irujo threatened to resign from the Cabinet. He was supported by Zugazagoitia, who denounced the activities of the director-general of the security police, the Communist Ortega. In the end, Ortega was dismissed, but Nin was not discovered. On 8 August 1937, the Madrid correspondent of the *New York Times* could write: 'Although everything is being done here to hush up the affair, everyone now knows that he was found dead in the suburbs of Madrid, murdered.'

The theory of Nin's friends—that he was kidnapped by the Soviet secret police, the NKVD—has now been confirmed by the revelations of Jesús Hernández. It was already known that, among the police who arrested the POUM leaders, was a Russian soldier, Leo Narvitch,[7] who a few weeks earlier had got in touch with Nin and Andrade by posing as a member of the Russian opposition serving as a technician in Spain. Jesús

Hernández completed the story: Nin, handed over to Orlov, head of the NKVD in Spain, by the Communist police who had arrested him, was imprisoned in a detention center, a villa in Alcalá de Henares. The idea was to wring from him 'confessions' that would permit a public trial similar to the one in Moscow and that would endorse Stalin's theory by once again affirming their opposition and 'Trotskyist' enemies' links with the Fascists. But Nin, though suffering from very poor health, resisted torture and refused to 'confess.' After that, it was impossible for him to reappear. Nin alive would have become a formidable accuser. But it was also impossible to announce his death in a detention center. According to Hernández, it was Major Carlos who, at the point when it had become necessary to conclude matters, had the idea of a scenario that would lend credit to the theory of Nin's escape through the intervention of 'members of the Gestapo' disguised as soldiers from the International Brigades. This would be the theory propounded by those in charge of the detention center to the official investigators. It is still not known, however, if Nin's corpse was eventually found or identified.

These official explanations deceived no one. After the murders of Berneri and Alfredo Martínez during the May days, it was clear that a similar 'police' were hounding Stalin's most feared enemies, both Spanish and foreign. The NKVD had its network in Spain, and though its leaders and its prisons were eventually known, it enjoyed complete freedom of action. The restoration of the state had done away with the *checas* of the parties, unions, and Committees, but the new legality put up with the existence of this all-powerful secret police force.

Dispersed after the dissolution of the POUM columns, isolated, jobless, the anti-Stalinist foreign revolutionaries were easy prey for Pedro's and Orlov's services, which implacably carried out the purge announced by *Pravda*. According to Georges Kopp, a Belgian Socialist whom the Communist press featured for a while as a top spy but whom a campaign by the foreign Socialist press later released,[8] it had many victims. Bob Smilie, delegate of the ILP Youth, died in a Valencia prison of suspected appendicitis. Others disappeared without trace: Kurt Landau, Austrian militant, former secretary of the international Left opposition, in alliance with the POUM against Trotsky, the young Russian Socialist Marc Rhein,[9] the Polish Trotskyist Freund, known as Moulin, the Czech Trotskyist Erwin Wolff, Trotsky's former secretary,[10] and José Robles, former professor at Johns Hopkins University and General Gorev's former secretary.[11] As well as the 'private' prisons, the state prisons were also filled with antifascists, mainly foreigners. In November 1937 the Commission of Investigation under Félicien Challaye and the Englishman McGovern was astonished to find itself welcomed at the Model Prison in Barcelona by the Internationale, sung by five hundred prisoners. It took a personal effort by Manuel de Irujo and an improvement in the prison system to end the hunger strike in Barcelona by antifascist prisoners urged on by Landau's wife.

The Dissolution of the Aragon Defense Council

The POUM and the anti-Stalinist Communists were not the only ones under fire from the 'government of victory.' It very soon became clear that the Aragon Defense Council could not retain the quasiautonomy that it had enjoyed under the Largo Caballero government and that had made it a bastion for CNT and FAI extremists. Its president, Joaquín Ascaso, was accused of having prompted the activities of certain unruly elements during the May days. Its liquidation, along with that of the Aragonese collectives, became a necessity for a government anxious to prove that it was ensuring law and order and respecting property. It was a guarantee made to all moderate Republicans as well as a blow struck against the CNT revolutionaries.

The campaign was skillfully handled. On 19 July, in a broadcast address, Joaquín Ascaso accused the government of deliberately neglecting the Aragon front and of refusing any help to the Council, though it was made up of representatives of all parties and unions, including the Communist party, the JSU, and the UGT. The fact was that Socialist, Communists, and Republicans had never yet managed to organize, from within, serious opposition to the CNT leadership, which completely dominated the Council. But with the formation of the Negrín government, conditions changed, and it became possible for them to rely on outside help. On 31 July the Communist newspaper *Frente Rojo* launched the first accusations against 'the extremists . . . of certain organizations . . . hand in glove with the Fifth Column.' A few days later, a meeting was held in Barbastro for the representatives of the Aragonese parties and unions hostile to domination by the CNT through the Council: the Republican party, the Communist party, and the UGT, in the name of the Popular Front, called for the dissolution of the Council because of its policy, 'equivocal and contrary to the interests of the region's economy,' and asked the government to send a 'federal governor' to represent it. On 10 August the decree for the dissolution of the Council was issued. 'Aragon,' it said in explaining its reasons, 'has remained aloof from the centralizing tendency to which we largely owe the victory promised us.' The Council's authority was replaced by that of a civil governor, the Republican Mantecón. Immediately, the Communist Major Lister's Eleventh Division, dispatched to the outskirts of Caspe by Prieto, went into action against the Committees, whose dissolution was unanimously called for by the Popular Front press. The Council's newspaper, *Nuevo Aragón*, was suppressed and replaced by the Communist *El Día*. The Local Committees were replaced by municipal councils set up by Lister's troops. The offices of the CNT and the Libertarian organizations were occupied by troops and then closed. Many leaders were arrested on 12 August, among them Joaquín Ascaso, accused of 'smuggling' and 'jewel thefts.'[12] On 18 September, thanks to the dismissal of the charge, he was released. By that date, the objective was attained, the remaining revolutionary power having been disposed of once and for all.

At the same time, the die-hard wing of the FAI and the CNT had been struck a decisive blow. After the May days, Santillán had tried to convince his friends García Oliver and Vázquez that the CNT and the FAI had been wrong in 'ceasing fire [in Barcelona] without settling the unresolved questions' and that there was still time to 'recover lost ground' by counterattacking. In the ensuing months, he held aloof from all confederal responsibility: the FAI, which shared his views, was powerless without the CNT, whose leadership, for want of another viewpoint, had been completely won over in favor of Negrín. At the height of the Libertarian movement in October 1938, Mariano Vázquez took issue with the unruly elements by condemning the activities of the Control Patrols, the 'quixotic stand' of the Aragon Council, and Joaquín Ascaso's 'trickery.' On 21 September 1937, guns and tanks, on government orders, took part in the attack on *Los Escolapios*, seat of the CNT–FAI Defense Committee, which was seized by the forces of order after several hours' fighting. In December the Libertarian Youth entered the Alliance of Antifascist Youth in company with the JSU. Fidel Miró, Alfredo Martínez's companion murdered in May, sat alongside Carrillo, moving spirit of the Alliance. From then on, the Revolutionary Youth Front was a thing of the past.

The Liquidation of the Loyal Opposition

Only one obstacle remained in the path of government authority, the opposition of Largo Caballero, still secretary of the UGT, whose influence in the party and the JSU was still considerable and was evident from the newspapers that his friends controlled, *Claridad*, the Valencian *Adelante*, and *La Correspondencia de Valencia*. The 'old man' resisted and tried to hold out against the combined forces of Prieto and the state in this struggle for the apparatus. But he avoided splitting the antifascist front in public; by the time he had decided to, it was too late.

The JSU minority was the first to be crushed. After the rebellion by Fernández and Gregori in the name of the federations of Asturias and the Levante, and strengthened by the appointment of the former JSU leaders, Leoncio Pérez, Martínez Dasi, and Tundidor López, it seemed at first to be developing along a twin line of opposition to the Communist party, on the one hand, and to the policy of Holy Alliance and struggle for internal power on the other. In June, it was fully on the offensive, anticipating the appearance of a weekly paper,

Renovación, and calling for a conference that would elect a leadership comprising representatives of all points of view. But the fall of Asturias was soon to deprive them of their bastion. Largo Caballero's silence left them reduced to their own forces, facing the government, which forbade them any public demonstrations. The JSU rebellion died out, for lack of support from outside.

Within the Socialist party, the battle was fought around the newspapers controlled by Largo Caballero and his friends. By May, Hernández Zancajo had ceased to be the director of *Claridad*; Carlos de Baraíbar and Araquistain were soon removed from the editorial committee. In July the UGT secretariat gave notice that *Claridad*, as well as the Barcelona *Las Noticias*, no longer represented the opinion of union headquarters. In mid-July the provincial plenum of the Valencia Socialist Federation announced the dissolution of all Liaison Committees with the Communist party as long as Jesús Hernández and La Pasionaria did not withdraw their accusations against Largo Caballero. On the twenty-sixth, through a decision by the National Executive Commission, the Socialist organization in Valencia seized the offices of the provincial federation. A commission, accompanied by the Socialist governor Molina Conejero, tried to seize the offices of the newspaper *Adelante*, mouthpiece of the provincial federation, loyal to Largo Caballero. The militants resisted: the newspaper was seized by force, on the orders of the Socialist minister of the interior, Zugazagoitia, by a detachment of *Asaltos*. An extraordinary plenum of the Socialist party approved the seizure. On the twenty-seventh, the editorship of *Adelante* was given to Prieto's former secretary, Cruz Salido, member of the executive.

Caballero now only had *La Correspondencia de Valencia*, the UGT evening newspaper. He was soon to lose it. Shortly after the formation of the Negrín government, in fact, the offensive against the leadership had begun within the UGT. On 28 May the National Committee, by 24 votes to 14, disapproved the executive's attitude during the crisis and its refusal to support a government without Largo Caballero as premier. The Communists exploited this vote, hostile to the leadership, in a very skillfully managed campaign for the reorganization of the controlling bodies through proportional representation of Communist, Socialist, and nonparty views. The executive resigned but reversed its decision, because the majority, which included not only the Communists but a large number of Socialists merely hostile to nonparticipation, was not ready to replace it. Yet on 1 August, the large Federations of Industry controlled by Communists and procommunists demanded a new meeting of the National Committee. The Caballero executive refused and hit back by expelling, for nonpayment of dues, such Federations of Industry as were at fault, 200,000 workers in all, including the miners, the leatherworkers, the gas and electricity workers, the teachers, and the bank employees. On 28 September the minority demanded the convocation, within forty-eight hours, of a national committee to discuss the expulsion 'of a third of the UGT federations.' *Adelante*, the Socialist party newspaper, announced the meeting of the national committee for 1 October. On 30 September Caballero and the executive denounced this convocation, which was an act of indiscipline. On 1 October the delegates of thirty-one federations out of forty-two, of which thirteen were suspended, met on the stairs in the executive offices, with Felipe Prctel, treasurer of the executive and secretary-general of the commissariat and Álvarez del Vayo's collaborator as chairman.

The assembly called itself the National Committee, cancelled the expulsions, elected a new executive[13] under González Peña's chairmanship, and declared its unconditional loyalty to the Negrín government. The minister of the interior suspended *La Correspondencia de Valencia*: workers demonstrated and protested in Valencia. On the sixth, the Caballero executive announced in a manifesto that it was preparing a national congress. It denounced the collusion between the 'secessionists' and the government: the minister Giner de los Ríos gave the postmen orders to redirect all the UGT's mail and to pay checks to the González Peña executive. The banks received similar orders. The Socialist party–Communist party Liaison Committee meanwhile denounced the 'secessionist and dictatorial conduct' of the Caballero executive and saluted the 'UGT

National Committee, which was ending the situation of violence and uncertainty' by 'rallying to the government.'

Henceforth the conflict was in the open: Largo Caballero announced that he was going to appeal to public opinion by means of a series of congresses to be held in the larger cities in Republican Spain. The government let it pass, hoping for failure in Madrid, where it was generally thought that the popularity of the 'old man' had slumped. On 17 October, when he spoke at the Pardinas cinema, the five larger rooms where his speech was being transmitted were crammed with people, and the crowd built up on the pavement around the loudspeakers. He described his dealings with the Communists, the way in which they had brought down his government, and denounced the coalition between the right-wing Socialists and the Communists and the use of state authority to dislodge him from control over the UGT. He fiercely criticized the Negrín government's policy, without however putting forward an alternative one and without launching any slogan. His speech was that of a loyal opponent who did not pose any threat to the regime.[14] Yet he made an enormous impression, judging from the response that he received. The government, alarmed, decided to stop him from carrying on: on the twenty-first, on his way to Alicante, he was arrested and taken to Valencia, where he was kept under guard at his home. His only protest was an open letter to the president of the Cortes: he was giving up the fight. The government now pressed home its advantage: on 28 November it recognized the dissident Executive Committee, under González Peña, as the sole legitimate authority. On the thirtieth it had *La Correspondencia de Valencia* seized. The Caballero executive, which was preparing to convene a congress, was practically outlawed. All that now remained was to have the new situation ratified by the International Federation of Trade Unions. In early January Léon Jouhaux, secretary-general of the French CGT, came to Valencia in the name of the federation to try and find a 'compromise' solution. On 2 January he succeeded: four Caballerists, Díaz Alor, Zabalza, Tomás, and Hernández Zancajo joined the executive under González Peña. The UGT 'secession' was over: there would be no congress. Largo Caballero was conclusively defeated and took no further part in Spanish political life.[15]

The Establishment of an Apparatus for Repression

The Negrín government, however, was busy setting up the machinery necessary to make an eventual repression effective. The minister of justice, Irujo, began by reorganizing the Popular Tribunals, reserving by decree the right to present jurymen only for the legal organizations from 16 February onward. The FAI was illegal and so found itself excluded from the Popular Tribunals. But the latter were still showing too much independence and were inclined to leniency when trying antifascist prisoners. The total liquidation of the opposition demanded a more willing instrument. A decree on 23 June 1937 therefore established special tribunals for repressing crimes of spying and high treason. They were made up of three civilian and two military judges, all appointed by the government. The definition 'offense of spying and high treason' was sufficiently elastic to permit the use of this fearsome weapon against any opponent, even a nonfascist one. In fact, among those regarded as such offenses were: 'committing acts hostile to the Republic, inside or outside national territory,' 'defending or propagating news or making judgments prejudicial to the conduct of war operations or to the credit and authority of the Republic,' and 'acts or demonstrations tending to weaken public morale, demoralize the Army, or diminish collective discipline.' The penalties varied from six days' detention to the death penalty. To make matters worse, they were the same for an actual offense as for 'an attempt and an abortive attempt, conspiracy and proposal, as well as complicity and protection.' The decree favored every kind of provocation and gave the police discretionary powers, because it provided that 'those who, after having agreed to commit one of these offenses, denounced it to the authorities before it was carried out, would be exempt from any penalty.'

This amounted to a ban on all opposition demonstrations and all criticism. It gave the government the chance to sentence for 'high treason' anyone who expressed disagreement with all or part of its policy. It was by virtue of this decree that the POUM leaders were tried for acts committed before it had been promulgated.

This policy of repression did not however come out into the open. As before the Revolution, trade-union meetings had to be authorized by the delegate for public order, after a request made at least three days in advance. As before the Revolution, censorship, justified at the outset by military necessity, was now imposed on political attitudes. On 18 May *Adelante* appeared with its first page blank, under the headline *¡Viva Largo Caballero!* On 18 June the government established a monopoly of radio broadcasts and seized transmitters from the various headquarters. On 7 August *Solidaridad Obrera* was given five days' suspension for committing a breach of the censorship's directives by appearing with 'blanks' to indicate censored passages: the censorship was working and demanded that no trace should remain of its activities. On 14 August a circular banned all criticism of the Russian government: 'With an insistence suggesting a plan specifically designed to offend an exceptionally friendly nation, thus creating difficulties for the government, various newspapers have treated the USSR in a way that cannot be allowed. . . . This utterly reprehensible license ought not to be permitted by the Council of Censors. . . . Any newspaper that does not conform will be suspended indefinitely, even if it has been censored, in which case the censor will be summoned before the special tribunal dealing with crimes of sabotage.' The censorship, like the police and the radio, played an active part in the secession of the UGT, systematically 'cutting' statements by the Caballero executive or articles by the CNT devoted to this question.

The SIM

A special role in this apparatus of repression was played by the SIM (*Servicio de Investigación Militar*), created on Indalecio Prieto's initiative by a decree on 15 August 1937. Initially a counterespionage service, it very soon became an all-powerful political police force, able to make arrests and grant releases without trial or investigation other than its own. After the

Republican Sayagües, it was run by the Socialist Uríbarri, a former officer in the Civil Guard, who worked closely with the Russians in the 'special services,' and then, after his escape to France,[16] by Santiago Garcés, who was regarded as one of the authors of Nin's murder. Prieto, creator of the SIM, has described at great length how the service came to fall from his clutches. Major Durán, a Communist and head of the Madrid SIM, appointed militant Communists to all the important posts, and the Russian 'technicians' protested when Prieto wanted to send them to the Army. A few months after its formation, the SIM, which was completely immune from the authority of the minister of war, had more than 6000 agents and was in control of prisons and concentration camps.[17]

The Strong State

This was how the 'democratic' state, built by Largo Caballero, became a strong state under Negrín. It still called itself 'democratic and parliamentary,' but the depleted Cortes was now a mere collection of walk-ons, and there was no question of elections, either in the Cortes or in the municipal councils.[18] No genuine opposition could declare itself openly and criticism was synonymous with treason. There was still talk of 'popular revolution,' but the reality was a continual reassessment of the revolutionary gains. The Negrín government came out in favor of freedom of worship and, at Irujo's patient instigation, managed to relax the pressure on the priests and the Catholic church. Many proprietors reported 'missing' returned; others were released from prison. All reclaimed their lands, seized in 1936: they had right and the law on their side, as well as government support.[19] In Catalonia, the application of the collectivization decree was suspended, because it was 'contrary to the spirit of the Constitution.' The decree of 28 August 1937 enabled the government, through *intervención*, to take over any metallurgical or mining concern. Soon afterward, on 26 February 1938, *The Economist* wrote: 'Intervention by the state in industry, as opposed to collectivization and workers' control, is reestablishing the principle of private property.'[20] Managers and directors recovered their posts. The state received into its coffers dividends on shares 'seized' from the factionists and paid out those of foreign capitalists.

Centralization was so great that the Catalan Autonomists and the Basque Nationalists finally quit the government.[21] The Popular Army changed definitively into a regular army of the traditional kind. The new military code of justice envisaged by Largo Caballero never saw the light of day and the old one remained in force. The Negrín government re-established a hierarchy with regard to pay.[22] Prieto forbade the 'workers' officers from rising above the rank of major. He restricted the powers and cut down on the numbers of the political Commissars[23] and forbade soldiers from taking part in political demonstrations (5 October 1937). The spirit of the officer caste was thus reborn, and Winston Churchill could write:

'During the past year, a marked advance towards an ordered system of government and war has simultaneously produced itself in the character of the Spanish Republican Government. . . . The Anarchists have been quelled by fire and steel. . . . An army which has a coherent entity, a strict organization and a hierarchy of command has been formed. . . . When in any country the whole structure of civilized and social life is destroyed by atavistic hatreds, the State can only be reconstituted upon a military framework. . . . In its new army, . . . the Spanish Republic has an instrument not only of military but of political significance. . . .'

The British Conservative leader concluded: 'Both sides have progressed steadily towards a coherent expression of the Spanish mind. Is not this the time when every effort should be made by all true friends of Spain to bring about a pacification?'[24] In a far-reaching article that made an assessment of Negrín's action on 8 November 1937, *The Times* wrote: 'Two new factors are gaining in importance: one concerns the character of the Revolution, the other the character of the war. The first consists of a strong reaction against violence from below; the second consists of the deep and broad working of that aspiration to independence which is one of the strongest latent feelings of the Spanish national character. The first, if it goes far enough, will change the character of the Revolution; the second, if it reaches its logical conclusion, must end by closely soldering together the parties at odds in Government Spain at the present moment.'

Was it a 'government of victory,' as the Communist party named it, or a 'government of national reconciliation,' as the English Conservatives hoped? At any rate, a new page had been turned. When the Cortes met again, on 1 October 1937, Caballero was not there, and naturally there was not a single Anarchist leader: in February 1938 they had no candidates or elected members. But the Conservative Miguel Maura was there, and so was Portela Valladares, back from France where he had sought refuge, who expressed his joy at seeing 'Spain moving towards profound and serious reconstruction.' When, a week later, the Nationalist press, in order to discredit him, exposed his offers of help to the 'national cause,' there was not much that could be answered from the Republican side: 'respectability' was paying off. The attacks by the CNT press on Maura and Valladares were censored, as was the speech by the ageing Pestaña denouncing Communist ascendancy and the ebbing of the Revolution.

The latter was in fact over. The state had been restored. A soldier who had 'abused' a superior officer now risked the death penalty. The workers in the factories were working under the strict discipline of 'militarization.' Two and a half galleries out of six in the Barcelona Model Prison were set aside for POUM and CNT prisoners.

Would those who had defeated the Revolution win the war? Only on this condition would the sacrifices and sufferings of the Spanish people have a meaning, and their own acts a justification. The men who had begun this war in chaos and enthusiasm, or at least those of them who remained, continued to fight: henceforth they did so in orderly and disciplined fashion, under a government that earned the praise of Winston Churchill and *The Times*. But, as for fighting against Franco and his allies, the 'democratic' and respectable Spain of 1937 was as isolated as the revolutionary Spain of 1936 had been.

Notes

[1] According to Largo Caballero, it was the only solution that would allow the preservation of a government for 16 May, the date fixed for the opening of the Estremadura offensive.

[2] See on this subject the article in *Le Temps*, 23 March, already quoted (chapter 11). Krivitsky said that Stashevsky, the Russian commercial attaché and Stalin's confidential agent, saw Juan Negrín as Largo Caballero's successor after November 1937 (General Walter Krivitsky, *Agent de Staline* [Paris: Corporation, 1940], p. 127; English translation, *I Was Stalin's Agent* [London: Hamish Hamilton, 1940]). Hernández (*Negro y rojo*, p. 71) described how he himself went and offered Negrín the Communist party's support.

[3] *Epistolario Prieto y Negrín* (Paris: Imprimerie Nouvelle, 1939), p. 41.

[4] It is not without interest to note that a great deal of this report was devoted to 'the infiltration of Trotskyist elements into the party's ranks.'

[5] Arquer was sentenced to eleven years, Escuder and Rebull acquitted. Largo Caballero and Federica Montseny had given evidence in favor of the accused.

[6] In the eyes of those who denounced it, the 'scandal' had two main aspects. From a simple democratic point of view, it was scandalous that, under a government that prided itself on having restored legality and put an end to violence, a prisoner could be handed over to killers by the police and that the authorities tried to conceal the truth. In addition, even after weeks of *paseos* and settlings of old scores, the Nin affair, because of the deliberately organized nature of his kidnapping and the stage management and orchestration that accompanied it, revealed the omnipotence of the NKVD and the determination of the Communists to stop at nothing in order to get rid of an enemy: other leaders of the antifascist coalition began to fear Nin's fate for themselves. Finally, in the eyes of many Communist sympathizers, the kidnapping and murder of a Communist dissident marked a real change in the nature of Stalinist Communism, whose death-blows had only been delivered at revolutionaries.

[7] Captain Narvitch was murdered in Barcelona and Munis accused of the murder. Munis's friends maintained that Narvitch was murdered by the NKVD because he knew too much. It seems that he was in fact murdered by the men of the POUM.

[8] Georges Kopp, who became a lieutenant colonel in Spain, had left Belgium after being sentenced to a long term of imprisonment for buying and dispatching arms to Spain.

[9] Marc Rhein was the son of the Russian Menshevik leader, Abramovitch. Correspondent for a Swedish Social-Democratic newspaper, he was fairly sympathetic to 'antifascist' theories.

[10] Erwin Wolff, in company with Leon Sedov, Trotsky's son, had contributed to the demolition of the prosecutor Vishinsky's theory about Piatakov's famous journey to Copenhagen, after the Moscow trials: the

Hotel Bristol, where Piatakov claimed to have met Leon Sedov, no longer existed.

[11] Fischer (*Men and Politics*, p. 429) wrote at length about the disappearance of Robles, whose son, shortly afterward, was sentenced to death by Franco. The writer John Dos Passos investigated his disappearance.

[12] This had to do with the sale of jewels seized on behalf of the Council of Aragon in autumn 1936.

[13] Edmundo Domínguez was vice-president, Rodríguez Vega secretary, and Pretel treasurer. They were all Socialists of the Del Vayo shade of opinion.

[14] He fully justified *The Times* commentator who wrote on 8 October that he represented 'a kind of opposition within the Popular Front that is ready to take over the government should fate so decree.'

[15] It is interesting to note on this point the total agreement of the Socialist and Communist leaders of the French CGT with Negrín against Caballero, whose defeat, inflicted through the state's intervention, was endorsed by Jouhaux's 'arbitration.' A few months later, Vincent Auriol tried in vain to persuade Largo Caballero to accept a reconciliation with Negrín.

[16] See Prieto's pamphlet, *Cómo y por que salí del Ministerio de Defensa Nacional* (Mexico City: Impresos y Papeles S. de R. L., 1940). Uríbarri began by complaining about pressure from the Russian 'specialists'; then he gave in and dealt with them directly, over the head of the minister. In early May 1938 he fled to France with a small fortune in jewels and gold stolen during the course of police activities. The Spanish government asked in vain for his extradition.

[17] After the Second World War, many writers compared the events in Eastern Europe, the grip of the Communist party and the USSR on the state, with what had happened in Republican Spain under the Negrín government. Julián Gorkin entitled an unpublished essay *L'Espagne, premier essai de démocratie populaire*. This comparison is equivocal, in the sense that the genesis of the popular democracies is ill known and is too often presented tendentiously, either as the result of a movement by the masses, a kind of revolution managed by the Communist party, or as the result of a direct conquest by the Red Army.

The resemblances are striking, but only if one confines oneself to indisputable facts, usually left in the shadows: (1) The countries of Eastern Europe first experienced a revolutionary upsurge in 1945. In Germany and Czechoslovakia, it came about through the formation of 'Workers' Councils' (see Benno Sarel, *La classe ouvrière d'Allemagne orientale*, pp. 17–49, and Paul Barton, *Prague à l'heure de Moscou*, pp. 120 ff.) (2) Then the Communist party, allied in a 'National Front' with the Social Democrats and with the Democratic Republicans whom it often revitalized, busied itself in destroying the Councils and restoring the state, in which it retained absolute control of the political police and, as far as possible, of the Army (see Barton, *Prague à l'heure de Moscou*, and François Fejtö, *Histoire des Démocraties populaires*, with a reference by Rakosi to police control on p. 107). (3) The third stage, the only one that is well known, was the 'salami' tactic described by Rakosi: the Communist party disposed of its recent allies in successive stages. Its apparatus controlled the unified party, formed by the Socialist-Communist alliance (German SED, Polish POUP, Hungarian Workers' party, etc.). It controlled its allies through personalities that it managed to win over and finally carried the day. (In Spain it used Prieto against Largo Caballero in this way, and then Negrín against Prieto).

[18] At the end of 1937 the Communist party fought a campaign at the general election. At this stage, it was a question of hitting back and a means of pressure on Prietos' attempts to reduce its influence.

[19] The Levante UGT Federation of Landworkers' nicknamed Uribe, minister of agriculture, 'public enemy number one.'

[20] The Labor Council, created by the Catalanist Ayguadé, consisted of thirty-one members, including seven representatives of the state, twelve of the employers, and twelve of the unions.

[21] Ayguadé and Irujo resigned on 11 August 1938 because they were in 'basic disagreement' with the government's policy on Catalonia. A Catalan and a Basque, Moix of the PSUC and Tomás Bilbao of the tiny *Acción Nacionalista Vasca*, took their place, but their presence had next to no significance.

[22] An ordinary soldier's pay went from 7 to 10 pesetas a day: a second lieutenant's to 25, a captain's to 50 and a lieutenant colonel's to 100.

[23] Only the commissars in brigades, divisions, and armies survived.

[24] *Step by Step*, pp. 189–191.

Part 2

CHAPTER 13

EUROPE AND THE WAR

'If democracy is defeated in this battle, if Fascism triumphs, His Majesty's government can claim this victory for its own.'[1] With these words, Lloyd George pointed out a new fact: in the view of the world, the Spanish Civil War had assumed the guise of an ideological war. Although no other nation was overtly engaged in the conflict it had become a European one. Henceforth, and especially after the weakening of the revolutionary parties on the Republican side, the Spanish Civil War was just another aspect of the struggle between the great powers in Europe. It was this struggle that had brought about the Italo-German *rapprochement* and the formation of the Rome–Berlin Axis, that cruelly showed up the uncertainties and contradictions of the Western democracies, France and Great Britain, and that in turn steered Russian policy toward cautious expectancy.

The European Balance and the Spanish Civil War

To understand to what point the Spanish Civil War had upset the European political balance, it must be remembered that in 1936 the German position in Europe was still precarious. After the accession of the Nazis to power in 1933, Germany had broken with the League of Nations. Hitler's rearmament and his territorial claims were giving the small neighboring countries cause for concern, though as yet they were not impressed by his power. Otherwise the diplomatic position of the Western powers appeared strong. The *entente* between France, Great Britain, and Belgium looked solid. French influence in the Balkans remained considerable, in spite of the murder of Alexander of Yugoslavia in Marseilles in 1934. Finally, the government of the Third Republic, faced with the danger of German rearmament, had just strengthened its system of alliances in the East: in 1935, mutual-aid pacts had been signed between the USSR and France on the one hand and the USSR and Czechoslovakia on the other. The re-establishment of German power greatly perturbed the Russians: hadn't Hitler indicated 'Bolshevism' as the first enemy to be fought?

The Italian Fascist government found itself in a difficult situation too. Its campaign against Abyssinia intended to create a veritable African 'empire,' had mainly proved its military inefficiency, and a large majority at the League of Nations had decided to take sanctions against the Mussolini government.

The Italian Fascist state and the German Nazi state, thus isolated in Europe, had found the opportunity for a *rapprochement* in the Spanish conflict. This war, by permitting a general political confrontation, had precipitated alliances and re-alignments; it had forced each power to take a stand. In this sense, it had created the political conditions for world war.

To the central European dictatorships, the Spanish conflict did not merely imply a trial of the democracies' weaknesses; it was the dress rehearsal, the first clash, the testing bench for their weapons against those from Russia and Czechoslovakia, the first use of material intended for bigger battlefields. One has only to read the countless articles and works written on this subject to judge the interest that this 'limited war' aroused on the military level.

By contrast, the strategic and economic significance of Spain now took second place; important as it was to have bases like Majorca and Ceuta, and still more so to make use of the tin and copper mines in Asturias and Rio Tinto, this factor could not be decisive to the point of seriously effecting the direction of international policy. With the grave events of summer 1938 and the Sudeten question, Spain became just one more pawn in the European game.

The Recognition of the Nationalist Government

How were the European powers to make their choice between the two camps pitted against each other in Spain?

Legally, the situation was simple. There was a properly elected Spanish Parliament, which had to appoint a government: these were the only bodies whose legality was indisputable. After the relative failure of 19 July, the Nationalists were simply military rebels in control of certain provinces. They were perfectly aware of this themselves, because in the early months all they did was to establish an authority officially intended to disappear after victory and make way for a proper government.[2] Their capital, Burgos, was ignored by the other countries, even those most actively sympathetic toward Nationalist Spain: when Franco, after his appointment as Spanish head of state in October 1936, sent a telegram of greetings to Hitler, the latter did not reply, thus showing that he did not consider it advisable to recognize Franco officially for the time being; when Welczeck, the German ambassador in Paris, took stock of the Spanish position in Berlin, he quite naturally contrasted the 'Spanish government' with the 'rebels.'[3]

But assuming that the European chancelleries refused to give the rebels belligerent rights, which could only be granted to a legal authority, they could not allow them to obtain supplies of war material from foreign states either. This situation was not long in hampering Italy, Germany, and Portugal considerably, and their chancelleries came to devise a whole string of arguments to justify their intervention: it was the Left that, by manipulating the electoral law and thereby encouraging the establishment of a Popular Front government, had created the revolutionary situation; the legal forms of government had themselves disappeared since the February 1936 elections, and the military leaders had revolted in order to reestablish them. We shall merely recall that the electoral law had been voted by a right-wing assembly that believed that it was thereby ensuring a long term of government for itself.

At any rate, such legal arguments were used only with caution; the Fascist governments preferred the method of the *fait accompli*. In order to give a respectable diplomatic form to the recognition of the Nationalist authorities as the government of Spain, the German and Italian foreign ministers, von Neurath and Ciano, wanted to wait for the fall of Madrid. A German plan for communication with the Spanish chargé d'affaires in Berlin, projected in late October 1936, began with these words: 'Now that General Franco has seized the Spanish capital of Madrid and his government thereby controls the greater part of the country. . . .'

For want of any other basis in law, the possession of the capital and its administrative buildings—*de facto* control—would make a distinction between the 'real country' and the 'legal country' possible. At any rate, a pretext would then exist in the form of a need to guarantee the 'defense of German interests.' The departure of the Republican government for Valencia seemed to anticipate this event, but the capital resisted, and the war threatened to go on. Now induced to take a firmer stand, the Germans and Italians finally decided, on 18 November, to go ahead with the *de jure* recognition of the Burgos government. Portugal followed suit.

Naturally the assertion that the Franco government controlled the lion's share of the territory seemed just as false in mid-November as the assertion that there was no longer any government authority in Republican Spain. Actual control over the territory by the Nationalists did not extend to any of the country's Mediterranean or Central provinces, and, although the situation was still fairly fluid in Loyalist Spain, the Caballero government certainly had far more authority than any of its predecessors. It was therefore paradoxical to maintain relations with the Spanish Republic in August and to break them off in November.

However, this change of attitude helped to clarify the international situation; the powers in sympathy with Franco thereby showed their willingness to regard Spain's legal government as an actual enemy. The breach created between the great European Powers was all the clearer because it coincided with the signing of a German-Italian-Japanese pact, prelude to the establishment of a formidable military bloc.

The Formation of the Axis

On the eve of the 18 July *pronunciamiento*, in spite of their similar political attitudes and their equal hostility to Socialism, the Fascist and Nazi governments were at odds on many points. The two powers had in fact betrayed expansionist ambitions that were likely to bring them frequently into competition.[4] Moreover Italy regarded the Mediterranean as a 'preserve' and was suspicious of an eventual German intervention in Spain.

But after August and September 1936, the firm attitude of the Central powers toward the Spanish question, in contrast to Western tergiversations, and their joint willingness to step up their military preparations had helped to settle their differences. The formation of an extreme right-wing government in Rumania under Antonescu was a prelude to negotiations that meant rupturing the balance in Central Europe in favor of Germany and Italy. It was during talks with Horthy, the regent of Hungary, that Hitler first called attention to the agreement between Rome and Berlin to back Franco. And the Hungarian government more or less had to support this joint action, as Budapest was at that time seeking, through a *rapprochement* with these two great powers, a guarantee in support of its own claims over Magyar minorities, especially in Rumania.

The improvement in Italo-German relations became clear at the end of September 1936, with a visit to Rome by the German minister of justice, Frank, received personally by the Duce. Frank pointed out on this occasion that the Führer regarded the Mediterranean as an 'Italian sea' and that his intervention in Spain was unconnected to any expanionist ambitions. When it was Mussolini's turn to state that he did not wish to alter 'the geographical positions,' he did however make one reservation in favor of the Balearic Islands, which had been saved by Italy. The key point in this conversation was stressed by Count Ciano: 'Two fronts have already been set up in Spain: on the one hand the German-Italian front, on the other the French-Belgian-Russian front. The Duce agrees with Hitler in the opinion that the definition of both fronts is henceforth a *fait accompli.*' The idea was launched of an alliance and a division of Europe into zones of influence.

The decisive move was not however made until the end of October, on a journey to Berlin by Count Ciano. The conversation between the two foreign ministers, von Neurath and Ciano, on 21 October, endorsed by a secret protocol and Hitler's reception of Count Ciano at Berchtesgaden, 'resulted in an *entente* between both countries on specific questions, of which some were in fact burning issues,' Mussolini stated in Milan on 1 November.[5] The most burning issue was of course the Spanish question. The main lines and even certain details of the joint move had been studied: they were, on the diplomatic level, the methods of recognizing the Franco government and, in the military field, the portion of the military effort to be contributed by each power, especially where aircraft were concerned. Germany and Italy took stock of the common ground between their interests. The enemy against which the Rome–Berlin Axis had officially been formed, Bolshevism, was at large in Spain; the idea was to rid the Iberian peninsula of 'every Communist [or even Marxist] threat.' To assert itself the Axis, Ciano told Hitler, had to 'deliver the *coup de grâce*' to the Madrid government.[6]

In fact, Rome and Berlin had promised to help the leaders of the *Movimiento* long before the insurrection had broken out. This support could, if necessary, be accepted by the other powers so long as there was no question of any large-scale traffic. But, on 31 July 1936, the announcement that some Savoïa-Marchetti planes had landed by accident in French Morocco revealed the extent of the Italian intervention and provoked a violent crisis between Paris and Rome.

In addition to this incident, there was the threat to Tangier posed by Franco's army. Tangier was under international control but surrounded by territories that had rallied to the Revolution. The French insisted that the Spanish government should have free use of the port. The Italians protested. This was a first and important diplomatic test, because the use of Tangier as a base would enable the Spanish government to hamper the passage of troops from Morocco through the straits of Gibraltar considerably. In the end, England's benevolent neutrality enabled the Italians to obtain satisfaction.[7]

The role of the English authorities, moderate and even favorable to Nationalism in this matter, clearly reflects the British government's opinion and the division among the Western countries. These were without doubt the two elements that determined the policy of nonintervention.

The French Position

There is a good deal of information about the origins of the French nonintervention proposal, especially in Léon Blum's statements to the Parliamentary Commission of Investigation in 1947, which have never, in their general outline, been refuted. We must not however forget that Léon Blum, aware of the bankruptcy of his Spanish policy, was less concerned with defending it than with justifying himself in an attempt to prove that, during the summer of 1936, there was no possible policy other than his own.

Faced with the Nationalist military *coup de force*, which Blum dubbed a '*coup de théâtre*,' the sympathies of the French Popular Front government were won over in advance to the Spanish Republican government. But could such sympathies remain platonic?

On 20 July Blum was faced with the problem raised by the request for material aid drawn up by the Giral government: 'Request you negotiate at once with us for supply of arms and planes.' There was nothing unusual about this telegram. In addition to the common interest between two Popular Front formations, it referred to a particular agreement according to which France had a monopoly for supplying arms to Spain. Not only could Giral apply to Paris, he was even obliged to do so by this commercial treaty. At the time, Blum had no hesitation. The conversations that he had between 20 and 22 July with Delbos, and in particular with Daladier, then minister of war, had the sole aim of working out the size of the aid to be given to the Spanish government and the means for accomplishing it. But between 22 and 25 July, the date of the Cabinet meeting that was to make an official decision about

French support for Republican Spain, several new facts emerged.

First was a fact of external policy, which was no doubt the most important because it had a considerable influence on Léon Blum. The French premier had noted, on a visit to London planned long before the events in Spain, the hostility of the Baldwin government to any intervention in the Spanish conflict, a hostility first indicated in a warning by the journalist Pertinax ('it is not well recorded here') and confirmed by the cautious advice of the English foreign secretary, Anthony Eden. Blum had been disagreeably surprised by this: his entire foreign policy was based on the Anglo-French *entente*, which seemed to him more necessary than ever in the face of German rearmament. To take action over the Spanish affair without the agreement and even against the wishes of England seemed difficult to him at first glance.

His return to France was the occasion of a new disappointment. A press campaign had been launched in *L'Echo de Paris* by Henry Kerillis, who had made public certain measures decided on in order to come to the aid of Spain. The offensive had begun with an article by Cartier, published on 23 July and entitled 'Will the French Popular Front dare to arm the Spanish Popular Front?' He ended on an extremely violent note: 'We are still reluctant to believe that the government could commit this crime against the nation.' The details mentioned in the articles in *L'Echo de Paris* concerned deliveries of planes and bombs, 75-mm field guns, and machine guns. It is interesting to note that there was an allusion in it to the principle of noninterference for which the French government had to take responsibility a week later.

No doubt the right-wing opposition should not have been expected to lighten the task of the French government. But Blum ran into opposition within the government itself, as well as in moderate parliamentary circles. The Senate, traditional soil for Conservative opposition, was undoubtedly the more affected: hence the vehement remarks of its president, Jeanneney: 'That we should be induced to make war over the affairs of Spain . . . is something no one can understand.'

The Radical attitude was even more disturbing: the Radicals in the French government held the two key posts of foreign minister and minister of war; their crossing over to the opposition would provoke a serious ministerial crisis. In such circumstances, one can imagine the impact of the intervention of Edouard Herriot, who added to the cautious advice of Eden and Jeanneney: 'Don't meddle.'[8]

How can one explain the panic in French political circles merely at the prospect of consignments of arms to the legal government of Spain? First by the pacifism of the period. The French Left, until about 1934, had never stopped proclaiming its love of peace and its desire to safeguard it by every means, as much on the Radical as on the Socialist side. France had accepted, without reacting, measures as serious as German rearmament and, more recently, the remilitarization of the Rhineland solely for fear of provoking a conflict. The hopes of many Socialists lay in a new Treaty of Locarno which they considered making with Germany and Fascist Italy. Such illusions were certainly not shared by Blum; he foresaw the conflict and agreed to undertake a French rearmament program that would enable France to catch up to some extent on German progress in the military field. But he himself was a moderate who could not have envisaged taking the risk of starting a war on his own. It has been added, and Blum himself has stated,[9] that the threat of foreign war was duplicated in France by the threat of civil war: 'In France we too were on the verge of experiencing a military coup d'état.' It must be conceded that a section at least of the Right, very nationalistic since 1919, had for some years exhibited a far less intransigent loyalty to the state; through sympathy for the German and Italian regimes, it preached in turn a pacifist policy, giving priority to its domestic troubles, aggravated by the social crisis of 1936 and the accession of the Popular Front, rather than to its foreign preoccupations. This right-wing opposition did not merely appear in the *Echo de Paris* articles. Blum said of the events of 1938: 'In the French Parliament there were some influential politicians who were representatives of Franco.'

In such unfavorable circumstances, the Cabinet, meeting on 25 July, no longer dared to consider aiding the Spanish Republicans openly but merely sought means of concealing arms deliveries; they used the method of imaginary sales to the Mexican government, which was free to use the arms thereby allocated to it for Spain. This was only the first setback. A few days later, the Savoïa-Marchetti incident would have enabled it to reconsider this concession. But Blum recalled that the press campaign launched against his government was being nurtured by many foreign articles, especially English and Belgian, which could not fail to affect public opinion. For Churchill, whose hostility toward Nazism during this period was beyond question, 'inflexible neutrality is the only solution for the moment.'[10]

A much more serious fact was that the French government was far from unanimous. The premier merely indicated that the ministers had been divided after the third Cabinet meeting about the Spanish question on 8 August. Furthermore, it may be said that the supporters of supplying arms, grouped around the Air minister, Pierre Cot, were in a minority against the coalition 'made up chiefly of Radicals and Socialists of the Paul Faure persuasion.'[11] To reverse this trend and to avoid at all costs the isolation in which a policy of intervention on behalf of Republican Spain threatened to place France, Blum saw only one recourse: to win over England.

This explains the friendly welcome he had given the Noel-Baker proposal to send Admiral Darlan, Navy chief of staff, who was regarded as a thoroughly Republican leader, on a mission to London. The mission entrusted to Darlan consisted of getting in touch with the permanent secretary of the Cabinet, Sir Maurice Hankey, through the First Lord of the Admiralty, Lord Chatfield, whom he knew personally. If Darlan managed to persuade him of the need to prevent Franco from seizing power, Hankey could then initiate a Cabinet meeting and possibly a modification of the English attitude.

In fact, it is doubtful if the British Cabinet meeting at the beginning of August would have altered its fixed attitude in any way; England saw too many drawbacks to taking part in the Spanish Civil War. Her mining interests on the mainland did not allow her to break with any of the enemies involved. Moreover, the English were contemplating a return to a *détente* in the Mediterranean after the period of tension typified by the Ethiopian affair in the preceding years. There were signs of a *rapprochement* with Rome and an Anglo-Italian naval pact was being drawn up. All reasons for not taking up an entrenched position diametrically opposed to Italy's. Finally, the British Conservatives sympathized far more with General Franco than with the 'Reds,' whose revolutionary excesses had been thoroughly reported by the Conservative press. Lord Chatfield's opinion of Franco as a 'good Spanish patriot' no doubt merely reflected that of most of the ministers. In such circumstances, the Darlan mission could only end in failure. Chatfield refused to intervene. English policy was not altered.

This abortive move was the last diplomatic effort made by the French government on behalf of Republican Spain. The 8 August Cabinet meeting took note of the isolation of France, which could count only on Czechoslovakia and the USSR in Europe. It must also be conceded that the Russian government was merely lavishing kind words on the Spanish Republicans and waiting for France to take the first step on the path of intervention. The French ministers, who accepted the principle of sending Spain some fifty consignments intended in any case for export, did not think that it was possible to send artillery or air-force equipment from the Army's reserves. Blum was justified in thinking that a policy based on a continuation of this sort of intervention would only create diplomatic embarrassments, without any worthwhile returns: the Spanish Republicans would receive very little material and probably not of the best quality. Blum then contemplated resignation and only gave up his plan at the insistence of his Spanish friends Fernando de los Rios and Jiménez de Asua.

Nonintervention

It was in such circumstances that the French premier took

the initiative with a proposal for noninterference in Spain's domestic affairs, a proposal that was to be put to all the great powers as well as to the lesser powers who were directly involved.

The policy of noninterference or, more precisely, of non-intervention was without doubt a generous idea, a liberal principle adopted by England at the beginning of the nineteenth century against the active interventionism of the Holy Alliance and the Metternich system. In the mind of the French premier it was also a political idea: to bind Germany and Italy with an international pact, which it would be difficult for them to break, and to prevent them from giving effective aid to Franco. The proposal made by the French government would either call attention to the bad faith of the Central powers and would indirectly give France far greater freedom of action, or would in fact halt the Italo-German intervention.

Moreover, if a decision were made not to fight a war, or if the capacity to fight it seemed lacking, wasn't it necessary to use every means to prevent it? 'When one has responsibility for peace and war,' Delbos said on 6 December, 'one has no right to give in to emotional impulses.' The following day, Blum pointed out: 'I believe that last August Europe was on the brink of war, and I believe that she was saved from war by French initiatives.'

In fact, the problem of an international pact on the Spanish question had been raised on 1 August. Count Welczeck, in a letter to his government on 2 August, envisaged a joint move by four European powers, Germany, Italy, Great Britain, and France, 'to call upon the Spanish combatants to lay down their arms.' This proposal was not followed up, but on 1 August the French government appealed to the other countries, inviting them to conclude a nonintervention pact regarding the Spanish conflict. This appeal was followed by diplomatic approaches to each of the capitals concerned.

Great Britain's support for this proposal had been secured in advance; in it she saw approval of the attitude of strict neutrality she had observed until then. The Conservative government's memorandum on this subject stated that 'the

British government would be happy to see the rapid conclusion of a pact between the powers likely to supply arms and ammunition to Spain, so that they will abstain from doing so and put a stop to the supply of arms and ammunition from their respective territories. However, the British government is of the opinion that a pact of this kind must, from the outset, be accepted simultaneously by the governments of countries such as France, Germany, Italy, Portugal, and Great Britain who have large material interests in Spain or are geographically close.'

But in order to obtain a simultaneous declaration, unreserved agreement from Germany and Italy was needed. Against all evidence, Count Ciano stated on 3 August that there had been 'no interference, even indirect, by the Fascist government' and, wanting a reason for refusing to sign the French declaration, took cover behind the need to consult the Duce, who was in fact absent. The German foreign minister, von Neurath, replied in kind that the German government, since it was not meddling in Spain's domestic affairs, had no statement to make and that, in any case, it would be necessary to include the USSR in an eventual pact. These prompt and possibly contrived answers paved the way to a series of confused negotiations and time-wasting schemes that were actually intended to win time and to enable Germany and Italy to supply the Nationalists with the arms necessary for winning a victory which it was then possible to imagine would be a rapid one. In the reply sent on 6 August by the Italian foreign minister to the French ambassador, Chambrun, Italy raised three questions.

First of all, what was to be understood by 'intervention'? Didn't 'the solidarity expressed through public demonstrations, press campaigns, subscriptions, and the enrollment of volunteers already amount to a blatant and dangerous form of intervention?' The Italians mentioned the attitude of the French and Russian press in this respect, thus trying to show that a Franco-Soviet bloc had been formed against which every measure taken would be a defensive one. Similarly, when the French ambassador, François-Poncet, remonstrated with the German foreign minister about the help given to the rebels, von Neurath kept reminding him 'of deliveries made to Spain.' The Central powers had scored an initial point: giving one's support to the legal government of Spain was placed on the same footing as giving it to the insurgents.

The second Italian question was an attempt to find out if the commitment made by the governments would be binding only on states or on individuals as well. Its interest lay in the fact that from the outset the German and Italian intervention had taken shelter behind the fiction of sales by individuals or private companies.

Finally the Italian government raised the question of 'methods of control.' This objection was far more serious. The French plan for a declaration in fact provided only for 'communications between governments,' which would not amount to real control over the measures adopted. Was this kind of control possible? Did the French government itself have complete faith in its effectiveness, or would it have been satisfied with a declaration of principle that would have reassured public opinion and made really large-scale aid to the Nationalists more embarrassing? At any rate, it can scarcely be doubted that neither the Italians nor the Germans would have accepted effective control. The basic aim of their requests was to drag the matter out.

Berlin also asked questions that the French government was incapable of answering. Since the French ambassador was counting on favorable replies from a certain number of governments, the Belgian, British, Dutch, Polish, Czech, and in particular the Soviet government, von Neurath insisted that promises should also be obtained from the United States, Sweden, and Switzerland, knowing that Switzerland would take shelter behind her neutrality and that the United States would always refuse a declaration of principle that would offend a number of American subjects. The government of the Third Reich also asked what would prevent the Comintern from taking action, even if Soviet Russia had entered into international agreements as far as she herself was concerned; what control was in fact to be exercised over an international body? Finally, how could it be guaranteed that arms and volunteers did not cross the French frontier? 'I explained,' Count Welczeck wrote on 10 August, 'that France, as a frontier state, was in a privileged position and that the export of arms as well as the crossing of passes in the Pyrenees by volunteers were very difficult for the government to control.'[12] In fact, the Portuguese frontier was just as important, but the French government apparently did not think it a good idea to raise this argument, no doubt through fear of revealing the ineffectiveness or inadequacy of its plan.

Moreover, in spite of these objections, it did not seem as if Germany or Italy wanted to offer formal opposition to a pact. Neither of these two powers seemed really anxious, at this point, to unleash a European conflict. Germany was not yet wholly committed to the Spanish Civil War. Hitler did not feel that in principle a ban could greatly hamper traffic with the rebellion. Thus, on 17 August, the German government declared itself ready to fall in with the proposed pact, on condition that the decision would be valid for the other states and for private firms.

To meet these continually renewed objections, diplomatic overtures were made by France. Switzerland and the USA, while refusing to sign any document, stated that they were prepared to apply the embargo. This left Italy, which sought to delay completion of the agreement but finished by accepting the French plan, though not without many reservations. Her acceptance in principle was handed to the French ambassador on 21 August. Thus the majority of European powers had subscribed to the principle of noninterference and had even officially announced a ban on the export of arms intended for Spain. The French moderates, like the British Conservatives, could count themselves satisfied: the risks of a general conflict had diminished.

But it was still necessary to answer the Italian objection on methods of control. The truth was that the Italian government took little interest in serious control. Also it confined itself to asking for the establishment of a commission made up of delegates from the various powers, with the task of supervising the application of the embargo. No one dreamed of pointing out that this commission would be taking on authority that belonged by right to an international organization, the League of Nations. Perhaps the League's failure over the Abyssinian question was too fresh in people's minds. It was, at any rate, a clear sign of the disrepute into which it had fallen.

The Nonintervention Committee

All the powers declared themselves in agreement on the principle of forming a committee. But its precise role had not been defined. For the French government, it had to permit the establishment of a permanent link, and consequently real control, between the different countries: it was therefore necessary to invest it with political powers. For the German and Italian governments, which had no intention of respecting the declarations on the embargo, it was, in Dieckhoff's words, necessary to avoid 'this institution's becoming a permanent political instrument likely to cause us trouble.'[13] There was a contradiction between these two attitudes, but an English move led to agreement. *Entente* was reached with the definition of the committee as 'a simple *de facto* meeting of diplomatic representatives,' and, as such, having no powers of decision. It was agreed by the powers concerned that the delegates would merely have 'exchanges of views,' which could, in certain cases, become a more detailed examination of complaints made. Finally, an additional satisfaction was given to Italy, with France's formal consent: the Nonintervention Committee was to sit in London, and not in Paris or Geneva. It is remarkable that the diplomatic move by the French government in early August slipped from its grasp and passed to the British. The committee and its powers according to the French chargé in Berlin, were more an English invention.[14]

In spite of the desire for appeasement shown by the Western governments, negotiations dragged on for over a month, and it was only on 9 September that the committee's inaugural session took place in London, in a hall symbolically named the Locarno Room. Twenty-five powers were represented at it, including Lithuania and Luxembourg, but not Portugal, though she had accepted the principle of nonintervention.

The only practical result of this first session was to give the committee its definitive name of 'International Committee for the Application of Nonintervention in Spain.' The German chargé in London, Prince Bismarck, retained the impression that what mattered to France and England was not so much 'a question of taking actual steps as of pacifying the aroused feelings of the Leftist parties in both countries.'[15] For all that, this task of appeasement should have been fairly easy in England where, on 10 September, the trade unions had come out against any intervention in Spain, on a motion by Sir Walter Citrine, secretary-general of the TUC, and Ernest Bevin, secretary of the Transport and General Workers' Union. At the beginning of October, the Labour party conference, held in Edinburgh, endorsed this attitude, proxy votes providing a crushing majority in favor of nonintervention.

Meanwhile, since early October 1936, the international situation had once again been growing tense, in spite of the precautions taken by the committee to sweeten the tone of the debates and not to provoke excessively violent quarrels. Reports had piled up, which pointed to constant intervention in the conflict by Italy and Portugal, in spite of pledges given. There was first and foremost the dossier compiled by the Spanish Republican government and handed to the League of Nations. There was the report published on 4 October by a commission led by three British MPs, indicating aid from Italy and Portugal after the formation of the committee. Finally there was the decision taken by the Soviet government to make public a violent attack on Germany, Italy, and Portugal, accusing them of violating the nonintervention pact and threatening to withdraw from the committee: 'The Soviet government cannot, in any event, let the nonintervention agreement be transformed by some of those taking part into a screen for concealing military aid to the rebels. . . . Consequently, the Soviet government finds itself obliged to state that, if such violations do not cease at once, it will consider itself freed from its obligations under the agreement.'[16]

This Russian statement was the first of a series of notes

officially drawn up for the Nonintervention Committee; it provoked a lively response. Yet there was nothing unjustifiable in this communiqué. The accusations contained in it cannot be denied, and its conclusion is perfectly logical. But it had been agreed that the work of the Nonintervention Committee should be carried on *in camera* in order to avoid unrest and the dangers of a public discussion; by publishing its communiqué Moscow broke this vow of silence, and did so deliberately.

On the other hand, the violations of the nonintervention agreement by the Fascist powers were already known through Spanish documents. The Russians were not producing anything new. Why then did they wait to make this outburst, whereas they had long been acquainted with the facts? This can only be explained by conceding a radical change in Russian policy toward the Spanish problem during the first fortnight of October.

Be that as it may, there was no breach during the 'full and stormy session'[17] on 10 October. The chairman of the Nonintervention Committee, Lord Plymouth, presented the documents that had been handed to him in his own name and in that of the British government. He came up against a stay of execution from the accused powers, who confined themselves to stating through their delegates that the facts contained in the Spanish and Soviet statements were pure fantasy. The Portuguese representative, who was now sitting on the committee, adopted an even more uncompromising attitude: he left the meeting hall, though he added that he would not thereby cease to take part in the committee. If the Russians had intended to demonstrate the complete impotence of the Nonintervention Committee, they had fully succeeded.

Once again it was the French delegate, Corbin, the French ambassador in London, who saved the committee through his moderation; he asked the Russian government to suggest 'the means that it envisaged for making control effective.' 'The French premier's zeal in preserving the nonintervention agreement cannot be doubted, and his representative has played an especially salutary role in the committee's recent discussions,' wrote *The Times* on 13 October. The session was adjourned without a date being fixed for the next meeting, because it was necessary to obtain replies from the three indicted governments in advance.

These replies took a long time coming. This was the time of Franco's greatest military successes, and any control, especially over the Portuguese frontier, threatened to compromise the rapid victory anticipated by the Nationalists by hampering the arrival of reinforcements and arms. On 6 October the Russian government had asked for the dispatch of a commission of investigation to the Spanish-Portuguese frontier, but, without acceptance by the Portuguese, such a measure would have been unenforceable, had it been adopted by the Nonintervention Committee. The Russian delegate then asked for a watch on the Portuguese coastline. This new demand met with a negative response from Lord Plymouth. In such circumstances, it was difficult to envisage a diplomatic solution.

The aid given to the Spanish Republicans by the Soviet government after October provided the Axis Powers with an excuse to revive the discussion. Henceforth, the meetings of the Nonintervention Committee were mainly taken up with the accusations hurled at each other by the delegates from Germany and Italy, on the one hand, and the Russian representative on the other. On 10 November, as an unexpected conclusion to these discussions, the committee decided that the accusations had not been proved. Who could take such an attitude seriously? One had only to read the newspapers to find plenty of information about landings of Italian troops, the arrival of international volunteers, and the dispatch of arms and ammunition to both sides. Noninterference had become a tragic farce.

Plans for Control

In order to try and return to the problem again, the British government submitted a plan to the committee for the control of war material destined for the two sides, which provided for supervision of land and sea cargoes. This plan, put forward on 12 November, was finally adopted on 2 December, in spite of

Portugal's abstention. The length of the negotiations was the result of a fresh maneuver by Germany and Italy; adopting tactics already used successfully, they claimed that the British proposals were inadequate and asked, in addition, for air control. It is pointless to emphasize the futility of this request in the absence of representatives of the Control Commission at airports. Since supervision would have had to be exercised on the land frontiers of Spain and in her ports, it would also have been necessary, once the principle of control had been accepted by the great powers, to obtain agreement from both Spanish governments, a thing that could hardly be counted on.

Moreover, during the course of the same session on 2 December a new problem had arisen, which from then on took priority in the negotiations: the problem of volunteers. 'There is an urgent need,' Blum told Welczeck, 'to halt the influx of troops and war material.'[18] This urgency must not have seemed so evident to the great powers, because discussions continued throughout December. This was not of course the fault of the French government; on the contrary, the latter stated that it was ready to agree to 'control not only of the Pyrenean frontier, but also of its troop locations and airports, and its arms factories and other installations.'[19] It was a worthless proposal, because France was the only power to consider such a sacrifice.

To settle things once and for all, the British government then temporarily abandoned its idea of control and confined itself to asking each government to ban its nationals from any military commitment in Spain, to take effect on 4 January 1937. Even this plan, so limited in application, did not succeed in winning approval. Russia refused to accept a decision without control. Germany, Italy, and Portugal stated that the problem of intervention ought not to be only partially solved. By the end of 1936, the failure of the talks was so complete that even the British stopped persisting in them within the Nonintervention Committee, and the German foreign minister considered 'generally ceasing to maintain the committee system.'

This lethargy did not prevent negotiations from reopening when, on 8 January, Germany and Italy, acting in full agreement, framed a reply in which they declared themselves 'willing to agree that the question of volunteers should be the object, as was asked, of a special agreement that would ban recruitment and departures from a date in the near future.' In fact, the Italian government was the only one that would have willingly continued its delaying tactics, but it was forced to reckon with its German ally. The latter did not seem prepared to push things too far. It felt that the Nonintervention Committee provided an excellent screen, which ought to be preserved from destruction. There were still many leaders in Berlin who approved of the English attitude and did not wish to provoke a quarrel with the government in London. Also, in a note issued on 25 January, the two governments stated that they had already introduced legislation 'empowering them to ban departures by volunteers': they were merely waiting for agreement among the powers in order to put it into effect. This goodwill was however qualified by the fact that Berlin refused to allow Control Commission officials to operate in German ports. Control within Spain was also out of the question because of negative replies from the Nationalists and the Republicans.

At any rate, it was at last possible to glimpse some upshot to the interminable discussions held since the committee's formation. The plan for air control was abandoned by common consent as impracticable. Control on land, like control at sea, had to be effective, and the German government, feeling that the German-Italian troop dispositions were adequate as they stood, now called for an increase in the number of officials and posts. Presumably the 150 inspectors scattered along the French frontier would not at any time have been able to prevent smuggling altogether. And this was even truer of the Portuguese frontier, easier to cross, longer than the French frontier, and watched by the same number of inspectors.

Maritime surveillance was entrusted to an international naval patrol.[20] But, instead of setting up joint control, the plan divided the Spanish coast into five sectors, each to be guarded by one of the great powers. On 26 February, the USSR, which had the job of watching the Bay of Biscay, stopped taking part in the patrol, no doubt through her anxiety not to commit her already inadequate naval forces to an obviously pointless task.

Moreover, to entrust Germany and Italy with surveillance at sea, while Italy in particular had contributed handsomely to supplying Franco's Spain with warships, could seem farcical.

But it was true that the establishment of control could restrict any too obvious forms of intervention, and for the first time there was good reason for taking the Nonintervention Committee seriously. Even Portugal finally conceded the need to accept control; as we have said, the Anglo-Portuguese agreement, made on 21 February, provided for the deployment of 150 observers in ports and at transit points. The date of 8 March was even fixed for the start of the application of control measures. In a first phase, officers with the task of supervising control would appear in their assigned spots, but their work would only become effective after all the necessary officials had been recruited.

To the British government, this was merely a first step. Halting the flow of volunteers to Spain in March and April 1937, when the war had been on almost nine months, was comparatively easy, because the majority of foreigners coming to fight in Spain had already crossed the frontier. England therefore proposed, in order that the principle of nonintervention should be genuinely respected, that the volunteers should be recalled to their countries of origin. On this point, all hopes of agreement swiftly vanished. The Italian representative, Grandi, whose excesses of language had already often helped to inflame discussions, stated coldly, at the full session of the committee, that the Italian volunteers 'would not quit Spanish soil before Franco's complete and final victory.' The news of the Italian defeat at Guadalajara merely hardened this stand, since Mussolini was unable to consider leaving Spain after such a humiliation.

Thus, only the acceptance of land and sea control could restrict the powers' intervention in the Spanish conflict. But the coming into force of control during the night of 19–20 April 1937 swiftly demonstrated the futility of this policy. The Civil War had begun nine months earlier. It had taken eight and a half months of negotiations to attain a result whose limitations escaped no one, and which was again put into question in May:

eight and a half months of abortive discussion to reach an agreement that lasted less than a month and a half!

Behind these futile talks was a far more disturbing diplomatic reality. We have seen two aspects of it: the formation of the Rome-Berlin Axis, soon to be followed by the signing of the Anticomintern Pact, which included Germany, Italy, and Japan; and the isolation of France, which hesitated to pursue the Russian alliance, and which sought frequently reluctant English support. By 7 December, Blum admitted that 'a certain number of our hopes and expectations have in fact been disappointed.' After December, the French political error became still clearer, in that German-Italian intervention merely increased.

Notes

[1] Speech by Lloyd George to the Commons, after the capture of Gijón. Quoted by Bowers.

[2] On the temporary political system and the formation of the February 1938 government, see below, chapters 5 and 6.

[3] Archives of the German Foreign Ministry.

[4] There was an old dispute between the Germans and the Italians about influence in the Balkans. The German threat against Austria had provoked a violent reaction from the Italian government, not altogether happy about the stationing of Nazi forces on the Brenner. There was a fear of a revival of disputes about the Tyrol.

[5] Speech from the Duomo.

[6] Count Galeazzo Ciano, *L'Europa verso la catastrofe* (Milan: Mondadori, 1948; translated into English as *Ciano's Diplomatic Papers*, ed. Malcolm Muggeridge (London: Odhams Press, 1948).

[7] See chapter 7.

[8] Statements by Blum to the Commission of Investigation.

[9] Ibid.

[10] Churchill, *Step by Step*.

[11] Colette Audry, *Léon Blum ou la politique du juste* (Paris, 1955).

[12] Archives of the German Foreign Ministry.

[13] Ibid.

[14] Ibid.

[15] Ibid.

[16] Note on 7 October 1936; meanwhile the Republican government's protests had been handed to the nonintervention Committee.

[17] See *Le Temps*.

[18] Archives of the German Foreign Ministry.

[19] Ibid.

[20] It should in theory have applied to the limits of territorial waters (three miles from the coast) and of the high seas (ten miles from the coast).

CHAPTER 14

GERMAN-ITALIAN INTERVENTION

In Spain, from the moment that a plot had been organized to overthrow the Republican regime, the Monarchists and soldiers had naturally considered the help that Fascist Italy could provide them. This was in spite of any repugnance that the Spanish Monarchists and Catholics might feel for a regime that had been forcibly imposed on royalty and whose relations with the Church still remained precarious. There was no question of an agreement on principle, but there was one of common interest; in other words, something much stronger.

The first contacts went back several years.[1] Ansaldo, who had piloted Sanjurjo at the time of his first attempt at a *pronunciamiento*, as he did again on 20 July 1936, had a meeting with Balbo in 1932, at which the latter promised him Italian support. After the failure of the *coup de force*, Ansaldo returned to Rome with Calvo Sotelo in 1933.

The same year, the Nazi party seized power in Germany. On the eve of the *Movimiento*, Sanjurjo traveled to Berlin to make sure of Hitler's support as well. There were certainly encouraging noises from Berlin, but German rearmament was still only in its infancy, and it seems that the Reich government cautiously promised its support only when the uprising had been under way for a few days. In spite of the wishes of Rome and Berlin to see a sympathetic regime installed in Madrid, it was clear that both governments were sizing up the risks of failure. Even Salazar's Portugal, which was more interested still in the disappearance of Republican Spain, and whose proximity enabled left-wing propaganda to be leveled dangerously against the presidential government, respected certain forms. The field where Sanjurjo's plane had been forced to land at the start of the uprising was a makeshift airstrip, which partly explains the accident that befell the leader of the *Movimiento.*

Italian Intervention

Italy, however, had given more serious assurances. On 31 March 1934, an agreement had been reached between the Spanish Monarchist leaders and representatives of the Fascist government, and promises had been made about supplying material. As soon as even partial success was assured for the rebel troops, the promised aid was not long in coming.

From the outset, Italian intervention was swift and massive. During the war, everything was done to help Franco and to ensure victory. The Fascist leaders in fact regarded the Nationalist venture as a personal affair. Mussolini saw action in Spain as a chance to exhibit his talents as a military leader. He stepped up military conferences and gave orders to the Italian Navy that 'submarines should prevent warships from arriving in Red ports.' His own son, Bruno, exhibited his talents as an aviator in the Balearics.

The Duce's government made victory in Spain a question of prestige. This war was an opportunity for Italian arms both to triumph over an enemy other than the tribes of Abyssinia and to establish some important strategic bases in the Mediterranean. Thus emerged the dual Italian policy, which tried to impose itself in the Balkans and in Spain, in the eastern as well as in the western Mediterranean. The weight of Italian intervention cannot be explained by ideological considerations. Of course the struggle against 'Bolshevism' was being carried on in Spain, and the Italian soldiers fighting there were represented as 'crusaders for an ideal.' But this was only a facade. To Mussolini, supremacy in the Mediterranean was vital. And the Rome-Berlin Axis could only be formed after assurances from the Germans that they had no ambitions in that area.

Important issues were at stake. A considerable effort had been made to convince the Italian population of this, but they remained frankly unenthusiastic. Even senior officials such as Cavagnari, the minister of the Navy, did not show the enthusiasm that the Duce wanted them to feel. Though Fascism had thrown itself wholeheartedly into the Spanish adventure, the Italian masses had not followed.

The troops sent to Spain could have been made up partly of volunteers, selected primarily from officers on the active list. Ciano's *Diaries* bear this out: 'Cupini asked me for a command in Spain, and I gave him satisfaction on the spot.' But the name given to the Italian forces, *Corpo Truppe Volontarie* (CTV), must be taken with a grain of salt: recruitment was organized quite officially in the military offices and the headquarters of the *Fascio*, where there was talk only of leaving for Abyssinia or for an 'unknown destination.' And most of the soldiers intended for Spain were probably detailed from previously trained troops; at the beginning, this had been mainly from those who had fought in the Abyssinian campaign.

At any rate, it was not a question of isolated groups but of a genuine expeditionary corps, with its flags and its leaders. At first General Roatta had command; he relinquished it during the Biscay campaign to Bastico, who was replaced first by Berti and then by Gambara. Although its deployment in the fighting was always under the control of the general staff in Salamanca, the CTV preserved its individuality.

The Italian soldiers did not reach Spain in large numbers until November 1936, when their presence became necessary to ensure rapid success for the Nationalists. But from then on, considerable efforts were made. On 29 December Hassell reported the departure of 3000 Black Shirts, along with a contingent of 1500 technicians. On 14 January 1937 he announced a further reinforcement of 4000 men. At the same time the dispatch of a division, to leave between 24 and 26 January, was under preparation.

These shipments brought more than 50,000 men to Spain before the start of February 1937 and enabled four divisions to be trained and equipped. Later on, the number of Italians fighting in Spain fell slightly. At the end of January 1938, Mussolini mentioned 44,000 men to Goering; on 1 July 1938, according to the German ambassador, they numbered 40,075, to which must be added 8000 men sent by way of reinforcement a few days later, for a total figure of almost 50,000. If we add an undisclosed number of technicians, and if we consider that the four divisions present at Guadalajara were later reduced to two, it must be conceded that in March 1937, when the Italians were at their most numerous, there could not have been fewer than 70,000 of them. Eden referred to 60,000, but this was certainly below the true figure. The Italian contribution was all the more important because the forces that Franco and Mola were able to put into the front line at that time could not have exceeded 250,000 men.

The technicians had been necessary at the start of the conflict for the handling of air equipment to enable Franco to cross the straits of Gibraltar. It was urgent, and there was no time to train the Spanish airmen. The transport planes and bombers that flowed into Morocco and then into Seville were accompanied by their crews. It is certain that the presence of these planes in comparatively large numbers—at one time there were six Caproni bombers on the Seville airfield[2]—in addition to some Italian submarines made an effective contribution to transporting Moorish troops and the Spanish foreign legion.

Moreover, it was the presence of Italian planes in the Balearics that enabled the Nationalists to repulse the attempt made by government troops, fairly well armed but without any antiaircraft defense, to recapture Majorca. From this moment, the island of Majorca became the chief base for the Italian 'legionary' planes, which should not be confused with the planes handed over to the Nationalists. The Italians, Mussolini pointed out to Ribbentrop, had three airfields and a few warships permanently in Majorca. The planes that carried out almost daily raids on Valencia and Barcelona from 1938 onward took off from there. Mussolini and Ciano had certainly regarded the occupation of Majorca as the establishment of a strategic base that, by virtue of its position, must have greatly strengthened Italian power in the Mediterranean. However, at no moment was there any question on the Spanish side of giving the island up; on the contrary, Franco made a point of indicating in all his statements that he would not tolerate any foreign encroachment on Spanish territory. Here without doubt was an initial misunderstanding, which helps to explain the many Italian complaints about expenses incurred on behalf of the Spanish Nationalists and never repaid.

Moreover, Italy did not confine herself to sending planes—Caproni and Savoïa-Marchetti bombers, Fiat and Arado fighters, more than 700 in all—whose presence, precious as it was, did not in itself suffice to bring victory to Franco's troops. After the initial failures, Rome became energetic in the naval field. On this last point, Italian aid increased markedly: two submarines and two destroyers were delivered at the end of August 1937, and four new submarines in September, etc., according to Ciano's *Diaries*. Although it is hardly possible, with sources that are too often contradictory, to compile a precise record of the material aid received by the Nationalists, certain figures quoted by Colonel Vivaldi may be used as a basis: 1930 field guns, more than 10,000 automatic weapons, and 950 tanks. Armor and artillery accompanied the troops committed after February 1937.

Participation by the Italians in Military Operations

The Italian divisions were assembled in Seville during the early months of 1937, before they were sent to the separate Madrid and southern fronts. Faupel, the German ambassador in Salamanca, noted on 7 January that there were 4000 Black Shirts in Seville; 2000 more were on their way to this rallying point. He estimated that the whole of these troops would be committed within a fortnight. In fact there was a slight delay, and Roatta could scarcely put more than 5000 men at the disposal of the southern general staff for the first operation in which CTV troops were to take part. It was only a small local maneuver, which led to the occupation of Estepona in the Málaga sector on 15 January and of Marbella on the seventeenth. The major operation planned against Málaga was put off, but for only a few days, because on 18 January Faupel reported 20,000 men with two artillery batteries and 1800 trucks around Seville.

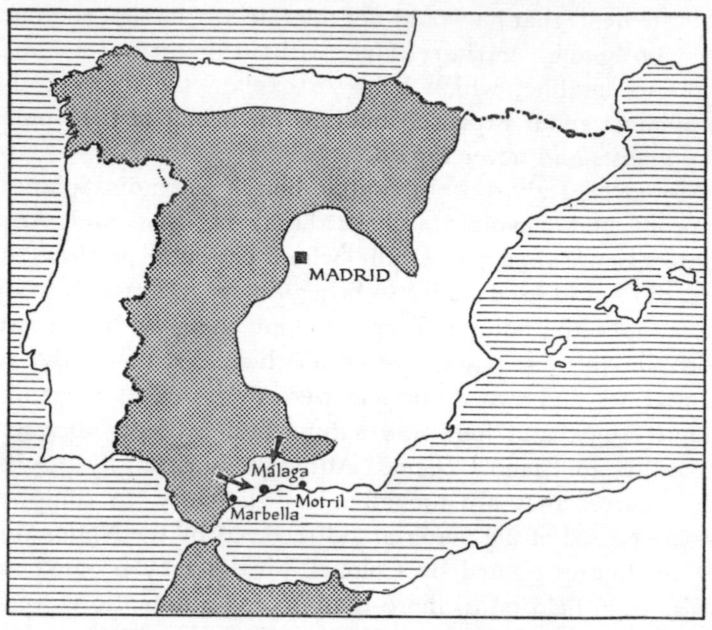

The Offensive against Málaga (February 1937)

It was natural that the Italians, armed and equipped in the South, should have been placed under General Queipo de Llano's command to take part in the only large-scale operation that was carried out in this sector during the whole of the war. On the other hand, the scheme, in the works since December, did not seem to present any major difficulties, in spite of the mountainous terrain; it was therefore an excellent test for Roatta's forces. Although Colonel Villalba, the defender of Málaga, did not have any well-organized troops and lacked arms and especially artillery, the Army of the South prepared its offensive with great care. The overambitious plan, directed at Motril, to try to encircle the defenders of Málaga had been abandoned in favor of a converging movement: the Spanish troops advanced along the coast, while three Italian columns from Antequera, where Roatta had set up his headquarters, Loja, and Alhama moved on the town from inland. The cruisers *Canarias* (from which Queipo supervised operations) and *Baleares* supported the offensive. The forces committed by Roatta were still limited to three Italian regiments, two mixed regiments, and two companies of tanks, supported by planes based in Seville.

The battle of Málaga may be regarded as one of the first successful lightning operations, thanks to the mechanized equipment at the attackers' disposal. The offensive had begun on 3 February, but there was no real contact before the fifth, proof of the weakness of the Republican defense. On the afternoon of the fifth, armored units made a deep thrust along the Antequera–Madrid road. In spite of the bad weather, which slowed down operations and prevented aircraft from intervening in the early stages, victory came extremely rapidly. On the morning of the eighth, the first Nationalist troops entered Málaga; on the tenth, Motril was occupied. With thousands of prisoners and tens of thousands of refugees blocking the roads and facilitating the Italian advance, there was a general stampede by the Republican Army, an encouraging result for the CTV. The occupation of Málaga was of great importance politically because it was a 'Red' town, and it was also an essential supply base. The Italians were in a better position to equip their divisions, now heading for Madrid.

The size of the Italian forces made it almost impossible to conceal the material and human aid now being supplied to Franco. In any case, after the capture of Málaga, Rome stopped disguising its intervention. On the contrary, it was stressed that the operation had been carried out by 'volunteers' and that the assault tanks and the Italian infantry had reached the town and left it behind. Even in cautious England, the *Manchester Guardian* did not hesitate to describe the battle of Málaga as an Italian victory.

On 9 March the attack began in the Guadalajara sector. Four exclusively Italian divisions, commanded by Generals Rossi, Coppi, Nuvolari, and Bergonzoli, were joined by mixed brigades of Arrows, Black Arrows and Blue Arrows, with Italian officers and NCOs. These Spanish contingents under Italian command survived until the end of the war. They remained in communication with the CTV to the extent that, in the closing months, the Arrows were incorporated into the CTV.

At the beginning of the battle of Guadalajara, the offensive was carried out by the Coppi and Nuvolari Divisions backed by the Spanish Moscardó Division, and with considerable armor, especially light tanks. The other two Italian divisions were held in reserve. But the maneuver grew in scope, and the whole of the CTV forces was soon involved, with 200 assault tanks. The result is known: failure and a rout, whose military consequences should not be exaggerated, but which dealt a severe blow to the morale of the Italians. Mussolini had expected much from the CTV. 'The rout of the international forces,' he wrote to Mancini, 'will be a triumph of great political as well as military bearing.' On 2 March, the Fascist Grand Council hailed the imminent victory that was to mark 'the end of all Bolshevik designs on the West.' And on 9 March the Italians jeered at their Spanish allies: 'Why so many months to take a defenseless town?'

But the enemy's bitter resistance and its propaganda by leaflet and loudspeaker soon affected the morale of the legionaries who thought they were all set for a triumphal march. On the sixteenth the officers were reminded of their responsibilities: 'The troops are lacking in dash' and 'tend to overestimate the enemy.' 'A state of exaltation' had to be created by showing them that their enemies were 'the brothers of those whom the Fascist squads had thrashed on the roads of Italy.' But, a few days later, the situation had worsened. Some Black Shirts inflicted wounds on themselves; others deserted. 'Even the best and bravest troops have cowards in their ranks.' It was too late to check their flight. The Italian command itself asked Franco to relieve the CTV.

This defeat, after the boasting of the Italian leaders, was the cue for jokes on the part of their allies; the Germans in Salamanca said that, Jews and Communists though they were, the men of the Eleventh Brigade had fought like Germans and were able to thrash the Italians. Moscardó's men sang:

Guadalajara is not Abyssinia.
The Spanish, though Red, are brave.
Less trucks and more balls.

But there were more serious things than songs or even the

incidents that broke out between Spaniards and legionaries—as in Tangier on 26 March. Guadalajara had been a grave defeat for Fascism. The Italians had shown that they were not prepared to die for Mussolini's ideal.

The Italian high command, disappointed, agreed to restrict the attacking power of the expeditionary corps. The four Italian divisions were reduced to two, the *Littorio* and the *23 March*; only the brigades of Arrows were kept as they were. The forces thereby reconstituted provided a greater capacity for resistance. The useless and incapable were no longer put in the front line. Henceforth Italy did not send any more large contingents, except to replace losses incurred. The latter were heavy: more than 1500 killed and wounded at Guadalajara. During the first twenty months of the war, the Italians lost 11,552 men killed, wounded, or missing in Spain.[3] The total dead was 6000.

Such casualties naturally added to the bitterness caused by the reverses. The Italian leaders and generals, who had advocated massive intervention in the hopes of a large military success and a rapid victory, were wondering if their troops should remain in Spain. They shed responsibility for the mistakes on the Spanish command. 'Our generals are worried, and they are right,' said Ciano.[4] Mussolini himself betrayed his impatience. On several occasions after December 1937 there was talk of withdrawing the volunteers. But these were mainly outbursts of bad temper. The Italian interest in this affair was too great for there to be any serious question of abandoning it. In the end, the CTV remained to the last, 'to give proof of Italian solidarity.'[5]

Italian Debts

The Italians shared in Franco's triumph. But they had paid heavily for it, not only in terms of human lives and by abandoning a large quantity of heavy equipment, but also by the considerable sums spent on the operation. 'Mancini told me,' Faupel reported on 18 January 1937, 'that Italy had invested up to 800 million lire in the Spanish affair.'[6] Mussolini himself stated, during a conversation with Goering, that expenditure by the end of the same year, 1937, was 4500 million lire.[7] By the end of the war, it had reached 14,000 million lire. Part of the sum thus spent was later repaid by the Nationalist government, but only part. At that time the Italians had contemplated seeking compensation in eventual economic advantages. But here too, results were disappointing. At the beginning of 1937, Mancini complained that Italy had not, 'so to speak, derived any profit from Spain.'[8]

Commercial relations improved later. In November 1937 Ciano noted with satisfaction the arrival of 100,000 tons of iron, of which the Italian war industry stood in particular need. Other compensations could also be envisaged: 'There is also,' said Mussolini, 'a political problem.'[9] The Italians wanted 'Nationalist Spain, saved exclusively by Italian and German aid, to remain closely linked with their system.' On the other hand, the financial aspect of the problem was also linked with the political aspect. 'Only if Spain remains within our system can we be fully compensated.' This system was the German-Italian Axis. Henceforth Mussolini looked to Nationalist Spain's entry into the Anticomintern Pact.

But on a practical level the results of political negotiations between Rome and Burgos were slender. Hopes of setting up strategic bases in Spain had been dashed. The only important point scored by Italy was the 28 November 1936 agreement, the official aim of which was to 'develop and strengthen' relations between both countries. The agreement consisted first of a Mediterranean pact: the two powers were to carry out a joint policy and give each other mutual aid in the western Mediterranean; along with this went a nonaggression pact, a promise of benevolent neutrality in the event of conflict, and finally a promise of economic *entente*, underwritten by the application of a preferential tariff to the cosignatory. It is none the less remarkable that the first undertaking to which Italy subscribed, by signing the protocol, was to give Spain 'her aid and support for the preservation of the country's independence and integrity, as much on the mainland as in the colonies.' Italy thereby relinquished all hope of receiving, in exchange for her unrepaid expenditure, any territorial compensation. 'We are giving our blood for Spain. Isn't that enough?' Ciano asked in March 1938. In fact, Italy had also given a lot of money, but in vain.

German Intervention

In this field at least, German moderation contrasted with the Fascist government's lack of caution. Naturally, Germany had far less immediate interest in the Mediterranean than Italy, and total victory by Franco was not absolutely necessary to her government. It is unquestionably true that Berlin was not seeking any political advantage in Spain, because the Germans had no illusions on this subject: they did not suppose that National Socialism could ever be introduced in Spain, and the German leaders' sympathies for Franco remained extremely delicate. Also it was felt in Berlin that an agreement that did away with the Extreme Left and steered Spain away from an alliance with the West would be a satisfactory solution. In the same way one of the considerations of the war was to expose the natural hostility that existed between Italy and France.

Moreover, German military circles did not have unlimited faith in the abilities of the Spanish generals, including Franco. On this point, the Italian and German general staffs were in complete agreement and did not hesitate to pass on to Burgos advice that was seldom heeded. In any case, the Wehrmacht was not anxious to commit excessively large forces to an adventure that it regarded as a dead end.

The Nazi government was unquestionably concerned with Franco's ultimate success. But its aid in terms of manpower was still slight. According to General Sperrle, 6500 Germans arrived in Cádiz in November 1936. But this mass arrival was exceptional. The Germans never totaled much more than 10,000 men. These were often specialists and cadres. Certain officers and NCOs were singled out to train Spanish cadres, and in particular to handle the training of Falangists. A letter written by Faupel from Salamanca on 10 December 1936 confirms this: 'I am asking with all urgency for the largest possible number of Spanish-speaking officers and NCOs. I am asking for Major von Issendorf to be released from his cavalry command to take over the training of the Falange. Also for retired Major von Frantzius, of the Spanish-American Institute,[10] to be sent as head of the infantry training school, and retired Major Siber to take over the training of intelligence units.' The arrival of these cadres, and no doubt of a few reinforcements, during the course of January 1937, explains the thanks sent by Franco to Rome and Berlin.

The officers in question were to serve in Spanish units. But the majority of the German technicians were together in a special formation, the Condor Legion. Organized after November 1936, when Republican resistance had intensified, it originated with the existence, earlier on, of a group of technicians, comprising in particular antiaircraft-artillery specialists and pilots. Berlin had agreed to send personnel but posed peremptory conditions: the German formations were to be put in the hands of a German commander, Franco's only adviser where they were concerned. A German command was in fact set up in the Hotel Maria-Christina in Seville, under Colonel Warlimont. Thus an effective force was built up, consisting mainly of aviation: a bomber group, a fighter group, and a strengthened reconnaissance unit. Three antiaircraft regiments, several signal units, a few detachments of marines, and four armored companies, each one having twelve tanks and a company of mine detectors, joined it. It was commanded by pilots: first Sperrle and then von Richthofen.

Its recruitment was carefully organized. There was a headheadquarters W... in Berlin under the Luftwaffe general Wilberg. The men of the Condor Legion were certainly detailed, but the advantages they received, good pay and the lure of adventure, often served as a decisive argument. The pilot Galland told how he had been selected for Spain, like many of his colleagues who suddenly disappeared over a period of six months. He was summoned to the W... office, which had the job of organizing the departure of the 'volunteers' and provided civilian clothing, papers, and the necessary money. The pilots left in the peaceful guise of tourists sent on leave by the 'Work through Joy' organization. Their postal address remained Berlin. Though detailed, Galland was none the less content with his lot and seemed to find it very interesting to take part in the Civil War. Arriving in Spain, once again in military olive drab, he was finally posted to the Condor Legion. With his fighter group, he moved from one front to another according to the fighting, wherever danger was most apparent: the German pilots had nicknamed themselves 'Franco's firemen.' Moreover, the Caudillo had recognized the importance of their aid; he made a special reference to it in a speech to the last commander of the Condor Legion, von Richthofen, at his farewell procession. The effectiveness of the German support, although it was less substantial than Italy's, was mainly accounted for by the perfect organization that ran this venture and the value of the material placed at the disposal of the Nationalist Army.

Arms aid by Germany evidently went further than the equipment of the Condor Legion. In fact, a large part of the material that the Nationalists possessed was German in origin. Franco had a confidential agent in Berlin with the job of supplying all the necessary details of Nationalist Spain's arms and ammunition requirements. The equipment arrived at first through the ports of Galicia and the South controlled by the Nationalists or else through Portugal, where the steamships *Kamerun* and *Wigbert* were sighted on 22 August 1936. After the proclamation of the embargo on arms for Spain, there was even talk of sending them through Holland. But such detours were very involved, whereas the German government had been informed of the urgency of the Nationalists' needs. 'It is material superiority that will carry the day,' Voelckers was writing by September 1936. Accordingly, the ammunition ships took a more direct route. Though, according to General Sperrle, in November 1936 there was only one squadron of Junkers 52 bombers, one of Heinkel 51 fighters, one of Heinkel seaplanes, and one battery of 88-mm antiaircraft guns, they were later joined by air groups (four squadrons of twelve bombers each, a fighter group of equal size, and twelve reconnaissance planes) companies of engineers, heavy antiaircraft batteries, and searchlight units.

This force, very useful in the early months of the war, became inadequate when Russian material began to reach the

Republicans. The first German planes were slow, and the Civil War fighting exposed their defects in comparison to the Russian planes, or even the Italian Savoïa-Marchettis. However, shortly after Galland's arrival in Spain, at the beginning of May 1937, new planes arrived from Germany. The bombers were Heinkel 111s and Dornier 17s, and the fighters, which gave the Nationalists overall air superiority, were the fastest and most easily handled planes used in the conflict, Messerschmitt 109s, which reappeared during the Polish and French campaigns.

HISMA

German material and munitions continued to be sent to Spain throughout the war, except during the brief period of the Czechoslovak crisis in September–October 1938. An actual business firm had been set up by the Germans, who took the opportunity of giving the Spanish affair a degree of profitability. Hitler of course directed operations personally and took the important decisions, as Mussolini did in Italy. But, once the orders were given, their execution was in the hands of the foreign organization, the *Auslandsorganisation*. Admiral Canaris, head of the *Abwehr*, that is, the German intelligence services, took charge of it, but it was a member of the *Auslandsorganisation*, Johannes Bernhardt, a businessman living in Morocco, who played the leading role in Spain. To make German aid to Franco easier, Bernhardt formed a transport company, the *Compania Hispano-Marroquí de Transportes* (HISMA Ltd. for short), whose first operation on 2 August was to transport Moroccan troops to Spain.

Corresponding to HISMA, operating in Spain, was an export firm set up in Germany with the help of General Goering,[11] ROWAK. The establishment of the HISMA–ROWAK tandem meant that a mass of overly obvious transactions and movements by the representatives of Franco and Mola in Berlin could be avoided. From now on, every shipment of material passed through these companies. HISMA in particular forwarded war material landed in Lisbon and the Nationalist ports. But the traffic soon increased beyond the scope of mere shipments of material, and the firm never stopped growing. In

October 1936, von Jagwitz, Goering's confidential agent, who ran ROWAK for the *Auslandsorganisation*, set up office in twelve rooms of the Columbus Haus in Berlin. Thus there was a fleet at the organization's disposal.

The power of this firm and Bernhardt's real authority in Berlin as well as in Nationalist circles enabled the HISMA representative in Spain to act in the best interests of Germany. One of the Berlin government's constant worries was in fact to make Franco recognize the debts that Burgos owed. In October 1937 von Stohrer reckoned up the monetary losses incurred by Germany until then, in order to present the bill to the Nationalist government: 'The costs incurred by the Germans are calculated at 90 million marks, plus a bill of 70 million marks for supplies to Spain.' Toward the end of the war, undersecretary Weizsäcker again reckoned up the costs involved. It was no longer a question of losses incurred by individuals, but of the expense of maintaining the Condor Legion up to November 1938 as well: on the one hand the cost of personnel, 75 million reichsmarks, and on the other the cost of material and equipment, far greater, since it totaled more than 190 million reichsmarks. It seems certain that this estimate was still well below the true figure, because a note from Sabath stated that the total expenditure rose to as much as 500 million reichsmarks.[12]

Berlin was as yet only asking for a recognition of debts. The Germans intended to be paid, but not necessarily in money. Besides, in 1939, Nationalist Spain was incapable of paying back the sums owed to Italy and Germany. All that she could do—and she did it for Berlin—was to accept the principle of repayment by annual installments. It is notable that in this respect Germany received greater satisfaction than Italy.

In reality, Berlin's aspirations were both vaguer and broader. It was a question of the 'restoration of Germanism in Spain.' A note by von Stohrer on 14 April 1939 drew up the balance of German infiltration into Spain: police agreement; cultural agreement of January 1939, which assured both parties of considerable advantages; establishment of cultural institutes enjoying financial subsidies; German schools in Spain that could issue diplomas equivalent to secondary schools in Germany; cultural cooperation fixed by exchanges of students, professors, and teachers; and exchange of radio broadcasts and films, but with an added guarantee that certain literary works banned for political reasons in one country would be banned in the other.

This positive record must also include the promise of preferential treatment for Germans returning to Spain to take up their work again, the Spanish-German friendship treaty to which we shall have occasion to return, and Spain's membership in the Anticomintern Pact, which was a joint success for Germany and Italy.

From the economic point of view, there was no treaty during the entire war that governed the exchange rates between Spain and Germany. The only existing agreement expired at the end of 1936 and was renewed only for a year.

In such conditions, all the negotiations that took place were based on a single document, very general in scope and significance, the 15 July 1937 protocol. The latter, signed by Ambassador Faupel and Minister Jordana, explained that 'both governments have a genuine desire to help each other in the provision of raw materials, foodstuffs, and manufactured and semimanufactured goods of special interest to the importing country. Similarly, both governments will take note as far as possible of the other's interests where exports are concerned.' All this remained very vague. Spain was mainly concerned with maintaining her balance of payments through the export of agricultural produce to Germany.

German-Nationalist Mining Agreements

The problem to which Berlin attached the most importance was that of the German-financed mining companies in Spain, which were supposed to send essential raw materials to Germany for her war industry. Since the beginning of the Civil War, the Germans had been interested in the mineral resources, copper, tungsten, and bronze, of Spain and Spanish Morocco. In January 1937 it was pointed out that the Zeghenghen iron-ore mines, near Melilla, were being worked by German staff.

The occupation of the Rio Tinto copper mines and the conquest of Asturias made the handling of Spanish ore the chief concern of the German authorities in Spain.

On 20 January Faupel wrote that HISMA had been promised that it would receive up to 60 percent of the output of the Rio Tinto copper mines. At the beginning of 1938, Bernhardt compiled a record of mining exports to Germany during the past year that showed that more than 2,500,000 tons had been sent, including 1,600,000 tons of iron ore, some of it already coming from Bilbao.[13] These figures were substantial ones; however, to be sure of maintaining them, Berlin not only needed a Spanish promise about exports, but control over production by the Germans themselves. It was to this end that Bernhardt was instructed to negotiate, on behalf of HISMA, the establishment and financial control of mining-development companies.

However, this time, German economic infiltration ran into serious resistance. The obstacle was a decree on 9 October 1937, issued under pressure from a group of Spanish technicians and financiers.[14] This decree annulled the mining concessions granted since the beginning of the Civil War. Officially, its aim was to denounce the concessions made by the authorities in Valencia. In reality, Germany was the target. The law prohibited foreigners from having more than a 30 percent financial interest in the mining companies. Possibly this decision should be seen in the light of the overtures made to Nationalist Spain at the same period by the Anglo-Saxon countries (before the war England received the lion's share of Spanish ore).

Germany then appealed to the Nationalists' sense of friendship. We are caught up, Bernhardt said in his report, 'in an economic war'; we are 'justified in expecting immediate supplies from Spain.'[15] The end in view was the forming of a HISMA-Montaña pirate firm, with the task of acquiring all or part of the shares in mining companies, whereby Germany would control their development. 'We must,' said Bernhardt, 'put our diplomatic, military, and cultural influence at the disposal of a single end, economic ascendancy.'

On 12 October 1937 the HISMA officials protested against the degree on the mining companies. This was the beginning of a series of diplomatic moves to obtain a share of at least 50 percent in these firms. An initial meeting took place on 20 October between Jordana and two delegates from HISMA, Pasch and Klingenberg; the Spanish rejected 'the parity of reciprocal treatment,' requested by the Germans. A conversation took place on 3 November 1937 between Bernhardt and the secretary-general, Nicolás Franco. Two sops were offered: first, a promise from the Burgos government that the demands made by HISMA would be examined upon the formation of a genuine government;[16] and secondly, the advice that an immediate request should be made to the Burgos Junta to obtain authorization to carry on with mining operations already in hand; moreover, that this request would be favorably received.

But Spanish-German relations had at this point entered a difficult phase. It was impossible, even for the ambassador, von Stohrer, to obtain firm promises from the Generalissimo. Besides, difficulties were being created by the entry of German goods into Spain,[17] and import licenses were being refused. Goering, supporter of strong-arm methods, then talked of sending von Jagwitz to Salamanca, in order to 'point a pistol at Franco's chest.' In fact, the prolongation of the war and Franco's material needs enabled Berlin to acquire in the long run what it had been unable to obtain at once.

Henceforth negotiations were handled simultaneously by Bernhardt, on behalf of HISMA–ROWAK, and by the new ambassador, von Stohrer, qualified for such a job by his past, a brilliant man but in the tradition of conspiratorial diplomats.[18] The joint move, which they made on 20 December to the Generalissimo, proved that 'HISMA and Reich representation are one and the same thing.[19] Franco's attitude during this meeting was not very encouraging: 'I am amazed,' he said, 'that HISMA, which I have instructed to regulate trading and payments, is also trying to acquire mining rights, and acquire them secretly.' Nevertheless, he agreed to the establishment of a mixed commission to study cases.

Finally, new legislation for mines in June 1938 gave the Germans satisfaction. Foreign ownership of the capital of Spanish mining companies was fixed at a maximum of 40 percent, and the possibility of an increase was not out of the question. 'The law,' said Bernhardt, 'makes it entirely possible for us to take part in the mining of the Spanish subsoil, as we wished.'

However, the decree was drawn up in such a way that it depended wholly on the goodwill of the Spanish for the Germans to be able to obtain the majority or the parity that they requested in the mining firms. Bernhardt then proposed that 20 percent of this capital should be open to public subscription and reacquired by Spanish figureheads in HISMA–Montaña. Naturally this solution could only work if the government agreed to close its eyes. Threats to suspend deliveries of arms and munitions were enough to make the Nationalists give way, since their supplies of material were completely dependent on Rome and Berlin. In November 1938 five anonymous companies obtained HISMA–Montaña mining rights.[20] According to the terms of the law, Germany had the right to 40 percent of the shares; in fact, an increase in German holdings was provided for, which could, in the Aralar company for instance, amount to as much as 35 percent of the capital.

At the same time, in view of the fact that the mining law was applicable only on the Spanish mainland and not in Morocco, HISMA–Montaña bought large holdings in the Rif mining-development companies, and the Nationalist government agreed to guarantee the establishment of a company called *Mauritania*, with its registered offices in Tetuán, which was to be exclusively German. Spanish-German economic negotiations also led to other substantial advantages, which HISMA obtained by means 'of various firms which it assumed control of.'[21]

A special role was entrusted to Nova, which was not only given the job of constructing the Spanish broadcasting network, but also contemplated playing an important part in Spain's postwar economic reconstruction, in aerial weaponry, army equipment, troopships, economic defense tasks, increased Spanish exports to Germany, and investments and supplies of machinery.

This was the record of the economic progress achieved.

Berlin had spent a lot of money and had made a large material contribution, but while part of this material was recoverable, the rest was altogether too obsolete to be of any use to the Wehrmacht. In the end, the lessons learned from the fighting and the fact that mining products essential to German rearmament were arriving and continued to arrive throughout the World War largely compensated for the expenses incurred.

Membership in the Anticomintern Pact

Politically, the results were less satisfying. Yet two agreements had been signed. The first was the 20 March 1937 protocol, which seemed to be largely inspired by the Spanish-Italian agreement; in it can in fact be found consultations on problems of common political concern, the principal of nonaggression, and the idea of benevolent neutrality in the event of war with a third power. But the Civil War had ended before a genuine friendship treaty was signed, to remain in force for five years beginning 31 March 1939, and couched in terms that were far more solid and precise than the 1937 protocol. There was however no question of an unconditional alliance.

On 27 March 1939 a protocol had been signed in Burgos by the ambassadors of Italy, Germany, and Japan, as well as by Jordana, then foreign minister in the Nationalist government: Nationalist Spain joined the Anticomintern Pact. As Mussolini had hoped in 1937, she entered the Axis's system of alliances. Whatever wrangles and difficulties might have arisen among the allies,[22] a financial and moral debt now bound Franco to his partners.

Notes

[1] These contacts are known mainly through Lizarza's *Memorias de la conspiración en Navarra* and through Juan Antonio Ansaldo's *Mémoires d'un monarchiste espagnol* (Monaco, 1953).

[2] Report by the German consul, Draeger.

[3] Including 2352 dead and 196 missing.

[4] Ciano, *Diaries*.

[5] It was involved in many operations, on the northern front at Bilbao and Santander, in the breakthrough to the north of Teruel, and in the

fighting in the Ebro loop. See extracts from the Italian press in March 1938 quoted by André Jacquelin, *Espagne et la liberté* (Paris: Kérénac, 1945).

[6] Archives of the German Foreign Ministry.

[7] Mussolini-Goering meeting in November 1937, reported by Ciano.

[8] Archives of the German Foreign Ministry.

[9] Quoted by Ciano.

[10] When he was chosen as ambassador to Spain, Faupel himself had been director of the Spanish-American Institute in Berlin since 1934. It is interesting to note that the recruitment of German agents began with official organizations.

[11] Goering however dealt personally with everything concerning the Spanish Civil War, economic negotiations as well as air support.

[12] It is true that the note from the legation adviser Sabath added 'both simple and compound interest' to the sum due for direct supplies to the Spanish Army.

[13] For the month of December alone, consignments of tin leaving Bilbao rose to 90,000 tons; exports originating from Morocco totaled 100,000 tons.

[14] Including Zabala, director of the Biscay mines.

[15] Bernhardt report on the Montaña project, 4 November 1937. Archives of the German Foreign Ministry.

[16] It was formed two months later.

[17] Stohrer's 27 November report.

[18] During the First World War he had been first secretary at the embassy in Madrid and had been removed because he was suspected of having taken part in a plot against the Count of Romanones.

[19] Archives of the German Foreign Ministry.

[20] They were: La Compañía de Explotaciones Mineras Aralar, in Tolosa; La Compañía Explotadora de Minas Montes de Galicia, in Orense; La Sociedad anónima de Estudios y Explotaciones Mineras Santa Tecla, in Vigo; La Compañía de Minas Sierra de Gredos SA, in Salamanca; and La Compañía Minera Montañas del Sur, in Seville.

[21] This was true of the Agro company, which bought and developed farms around Seville, and especially the *Sofindus*, which owned 90 percent of the shares in a cork factory, the Corchos zum Hingste, as well as the Compañía General de Lanas, the Sociedad Exportadora de Pieles, and the Marion transport company, which had sole charge of Sofindus transport.

[22] The meeting that should have taken place between General Franco and Goering in May 1939 was in actual fact the occasion of a series of difficulties between Spain and Germany and led to the prompt recall of Bernhardt.

CHAPTER 15

RUSSIAN AID AND THE INTERNATIONAL BRIGADES

To the Russians, as to the Italians and Germans, Spain had been a testing ground. The test had been mainly one of material. They had succeeded in gaining precious information about the value of their arms compared to those of the Fascist powers, Russian Ratos compared to Messerschmitts, for instance. They had learned valuable lessons from the experience of war: the use of artillery barrages, the need for maneuver in depth in a manner adapted to new fighting techniques, and the use of guerrillas against an organized army. A large number of Russian army cadres had enjoyed a highly informative stay in Spain.

On the other hand, it should be pointed out right away that without the contribution of Russian material Republican resistance could not have continued beyond 1936.

Stalin's Russia and the Spanish Civil War

This indispensable aid, however, was never adequate. The Republican troops continued to be short of air equipment, antiaircraft weapons, and even small arms throughout the entire conflict. With this in mind, it is impossible to present as a wholehearted attempt at solidarity help that for a long time had been enough to carry on the struggle but that, had it been more generous, would undoubtedly have tipped the scales conclusively in favor of Republican Spain. This fact has even prompted politicians and especially former Spanish Communists to attribute an extraordinary Machiavellism to the Russian leaders, lastly crediting Stalin's policy with a simplicity and continuity[1] that were persistently contradicted by the facts during this period.

Without considering any problems but those raised by the Spanish conflict, it is possible to distinguish three successive attitudes in the USSR's policy during this period: first, a *de facto* position of neutrality, accompanied by clear-cut evidence of sympathy and solidarity; after October 1936, a substantial contribution in military aid, with a correspondingly vigorous attitude in favor of the Republic on the Nonintervention Committee; finally, after summer 1938, a gradual slowing down of military aid, ending in the total abandonment of the Republic.

Initial Neutrality

During the early months of the conflict, the USSR refused to intervene on the side of the Spanish Revolution. In fact, Stalin's government had no reason either to encourage or to aid the revolutionary organizations, the CNT–FAI and the POUM, whose role was vital at that stage, and which did not have any particular sympathy for the Russian political regime. Furthermore, there were still no diplomatic relations between the USSR and Spain. There was talk of opening them, but five years of a Republic had not been enough to produce even so slender a result. Finally, Spain was in Stalin's view only a very minor element in a disturbing international situation. Russia did not wish to be involved in any conflict. She was afraid of isolation and was still caught up in memories of the prewar years, which, with the failure of the revolution in Hungary and Germany, had aligned the Western powers against 'Bolshevism.' Renouncing the spread of world revolution, with Stalin the USSR was trying to build Socialism in one country, and at the same time protect herself by a system of foreign alliances. Hitler's accession to power was a direct threat. The conclusion of the Franco-Soviet (Laval-Stalin) pact in 1934 was a riposte, a first step toward security. Yet this alliance remained tenuous and could not be regarded as effective unless it extended to Great Britain, which did not seem altogether taken with the idea. The Léon Blum government's vacillating attitude and its eventual position of cautious neutrality were not exactly calculated to encourage Stalin to embark on a hazardous adventure in Spain. Thus, when the nonintervention campaign was launched, the USSR joined it without hesitation. On 31 August the decree, banning 'the export, the reexport, and the shipment to Spain of all types of arms, munitions, war material, planes, and warships' was made public in Moscow, as well as in the West. As it turned out, this decree was respected for only a month at the most. In mid-October, Russian material, loaded on Russian and foreign ships, was already beginning to arrive in Spain.

The Turning Point in Autumn 1936

There had thus been a first turning point, due to various factors that had all ultimately conspired to modify Russian policy in the same direction. Initially there was the general emotion that the Nationalist *pronunciamiento* and the popular reaction aroused in the world, and more particularly in left-wing circles in Western countries. It seemed impossible that the 'country of Socialism' should hold aloof from the general move to help Spain, at the risk of losing many of her foreign supporters. It was said over and over again that the leaders of the Western Communist parties, and especially Maurice Thorez, were echoing the misgivings of the militants at the imminent defeat of the Spanish Popular Front, which, after the failure of left-wing forces in Italy and Germany, had inspired them with great hope.

But most important, the Spanish conflict had become too widespread for the Moscow government to remain in the wings, in spite of the moderation it had shown. The intervention of the Nazis and especially of the Italian Fascists was too obvious. General Franco's victory would look to everyone like their victory, and consequently like the failure of the USSR's policy, the more so as Russian intervention was striving at that time to appear in the eyes of the London and Paris governments as

9. Militiamen patrolling a street in Madrid

10. Observing the fall of Barcelona

a move in support of the European *status quo*, for the sake of democracy and peace.[2]

It is also perhaps advisable to indicate a reason deriving from domestic policy. The Spanish epic was diverting the attention of part of the militant opinion in the USSR from the purges aimed at Stalin's enemies;[3] furthermore, under cover of aid to Republican Spain, it would be possible to ask the Russian workers for an extra effort to raise production, which could not fail to contribute toward the achievement of the objectives set by the Five-Year Plan of 1933.

Be that as it may, the decision to intervene in Spain had been announced at the beginning of September, according to Krivitsky, at a conference of senior officials in Lubianka, attended by Orlov, who was one of the all-powerful official representatives of Stalin's police in Spain. Since this decision was contrary to the principles affirmed by the USSR and the other powers on the Nonintervention Committee, it had to remain as discreet as possible; private firms had been formed by the beginning of the same month to handle the purchase and transport of arms from Russia via Odessa to Spain.

Material Aid

Shipments followed each other between October 1936 and February–March 1937 at the rate of thirty to forty ships of varying tonnages per month. Consignments of clothes and foodstuffs, substantial even before October, increased with the considerable growth in the activities of the Internal Committee for Aid to the Spanish People. The USSR sent some gasoline and trucks, which the nonintervention agreement did not in fact prohibit, but mainly arms and planes. More than 50 percent of the planes used by the Republicans between August 1936 and April 1937 came from the USSR. According to an American State Department document (25 March 1937), out of 460 Republican planes, there were 200 Russian fighters, 150 Russian bombers, and 70 Russian reconnaissance planes. They were mainly Katyusha bombers and I.15 and I.16 fighters, superior to the early German planes, but far inferior to the Messerschmitts. Almost all the tanks were also of Russian origin: the 12- and 18-ton tanks were fast and well armed.[4] However, there were not enough of them, and most of the time they were mishandled, although they were at least as valuable as the enemy's tanks from Germany and Italy. Artillery, which was in short supply, consisted mainly of 76-mm field guns and heavy guns, which the Republican Army lacked.

Moreover, not all the material coming from Russia was brought by Russian ships, nor was it necessarily Russian material. Neither was it always of the best quality: President Aguirre mentioned rifles 'dating back to the Crimean War,' and Krivitsky, referring to purchases made in Poland, Czechoslovakia, and even Germany, spoke of 'old but useful material.' There was nothing remarkable about this: the French material that crossed the frontier during the early weeks was also old and sometimes in poor condition. Spain was not merely a testing ground for new weapons; she also provided the means of selling off old material that was cluttering up military supply dumps at a good price. It should not be forgotten that there was a commercial aspect to this traffic. The USSR did not give away its arms to Spain, any more than Germany did to Franco: from the earliest negotiations, it had been assumed that the Bank of Spain would finance these supplies.

The dispatch of most of Spain's gold to Russia later gave rise to violent controversies among the Republican leaders. Today, they can be boiled down to one question: did responsibility for the operation rest solely on Negrín, minister of finance at the time, or did he share it with others, Largo Caballero, the premier, and Prieto, minister of war? At the time of the Nationalist advance on Madrid, a Cabinet meeting decided to place the Bank of Spain's gold in safekeeping. An initial transfer took place, from Madrid to Cartagena. On 25 October 1936 the gold, estimated at 510,079,529 grams, was sent to Odessa under the surveillance of four Spanish officials. Prieto had saddled Negrín with responsibility for this consignment. Álvarez del Vayo replied that the decision had been taken by Largo Caballero and Negrín and that Prieto had been in the know. It is certain in any case that the initial transfer to Cartagena had been made with the approval of the ministers, and it is hardly likely that so important a decision as the departure of Spain's gold could have been taken without the premier's agreement.[5]

The dispatch of the gold to Russia came at the time when Russian aid was greatest. It is more than likely that a large part of it was in fact used to pay for arms purchases abroad. Moreover, the traffic created by the Spanish Civil War was far from negligible for a modest export trade such as Soviet Russia's: Spain became her second-best customer, and the turnover in this trade was twenty times what it was before the war.

Naturally, this traffic was very difficult to conceal: the length of the crossing meant that convoys could easily be spotted, and Italian submarines had no trouble observing their movements through the central Mediterranean. Russia's aid provided Germany and Italy with an excuse to counterattack on the Nonintervention Committee and to try to set the USSR at odds with the Western countries. It also enabled England to maintain a fictional neutrality, by claiming that she was thereby preserving an equal balance between the two belligerents. Stalin was afraid of finding himself isolated in diplomatic talks, as too often happened to his representatives on the committee. On the other hand, after Franco's reverses at Madrid, hopes of a rapid Nationalist victory had vanished. The prolongation of the war was probably favorable to the policy of the USSR, which saw the Spanish conflict as a running sore that was diverting part of the German and Italian forces.

This explains both the continuation of and the reduction in Russian aid. Moreover, the application of maritime control measures by the powers on the Nonintervention Committee hampered the arrival of material and led to a definite falling off of consignments by spring 1937. The USSR, which did not have large naval resources and was not anxious to commit them rashly, refused to take part in the control but as a consequence found Republican Spain's Mediterranean coasts guarded by German and Italian warships. Finally, after December 1936, in order to change the measures for restricting the arms trade to Spain into a virtual blockade, Italy resorted to actual piracy against Russian ships and any ships that might be transporting war material from Russia. The first ship to be torpedoed in these circumstances seems to have been the *Komsomol*, although it is hard to tell if responsibility for it should be attributed to the Spanish Nationalists equipped with submarines or to the Italian Navy itself.

Russian Aid: Men

While it is necessary to stress the reduction in Russian aid starting in 1937, it must also be remembered that, no matter how restricted it was, it had enabled the Valencia government to continue its resistance. On different occasions, even during 1938, and especially during the battle of Aragon, Russian material represented the only substantial outside aid. This fact alone could suffice to explain the immense influence won by Russian advisers over the political and military development of Loyalist Spain. It also enabled her enemies to accuse Negrín of being Russia's agent. The premier had made a political choice and justified himself by refusing to fall out with the only state that was at that time supplying substantial aid to Spain.

Mention must also be made of the work of Nationalist propaganda, which had systematically 'inflated' Russian aid. Even ignoring certain gross exaggerations, it was not uncommon to hear talk on the Nationalist side of thousands of men sent to Spain. What is actually remarkable is the numerical weakness of the Russian troops in Spain. In 1939 Brasillach and Bardèche estimated that there had never been more than 500 of them. Others, such as Krivitsky and Cattell, conceded slightly larger figures; at any rate, the Russians had never totaled more than 1000, mainly specialists, tank crews, and airmen, retaining, like the Germans on the Nationalist side, their own command and installations, at a distance from the civilian population.

This of course left the role of the 'Russian technicians.' The diplomats first of all were, it seems, genuinely devoted to the Spanish cause, but nearly all of them had been recalled during 1937 and had disappeared afterwards, imprisoned or executed. Among those who had disappeared were Marcel Rosenberg, the USSR's first ambassador to Madrid, Antonov-Ovseyenko, consul in Barcelona, Stashevsky,[6] the commercial attaché who negotiated the arms deliveries, and Mikhail Koltsov,[7] as though the idea were that no one should survive who could testify to this political intervention, unless it was that their disappearance had seemed a necessary prelude to the abandonment of Spain. With the diplomats or immediately after them came the military advisers, numerous and influential but little known, whose true identities were only rarely disclosed: Generals Gorev, organizer of the defence of Madrid, who aroused nothing but sympathy in those who were close to him, Grigorovitch, Douglas, commander of the airmen, Pavlov, commander of the tank crews, and Kolya, who commanded the sailors. Among them, under borrowed names, were some of the great military leaders of the 1939–1945 war. A first group had arrived on 28 August with Rosenberg, another in September, and a third in October. 'The generals are always changing,' Koltsov told Regler, 'they come to learn their trade, and since defeats are more instructive than victories, they do not remain long.' It seems at any rate that apart from the headquarters where the Russian mission worked, all the top Republican leaders had had at least one Russian technical adviser on their staffs.[8] All had been under constant supervision from agents of the NKVD, the all-powerful political police, in Spain under Orlov.[9] The NKVD must also be credited with a large number of foreign Communist militants who came from Russia with the Comintern apparatus, such as Gerö and a few others, whose activities were more police ones than political or military.[10]

The First International Volunteers

Apart from Russian troops, there were foreign Communists trained in the Soviet Union who played a vital role in the organization and officering of the International Brigades, because there were practically no Russians in the brigades except, paradoxically, White Russians.[11]

In fact, along with intervention by foreign troops on the side of the Spanish Republic, the aid that came from outside was in the long run merely the result of a large number of individual contributions. In contrast to what happened on the Nationalist side, where the German and Italian leaders prepared and organized the dispatch of armed contingents, no government, except that of the USSR—we have seen to what extent—played a vital part in the struggle on the Republican side. However, it was mainly on the Comintern's initiative that it was possible to organize this aid.

No doubt, during the early months of the war, at the time of the revolutionary militias, a small number of foreigners had come of their own accord to fight in the Republican ranks: foreigners already living in Spain such as the Italian Socialist De Rosa, or who had been there for one reason or another when the uprising occurred, such as those taking part in the Spartacist games in Barcelona, who had immediately supported the Catalan workers. This was how the first groups of foreign volunteers were formed, and they were joined by Italian, German, French, and Belgian antifascist militants from France. This was also true of the small group that formed on the northern front and which took part in the defense of Irún, Germans from the Thaelmann Centuria, Italians from the Rosselli Column, French from the Commune de Paris Centuria, Italians from the Gastone Sozzi Centuria, who defended Madrid on the sierra, and foreigners who joined the Durruti Column.[12]

But the first instance of a sizable organization was the international airforce established by André Malraux. The *España* Squadron made a huge contribution, at least in the early months of the war, at a time when the government's bomber force was completely nonexistent. In spite of their small number of planes—about twenty—the men of the International Brigade were the only ones whose actions had some effect, especially with the bombing of the Nationalist Column in Medellin, which, as its head pointed out, was the only operation carried out in the grand manner by the Republicans during the first part of the war. In the same way, their fighter force—some forty planes—effectually relieved the Republican air force, which only had some old Bréguets. Yet these improvised squadrons could not contend with the more modern and of course faster German and Italian planes. The *España* Squadron completed its final mission with an attempt to protect the retreat from the machine guns of the enemy fighters.[13]

The International Brigades

In November 1936 the first Russian planes that could bear comparison with the enemy's appeared. It was also in November that the International Brigades were committed to the Spanish front. Whatever their political views, journalists and writers have always stressed the influence of the commitment of the International Brigades on the stiffening of Republican resistance. They formed a *corps d'élite* involved in all fighting of any importance until the end of 1938. On 7 November they were in Madrid, and on the thirteenth they took part in the fighting on the Cerro de los Angeles: in December, they turned up in Teruel and Lopera, on the Cordova front. In February–March 1937 they fought on the Jarama, at Málaga, and at Guadalajara. They were later involved in all the major offensives, at Brunete and Belchite, at Teruel, and finally at the battle of the Ebro, where they took part in the last Republican offensive.

The decisive role they played in all the theaters of the war may have given rise to the belief in the existence of a numerically very substantial force. There is talk in Spain, even today, of hundreds of thousands of foreign volunteers in the brigades. Without its being possible always to determine figures and to go into fighting conditions, a more serious study reveals infinitely lower numbers.

Who were these combatants? Where did they come from? How were they prepared and launched into battle? At the start, it seems, only individuals enlisted in the Republican militias. Then the foreigners gradually regrouped in separately organized units. These combatants were antifascists, mainly Germans and Italians, expelled from their countries by the Hitler and Mussolini regimes, who chose this occasion to renew their struggle against the dictators, but also some Frenchmen, numerous because of the proximity of the country, the ease of crossing the frontier, and the natural *rapprochement* that existed between the two countries where the Popular Front had just triumphed. In fact, these individual enlistments could not have had a serious bearing on the balance of military forces and, more often, merely added yet another heterogeneous element to an already very ill-assorted army.

By the end of September aid to Spain had its first taste of organization, especially in the recruitment and dispatching of volunteers. The governing cell was recruited from leaders of the French Communist party and Italian political refugees. The committee in charge of recruitment was, according to Longo, run by Giulio Ceretti, known as Allard. Another Communist, Josip Broz, later Marshal Tito, organized the dispatching of volunteers from central Europe.[14] Luigi Longo, known as Gallo, shared responsibility with the French Communist party apparatus for getting the volunteers across. A large number had already passed through the organized channels by 22 October, when the brigades were officially born. At the beginning of the month, a delegation made up of three Communists, an Italian, Longo, a Pole, Wizniewski, and a Frenchman, Rebière, was received by Azaña and later by Largo Caballero.[15] The three men were finally sent to Martínez Barrio, who was in charge of organizing the first brigades of the Republican Army. Agreement was easily reached, and thus it was that the first International Brigades appeared in November 1936.

Recruitment of the Brigades

Of course, recruitment remained an individual matter. The volunteers from all countries assembled in France, after which they arrived in small groups, across the Pyrenean frontier. In fact, in spite of the diversity of the organizations in charge of enrollment—enlistment took place in offices established on the premises of trade-union organizations or left-wing parties—it was the Communist party that had overall control of the operation. It was also in charge of the dispatching of the volunteers as far as Spain. Moreover, there were no obstacles to crossing the frontier, even though it was officially prohibited.[16] In Perpignan there was actually a barracks for the international volunteers, who moved freely about the town. In February alone, more than thirty-five trucks crossed the frontier without running into difficulties. Moreover, the French Communist party had duplicated the frontier convoys by means of boats that under cover of a shipping company, France-Navigation, transported the volunteers. Longo, referring to the first volunteers, stated that 500 came through Figueras and 500 from Marseilles to Alicante on the *Ciudad de Barcelona.* Delegations for the brigades were set up in all large Spanish towns to welcome the newcomers. But, while the question of transit was thus solved, the organization of the original force, as constituted by an international army of volunteers, raised special problems.

It is very difficult, as we saw, to determine with any precision how many men were in the brigades; most of the documents have disappeared and even former leaders cannot agree on the figures. Without doubt the most common tendency is to exaggerate them: the Fascist countries have tried systematically to inflate the numbers of what they called Red volunteers, and the antifascist parties and national groups have themselves tended to present their contribution as greater than it actually was. According to Victor Alba, in June 1937 there were 25,000 French, 5000 Poles, 5000 English and Americans, 3000 Belgians, 2000 'Balkaners,' and 5000 Germans and Italians, making a total of at least 30,000. Taking into account the continual coming and going, and the fact that the volunteers kept arriving until the beginning of 1938, a total figure of fewer than 50,000 men can hardly be advanced; in practice this figure is probably greater than the true one. If the number of men in a brigade is calculated at a maximum of 3500, since the brigades were rarely at full strength, this makes a total figure of 30,000. And probably even this was not attained. Malraux's opinion is that the total number of volunteers did not exceed 25,000 men. This is also the view, a very well-founded one, of Vidal Gayman. According to him, there were never more than 15,000 men in action at any one time, of whom about some 10,000 were combatants, at the point when the brigades were at their greatest strength, in the spring and summer of 1937. This number later fell: casualties were heavy—the number killed was about 2000—and many of the volunteers, wounded, weary or disheartened, left without being replaced by the same number of new arrivals.

Of this total of 25,000, the French were unquestionably the most numerous, although their fighting quality was often inferior to that of the German or Italian contingents, recruited from *émigrés* who had already paid for fighting for the cause in their native lands with exile. As the result of an economic crisis that had shaken Europe and whose repercussions could still be felt in spite of an economic recovery stimulated by the manufacture of war material, there was still a lumpen proletariat in France that enlisted to fight in Spain for not always disinterested motives. This explains certain statements made in France to the pro-Nationalist press by men who left without being very sure of themselves and who were quickly disheartened by the severity of the fighting. The number of French volunteers also varied the most, along with opinions of their conduct. The Fourteenth and Fourteenth A Brigades were mainly French, but there were other Frenchmen in the Commune de Paris Battalion in the Eleventh Brigade, the Franco-Belgian Battalion in the Twelfth Brigade, and the Henri Vuillemin Battalion in the Thirteenth Brigade. Once again a classification of this sort is difficult, because these battalions were constantly being reshuffled and integrated with new units, according to the needs of the moment or the casualities incurred. The work carried out by the Association of Volunteers for Republican Spain to try to discover the exact strength of the brigades showed about one-third of the volunteers as French, certainly fewer than 10,000 men and often confused with the Belgian volunteers. To this Franco-Belgian group may be added a Polish one, mainly recruited from the mining areas of France and Belgium.[17] Thanks to their contribution, the total number of Poles who fought in Spain was certainly more than 4000 men.

Another substantial contingent of volunteers was supplied by German and Italian *émigrés*. They played an especially important role in the officering of the brigades. Among them were some political cadres, mainly Communists. The Italians and Germans sent nearly all their leaders: the Socialist Pietro Nenni, the Communists Luigi Longo (Gallo) and Di Vittorio (Nicoletti), and the Republican Pacciardi, among the Italians; the Austrian Socialist Julius Deutsch; and the German Communists Hans Beimler and Franz Dahlem. Other countries sent few 'national' leaders, with the exception of André Marty, but many 'middle-level cadres' and, especially in the case of the French, leaders of the Communist Youth.

This leaves the volunteers from the Anglo-Saxon countries, the English, Canadians, and Americans in the Lincoln Battalion, a few hundred men of each nationality; from central Europe mainly Yugoslavs, but also Hungarians, Czechs, Bulgarians, and even Albanians, arriving by every known means, even on foot. Others came from even further afield, from Asia and Africa. Altogether, fifty-three countries were represented in the brigades.[18]

The senior cadres, like the troops, were of all nationalities, French and Italian of course, but also Germans, Hungarians, and Poles. The officers with the most important posts were more often than might be expected of central European origin. The Communists were in the majority, which made a Nenni or a Pacciardi stand out all the more.[19] Many of them had fought in the Great War, some had been regular officers, and others had received their military training in Moscow. Sometimes they had undergone both kinds of training: such as Hans Kahle (Lieutenant Colonel Hans), Wilhelm Zaisser (General Gómez), the Hungarian Mata Zalka (General Lukacz), the Pole Karol Swierczewski (General Walter), all combatants in the Great War who had become Communist militants and had sometimes taken courses at military academies in the USSR. The same was true of some former combatants with more limited political responsibilities, the Frenchman Dumont,[20] the German writer Ludwig Renn, Gustav Regler, and the Hungarian Colonel Gal, Bela Kun's one-time companion; and of the most mysterious and most famous of all the leaders of the International Brigades, General Kléber, whom many contemporaries regarded as the hero of Madrid's defense.[21]

The Base at Albacete

The first problem facing the organizers of the brigades was to give a certain unity to such heterogeneous forces in order to integrate them into the Spanish Army later on. The volunteers, on arriving in Spain, had to find assembly and training centers, which would enable them to be split up according to their origins and their abilities. It was to perform this role that the center in Albacete was initially set up.

The town had not been chosen at random: the Fifth Regiment, in fact, already had a base there. Longo, helped by Vidali (Major Carlos), had got ready the premises that were to receive the first men of the International Brigades. A headquarters was improvised there that, with the collaboration of the Spanish, had mainly to procure the necessary material for quartering and feeding the men who were arriving in ever greater numbers. Everything was not perfect in the early days, and they were even short of water for washing. Gradually, however, the most urgent problems were solved.

The Albacete headquarters, composed mainly of Frenchmen, worked in constant liaison with the Spanish military authorities. The men of the International Brigades were sent wherever the danger was most pressing, at the request and on the orders of the Spanish command. Naturally, the duality of power between military command and commissariat, familiar in the Popular Army, was met with again at Albacete. Military questions fell within the scope of the French officers, especially Vidal Gayman, 'Major Vidal,' and the political leadership was in the hands of Di Vittorio, Longo, and, in particular, André Marty. The latter owed this crucial post of 'leader of men' to his career as a militant and to his reputation as an old revolutionary. But the man who had long been 'the Black Sea mutineer,' and no doubt a victim of his own legend, became, to many of his detractors, 'the butcher of Albacete.'[22] Even if most of his crimes are to be believed, it must be admitted that this pugnacious old grumbler was not the ideal leader for such a composite troop. However, Gayman stated that he never departed from his political functions and meddled neither with the appointment of officers nor with the handling of operations.

The base rapidly ceased to be merely a reception center for freedom fighters. On the one hand it became a mobilization center for units at the front or in the process of being constituted, and on the other hand it became a center for training and general control of the services. Training camps were set up in the neighborhood, as well as a military academy for officers and political commissars. There were many and diverse services, because it contained a workshop for repairing equipment and, later, a grenade factory. There was even, for a certain time, a stockyard full of beasts abandoned at the start of the Civil War and brought from Estremadura, where they had been wandering for months. More essential, however, were the postal and transport services. Postal censorship of letters written in some forty languages posed a complicated problem. Means of transport, almost nonexistent at the start—'three motorcycles and a few old cars'—were improved. The car-park was well maintained by volunteers, former Renault and Citroën workers.

The health service was the most important. Of course, there were Spanish hospitals, but they were concentrated in Madrid, which caused real difficulties because of the bombing of the capital. The isolation of wounded members of the International Brigades among Spaniards, whom they very often did not understand, had unfortunate repercussions on their morale. At first they were given private rooms in Madrid hospitals. Then an attempt was made to put them together. By October six doctors, under Dr. Rouques and then Dr. Neumann, had organized the medical service: field hospitals, ambulances, and mobile evacuation groups. A woman doctor, Struzelska, organized the Murcia International Hospital and four hundred annexes in the region. Rest and convalescence centers were set up. Ambulances and medical equipment came from Paris. To finance these achievements, the volunteers temporarily gave up two-thirds of their pay.[23]

Organization of the Brigades

We have dwelt here solely on the problems peculiar to the brigades, since their organization and the difficulties of arming them were the same as those of the other Republican troops. We shall merely note that, in addition to the infantry brigades, there were some international artillery groups, the Gramsci Battery, the Anna Pauker Battery, and the Skoda Battery, the oldest.

As to the command, there had never been, any more than in the whole of the Republican Army, a very clear-cut distinction between the political commissar and the unit commander. The commissar's role was initially that of a supervisor: he wore a special uniform. The importance of his role varied according to his personality. It was a remarkable fact that, although the commissar at first had to devote himself mainly to human problems, especially complex in the brigades, he ended by becoming the commander's deputy, relieving him of material questions, the evacuation of the wounded, medical and postal services, and food problems. Toward the end of the war, political commissariat and command finally merged everywhere, thus reestablishing the unilateral command of classic armies, rather more clear-cut than in the rest of the Republican Army.

The experienced officers who ran the brigade also made a substantial contribution to the training of Spanish soldiers, many of whom eventually served in international units. This was because they changed progressively, first by organizing themselves according to the needs of the moment and the growing number of volunteers, then because the volunteers became less and less numerous. From the outset, in the interests of training and command, the general staff of the brigades tried to group the men according to their countries of origin. It was thus that the Thaelmann and Edgar André Battalions were made up of Germans and a few Austrians. The Garibaldi Battalion, one of the first combatant groups, which played a decisive role at Guadalajara, was exclusively made up of Italians. However it was not always possible to group the combatants in this way, the number of nationals from certain countries making it difficult to form homogeneous units. On the other hand, the volunteers had to be integrated as they arrived, and this could only happen in training units. In this way the Gastone Sozzi Battalion included Italians and Poles. The Ninth Battalion of the Fourteenth Brigade was known as the 'battalion of nine nationalities.' The Italian Pencheniati told us about the Dimitrov Battalion, whose commander was the Bulgarian Grebenarov, and whose political commissar was the German Furman.[24] Difficulties were even greater in the case of large units, the brigades themselves sometimes being hastily formed to go up to the front with the least possible delay. In this way the Twelfth Brigade, on its formation, included a German battalion, the Thaelmann Battalion, an Italian one, the Garibaldi Battalion, and a Franco-Belgian one. Later on, there was an attempt at regrouping, with the Thaelmann and Edgar André Battalions transferred to the Eleventh, and the Fourteenth being almost exclusively made up of French battalions. The heavy casualties incurred in the early fighting speeded up this tendency, forcing the Albacete headquarters to make a complete reshuffle. By November 1936 the Commune de Paris Battalion had lost the equivalent of two platoons. In Teruel, between 28 and 31 December 1937, the Twelfth Brigade lost half its men. Thus units disappeared: the Louise Michel Battalion was merged with the Henri Vuillemin after the initial clashes. Taking these reshuffles into account, and relying on the table of international units compiled by the AVER,[25] the permanent presence of five brigades can be established: the Eleventh, whose commander was Kléber and whose commissar was Beimler, the Twelfth, whose commander was Lukacz and whose commissar was Longo-Gallo, the Thirteenth under Zaisser-Gómez, the Fourteenth under Walter, and the Fifteenth under Gal. Some of the international elements were merged directly with the Spanish Army, while Spanish recruits were incorporated with brigades. According to Longo, this merger became necessary in March 1937.

This was how the dual role of the brigades in the Republican Army emerged. With their gallantry and enthusiasm, they formed an élite troop ready to be assigned to the toughest fighting. With their capacity for resistance and their aggressiveness, they served as an example and, in some respects, as a school. Their small numbers, however, meant that they could only be committed on limited fronts. Their efforts were in vain, especially after the collapse of the North. Besides, the great international surge to the defense of the Spanish Republic in 1936–1937 did not reoccur: from 1937 on, the Communist parties dissociated themselves from mobilization in the name of antifascism. The fact remains that the brigades existed, and that they played a crucial role in several decisive battles. It is for this reason, among others, that a man like Gustav Regler, after his split with the Communist party and the collapse of the illusions on which he had based his life as an outlaw, can, even today, rejoice wholeheartedly at the memory of the enthusiastic brotherhood of the International Brigades.

Notes

[1] Thus, to Jesús Hernández, Stalin was capable of deciding the exact date of the fall of Largo Caballero's government and even that of the final defeat later on.

[2] Significant in this respect was the speech made at the *Monumental* cinema meeting on 30 October 1936 by Marcel Rosenberg: 'I am not inviting anyone to take part in a crusade against one or another regime, because it would be contrary to our very conception of democracy to want to impose our way of thinking on others by force. It is merely a question of acting in such a way that the democracies that are fighting for peace may work together and unite.' See also José Díaz's speech to the Cortes on 1 December 1936 (*Tres años de lucha*, pp. 227 ff.), and his appeal to the democratic governments of France and Britain, threatened by the preparations of Germany and Italy for world war. The propaganda of the Western Communist parties took up the same theme: *L'Humanité*, at the end of August 1936, adopted the rallying cry: 'With Spain, for the safety of France.'

[3] The existence of the Spanish Revolution and the help that the USSR gave it were to many militants pressing reasons for silently accepting the bloody purges in Moscow. André Gide described the pressures that were put on him, in the name of the Spanish militiamen, to stop publication of his *Retour de l'USSR*. At the time, fellow travelers such as André Malraux and Louis Fischer justified their silence over the Moscow trials by the need not to imperil the unity of Spain's defenders.

[4] We have followed fairly closely here the figures compiled by David Cattell, *Soviet Diplomacy and the Spanish Civil War* (Berkeley: University of California Press, 1957).

[5] The Russian government's version was that the gold had been entirely consumed in feeding and arming Spain. After Negrín's death and, it seems, on his instructions, his family handed the receipt for this gold to Franco's government.

[6] It is interesting to note that Marcel Rosenberg and Antonov-Ovseyenko were both former Trotskyists. Antonov-Ovseyenko, former colleague of Trotsky, former commissar-general of the Red Army, had been one of the leaders of the 1923 opposition. The choice of these men gave rise to much discussion. Was Stalin setting a trap for them? Was he trying to compromise them by putting them under close supervision? (It was said in Barcelona that Antonov was scared of Gerö.) Did he want to test out a

11. Refugees resting on their way to France, February 1939

12. Republican troops entering France at La Perthus, 7th February 1939

loyalty whose sincerity he doubted? Shot on Stalin's orders, Antonov-Ovseyenko was one of the first Communists rehabilitated by Khrushchev.

As for Stashevsky, Krivitsky regarded him as the man actually responsible for Russian policy in Spain and stated that it was he who put forward Negrín's name as Largo Caballero's successor. Álvarez del Vayo confirmed Stashevsky's excellent relations with Negrín, easily explained by the fact that in 1936 Negrín was minister of finance and Stashevsky commercial attaché.

[7] We have already indicated, in chapter 10, the substantial political and probably military role played in Spain by Mikhail Koltsov, whose brilliant intelligence no enemy disputed. His somewhat complicated psychology as a 'lucid Stalinist' can be glimpsed through the autobiography of Regler, who remained loyally attached to him. Like Rosenberg and Antonov-Ovseyenko, Koltsov disappeared, liquidated without trial in the great 1938 purges. The disappearance of his name from all official works was however the only evidence of his condemnation by Stalin. He too was rehabilitated by Khrushchev, and his Spanish diary republished: the official version of his death today is 'exhaustion due to overwork.' The death of Koltsov and of the entire team that accompanied him doubtless meant the liquidation of the antifascist line so remarkably expounded in his book.

[8] The true identities of the Russian officers was a well-kept secret, as were the exact dates of their stays. Krivitsky said that the head of the Russian mission was General Berzin, whose true identity was known only by half a dozen Spaniards. But he did not mention his *nom de guerre*. Berzin, according to him, was recalled and shot in Moscow. For the period 1936–1937, Álvarez del Vayo mentioned General Grigorovitch. Louis Fischer, Barea, and most former Spanish Communists stressed the role played by General Gorev, and Colodny even suggested the hypothesis that Grigorovitch and Gorev were two pseudonyms for the same officer, Berzin. But a reading of Fischer, who knew Gorev and Grigorovitch, rules out this supposition. All one can say is that Berzin was perhaps the man known as Gorev.

Witnesses concur about Gorev's role in the defense of Madrid. He is clearly the same man mentioned by Hernández, Castro, Fischer, and Arturo Barea, who described him as 'a handsome man, tall and strong, with high cheek-bones, ice-blue eyes, a facade of calm, and behind it constant tension.' According to Fischer, Gorev was recalled and shot in 1937 or 1938, which does not weaken the hypothesis that he was really Berzin.

Grigorovitch was, according to the official Russian source, *Questions d'Histoire*, General Stern. Castro had said so beforehand, and this identification can be regarded as certain. Again, according to Fischer, Grigorovitch was replaced by General Grishin, and then by General Maximov—probably the General Maximovich mentioned by Gustav Regler.

Among the other Russian officers, Fischer, who visited them a lot, mentioned Colonel Valois, alias Simonov, adviser to the International Brigades; Nicolas Kusnetsov, known as Kolya, head of the naval mission, later admiral and commissar to the Navy, and 'Fritz,' Lister's adviser. He also stated that the future Marshal Zhukov fought in Madrid during the winter of 1936–1937. All of them refer to General Kulik, known as Kupper, Pozas's adviser, though with much less sympathy. El Campesino mentioned Malinovsky, alias Colonel Manolito, Rokossovsky, and Konev. General von Thoma told Liddell Hart that he had already fought Konev in Spain—was this the tank expert with the shaven head who was Gorev's aide and who turned up under various names, such as Pavlov, Pablo, and Konev? Possibly. *Questions d'Histoire* confirmed Malinovsky's presence, adding Meretskov and Rodimtsev, then a captain. It pointed out that Comrade Douglas, the air chief, was in fact General Smushkevich. President Aguirre preserved an excellent memory of General Jansen, who was in command of the Russian airmen in the North.

[9] Gustav Regler was however struck by the atmosphere of the Russian mission: 'No hint of Muscovite suspicion; the Fascist raids erased the memories of revolver shots in the back of the neck and OGPU arrests. The Revolution bred confidence. Heroic Spain gave these men the souls of partisans' (*The Great Crusade* [New York: Longmans, 1940], pp. 326–327). He discovered to his stupefaction that they were celebrating with champagne the departure of an engineer of whom it was common knowledge—Koltsov was to tell him—that he had been recalled to be shot. Koltsov was always saying: 'If one day I have to be shot . . .' (ibid.). The NKVD network in Spain was, according to Krivitsky, set up by Sloutsky. According to Ettore Vanni, its senior official was Velayev. Fischer knew Velayev and Orlov, both attached to the embassy.

[10] The intervention by the NKVD in Spain provoked, even within its own ranks, a very serious crisis, of which Krivitsky's split was but one manifestation. Before him, one of the most important agents in Western Europe, Ignace Reiss, a Polish Communist known in the service as Ludwig, had broken publicly with Stalin and joined Trotsky's Fourth International. It was he who had warned Trotsky, Victor Serge, and their friends of the decision taken in Moscow to exterminate Trotskyists and POUM members in Spain. He was murdered at the beginning of September 1937 near Lausanne, on the eve of a meeting in France with Victor Serge and his friends. The inquiry later examined foreign Communists and officials of the Russian trade mission in Paris, including Lydia Grosovskaya, who was released on bail and took advantage of it to disappear.

[11] Such as the former general in Wrangel's army who became a groom in exile and who enlisted in the brigades in the hope of earning a return to his country, serving under Walter, his enemy during the Civil War. A platoon commander, he met his death in action.

[12] Note among these volunteers Simone Weil in the Durruti Column. However, her career as a militiawoman was cut short very soon by a serious accident.

[13] André Malraux gave a remarkable description in *L'Espoir* of the difficulties of his task, first because of the poor quality of the planes, which were often damaged surplus, but also because of the men, with the volunteers, the great majority, at odds with the mercenaries.

[14] It should be pointed out in this respect that, contrary to what has often been asserted, even by veterans of the brigades, Tito never fought in Spain.

[15] According to Luigi Longo, Largo Caballero's welcome was a rather cool one.

[16] No doubt the French newspapers regularly noted frontier arrests, but it seems that they were more or less symbolic.

[17] These recent immigrants, feeling alien in their adoptive country, often found a framework for their lives only in a union or party.

[18] Many veterans of the brigades later rose in the apparatus of their party or in that of the state after their party's victory. For instance, among the present German leaders of the DDR, there are Heinrich Rau and General Staimer, police general and 'Richard' in Spain. Among the Hungarians were Laslo Rajk, who was minister of the interior in his country before being hanged after a celebrated trial, and who had been a lieutenant and political commissar in Spain under the name Firtos; the Hungarian General Szalval who was Major Chapayev in Spain; and the premier of Hungary from 1958 to 1961, Ferenc Münnich. Among the Poles, General Komar, who, as Vacek, commanded a battalion and played a decisive role in 1956 at the head of the security troops in the events that brought Gomulka to power. Veterans of the brigades, in company with Gosnjak, Rankovich, and Vlahovich, formed the political and military officer strength of the Yugoslav partisans. Others, Frenchmen, made up the nucleus of the *Francs-Tireurs et Partisans*. Rebière, shot in 1942; Pierre Georges, a lieutenant in Spain and later Colonel Fabien; Tanguy, political commissar, later Colonel Rol; François Vittori, an organizer in the National Front of the Corsican uprising in 1944. Also worthy of mention, in the case of France, is the then-future secretary-general of the Communist party, since expelled, Auguste Lecoeur, and the future senator Jean Chaintron (Bethel).

[19] The dismissal of Randolfo Pacciardi, 'that great Republican lord' as Regler called him, and his departure from Spain, were in the view of many combatants proof of the grip, now undisguised, of the Communists over the brigades. By means of accounts from his own militiamen and accusations leveled by them, Antonia Stern was able to ascertain that Hans Beimler was murdered at the instigation of the NKVD. From documents she collected, it turns out that Beimler was in effective contact with German opposition members, freely critical of the leadership, and very hostile to the special services: in such circumstances, the hypothesis of murder is quite a likely one. It has not however been backed by hard evidence.

[20] Hans Kahle, was a former officer, a Communist militant since 1919; Zaisser, an officer who went over to the Russian revolutionaries in the Ukraine at the head of his troops. Both had stayed in Russia and had held senior posts in the secret Communist military apparatus in Germany. Zalka, former First World War officer, a comrade of Bela Kun in the 1919 Hungarian revolution, had served in China as military adviser with Gallen and Borodin. Jules Dumont, a late convert to Communism and a former captain, had previously served in Abyssinia against the Duce's troops.

[21] The man who enjoyed success in Spain under the name General

Kléber seems in fact to have been called Lazar Stern. According to Ypsilon, he was a former Austrian officer, prisoner in Russia during the Great War where he was converted to Communism, militant in the secret military apparatus in Germany, military adviser in China in 1927, and then commander of the Far East troops against the Japanese in 1935. Cox credited him with the same life history, but made him an Austrian, later a naturalized Canadian, who went to Russia in 1919 with the Allied Expeditionary Corps. Pacciardi wrote that he said he was Canadian but seemed to be German. According to Fischer, he was liquidated during the prewar Moscow purges, whereas Colodny maintained that he was the leader of the Russian troops who broke through the Mannerheim line during the 1940 Russo-Finnish War. But surely he was confusing him with the other General Stern, named Grigorovitch, who was not purged?

[22] The Belgian volunteer Nick Gillain, in his book *Le mercenaire* (Paris: Librairie Arthème Fayard, 1938) accused him of being president of a war council that sentenced and executed without cause—possibly for having been in touch with the CNT columns—a French officer, Major Delesalle. Pencheniati accused him of having personally shot four soldiers in Cambrils who protested because he had showered them with insults for giving ground. Ernest Hemingway, in *For Whom the Bell Tolls*, drew, under the transparent pseudonym Massart, a rather unflattering portrait of him as a suspicious brute, a bungler, and a bully. Fischer, who worked under him at Albacete, was equally harsh, while Regler wrote: 'He concealed his perfectly excusable incompetence beneath an incurable distrust.' It would be even more difficult to establish the truth about André Marty because the Communists, after his expulsion, joined in the concert of blame, too.

[23] The essential part of this information is taken from Longo's book.

[24] To understand each other, they were obliged to talk Russian.

[25] Former volunteers in Republican Spain.

CHAPTER 16

THE CONQUEST OF THE NORTH

After the fall of San Sebastián and Irún, which deprived the northern front of any chance of getting food supplies across the French frontier, no attack of any importance was attempted against the Basque provinces. Mola's best organized forces were directed against Madrid. Neither on the Republican nor the Nationalist side were there large numbers of well-armed troops for some months. There were not enough combatants to hold a continuous front from the Bay of Biscay to Galicia. Fighting flared up in one sector, then in another. Biscay, Santander, Asturias—their conquest, one by one, during the course of the year, marked the stages of the Nationalist offensive.

The Northern Front

It is immediately obvious that the Nationalists were confronted by two areas of solid resistance, though their political regimes were diametrically opposed: the Basque provinces, conservative and Catholic, whose national aspirations had rallied them to the side of the Republic, and working-class Asturias, bastion of the Revolution in October 1934 and again in July 1936. In the Center, on the other hand, was an area of weakness, the Santander region, where the War Committee was faced with an insoluble problem, defending the broadest part of the front with a very small number of ill-armed troops. The brittleness of the sector was further increased by dissension between Socialists and Anarchists.

The fact that the decisive fighting took place around Bilbao and the influence of Basque resistance and its repercussions abroad kept the simultaneous existence between these three centers hidden. However, it was the middle of 1937 before the military command was unified, adequate proof that there was no real *entente*, even in this field. The officers sent by Caballero, Captain Ciutat to Asturias and General Llano de la Encomienda to the Basque provinces, had attempted in vain to achieve unity with the help of Russian technicians. Though as 'militarized' units their names were similar, the troops remained different: the 'Basque militias' were uniformed units with a stiffening of chaplains, without *monos* and political commissars, while in the 'Asturian militias,' parties and trade unions retained control.[1]

Not only was there no unilateral military command for the three zones, but one area was hostile to and suspicious of the next: the Asturian revolutionaries were hostile to the 'conservative' Basques, and the Basques had reservations about the 'anarchism' of Santander and Gijón.

Already in August 1936 there were difficulties. In Asturias there was a witch-hunt against priests and nuns. The churches had been destroyed or closed and worship forbidden. In the Basque provinces, on the contrary, the Church still enjoyed all its freedoms and continued to have a profound influence not only on the people but also within the government, which included several Catholic ministers. The oath sworn by Aguirre stressed that the president would conduct himself 'as a believer, a people's magistrate, and a Basque.' Priests and disciples, persecuted in Asturias, sought refuge in the Basque provinces, where CNT militants protested violently against the decree making Good Friday a feast day. In Asturias, mines and factories were controlled, and many business firms, even in minor industries, were collectivized. In the Basque provinces property had remained untouched. Whereas the Government Committees were leading the Revolution in Asturias, the Euzkadi Defense Juntas were busy restoring *normalidad* everywhere. Few Civil Guards remained in Asturias, except in Gijón, whereas there were plenty in Santander and the Basque provinces. After the regional powers had been integrated into the

Republican state, the Asturias Council still included Anarchists; there were never any in the Basque government.[2] The Aguirre government had fought against the Revolution. Though there had been a harsh purge in Asturias, the Euzkadi government had set itself the objective of guaranteeing 'the safety of individuals and their possessions.' It had disarmed the rear, with a ban on the carrying of arms applying to anyone not in the Army or the police, and it acquired the right to recruit as many police forces as 'the situation required.'

It is not surprising that in such circumstances collaboration between the two territories in what may be called the 'Spanish Confederation' became difficult.[3] With no coordination achieved in the military field as long as the inferiority of the Republican forces was not yet obvious, the scattering of effort put a brake on all initiative. The Basques reproved the Asturians for not backing the operation in October against Alasua, intended to relieve Madrid. The Asturians retorted that, with munitions and a little heavy equipment, they would have taken Oviedo in October, before the Solchaga Column came to its rescue. Certainly, Basque battalions took part in the major attack by the Asturians against Oviedo[4] in February, but the calm of the rest of the northern front enabled the Nationalists to contain this attack successfully.

There was no collaboration in the economic field either. Yet the North was the only industrial region where conversion of factories could have established a strong war industry. But the Asturians had the coal and the Basques the iron: precious months were lost in talks and recrimination.

The central government undoubtedly strove to settle their differences. On several occasions it was suggested to Aguirre that he should admit CNT representatives to his Cabinet. And the CNT leaders asked their Euzkadi comrades to avoid 'blunders.' But the North did not receive any material aid, which deprived the Councils of Madrid and Valencia of any effectiveness. Caballero in *Mis recuerdos* recalled anguished telegrams from Aguirre calling for air support and referred to the Basque president's 'despair.' The Asturians also stated that they had been defeated through lack of war material. The only appreciable contribution was the arrival of Russian arms: 15 fighters, 5 field guns, 15 tanks, 200 machine guns, and 15,000 rifles 'dating back to the Crimean War,'[5] which was little for 35,000 soldiers and proved absurdly inadequate in the 1937 offensive.

Faced with imminent danger, the attitudes of the Basques and the Asturians were radically different. The Asturian militias, like all the rest, fought badly in open country. But in street fighting they knew how to hang on to every house in the towns and villages. The struggle entered on was to them a matter of life and death, and dynamite was their supreme argument.[6] They were not afraid of destruction and intended to leave only ruins in the hands of the Nationalists. In their view, terror was the only means of holding the rear. They never hesitated to kill anyone who mentioned surrender on the spot. They were prepared to answer bombing raids with mass executions of 'hostages,' either rebel sympathizers or simply suspects.

The Basques, in similar circumstances, had very different reactions. Respectful of religious beliefs and political opinions, and anxious to behave like 'good Catholics,' they preferred to release a guilty man rather than execute an innocent one; they retained suspect or merely halfhearted persons in key posts[7] and were as concerned with preserving the lives of 'hostages' captured by their neighbors as with holding the front.[8] More important, the stakes in the war were not the same in their case; temporary allies of the Popular Front, the leaders of the Basque Nationalist Party, their financial backers, and their troops shared neither the ideology nor the outlook of the other antifascist combatants. They were fighting for the Basque provinces in themselves, and for their liberties, refusing to let everything be destroyed in futile combat. The Basque bourgeoisie knew that the future would not be wholly denied to them in the event of a Nationalist victory and that their services would be needed when the factories and mines that had escaped destruction were functioning again. They were relying on their British associates to protect them. Finally, Catholic solidarity gave them hope, if not of a compromise, at least of some consideration from the rebels, and the chance of safe-guarding part at least of their interests.

The struggle on two fronts had its own logic. The desire not to yield to the Revolution, and not to subject the populations of towns, monuments, and industrial installations to the atrocities of street fighting and to the inevitable reprisals, induced some of the Basques to oppose, by force if necessary, the advocates of last-ditch resistance and destruction. In this task, they were sometimes outstripped by disguised Falangists and opportunists, who saw in it a means of hastening the Republican rout.

The Campaign for Bilbao

The prospect of an easy victory would alone have been enough to persuade Franco to turn toward the North, after his successive failures at Madrid. But other factors were certainly

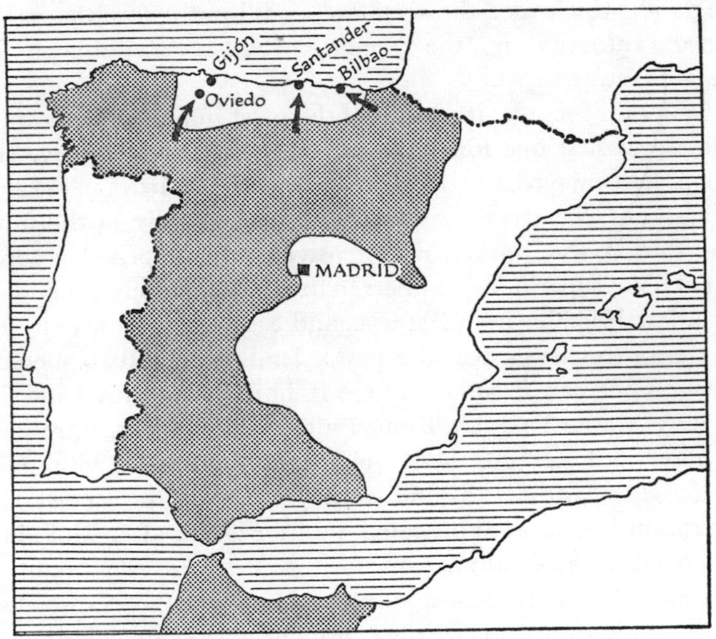

The Offensive against the North (March–September 1937)

operating: in the first place, the battle of Madrid had proved that it was advisable to prepare for a long war. A Republican Army was now in existence.

Franco, who did not have the means to carry the day by seizing the capital, could not hope to win by a general offensive. His reserves were too weak, and the casualties incurred in the recent fighting had temporarily dispelled the idea of a war of attrition. The tactics employed until the cessation of hostilities consisted of attacking and reducing Republican Spain region by region, which meant that substantial material could be concentrated on a limited front. The isolation of the North naturally made it the ideal sector for such a venture. Moreover, the fall of the North had an economic value that could be crucial for the latter part of the war: the lion's share of the Spanish metal industry was there. Finally, its possession was important for future international negotiations. Germany, which needed Cantabrian iron ore, had to support such an operation. England, which used the same ore, could not ignore the established authority in the region, whether Republican or Nationalist.

General Mola was in charge of the most important operation and the easiest one to carry out, the conquest of Biscay. His troops had enjoyed a period of calm and reorganization in early 1937. Four Navarrese brigades[9] were continually in the front line during the Nationalist offensive and comprised a force equal if not superior in numbers to the Basque troops, reinforced by a few brigades from Asturias and Santander, concentrated in the sierras to protect the passes leading to Bilbao. Behind General Solchaga's Navarrese the Italian Black Arrows and the new 23 March Division, formed after Guadalajara, were held in reserve. Later on, Mola reinforced his troops with units composed of Moroccans and contingents from the *Tercio*. The operation began, as anticipated, on 31 March, after Mola had delivered a final ultimatum to the Basques. The fighting methods that were continually employed by the Nationalists during this campaign at once became clear: exploitation of overwhelming material superiority and intensive artillery barrages, followed by air attacks.[10] Their effectiveness emerged at once from the results obtained in the first five days of the offensive, in spite of frequent and courageous counterattacks by the Basques; however, the occupation of the mountain passes had not brought the Nationalists into contact with the Iron Ring, Bilbao's defense line. Aznar invoked the bad weather, which had certainly slowed down operations by ruling out air attacks at a crucial moment. But the Basque Army, in spite of its losses and its paucity of material, was still capable of hitting back dangerously. This explains the harsh fighting around Mount Sabigan, captured and recaptured several times between 11 and 15 April. At that point, what was needed was a diversion from outside, forcing Franco to switch part of his troops and air force to another sector. But efforts in this direction were, as we shall see, too late and too feebly carried out.

The first stage of the Biscay campaign had been completed by the end of April with the occupation of Durango, Eibar, and Guernica. The Navarrese brigades were at last in contact with the heights that protected and dominated the Iron Ring. These last operations were notable for a massive use of planes, which terrorized and pulverized not only the defense lines but towns and villages too. The most famous incident in this respect was the destruction of Guernica on 26 April by German aircraft; this raid had tremendous repercussions abroad. Nowadays, after Rotterdam and Coventry, after the destruction of Warsaw and the atom bomb at Hiroshima, people are almost surprised by the importance attached to this attack. But this was because Guernica was the religious capital of the Basque provinces. The emotions of the Catholic world, especially in France, were greatly aroused. And then the affair had an international aspect to it, because it was the Germans who were justly accused of being responsible: the evidence of the inhabitants who fled Guernica, burned and threatened by the rebels, was irrefutable. The pilot Galland merely said that it was a regrettable mistake. But faced with public strictures and the feelings of the House of Commons, where Eden had been challenged, Germany asked Franco for 'a vigorous denial.' Hence the Nationalist version: 'Guernica was burned by . . . Red hordes. Aguirre devised a satanic plan for the destruction of Guernica,'[11] which was carried out by Asturian *dinamiteros*. This interpretation still holds good today in Spain.[12]

Meanwhile, the Nationalist forces needed reorganization and reinforcement before attacking the fortifications of Bilbao. Faupel reported that General Franco had asked the Italians to commit the Littorio Division to these crucial operations. But the latter were less enthusiastic since Guadalajara, especially since a new emergency, due to recklessness, revived unhappy memories. After the occupation of Guernica, the Black Arrows made rapid progress along the coast and reached Bermeo, leaving their left flank exposed; a Republican counterattack cut them off for a few days, and the 23 March Division and a Navarrese brigade had to be sent to rescue them.

May was spent in preparations for the decisive battle. The two adversaries strengthened their positions around the Iron Ring. The ineffectiveness of this line of fortifications, famous until it was put to the test, was to be swiftly demonstrated: it was not garrisoned by enough men, and it was dominated by heights that, once they were occupied by the enemy, made its long-term defense impossible. Also, the Republicans persisted in defending these strategic points, thereby delaying the Nationalist offensive.

However, Mola's replacement by Dávila, who faithfully carried out Franco's orders, strengthened the unity of the Nationalist command. The casualties incurred by the Basques during the counterattacks had been enormous. Finally, the plan of the Iron Ring[13] had been handed over to the Nationalists by Captain Goicoechea,[14] which explains the remarkable accuracy of the artillery barrage that preceded the assault.

Henceforth, the breaching of the fortified line was inevitable. The decisive attack began on 12 June, and the Iron Ring was broken over a two-mile front that day. The rest of the defenses were taken from the rear.

The Basques, who until then had fought well, now felt that there was no way of resisting. Possibly they could have prolonged the struggle by agreeing to fight in the streets, but this would have led to the destruction of their city. By evacuating Bilbao almost without a struggle, the Basques unquestionably brought the Nationalist victory nearer, but they prevented destruction that seemed pointless to them by then. Here, as at San Sebastián, two conceptions of war were at odds: the Basques did not hesitate to disarm the Asturian militias that had set up barricades in the streets of the new town. On the sixteenth, Colonel Bengoa fled to France; in his view, Bilbao was undergoing a genuine 'collapse of authority.' He was afraid that, since no one was exercising any authority there any longer, the city would be unable to surrender. On the seventeenth, the Basque governor quit the capital, leaving a Defense Junta including Leizaola, Aznar (Socialist), Astigarrabía (Communist), and General Ulíbarri. It is very difficult to say if it had any real authority. According to *Le Temps*, on the evening of the seventeenth shooting broke out between the Basques, in favor of surrender,[15] and the 'extremists, in favor of resistance to the bitter end.' The Anarchists blew up bridges and summarily executed some of those favoring surrender. A Basque unit of 1200 militiamen who had been soldiers in the regular army before the war then went into action, supported by the police, the *Asaltos*, and the Civil Guards. The militiamen from Santander and Asturias were attacked and disarmed, and the white flag was hoisted on the Telephone Exchange. Emissaries were sent to the Nationalists, and Basque units occupied public buildings and restored order. The police, now wearing the Carlist beret, carried on with its work after the entry of Dávila's troops.

While the Nationalists were occupying Bilbao, the Basque Army was retreating toward the west. Almost without resistance, all the rest of Biscay fell into the hands of the Nationalists. Aznar estimated the losses suffered by the Basques during the campaign at 30,000 men.

However, it took the Nationalist general staff eleven weeks to wind up the campaign. Natural conditions and Basque resistance are not enough to account for the length of the fighting. There were mistakes by the Nationalists and, in particular, a misunderstanding between the Spaniards and the Italians: General Duria was even forced, after the setback at

Bermeo, to do without the active participation of the CTV in the campaign.

The Diversion: Brunete

The Republicans had been unable to take advantage of the delay. A powerful attack from the central zone could have interrupted the Nationalist offensive. But the two attempts at a diversion that were made from the central front in May and June lacked scope. They were undertaken without conviction and with inadequate means. At Balsain, in Old Castile, the attack had the immediate aim of seizing La Granja; it was not even supported by assault tanks. At Huesca, where the offensive was to have led to the occupation of the town, the attackers had only three batteries of artillery. In both cases, the enemy seemed to be on his guard, and the first attackers met with a lively response.

The very day after the final attempt on the Huesca front, the occupation of Bilbao by the Nationalists marked the end of the Biscay campaign. Of course, the struggle could have gone on longer, but it was necessary, in order to free the North, to act swiftly with a large tactical force.

Meanwhile, the elimination of the revolutionary opposition had meant the creation, at least in appearance, of political unity. The Negrín government, the 'government of victory,' was relying on an army that was progressively losing its revolutionary character and coming to resemble a regular army. The autonomous militias were disappearing. The military technicians, who had the government's confidence, were pushing the political ones into the background. In the central sector, the chief role was played by Vicente Rojo; on the northern front, Gamir Ulíbarri, former professor at the Toledo Military Academy like Rojo, was given control of the whole of the Republican zone, thus achieving, though belatedly, unity of command in this region. At the instigation of these technicians, a total reorganization of the Army was envisaged. The troops, whatever their origin and initial training, were divided into armies, army corps, brigades, and battalions. This reorganization, useful wherever a long period of calm allowed it to be completed, had little significance on the northern front, where more immediate defense tasks were imposed on the command.

It was one thing to organize such army corps theoretically, but another to provide them with the capacity to resist and to prepare them for an offensive action. The men had to be instructed; the Fifth Army Corps, made up chiefly of troops of the old Fifth Regiment, was both example and model. It provided the first tactical force in the summer 1937 offensives.

The second problem, even more awkward for the Republicans to solve, was that of arms. The provision of arms had become more and more difficult since border and sea coast controls had come into effect on 19 April. The units' complement of heavy arms and assault tanks, which played an important part in a breakthrough, was quite inadequate. The supply of Russian planes was far from being great enough to permit a massive use of aircraft, especially attack planes.

This material inferiority was less obvious around Madrid than in the other combat sectors, since the mass of organized troops had been concentrated on that part of the front during the first three months of 1937. This was no doubt one of the reasons that determined the choice of Brunete for the large diversionary offensive launched in early July. It seems that there was a fairly serious discussion before the choice of the attack sector, which was finally made for political rather than military considerations.

Two possibilities were in fact open to the government forces: the first was an offensive in Estremadura, in the Mérida area. A glance at the map shows that the advantages of such a move were obvious. Its success would have confronted the Nationalist Army with its greatest danger, by directly threatening Badajoz and the Portuguese frontier and consequently severing communications with the Moroccan and southern bases. Moreover, there were far fewer forces defending this area than on the Madrid front. All these considerations had raised the possibility of an attack in this sector long before; this was the particular brainchild of Colonel Asensio Torrado, Largo Caballero's technician. During 1938, the Republican military leaders reexamined this plan, but, everything considered, it was never carried out with the means necessary to ensure its success.[16]

In the end it was the second offensive solution that prevailed: an attack in the Madrid sector. The decision for launching a military operation of this scope lay with the government, and especially with the war minister, Indalecio Prieto. The latter had insisted on personally attending the opening of the offensive against Brunete. Ultimately, in agreement with the Russian technicians, Miaja and Rojo took the step of choosing the Madrid front. Rojo explained its military advantages: the Nationalist forces were weaker because they had had to dispatch troops from this sector to the northern front; they were morally weakened because of their failure at the capital. But above all, the reserves of manpower were in place there; no great troop movements were necessary. The effect of surprise could be more easily achieved than on the southern front, toward which large-scale troop movements could not be long concealed. At all events, there was no question of depleting the Madrid front, symbol of Republican Spain's resistance.

On the other hand, the Republican general staff was convinced that the only way of winning was to breach the line of battle with a heavy concentration of troops and artillery, which meant an attempted breakthrough on an extremely limited front. The choice of Brunete answered these imperatives.

The Battle of Brunete

The operation had a twofold aim: to halt the Nationalist offensive in the North by forcing Franco to recall part of the forces involved in Biscay, and, in reaching the communications network of Navalcarnero by an attack to the west of Madrid, to make the Nationalists withdraw to the Tagus and to isolate the troops positioned on the immediate outskirts of the capital. The success of this scheme, even if the enemy managed to avoid encirclement, would force him into a hasty retreat and relieve Madrid. In this way all the Nationalist successes would be threatened.

To carry out this scheme of encirclement, a two-pronged

attack was envisaged. The major one was to bring about the capture of Brunete and the occupation of the mountainous ridge overlooking Navalcarnero. The subsidiary attack's objective was a breakthrough in the direction of Alcorcón, to the south of Madrid. The main attack was entrusted to the Fifth Army Corps under Modesto, and to the eighteenth under Jurado. The best of the Republican troops were there: the Lister Division, the Thirteenth and Fifteenth International Brigades. The subsidiary attack was led by the Madrid reserves, including the Kléber and Durán Divisions and the Second Army Corps under Romero.

The means allotted to the Republican general staff were the greatest so far employed. Aznar estimated the government forces at 47,000 men, and all observers reported the exceptional weight of the artillery, especially of antiaircraft guns.[17]

By contrast, the Nationalist forces that could immediately be committed were weak: two *banderas* of the Falange, three centurias, and the San Quintin Battalion, plus the subsector services concentrated on Brunete. Some reserves were thrown in early on to help the defense, but the whole force was clearly inadequate to prevent an attack in depth. The fighting conditions were therefore as good as they could be for the Republicans. Rojo estimated that, apart from the battle of the Ebro, Brunete was 'the only operation perfectly prepared by the Republican side.' The secret was perfectly kept, which was quite exceptional.

Roughly speaking, the battle consisted of two phases: the Republican offensive took place between 5 and 13 July; the Nationalist counteroffensive lasted from the fifteenth to the end of the month.

On 5 July the general offensive was preceded by attacks in the direction of Aranjuez. During the night between the fifth and the sixth, the assault was successfully launched. The anticipated breakthrough was achieved; in the center, the Lister Division, making a deep thrust, occupied Brunete. The gains made were such that it was possible to anticipate a great victory.

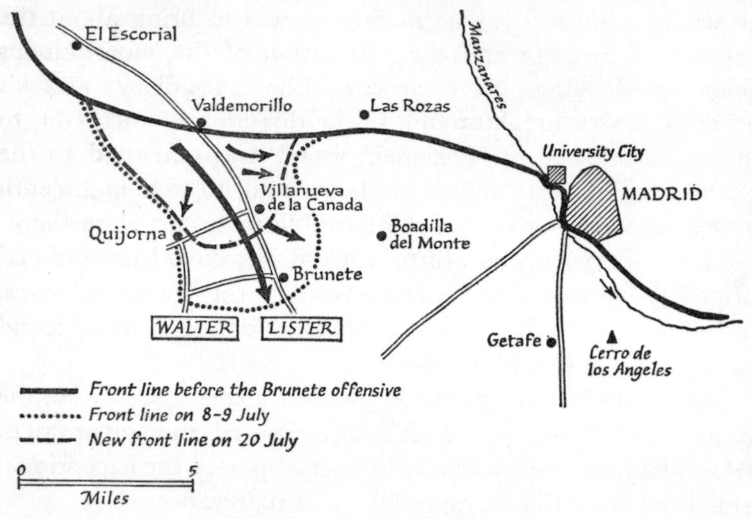

Brunete (July 1937)

But by 7 July the offensive was slowing down, and the fresh advances made were purely local and lacking in scope: it was clearly running out of steam. The occupation of Villafranca del Castillo, to the extreme east of the positions, lasted barely a day, the Moroccan *tabors* managing to retake the village on the twelfth. From then on, the Republicans confined themselves to limiting the Nationalist counterattacks as far as possible. All in all, on the operational level, it amounted to failure. To explain this, both the lack of means and the government's blunders must be taken into account.

The obvious mistake was not to have exploited the initial success by broadening the scope of the attack. While the Lister Division was holding the positions gained on the sixth and seventh, the Republican command spent itself on villages that a handful of Nationalists defended with desperate energy. By wasting four days on these positions, the Republicans allowed the Nationalist reinforcements to arrive; on the other hand, by persisting, they suffered very heavy casualties and also weakened their military potential. These two features kept recurring during the war: on the one hand the command's timorous character and its lack of a broad overall conception,[18] and on the other, the slowness of operations, which cannot be explained solely by the resistance encountered but must also take account of the violent and unexpected reactions of the troops involved. This, in particular, accounts for the failure of the subsidiary attack, which should have led to the forward troops were often seized with panic and obliged the the encirclement of the Nationalists to the south of Madrid; whole of the forces grouped in that sector to withdraw to their original positions. These sudden retreats, so frequent in the major Republican campaigns, often made a large-scale movement impossible, especially at Brunete.

In fact, things nearly turned to disaster there, because the front suddenly found itself completely depleted at one point as the result of a fresh panic. In the end, however, the counter-attack launched by General Varela was halted.

Ultimately, Brunete was a half-success for the government forces. A small number of their initial objectives had been attained. The pocket created to the north of Brunete, which merely succeeded in lengthening the front, cannot be considered a significant advance. More important were the troop movements that Franco had been forced into. He had had to recall two Navarrese brigades and most of the Air Force from the northern front.[19] it was, moreover, the air superiority of the Nationalists that had been the deciding factor in the struggle. The almost incessant machine-gunning by day and bombing raids by night[20] broke the offensive and managed to foil the Republican move.

Certainly respite had been won for organizing the defense of Santander. But this respite was short lived. By the end of July, part of the troops engaged at Brunete were able to return to the north[21] to take part in a new and decisive assault, which was working toward the collapse of the northern front and the fall of the Asturian industrial area.

The Campaign against Santander

In fact, there was only a fortnight's calm between the end of the battle of Brunete and the beginning of the new offensive against Santander. This scarcely left time to put an attacking force in position. The two essential factors were, as at Bilbao, the Navarrese brigades and the whole complement of Italian troops, CTV and Black Arrows, now reorganized; all these forces were placed under General Dávila. The battalions' allocation of artillery was strengthened, and the Air Force was again concentrated in the North. Franco hoped to be able to make a great effort in August and September, in such a way as to be done with Santander and Asturias by the end of the summer, before the rainy season slowed down operations in the mountainous area.

On the Republican side, Ulíbarri, appointed as commander of the troops on the northern front, theoretically had four army corps. But the Basque army corps was made up of troops sorely tested by the earlier fighting, who had fallen back on the province of Santander. They had even stopped fighting to defend their territory; they were morally and materially weakened. Yet they were entrusted with the whole of the eastern sector. The two Asturian army corps (the Sixteenth and the Seventeenth) were only partially committed in the Santander operations.

In the end, the defense of Santander was far harder to organize than that of Bilbao. Though the province is protected to the south by a mountain barrier beyond the passes of Los Torros, Escudo, and Reinosa, no obstacle of any importance bars the way to the coast. Nor were there any fortifications similar to the Iron Ring. To fill this gap, men born between 1913 and 1920 were mobilized and enrolled in labor battalions, with the job of building a second line of entrenchments behind the one completed by the disciplinary companies and the frontline troops. However, the lack of organization and the scale of the work to be accomplished made this a hazardous task.

The lack of improvement of arms supplies meant that it took time to get organized. Ulíbarri tried to gain the necessary respite by launching an offensive from the pocket on the front to the south of Reinosa. But the attack, made by an Asturian army corps, was swiftly halted. A failure of this sort coupled with the halting of the Brunete offensive merely emphasized the feeling of isolation that pervaded the northern region. Santander had only two destroyers, the *Ciscar* and the *Jose Luis Diez*, to protect its communications with the outside world by sea. Moreover, these warships were quite ineffectual: the blockade, already decided on and organized by the Nationalist command on the Biscay coast, worked even better during the Santander campaign.

It was not surprising, in such circumstances, that there was a lightning campaign. Fighting was widespread only during the first three or four days, and the fate of the campaign was decided within a few hours. The two main positions, on the Escudo and Reinosa passes, were attacked, the first by the CTV, with the Littorio Division in reserve, the second by three Navarrese brigades. In spite of the ease of defense in this mountainous sector, success was complete and rapid, and the use of motorized units further accentuated how crushing was the Nationalist advance.

On 14 August, the first evening of the fighting, the order was given to the men furthest forward in the Reinosa pocket to withdraw, in order to avoid being encircled. Within forty-eight hours, the Navarrese had taken Reinosa, after destroying the only serious resistance they had met, and had occupied a naval artillery factory, where guns in process of manufacture were seized. Reinosa did not hold out: only one Asturian battalion resisted for a few hours in the streets of the town. Meanwhile, the Italians, after a mass tank attack, occupied Escudo; the motorized column that was advancing to the south linked up with the Navarrese. Once again, material superiority had been decisive; there was now no serious obstacle before the Nationalists. There was a little sporadic resistance, such as that by the Asturians who left Corconte a mere heap of rubble. But many Basque battalions surrendered, and contrary to orders from Ulíbarri, who had called for a withdrawal to Asturias, the Basque troops began to concentrate around Santona.

By 17 August the second phase of the operation was in motion: a rapid, mass advance, which led to the wiping out of the defenses of Santander province in about ten days. On the twenty-fifth the British warship *Keith* took on board there the seventeen hostages that remained from Bilbao, with their guards and a certain number of Basque leaders, whom Aguirre, arriving from the central zone, joined in Bayonne; Juan Ruiz, the Socialist governor, and General Ulíbarri left in the evening aboard a submarine; Civil Guards, *Asaltos*, and *Carabineros* revolted. Their leaders[22] made contact with the Nationalists, informing them that they were ready to surrender the town, where only the men of the CNT–FAI showed any inclination to resist.[23] A communiqué from the Nationalist command on the twenty-seventh announced that the entry of the troops, planned for the twenty-sixth, had been delayed twenty-four hours, 'law and order in Santander henceforth being maintained by the population.' The alliance of the Army and police leaders with the Nationalist sympathizers made surrender inevitable. As the Santander front crumbled, the Basques in Laredo capitulated.

Capitulation by the Basques

The capitulation by the Basques in Laredo, following an agreement in due form, raised problems of every kind. The simplest was that of relations within the Republican coalition; the others involved both Franco's policy with regard to an eventual reconciliation and his relations with his Italian allies. Finally, and less obviously, British policy now began to make itself felt.[24]

Without retracing the history of the diplomatic contacts made with a view to a political settlement of the conflict, it must be noted that, since the beginning of the Civil War, several approaches had been made to the Basques. Their political and material isolation must in fact have prompted some of their leaders to examine the possibilities of an honorable settlement.

According to Cantalupo, the first attempt at separate negotiation took place at his instigation immediately after Guadalajara. The Italian consul in San Sebastián, Cavaletti, made the first move and was informed by the Jesuit Father Pereda of the guarantees requested by Aguirre and Jáuregui:

opportunity for the leaders to leave Spain, no reprisals against the civilian population except where common-law offenses were involved, and lastly exclusively Italian mediation, which implied control of the surrender operations and of the conditions for repression by the Italian command, in order to avoid massacres similar to those that had occurred at Badajoz and Málaga. It was this last point that led to the failure of the move, because the Nationalist command found it hard to accept Italian control, which could have spread to the whole of Spain. Besides, what would guarantees made by Franco have been worth?

These negotiations seemed to drag on into May. Aguirre confirmed that he was sounded out in Bilbao by an emissary, but without any result. Faupel, the German ambassador, attributed the failure of the talks to opposition from Franco. But the fall of Bilbao, the heavy losses of the Basques, and constant pressure from the Vatican[25] led to renewed contacts. Von Hassell, the German ambassador in Rome, telegraphed on 7 July, just as the offensive against Santander was under preparation, that 'delegates from the Basques are negotiating surrender' and that 'the Italian government is using its influence over Franco to obtain lenient conditions.' The Basques, who had fought bravely to defend their country, now felt as if they were fighting for people who were strangers to them, and for an ideology that was not theirs. After the loss of Biscay, they had stopped taking a serious part in the fighting. Their withdrawal to Santona was a prelude to their capitulation. The president of the Basque Nationalist party, Juan de Achuriaguera, negotiated with General Mancini and signed the pact of Laredo: the Basques handed over their arms to the Italians, released political prisoners, and promised to maintain law and order in the zone they controlled until they were 'relieved' by the Italians. In return, the latter guaranteed the lives of combatants and authorized the Basque leaders who were in the territory to leave. But these guarantees were made only to Basques: the non-Basque combatants in the Santona area were thus caught in a real trap, under the surveillance of the Basques, who were 'maintaining law and order.'

The capitulation took effect on 25 August. The Italians occupied Laredo on the twenty-fifth and Santona on the twenty-sixth. The embarkation of the leaders began on the twenty-seventh on two British vessels, the *Bobie* and the *Seven Seas Spray*, under the direct supervision of the Italians. The Spanish official arrived with orders from Franco banning all departures: the Basque leaders, the members of the Defense Junta who had organized 'the capitulation in good order' were arrested. The pact was torn up; Franco ignored the word of the Italian officers.[26] It was the Basques who were now caught in a trap.

Only a semblance of an army now remained in Santander province, which the Asturian militias hastily evacuated; in five days, the Nationalist troops had advanced twenty-five miles beyond Santander.

The End of Asturias

However, a front was formed again in the coastal area, stretching from Santander to Gijón; moreover, the mountainous area formed a solid rampart that the Asturias militiamen exploited admirably.[27]

Moreover, it was not long before the advance of the Navarrese slowed down. It took them over a month of fighting to cover the twenty-five miles between Ridesella and Villaviciosa; at this point, on 19 October, Gijón was directly threatened. Could resistance continue, and, more important, could it last until winter, as the Madrid government was asking?

The *New York Times* correspondent wrote: 'The retreating Asturians seem determined to leave behind them only smoking ruins and desolation when they are finally obliged to abandon a town or village. . . . The rebels generally find them dynamited and burnt to the ground.' On 19 October Franco did not hesitate, in the face of such stubborn resistance, to wire Mussolini to dispatch a new division in order to liquidate the front before winter.

However, resistance collapsed within forty-eight hours. On 20 October, at 2 A.M., Colonel Pradas reported to a meeting of the Council of Asturias on the military situation, which he considered gravely imperiled and almost desperate. The material and munitions requested from Madrid had not arrived, and the morale of the troops was low, worsened by pessimism in the rear. In his view, all resistance was impossible. They could hold on, if they wanted, until they were crushed, in which case the members of the Council might as well leave for the front. However, he thought that it was possible to save part of the Army by ordering a withdrawal to the ports of Gijón, Avilés, and Candás, on condition that it was carried out that day: 'Tomorrow, it will be too late.' The Council was divided. Negrín's orders were categorical; they must hold out to the end. But only the Communists Ambou and Roces pleaded for obedience. The majority came out in favor of withdrawal; the Council proclaimed its sovereignty, which relieved it of any tie of obedience to Madrid, and ordered a departure by sea, using every possible means.[28]

Colonel Pradas felt that he could complete this operation within twenty-four hours. Only part of it was achieved. Five planes landed at Bayonne during the day of the twentieth; in them were officers, who said they had received orders to evacuate the staff. Russian officers also arrived at Bayonne in an *Air-Pyrénées* plane. At 5 A.M., the Communist leaders left in a motorboat. At eight, Belarmino Tomás went aboard a fishing boat, *L'Abascal*, with the other members of the Council, including Segundo Blanco, who had returned from the central zone the previous day by plane.

During the night, a revolt broke out, of which Colonel Pradas had no doubt got wind. Colonel Franco,[29] commander of the Gijón garrison, backed by the Civil Guard and the *Carabineros*, took control of the town and immediately made contact with the Navarrese, whom he begged to speed up their march on the city, where he feared 'an Anarchist uprising.' On the twenty-first, at 10 A.M., the radio announced: 'We are waiting impatiently. . . . Long live Franco.' Thousands of militiamen, deserted by their leaders and disarmed by the Civil Guards, were already prisoner when the Navarrese arrived.[30]

After the fall of Gijón, the northern front ceased to exist.

However, all resistance had not ended.[31] Mopping-up operations there went on much longer than in Biscay and in Santander province, and consequently Franco was unable to immediately transfer all of the troops engaged there to the central front. The conquest of the North had ultimately been only one phase of the war.

Belchite

However, to the rebels, this was their greatest victory since the battle at Madrid had altered in character. It was doubly important. Economically, it gave Franco some of the most important Spanish provinces, the only ones at any rate where the Republicans could have established a war industry; it provided the essential commercial product of iron ore. Militarily, it not only revealed the superiority of the Nationalist Army over the divided and badly armed Basque and Asturian troops, it also proved that, at that stage at least, the army of Valencia and Madrid was incapable of effectively halting a Nationalist offensive. Brunete had been only a half-success: the second major attempt, at Belchite, was a total failure.

The choice of Belchite was justified by considerations diametrically opposed to those at Brunete. The front had not undergone any reorganization there. The soldiers, said Rojo, 'are hunters rather than soldiers,' which meant that they operated in small groups, isolated or linked with the rest of the front by observation posts. But the enemy soldiers were no better off. It therefore seemed easy to breach the front. On the other hand, the maneuver could be extended with relatively limited numbers. The objectives were as follows: to take Saragossa by a three-pronged attack on Zuera, to the north of the Ebro, and on Saragossa itself, and to the south to reduce the pocket formed by the front between Quinto and Belchite. At the same time, the Republican command obviously hoped to force the Nationalists to defer their offensive in the North.

But the offensive began very late, on 29 August, several days after the capture of Santander. Most of the troops involved had had to be transported to the sector of attack, along bad roads and amidst immense confusion.[32] Finally, the unmaneuverability of the Republican troops was once again amply demonstrated. There was only one success, the capture of Quinto and Belchite; it took another twelve days for Belchite to fall. The lofty ambitions of the offensive against Saragossa were abandoned after a fruitless attempt north of the Ebro. Belchite was a failure, because none of the vital objectives had been attained. The conquest of the North by the Nationalists had not been delayed by a single day.

Henceforth, the map showed two Spains in conflict. The Nationalists dominated the whole of the west and northwest part of the country; their territory formed a single bloc, from Galicia to Aragon, from Gibraltar to the Gulf of Gascony.

Notes

[1] The Asturian Defense Department was run by the Communist Ambou, and the general staff by Ciutat. González Peña (Socialist), Juan José Manso (Communist), and González Mallada (CNT) were commissars.

[2] The Basque government consisted of four Nationalists, three Socialists, and a Communist; the Council of Asturias, four Anarchists (two CNT, one FAI, and one Libertarian Youth), four Republicans, two Socialists, two Communists, and two JSU members.

[3] See Rama, *La crisis española del siglo XX*.

[4] On 1 March the organizer of the Basque militias, Candido Saseta Echevarría, was killed at Oviedo. Lizarra, commenting on his death, did not conceal the Basques' lack of enthusiasm for fighting with the Asturians.

[5] According to Aguirre, the Basque president did however stress the bravery of the Russian pilots and of their leader, General Jansen.

In addition, the Basque Nationalist leader Monzón managed to buy 5000 Czech rifles and 5 million bullets in Hamburg in October. We do not have any figures for the arms of the Asturians, who were probably even less equipped than the Basques, and on whom the siege of Oviedo was a constant drain. They received mainly Czech arms, mostly rifles sent through Mexico, and on 19 October a load of old French rifles brought by the steamship *Reina*.

[6] See the letter from an Asturian militiaman quoted in *La Dépêche de Toulouse* (4 October 1937): 'What does death matter, so long as they don't pass, and if they do pass, well, what does death matter then?'

[7] See the episode quoted by Steer about Colonel Annex, head of military censorship, who declared, as the enemy closed on Bilbao, 'What's the point of getting killed?' and retained his post by crossing over into the enemy ranks.

[8] According to *The Times*.

[9] See Manuel Aznar, *Historia militar de la guerra de España*, 3 vols., 3rd ed.

(Madrid: Editora Nacional, 1958–1963): First Brigade, Colonel García Valiño; Second Brigade, Colonel Cayuela; Third Brigade, Colonel Latorre; Fourth Brigade, Colonel Alonso Vega.

[10] The shelling on 31 March that preceded the Nationalist attack was carried out by thirty-five artillery batteries, twice as many as the Basques could bring up.

[11] Denial published on 29 April by the Nationalist press office (see Archives of the German Foreign Ministry).

[12] See Aznar, *Historia militar de la guerra de España.*

[13] The defense was made up of three lines of trenches, five barbed-wire entanglements, underground shelters, and machine-gun nests.

[14] See George L. Steer, *The Tree of Gernika* (London: Hodder, 1938).

[15] On the eighteenth 1500 Nationalist prisoners armed with picks and shovels were led in ranks to the Nationalist forward positions, on the pretext of going to dig trenches.

[16] It is probable that the Russian military advisers were opposed to this operation in 1937.

[17] So great a concentration of material was achieved only twice during the entire war on the Republican side, at Brunete and at Teruel.

[18] Rojo wrote that 'the forward troops' divisional commanders were afraid of advancing more deeply and leaving themselves open to encirclement.'

[19] Especially the Italian Legion Air Force and the Condor Legion

[20] Rojo noted that, for the first time, night sorties were being made.

[21] According to Aznar, after 3 August the Fifth Navarrese Brigade was concentrated in the Alguilar del Campo and Ala del Rey areas.

[22] According to *Independent News,* quoting an agency dispatch, they were the commander of the Civil Guard, Pedro Vega, the commander of the Basque troops, Angel Botella, and Staff Captain Luis Térez.

[23] A report by the FAI Mainland Committee mentioned Battalions 122 and 136 and referred to 'POUM militants at their sides'; according to *Fragua Social,* the doctor and POUM militant, José Luis Arenillas, head of the medical corps in the Army of the North, tried to organize resistance at the last moment. Taken prisoner, he was hanged. He was the author of a severe critique of the Euzkadi government's policy, which appeared in *Nueva Era* in January 1937.

[24] In particular, in June the press noted a journey to London by Constantino Zabala, Aguirre's father-in-law.

[25] See Hassell's note (13 January): 'Negotiations are under way with the Basque Separatists, with the Vatican as intermediary.' Cardinal Pacelli—the future Pope Pius XIII—was the intermediary, according to Largo Caballero and Aguirre.

[26] Nationalist historians have generally kept silent about this episode, as have many Republicans, too.

[27] Castro Delgado (*Hombres made in Moscú,* pp. 571–572) estimated the Fourteenth and Seventeenth Corps, which were defending Asturias, at 45,000 men, with 850 machine guns, 180 field guns, and 6 antiaircraft guns.

[28] See the minutes of the last meeting of the Council of Asturias, as they were published in the note from the Council in reply to Negrín. This text,

whose publication was banned by the Republican censorship, appeared in *Independent News*, and its authenticity has been confirmed by members of the Council: Julián Zugazagoitia pointed out that it was on 29 April that the Provincial Council decided to transform itself into a sovereign council (*Historia de la guerra en España* [Buenos Aires: La Vanguardia, 1940], p. 314). It forbade anyone to leave: 'De aquí sale ni Dios.' Castro Delgado (*Hombres made in Moscú*, pp. 573 ff.) stated that Amador Fernández went afterward to France to obtain a compromise: authorization to evacuate the Army in exchange for the nondestruction of industrial installations.

[29] According to Castro Delgado (*Hombres made in Moscú*, pp. 576–577), Colonel Franco, long since accused of sabotage by the Communists, had attended the last meeting of the Council.

[30] Most of the Asturian leaders managed to escape: members of the Council, president of the Popular Tribunal, prominent militants, such as Javier Bueno, military leaders, such as Colonels Pradas, Linares, Ciutat, and Galán, and Admiral Fuentes. But thousands of combatants were taken prisoner, and many of them were shot. Among them was the metalworker Carrocerra, who was in command of a brigade. Zugazagoitia (*Historia de la guerra en España*, p. 319) described how this CNT militant refused to embark without his men and thus deliberately chose death.

[31] See Stohrer's note on 4 March 1938, quoting Franco: 'The guerrillas have been hounded in Asturias until quite recently. After the capture of Gijón, there were still 18,000 armed men scattered about the region; it was only recently that we took the last of them prisoner, some 2000 men, with 18 machine guns and 1500 rifles.'

[32] A little shelling of the zones of concentration would have brought everything to a halt, according to Rojo.

CHAPTER 17

POLITICAL EVOLUTION IN NATIONALIST SPAIN

The conquest of the North did not only give the Nationalists economic and strategic advantages. It provided an assurance for foreign states that the *Movimiento* could not be defeated by force of arms. It affirmed Franco's military superiority at a time when he was becoming, in the view of everyone in rebel Spain, the uncontested leader of the crusade.

The Army's dominance had at once imposed 'law and order' through fear. Nevertheless, the political situation in Nationalist Spain had remained extraordinarily confused during the early months. During this period, in fact, and until October 1936, the leaders of the rebellion had not considered a political organization necessary in that zone. They devoted all their efforts to the pursuit of a war that they thought would be short lived. They were content to secure their rear by means of forceful measures.

Thus they could not and did not allow any opposition party to linger on. The proclamation of a state of siege put the means of breaking all resistance in the hands of the military authorities. There were no longer any trade unions nor workers' or Republican parties, and the other parties no longer showed signs of any serious activity. Moreover, a decision on 25 September 1936 banned all political and trade-union activity. Though a worker and peasant resistance existed in Andalusia and particularly in Estremadura, it had been decapitated after the initial Nationalist victories and the violent repression that had followed them. It was barely visible except through acts of sabotage in factories and guerrillas who harried the Nationalists, without constituting a very serious threat to their safety.

But the military dictatorship was unable to conceal the disparity between the forces that had taken part in the *Movimiento* and the lack of qualified political personnel. Outside the regular forces, there was, as in Republican Spain in the early days of the uprising, a diversity of uniforms symbolizing political differences. A report in *Le Temps* on 8 October, overtly favorable to the rebels, emphasized the cheerful disorder that prevailed in the Pamplona and Vitoria area; the clothes worn by the *Flechas*, young boys in the Falangist Youth, and the *Pelayos*, the young Carlists, injected a strange note, the black trousers, blue shirts, and police caps of the former contrasting with the khaki uniforms and red berets of the latter. One or another faction prevailed in a particular sector. In this way, the 'Albiñanists'[1] were mainly recruited from the Burgos region; there were large numbers of Falangists in Salamanca, 'the blue town,' and in Valladolid; the *Requetés*, who were the most picturesque, were manifestly dominant in Navarre, where the red *boina*, the Carlist beret, acted as a rallying sign.

Thus declarations of apoliticality in the early days were merely on principle. They emphasized the transitory character of the period, leaving uncertainty about the future. Was military dictatorship an expedient or would it continue? Which of the predominant political forces, whose aims were not always similar, the traditionalist Monarchists or the Falangists, were to prevail? At the outset, the question had been deliberately avoided. In the early days of the uprising, the flags of the Republic could be seen floating alongside Monarchist flags. Finally, the royal colors had been readopted, though it did not imply that the Monarchy would be the permanent regime in Spain.

The Men of the New Regime

Since the insurgent country needed a central body all the

same, a Provisional Junta had been established. Its official head was the ageing General Cabanellas, of the noble beard and limited ability, no doubt with the intention of avoiding a difficult choice between the leaders of the uprising after Sanjurjo's death. But real power was quickly seized by the Queipo de Llano–Mola–Franco triumvirate. When it became necessary to establish, along with unity of military command, absolute political authority, it was entrusted to General Franco.

Most of the men who could have vied with him were dead. Sanjurjo, who was the real leader of the uprising, had disappeared at its outset. Of the other military leaders, only Queipo and Mola had authority comparable to Franco's.

However, Queipo, the dictator of the South, did not have the breadth of a political leader. He lacked both subtlety and caution in his opinions. Before the Civil War, he had compromised himself by his attitude as a 'Republican' and 'Masonic' leader, and the Republican government had even contemplated entrusting him with the repression of the insurgent movement. Later on, nicknamed the 'social general' because he had had workers' cities built during the war, he acquired rather spurious popularity by his blusterings on the radio and his excesses of language. But his unexpected success in the early weeks of the uprising and the decisive role that Seville played in later operations had made him one of the *Movimiento*'s leaders. Later on, his political role continued to wane, and, after the capture of Málaga, an Italian success rather than a Spanish one, he never again had the opportunity of launching an important military operation.

Emilio Mola, because of his past and his qualities, enjoyed far greater prestige. Until his death in a plane accident during the campaign in the North, he was the only military leader with great authority who had his own ideas about the conduct of the war and policy, making him a frequent opponent of Franco; according to the latter, he was too stubborn to bend to another's will. His influence in the northern zone, fief of the *Requetés*, made him a rallying point for Monarchist intrigue. Moreover, after his death, in order to demonstrate that no one could take the place of the missing leader, Franco made a point of exercising direct control over operations on the northern front, and Dávila, who had effective command, always remained a subordinate.

The political leaders of the uprising had also disappeared or had proved incapable of imposing their views. Calvo Sotelo, the Monarchist, had died in circumstances that are already known. Of the other Monarchist leaders, Gil Robles seemed timorous and ineffectual faced with the violence of events, in which moreover he had not taken an active part. Manuel Fal Conde, the head of the Traditionalist Commune, was too politically inflexible to hope to establish unity around his party. The early leaders of the Falange had also disappeared: José Antonio Primo de Rivera, who had been shot in Alicante, was still the 'Absent One,' the *Ausente*, to his supporters, which was a way of regarding him as irreplaceable. Ruiz de Alda, the pilot, was dead, too. Onésimo Redondo had been killed in the early fighting. Fernández Cuesta was in a Republican prison. The only ones who were still there to run the Falange were second raters, like Manuel Hedilla, chairman of the Provisional Junta, and its secretary, Francisco Bravo; both were *Camisas Viejas*, former militants, by contrast with the thousands of men who had turned Falangist between February and July 1936, in order to find a framework for action against the Left, or shortly after the uprising, in order to obtain the precious safe-conduct of a party card.

Although they did not have leaders capable of asserting themselves, the Falangists, like the *Requetés*, and often in spite of them, were one of the dynamic forces in the *Movimiento*. Unity between the two groups was clearly difficult to achieve and demanded, if they were to survive a long war victoriously, the existence of a political arbiter; in the same way, rivalry between the military leaders had to give way to unified military command.

This arbiter, who quickly asserted himself as an authoritarian and obeyed leader, was General Franco. This took place gradually between July 1936 and June 1937.

On 1 October 1936, after the linkup between the forces in

the North and the South, Franco became Generalissimo and head of state. These powers had been entrusted to him by the other military leaders, after a meeting held in Salamanca on 29 September 1936.[2] No doubt this was merely a restricted and provisional authority, which was extended to the beginning of 1937 after the failure at Madrid. But the authority that was conferred on him in October 1936 was political as much as military: 'I entrust you,' said Cabanellas at the official ceremony for the transfer of functions, 'with the absolute powers of the state.'

The Nationalist Provisional Government

The system that was then functioning in Nationalist Spain remained a provisional one. It answered the needs of the moment. It was useful, because it set aside problems that could have been the cause of divisions, and because it enabled the energies of the leaders and troops to be devoted wholeheartedly to the primary task of handling the war. It was necessary, because there were too few officials and technicians to ensure the smooth working of the government apparatus; some of them had remained loyal to the Republican government, many had been dismissed, sentenced, or were merely under suspicion; only the diplomatic corps was mainly favorable to the uprising. A considerable number of military men held posts as officials.

This political system should normally have ended with the entry of Nationalist troops into Madrid. The provisional capital was Burgos, but Franco was more often in residence at Salamanca, where the general staff had its quarters. Also in Salamanca was the Generalissimo's eldest brother and the strong man of the new regime, Nicolás Franco, with the title of secretary-general to the head of state. He was in charge of the war economy, public order, and also foreign relations. He was therefore a very powerful individual.[3] At that period, the Generalissimo could in fact only supervise political questions, since he was absorbed with the running of military operations. At least he was assured of sharing power only with reliable men.

The third man in the provisional government was General Sangróniz, the Generalissimo's principal private secretary. Sangróniz had been Franco's disciple from the very start; he had been in his liaison between the Canaries and Spain.[4]

These two organs, the Secretariat-General and the Generalissimo's Secretariat, were completed by new departments created before the end of 1936. These were rough sketches for future ministries in the Nationalist government: the Secretariat for Foreign Affairs, initially under the former Spanish minister in Vienna, Francisco Serrat, the Secretariat of War, entrusted to General Gil Yuste, and the task of governor-general, given to another soldier, General Francisco Fermoso, whose functions were however as broad as they were vague: administrative control of the provinces, appointments, and relations with provincial deputations.

The offices of public security were installed in Valladolid. A press and propaganda office was opened in Salamanca; it was directed by Millán Astray, the founder of the *Tercio*, and remained closely linked with the departments of the Secretariat-General. It was however intended as much to 'orient' the Nationalist press as to 'inform' foreign correspondents visiting Nationalist Spain.

Finally, alongside the essential organs of the new Franco regime, were installed the departments of the Technical Junta, whose role was to prepare the decrees submitted to the head of the Government for his signature: finance, justice, industry, trade and food supplies, agriculture, labor, education, public works and communications.

Within the framework of the Technical Junta were the bureaux and offices that, in the style of a totalitarian system, were to control the whole of the country's activities and operate the war economy. This was a difficult task, the running of which fell to General Dávila. The latter was, like Sangróniz, one of the officers who enjoyed the Generalissimo's complete confidence. Although he was playing a second-rate role, it was a substantial one. At the same time as he was superintending the work of the Junta, he was Army chief of staff.

Consequently, Franco exercised power directly or through

his friends. But it seems that in October–November he had not yet made a choice about the future. The provisional government's program, which should have reflected its political tendencies, did not produce any original ideas. It was a compromise between Fal Conde's ideas and the theories of the Falangists.

Traditionalist survivals included the establishment of a government of totalitarian character, the chance of a Monarchist restoration, and above all the idea of national unity, which was one of the recurring themes of Nationalist propaganda and of Franco's speeches: 'The Spanish Civil War,' he declared, 'is a fight of Unity against Secession.'

Certain principles emerged from the Falange program, such as compulsory work ('The new state cannot allow parasitical citizens'), but guaranteed and protected against 'the abuses of capitalism,' fair wages for labor, and finally the possibility of profit-sharing.

In thus borrowing from everyone, Franco gave the impression of merely having sought at the time to play the role of indispensable arbiter. The rapid victory expected by the Nationalists would undoubtedly have raised the problem of what direction to give the regime. The failure at Madrid completely altered the question. It was necessary to maintain a strong authority in the face of an uncertain military situation, to avoid internal quarrels and, consequently, to put off the choice for or against the Monarchy. The provisional *status quo* was no longer adequate. It was necessary, in Suñer's words,[5] 'to give the movement the character and appearance of a state.' Franco was no longer merely the Generalissimo, he became the inspired leader of the *Movimiento*, the Caudillo.[6]

General Franco

Thus an initial political evolution was achieved: the man who had merely been one of the principal leaders of the *Movimiento* had become supreme military leader. It was not long before General Franco transformed himself into a master and a savior.

Yet this small, stocky man, 'plump, spruce, and overbearing,' with a round face and a black moustache, was not very impressive physically; on photographs, his dumpiness and his premature paunch contrasted with Mola and Kindelán. But this lack of bearing had not prevented him from enjoying an extremely brilliant political career, a captain at twenty-one and a general at thirty-two. This was exceptional, even in the Spanish Army.

Born on 3 December 1892, Francisco Franco y Bahamonde,[7] was the second child of Nicolás Franco, a naval paymaster from El Ferrol.[8] His studies, at the Sacré-Coeur in El Ferrol, then at the Naval College, earmarked him, like his father and his maternal grandfather, for a naval career. But fate intervened, because there was no room at the Naval Cadet School, and Francisco became an officer cadet at the Infantry Academy in Toledo. He left it a second lieutenant in 1910, but his real career began after two years on garrison duty, when he was sent to Morocco to take part in the battle around the old *presidios*,[9] Melilla, Ceuta, and Larache. In the harsh and inglorious initial fighting, casualties were heavy, and he was one of the few who remained unscarred by four years of war. He was wounded in 1916; by that time he was already a major. After a long interval, he returned to Morocco and was attached to the Spanish foreign legion, which was then being organized by Millán Astray. His reputation as a military leader and an organizer began as a result of his part in the *Tercio*'s battles from 1920 to 1924. His biographers have credited him with the leading role in the landing at Alhucemas Bay, which, coming after a series of reverses, put new heart into the Army of Africa. He was showered with honors and became the youngest general in the Army, and Millán Astray's successor at the head of the legion. Finally, on his return to Spain, he was given the directorship of the General Military Academy, which had just been founded in Saragossa.

He was therefore one of the most highly regarded military leaders when the 1931 revolution broke out. The rest of his story is bound up with the Republic's. Sometimes he was out of favor, sometimes at the top of the honors list. It is certain that he hesitated for a long while before joining the plot against the

Republican government. He approached Pozas and then Azaña, between February and July 1936, to ask them to crush the Revolution. This may be regarded as a manifestation of his hostility to the revolutionary Left, but it was also evidence that he wished to give the Republic a chance—even if he later fought it bitterly until it was utterly defeated.

Although Franco was slow and cautious in his decisions, he stuck to them afterward with a determination and even a stubbornness that was one of the outstanding features of his character. He undoubtedly had exceptional qualities, real intelligence, and great shrewdness, which made him as good a politician as a soldier, if not better. He was adept at concealing his views. He was calm, tactful, and sparing of words, which does not altogether square with his Spanish temperament (though it must be remembered that he was a Galician). He knew exactly how to make use of the opportunities given him.

Many lucky chances came General Franco's way. His entry into the Army, the war in the Riff, and the disappearance of the original leaders of the uprising were all factors that explain the great self-confidence with which observers credited him. But Francisco Franco was also a deeply Catholic officer. His education, the influence exerted on him by a Monarchist environment, and his respect for established religion certainly alienated him from so-called Fascism. Franco was a conservative in the military and Catholic tradition. The position he had come to occupy instilled in him the idea that he had been appointed by God to save Spain from anarchy, atheism, and revolution in all its manifestations. Long regarded as a Royalist,[10] although he had agreed to be a senior official in the Republican regime, brought up in a charismatic tradition, he regarded himself as chosen, even sacred. As a realist, however, he did not believe in the possibility of immediately reestablishing the Monarchy in its traditional form, which would have split the supporters of the *Movimiento*. He was also a realist in refusing, as he did, any compromise with the 'Reds,' because the rift between the two parties could not have been bridged by negotiation.

In short, the war provided him with the opportunity to develop his political qualities; a calm man and a player for time, he was not given to outbursts or strokes of genius, but after the humiliation of Madrid, he managed to adapt himself to a long war.

In the conduct and winning of this war, he held many trumps. First was the territory he controlled: the Nationalist government was much more favored than the Republican government. The resources in these areas complemented each other, the flocks of Estremadura and the farmlands of the big Andalusian estates, the corn of Castile and the vegetables of Galicia. In contrast, the large, densely populated cities, which had to be fed, were on the Republican side. Financially, in the absence of the Bank of Spain's resources, Franco had access to his supporters' wealth, capital smuggled out of Republican Spain and substantial foreign backing, whose interests Juan March represented. On the other hand, the exploitation of the Moroccan and Rio Tinto mines, seized by the rebels at the start of the *Movimiento*, and, after August 1937, effective control of the Basque provinces and the Santander area guaranteed an exchange currency indispensable to a stable economy. Also Nationalist Spain did not undergo any serious economic crisis.

But General Franco had to resolve the profound contradictions between the political forces that he was relying on. So that his absolute authority should not remain nominal, he had to reconcile the conservative tendencies of the Traditionalists with the Falangist ideas that sought a complete transformation of the state.

The Single Party

To achieve this goal, he used a radical method, the formation of a single party, of which he was to be indisputable leader, in imitation of what had happened in Germany and Italy. The task was a difficult one. The Monarchists had a strong political organization. Their differences had been erased in action, and the dominant part played in the uprising by the Traditionalist Commune enabled it to absorb a large number of *Acción Popular* forces. Heavily represented in Castile, it was mainly dominant in Navarre and Aragon, bastions of the uprising. Its leaders enjoyed considerable help and friendship from abroad. Faced with the protraction of the conflict, they declared their feelings openly; they demonstrated at San Sebastián in February, and Fal Conde came out publicly for an immediate restoration of the Monarchy. Franco regarded this as a fairly serious threat. He wondered if it were not advisable 'to have Fal Conde shot for the crime of high treason.'[11] At any rate, the Carlist leader was obliged to make for Portugal.

The Falange, too, had become a prominent political force. It had rallied a great number of persons, who were attracted by its dynamism or who saw it as a progressive force, as opposed to the conservatism of the *Requetés*. The Falangists, often of Republican and trade-union origin, demanded that the 'social problem' should be raised and solved. They had considerable military forces, organized into militias in Castile, Estremadura, and Andalusia. Lacking direct support, they enjoyed the sympathy of the Burgos government's Italian and German allies. But the Falange remained a party without a worthy leader.

Moreover, the political parties in view were not alone in playing a role. Franco managed to use the Army by placing it in the front rank. The military leaders were undoubtedly not always in agreement with him, and opponents emerged who were overtly hoping for a government led by Mola; most of the officers clearly did not have very dogmatic political viewpoints and were merely exhibiting their wish to support an authoritarian government. But the Army existed as a political force and was in no mood to have its political powers reduced. It was a power on which the Generalissimo could rely.

The single-party principle and the reforms that derived from it had long been accepted by Franco. Their application had at first been delayed by the Caudillo's wishes in order to obtain universal consent through negotiation. It was a question of not giving offense. The drawing up of a plan for a decree was announced in early February 1937. The easiest part had been to obtain the dissolution of the old right-wing parties, which had lost a great deal of their influence. Gil Robles's *Acción Popular* had disappeared by 10 February; a few days afterward, Robles, who had not made a move since the start of the uprising, confirmed that he was giving up all political activity. At the same time, Goicoechea announced that the other Monarchist party, *Renovación Española*, had also disappeared. Such encouraging statements were not however enough to establish the desired unity. No *entente* between the Falange and the Traditionalists could be obtained by negotiation. Reforms therefore had to be imposed.

There remained the question of finding an excuse. The one that was invoked was an incident between rival Falangist groups in Salamanca. As the decree stated, 'minor dissensions within organizations, reviving old political intrigues, threatened to disrupt organizations and authority.' The 19 April unification decree was presented as an act of peace. Franco had given careful attention to the text of this edict. According to Serrano Suñer, who claimed to have drawn up the final text, Franco took special pains to work on and annotate the Falange statutes and sought to harmonize the language of the Traditionalist Pradera with that of José Antonio. He finally submitted the decree to the approval of Queipo and Mola. Both accepted the text unreservedly. Mola's only objection was a grammatical one. However, Queipo asked for its publication to be put off for a month, on the pretext of waiting for the fall of Madrid.

'There is an urgent need,' said the preamble to the unification decree, 'to accomplish the great task of peace, crystalizing in the new state the ideas and the style of our Revolution.' This phrase alone established the importance of the text. In it, first of all, could be seen the formation of a single party: 'It is indispensable that everyone should expunge personal differences from his heart.'[12] It was equally easy to find in it previously stated principles, a legacy of the *Requetés* and the Falange. But the decree also stressed the reasons that had made its promulgation necessary: the political parties 'are wearing themselves out in sterile conflict'; by acting in this way, the leaders were betraying the masses of their supporters 'who are moved by a pure ideal.' It was therefore as well to safeguard this ideal, accepted by everyone and proclaimed by the state. The new party was to be a link between state and society, 'guarantee of the people's vigorous adherence to the state,' a link between traditional forces and new ones.[13] 'The Falange is bringing, with its program for the youthful masses, a new style of propaganda, a political and heroic form for the present; the *Requetés* have brought the sacred trust of Spanish tradition, tenaciously preserved, with its Catholic spirituality.' A profound idea emerged here, the determination to create not only a genuine party, that is, a political organization that could be used by the government, but a *hermandad*, a fraternal society, of the sort that Spanish tradition could inspire, along the lines of the half-secular, half-religious organizations formed by the Catholic kings. To link the present with the past, reviving Spain's glory in a 'new form,' such was the task of the crusade, at least for the immediate future. This was because the Caudillo refused to be a prisoner of his own decisions and was already starting to consider the possibility of modifying the edict: 'This will not be a rigid thing, but one subject to a task of revision and improvement.'

The actual decree contained three articles:

> *Article I:* The Spanish Falange and the *Requetés*, with their services and their present members, are being merged, under my command, into a single political authority of national character, which will be known as the *Falange Española Tradicionalista y de los Juntas de Ofensiva Nacional-Sindicalista.* The principal mission of this organization, halfway between society and the state, is to communicate the feelings of the people to the state and to convey to them the thinking of the state, through the politico-moral virtues of service, hierarchy, and brotherhood. All those who, on the publication day of the decree, hold a Falange or Traditional Community card, are officially affiliated with the new organization, and all Spaniards who wish to join may do so.

In appearance this article gave satisfaction to the Falange by introducing the idea of a political morality, and especially by retaining the essential part of the Falange's name to denote the new party. Franco had, moreover, intimated before 19 April that the Falange 'would be the basis of the single party.' But the two ensuing articles revealed the true meaning of the decree, which was intended to muzzle all opposition and to destroy all possibilities of a military action or a simple *coup de force* by malcontents.

> *Article II:* Governing agents of the new politico-national ensemble will be the head of state, a secretariat or Political Junta, and the National Council. The secretariat or junta corresponds to the establishment of the internal constitution of the ensemble, for the accomplishment of its principal aim: to help its leader in the preparation of the state's organic and functional structure, and to collaborate, in any case, with the government's activities. Half of its members will be appointed by the head of state and the other half elected by the National Council. The National Council will handle major national problems that the head of state submits to it in terms that will be established in accordance with subsequent arrangements.
>
> *Article III:* The militias of the Falange and the *Requetés* will be merged into a single National Militia, preserving their emblems and their insignia; the National Militia is subordinate to the Army. The head of state is the supreme head of the militia, and the direct head will be an Army general. . . .

Although General Franco thus allowed signs and symbols to survive he took care to empty them of their real meaning. A peacemaker and diplomat, he was always amenable to superficial concessions. Thus, in order to conciliate the *Requetés*, he had the ancient emblem of Navarre added to the new arms of Spain; he also had the entrance to his headquarters guarded by *Requetés*. In fact, the last two articles of the 19 April decree were a decisive step on the path to the establishment of a new regime. The second ratified the political authority of the Caudillo, who was building and consequently could always modify the structure of the state; he appointed the majority of the leaders of the single party. All the members of the first National Council were directly nominated by him. Article III contrived to give him total military authority by making him sole head of the National Militia, which had been deliberately merged with the regular army and was subordinate to it. The new party thus constituted was therefore to be the instrument of government and to be used by Francisco Franco, head of state, head of the government, national head of the *Movimiento*, and Generalissimo; his authority had been most vigorously asserted in every field.

But it was advisable to ensure this authority and the organization of the new state in actual practice. For this newly established political system to function normally, it was necessary not only to launch the idea of national unity, but also to achieve this unity and to crush all opposition. All these steps were taken with an apparent view to conciliation. The formation of the Falange's National Council was evidence of such astute distributive justice, which aimed at preserving, around the Caudillo's own person, genuine unity among the political elements that had taken part in the *Movimiento*. The council was made up of a shrewd admixture of former Falangists such as Fernández Cuesta and Agustín Aznar, of Monarchists such as Esteban Bilbao and Fal Conde, who in this way was making his political comeback, and also of soldiers such as Francisco Gómez Jordana, and proven men, including Serrano Suñer.

The danger clearly lay in displeasing all those in both parties who rightly feared that it would be impossible to find a common ground. Though Catholic support and the Caudillo's astuteness had reduced Monarchist reactions to the minimum, it had not been so on the Falangist side.

The chances of persons overtly hostile to the Falange's revolutionary program or of General Franco's friends entering the Party Junta worried the *Camisas Viejas*. The supreme power granted to Franco, whose past, education, and friendships were highly suspect, seemed even more dangerous to some of them. In such circumstances, to wait for the end of the war to bring about the triumph of the Falange ideal was very risky. The discontent of these Falangists soon came out in the open: this was the Hedilla plot.

Political Resistance

Manuel Hedilla took over the leadership of the Falange, with the title of secretary-general. He had been one of José Antonio's close collaborators. His past as a manual worker—he had been a dock worker—was the guarantee of his 'social attitude.' But he had no political training. Hughes described him as 'crude, violent and immoderate.' The plot that he organized seems, as far as one can tell, simplistic and even naïve: to prepare demonstrations throughout the country to reveal the Falange's discontent, to surround Franco's headquarters and take it by storm, and finally to proclaim a revolutionary political junta made up of Hedilla and his friends. This junta would, according to Suñer, have consisted of Pilar Primo de Rivera, sister of the former head of the Falange, General Yagüe, whose sympathies for the Falange had long been known, Dionisio Ridruejo, and José Sáinz, among others. We are, however, reduced to supposition as to the details of this affair. The transcripts of the trial have never been made public; all we know are the charges against the Falangists arrested. The most serious was unquestionably the attempt at military revolt. Possibly the importance of these activities has been deliberately exaggerated on the Franco side. Suñer accused Major Doval, in charge of public order at the Salamanca headquarters, of being a sensation seeker. It seems at any rate that the plot was very clumsily executed. Hedilla committed folly upon folly: emissaries sent to the provinces, telegrams in code to the provincial delegations inciting them to resist the unification decree, orders passed on by the provincial leader in Zamora to the local leaders, all fully justified his arrest and trial. It is clear that there were a considerable number of arrests and that measures such as the provisional one banning Falangists from entering Salamanca tended to demonstrate publicly that the new regime would not shrink from any decision, however serious, in order to impose its will.

But what was really behind the plot? It is difficult to believe that Franco's government had been seriously threatened by this narrow-minded illiterate, of whom Franco complacently remarked to Faupel that 'he fell short of the abilities required of a head of the Falange.' In the same conversation, the Caudillo had alluded to 'a clutch of ambitious young men, who were exerting their influence on him,' without however going into any further details. It is certain that Hedilla was prompted by others and that he was merely a front for them. In this respect, it is curious to note that permanent hostility to the regime in Pilar Primo de Rivera's circle continued. This woman, who was anxious to embody the spirit of the Falange after her brother's death, seems to have been at the heart of the opposition of the *Camisas Viejas* to the Franco government.[14] But her name protected her from police measures.

By deliberately exaggerating and harshly repressing a clumsy plot, Franco clearly intended to impress more dangerous opponents than Hedilla. The 'young men' to whom the Generalissimo referred had been encouraged from outside. The sympathy that the Falange had always met in Rome and Berlin had increased since the arrival of ambassadors from the Axis powers. Though the first Italian ambassador, Cantalupo, whose mission was incidentally extremely brief, did not look very closely at the domestic politics of Nationalist Spain, this was not true of his successor, Count Viola, and the German representative. Wilhelm von Faupel made no secret of his friendship for the *Camisas Viejas*; he was certainly in the know about the plot and may have supplied arms to the conspirators. Was Franco joking when he suggested to Faupel that he should send Hedilla 'to Germany and Italy for a few months, so that he can learn something and afterwards make use of his experiences in working for the country's recovery?'[15]

In fact, Hedilla was soon to learn the outcome of his trial: the guilt of the accused was unanimously recognized. Four death sentences were pronounced, including one on the former leader of the Falange.[16] According to Suñer, who does not usually sin through overgenerosity, the sentences were very harsh. Faupel, no doubt afraid of being regarded as responsible for the situation, tried to save Hedilla's life. He asked his government for instructions on what attitude to adopt toward the affair, while at the same time suggesting direct intervention and an appeal for clemency. He even suggested that a memorandum should be sent to the Generalissimo according to which 'the execution of Hedilla and his companions, at the present moment, is a step that seems open to criticism for political and social reasons.' We do not know what reply Wilhelmstrasse made to its ambassador on this subject, nor if there was, as seems probable, an Italian move on behalf of Hedilla, but the death sentences were commuted to life imprisonment.[17] A pardon of this kind would not have weakened General Franco's position—quite the contrary. Besides, the need to safeguard national unity during the fighting ensured him a good deal of support. He claimed to have received, on 5 May, 'sixty thousand telegrams of congratulation and approval.'

In spite of this official optimism, it is certain that the spirit of opposition had survived in a number of Falangist circles; it surged up from time to time and showed itself all the more violently because any form of hostility to the regime was stifled by continual repression. The most typical incident in this respect was the speech made on 19 April 1938 in Burgos by General Yagüe. Yagüe was one of the most popular Nationalist military leaders. His substantial contribution to the war since the uprising in Morocco, his reputation as a 'social' leader, and his personal friendships with the *Camisas Viejas* had made him 'the Falange general,' which explains why his name came up in Hedilla's plot. The criticisms that he made in his speech at Burgos seemed an echo of Falangist disillusion as a result of the measures for social conservation taken by the Nationalist government: it is necessary, said Yagüe, to make a few social reforms; justice must be made truly just and its partiality eliminated. The implications of these reproaches were in fact limited, and the incident did not have any serious repercussions. Naturally, sanctions were taken against Yagüe, but, although he was relieved of his command, it was not long before he returned to favor and received another appointment.

The plot organized by Vélez and Aznar was far more serious. Although the sentences passed on them were relatively light,[18] this was because the regime was now secure, and it was not necessary to strike so hard as at the time of the Hedilla plot. On the contrary, it would have been dangerous to drive part of the Falange Old Guard into the opposition ranks, and Franco was too diplomatic to do so. The important role in the Falange played by the two men implicated in the new plot in fact made them well-known figures in the *Movimiento*. Vélez was certainly the more involved. A former member of the Moroccan branch of the Falange and a national councillor like Aznar, he really seems to have sought the sympathies of several military leaders for a *coup de force*. Agustín Aznar, more cautious, merely attacked the leadership of the new regime with words; a former companion of José Antonio and friend of Fernández Cuesta, who did not follow him along this path, Aznar meant to stand for 'pure Falangism,' doctrinal intransigence. Head of the Falangist Militia before the war, which had induced him to take responsibility for the armed attacks in Madrid between February and July 1936, he was afterwards appointed Inspector-General of the Militias.

In fact, to the Falangists, the real enemy was not Franco but the conservative forces, the Church and the Monarchists. Opposition sometimes turned into brawls. Stohrer reported[19] skirmishes in Seville in early November 1938 'between the Falange and the clergy.' Moreover, the Falangists identified the Church with Monarchist reaction. Also, they were equally hostile to any attempt at a restoration.

A number of Monarchists felt after the war that Franco had bluffed them; Ansaldo testified to the constant hope of a restoration. In fact, the Generalissimo had never given a commitment to the *Requetés* and Mola himself had refused to decide in advance on the regime that the *Movimiento* would impose on Spain. Many Royalists served the new state loyally and even did it considerable service: thus Antonio Goicoechea became a respected figure in the Nationalist system and the Duke of Alba was an effective ambassador in London. Though restrained by discipline, Generals Ponte and Kindelán did not hide the fact that they were favorable to a restoration. Not a month passed without an eventual return to Monarchy being envisaged; there was even speculation about making it easier by replacing Alfonso XIII with his son Don Juan. Franco never came out directly against such schemes. He merely kept his distance from them, pointing out that Spain must not be divided any further and that he must first safeguard the unity of the *Movimiento*, guarantee of national unity.

The organization of the single party gave him the means of control and influence over all activity in Spain. This was the decisive step toward the realization of the new Spanish state, dictatorial in structure. But it was not until the early days of 1938 that a government was formed.

Meantime, two important events occurred, which also contributed to strengthening the Caudillo's position: the first was the decisive victory won in the North, and the second was the official rallying of the clergy and the unreserved support that it brought to the new regime.

The Church's Involvement

There is no doubt that, since the beginning of the war, the majority of the priests had taken sides, often in an active and even violent manner, in favor of the rebellion. But the Catholic hierarchy, while showing its sympathy, had refused to give official endorsement to a movement of revolt. The uncertainty of the early days, the concern not to break the Church's unity, and the fact that a large part of the clergy remained loyal to the government explain this waiting game. The way the situation developed during 1937 led to a radical change in this position. The reasons for it appear simple: the protraction of the war, whose outcome seemed further and further away, led to making official a choice that was already evident in practice; the successes of the Nationalists had improved the diplomatic position of the Burgos government and the logic of events pointed toward the establishment of relations with the Vatican; finally, the Biscay campaign resolved the problem posed by the existence of a Catholic minority within the Republican camp. Moreover, on 7 October 1937 the papal nuncio, Antoniutti, presented his credentials to General Franco. A few months earlier, a stand taken by the majority of Spanish prelates had anticipated this move. Constant references by Nationalists to the Catholic tradition and the work of the Catholic kings, and the personal influence of certain bishops, in particular the Cardinal-Archbishop of Toledo, Goma y Tomás, had largely contributed to sway the ecclesiastical hierarchy in this direction.

On 1 July 1937 the 'Collective Letter from the Spanish Bishops' was published. It removed all ambiguity on the subject. Signed by forty-three bishops and five capitular vicars led by Cardinal Goma and Cardinal Ilundaín, archbishop of Seville, this text owed its importance not only to the fact that it was an explanation of the attitude of the clergy and the Spanish Catholics, but in particular to the fact that it was one of the few that tried to justify the *Movimiento* in a rational and intelligent way.

First of all, the bishops' letter claimed to justify the Church's position by justifying the war. Although in some foreign countries, and more especially in certain French Catholic circles, there had been indignation at the religious persecutions in Republican Spain, there was also evident concern at the very 'active' outlook of many Spanish priests in the conflict. Moreover, the bishops stated peremptorily that 'the Church did not want the war.' It had not wanted it, but it had accepted it, because it had been compelled to do so. Recourse to force, in such circumstances, was legitimate.[20]

The text went on to say that there had been a threat to the very existence of the common good; first a threat to the Fatherland, because the orientation of the Popular Front's policy was quite 'contrary to the nature and requirements of the national spirit.' There had been threats to the religious spirit, too; thus secular laws were dubbed 'iniquitous,' attacks on 'Christian' liberty of conscience; afterward, there were attacks on the churches of a more material and less debatable kind.[21] Finally, a threat to established Society was conjured up indirectly, because there are constant references in the text of the danger of 'destructive Communism' and of the 'anti-divine' Revolution. It was therefore essential to fight, because it was a question of 'perishing under the assault of Communism or attempting to overcome it.' The war was depicted as a salutary reaction, as a 'heroic remedy' against a public danger; those who had revolted were making patriotism and the religious spirit imperatives that the Church could not repudiate.

On the other hand, it was taken for granted that 'the whole body of social authorities and men of learning recognize the public danger' and that 'the conviction of learned men about the legitimacy of their triumph' was absolute.

Since this war was just and necessary, the Church could not remain indifferent; because those who were fighting were supporting a sacred cause, the battle had to be made into a holy struggle. Hence the second purpose that may be assigned to the bishops' Letter: to indicate in which direction the conflict should be oriented, what character it should be given. This conflict, 'a reaction by a religious order,' was a crusade, and those taking part could be compared with the friar-knights of the military orders. The cause they were defending was first of all that of Spain, but also that of all Christendom. These soldiers of God were fighting 'for the fundamental principles of every civilized society.' It was, moreover, quite remarkable that the text began with a 'summons to the aid of Catholic people.' This summons was unquestionably meant for the French Catholics, but also to those in South America; the reminder of a common civilization, of their adherence to *Hispanidad*, would make it easier to rally them to the cause.

Finally, the letter refuted the idea that the war was setting the Church against the powers that be. Public authority was in ruins; to reestablish it, the leaders of the uprising had had recourse to 'an armed plebiscite.' Once again we find here the argument invoked by its supporters ever since the beginning of the *Movimiento*.

The fact remains that the representatives of the Spanish Church categorically refused to answer for everything that was covered by the *Movimiento*. One paragraph was particularly significant: it stated that the Church was not responsible for 'trends or intentions that could, in the future, disfigure the noble mien of the National Movement,' thus adding to the text a polemical element, clearly aimed at the Falange.

It cannot be emphasized too strongly that this letter was designed for export. The stand taken by the bishops meant nothing to those who were caught up in the Spanish conflict. By contrast, its official air and its categorical tone made it a key text in the eyes of foreigners: 'the real face' of the Spanish Civil War was being presented to the foreign chancelleries. Hence the text's insistence on stressing the 'collective savagery' of the Revolution and the antireligious persecutions, and hence the deliberate distortion that consisted in presenting the Revolution as a Communist uprising, without worrying about confusing the terms.[22] The idea was to remind everyone that what was happening in Spain went beyond the context of an ordinary civil war, because 'God has permitted our country to be a testing ground for the ideas and systems that aspire to conquer the world.'

Henceforth, the Church had taken its stand in the struggle. Its activities helped to give the regime its permanent orientation. Even more than the Jesuits, whose return at this period was significant, the Dominicans seem to have wielded considerable influence over the Nationalist leaders. Stohrer noted, among Franco's personal advisers, Father Menéndez Reigada. The Church's influence was not merely being wielded over the General, but also over his intimates, especially his brother-in-law, Ramón Serrano Suñer. Ever since the latter had escaped from Republican Spain in February 1937, his influence had continued to grow. Faces changed: when the first real government was formed, Suñer joined it, while Nicolás Franco was sent as ambassador to Portugal.

The New Nationalist Faces

At the time of the proclamation of the unification decree, Suñer had just arrived in Salamanca. He at once gained an ascendancy over the General that never slackened. He was small but quite strong, 'very correct, even elegant, in his dress'; he was remarkable for his prematurely white hair, his quick gestures, and his 'perpetual state of excitement'; very highly strung, switching from one extreme to another, at times charming and eager to please, at others brusque and even rude. He had studied at the Spanish Institute in Bologna. An able lawyer, he had lived for a long while in Saragossa. His relations with Franco dated back to his marriage, because the two men had married sisters. At the time of the uprising he had been in Madrid. His political views—he had belonged to the CEDA—and his family relationship with the leader of the uprising made him one of the most direct targets of the popular revolution; he was arrested, incarcerated in the Model Prison, and then transferred to a clinic on Irujo's intervention; he then managed to take refuge in a legation, probably the Dutch Legation. With the help of the Argentine ambassador, he boarded the *Tucuman* for Marseilles. But his two brothers had not been so fortunate, and Suñer still harbored resentment toward England over their deaths, responsibility for which he partly attributed to the British Embassy's bad faith.

A pupil of the Jesuits and an uncompromising defender of the Church, he remained deeply marked by his Catholic education. Friendly to Germany, he still preserved a certain mistrust of Hitler, whose policy of hostility to Christianity offended him. Also he was regarded more as a friend of Italy, and with good reason. Outspoken, violent, 'a pocket Robespierre,'[23] all those who had dealings with him were agreed in calling him a fanatic.[24] His mysticism, his hatred of the liberal spirit and consequently for the democratic system were other features of his character. His admiration for authoritarian regimes and especially for Fascism led him to steer clear of Monarchist elements, whose moderantism he criticized. His friendships had always been most eclectic; he was on good terms with certain Traditionalist leaders, such as Rodezno and Sáinz Rodríguez, but he was also a personal friend of José Antonio[25] and got along well with the new leaders of the Falange, Amado and Hedilla. His political evolution had impelled him to propose the idea of a permanent regime, led by Franco as head of state. Although he was not categorically opposed to the restitution of the monarchy, he no longer envisaged an immediate restitution. In twenty years' time, 'Spain might need a king'; in the meantime, it is highly probable that he encouraged his brother-in-law in the establishment of a personal dictatorship.

With the formation of the new government on 1 February

1938, Suñer's ideas seemed to be in the ascendancy. He was minister of the interior, minister of the press and propaganda, and he became the new regime's theoretician. The most politically inflexible leaders of the Monarchists and the Falange were not in the Cabinet. On the other hand, there were five soldiers among the principal ministers; there were three posts for technicians,[26] and General Jordana was foreign minister. Suñer, who did not care for him, dubbed him a liberal, while Hayes called him a traditionalist. He was friendly to England. General Martínez Anido was in charge of public order. It is usual to see him rather than Suñer pictured as the true leader of the repression in Nationalist Spain, although political responsibilities, and especially police measures, sometimes lay with the minister of the interior and sometimes with the minister of public order. This state of affairs, moreover, gave rise to hostility between the two men, equally authoritarian in character. Ministerial meetings in 1938 were enlivened by this quarrel.[27]

The other ministers were technicians rather than politicians: Andrés Amado, Calvo Sotelo's former collaborator, was finance minister; Suanzes, a naval architect, was minister of industry and commerce.

Soldiers and technicians were at loggerheads because of their personalities and their political views; in addition, the formation of the ministry was another step toward dictatorship by General Franco. Indispensable reforms had in fact to be imposed on Monarchist opponents: the first government message was a reminder of the urgency of social change and proclaimed the need for a trade-union organization combining employers, technicians, and workers. On the other hand, it was time to inform the Falangists that the revolution was a danger and that Spain had to revert to her great traditions.[28] Everyone had to be told that the moment had come to rebuild the state. In everyone's view the Caudillo had to be the head of this *Movimiento* and the reorganizer of the country. On 19 July 1938 a decree gave Francisco Franco the imposing title of Captain-General of the Army and the Navy. This title meant nothing in itself. Its value was purely symbolic. In Spain it had been granted only to kings. It made anyone who received it a veritable uncrowned sovereign and set the seal on the General's political victory. Two years after the 1936 *pronunciamiento*, Franco became the successor to the Catholic kings. Superiority of arms had brought him close to the total domination of the country. On 20 July he stated: 'We have won the war.' But it was in vain that he spoke of a 'fruitful peace' and the disappearance of privilege; it did not seem as if his government's efforts would be sufficient to rally its opponents. 'It is not enough to win,' said Miguel de Unamuno,[29] 'we must convince.'

Notes

[1] Supporters of Dr. Albiñana, head of a small extreme right-wing group.

[2] The meeting took place at the Nuñodono camp; those taking part were Cabanellas, Mola, Queipo, Yuste, Orgaz, Kindelán, Saliquet, Dávila, and Colonels Moreno Calderón and Montáner (the last, secretary of the Cabanellas Junta).

[3] Administrative dispersion however persisted until the end of the war. For a few months, the power of the secretary-general was so great that the government could be regarded as a two-headed dictatorship; when the Germans wanted to enter into negotiations with Nationalist Spain, they had to admit that the only way of obtaining an important decision was to apply either to the Generalissimo or to Nicolás Franco.

[4] In particular, on 14 July 1936, Sangróniz reported to Franco on the measures adopted for the uprising.

[5] The Generalissimo's brother-in-law, whose political activity had been considerable since his return to Nationalist Spain.

[6] Like the Duce in Italy, he was both leader and 'guide.'

[7] From his exact name, Francisco Paulino Hermenegildo Theodulo Franco y Bahamonde.

[8] His five children were Nicolás, Francisco, Pilar, Ramón (the pilot, killed during the war), and Pacita.

[9] Former Spanish enclaves on the coast of North Africa.

[10] The best man at his wedding had been the King, who was represented by the governor of Oviedo.

[11] Letter from Faupel, 14 April.

[12] Franco's speech announcing the 19 April decree.

[13] Franco had prepared public opinion for such a move on several occasions. Thus, when he came to Málaga after the town's capture, he appeared to the crowd between the local chiefs of the Falange and the *Requetés*.

[14] Suñer refers to the Salamanca group formed around Pilar Primo de Rivera.

[15] Archives of the German Foreign Ministry.

[16] Other sentences were pronounced for various terms of imprisonment, including one on José Luis Arrese, who a few years later became secretary-general of the Falange.

[17] Hedilla later benefited from a new act of pardon.

[18] Five and a half years at hard labor.

[19] Report of 19 November 1938.

[20] The Spanish bishops appealed to the authority of St. Thomas on this point.

[21] According to this text, 411 churches were destroyed and desecrated between February and July 1936.

[22] Thus, in a paragraph devoted to the 'character of the Communist revolution,' there is mention of the 'Anarchist revolution.'

[23] See Samuel Hoare, *Nine Troubled Years* (Toronto: Collins, 1954), letter of 15 October 1942.

[24] See Stohrer, in the Archives of the German Foreign Ministry.

[25] He was one of his executors.

[26] General Orgaz at the Ministry of War, Vice-Admiral Cervera at the Naval Ministry, and General Kindelán at the Air Ministry.

[27] On Martínez Anido's death, the Ministry of Public Order reverted to another soldier, General Álvarez Arenas.

[28] The coat of arms of the Catholic kings was adopted on 5 February.

[29] Unamuno had joined the *Movimiento* after the early days of the Civil War, but it was not long before he dissociated himself from the Nationalist regime, whose police excesses and absolute conservatism he disapproved of.

CHAPTER 18

THE ORGANIZATION OF THE NEW STATE

A few words keep recurring in the basic texts of the National-Syndicalist state: authority, hierarchy, and order. These terms, and the presence of the Army and of officers in every branch of the administration remind us that the Caudillo was a soldier and intended, in Marcotte's words, to instill the state with 'a discipline similar to that of armies.' Once the early days of excitement and color were over, observers agreed in recognizing that Nationalist Spain wore an appearance of calm and even, in certain regions, of peace, inconceivable at that time in Republican Spain.

The Maintenance of Law and Order

It was astonishing to note this peace and calm in areas like Andalusia and Estremadura, which had been more Red than most before July 1936. Without doubt, the repression of the revolutionary unrest here had been particularly bloody. But violent and sporadic measures did not usually succeed in crushing every visible form of opposition. To achieve this it would have been necessary to set up an actual organization for repression. The Nationalists first destroyed the cadres of Republican or revolutionary opposition; steps had been taken to render harmless all individuals regarded as dangerous, christened, somewhat oddly, as 'rebels' by the military leaders. As in Republican Spain, there had been a switch where repression was concerned from organized terror to a semblance of justice. Bahamonde gave a good description of this evolution, which progressed from mass shootings at the outset to 'summary procedure,' then, after February 1937, to systematic action by war councils. The latter were competent to judge 'offenses of rebellion, sedition, resistance, and disobedience to Authority,'[1] a definition already dangerous in its vagueness. The few details provided only made it all the more fearsome. Thus, sentence could be passed not only on those in possession of firearms, but, for instance, on those who 'interfered with the freedom to work' or who 'spread tendentious news likely to affect the prestige of the Army.' Any person who insulted or attacked a soldier or an official was liable to punishment. It is true that this was merely the tenor, while it is only the effect that should interest us. But in Nationalist Spain repression was in fact a daily reality: 'We shall be pitiless,' Queipo stated, 'to murderers who have sacrificed women, children, and old people to political fury. As for members of the Republican Union party, they are too close to the Popular Front to be treated separately.'[2] Thus all those who had supported the Republic at some point after 18 July, however briefly, were threatened. Even if they later rallied to the Nationalist cause it did not necessarily guarantee them impunity: the former deputy, Rosado Gil, who had been unfortunate enough to ask for a vote of confidence in the Madrid government on 1 October 1936, was sentenced to three months' imprisonment for this crime, although he had fled to Nationalist Spain a few months afterward. Even some supporters of the *Movimiento*, whose attitude was regarded as subversive, were hounded down: in July 1938, the Marquis de Carvajal had his property confiscated by the Saragossa courts for defeatism.[3] Furthermore, in the abovementioned cases, only minor crimes and comparatively moderate punishments were involved. Imprisonments and executions followed on each other's heels and the repression, often accompanied by violence and torture, gathered steam under the regime established by the minister of public order, General Martínez Anido. This earned him many attacks, especially from the *Camisas Viejas*, but his death did not put an end to these measures.[4]

Sentences,[5] purges, and surveillance were stepped up and persisted after the end of the war. It was only in January 1939 that the law on political responsibility was published, which was meant to eliminate 'the political failings of those who had contributed by acts of commission or omission to aiding or abetting Red subversion.' It sought to repress not only acts committed during the Civil War, but also those during the preceding period by members and leaders of unions, parties, and lodges. Thus 'those who had organized the 1936 elections, those who had been candidates for the government in the 1936 Cortes,' and 'those who, from 1934 to 1936, had contributed to subversion' in a general way were regarded as liable. Such offenses, which were subject to punishment ranging from prison to the confiscation of property, were to be judged by a special court known as the National Tribunal for Political Responsibility, which did not interfere in any way with the work of the war councils.

Purges and Surveillance

The purges were equally radical. These were aimed especially at the officials who had not rallied to the *Movimiento*.[6] In the area under the immediate control of the Nationalists, the problem was solved in a simple way: the new authorities gave orders to all agents of the state who were not in their assigned spots to present themselves to the military authority nearest their homes. Those who did not do so were regarded as rebels. Elsewhere, purges were carried out as new conquests were made. For instance, after the occupation of Biscay a decree on 3 July 1937 temporarily suspended all teaching staff; those who wished could 'apply to the rectorate of Valladolid for reappointment.' All they had to do was to fill in forms on which they indicated the offices that they had held under the Republic, 'the political groups or parties to which they had belonged,' and the names of persons who 'could thoroughly vouch for their attitude.' At the end of the war, the purge of officials was extended and generalized: to fall foul of the law, it was enough 'to have exercised functions unrelated to administrative activity, to have accepted exceptional promotion,' or merely not to have supported the uprising to the best of one's ability.

The measures that established the system of constant and total surveillance of the population were too numerous and too disparate to be summed up in a few words.[7] Identity cards were compulsory over the age of sixteen, a usual measure in authoritarian regimes. The formation of an Identification Department was especially helpful to the police force, or rather to the police forces, because, along with the old Civil Guard, the *Seguridad* (security police) continued to exist, as well as the secret police; shortly after the formation of the single party, the Falange had its own police force, too. It was difficult to elude such a sizable police apparatus.

The measures of surveillance did not merely affect individuals. They were extended to all the means of disseminating propaganda and information: radio, cinema, and especially the press. The war emergency law had already put a ban on the use of radio transmitters and permitted the establishment of a censorship, in theory exclusively military. Gradually, national censorship became organized: two commissions were in operation by May 1937, in Seville and in Corunna.[8] They included representatives from the military authorities but also, which is a fair indication of the scope of its powers, delegates from the society of authors, film companies, cultural centers, and heads of families. These initial arrangements were completed by a series of measures aimed at controlling the production of films, books, and newspapers. The minister of the interior, through the civil governors, was responsible for the censorship of films. On 23 December 1936 the 'publication and circulation of pornographic, Marxist, and disruptive books and printed matter'[9] was banned.

The press was even more dangerous because of the daily influence it wielded over the masses. Moreover, General Franco had always allocated an especially important role to the delegation for the press and propaganda, whose aim was 'to use the press to publicize the characteristic features of the *Movimiento*, its work and its future potential.' The head of the press department ran[10] the censorship and acted as a link with the newspaper publishers; the latter became true wielders of power. In practice appointed by the Falange, they were responsible for everything and could be removed and even struck off the register for a single mistake. Also, the information distributed in Nationalist Spain was strictly controlled in advance of publication.

As a result, it is just as well not to attach too much importance to enthusiastic descriptions made at this period by journalists in political sympathy with Franco, who in reality were content with information provided by the press office intended for foreign journalists. It was easy to find clouds on the horizon. Seville had the look of a peaceful city, wrote Antonio Bahamonde,[11] but convoys of wounded were arriving at night, and to spare the population a painful spectacle Queipo had the alert sounded during this period. In October 1937 'traffic was halted after 8 P.M. at the very gates of Seville.' The *guerrilleros* continued to hold out for a long while in Andalusia and were still taking huge risks. Bahamonde mentioned an attack on the Civil Guards in broad daylight. In May 1938, although pacification seemed almost complete, Stohrer noted similar activities near Cáceres and in Asturias. In the same report, the German ambassador estimated the share of the population in Nationalist Spain which he regarded as 'politically unstable' at 40 percent: the omnipotence of the Nationalist authorities could not wholly conceal the opinions of certain groups in the population who were in sympathy with the Reds.

It is difficult to make out to what extent the civilian and military authorities with the task of maintaining order co-operated with or thwarted each other. In the areas near the front the problem did not arise: all power was in the hands of the military. The civilian delegates appointed and installed by the officers remained mere subordinates. Later on, when the region had been pacified, the functions were gradually handed back to civil governors, to established control commissions, or in certain cases, to mayors who had been able to perform their duties. In theory, the civil governors were responsible to the minister of the interior. In reality, they had to deal with the military authorities who were still further up in the hierarchy and for a long while preserved sole responsibility for public order. The military had the right to evaluate 'the lack of ability' or the 'moral errors' of the civilians and to replace them, when they felt it absolutely necessary, by a delegate for public order.

Moreover, the lack of reliable officials often meant choosing 'civil' governors from the officers. In Málaga, for instance, after the Nationalist victory, the civil governor was Captain García Alfed, who gave the Italian troops free rein and demonstrated his political views in a spectacular fashion by wearing the uniform of the Falange.

It was natural, in such circumstances, that the only genuinely respected power was the Army and that there were clashes between the civilian and military authorities.[12]

Apart from the application of the measures decreed by the government, the major preoccupation of the civil governors and the local administrations was feeding the Army and the population. This was however easily accomplished, since the shops were always full and the stores even had English cloth on sale. Only rice, tea, and coffee were rationed in 1937–1938. The Nationalists were even able to export part of their farm produce and still maintain reserves. But they fell rapidly after the occupation of the large cities. After the fall of Barcelona, it became necessary to feed a population that had been undernourished for months. Economic problems were far more awkward once the war was over.

Prices had risen during the Civil War but had maintained a reasonable level. Every increase had to be authorized, and it was quite common to see a shop closed for contravening the price laws. In this way, the authoritarian regime prevented the living standards of the population from falling too low. Obviously it did not inhibit all speculation. According to Courmont, who was wholly on the side of the Nationalists, the price of cloth 'took a great leap,' and between October 1936 and May 1938 beef went up 37 percent and wine 48 percent.

Moreover, in spite of the apparent plenty, the regime

remained one of *austeridad*, officially explained by the demands of the war economy. In order to publicize the sacrifices made by everyone to the common cause, the regime invented the 'single course' system. On Fridays, at the beginning of the war, and then on Thursdays, everybody had to settle for a one-course meal. Yet, in practice, how could such an institution be controlled? It must be granted that this was all very utopian, except, of course, for those who ate in restaurants, who also had to agree to 'go without dessert' on Mondays. In fact, this was a question of platonic demonstrations, intended mainly to impress foreigners who would thereby be convinced of the discipline and voluntary sacrifices of the country at war. The poverty of the population was the real cause of austerity.

The calm and prosperity was therefore only a facade. For those who genuinely wish to understand the new state, it is necessary to examine its institutions in detail.

The National-Syndicalist State

Apart from the officers, whose loyalty and discipline were precious to Franco and who were indispensable, the new cadres of the political system were supplied by Falangists from the single party. This was the National-Syndicalist state's 'blue period.' The Falange was 'the inspiration and basis of the Spanish state,' according to the first sentence in its articles,[13] which reiterated and set out in detail the principles of political morality enunciated in the 19 April decree: individual interests had to bow to the 'service of the state, social justice, and the Christian freedom of the individual.' Thus, to the concept of political and social freedom, about which there was no longer any question, was opposed the principle of Christian freedom, which was simply a moral freedom. What counted, in fact, was respect for 'the fatherland's eternal values' and the social hierarchy. This notion of hierarchy inspired every party organization, from local Falanges to the Caudillo. The national leader of the *Movimiento* had, as we saw, the real power. It was he who chose the members of the first National Council, appointed the president of the Political Junta, and named five of the ten national councillors who took part in it.[14] He was the supreme head of the Falange militias, selected and dismissed the provincial leaders, and decided on regional inspections. He had the supreme power of both decision and appeal.

The Political Junta was therefore only a council with political powers in the view of the national leader; it met at least once a month, to study the proposals to be made to the head of state and to examine the accounts of the *Movimiento*. Orders were handed down from the top, from the junta or the National Council, to provincial commanders and local Falanges.

A local Falange was made up of at least twenty 'militant associates.' There could be no question of everyone who applied being admitted into the party. But neither was goodwill to be discouraged; hence the distinction between 'supporters' and 'militants,' which irresistibly brought to mind the organization of certain religious orders, and especially that of the Jesuits. The supporters were not members of the Falange. However, they had to subscribe to the formula of membership and allegiance established by the national *Jefatura* and to pay dues. The title of militant was given to supporters who had five years' membership, to former members of the Falange and the *Requetés*, and to generals, officers on active duty or serving in combat, as well as to 'those who obtained this title through a personal decision by the Caudillo or through a proposal by the provincial *Jefaturas*.' Each section had a similar hierarchy, with a local leader, a secretary, a treasurer, and a local head of militias; in the large towns, the municipal *Jefatura* had under its supervision 'heads of districts, subdistricts, blocks, and houses.' In this way a network was set up from which there was no escape, which was more efficient than any police force.

The Falange was, in every field, the instrument of totalitarian power. It existed under every form, such as women's movements and youth movements (*Flechas*); it led the youth in the universities by creating the *Sindicato Español Universitario*, a single, compulsory student organization, meant to 'instill the intellectual profession with a deeply Catholic and Spanish feeling.' Like the Falange, it was organized on a hierarchical basis, with a national leader appointed by the Caudillo and invested with supreme authority at its head. Apart from the students who were normally part of the SEU and who paid their dues, subscribed to the rules of membership—which implied unconditional obedience—and wore the five arrows and the yoke, emblems of the Falange, there were two unusual categories of associate member, honorary members who, without being students, had contributed, through intellectual work, to Spain's greatness, and patrons, who had helped the development of the SEU with gifts or financial aid.

From 1938, the Falangist state became the National-Syndicalist state. The Suñer group, which included, in the government, Fernández Cuesta, Amado, and the minister for trade-union affairs, González Bueno, felt that it was not possible to abandon the positive side of the Falangist program. First they wanted to obtain an affirmation of principle: the new state had to demonstrate its social vocation to everyone. The Labor Charter in fact began with a twofold statement: 'Work will be required of everyone,' but 'everyone has the right to work.' It also contained a number of promises: the length of the workday was not to be excessive; married women would be 'freed from the workshop and the factory'; a public holiday would be created that, in contrast to the Reds' 1 May, would be on 18 July, anniversary of the glorious uprising, and would be called the holiday for the glorification of work. There was even mention of holidays with pay and institutions for workers' leisure hours. However it is necessary to note the extremely vague nature of these provisions. For instance, at what point can the working day be regarded as 'excessive'? The text mentioned holidays with pay but did not fix their length for the time being. Later on, there was talk of a week, but it had still not been granted in 1938. The war provided an excuse for putting off 'social' achievements. In the meantime, some of the advantages gained were lost. The work week in metalworks, ironworks, and factories making electrical and scientific equipment rose from forty-four to forty-eight hours, and in the Huelva mines, in the first six months of 1938, the work week was increased by an hour.

Also, without dwelling on the hypothetical benefits granted to the workers by the *Fuero del Trabajo,* it is necessary to consider the deep-seated principles that had guided the legislators in the Falange National Council. Courmont recalled that 'the state's National-Syndicalist organization is inspired by the principles of Unity, Totality, and Hierarchy.' We shall merely follow his analysis of the charter and of the formation of vertical trade unions.

The Principle of Unity

The principle of unity meant that 'outside the trade union, there is nothing.' Joining a union was in fact compulsory: the issue of union cards, a Falange monopoly, was, in the hands of the single party, an important new means of control. The totalitarian idea was clear from the union's very organization: 'All productive forces are united.' In fact, in contrast to the affirmation of the class struggle that was at the basis of 'Marxist materialism,' the National-Syndicalist state claimed to have overcome the differences between social categories. Moreover, the union was to group employers, employees, and technicians in the same bodies. The unions were in fact strictly hierarchical. 'All union groups are subject to the authority of their leaders,' the latter being, of course, chosen by the Falange, which provided cadres for the workers as it did for the rest of the population. The state promised that it would grant aid and protection and that it would act faithfully toward the workers. In return, it required unconditional loyalty and obedience.

Finally, the Falange intervened in the country's life by means of social work, which it is more tempting to call charitable work, and which it alone organized. The essential achievement in this respect was *Auxilio Social*, founded in autumn 1936 by Mercedes Sanz Bachiller, the widow of the Falangist leader Onésimo Redondo, but which was in fact run by Pilar Primo de Rivera. *Auxilio Social* had begun as an organization for winter aid: initially, it had provided three dining halls for orphans. Later, aid was extended to refugees: these were 'brotherhood kitchens,' a name beloved by the regime. Later on, help was organized for sick and aged workers. The headquarters of *Auxilio Social* was in Valladolid.[15] Its means were provided by the efforts of Falangist women and later on by the Social

Service, the equivalent for women from seventeen to thirty-five of what military service was for men. This also was to help establish an atmosphere of brotherhood: married women, widows, and disabled women were exempt from it.[16] In theory it was voluntary, but a woman could not take an examination or get a job in the administration if she had not served in it.[17]

The distribution of this substantial aid required considerable financial means, and government contributions were quite inadequate. The necessary resources were supplied by fortnightly collections, the sale of *Auxilio Social* stamps, and in particular by 'blue forms,' whose signers committed themselves to regular payments.[18]

Elsewhere, independently of the Falange, the Nationalist government was particularly concerned with two problems arising from the war: help for the families of combatants, for whom a 'relief fund' was set up and maintained by a 10 percent tax on luxury goods,[19] and the *Colocación Familiar de Niños*, typical of the kind of poverty created by the war. The task of this organization was to search every locality for families able to provide orphans or children separated from their parents by the war with 'the sacred warmth of a family.' They also had to be able to give them a good education. Moreover, the official wording provided that they had to be models 'of behavior, religion, and morality,' in order to give the rescued children 'a Christian education and the holy love of the fatherland.'[20] They were chosen with great care: a local junta, including the *alcade*, the doyen of the priests, and a municipal health officer, appointed guardians and supplied detailed information about them supporting their applications;[21] moreover, it had to make sure that such guardians 'carried out their duties.'

In all such institutions, hand in hand with a charitable spirit went the desire for law and order and the wish to struggle for the triumph of official morality, which was both Christian morality and the Falange's political morality. In spite of declarations of social intent by the state, the fact was that the only achievements were exclusively charitable measures, making use of goodwill and private contributions. The *benefico-social* welfare fund was kept going by profits made during the single-course day, the result of public collections authorized by the state, and, finally, but as a last resort, by contributions from the state.

As to social justice, profit sharing, and the other promises in the Labor Charter, not one had even begun to be put into effect by 1939. The only serious attempt made had been the introduction of the *subsidio familiar*, a family grant made to the head of the family from a fund maintained by workers' and measures preached by the Falange, but this aid for families was mainly the result of the considerable influence of the Catholic Church.

The Church and the New State

'Perhaps the only thing that is certain in the present state of affairs,' Stohrer said in 1938, 'is that, under the present regime, the influence of the Catholic Church has greatly increased in Nationalist Spain.'

We have already pointed out that a large number of Spanish priests had approved and supported the rebellion from the outset. Cardinal Segura, whose differences with the Falange were later to take a most violent turn—he was even induced to quit Spanish soil for a while—had fought against the Popular Front. Cardinal Goma y Tomás tried to convince the French episcopate of the sanctity of the crusade. On 15 August 1936, Cardinal Ilundaín presided over an official ceremony alongside Queipo de Llano. Some lesser religious personalities adopted very violent attitudes in their speeches. Bahamonde quoted a sermon by a priest from Rota: 'All this filth must be swept away. . . . I am warning you: Everyone to Mass. I am not accepting any excuses!' Georges Bernanos testified that compulsory attendance at Mass was backed, at least in the early months of the war, by serious threats. However, it must be pointed out that certain priests had had the courage to protest against mass executions, even at the risk of themselves becoming victims of *paseos*: Bahamonde quoted the case of a priest from Carmona, killed for protesting against the Falange's crimes.

The Church's influence, however, did not cease growing. One of the reasons that had prompted several Monarchist leaders to rally to the new regime—among them Rodezno, later minister of justice—was quite clearly the government's alliance with the Vatican, accompanied by the abolition of the secular measures taken by the Republicans: it was thus that the legislation on divorce was suppressed, the 2 March 1938 decree authorizing only the investigation of 'requests concerning preventive moves against separations of husbands and wives.'

The measure that made the greatest impact in this respect was the 3 May 1938 decree authorizing the return of the Jesuits to Spain. This move was not presented as a move in favor of the Catholic Church but as a reparation. In the government's view, two motives justified it: first, it was an 'eminently Spanish' order, and it was natural, at a time when *Hispanidad* was being rediscovered, that the Jesuits should recover their rights and property. This was part of the return to tradition. The other reason was 'the enormous cultural contribution' made to the country by the Jesuits. At a time when the influence of Marxist intellectuals had to be destroyed, the Jesuits would naturally help to make Spain a country united in its Catholicity. Their role was at any rate debated: Bahamonde saw them as 'the most violent instigators of repression.'

The Church was present everywhere in the new state, first of all in the Army. Military chaplains were restored at the end of 1936, and a decree in May 1937 completed the organization of 'Catholic spiritual aid in war units,' under the guidance of the cardinal-archbishop of Toledo, the pontifical delegate. The staff were recruited from mobilized priests.

The Church and Education

But it was in the field of education that the activities of the clergy had most effect, particularly after 1938, when Franco called in Sáinz Rodríguez as minister of education. Suñer, though a fervent Catholic, said the new minister was 'the most Vatican-minded legislator that Spain has known.' The secular teaching staff had on the whole been loyal to the Republic; on several occasions, Franco's government had had to close the secondary schools, for lack of staff. Thus, in 1937, the national schools in Santander, Mérida, and Talavera had been temporarily closed; the premises were usually occupied afterward by the Army. When there was staff available, it had to be very carefully integrated. Teachers who had been kept in their posts by the purge commissions were regarded as still in need of fresh control and training. Thus, special courses were organized during the summer for their benefit in all provincial capitals. In the first week, they attended conferences on religion, the fatherland, man, and master; during the second week, subjects treated were classified under such headings as: 'Pedagogy of Religion,' 'History of the Fatherland,' 'Children,' and 'School.' The lecturers in charge of religious courses were appointed by the bishop. The titles of their lessons were significant: one was devoted to demonstrating 'the superiority of the Christian religion over Eastern-style religions.' Another lesson dealt with 'the Catholic conception of the master, according to Pope Pius XI's encyclical.' Concessions to modernity that permitted references to 'psychology' and 'psychopathology' did not rule out constant and basic intervention by the Church in teacher training.

Religious instruction was made compulsory in primary as well as in secondary education. The only ones exempt were 'natives in the protectorate of Morocco and the African colonies,' whom it was advisable not to shock by clumsy proselytism. Elsewhere and for everyone else, religious instruction ranged from a simple knowledge of the catechism and religious history in the early years to more complicated lessons in the form of 'broad-minded' explanations of Catholic dogma. It ended, in the fifth year of secondary education, with some training in apologetics.

Quite apart from these lessons, religion was ever-present. Thus, there was exaggerated respect in the schools for 'rules of devotion to the Virgin Mary': a decree in April 1937 compelled masters to place a picture of the Virgin, 'preferably under the typically Spanish invocation of the Immaculate Conception,' in their classrooms, in such a way that the pupils, entering and leaving, could see her while exchanging the ritual phrases with their master: '*Ave Maria purissima, sin pecado concebida. . . .*' Moreover, a special invocation was repeated each day throughout the war. Of course, this was, according to the legislators, a case of returning to the traditions of the 'spirit of the people.' But, in reality, it was teaching with a well-defined orientation, intended to mold citizens who were at the same time practicing Christians.

Starting with primary school, it was, according to the official instructions, necessary 'for every scholastic environment to be subjected to the influence of Catholic doctrine.' Purely religious manifestations increased: an order in February 1938 established a holiday for the feast of St. Thomas Aquinas and organized a commemorative ceremony 'to perpetuate this model of saintliness in the minds of generations of pupils.' All the academic authorities were present, and the students were represented by the SEU. Similarly, it became obligatory for the 'holy crucifix' to be placed in intermediate teaching colleges and universities. Everything had to testify to the radical change: lay schools were those with a 'soviet regime'; national education had to be Christian, and the teaching of 'social brotherhood,' as proclaimed by the Church, was to do away with 'odious materialism.' This was an education in depth that did not end at the school gates. It was not enough for children to attend Mass in a group, led by their masters. The recommendations made to inspectors of primary education reminded them that school was an institution that helped to 'dignify the religious spirit,' that it was 'educational and formed good patriots,' and finally that in it young girls were to learn 'their lofty duties in family and home.'

In this way the forms of religious, civic, and patriotic education were closely linked. To maintain this atmosphere, the use of 'popular songs, and patriotic anthems and biographies' was recommended, as well as the 'reading of newspapers and commentaries on news items,' which was evidently an original conception of the study of history. And since this education was meant for everyone, adults, too, would learn what the 'National Movement' was, in their own classes.

The aim of all this was to spread the idea that life is 'combat, sacrifice, discipline, struggle, and austerity.'

But the discipline promised to everyone had to be imposed on everyone. Nationalist society was Christian and hierarchical. The oath of loyalty, sworn according to various formulae, was evidence of it. Thus, magistrates taking office stood and swore the oath before the holy crucifix. To the formula, 'Do you swear before God and the holy Gospels to give unconditional support to the Caudillo of Spain, to render honest and impartial justice, to obey the laws and provisions pertaining to the exercise of your office, without other motive than the faithful accomplishment of your duty and the good of Spain?', the judge replied with the sacred formula.

The formula for academic oaths was even more original and symbolic. Before a desk on which were placed 'a copy of the Gospels in the Vulgate' (the cover decorated with the sign of the cross) and 'a copy of Don Quixote' (the cover decorated with the Falange arms), the academician had to swear 'before God and his guardian angel' to 'serve Spain continually and loyally, under the authority and rule of its living tradition, its Catholicity as embodied by the Roman pontiff, and its continuity as represented by the Caudillo.'

Hispanidad

The foundation of the Spanish Institute served a twofold aim: to conserve national wealth and to preserve and propagate tradition. Although its president was the great musician Manuel de Falla, the list of presidents of learned societies was revelatory of a state of mind, because it contained the most eminent representatives of conservative opinion: Pemartín, the Duke of Alba, the Count of Romanones, and Goicoechea. With the foundation of the Institute, the protection bestowed on the arts was to restore Spain's prestige in such a way that she would rapidly recover the leadership of all Spanish-speaking nations. *Hispanidad* was to be achieved by union between Spain and the Latin-American states. Students in the SEU were advised to make every effort to establish links with those in Latin America. Thus the imperial vocation, a favorite theme of the Falangists, was on the way to being achieved. It was in this spirit that the order of Alfonso X, the Wise, designed to reward 'Spaniards who have distinguished themselves in the sciences, education, literature, or the arts,' and the imperial order of the Red Arrows, which, in a vague way, was to reward national merit, were founded. Naturally, such a policy contained dangers, especially that of displeasing allies. Some young Falangists had vociferously demonstrated their wish to rebuild a great Iberian power, which could not fail to antagonize Portugal. But the Nationalist government took care to modify such intemperance.

It was therefore more out of an intellectual game than out of living reality that Franco's Spain projected herself as the successor to the Spain of the Catholic kings, of Charles V and Philip II. It was advisable to convince all Spaniards that, if they accepted the trials and tribulations of the war, it was in order to achieve a great ideal, so that Spain could re-echo the royal motto, 'One, great, free.' In the meantime, lacking real power, the Nationalists had to make do with affirmations of principle and symbolic gestures, such as reestablishing the order of Isabella the Catholic, of which the head of state became grand master. Such decorations, and the ceremonies that commemorated the glorious anniversaries of Calvo Sotelo's death and the 18 July uprising, were primarily intended to preserve the Nationalist Army's determination to fight.

The Nationalist Army

The spirit of sacrifice and the military qualities of the Nationalist troops were indisputable. There were occasions when Italian or German allies questioned the decisions of the Spanish command or the unpreparedness of the troops in action; they never complained of lack of courage. This was necessary in a war that grew in bitterness. According to General Walch, in 1938 the 'average life expectancy of a lieutenant from the Military Academy' was forty-three days. However, the cadres maintained their level of ability, because a special effort had been made in this field. Since the end of 1936, recruitment, organization, and training of troops had been entrusted to General Orgaz. His first concern had been to establish schools and courses for officer training. Military academies increased: there were three for infantry, one for cavalry, one for supply, and one for engineers.[22] Specialists were harder to recruit, and in January 1937, radio operators were mobilized. Then an Air School was created; flight and ground-staff bonuses were freely distributed.

There was never any general mobilization: young men in civilian clothes were still to be seen in Nationalist Spain. It is certain that the government had hesitated at the beginning before calling up a mass of politically undecided and, in certain regions, even hostile men. The superiority of the regular army then seemed adequate enough for the recourse to mobilization to be avoided. At the time of the big battle at Madrid, the Nationalist Army consisted of barely more than 250,000 men, a large part of which was made up of the Spanish foreign legion and Moorish troops. There were still many recruits from Morocco, helped by General Franco's clever treatment of natives. The Caudillo had always been at pains to distinguish between the laws applying to the homeland and the ones that had been created for the Riff areas. Although he had made certain special disciplinary provisions for the Moorish troops, such as a ban on frequenting taverns, he had also adopted special measures for financial aid to the wounded and their families. A veteran of the Riff war, he had been adept at wining over troops and had chosen his honor guard there. He never lost sight of the need for substantial military recruitment in Morocco and was constantly humoring the Moroccan Nationalists in spite of noisy affirmations of principle about the nation and the empire.

However, after 1937, the Army was strengthened. The formation of a 'Red' Army capable of fighting forced the Nationalists to levy fresh troops. At the time of the battle of Teruel, the Nationalist Army comprised 600,000 men; after the end of 1937, it merged regular troops and militias into a single force. Sixty-six *banderas* from the Falange, thirty-one *Tercios* from the *Requetés*, and thirty-six battalions from various political organizations were brought into the new single-party militias. The new head of the militias, Colonel Monasterio, one of the leaders of the Army of the South, had played an important part in the early fighting. In this way, not only had the political parties disappeared, but also their chances of one day being revived as combat forces.

The party, the Church, the Army: these were the three forces in the new Spain, the pillars of the National-Syndicalist state. It was a totalitarian state, which crushed opposition, possessed a remarkable police apparatus, and imposed obedience through a powerful state bureaucracy. But it was not a Fascist power. It had retained only the forms, the cadres, and the appeal to nationalism of Fascism, a simple means of channeling minds toward dreams of greatness and conquest, because Spain, poor before the war and ruined after it, could only dream of greatness, without any hope of attaining it. There was no question of any 'social' achievements here, such as existed in Italy and especially in Germany. The workers' and peasants' living conditions were as bad as ever. The indispensable agrarian reforms had not even been contemplated.

This was because in reality, behind the dictatorship of the Church and the Army, and behind Franco's dictatorship, lay the domination of a class, or more precisely of a social caste. Franco's Spain was the Spain of the big landowners, of the old aristocracy, the Spain of the oligarchs. The Army and the party were merely instruments of their authority, and they exercised their power all the more rigorously in that they had been afraid of losing it when the Revolution had roused the popular masses, and in that they had to fight long and hard to carry the day. At the end of 1937, in spite of their successes, they were not yet certain of victory.

Notes

[1] Decree of 28 July 1936.

[2] See *Le Temps*, 28 July 1938.

[3] According to *Le Temps*, 2 July, he was reproached for having stated: 'An armistice seems not inconceivable, and still less improbable.'

[4] General Martínez Anido, as governor of Catalonia, had led his *pistoleros* in attacking the cadres of the CNT in 1921. He had also been the first

minister of the interior in Primo de Rivera's Military Directorate. His past made him the symbol of the harshest kind of repression against workers and revolutionaries. This partly explains the attacks by the *Camisas Viejas*.

[5] As soon as a province was pacified, war councils began to operate. After the fall of Catalonia, *Le Temps* on 15 February 1939 reported as sentenced to death Ventura, former president of the revolutionary tribunal of the *Uruguay* (the boat having acted as a court since the beginning of the war), who had sentenced General Goded to death; Garrigo López, president of the first Workers' Committee of General Motors, and the auto-worker trade unionist Emilio Morales.

[6] Specific measures were taken regarding the diplomatic corps, whose position abroad was obviously a special one.

[7] Foremost among these were errors leading to final dismissal or temporary suspension, removal from office, or a ban on being appointed to management.

[8] The Seville commission was presided over by Carlos Pedro Quintana, and the Corunna commission by Francisco de la Rocha.

[9] A remarkable association of ideas of which the authors never wearied, because it recurred in the acts controlling literature in Nationalist Spain, such as the astonishing organization of libraries, not a temporary censorship explicable by the war, but the preparation of a systematic control intended to eliminate once and for all 'disruptive literature' in public libraries and cultural centers. In each university district a commission was set up consisting of 'the rector or his deputy, a professor from the faculty of philosophy or literature, and a delegate from the library and archaeological archivists,' who were the delegates of the lay professors, but also 'a representative from the ecclesiastical authority, one from the military authority, one appointed by the Falange's Cultural Delegation, and finally a family man appointed by the Catholic association of family men.' It was up to each authority to denounce, among publications regarded as dangerous, the ones that represented 'disparagement of the Catholic religion,' lack of respect 'for the dignity of our glorious Army,' and an 'outrage to the unity of the fatherland.' To be more precise, it was recommended that works that were 'pornographic and void of literary quality' or revolutionary 'without essentially worthwhile ideological content' should be destroyed, pure and simple. Worthwhile works could be preserved, but to avoid their falling into the hands of 'innocent readers,' they would be accessible only to readers provided with a special authorization from the Cultural Commission.

[10] During the war, this was Juan Pujol, whose abilities were generally recognized.

[11] *Un año con Queipo de Llano* (Barcelona: Ediciones Españolas, 1938; translated into English as *Memoirs of a Spanish Nationalist* [London: United Editorial, 1939]).

[12] Bahamonde (ibid.) described a very serious conflict that broke out in Badajoz. The origin of it involved the organization of one of the innumerable funds launched by the regime, but it degenerated into a real trial of strength between the military governor, Canizarés, and the 'civil' governor, Díaz de Llano. The Army and the Falange together finally imposed their will, and the civil governor had to give way.

[13] Statutes of the *Federación Española Tradicionalista* and the JONS, decree of 4 August 1937.

[14] The other five were nominated by the council at the Caudillo's suggestion.

[15] The decree of 7 October 1937, which instituted it, claimed to be a contribution to 'the achievement of the Falange's program.'

[16] For widows, on condition that they had at least one child.

[17] The service required a minimum of six months' continuous service or six successive periods of at least a month.

[18] See V. A. Marcotte, *L'Espagne Nationale-Syndicaliste* (Brussels: Imprimerie Puvrez, 1948).

[19] The tax was levied on the sale of tobacco, entrance fees to places of entertainment, bills in cafés and restaurants, and the sale of perfume.

[20] Official Bulletin, 2 January 1937.

[21] The following information in particular had to be given about the guardian's family: moral, religious, and economic standing, indication of resources, and health report.

[22] For the German staff, see chapter 14.

CHAPTER 19

TERUEL, TURNING POINT OF THE WAR

We have seen that, during the course of 1937, there was a parallel political evolution in the two camps. In both Valencia and Burgos, the forces of strength prevailed over the elements tending toward dispersion, the official authority over the supporters of the movement. The evolution thus set in motion seemed irreversible. It was impossible to envisage a violent political reversal in Nationalist Spain after the *Camisas Viejas* were brought to heel, any more than in Republican Spain after the May days. Thus there was a return to the conditions of a war in the traditional mold. However, an examination of events on the military level reveals an evolution unfavorable to the Valencia government.

Conditions for the Offensive

It is indisputable that the military situation at the end of 1937 gave the Republicans great cause for concern. The chief feeling after the fall of the North was one of total impotence. Every attempt to restrict the scope of the Nationalist successes had failed in the end. There had certainly been an attempt at reorganization: Rojo listed five army corps, trained and on a war footing. But their equipment was still inadequate, and, more important, they lacked faith in their means. Moreover, the end of the fighting in Asturias released a large number of well-trained Nationalist troops.

These reinforcements made a profound change in the balance

of forces on the part of the front where they were deployed. In fact, Franco now had almost 600,000 men, about a third of whom could be held in reserve. The Navarrese forces, which alone had preserved their original organization in brigades, had been reorganized into divisions after 9 November.

Of the three sectors from which the Nationalists could choose to launch a new offensive, two were held by forces relatively weak in number, the one in the South, still under Queipo, and the one in the North, under Dávila. The heaviest concentration of troops was around Madrid. It therefore seemed to the Nationalist general staff that, in order to achieve a conclusive victory, it had to be won in this sector, by far the most important. For the first time since Guadalajara, Franco felt ready to strike hard in the direction of the capital. There was however no question of a frontal offensive, which would risk coming to grief at the hands of a well-organized defense, and would at any rate cause heavy casualties. It was therefore better to revert to the principle of a flank attack; the offensive had to be on as broad a scale as possible to make maximum use of the numerical and material superiority of the Nationalists. Opinion favored a pincer movement on Alcalá de Henares. The Moroccan army corps was, according to Díaz de Villegas, to move down the Henares, the CTV to advance along the Tajuna, and the Castilian army corps along the Tagus. This vast maneuver naturally called for fairly lengthy preparation; moreover, such a substantial concentration of troops could hardly fail to pass unnoticed.

Meanwhile the Republican general staff was aware that, if it once again let the Nationalists take the initiative in operations, it stood in danger of defeat. The Republican government was in dire need of a success to boost the morale of its supporters and to justify its actions by a demonstration of effectiveness. By the end of 1937, Negrín was in a position of political strength: his friends had taken over the UGT leadership. He transferred ministries and central administrative offices from Valencia to Barcelona. The premier explained this transfer, inconceivable at the beginning of the year: 'It is an old idea of the previous government's. The government's residence in Valencia had been determined by the need to organize supplies and military operations for the central and eastern fronts. The government is convinced that the Levante area will retain its enthusiasm. Economic and strategic considerations have demanded that the government have its seat in Barcelona ever since the *Movimiento* began.' The motives advanced were not new ones. The transfer had not been made any earlier because the strength of the CNT and of the Autonomists had made the installation of the government in Barcelona difficult. Now, Negrín could refer in his speech to 'cordial relations with the Generalidad.' In this sense, it was possible to talk of a strengthening of unity in the Republican camp. However, political unity could only really be forged by a military victory.

The Battle of Teruel

The Republican general staff was therefore forced onto the offensive. On 8 December, the Supreme War Council approved the choice of Teruel as an objective. The positions seemed to favor an attack. The front was shaped like a big loop that came to a point around the town, forming a salient in the Republican lines. To the north it followed the mountainous area overlooking the Alfambra, bending sharply and moving southeast-northwest between Teruel and Albarracín, north of the Montes Universales. The government troops therefore held positions dominating the town on two sides. Moreover, against the modest forces that the Nationalists had there, as they had along the whole of the northern front—2500 men to defend Teruel at the start of the battle—the Republicans committed substantial forces, 40,000 men in a very limited sector of the attack. The three army corps that made up the striking force were supported by troops from the Levante that had been holding the sector until then. The Twenty-second Army Corps, under Ibarrola, was to attack in the north, the Twentieth, under Menéndez, in the southeast, and the Eighteenth, under Herédia, in the south. The first aim of the maneuver was to effect a link, beyond Teruel, between the troops of the Eighteenth and the Twenty-second Army Corps, thus isolating the town's defenders and simultaneously reducing the salient.

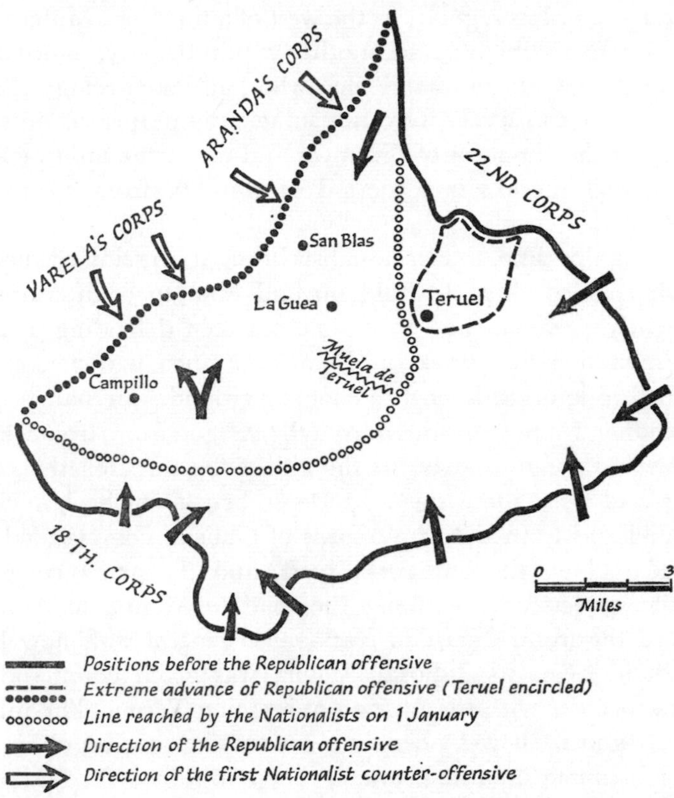

Map of the Battle of Teruel (December 1937–January 1938)

The offensive began on 15 December. For a week, from the fifteenth to the twenty-second, it achieved considerable success. From the start, it was clear that the enveloping movement was working. Campillo, which had resisted, and San Blas fell. Even so there were substantial pockets of resistance in the rear which had to be wiped out one by one. On the eighteenth, the Muela de Teruel, which dominated the town to the southwest, fell. Its defenders, fighting as they retreated, had taken refuge in the town, which two Republican divisions entered on the twenty-second. The Nationalists, under Colonel Rey D'Harcourt, had entrenched themselves in the civil government buildings, the Bank of Spain, the seminary, and the convents of Santa Clara and Santa Teresa. Two fronts were thus organized: an external front, more or less regular, to the west of a line from Muleton to San Blas and Rubiales, and another within the city, in order to reduce the several thousand men who had taken refuge there. The Republican forces were not sufficiently numerous both to carry out the conquest of the town and to pursue an attack in depth, and there was a period of stability from 23 to 28 December.

During this time, the Nationalists brought up reinforcements, which enabled them to hold on and even to counterattack. Evidently they had had to choose between defending Teruel and mounting an attack on Madrid. Franco had personally decided to join battle on the enemy's ground.[1] He had begun by sending troops withdrawn from the Aragon front, from which they could come quickly, to the aid of the threatened sector. They had been there since 17 December. Then he launched the divisions from the army corps of Galicia, commanded by Aranda, along the Saragossa road, and the army corps of Castile, under Varela, along the road to Molina in Aragon toward the front line. The Nationalist general staff now had ten divisions at its disposal. Dávila was given command of them, together with the mission of rescuing Teruel. The influx of troops in itself was already a success for the Republicans: more fortunate than at Brunete, they had forced the Nationalists to alter their plans and to give up their large-scale offensive against Madrid, of which moreover there was no further question until the end of the war. There was great disappointment among Franco's allies, as witnessed by this note from Schwendemann: 'Hopes before the events at Teruel of seeing Franco end the war with an offensive in the grand style were ill founded.'[2] On 20 December Count Ciano was telling himself that 'the offensive against Guadalajara has been indefinitely postponed because of the Nationalist command's hesitancy and the preventive offensive by the Reds.' The failure of the Nationalist counteroffensive justified the fears of the Italian generals. In spite of the accumulation of material, air superiority, the vast concentration of artillery,[3] and, finally, the violence of the attacks, only part of the objectives had been attained. At first, there were a few successes: the Republican

Twentieth Army Corps retreated in disorder. Aranda's troops advanced toward Teruel and recaptured La Muela; they dominated the town and were so certain of taking it that the Nationalist radio announced it as a *fait accompli*. Yet at the beginning of January a new front line had emerged: it barely altered for a month.

How can this Nationalist failure be explained? First, by the scope and bitterness of the fighting. In order to hold the line, fresh troops and material were brought up on both sides. The figure of 180,000 soldiers that has been advanced may be taken as a likely one: it was the largest concentration of men in so confined a space throughout the entire war. But the battle was also one of material: the amount of artillery involved was so great that the infantry had to dig in, and reinforcements came up only at night. Fighting conditions had become remarkably difficult, the more so because, in this part of the interior where the climate was harsh, the cold had reappeared with an intensity all its own. Soldiers had to be relieved every quarter of an hour, and, at –4°, entrenched men first had to protect themselves from cold, snow, and wind. Framed against the snow, everything became a target, and attacks grew rarer: even night convoys found it difficult to arrive in the frost. 'The trenches are strewn with iron carcasses.'[4] The Nationalists' air superiority could not be fully exploited, because the weather did not always permit sorties. Ansaldo referred to 'mornings at the new Burgos airport' when you had to 'remove a thick layer of ice from the fuselage.' Moreover, the Republicans had made considerable efforts, too, and the narrowness of the front contributed to an effective use of antiaircraft defenses.[5]

In spite of these difficult conditions, the Nationalists kept up their attacks during the first week of January. Finally, on 7 January, calm was restored. The pursuit of the offensive no longer had any meaning, because the defenders of the town had surrendered: Teruel was completely in the hands of the Republicans. The struggle had been long and harsh; one after another, the buildings in which the Nationalists were sheltering had been destroyed. The seminary had been fired, and government troops had blown up the Bank of Spain. Hopes of making

Teruel another Alcázar were in vain. The defenders were cut off from each other, and the Convent of Santa Clara surrendered only on the eighth—twenty-four hours after Rey D'Harcourt had capitulated with 1500 men. An official communiqué announced: 'The whole of Teruel belongs to the Republic.' This was not however a remarkable success; the center of the town was in ruins, and it took a fortnight to eliminate all the snipers. This was because the defense had been courageous, in spite of what Queipo had asserted on Radio Seville about the 'betrayal by scum' that alone had caused the fall of the town. But this very anger clearly indicated the importance of the capture of Teruel to the Republicans. It was the first and only important town that they had managed to recapture during the war. Although it was incorrect to state, as Rojo did, that 'Teruel changed the face of the war,'[6] at least it can be conceded that it gave the impression of having done so. With the outcome of this terrible battle, it was the Republican Army that appeared the victor. After the depressing communiqués that had announced in turn the loss of Bilbao, Santander, and Gijón, here at last was a hopeful one.

But this victory was limited. The question had been raised[7]—as with all the Republican successes— as to whether it would have been possible to exploit the initial success better. The answer was in the negative: there was a lack of reserves. All in all, the Republicans were numerically weaker than their opponents, when in order to make up for their inferiority in arms and equipment they needed at least a numerical superiority in men. They succeeded in this only for a few days, long enough for the enemy to bring up reinforcements. In such circumstances, it was a real triumph for the Republican general staff to have been able to hold on to the positions gained. But this was also why Franco could not pause at a defeat that he had good reason to believe was only temporary. In fact, the Republican leaders ought not to have forgotten, in the euphoria of success, that even there they had at one point been on the brink of disaster: on the twenty-ninth, their lines had been breached. That day, in Teruel, as earlier at Brunete, there had been a moment of panic for which no one could give a reasonable explanation. It had been necessary to rush up reinforcements to restore the front line and to prevent Aranda's troops from linking up with the ones under siege in the town.[8]

The Nationalist Counteroffensive

After 15 January the weather grew milder, and the Nationalists were once again able to show their air superiority. Aranda was mounting an attack, not against Teruel, because an advance across the plain presented too many dangers, but against the positions that dominated it, especially to the north. His men thus managed to seize some important observation posts, including the one at Muleton, which endangered the positions of the Republican forces. Thus they had a launching base for operations, which now shifted to the north, around the Alfambra River.

But it was first necessary to break up fresh Republican attacks, which lasted five days, from 25 to 30 January, and produced no results. It was then necessary to concentrate the forces designed to pierce the Republican front to the west of the Alfambra, and to dislodge the troops who were holding strong positions in the Sierra Palomera; this was where the victorious December offensive opened. But the Nationalist command was even more ambitious. Its plan consisted of pushing back the front toward the east, in such a way as to outflank Teruel and the Republican positions to the north. Eventually, during the course of operations, it envisaged a pincer movement by the Twenty-third Army Corps, which was covering this sector. The attack was therefore directed against the two far ends of the Nationalist positions: to the north, under Yagüe, the Moroccan army corps, supported by the Navarrese, was to advance in the direction of Viver del Rio. To the south, the army corps of Galicia, reinforced by Muñoz Grandes's 150th Division, was to breach the front in the mountainous area between Teruel and Celados and to cross the Alfambra. The center of the line was weakest; it was manned by Colonel Monasterio's First Division.

The two-pronged attack opened on 5 February and managed to win an initial success. Yagüe's troops had broken through the front and had managed to outflank the Republican positions as far as the Alhambra. To the south, however, Aranda's advance was slower. Apparently the river had been reached and Celados occupied. But the immediate danger to Teruel led to a stiffening of the Republican defense. More bad weather once again slowed down the fighting, and the offensive came to a halt about 15 February, hindered by wind and rain. The pincer movement had not succeeded, but the Nationalists had on the whole improved their positions. From then on the front consisted of an almost continuous line between Teruel and Belchite to the south of the Ebro. The Republicans had been sorely tried by the battle of attrition that they had been enduring for almost two months, and when the Nationalists took to the offensive again, on the eighteenth, their defensive position was at once breached. Teruel was virtually outflanked by the forward troops, who cut the Sagunto road to the east on the twentieth. For another two days, there was fighting in Teruel. But it was only halfhearted. On 22 February the Republicans evacuated the town completely. The battle was over.

Just as the occupation of Teruel had at one point contributed to restoring the faith of the Republican troops, its loss could be regarded as a very serious turning point in the course of the Civil War. Both sides began furiously disputing the ruins; the successful raid became a protracted battle, a battle of destruction in which material superiority ultimately prevailed. Teruel was perhaps, as Rojo put it, the 'revelation of the moral grandeur' of the Spanish soldier. But the bravery and persistence of the men were not in themselves enough to bring about victory. Teruel had proved that, too. The end of the battle in fact marked the beginning of a new phase in the war. Until then, there had been a certain balance from the military point of view. In Teruel, masses of men had faced each other for months without managing to win a decisive success; suddenly, the Republican lines gave way, and the Nationalist offensive spread irresistibly. The balance of forces had been conclusively destroyed.

The Battle of Aragon

Meanwhile, in Republican Spain, the authority of the Negrín

government seemed to have strengthened progressively since July 1937. The CNT had given up all idea of serious opposition. The UGT leadership was solidly behind Negrín. But the government's political program, based on the imperative of 'Defeat Franco first,' made it absolutely necessary for him to win military victories. The loss of the North, which followed closely on the heels of his accession to power, and which he was unable either to prevent or to delay, dealt a harsh blow to his prestige. The Aragon disaster affected it even more. From then on, military and civil crises developed side by side, both of them weakening Republican Spain.

Of course, it must be allowed that the Negrín government had barely had time, before the first fighting of any scope, to take over the organization of the war. Yet a huge effort had been made in the military field in 1937. The reorganization, undertaken at the beginning of the year, had made it possible to train and equip troops who had given proof of their fighting ability at Teruel and Belchite. But there had always been a lack of reserves, and the best troops, barely trained, had been used at once. The offensives at Brunete and Belchite had been costly in human lives. The battle of attrition at Teruel had tired and tested the men, obliged to fight too many days on end without being relieved. Finally, the slowing down of deliveries of foreign war material put a heavy strain on the troops' equipment. Republican Spain was suffering from the blockade, broken only in September 1937. From the end of the year, in spite of the steps taken by the Western powers, ships had to run heavy risks to enter government ports. The only route left open was the Pyrenean frontier, which explains the government's constant anxiety not to be cut off from France. This was one of the arguments put forward by Negrín to explain the transfer of the government to Barcelona. It was this too that persuaded the Republican ministers to remain in the Catalan capital when the Republican territory was split in half by the Nationalist offensive.

But Catalonia was only defended by a small proportion of the Republican forces. The battle of Teruel had forced the Nationalists to mass the majority of their troops on both sides of the town and, further north, from the Maestrazgo to the Ebro. Although the Caudillo's plans had been upset and there was no longer any question of launching a major offensive against Madrid in order to decide the issue, the concentration of troops on the Aragon front after the victory at Teruel put an undeniably superior striking force at the Nationalist command's disposal: three army corps against one, the Twelfth Republican Army Corps.

With the Aragon offensive in particular, the war changed in character. The war of static positions was over: the breakthrough was followed at once by a general offensive. And in this new mobile war, motorized troops and armor, advancing in mass formations, played a decisive role.

The attack had opened on 9 March 1938. The terrain, mostly open ground, was that on which the battle of Belchite had been fought, a region suitable for a large-scale offensive because there were no obstacles over a large radius, and because it lent itself admirably to the esu of tanks and sweeping movements. Franco had concentrated huge numbers of troops there. The Galician army corps, to the south, was to attack in the direction of Montalbán, and the *Corpo Truppe Volontarie* in the Llanos area toward Alcañiz. The Moroccan army corps, to the north, operating from Belchite, had as its objective the right bank of the Ebro, toward Caspe. The aim of the offensive led by Aranda was to pierce the front held by the Twelfth Republican Army Corps and to reach the Guadalupe on the Caspe–Alcañiz line. In this way, a huge pocket would be formed in the Republican front, driving the Army of the East north of the Ebro, and threatening to outflank the forces concentrated around Teruel to their right. The occupation of the positions aimed at to the south and southwest of Montalbán would also enable the Nationalists to control the approaches to the nonmountainous region of the Maestrazgo. Beyond the Caspe–Alcañiz line, the Nationalist general staff was in fact aiming for the Mediterranean and was trying to cut Republican Spain in half.

The Nationalist attack was not, strictly speaking, a surprise, but it caught the Republican forces in the middle of reorganization. The Eighteenth Army Corps, which was in reserve, could

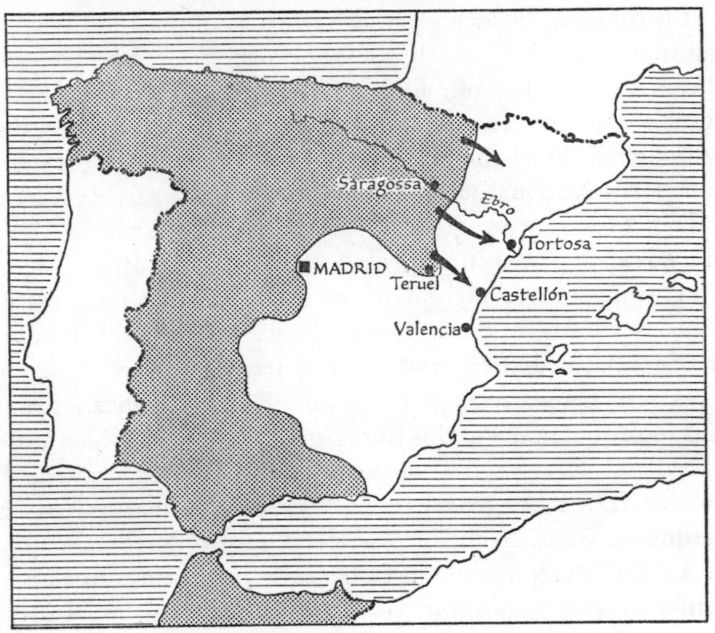

The Aragon Offensive (March 1938)

not even intervene; for the first time since the beginning of the war, there was an actual collapse of the front, quite unlike the local panics that had been a feature of such operations. The Italian and Moroccan motorized columns advanced without meeting practically any resistance. The best-organized Republican troops fell back to the north of the Ebro. The rest were little more than a mass of leaderless fugitives; ill-equipped and ill-armed, they could not hold out in the face of such a large-scale operation. The Twenty-first Army Corps, which had at first contained the Galicians, had to fall back because of the threat north of its positions. From then on, a vast area lay open and defenseless to the enemy's advance. 'On 15 March,' Rojo wrote, 'in the vast area stretching from Caspe to Calanda, there was only one organized unit left, there was no longer any link between the Army of the East and the tactical reserve, and a thirty-mile front lay completely exposed to the invasion as far as the coast.' In six days, the CTV covered half the distance that separated it from the Mediterranean.

It is difficult, in such circumstances, to understand why this lightning offensive, which slowed down between 15 and 21 March, was called off. Only the official communiqués and Ciano's optimism can explain the halt on the positions gained by the need 'to let the Nationalist troops support the Italians.' In fact, the Nationalists had been the first to be surprised by the scale of their success. 'The troops,' Ciano noted on 14 March, 'are advancing with unexpected rapidity.' But after five days of lightning progress, the pace of the motorized columns had to be cut down. Reserves were inadequate to exploit the initial successes immediately, and it was necessary to wait for the Navarrese before setting off again. The Republican general staff took advantage of this to regroup a few units which it used on suicide missions for harassing and delaying actions. On 20 March, it managed to reestablish an undeniably weak but continuous front. In the brief respite that the Nationalist pause gave them, the government forces saw fit to bring up as many reinforcements as possible to 'plug the gap' and, more important, to defend Catalonia. In fact, Prieto told the Cabinet: 'If the rebels reach the Mediterranean, four-fifths of the Army will be in the southern zone.' Between 15 March and 15 April, the date on which the Nationalists reached the sea at Vinaroz, the Barcelona general staff tried to slip through as many troops as possible along the Tortosa coast road. This explains the bitterness of the Republican resistance, first on the Caspe–Alcañiz line and then, after it was breached, at Tortosa. But in the end this resistance had only been—and could only be—sporadic.

In fact, the first Nationalist offensive had achieved far-reaching consequences. The disorganization that it had caused could not have been put right in a few days. Moreover, the resumption of the offensive would not have permitted it. Confusion among the Republicans was so great that the exact positions of the Nationalists were not known. Two officers from the International Brigades were captured in Gandesa, not realizing that it had fallen. The remnants of various units made their way to the right bank of the Ebro, where they were joined by reinforcements from the central zone. Perhaps for the first time, in the face of such a large-scale debacle, there were some who envisioned the approaching end of the conflict. Staff officers had to go up into the front line to try to take a grip on their troops and to improvise a defense as best they could.

Generalization of the Offensive

But above all else it was the generalization of the offensive that gave the Aragon defeat its disastrous character. After the attack on Caspe, six Nationalist army corps were in action. In the North, the idea was to prevent the Tenth and Eleventh Republican Army Corps, spread out from the Ebro to the Pyrenees, from coming to the help of the scattered and defeated forces to the south of the river. The Nationalist success was clinched through a surprise attack by the Moroccan army corps, which suddenly crossed the river along which it had until then been deployed: the Tenth and Eleventh Republican Army Corps met a fate similar to that of the Twelfth a few days earlier, though on terrain less favorable to a combined attack. There, too, resistance was practically nonexistent. The only serious opposition in ten days was that met by the Nationalists at Lérida, which fell on 3 April. The front was stabilized in this sector. But in the meantime the offensive had spread to both sides of the river, with the Aragon and Moroccan army corps and Urgel's recently formed Army Corps. The Republicans could only reestablish themselves on a line from the Ebro to the Pyrenees, along the Segre and the Noguera, natural defenses behind which the remains of the two defeated army corps could withdraw. Rojo made special mention of Colonel Beltrán's Forty-third Division, which, isolated after the breach of the front, fought a three-month delaying action by hugging the Pyrenean foothills before being interned in France, where it passed with the greater part of its equipment. But isolated resistance of this kind could only slow down the Nationalist advance, not halt it, the more so because Franco had decided to strike in the South and join battle in the Levante, where the three army corps were reaching the Mediterranean. At the Nationalist headquarters, there was talk about whether it was desirable to make a fresh effort in Catalonia, which was held by sorely tried troops, or whether it was necessary to try to crush the enemy by attacking the Republican striking force, whose lines were dangerously stretched. The second solution was the one chosen.

It was in practice the more difficult operation: the mountainous area from the Maestrazgo to the sea, the slopes of the Sierra de Javalambre, which rose to as much as 5000 to 6000 feet above sea level, and, to a lesser degree, of the Sierra de Espadán, between Castellón and Valencia, were uniquely easy to defend. Moreover, the government forces were fortifying a line from Viver to Segorbe. Their troops there were fresher. Against them, far more men and material had to be concentrated in a much more restricted area during the early part of the offensive. While the Moroccan army corps was covering the sector from the Ebro to the delta, the Navarrese and Galicians under Aranda switched back to the south and advanced along the coast, occupying Castellón without difficulty. At the same time, Varela was drawing up the Castilian army corps and the CTV, whose motorized units were once again to play a decisive role. This meant a new breakthrough; the forces concentrated by the Republicans to save Valencia were the last available to Miaja, appointed commander of the central-southern zone. There were no reserves left. The sole reinforcements, necessary as they were, could only have been procured from the Army of the Center, which would have meant dangerously stripping Madrid of its defenses for the first time. Franco was counting on the imminent fall of Valencia, the third largest city in Spain and till recently the seat of government, a moral success at least as important as the conquest of the Levante. The latter would deprive the central-southern zone, where the food situation was always uncertain, of an area indispensable to its supplies. But the difficulties of the operation required two months of preparation; the battle of the Levante was not joined until the summer. On 15 July, it was launched with enormous material support, on both sides of Teruel. On the thirteenth and the seventeenth, Republican army corps had to withdraw: the armies of Varela and Aranda linked up and reached the Viver–Segorbe line. From the twentieth to the twenty-third, after intense artillery preparation, there followed attacks by tanks and infantry on the fortified line. But in the end the offensive failed.

Between May and July, aware of the danger courted by the southern zone, the Republican general staff regrouped its forces and launched a counterattack from the Ebro that forced the Nationalist general staff to relax its grip on the Levante. Valencia was temporarily saved. However, since July 1938, the Republicans' military situation had taken a considerable turn for the worse. Aragon was lost, and the defense of the Maestrazgo remained uncertain. The Nationalists' material superiority was definitely proven, and their command's ability to fight the war with the modern means at its disposal. Finally, the division of Republican Spain into two zones was very serious, not only because it made an overall strategy difficult, but because it undermined the very basis of the political regime imposed by the Negrín government, obliged to delegate its powers to military authorities over a substantial part of its territory. Separated, the two zones developed differently in the political field, and the central-southern zone was soon without direct influence from the government. Meanwhile, the Aragon disaster had had a direct political consequence: a crisis in the very heart of the government.

The Dismissal of Prieto

The departure of Prieto from the Ministry of National Defence was in fact the most important event that had occurred in Republican Spain since the fall of Largo Caballero. It intruded a note of discord into the atmosphere of relative political calm and 'holy union' that had followed the events of spring 1937.

Its importance derived first of all from the minister's personality. Prieto was well known abroad and was regarded by many as England's friend. He was a Socialist who enjoyed the trust of the Republicans and even a certain respect in Nationalist Spain, where historians went so far as to regard him as the only politician of worth in the 'Red' zone. He had long been regarded as the strong man of the Negrín government. The old friendship that bound him to the premier, whose candidacy he had supported after the crisis, was common knowledge. It was even thought that he would govern under Negrín's name. In fact, Negrín had taken his task seriously, deciding all the essential questions himself and not shirking any responsibility. Very soon, the two men experienced differences of opinion. They did not have the same conception of how the war should be handled, nor, more important, the same outlook, the same hopes for a happy outcome to the conflict. Their postwar disputes also betrayed a lively personal hostility. Though it was not yet March 1938, their relations had nevertheless worsened enough for Prieto to be removed from the key post he had held ever since the formation of the 'government of victory.'

Negrín's theory was that, faced with the seriousness of the military situation after the fall of Teruel and the Aragon disaster, he should have strengthened the executive in order to strengthen the wish and the determination to fight on. In his view, Prieto's pessimism did not make him a fit person to carry out the functions of minister of national defense in these circumstances. How could he entrust the control of the war to a man who did not believe in victory? In fact, it was to strengthen the Executive that Negrín did not turn the Ministry of National Defense over to someone else but took charge of it himself, thus adding it to the premiership.

Although Negrín claimed that in March there was a conflict within the government and that this conflict was due to Prieto's pessimism, the latter merely observed that his feelings had not altered and that they were known to everyone, especially Negrín, who had not however hesitated to appoint him minister of national defense the previous year. In fact, when Prieto left the ministry in March 1938, it was not his views on the prospects of a military victory but the military situation in Republican Spain that had changed. The loss of the North and the Aragon disaster led to political options that revolved around the dilemma of whether to resist or to negotiate. But Prieto claimed that this was not the motive behind his dismissal.

In fact, in his view, responsibility for the crisis lay on the Communists: it was they who had asked for his departure.

Their determination to remove him was the one and only cause of it. According to him there was only one conflict: the one that pitted him against the Communist party. The Communist ministers Uribe and Hernández had tried to associate him with the leadership of a Socialist-Communist splinter group in the government, and his denial had made them determined to fight him. It was indisputably the public attacks by La Pasionaria, followed by the articles by Hernández in *La Vanguardia* and *Frente Rojo* signed Juan Ventura, that provoked the crisis, Prieto's protest to Negrín against this breach of ministerial solidarity, and then the reshuffle and the exclusion of Prieto. But, as Prieto vigorously repeated, he did not resign, he was dismissed.

It is still not known whether, as he claimed, the decision to dismiss him was imposed on the premier by the Communist party. There can be no doubt that the Communist party leaders had used all their influence, which was in fact great, to work for his removal. He had long been one of their most valuable allies; in the struggle against Largo Caballero and over long months in the Negrín government, they had stood by him because he was a man of order whose views coincided with theirs, because he was the only politician capable of winning the active sympathy of the Western powers, and finally because he was a resolute supporter of Socialist-Communist unity.[9] Now it turned out that this ally refused to become a tool. He rejected the alliance that was offered him in the government. As minister of national defense, he was infuriated by the Russian technicians' interference and did not hesitate to make direct attacks on the Communist party and its influence in certain sectors,[10] deliberately advertizing his intention to make it bend to that iron discipline he had so often imposed. Prieto did not deny this; on the contrary, he recited at great length the tale of all the clashes that had brought him out against the Communists and the Russian advisers.[11] However, he kept quiet about the reasons behind a change of course that he could hardly admit, in that he would have been obliged at the same time to recognize his long alliance with the Communist party. Prieto's motives were clear: they were bound up with the evolution of political and military events since the establishment of the government he had sponsored. In his view, Communist support had been indispensable for the restoration of the state, just as Largo Caballero's had been at the outset. The state restored, the Communist hold over the Army and the police struck him as dangerous in many respects. In the domestic field, Prieto had witnessed the defection of many of his disciples: after the break-away of the left wing, which followed Álvarez del Vayo, an important section of the right wing, drawn by him into the antifascist coalition, seemed to follow Negrín in identifying itself on every point with the Communist 'ally' whose power constituted, as we have seen, a state within a state. In the foreign field, he was apparently very disillusioned by the attitude of the Communists and the counsels of prudence from the Russians after the shelling of Almería;[12] undoubtedly he lost some of his illusions on that occasion, when he had recognized the limitations of Russian aid. Thus, from then on, he lent more and more attention and importance to the attitudes of London and Paris, which were clearly not based on the same grounds as Moscow's. Certainly Prieto was not as much a friend of England as was claimed, but he was undeniably in favor of a negotiated peace for which England could have acted as agent. In May 1937 he tried to get in touch with the Nationalists to study the possibilities of negotiation.[13] A few months later, taking advantage of the exchange of prisoners that released Fernández Cuesta to rejoin Franco, he had several meetings with the Falangist leader on this subject. When the former prisoner became a minister in Burgos, he tried to renew contact with him,[14] but the strong position of the Communists in the Republican state was an obstacle to negotiations, whether they involved Franco or London.

After the Aragon disaster, Negrín's chief concern was to stiffen resistance. Prieto no longer had faith in anything besides negotiation. It is probable that Negrín did not have to yield to pressure from the Communists: the logic of his policy compelled the departure of Prieto, who was now both his and the Communist party's enemy.

Would an increase in the number of seats in the government

through the return of union representatives have led, as Negrín's friends claimed, to the strengthening of his authority, in spite of Prieto's departure?[15] It is open to doubt, because Prieto left at the very moment that the Nationalists reached the Mediterranean and cut the Republic's territory in half. Negrín had to telephone General Miaja in order to assign him the responsibility for political and military power in the central-southern zone: the political coalition in power relied more and more on agreement and collaboration with the Army leaders, who were soon to revolt against it.

For the time being, in spite of the Aragon disaster, Negrín had opted for resistance. Álvarez del Vayo, his right-hand man, stated: 'Thanks to the energy and presence of mind shown by the premier during these anxious days, the consequences of the disaster were considerably reduced.' And he added this homage to the man whose faithful lieutenant he was: 'Dr. Negrín cannot be denied the merit of having saved the situation in 1938 and of having made the continuation of the war for another year possible.' In effect, Negrín and Del Vayo thought, in April 1938, that the mere fact of holding on still gave the Republic a chance of winning. Both believed that a European war was around the corner and that it could save Spain. On one condition, however: that the Republic had not been completely abandoned beforehand.

Notes

[1] It had always been typical of Franco to refuse to concede a defeat that would affect his prestige. At Teruel, and later on at the Ebro, he committed himself completely, even if it was only a matter of rectifying a local failure. His caution, on the other hand, prevented him from launching a large-scale attack at any point, so long as the front was threatened elsewhere.

[2] Archives of the German Foreign Ministry, 28 January 1938.

[3] Aranda had 300 batteries at his disposal.

[4] Details taken from Vicente Rojo, *España heroica* (Mexico City: Ediciones Era, 1961), and from newspaper articles, especially from *Le Temps*.

[5] Galland reported the first appearance of 20-mm guns with quadruple mountings on the Teruel front.

[6] *Le Temps*, 6 January 1938.

[7] See on this subject the criticisms issued by the leading circles of the

Libertarian movement, especially the document signed by Mariano Vázquez, entitled *Critique de la prise de Teruel*, quoted by Peirats.

[8] Rojo reported that for four hours, on 31 December, Teruel was to all intents and purposes lost by the Republicans.

[9] After the war, Prieto tried to draw a veil over this alliance, which embarrassed him. In addition, he always minimized his own role and exaggerated the Communist party's, saddling the Communists alone with responsibilities that in fact he had shared with them. For instance, many writers imputed to the Communist Lister responsibility for the repression of the Aragon collectives, whereas it is certain that Lister was acting on the orders of his minister.

[10] See Prieto's polemical pamphlets. It was the Communists who, according to him, prevented the *Ciscar* from leaving the North and therefore bore responsibility for an act of disobedience that led to the loss of the Russian warship. According to Prieto, the Russian technicians dealt with Uríbarri over his head. He also wrote at length about his dealings with Major Durán, a Communist, head of the SIM in Madrid and protected by the Russian technicians. The Antón incident was also very significant. This member of the Political Bureau, probably La Pasionaria's lover, held an important post in the Madrid commissariat. He belonged to a mobilized class and for this reason should have left the bureau and been posted to a fighting unit. The Communist party asked for him to be exempted, but Prieto refused. It is however interesting to note, again according to Prieto, that in the end it was the Communists who had the last word: Antón was never posted to a fighting unit.

[11] It is in this light that the measures taken by Prieto after the fall of the North must be seen; such as the restrictions on the number and role of commissars and the ban on officers and units of the Popular Army from taking part in political demonstrations without his authorization, among others.

[12] See chapter 20.

[13] See in the Archives of the German Foreign Ministry a report by Faupel about a meeting with Franco; according to the latter, Prieto got in touch with Blum after the May days in order to seek American mediation. According to Stohrer, in a note on 3 December, Prieto tried to get in touch with the commander of Irún using one of his secretaries as a middleman.

[14] See on this subject *Palabras al viento* (Mexico City: Ediciones Minerva, 1942), pp. 233–238. Prieto pointed out that the exchange between Fernández Cuesta and the Republican Justino Azcárate was suggested by Giral, and that he personally was opposed to it. He only agreed in the end because he was counting on the influence that Fernández Cuesta, once released, could exert over the Nationalists for negotiations. It was after his departure from the government that he made an attempt to renew contact with the Falangist leader. He gave up after a meeting with Negrín, who refused to cover him.

[15] In the interests of parliamentary balance, Negrín removed the Communist minister who had been at the source of the incidents at the same time as Prieto. Jesús Hernández became deputy commissar-general of the Army of the Center. The premier's enemies pointed out that it was actually a more

important post than that of minister; appearances, at least, were saved. On the other hand, it is impossible to follow Negrín's friends in attributing great significance to the entry into the government of delegates from the CNT and the UGT. In fact, González Peña of the UGT and Segundo Blanco of the CNT were regarded in their organizations as Negrín's men. Their entry into the government could not have signified the unions' adherence to Negrín's policy; it merely put an official seal on their submission.

CHAPTER 20

THE ABANDONMENT OF THE REPUBLIC

In spite of a considerable delay, the application of the non-intervention agreement on 19 April gave the Western governments great hope. For the first time, it seemed that effective cooperation was shortly, to come into being and bring about a solution to the problem raised by the internationalization of the war; for the first time, there was to be control, which would at least localize the conflict. Naturally, if it had been possible to obtain a faithful application of control by all concerned, the difficulties inherent in all international cooperation could have finally been overcome. But from the earliest days, the ill will of the Axis powers was made abundantly clear. In fact, after dragging out the talks, they only accepted control in the hopes of seeing the war brought to a rapid conclusion. After Guadalajara, the protraction of the war threatened the whole of the system painfully worked out by the Nonintervention Committee. Although no serious incident troubled the border patrols, which were anyway very lax, on the other hand, the sea patrols led to violent quarrels.

The Deutschland *Affair*

Even before the application of the control system, various incidents had already occurred, and British and French ships had been stopped and searched. But the only consequences had been protest notes from the governments concerned.[1] The *Deutschland* affair had different repercussions.

The powers that were supposed to be taking part in the patrols had sent warships to the Mediterranean. The latter refueled in friendly Spanish ports. Thus the naval base at Ibiza, in the Balearic Islands, acted as a gathering place for German warships. After various incidents in May 1937, the German pocket battleship *Deutschland* was seriously damaged during an attack on Ibiza by Republican aircraft; there were a number of killed and wounded. The Berlin government reacted vigorously. It was not content, like the others, with a note handed to the powers in charge of control; it intended to profit by the occasion and make a show of force.

A naval action by Germany in the early months of the Civil War could have provoked a general conflict, but at the beginning of 1937 the atmosphere was relaxed. Great Britain and France had already made enough concessions; they no longer believed in the imminence of a world war.

On 31 May three German warships, the pocket battleship *Admiral Scheer* and two destroyers, on orders from Berlin, shelled the port of Almería. This shelling was presented as a simple reprisal raid. But there was no connection between the two incidents: on the one hand, a bombing raid within a war zone on enemy territory, and on the other, a spectacular operation deliberately carried out by a neutral power and taking the most shock form possible, that of an attack on an ill-defended town. It was in fact a genuine act of aggression by one of the powers entrusted with control at sea.

Violent reactions were to be expected, from the Spanish Republicans as well as from the Western democracies. The tone of the press grew shriller. In Valencia, the Republican Cabinet heard Prieto, the minister of national defense, propose a bombing attack on the German fleet in the Mediterranean. Such a retaliation meant war with Germany. Prieto realized this, but he hoped that a European war would follow, the only way, in his view, of saving Spain. However, most of the members of the Republican government[2] refused to accept responsibility for such a conflict. In the end, since France and Britain eschewed any positive reaction, the German provocation remained unanswered. What is more, it was the Germans and Italians who voiced their indignation; their representatives on the Nonintervention Committee stormed out. They returned in early June.

After the bombing of the *Deutschland* came the incident of the *Leipzig*, attacked, according to the German government, by a submarine. Germany and Italy proposed a joint move against Valencia by the countries entrusted with control. France and Great Britain agreed to ask both Spanish sides to respect the warships, but they refused to be associated with a military action, claiming that in any case it had been impossible to identify the *Leipzig*'s aggressor. They then suggested a commission of investigation, but ran into virtuous indigation from Berlin and Rome; the Axis delegates realized the impossibility of ensuring effective naval control and on 23 June decided to give it up altogether.

In such circumstances, border controls no longer made sense. Thus, on 1 July, in conjunction with the Axis countries, Portugal decided to do away with 'the facilities granted for the control of frontiers.' France, in desperation, followed suit on 10 July. The control plan, which the Nonintervention Committee powers had taken seven and a half months to work out, had lasted precisely a month and a half. In the meantime, after the failure of its foreign policy, the Blum government had fallen.

Certainly the Nonintervention Committee still existed, but it had lost the little authority it had. These two months had been the only ones in nearly three years of war in which it had played an even slightly effective role. Its failure amounted to a fresh defeat for the Western democracies. Faced with men who proudly boasted of practicing only 'the Fascist law of the *fait accompli*,'[3] they had again proved by their neglect that they were ready to pay any price in order to keep the peace.

Piracy in the Mediterranean

The summer of 1937 had been notable for a fresh series of naval incidents, attacks on Spanish and neutral merchant ships and warships on the high seas by planes and then by submarines. In August 1937, international relations were once again strained by the increase of such acts of piracy. A glance through the newspapers would produce details of this sort almost every day. On 6 August, the British tanker *British Corporal* and the French liner *Djebel Amour* were bombed by planes. On 11 August there was an attack on a British warship, the destroyer *Foxhound*, off the northern coast of Spain. On 13 August the *Edith*, a Danish ship, went down. On 15 August the Panamanian tanker *George McKnight* was set on fire by a warship. Some Spanish government warships (like the *Ciudad de Cádiz*, sunk on 16 August) were simultaneously attacked and torpedoed by submarines 'of unknown nationality,' throughout the Mediterranean and as far away as the Dardanelles.

Where did these attacks come from? The two Spanish governments mutually disclaimed any responsibility for them. In fact, the majority of the victims were either Spanish government ships or neutral ships, especially Soviet ones, belonging to powers in sympathy with the Spanish Republic; some were transporting material destined for Republican Spain. Very quickly, a section of the press, in particular the British newspapers, named the aggressor. The planes that attacked the neutral warships turned out, in spite of vehement protests from Franco's general staff, to be Nationalist planes, and the submarines probably were, too; there was even reference, at the time, to the Italian nationality of some of the aggressors. This hypothesis was later confirmed in Count Ciano's diaries. The latter stated unflinchingly that the authors of these acts of aggression were Italian warships, whether under the Nationalist flag or not. On 31 August Ciano drew up a provisional balance sheet on this matter: 'Four Russian or Red ships sunk, one Greek ship captured, one Spanish ship bombed and forced to seek refuge in a French port.'

The objective in question was the sea blockade of Republican Spain; Franco himself explained this, when he stated that 'the halting of ships transporting arms in the Mediterranean and the prevention of unloading in Red ports were, for those nations concerned to see the war over, the most effective means of shortening it.'[4] In fact, it was privateering in a new guise, during peacetime. Tolerant as the Western powers were, it was difficult for them not to react.

'The full Franco-Russo-British orchestra. The theme: Piracy in the Mediterranean. Guilty: the Fascists.' At the time when Ciano wrote these lines, international opinion seemed to have been effectively aroused. This was because of a fresh naval incident: an attempt by a submarine 'of unknown nationality' to torpedo the British destroyer *Havock*. Actually, it was another Italian move, whose source Ciano indicated: 'The torpedo was fired by the *Iride*.'

This time it seems that London was no longer in a mood to settle for moral protests. Tension rose between Britain and Italy. The French government was also bent on showing greater firmness and decided to have its freighters in the Mediterranean escorted by warships. The Fascist leaders were for the first time nonplussed. 'I have arranged,' said Ciano, 'for the dispatch of reinforcements to Spain to be deferred.' And on 4 September, he noted: 'I have ordered Cavagnari[5] to suspend all naval activities until further notice.' Thus, the first firm reaction by the Western governments was sufficient to check the inflammatory Italian policy, in spite of the pressure put on Rome by Nationalist Spain. 'Franco says that the blockade will be decisive if it lasts all September. This is true; however, we must suspend it.' Could there have been a clearer statement of Italy's determination not to become involved in a European war at this stage and under these conditions?

However, neither the French government, in which Socialist influence had declined, nor the British government, now led by Chamberlain,[6] were anxious to go too far. They merely put to the Nonintervention Committee a proposal for a conference to be held at Nyon on 10 September; the powers invited would all be states bordering the Mediterranean and the Black Sea,[7] plus Germany and minus the two Spains. The official aim was to discuss means of ending piracy in the Mediterranean. But in a conference of this sort, procedure was as important as the problems broached. It was essential to know whether Italy would take part in the debate of her own free will and whether she would accept the role of the accused. The Russian government took advantage of the situation to prepare an extremely violent note attacking the Fascist government. It was a genuine indictment. The motive invoked was the torpedoing of a Russian warship for which the Soviet Union was claiming reparation. Italy then refused to take part; Germany and Albania followed suit. The leaders of these countries asserted that, if the conference failed, it would be solely the fault of the USSR.

However, the meeting opened on the agreed date. Was it a success? The Western states claimed that it was. Their press hailed the Nyon agreement as a diplomatic triumph after the long series of reverses suffered in the preceding months. The decision taken to 'entrust the fight against piracy to the French and British fleets' seemed to herald a radical change in attitude toward Italy, and consequently a new stand in the Spanish conflict. The Duce, on hearing these decisions, flew into a violent rage. But not too much notice needed to be taken of Mussolini's temper, because he was inclined to react violently to first impressions. The Western powers took up a forceful position at Nyon mainly in order to have a basis for negotiations. An initial sop was immediately given to the Italians: the USSR was excluded from control.

Moreover, the British and French governments sought to obtain the participation of Italy herself in the agreement. Possibly, by making overtures to Italy and not to Germany, they hoped to set the two powers against each other, but this was to misunderstand an alliance based both on complementary interests and on a mutual need for security. Italy could take part in control of the Mediterranean without weakening the Rome-Berlin Axis. When approached, she made one condition: equality with France and Britain in the controls. 'We are shifting,' Ciano wrote in his diary, 'from the role of torpedo launchers which had been allotted to us to that of Mediterranean policemen, whereas the Russians, sunk without trace, are excluded from control.'

Italian piracy did not in the end persuade the Western powers to make a gesture in support of the Spanish Republic any more than the shelling of Almería. Russia's political isolation, which the London discussions had underlined, was further aggravated. This was undoubtedly one of the reasons behind the diplomatic change of course taken by Stalin, who was convinced that he had nothing to expect from the Western democracies. This was the outcome of Great Britain's pacifist policy.

The Triumph of Chamberlain's Policy

British policy had not, since the beginning of the war, supported the Republican government. Eden did not show, any more than Baldwin, the slightest understanding of the Spanish ambassador Azcárate's requests. At least the British government had observed the forms of strict neutrality. But the British Conservatives were no friendlier than Franco's supporters to those whom they still regarded as 'Reds.' In the beginning, they were mainly concerned with bringing about a mediation that would lead to a compromise peace. Since this peace could only be guaranteed by an international *entente*, or rather by a Mediterranean *entente*, the aim of British diplomacy was therefore to ensure peace in the Mediterranean by maintaining the *status quo*.

These views were in no sense inimical to those of Franco who, in the face of his Italian allies, insisted imperatively on the maintenance of the integrity of Spanish territory. By the end of 1936, the Ciano-Drummond talks made it clear that nothing could be done to alter the existing situation in the Mediterranean. It was without doubt the crisis brought about by piracy in the Mediterranean that had broken off Anglo-Italian relations. But they were renewed in November 1937, through the efforts of the British premier, Chamberlain. On 16 November the British government had decided, in order to 'protect its interests,' to make a *de facto* recognition of the Burgos government.

It therefore sent a representative to Nationalist Spain, Robert Hodgson, who in practice carried out the functions of an ambassador; similarly, the 'agents' posted to Spanish towns held the rank of consul. Franco was represented in Great

Britain by one of the leading figures in the regime, the Duke of Alba, who arrived in London on 22 November. This exchange of plenipotentiaries heralded a *rapprochement* between Britain and Nationalist Spain already initiated in the commercial field. The conquest of the North, where the British had vast interests, had undoubtedly been the decisive factor explaining this evolution. It was not long before Hodgson was wielding real influence in Burgos, and from then on efforts to reach a compromise peace were directed at securing a Nationalist victory under the least violent conditions possible.

But this was where the differences between the British leaders began. Although they all regarded a Franco victory as inevitable and thought that, after all, it was convenient, there was a minority within the government, whose most influential member was Anthony Eden, who felt that an *entente* with Fascism in the Mediterranean was a delusion. The application of a diplomatic agreement between Britain and Italy meant the elimination of this minority. After a meeting between Grandi, the Italian ambassador in London, Eden, and Chamberlain, the differences between the last two became obvious, especially on the question of foreign volunteers in Spain. Eden had to resign, which was hailed by the Axis diplomats as a victory. Great Britain's policy took a final turn: an agreement between Britain and Italy was drawn up by Count Ciano and Lord Perth, the British chargé in Rome. Ciano wanted to avoid making difficulties for the Chamberlain government and was therefore ready to make concessions. The *entente* was concluded at the end of 1937, in spite of fresh incidents in the Mediterranean. But for the agreement to be applied, the war had to end. At the beginning of 1938, the Republican disaster in Aragon seemed to reinforce this prospect.

France's Final Hesitations

The Barcelona government had not yet given up all hope; nor had it surrendered all its claims to help from outside. French support was still conceivable, especially in March 1938, with Blum's return to the government. According to

Negrín, Blum, even before taking over the Cabinet, had asked him to come to Paris and discuss methods of material aid with certain influential Frenchmen. Negrín had made the journey and had met Blum, Daladier, and Paul-Boncour. An agreement had then been reached on arms supplies.

In fact, at the time of the Aragon campaign, the second Blum government had considered going further in terms of intervention. With the Republican collapse, when a general advance by the Nationalists in Catalonia was to be expected, there had been serious talk in France of a military intervention that would take the form of occupying this province of Spain. The French government was no doubt relying on thus having a pawn for political negotiations. The ministers had envisaged, according to Blum himself, a rapid move carried out by mechanized units.[8] But at a meeting of the French National Defense Council, the French military leaders had stated that they could not act without a mobilization order. On the other hand, there is no doubt that such a step would have seriously risked setting off a European conflict. If France sent '*in articulo mortis* men and air material, we would intervene in force,' said Ciano.

Thus Blum was faced for the second time with the alternatives of peace or war. When Morell,[9] the French military attaché in Madrid, was consulted by the premier as to the possibilities of military action, he replied: 'I have only one thing to tell you: a king of France would go to war.' But, said Blum, 'I was not the King of France.'

By giving up the idea of direct intervention for the second time, the French government, in March 1938, also gave up the idea of effectively defending the Spanish Republican government. The dispatch of French arms and the free passage permitted to cargoes of foreign material were not enough to alter the course of events. The Blum government was replaced in April by a Daladier ministry, which was joined by Georges Bonnet, supporter of an *entente* with the Axis powers. France, in her turn, was preparing to abandon the Barcelona government. However, it was advisable to preserve appearances, to show that an international agreement could restore the conflict's truly Spanish character, and finally to reach agreement on the withdrawal of volunteers, which had been fruitlessly discussed ever since the establishment of the Non-intervention Committee.

The London Plan

During the course of summer 1937, the British government tried to revive discussion on this subject. A plan was communicated on 14 July to the powers concerned, which contained four points: (1) Renewal of control according to a different system: stationing of neutral agents in Spanish ports to exercise control previously entrusted to the Navy, and the reestablishment of border controls. (2) Since it was necessary for both sides to undertake to permit neutral observers to operate, belligerent rights would be granted to them both. (3) Both sides would proceed to the withdrawal of foreign nationals under supervision by the commission. (4) These operations would take place in the following order: stationing of international officials in foreign ports, withdrawal of volunteers, recognition of belligerent rights.

In this way, the issue of the withdrawal of volunteers and the issue of belligerent rights were linked, as Italy and Germany had been requesting since 1936. But what at the beginning of the conflict would have represented a serious problem of equity had only a limited interest and bearing in July 1937. Once again the Axis powers found it necessary to drag out the talks: the British plan was merely a 'basis for negotiations.' But why did the French government agree to let itself be led on in this way from discussion to discussion over months and years? The Civil War had begun in July 1936, and the British control plan had been put forward one year later; and on 9 November 1938, in an article in *Le Populaire*, Blum once again raised the question, 'Must the London plan be applied?'

The London plan was never applied, mainly because of Russian opposition, hostile to any form of recognition of the Burgos government, a position that the USSR confirmed at a meeting of the Nonintervention Committee in late October 1937. Italy, Portugal, and Germany took advantage of it to state that they could not vote for the resolution until unanimity had been reached.

Faithful, nevertheless, to the attitude that had been theirs from the start, the Axis powers were still trying to get the talks going again. The German government proposed a compromise, 'a symbolic gesture' consisting of withdrawing a certain number of volunteers from each side. The theoretical nature of this proposal did not arouse great enthusiasm at the time; once again there was *impasse.*

However, during the course of summer 1938, a change of tack occurred. The delegates on the committee agreed to work out the application of the British plan. Britain congratulated herself. 'The policy of nonintervention has achieved its goal,' declared Chamberlain,[10] while Butler announced to the House of Commons: 'The system of surveillance will be reestablished, and the system of naval control come into force under its new formula when the International Commission for controlling the withdrawal of volunteers is ready to start its enumeration.'[11]

The new factor was the unanimity achieved by the Non-intervention Committee. This was due basically to the shift in Russian policy. Moscow was now actually in favor of the plan for naval control. The explanation for this change was given in detail by Schulemburg, the German ambassador in Moscow:

'The Soviet government feels that a victory by the Reds is quite unlikely and consequently believes it preferable to prepare public opinion for a negotiated peace.'[12] This explanation was doubtless only a partial one. Certainly the Republican defeats must have induced the USSR to adopt an increasingly cautious attitude, but it is likely that the shift initially derived from overall Russian policy. This was the starting point of an evolution that led, a year after the 'dropping' of Spain, to the signing of the Soviet–German pact. In the meantime, the prolongation of the war deferred the threat of a conflict in central Europe. With such future dangers in mind, the USSR was not anxious to become openly divorced from the Western democracies, with which she had common interests.

The Withdrawal of the Volunteers

Be that as it may, on 5 July an agreement was reached by the Nonintervention Committee on the plan for the withdrawal of volunteers: as Germany had requested, the belligerent rights of both parties would be recognized as soon as 10,000 men had been withdrawn from each side. Two commissions stood ready. The first had to find a way of counting the volunteers still scattered about both Spains. The general secretary of the committee, Hemming, was given the task of obtaining agreement from the Spanish authorities. But Franco's clear-cut hostility[13] prevented him from completing his mission.

The second commission, far more active, moved into Toulouse in August. This was the Commission for the Exchange of Prisoners, led by Field Marshal Sir Philip Chetwode. It contributed to the organization of many exchanges, and it is probable that Chetwode and his colleagues, Cowan in Republican Spain and Mosley in Nationalist Spain, made an effective contribution toward preparations for the end of the conflict.

By contrast, the evacuation of foreigners fighting in Spain produced a diplomatic comedy on both sides. It was carried out without any supervision, but to the accompaniment of spectacular ceremonies, processions, and moving farewells. Negrín spoke to the men of the International Brigades. The members of the CTV evacuated from Spain were given a resounding welcome on their arrival in Naples, but the troops evacuated in fact consisted only of sick and wounded, or at least of weary men who, on the Italian side, were at once replaced by fresh troops.

No one, however, was taken in: the Germans and Italians accused the Republicans of having taken steps to 'camouflage' their volunteers, and Weizsäcker wrote: 'In fact, no evacuation of Red volunteers has occurred, whatever may have been said. Only the French wounded have been taken charge of by France.'[14] The Axis spokesmen contrasted the Italian attitude with this breach of the commitments made. It was true that a certain number of Italians had been evacuated—11,000 apparently—but it must be mentioned in precisely what conditions. According to a note from the Wilhelmstrasse, Berti, the commander in chief of the Italians, gave Franco the choice of three proposals: the dispatch of two to three new divisions, the dispatch of 10,000 men to compensate for losses, or the total or partial withdrawal of the Italians; this final measure was feasible because the military capacity of the Nationalist Army had been strengthened. But total withdrawal was not to Franco's taste, nor to Mussolini's. Thus they insisted on a measure that could not weaken the Nationalist war potential: the departure of part of the infantry would be compensated by the reinforcement of the specialist troops and the Air Force. It was only after this agreement that a token evacuation took place. The Germans, who had not been involved in these dealings, had completely reformed the Condor Legion since July 1938.

In this way discussions on volunteers ended. The Non-intervention Committee still existed, but its role was negligible. Its thirtieth and last sitting took place on 19 May 1939, after the end of the conflict. Conscious of its futility, it proceeded to dissolve itself.

Munich and Spain: The Spaniards and the European Crisis

The death sentence on Republican Spain, accepted since summer 1938 by France and Russia, became final after Munich. At this point, Negrín and Del Vayo, like Prieto at the time of Almería, felt that the European war was inevitable and that it was the Republic's only hope of victory. Although the Spanish Republic's diplomatic position had been weakened, the chances of an international conflict had greatly increased.

The *Anschluss* had been a prelude to Hitler's widespread annexations. Then came the territorial claims on the Sudetenland. Italy was certainly ill prepared for war and weakened by the Spanish adventure. But her alliance with Germany was firmer than ever. France and Britain had drawn closer together and had guaranteed Czechoslovakia's frontiers. The political situation in Europe was so tense that the Spanish question had slipped to second place among international preoccupations.

However, in the event of war, the Negrín government had made up its mind to take a stand at once and to force the hand of France and Britain by siding with them and declaring war on Germany and Italy, whose troops were occupying part of its territory. It was in fact left to the Republic to reverse a situation that daily grew worse. Its political abandonment by the great powers led to a change of attitude among the smaller states, which naturally turned to the strongest. Until then, Germany, Italy, and Portugal had been isolated and in a minority of the Nonintervention Committee; in January 1938, Hungary, Austria, and Albania, future victims of Fascist ambitions, took sides with them. Eleven states had now given General Franco's regime *de jure* or *de facto* recognition.[15]

The Republicans wanted to convince the Western powers that they did not represent a dangerous revolutionary force and that the period of anarchy was now over. The Negrín government symbolized the maintenance of authority; there had been no opposition since Prieto's departure. Negrín was himself shouldering the essential responsibilities of the state. He was not only premier, but also foreign minister, minister of national defense, and minister of the interior. His friends liked to compare him to Clemenceau, and he undeniably had the same determination to identify himself with the country at war. Authority and national unity were being maintained at the expense of the Basque and Catalan autonomist movements: in August 1938, the resignation of the Catalan minister Ayguadé and the Basque Irujo, replaced by Moix Regas of the PSUC and the Socialist Bilbao Hospitalet, clearly indicated, in spite of official protests,[16] the strengthening of the central authority.

In the same way, the policy of religious tolerance practiced by Negrín was inspired by the wish to win the sympathy of the Western world. While Irujo was a minister, he fought for freedom of worship; he had very soon forced the concession that 'the denunciation of priests for the mere fact of practicing the priesthood' should be regarded as an offense.[17] Private masses were authorized and on 15 August 1937 the first official mass was celebrated in the building of the Basque

Delegation in Valencia. Of course this did not mean that the Catholic Church had had its prerogatives restored: the first publicly authorized religious burial was regarded as a magnificent proof of the government's tolerance. But less spectacular measures were effective in other ways, such as the decision by Negrín to 'exempt religious objects from the general rules governing the requisition of precious metals,' and in particular the 1938 measures, which exempted priests from active duty and drafted them into medical and welfare services, and which authorized them to enter prisons to minister to the men there, especially the condemned men. All these decisions tended to reassure foreigners. It was possible to get along with such a regime, to help it to win or at least retain the essentials by means of an honorable compromise.

Moreover, the Czech crisis roused great hope among the Republicans. In the event of a conflict, Franco's Spain would soon find herself in an untenable military situation. The Nationalists did not have adequate reserves to hold an additional front. According to von Funk, the German military attaché in San Sebastián, Franco himself had stated 'that he had never had any reserves, and that with every attack by the Reds, he had had to call a halt to the offensive in order to meet them.'[18] Certainly the Pyrenees provided a natural defense, but Franco knew quite well that it was not adequate. He had sent thousands of prisoners to the two frontiers in the North and the South to prepare fortifications. On the other hand, his army still depended on supplies of material from Italy and Germany. The halting of deliveries of ammunition during the Czech crisis had already put his troops in a difficult situation. Quite clearly, in the event of a European conflict, the collapse of Spain within a short space of time was to be expected. Even Franco's supporters knew this, and the Germans thought that the Caudillo would then be 'reduced to retiring and handing over to a more moderate figure the task of winding up the Civil War.'[19]

Franco had stopped receiving encouragement and promises from his allies; he was not even kept abreast of the political situation by the German government. Anxiety increased at

Nationalist headquarters. 'Franco's general staff is very depressed,' said Stohrer, 'and is unable to conceal its displeasure with us.'[20] To this displeasure must be added the displays of bad temper against Suñer, which inspired fears of a revived opposition in Nationalist Spain. To ensure victory, Franco had to make absolutely certain, in the event of a European conflagration, of the neutrality of the great powers, and in particular of France.

Nationalist Neutrality in the Czech Crisis

From 18 to 28 September the diplomatic efforts of Nationalist Spain were aimed at getting the Western powers to agree first to keep the Spanish affair separate from the impending European war, and afterward to accept the Nationalist government's neutrality, which would be equivalent on their side to a final refusal to support the Spanish Republic.

The Western powers' position was precarious. They did not have a united front. The Chamberlain government would only go to war against the Axis as a last resort. Russian aid to Czechoslovakia was problematical. France would therefore be isolated in the event of war and obliged to divest its eastern frontiers in order to launch the anticipated twofold attack against Nationalist Spain through Catalonia and Morocco. The French general staff would unquestionably prefer not to have to fight an additional enemy. Thus, when Jordana and Franco undertook to observe the strictest neutrality in the event of a European conflict, the British and French governments showed satisfaction at the promises made directly by the Caudillo and passed on to Paris and London by Quinones de León and the Duke of Alba.

This declaration of neutrality still had to be accepted by the Axis powers, and this was a very difficult matter. Nationalist diplomacy had exhibited great shrewdness in this respect. First it had deliberately revealed its fear of a war that might do it harm; then it had deplored the fact that its allies left it in ignorance of how the political situation was developing. On this point, however, Franco had no difficulty in finding cause for complaint.

In reality, Franco was not afraid that Spain would be neglected, but that too much attention would be paid to her during the course of negotiations at which he would not be represented; it was not impossible that the Axis powers would abandon their Spanish ally or that Germany would make use of her forces in Spain and the Mediterranean for military action in the event of war. The arrival of the *Deutschland* in Vigo, like the presence of the Italians in Majorca, could legitimately give rise to fears in this respect. Finally, the European political crisis, by reviving hopes in the Republican camp, could provoke disturbances and even actual revolts in Nationalist Spain.

These fears explain the Burgos government's neutralist attitude. On 26 September the German leaders were told about it; on the twenty-seventh, Jordana officially passed on this decision to the German and Italian ambassadors. Apparently, it was a question of benevolent neutrality. But the fact remains that Franco had presented his allies with a *fait accompli*. He expected to be approved, but he only informed them once his decision had been taken.

How, in such circumstances, could there have been surprise at the violent reactions from German and Italian diplomats? The Italians were especially furious; their leaders felt that the sacrifices made for the Nationalist cause ought to be repaid there and then. 'Our dead should be turning in their graves,' wrote Ciano. The Germans were more reserved, but no less shocked at the Spaniards' haste in proclaiming their neutrality; they considered the move premature, to say the least. The Italians and Germans were also anxious about the fate that awaited their troops fighting in Spain in the event of war. No doubt Jordana had stated that these troops would be regarded and treated as Spanish soldiers. But could it be believed that France, at war with Germany, would tolerate the presence of enemy soldiers in a so-called neutral country? On receiving the news of Spanish neutrality, Ciano's instinctive reaction was to consider the immediate evacuation of the Italian troops.

In spite of the precautions taken by the Nationalist government, it was clear that a European conflict would threaten all the successes won up till then. And the representatives of both Spains were perfectly aware that their fate hung in the balance beyond their own frontiers.

Once again the reluctance of the Western powers determined Spain's fate. In August–September 1936, the comedy of nonintervention had played into the hands of the Fascist states. In September 1938, the Munich capitulation did not merely deliver up Czechoslovakia to Hitler, it utterly extinguished the last hope of Spanish democracy: 'This dawn of peace has sounded the knell of Red tyranny. The efforts of our armies will soon lead to victorious peace.'[21]

From this point on, in fact, the great powers' first preoccupation was to put an end to the Civil War. The winners at Munich had realized that, in the event of a general conflict, Nationalist Spain would be a millstone around their necks if the Civil War continued. The Western powers had not been altogether unhappy about Franco's attitude at the time of the Munich crisis. Russia was pulling out for good. France herself, reassured by the Caudillo's position, was considering establishing diplomatic relations with the Nationalists. In early 1939, Léon Bérard was given the task of negotiating *de facto* recognition of the Burgos government. In spite of his known sympathy for the Nationalists, he ran into unconcealed ill will; Franco demanded *de jure* recognition and asked the French to hand over to him Spanish property in France, war material, and the gold in the Bank of Spain, among other things.

For the time being, negotiations were suspended. At the end of the Civil War, however, the Pétain mission renewed apparently cordial relations, and finally all the Nationalist government's requests were accepted.

By October 1938 the only question was to know how Franco's final victory could be assured. Stohrer explained how the intervention of the powers could induce 'the moderate elements among the Reds to lay down their arms,'[22] which seemed to anticipate by a few months the action of the Casado Junta in destroying the Republican positions.

The Stohrer plan excluded the Communists from negotiations and seemed to exclude Negrín. However, the latter did not close the door on a peaceful solution of the conflict. In a thirteen-point speech, he outlined the conditions required for a compromise between the two sides. On 1 October 1938, in a speech to the Cortes, he accepted the principle of mediation. A few days later he admitted that a plebiscite could be a solution. But could a compromise acceptable to all Spaniards really be found? The mere word 'mediation' or 'compromise' provoked a violent reaction from many of the leaders in Nationalist Spain. Each time he had spoken on this subject, Franco had been categorical: there was no question of anything but capitulation. And the San Sebastián *Diario Vasco* came up with this colorful formula, which put Nationalist thinking in a nutshell: 'We do not want a pact with the devil, we want the peace of Conquest.'[23]

Notes

[1] Only on 1 April 1937 did *Le Temps* record the boarding of the *Magdalena* and the *Cap Falcón* by Nationalist warships, the French government reacting solely with a formal protest.

[2] Among them, according to Prieto, were the Communist ministers.

[3] Ciano, *Diary, 1937–1938.*

[4] Archives of the German Foreign Ministry.

[5] Italian minister of the Navy.

[6] Chamberlain succeeded Baldwin on 28 May 1937 as a result of the British dynastic crisis provoked by Edward VIII's marriage.

[7] So as to include the USSR.

[8] Blum's statements to the Commission of Investigation.

[9] In spite of his *Action Française* views, he was one of the most loyal supporters of Republican Spain, in the interest of French security.

[10] Quoted by *Le Temps*, 4 July.

[11] See *Le Temps*, 1 July.

[12] Note on 5 July 1938, Archives of the German Foreign Ministry.

[13] It was only on 8 October 1938 that Hemming was able to go to Burgos, accompanied by Vice Admiral Waterhouse and Captain Mackey-Hodge.

[14] Archives of the German Foreign Ministry.

[15] They were: Germany, Italy, Portugal, Guatemala, San Salvador, Nicaragua, Albania, the Vatican, Japan, Manchukuo, Austria, and Hungary.

[16] The pretext for this was the disagreements that followed the decrees regulating the war industry and the administration of justice.

[17] See Garrido's article in *El Socialista*.
[18] Archives of the German Foreign Ministry.
[19] Ibid.
[20] Ibid.
[21] Franco's speech at Burgos on the Caudillo's celebration day (1 October 1938).
[22] Archives of the German Foreign Ministry.
[23] Quoted by *Le Temps*, 13 October 1938.

CHAPTER 21

THE BATTLE OF THE EBRO AND THE CAMPAIGN IN CATALONIA

The Offensive: A Political Necessity

The final abandonment of the Republic had coincided with the fall of the second Blum government; at that point, the Nationalists' victory in Aragon, severing Catalonia from the Republic, gave the impression that a collapse might occur at any time, shattering the Republican front. It is true that the offensive in the direction of Valencia had slowed in front of the line at Viver, but after a big military thrust a period of regrouping and readaptation is always to be expected. Moreover, the attacks on Viver did not cease until 23 July, granting no respite to the weary government troops, morally weakened by retreat and by the certainty of fighting on their last line of defense from then on. Their severance from Catalonia prevented any material aid from being brought across the French frontier: to become involved in fighting in such circumstances could have been disastrous. It was at this juncture that, in order to save Valencia and make a final effort to regroup the Republican forces, the Republican general staff tried to recover the initiative. This was the Ebro offensive, whose launching surprised not only the Spanish, but also the foreign powers, who were scarcely counting on another large-scale Republican action.

Rojo observed that it had become necessary 'to make a gigantic effort in the military as well as in the international field.' Since the beginning of 1938, tension had once again built up between the Western powers and Germany. As the first typical Hitler annexation, the *Anschluss* heralded further territorial claims. The European war was being prepared in central Europe. At the same time, the Negrín government once again saw a chance of internationalizing the conflict. Once again it was necessary to prove to Europe and the world that the reverses they had suffered had not shaken the Republicans' determination to fight on, that the morale of the troops was still intact; in short, that the movement that had aroused the Spanish people in 1936 had been able to resist both time and the hardships of war. Possibly Negrín also had it in mind to prove that the outcome of the struggle was still a long way off, and that the adversaries had to accept a compromise. The Ebro offensive was therefore as much a political as a military operation.

But why choose the Ebro sector, which, by requiring the crossing of the river at a difficult place, presented an additional danger? There were in fact only two means of saving Valencia: either a direct counterattack to the north of Sagunto, leading to the recapture of part of the land lost during the preceding months and the relief of the capital of the Levante (but this operation would have been seriously compromised from the start by the weariness of the troops involved, the lack of reserves, and the gaps already made in the Madrid, Estremaduran, and Andalusian fronts); or else a large-scale action in another vital sector, preventing the resumption of the Nationalist offensive against Valencia. The first objective of the Republican general staff was to force the Nationalists to divert their attention from the Levante to Catalonia.

The forces that were to take part in the attack had been regrouped in the North; they were still well organized and admirably prepared for the surprise action that had to be carried out before the crossing of the river. Certain problems were obviously difficult to solve, especially the need to cross the Ebro with heavy equipment in order to achieve the second objective, a breach of the Nationalist front, leading to the recovery of part of the Mediterranean coast. In fact, only total success could prove that the Republican Army was still capable of winning. But if the operation miscarried from the start, a setback like this threatened to end in disaster. The general staff had certainly taken a risk, but it was a calculated risk. It was in fact no longer possible to remain passive: a complete victory was unthinkable, given the balance of power, but a local success was both necessary and possible.

The Crossing of the Ebro

The place where the offensive was to be launched had been fixed since June. General Rojo pointed out in this regard that the general staff's initially lofty ambitions had eventually been confined to the following objective: forcing a crossing of the Ebro on both sides of the loop, occupying the heights to the south, and making a deep thrust.

Two complementary actions were to accompany this main though limited action, one toward the west on the Fayón–Mequinenza axis, in a move to sever the communications of the Nationalist troops and to hamper the arrival of reinforcements, and the other toward the coast, which would merely be a diversion. On the whole, the government ambitions were relatively modest, although substantial forces were committed—the Army of the Ebro, reinforced by a certain number of divisions from the Army of the East.[1] But the delays necessary for concentrating men and arms for collecting the boats that were to aid the first crossings, and for the arrival of the component parts of the bridges that were to be thrown across the river meant that the start of the offensive had to be deferred. All this dragged on for about two months. In spite of everything, the element of surprise was almost complete.

On the night of 24–25 July the boats were discreetly positioned. The attack by small assault groups with a commando mission reflected both the means and the best utilization of the Republican soldiers. Success was nearly complete, although the technical services, as always in the Republican Army, proved inadequate; thus, communications between the general staff, posted a few miles from the river, and the Fifth Army Corps were severed during the early hours of the attack.

The news of the attack, during the same night, was good: bridgeheads had been established, footbridges and transport

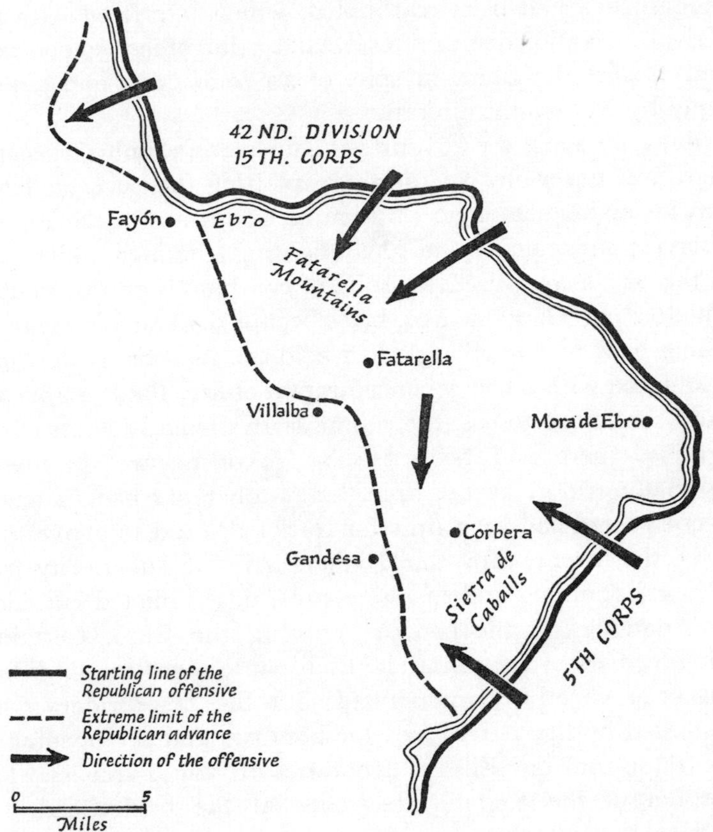

The Republican Offensive on the Ebro (July–August 1938)

bridges had been put in position, and the crossing of the river, at two points, began at dawn. Thrusting toward Villalba on the one side and toward Gandesa and Corbera on the other, the two pincers of the Republican offensive closed on a pocket occupying the furthest point of the loop, with its center at Mora del Ebro. On the twenty-sixth, Corbera was occupied and the outskirts of Villalba and Gandesa reached. The pocket at Mora del Ebro was wiped out in a few days. The bridgehead across the Ebro was then twelve miles deep and eighteen miles wide. To the north, the crossing by the Forty-second Division meant that a subsidiary bridgehead between Fayón and

Mequinenza had been established, which interfered with the arrival of Nationalist reinforcements. Altogether, 50,000 men had crossed the Ebro, in spite of an immediate and violent reply by Nationalist aircraft.

But once again the advantages gained were limited, because there was never any question of exploiting this success. There was an inadequate concentration of troops and a shortage of reserves; after five days of tough fighting, the men taking part in the battle were tired. In spite of continuous efforts, neither Villalba nor Gandesa had been occupied. The Nationalists, falling back on the villages, had held on. As soon as they had been faced with a heavy concentration of fire, the Republicans had been forced to halt their attacks. In the early hours of the fighting, there had been a shortage of heavy equipment, especially armor. By the time the 24-ton tanks had managed to cross there had been time for Nationalist aid to arrive.

By the twenty-fifth the Nationalists' air superiority was obvious. Bombing and machine-gun raids[2] inflicted considerable damage on the convoys crossing the Ebro. Certainly reinforcements were still arriving, because night crossings had not been effectively interrupted, but the first bridges were destroyed by the activities of the bombers and the opening of the dams on the Ebro's tributaries in the Pyrenees. The position of the Republican troops in the bridgehead was constantly being threatened.

The Battle of Attrition

On 1 August the real battle began. The Nationalists were intent on hurling their opponents back across the river; the Republicans were determined to hold on. The fighting that ensued went on until 15 November; the government forces showed, as they had at Teruel, that they were capable of tenacity in the most difficult of circumstances.

But the Army of the Ebro had to embark on a battle of attrition, a battle of equipment. However much courage it showed, it could not emerge victorious from such a confrontation. It was, said Rojo, 'a fight between plenty and poverty.' The protraction of the fighting had only one meaning: to give foreigners the idea that there was still a balance of forces in Spain, at a time when the Czech crisis was breaking in Europe.

At this point European reconciliation was brought about in Munich, and hopes of foreign intervention vanished. Henceforth, the battle of the Ebro became not only pointless but dangerous for the Republicans: 'The loss of Catalonia,' wrote Ulíbarri, 'was determined on the Ebro.' Without doubt, a withdrawal to the left bank in the early days of August would have avoided more serious reverses and the enormous casualties incurred afterward by the Republicans. But the respite given to the armies in the Center had been too brief, and, more important, the abandonment of the bridgehead, after the blaring victory communiqués, would have caused a reaction disastrous for the morale of the Army and the rear.

Also, in spite of the presence of substantial forces on the Nationalist side, the Barcelona general staff dug in its heels and resisted. Possibly the Republican command was more willing to accept a defensive war than broadscale maneuvers. The troops that were holding the bridgehead had gained certain advantages, in particular, the possession of the main observation points in the area strengthened their position. The successes won in the early days and the confusion and irresolution that they had noticed among the enemy increased their courage and tenacity.

At the start of the offensive they were faced by comparatively limited forces. Thus, with the exception of Amposta, the whole zone of attack was protected solely by the Fiftieth Division. The Nationalist general staff was relying mainly on the natural protection afforded by the river and the normal sluggishness of government operations. It was deceived on both these points. Although, in the early stages of the offensive, certain Nationalist officers had been optimistic, by the dawn of the twenty-fifth the tone of the communiqués had changed; the news had become frankly bad. In spite of the mass of material flung hurriedly into the battle, all the available artillery and aircraft, it took a week to reestablish 'normal battle conditions' and to stabilize the front.

Seven divisions[3] had been successively placed at the disposal of the Moroccan army corps in order to restore the situation. General Franco had been forced to withdraw troops from the Levante and even from some other sectors on the central front, and to transfer them to the Ebro. As at Teruel, he had agreed to fight on the terrain chosen by his enemies. But he accepted this challenge because he was confident of his daily increasing material superiority. On such a narrow front, victory could only be won by pounding the enemy with artillery fire and aircraft. Franco felt that this was now possible.

The Republicans had hung on too and had moved up reinforcements. For weeks, the adversaries persisted, bringing up new means and fresh troops, until the point when the terrible casualties incurred by both sides forced one of the combatants to leave the field. The battle of the Ebro had been even bloodier than Teruel. It too had changed into a battle of annihilation, but this time the fighting was to be decisive.

To start with, the Nationalist counteroffensive worked out well. The Fayón bridgehead had been reduced; the concentration of troops and especially of artillery, its extraordinary density, pointed to a rapid victory. The Republican Forty-second Division was practically annihilated.

But this was only a local success. The decisive battle took place around the Gandesa bridgehead. The Nationalists met with an initial failure here: the attack launched before 10 August against the Sierra de Pandols met with bitter resistance, 'unlike anything else in the whole of the war,' said Aznar; in practical terms the gains made were nonexistent. In August and September the attacks continued, barely interrupted by a few periods of calm, which enabled the troops, who had suffered heavy casualties on each occasion, to reform. There were four offensives before October. These were not, strictly speaking, large-scale military actions, but localized actions around several points that were taken and retaken. More than at Teruel, where the harshness of the fighting was due mainly to weather conditions, the battle of the Ebro, because of its length, its harshness, and its stubbornness, revived memories of the fighting in the Great War. It was the Spanish Verdun.

But the adversaries could not endure such a cadence of almost uninterrupted destruction indefinitely. The enormous losses of men and material eventually led to the exhaustion of the Republican forces. By the end of October, reserves had become inadequate. On the Nationalist side, on the other hand, it had been possible to prepare reinforcements. A new army corps of the Maestrazgo was formed; led by General García Valino, it consisted of five divisions.

On 24 October General Order No. 44 to the Nationalists ordered them to 'reduce the pocket formed on the Ebro.' In fact, the attack only really began after 1 November. The scaling of the Republican positions in the Sierra de Caballs was managed by surprise. Between 1 and 8 November the whole of the southeastern part of the bridgehead as far as Mora del Ebro was occupied. The second phase of the offensive ended on 15 November. The government forces had lost all the ground won since the beginning of the fighting. The Republican Army had proved that it was capable of fighting and holding on, in spite of its material inferiority, but the casualties incurred, possibly some 100,000 men killed, wounded, and taken prisoner,[4] had bled it white and had undeniably opened the way to defeat.

There is no doubt that the front stabilized itself after 15 November. On the other hand, the offensive launched in Estremadura in the direction of Cabeza del Buey and Almadén, an offensive that had made rapid progress during August, was finally blocked by the Republicans, thanks to support by troops from the Levante. The battle of the Ebro, by luring away the best Nationalist troops, had given the central zone an appreciable respite; Miaja had taken advantage of it to reorganize his troops.

But since Franco's victory in Aragon, Spain had been divided. The troops in Catalonia had had no relief; they were exhausted by the fighting they had had to endure. They needed a long period of calm and arms reinforcements to be able to meet a vast Nationalist offensive with a single solid front, but this was not to be. The weariness caused by the war became more and more obvious with each military failure. The successes won on the Ebro in July had boosted the morale of the rear for a while, but since then, the ground won had been retaken by the Nationalists. Hopes of aid from outside had ended with Munich. Prieto's theory, 'Europe has betrayed us,' was agreed to by many.

To Catalonia, which had been the home of the Anarchist revolution and the scene of the May days, Europe's 'betrayal' was like the condemnation of Negrín's policy. The Revolution had been abandoned, and Europe was now backing Franco.

For the first time in Catalonia, the rear began to weaken. To make Barcelona another Madrid was now impossible. Conditions were no longer what they had been in 1936. Nor was faith.

Catalonia before the Attack

Can it at least be said that the government had gained in authority what it had lost in popularity? Even this is disputable. The Socialist party was deeply divided in spite of the apparent reconciliation among its various shades of opinion. The Communist upsurge had crystallized the hostility of the other parties toward this encroaching partner. The Army had never stopped being influenced by politics. On the other hand, the lack of imported goods, the progressive halting of trade as a result of the blockade, lack of money, and the ill will of foreign countries slowly paralyzed life in Catalonia. Just when industry should have been developed to the full, production was slowing down: there were not enough raw materials. Agricultural production was also slipping back; many peasants were at the front, others were not delivering their goods. Food supplies became more and more difficult to obtain. In November, faced with the difficulties that another winter of war presaged, the government had created, under the chairmanship of the minister of national defense, a Food-Supply Coordinating Committee, which was to coordinate 'all activities dealing with production, the sale of foodstuffs, and essential clothing.' It was a question of distributing food, giving priority to the fighting men, then to the armed forces in the rear, and finally to the civilian population, beginning with children, the sick, and workers in war industries. But this organ soon found itself up against insurmountable obstacles.

It should be added that throughout Catalonia, and especially in Barcelona, Franco's supporters were still numerous and active. With the collapse of Catalonia, this Fifth Column showed its face, especially in the last hours of the defense of Barcelona. Finally, morale in the rear was sapped by incessant bombing raids on the Catalan capital. Everything was conspiring toward the defeat of the Republic in Catalonia.

The Nationalist army corps[5] were deployed on a front running along the Ebro to the tributary of the Segre, and then rising toward the Pyrenees, following the Segre and the Noguera, because the towns staked out by this front line, Lérida, Balaguer, and Tremp, were in Nationalist hands.

The Loss of Barcelona

On 23 December the offensive against Catalonia opened. In theory, the Republican forces were still made up of two armies: in the North starting from the French frontier, the Army of the East;[6] in the South, the Army of the Ebro. Their inferiority in men and material was such that, after the battle of the Ebro, the Republicans were almost incapable of carrying out any sort of offensive action. According to Ulíbarri, each brigade lacked from 600 to 1000 men of the 3600 that made up their full strength. All in all, the Republican command could put 90,000 men on the front but did not have any reserves.

The Eleventh and Twelfth Army Corps of the Army of the East had to bear the full brunt of the attack. A two-pronged Nationalist assault made a breach in the Segre front. After a weak artillery barrage, an attack by Italian armor provoked a stampede; the Sixteenth Division, held in reserve, retreated instead of defending its positions. The breach thus created made a large-scale counterattack difficult. The attempt made on 25 December led to almost total failure; its only result was slightly to slow down the advance of the CTV and the Navarrese. Finally, in order to attempt a new offensive action, the Army of the Ebro had to be reinforced with contingents from the Army of the East. And this led to another failure.

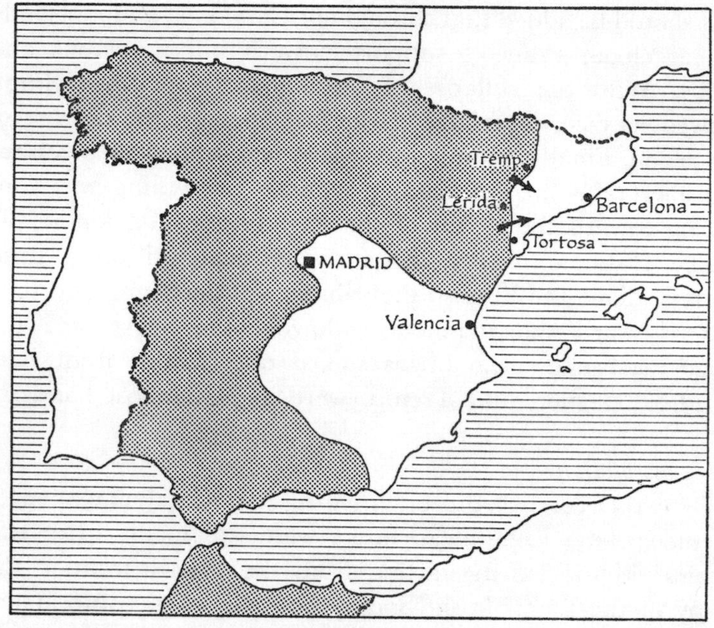

The Campaign in Catalonia (January–February 1939)

The fighting had now been going on for ten days. It was practically impossible, in the Republican Army, to relieve the fighting units. Weariness and a sense of impotence were now added to material inferiority. The fighters no longer even tried to hinder the Nationalist air raids and only appeared after the fighting: the inhabitants of Barcelona christened them the *Arco de Iris*, the Rainbow. The morale of the troops, especially that of the new recruits, slumped daily.

The collapse occurred in the early days of January. While the Italian attack resulted in a breakthrough toward Borjas Blancas, the Nationalist army corps of Aragon and the Maestrazgo made rapid progress in the Tremp area, threatening to isolate the Republican forces in their positions facing Lérida. All the power stations in the Lérida area, the most important in Spain, fell into Nationalist hands. The Barcelona general staff gave the order to fall back. The front line literally burst open. The Nationalist offensive became a general one; the six army corps fanned out, making use of armor. By 6 January there was no longer any question of offensive action. 'All we can do,' said Rojo, 'is defend.' In fact, it was mainly a question of knowing how long the Republicans could resist, avoid encirclement and isolation, and protect the roads that led to the Pyrenean frontier. The Nationalists did not even need to initiate a breakthrough, as before; with six army corps in the line, they were already vastly superior in numbers to the forces mustered by the seven Republican army corps, and they gave proof of a daily more overwhelming material superiority. The Republican artillery was, according to Rojo, reduced to a sixth of the opposing artillery. Individual arms were in short supply: 60,000 rifles, insufficient to arm all the combatants.

Certainly, an effort was still possible; the Barcelona government attempted one by mobilizing all men of fighting age, but this mobilization, even if it had been completed, would have barely altered the situation, because there were no arms to be issued. And then this mass levy had an absurd side to it: under pretext of bringing up to the front troops whom it was not even possible to use, the firemen were mobilized in Barcelona, a town bombed daily and that had as many as five or six alerts a day. From 20 to 26 January the life of the city was completely disrupted.

In fact, the battle that took place for the possession of the town had been lost in advance. The Army of the Ebro, heavily committed to the south, had to abandon the southern triangle defended by Tarragona in order to avoid encirclement; the loss of this town was the prelude to the collapse of the front. It added to the immense chaos by forcing droves of refugees to the north, who encumbered the roads of Catalonia. They were already crowding into Barcelona, even sleeping on the platforms of the subway, which was being used both as shelters and dormitories.

Evidently, the military leaders, the commissars, and the representatives of the parties and unions still hoped, on 24 January, to sustain a long defense. A substantial propaganda campaign had been waged. Everywhere streamers were hung and posters were put up: 'Catalonia is in danger. Everyone to arms!', or 'Win this battle and we shall win the war!' To win the battle, it was first necessary to join it. The forces with the task of defending the square were plainly inadequate. Colonel Romero had barely a few thousand men, either from rear battalions of dubious quality or from troops on the retreat since the opening of the Nationalist offensive, who could not be expected to have remarkable morale. Moreover, the *Asaltos* deserted the front on the morning of 21 January.

Finally, the population of the town was not prepared for genuine resistance. Excluding those in sympathy with Nationalism, the vast majority of the inhabitants were clearly worn out and had stopped believing in the victory they had waited for so long. Survival had become the main problem in Barcelona. Everything was in short supply; there was no more coal or electricity. The shops were empty; even on the black market scarcity was the rule. Government deliveries were irregular and too small. Markets stopped receiving supplies; sugar was replaced by saccharine; there was practically no oil. Only bread was not short, except during the three days before the city's capture, but 300 grams of gray bread did not satisfy hunger. The city's desolate look, in contrast to the gaiety and color of the early days of the Revolution on the Ramblas, showed how far things had gone. Places of entertainment closed their doors, first nightclubs and dance halls, then, after 14 January, theaters, cinemas, and even cafés, where people sat out of sheer habit. The last shops had closed their iron shutters. 'Barcelona forty-eight hours before the entry of the enemy,' said Rojo, 'is like a city of the dead.'

The last line of defense protecting the city was the Tibidabo mountain range. It was not seriously defended. On the twenty-third the Llobregat front was breached. In three days, disobedience and desertion were rife. On the morning of the twenty-sixth, there was an almost wholesale stampede; the heroic devotion of a few groups,[7] which were massacred on the spot, was completely pointless. The port area was bombed by Nationalist aircraft, artillery, and warships. The troops of

Solchaga and Yagüe that converged on the city occupied the military districts on the outskirts. In the early afternoon, tanks appeared at the harbor. By evening, all resistance had ceased. The actual occupation of the town had cost the Nationalists only a single life.

The capital's last defenders had withdrawn, mainly anxious not to be outflanked to the north. On 23 January Negrín and his government, the embassies, and the ministries had left Barcelona. However, it had not been possible to evacuate everything; part of the archives had been destroyed. And when the Nationalists had entered the city, they had not found it void of its inhabitants. Many, like the former town clerk, had preferred to wait for the victors. The city's new mayor, Miguel Mateu Plá, president of the Hispano-Suiza company, was soon able to restore the essential services. The most difficult thing was to reorganize food supplies.

The loss of Barcelona was not of enormous strategic importance to the Republicans, but the unconditional surrender of the Catalonian capital had a decisive effect on the morale of the population throughout Republican Spain. The death throes of the Republic began that day.

The Flight toward the Frontier

The collapse of the front and the rumors that accompany every catastrophe drove onto the roads a horde of refugees who were heading in disorder for all the French frontier crossings. According to *Le Temps* on 6 February, 100,000 had already crossed it. Rojo estimated those thronging the border posts at some hundreds of thousands. 'It is chaos,' he said. Mingled with the civilian population fleeing the Nationalist advance, a wretched crowd encumbered with a few belongings, were thousands of soldiers who had deserted the fighting area. They added to the panic by peddling the most unlikely rumors. Armed men commandeered cars and then abandoned them at the frontier. There was no longer any law and order or police, only total anarchy. It was the chaos of defeat and despair. But why shouldn't the crowd have taken to its heels? Since the end of January not a day had gone by without a report of some well-known figure crossing into France, Giral, Caballero, and Araquistain. These facts were common knowledge and, in the general panic, were even grossly exaggerated.

The French authorities were overwhelmed by the mass of fugitives. To begin with, they had admitted the refugees, but very soon it had become impossible to register tens of thousands of refugees and disperse them about the country. On 30 January the French authorities decided not to let able-bodied men cross for a while and to grant right of asylum only to women and children. The men who had already crossed the frontier and had not yet been directed to a particular place were massed in a detention camp at Argelès, in the Pyrenées-Orientales. At the time, this decision sowed fresh panic among the Spaniards who were waiting at the frontier posts in Perthus and Boulou. Some of the fugitives streamed back into still unoccupied Catalonia. Others tried to enter France by stealth, and many succeeded, in spite of the presence of Senegalese troops with the task of surveillance. This situation merely complicated the task of the French authorities. Also, from 5 to 9 February, the frontier was once again officially opened to Spanish soldiers. Rojo had promised that crossings of the frontier would be made in good order.

In fact, although a stampede by some elements proved unavoidable, it is only fair to point out—because it was a success that testified, amid general anarchy, to the real worth of these troops—that the last armed contingents to cross the frontier had retreated in good order. French journalists noted that their morale was better and that they did not have the look of a routed army. Among them were 700 of the surviving members of the International Brigades, who had remained in Catalonia until the last moment and crossed the frontier only on 7 February.

According to the agreements reached with the Republican general staff, once the men had crossed the frontier they were no longer regarded as soldiers, but as refugees; they were disarmed, underwent a formal search, and were immediately sent on to assembly centers, the chief of which was still at Argelès. The latter soon proved inadequate to take in everyone; another had to be created, not far away, in Saint-Cyprien.

War material was confiscated by the French government; though some Spanish leaders were under the illusion that they could transport such equipment to the central zone, they were soon obliged to bow to the facts: if the central zone went on fighting, it would do so with its own forces.

During the final days, the leaders of the Republic had crossed the frontier too. President Azaña arrived in France on the morning of 5 February, three days after the remaining members of the government and Negrín himself. But differences were already emerging between the president of the Republic and the head of the government on what attitude was to be adopted after the loss of Catalonia.

Negrín and his staff had striven to maintain some slight order and discipline. They may have contemplated a degree of resistance in the extreme north of the country, around Gerona and Figueras, relying on the French frontier. But it was difficult to imagine that a regular front could be held by troops that were melting away daily. The information services had stopped functioning; though the advance of the Nationalist troops could be contained in the mountainous sector, it had not ceased along the coast. The command itself did not seem up to its task, and it had been necessary to replace it in the final days. General Jurado took over from Sarabia at the head of what remained of the group of armies. In spite of all its efforts to maintain discipline, the general staff could not avoid localized panic; units of *Carabineros* and security forces, incorporated in the Army, had given the signal for a stampede. The steps that had been taken in Figueras to try to organize the retreating troops were nothing but totally inadequate palliatives. Air raids and the fear of a Nationalist landing in the rear contrived to make any organization of defense impracticable. The ministerial meetings that Negrín held in Figueras no longer had any rhyme or reason: what was the point of decisions that could not be carried out? What had disappeared or had become unusable was not the government, but the organs of the government and the executive. The small towns of Figueras and Gerona could not shelter them. There was not even room there to set up offices; the arrival of processions of official cars merely brought the traffic to a standstill. Many Barcelona officials, who no longer had the least confidence in the outcome of the war, had not even waited for orders from the government to make for the frontier. In short, though there was still a government, the state had already ceased to exist.

On 8 February the general staff moved to Perthus and on the ninth Rojo crossed to Boulou in French territory. The same day, at 1:50 P.M., the Nationalists reached the frontier at Perthus. The remaining organized Republican troops crossed into France on 9 and 10 February. There was no longer any Army of Catalonia.

The Capitulation of Minorca

At the same time, the capitulation of Minorca introduced a new element, British mediation.

The island had been completely isolated since Nationalist Spain had showed its naval superiority. On 8 February the English cruiser *Devonshire* brought a Nationalist representative, Colonel San Luis, to Port Mahon. An initial meeting took place between the governor of Minorca, González Ubieta, and the captain of the *Devonshire*, Muirhead-Gould. Ubieta agreed to work out the lines along which a surrender could be negotiated with Colonel San Luis. During the course of two meetings, which the commander of the *Devonshire* attended, the two sides agreed that the lives of the Republican officers and officials should be spared and that the evacuation of those who wished to escape Nationalist domination would be guaranteed. The *Devonshire* took on board 300 men, 100 women, and 50 children.

Yet everything nearly fell through at the last moment, as a result of a Nationalist air raid that took place on 9 February, after the Port Mahon agreement. This was regarded as a betrayal on the part of the Nationalists. The Nationalist base in Palma described this raid as a 'mistake.' This was doubtful: the base at Palma was, in spite of its Spanish command, controlled by the Italians, hostile to any agreement made under the aegis of Great Britain. Indeed, the British radio denied that the British government had taken part in an agreement and stated that the commander of the *Devonshire* had acted on his own initiative, while Jordana told the German ambassador that there had been no Anglo-Spanish agreement over Minorca. But these were diplomatic statements. Great Britain was obviously not proud of an intervention that could be regarded as an interference in Spanish affairs, and the Nationalists set too much store by the Italian-German alliance openly to displease the governments of those countries.

But the Minorca agreements were significant: after the fall of Catalonia, the end of the war was in sight.

The Negrín Government and the Problem of Peace

In the middle of the disaster there arose the basic problem of peace, which was a political problem. On 1 February the Cortes, or what remained of it, had met in Figueras. Negrín had put to them in no uncertain manner the possibility of a restoration of the peace. But with a defeated army and a state in the process of breaking up, there was no longer any question of negotiation between equals. In spite of their moderation, the thirteen points that Negrín had set out as his minimum program in 1938 were now superseded. There were only three points that he still considered as conditions for peace: the guarantee of independence and national integrity; the guarantee of freedom for the Spanish people to choose its destiny; the guarantee that a policy of authority would put a stop to persecutions after the war.

It was still obvious that it would be difficult, in negotiations, to obtain satisfaction on the second point. Negrín did not seem to wish to confine himself to a simple statement of these conditions. For the first time, British mediation was officially considered by the Republican government. Del Vayo told how a meeting had taken place in Agullana between the British chargé, Stevenson, the French ambassador, Jules Henry, Negrín, and himself. During the course of this meeting, Negrín had explained what the three guarantees meant to him. The first concerned 'the evacuation of all foreign elements from Spanish territory'; the second meant that 'the Spanish people would freely decide on its political system, without any foreign pressure.' Del Vayo explained that Franco would probably not accept these two proposals. Negrín conceded that they could be dropped during the course of negotiations: even if an approval in principle was received from the Burgos government, it would have little chance of being respected afterward. All that then remained was the third condition, which Del Vayo interpreted with the help of this concise formula: 'No reprisals.' It was difficult to be more conciliatory.

Rojo seemed to confirm what Del Vayo had said when he referred to ending the war in the most dignified way and saving the largest number of people. But there was already a word in Rojo's text that pointed to the growing dissension between the Army and the premier; the general was actually referring to a future political formula. It may be that he was in fact agreed on preparing a capitulation by removing those who presented an obstacle to peace. Negrín, on the other hand, intended to hold government-to-government negotiations, which Franco would never accept. In the event of negotiations breaking down, Negrín gave the order to resist. 'What shall we resist with? Why are we going to resist?' asked Rojo.

In effect, for many of the soldiers, the war was over. *Le Temps* on 9 February referred to the choice made by the officers in Azaña's military bureau: they had decided to join Nationalist Spain. Any *entente* between the military leaders, who acknowledged defeat, and the government, which was still contemplating resistance, was impossible.

Notes

[1] The Army of the Ebro, which was to be entrusted with the crucial attack, contained Lister's Fifth Army Corps, Vega's Twelfth Army Corps, and Tagüeña's Fifteenth Army Corps. Contingents in the Army of the East included the Twenty-seventh, Forty-third, and Sixtieth Divisions.

[2] Rojo noted the appearance of 200 bombers and 96 fighters on 31 July alone.

[3] The Thirteenth Division (Barrón), the Eighty-fourth (Galera), the Eighth (Delgado Serrano), the 152nd (Rada), the Fourth Navarrese (Alonso Vega), the 102nd (Castejón), and the Seventy-fourth (Ariás). Around the main bridgehead were grouped the Eighth and the 102nd under Delgado Serrano, the Thirteenth and the Seventy-fourth commanded by

Barrón, the Fourth, and the Eighty-fourth. The 105th Division held the front as far as the mouth of the Ebro.

[4] This was the figure given by the Nationalists.

[5] Moroccan, Navarrese, and Italian army corps, and those of Aragon, the Maestrazgo, and Urgel.

[6] Its headquarters was in Solsone. It consisted of the Tenth, Eleventh, and Eighteenth Army Corps. The Army of the Ebro included the Thirteenth, Fifteenth, and Twenty-fourth Army Corps.

[7] The 125th Machine-Gun Battalion, the 151st Mixed Brigade.

CHAPTER 22

THE CASADO JUNTA AND THE WINDING UP OF THE REPUBLIC

The fall of Catalonia stirred up antagonisms, hatreds, and jealousies, as had occurred months earlier in the defeated cities of Málaga, Bilbao, and Barcelona. Advocates of resistance and capitulation were at each other's throats. People snatched at any means of flight. There were mutual accusations of the wish for futile slaughter and attempts at betrayal. The Republican officers were hoping that those in the opposite camp would act mildly toward them and contemplated the possibility of an honorable surrender. Foreign agents, members of the Fifth Column, wove intrigues. Eventually a struggle took place between those who were still talking of resistance and those who wanted immediate peace.

No period of the Civil War produced a more copious and questionable supply of literature, memoirs, accusations, polemics, and special pleading. Paradoxically, the task of the historian is complicated by the abundance of material too obviously destined for him. Many of the witnesses seem primarily concerned with saving their own skins and their future political careers.

The Negrín Government in France

Henceforth, the fate of Republican territory was debated not in Spain but in France, at the Spanish consulate in Toulouse, where the Negrín government had sought asylum after the rout in Catalonia. President Azaña, like his entourage, no longer believed in the possibility of prolonging the struggle, and it was in vain that Negrín stepped up his efforts to persuade him that it was his duty to return with him to Spain. The government's absence did in fact have a lot to do with the demoralization. Such interminable discussions only confirmed the feeling in Republican Spain that all was lost. In fact, the situation was worsening daily: incessant bombing raids were terrorizing the urban populations; the problem of food supplies had reached tragic proportions. Many people were trying desperately to find a way out of the trap of the central-southern zone. The problem of evacuation was on top of the list of government tasks; Negrín devoted part of his activities to it in Toulouse. Mexico offered to take in 30,000 families. Lord Halifax promised British aid to evacuate the threatened refugees. The Mid-Atlantic Company signed a contract for the lease of the 150,000 tons of shipping in its transport fleet. Two government commissions were permanently engaged on both aspects of the problem: means of transport and the persons to be evacuated.

However, the Negrín government did not regard evacuation as the most urgent task. At dramatic meetings of the Toulouse Cabinet, the premier, Del Vayo, and the Communists imposed their point of view: with or without Azaña, the government was to return to Spain to organize last-ditch resistance there. Why this decision?

No doubt, according to Segundo Blanco, 'the government is doing what it can, no more and no less.' In fact, Franco did not wish to negotiate with it. He had refused to parley on the basis of Negrín's three points. There was therefore nothing for it but to resist. This alone could induce the Nationalists to moderate their demands and to talk, as the British so earnestly wished. Resistance was the only way of avoiding unconditional surrender. This was what Álvarez de Vayo was attempting to prove. To him, Negrín and his friends obviously no longer believed in an imminent military victory but considered that the armed forces in the central-southern zone were sufficient to go on resisting for a few months; even if Madrid fell, the Republican troops could hold out for a long while in the southeastern mountainous sector. According to them, war had been inevitable in Europe ever since Munich. It could still save the Republic by providing her with allies.

Even admitting that this theory was correct,[1] the most difficult task remained: convincing the Spanish themselves of the possibility and necessity of resistance. The ministers present in Toulouse agreed to return, except for Giral. But Azaña remained in Paris and replied to Álvarez de Vayo, 'No one believes in our ability to resist, and those who believe in it least are our own generals.' He resigned on 2 March. His 'legitimate' successor, Martínez Barrio, the president of the Cortes, would not grant Negrín legal ratification of his premiership and refused to return to Spain.

The Government's Return to Spain

On his arrival at the Los Llanos airport, Negrín summoned the military leaders. This conference was to help him assess the difficulties of the mission that he had undertaken. After his statement, all the military leaders except Miaja declared that from now on resistance was impossible; they had to negotiate to avoid disaster. In addition to the demoralization of the rear and of the soldiers, Negrín was faced with a new obstacle to his policy, the defeatism of the Army leaders, as it had been expressed for several months through the political activities of the commander of the Army of the Center, Colonel Casado.

A long-standing Republican officer and former commander of the presidential guard, Casado was one of the professional soldiers who made up Largo Caballero's general staff. He was regarded as a man of the Left and had connections with certain Socialists and Anarchists, but he remained an officer, convinced of the importance of his 'mission as a soldier' and persuaded that he was 'respected in the enemy camp.'[2] He was very hostile to the Communist party and felt that it was 'the excess of Communist commands' that had led the Western democracies to abandon the Republic. As a soldier, he considered resistance out of the question. Franco would not negotiate as long as Negrín, Del Vayo, and the Communists were dominant in the Republic. They therefore had to be removed in order to obtain an honorable peace.[3] Casado was convinced that the advocates of negotiation would benefit from British support as soon as Communist influence had disappeared. It was necessary, he told Negrín, to obtain Azaña's return and to form a new government of Republicans and Socialists, but excluding the Communist party.

In fact, at that date it had already been several weeks since he had made certain political contacts with a view to overthrowing the government. Among the Anarchists, he had close ties with Cipriano Mera,[4] who had command of an army corps, and with García Pradas, whose hostility to the Communist party had never wavered. Naturally the CNT continued to support Negrín, for whom Segundo Blanco became spokesman within the Libertarian movement. But the hostility of the FAI prevailed at a meeting of the Liaison Committee of the CNT–FAI Libertarian Youth, who asked on 25 February for the formation 'of a new government or a new Defense Junta.' Of the Socialists, Caballero's friend Wenceslao Carrillo was also in on the colonel's plans and approved of them. He mustered his friends in Madrid in order to try to wrest the leadership of the Socialist party and the UGT from Negrín's supporters who had remained close to him in France: after their return, he stepped up his attacks on González Peña. Another Socialist lent his support to the Casado movement: Julián Besteiro was neither a militant nor a man of action, but the incarnation of Republican Socialism. Classed on the Extreme Right of the Socialist party, this university professor had played no important role since the beginning of the war. He had been regarded as a man of compromise ever since Azaña had given him the task of seeking a basis for mediation in London. He was 'highly regarded' in London and Paris.

Finally, Casado had undoubtedly been in touch with foreign diplomats, especially British ones. Domínguez said[5] that he had frequent contacts with Cowan, who seems to have been the actual instigator of the plot, even advising the colonel in the choice of his collaborators. Hidalgo de Cisneros told Del Vayo that the colonel had dropped hints to him about British promises.[6]

The Negrín government was acquainted with the situation and the dangers inherent in it. It tried both to win over and intimidate its obviously vacillating enemies. Behind Negrín was the substantial power of the Communist party, its military units, and its police force. But the Anarchists wanted to wring concessions from Negrín and to persuade him to share certain responsibilities with them. According to them, the government that was installed 'somewhere in Republican Spain' had in fact been reduced to the Negrín–Del Vayo–Uribe triumvirate. They regarded as a provocation its appointment of the leader of the SIM, Garcés, to the head of the commission that was to select the people to be evacuated; they insisted that control of the evacuation operations should not remain 'in the hands of Negrín and Vayo' and expressed the fear that senior officials would be evacuated first. On 3 March they were still hoping to take part in organizing the evacuation and put forward one of their own men, González Entrialgo, for the vital post of commander of the naval base at Cartagena. On several occasions, they repeated to Negrín that they were not eager to see Communist power increase through the allocation of new commands. On 2 March, Negrín had made his choice, and the Cabinet confirmed a series of promotions and transfers in the high command. Casado was appointed a general but replaced at the head of the Army of the Center by the Communist Modesto, also promoted to general. Miaja[7] was honorably retired with the title of Inspector-General of the Army. The creation of 'mobile shock units,' intended to reform fighting methods, was accompanied by promotions of Communist officers: Lister, Galán, and Márquez were appointed colonels. The Communists eventually received command of the ports, Vega in Alicante, Tagüeña in Murcia, and most important, Francisco 'Paco' Galán in Caragena, a post coveted by everyone, which gave him the upper hand over what remained of the fleet.

To those who accused him of having thus carried out an actual *coup d'état* and handing power over to the Communists, Negrín replied that, since the government had decided on resistance, its duty was to appoint advocates of resistance to positions of command. The preponderance of Communists was merely a reflection of their wholehearted adherence to Negrín's policy. But to the government's enemies, the measures adopted had only one meaning: from now on it was the Communist party that had sole control of the evacuation and that alone held power.

A New Civil War?

The reshuffles decided by the government were badly received. Not only the military technicians, but the party and union cadres and a large part of the population regarded it as a seizure by a party whose actions had aroused great hatred and resentment. This was an unexpected opportunity for the conspirators, who thereby showed their antagonism toward a Communist *coup d'état* and to a pointless continuation of the war with its massacres and its sufferings. Increasing irritation with this government of the defeated, after three years of civil war, was to provoke an explosion of anger against Negrín.

The Anarchists and left-wing Socialists who had had to relinquish their revolutionary ambitions were at last enjoying their revenge on the party of law and order. Senior officials and regular officers were quick to seize the opportunity for an honorable peace. They were hoping for a compromise by which Franco would acknowledge their standing in the social hierarchy. The party and union leaders wanted guarantees that they would be able to leave the country. The mass of the population, which no longer had faith in anything, turned on those who wanted to accumulate pointless suffering and on the privileged members of the new authority; it had one desire, to put an end to the war as quickly as possible. There were vague hopes that Franco would be more disposed to clemency once the Communists had been removed. Nationalist agents, growing in numbers daily, caused friction.

The first trouble broke out in Cartagena, amid total confusion. Admiral Buiza had already informed Negrín that the fleet would leave the country if he did not decide to negotiate. In spite of a special journey by Paulino Gómez, the minister of the interior, with the task of preparing the ground beforehand,

Galán's appointment caused an explosion. Part of the garrison revolted under a senior artillery officer, Colonel Armentía, and challenged the instatement of the new commander. The Falangists, mixing with the insurgents, seized the radio station and put out false rumors. The fleet took to sea to avoid falling into their hands. Yet the uprising failed. Colonel Armentía, after much hesitation, surrendered and then took his life. The Tenth Division, under the Communist De Frutos, marched on Cartagena; within a few hours, the Communist Rodríguez, at the head of the Eleventh Brigade, had crushed the uprising. But the fleet did not return, finally deciding, on the injunction of the French admiralty, to head for Bizerta, where the crews were interned: thus one of the means of evacuation disappeared. The government seemed to be panic-stricken: Hernández, the commissar-general, hit back on his own initiative.

Meanwhile, in Madrid, the situation took a sudden turn for the worse. Casado had in fact made up his mind: informed by Gómez Ossorio, governor of Madrid, as to the tenor of the decrees, he immediately got in touch with the parties and set up a Defense Committee in which he himself would represent the armed forces. Menéndez, in the Levante, was in agreement with him, and so was Matallana. Miaja joined the movement, adding his prestige to it. García Pradas drew up the revolutionaries' manifesto. Pedrero, of the SIM, and the Socialist Giranta, director-general of the security police, were in the plot. Mera brough the support of the Fourth Army Corps and the Socialist Francisco Castro that of a brigade of *Carabineros*. Nearly all the *Asalto* officers joined in.

The Casado Junta

Meeting in the cellars of the Ministry of Finance, the conspirators spent the evening of the fifth waiting for the *coup d'état*. The Ninetieth Brigade, led by the Anarchist Bernabé López, occupied the capital's strategic points. When his men had completed their moves, the proclamation of the Junta was broadcast over the radio. Besteiro spoke first and asked the Negrín government to stand down: 'The Army of the Republic, with indisputable authority, is undertaking the settlement of a very serious problem, basically a military one.' Criticizing Negrín's policy, he accused him of merely seeking to gain time, in 'the morbid belief that the growing complication of international events will lead to a catastrophe of universal proportions.' He asked all Spaniards to support 'the legitimate government of the Republic, which is, for the time being, nothing but the Army.' Casado then addressed Spaniards 'beyond the trenches.' He offered the choice, 'either peace for Spain or a fight to the death.' Mera said that the Junta's mission was to obtain 'an honorable peace, based on justice and brotherhood.' Then the composition of the Junta was announced: General Miaja as president, Besteiro as foreign minister, Casado as minister of defense, Carrillo as minister of the interior, and Eduardo Val as minister of communications; another Anarchist, González Marín, survivor of the 1937 Junta, Antonio Pérez of the UGT, and the Republicans San Andrés and José del Río completed the lineup, of which the 'Syndicalist' Sánchez Requena was appointed secretary. All the Popular Front unions and parties were represented in it, with the exception of the Communist party.

The Negrín government, which was in Elda in total isolation, protected by a detachment of eighty soldiers led by Communist officers, embarked on a discussion on 5 March that lasted until the evening of the sixth. On paper, it still possessed considerable means: three out of the four army corps of the Center were commanded by Communists: Barceló, Bueno, and Ortega. Similarly, in the Levante, there were three army corps to challenge Menéndez, three divisions in Estremadura, and Communist officers in all the units. In spite of this, Negrín did not attempt to resist; he made a solemn appeal to Casado in order to avoid bloodshed and offered to appoint delegates to 'resolve all differences.' Casado replied by threatening to have all the members of the government shot if General Matallana, detained in Elda, was not released within three hours. As the Communist officers took up arms in Madrid against the Junta, the government left Spain. Negrín and Álvarez del Vayo took the plane for France. With them went the Communist leaders, political ones such as La Pasionaria and Uribe, and military ones such as Lister, Modesto, Hidalgo de Cisneros, and Núñez Mazas. But the government's flight did not prevent the bloodshed that it had seemed anxious to avoid.

In Madrid, Major Ascanio, at the head of the Eighth Army Corps (he had taken over from Bueno, who was sick), tried to sever the capital, to the north, from the rest of Republican Spain. A three-sided struggle now ensued, with the Nationalists exploiting the situation, and the Communists and Casadists accusing each other, justifiably it would seem, of neglecting the front in order to settle old scores.

On the seventh, Barceló seized Casado's headquarters, where he was attacked by Mera. On the tenth, Colonel Ortega, suspect in the eyes of the Junta, surrendered to Casado's troops. As a result of his mediation, negotiations were opened between the Communist party, represented by Diéguez, and Casado. The Communist party asked for a guarantee of freedom for its militants and its press, and for a Communist to join the Junta. Casado agreed in principle not to indulge in reprisals but shot Lieutenant-Colonel Barceló[8] and the Communist commissar Conesa, whom he held responsible for the execution, after the capture of his headquarters, of several officers, including Colonels Gazolo and Otero. On the twelfth, a Communist party leaflet called for an end to fratricidal strife: 'Not only are we giving up all resistance to the constituted authority, but the Communists, at the front, in the rear, and in their working and fighting posts, will continue to set an example of self-abnegation and sacrifice, and of heroism and discipline.'

This week of civil war had caused 2000 deaths. Yet there had not been any real fighting except around Madrid. In the Levante, troops loyal to Menéndez had had several clashes with Major Sendin's armor, which was standing by to sever communications with Madrid. But the Forty-fifth Division, on the Junta's orders, had occupied the Communist party's offices and had arrested its leaders. The Republican Julio Just negotiated the settlement between Casadists and Communists. In Estremadura, the Communists Teral and Martínez Cartón were in a state of readiness; the only serious incidents had occurred at Ciudad Real, where the governor, Antona, shelled a Communist party building and arrested Mangada, in spite of his membership in the Junta.

All in all, there was nothing to show that the Communist party wished to get rid of the Casado Junta. Only the units led by Ascanio had attacked Casadist troops. Elsewhere, troops led by Communists had been content to defend themselves. The efforts of Castro Delgado and Jesús Hernández in Valencia had been in vain. The departure of the Communist general staff on 6 March proved that the Communist party had backed down and that it too now regarded defeat as inevitable. Togliatti, Checa, and Clandin of the JSU, who had stayed on in Spain after the sixth, had been arrested and then released on the orders of General Hernández Sarabia. Their only mission seems to have been that of evacuating the cadres; a group of about fifty militants took off on 25 March from a small airport near Cartagena.[9]

Failure of Negotiations for an Honorable Peace

This 'civil war' had had at least one result, that of compromising once and for all the fulfillment of the objective common to both sides: Negrín's friends had in fact even noted that the Casado Junta had merely taken over the premier's policy, minus the chances of putting it into practice, because it had given up blackmail over the protraction of the fighting. Casado's supporters then retorted that it was the Communist uprising that had dealt a mortal blow to the slender possibilities of resistance. Be that as it may, the fact remains that it was no longer possible.

At any rate, its internal struggles over, the Junta had a free hand to negotiate. It proposed to do so on the following grounds: (1) affirmation of national integrity and sovereignty; (2) respect for all combatants whose motives were 'sincere' and 'honorable'; (3) guarantees that there would be no reprisals apart from normal trials, and that political offences would be distinguished from common-law ones; (4) respect for the lives and liberties of soldiers, militiamen, and commissars who had not committed any criminal acts; (5) respect for the lives, liberties, and careers of professional soldiers; (6) same guarantees for officials; (7) twenty-five days' grace for anyone wishing to leave Spain freely; (8) no Italian or Moroccan soldiers in former Republican Spain.

These were clearly extravagant claims, given the circumstances in which they were formulated. The most important part of the document was the request for guarantees for soldiers and officials: it amounted to sealing a reconciliation between enemies of the same class over the heads of the combatants. But, on the whole, the Junta was in for disillusion after disillusion. It wanted negotiations: Franco wanted a capitulation. It wanted a treaty: Franco did not wish to sign anything. There was an initial affront: Franco's plenipotentiary was a 'Republican' officer from the Army of the Center, a subordinate of Casado's (who momentarily considered having him shot), Colonel Centaños; he knew, before Casado handed it to him, the text of the memorandum. Second affront: Franco refused to negotiate with Casado and Matallana; he was interested only in surrender and insisted on dealing with lower-ranking officers. Casado gave way and selected two staff officers, Major Leopoldo Ortega and Lieutenant-Colonel Antonio Garijo, attached to Miaja for many years (but whom Franco later rewarded for services rendered to the national cause). On 23 March the two plenipotentaries were in Burgos. Their proposals were not even studied. Franco wanted the Air Force to surrender on the twenty-fifth and the whole of the rest of the Army on the twenty-seventh. His representatives, Colonels Ungría, director-general of the security police, and Vittoria made several verbal promises: application of the code of justice, no 'political' reprisals, and the opportunity for some to leave the country.

The Junta's reactions were violent: Carrillo said that the Republicans could not accept anything without a written text. Besteiro retorted: 'I did not come here to pursue the war.' Carrillo added: 'Nor I to betray.'

On the twenty-fifth, Ortega and Garijo, again in Burgos, hoped to convince their opposites that the Junta could go no further. But an order from Franco broke off negotiations: the Air Force had not surrendered as he had requested. The Junta had its back to the wall; certain Anarchists wanted to resist; the military were against it. Casado thought that he could evacuate Madrid in three days. On the twenty-sixth, the Junta announced to Franco that the Air Force would surrender on the twenty-seventh and asked for the date of the capitulation to be decided. Franco's laconic reply brooked no response: the Nationalist troops were about to attack; the Republican troops were to fly the white flag and carry out a 'spontaneous surrender,' following as closely as possible instructions provided by the Nationalist envoys, with the soldiers assembled in brigades after surrendering their arms.

There was no need of a government for this sort of capitulation. Moreover, the Junta no longer was one. The Republican state had been dissolved: no police official had been found to obey the order to arrest the Falangist Valdés, released since the beginning of March, in Madrid. In the succeeding hours, all that the advisers could do was to try to complete the evacuation as quickly and as thoroughly as possible. 'Our preoccupation,' the Junta stated during the night following the twenty-sixth, is 'the evacuation from Republican Spain of citizens who have to leave the country.' The governors were invited to issue safe-conducts to all threatened citizens. The Junta asked for ships from abroad, especially from London and Paris.

But the breakup was too far gone for this final operation to be carried out. The ships booked by Negrín did not come, on the excuse that advance payments had not been made, and the Mid-Atlantic handed over its contract to Burgos. London and Paris stood idly by. While 45,000 persons were crammed together in Alicante, a single French boat left with forty passengers.

There was no longer any Army or any authority. From 27 to 30 March, there was a mad dash to the sea by all who had remained till the last moment and were trying to escape from the enemy.

The Junta held its last meeting on the evening of the twenty-seventh: everything was over. Carrillo and some other councillors left for Valencia during the night. Casado, who had wanted to control the evacuation of Madrid in the days to come, finally went ahead of them by plane. Bands of young men were sporting Nationalist emblems and chanting Franco's name in the streets. What was left of authority in Republican Spain was taken up with ensuring the peaceful transfer of power, as in Valencia, where the council members were dealing with a representative of the Fifth Column. Casado announced this agreement on the radio to try to obtain calm. On the evening of the twenty-ninth, General Miaja left Spain. Casado and the remaining council members around him took passage, after long discussions, on the *Galatea*, an English warship. The Nationalists made no attempt to stop them. But they arrested Besteiro, who had stayed in Madrid, and Sánchez Requena in Valencia. Here and there, a few hundred combatants were killed or took their own lives. A few hundred thousand had abandoned the front, but the vast majority were eventually captured. Franco's domination spread to the whole of Spain. The Civil War was ended.

Notes

[1] The reasoning of Negrín and Álvarez del Vayo seems justified in retrospect by the outbreak of the Second World War in September 1939. In February, however, it was based only on flimsy theories. Even in the event of war, there was nothing to prove that the Western countries could or even would bring real aid to the Republic. Moreover, the Spanish leaders were counting on the fact that the USSR would be in the 'democratic' camp: the Soviet-German nonaggression pact dashed such hopes. The international alliance from which Negrín and Del Vayo were hoping for salvation only took place in 1942. To follow Del Vayo, it would have been necessary to concede that the Republic could have held on or that the Spanish Communists, unlike all the rest, would have agreed, ignoring the pact, to have allied themselves from 1939 to 1942 with the camp of the democracies.

[2] Colonel Segismundo Casado, *The Last Days of Madrid* (London: Peter Davies, 1939).

[3] 'Negrín ended by telling us that he had failed in his efforts for peace and that therefore there was nothing to do but to resist. It did not occur to him to tell us that having failed in his intention he had decided to resign, so that a government might be formed which could achieve what he was unable to achieve.' (*The Last Days of Madrid*, p. 119.)

[4] On 16 February, in Madrid, there was a meeting of the Liaison Committee dealing with the Mera affair; his comrades blamed him for joining with Casado and risking a 'precipitous act' or a '*faux pas*' (Peirats, *La CNT en la Revolución española*, 3:358).

[5] Domínguez, *Los vencedores de Negrín.*

[6] Álvarez del Vayo, *La guerra empezó in España*, p. 307.

[7] The latter too had just emerged as an advocate of negotiation.

[8] Eduardo Barceló Llacuri, a regular officer, belonged to a nucleus of officers from ministerial offices who had worked at the Ministry of War in August 1936. Commander of the troops at the Alcázar, he was later one of the leaders of the Fifth Regiment. The Communists were not alone in presenting him as an honest man. Peirats recalled however that, as commander of the Fourteenth Brigade, he was accused by the divisional commander of the murder of two of his soldiers. Charged with these actions and imprisoned in Barcelona, he was released on Cordón's intervention.

[9] Castro and Hernández seem to have taken a stand at the time against their leadership's attitude in favor of capitulation and especially against La Pasionaria's flight. Discussion on this point was never broached in Moscow: they had the support of José Díaz, but La Pasionaria had Stalin's. Both swore that the Communists were waiting for Casado's move and were prepared for it. According to Hernández, Togliatti thought that the uprising would be snuffed out in half an hour. Diéguez, according to Vanni, said that the Communists could have crushed the Junta, and claimed that the order for final liquidation was brought on 12 March by Rita Montagnana, Togliatti's wife. Be that as it may, it seems that the USSR had no interest in drawing out a lost battle that was hindering her nascent reconciliation with Germany, and that the Communist party, actually in favor of halting the war, had been shrewd enough to utilize the spontaneous reaction of the Madrid Communists without provoking it. However it is reasonable to think that the Party's leadership was preoccupied at the same time with not 'risking the loss' of leaders, as the Ferraras, Togliatti's biographers, modestly put it.

EPILOGUE

It is impossible to give the exact number of refugees who had left the central zone in the second fortnight of March for France and North Africa. In his indictment of Casado, Álvarez del Vayo said that only 2000 had left, whereas 30,000 should have been able to do so, but his argument was based on the assumption that the Negrín government enjoyed an authority superior to the Casado Junta's, which is doubtful. The aid that the Republicans needed ought to have been both rapid and massive; the French and British governments had not responded as was hoped to the appeals from Madrid. The French government in particular, which had already welcomed Basque and Catalan refugees, now acted very reticent: few French ships responded to the appeal by the Republicans; many men had to take flight at the last moment with whatever means came to hand.

Exile

The terrible ordeal of exile for all these refugees now began. In North Africa and in France, they were interned in camps where they endured very harsh moral and physical conditions while awaiting the welcome of a foreign country or authorization to remain in France. Though unenthusiastic and even ill-mannered, the French authorities nevertheless granted the exile that the defeated Republicans asked them for. They did not exercise any political discrimination. But in the Second World War a large proportion of the refugees found themselves back in camps. The Pétain government agreed to hand them over to Germany: several thousand Spaniards[1] thus endured deportation and death camps. Others, more numerous, especially in the southwest, took part in the Resistance with the French *maquisards*.

However, the United States, the majority of whose population had condemned the Nationalists, only accepted a very small batch of refugees.

Equally, the USSR was cruelly disillusioning to its Spanish supporters. The Russian government did indeed agree to take in a large number of them, but although it offered certain leaders of the Spanish Communist party privileged living conditions, the rest, finding themselves in new living conditions, in a country alien both in language and spirit, ran into great difficulties. Not only did they not find in the Russia of 1939 the paradise promised by their leaders, but they were often dispersed, isolated, and settled in working conditions made even more irksome by the climate, hard for Mediterraneans to endure. The evidence that we have about their fate may be suspect of partiality because it originates from former Communists who had broken with their party; it nevertheless explains the disenchantment that, for some, turned to systematic hostility and refueled the dissensions of exile.

Such uneasy welcomes, the result of selfish or vindictive motives, only heightened the goodwill and generosity shown by the Mexican government, which opened its frontiers liberally to all who wished to seek refuge in that country.[2]

With exile came the age of controversy. Certainly, the Republican parties had long since given up hiding their differences. At least they had pretended, while the war had lasted, to believe in unity during a struggle against a common enemy, Nationalism. With defeat, this bond had disappeared. On the contrary, politicians and soldiers found themselves faced with a disaster that they had to explain. It was a time of justification. Censorship and the concern to prevent the enemy from exploiting dissension in the Republican camp had concealed many differences from the general public, but defeat disposed of scruples of this order, and discussions among the former allies became bitter, even within the parties themselves, which suffered comparatively deep and lasting rifts with emigration.

Quarrels between *émigrés* are always painful; in this case at least they were explained by the persistence of illusions about the 'democracies' among most of the political leaders in exile and the hopes nurtured over the years of bringing about the collapse of Franco's Spain from outside. Of course, neither the political activities of governments in exile nor even the guerrillas who held out or were still turning up several years after the end of the Civil War in themselves justified their faith in the future of emigration; but everyone knew that after the World War, the Western powers, if they had wanted, could have overthrown Franco, to whom military victory had been only the beginning of serious political and economic difficulties.

Spain after the War

Be that as it may, in March 1939 all that remained of Republican Spain was occupied within a week. Franco had announced an offensive for 26 March, but he was no longer confronted by an organized force. There was no longer a fight but a simple occupation of abandoned positions. The Nationalists could have made an immediate entry into Madrid. They had waited several hours to lend greater solemnity to the taking over of the city. In Madrid, symbol of Republican resistance and the restored capital of Spain, the victory procession took place along the Pasco de la Castellana. Honor was rendered to the German and Italian allies, whose troops were at the head of the procession. Moreover, everywhere the occupation went off without difficulty, to the accompaniment of cheers and religious ceremonies.

The Caudillo had not made the conciliatory gestures that some of those in the enemy camp had expected from him: repression had not ceased with his victory. On the contrary, the application of the law on political responsibility and the establishment of war councils throughout the whole of former Republican Spain strengthened reactionary measures. Arrests and sentences multiplied. It was a question, according to Ciano, 'of a serious and most rigorous purge.' Moderantism was not regarded as a mitigating circumstance; Besteiro, who had intended to spare Spain violence, was himself sentenced to thirty years' imprisonment.[3] Tens of thousands of prisoners attested to the power of the new state over the years. The Army, the police, and the Falangist militia ensured the stability of a 'strong' regime. Everyone was inculcated with a hatred of the 'Red revolution' and even of a liberal system condemned by the Church. Although certain Falangists preserved the hope of one day seeing the triumph of the National-Socialist regime, which would perhaps mean social progress, and although certain 'liberals' went so far, through hostility to the regime, as to hope for the coming of the Monarchy, even if all the signs indicated that it would preserve an absolutist character, the true victors—and this became clearer daily—were the Army and the Church. *Acción Católica* had in fact wasted no time in recovering all its power: after having been content to support the system from outside, it had agreed to take part in the government. It was true that there had several times been question of a liberalization of the regime, that the frontiers had been easier to cross, and that a certain number of political exiles had been able to return. But in its essentials, the system remained immutable. This was because the regime, product of the purest political conservatism, had been unable to resolve its economic problems.

Insolvent and impoverished, Spain had, during the war, lost part of the livestock that made up her wealth. In 1939 only 60 per cent of the horses, 72 per cent of the mules, and 73 per cent of the oxen remained of the ones that had been there in 1935. With crops, there was a fall in production, calculated on the same years, of about 30 per cent for corn, 35 percent for barley, tobacco, and olives,[4] and 65 per cent for beetroot. Although the production of maize had increased, this was because it had been an exceptionally good year. The drop in essential goods was spectacular and corresponded to a falling off in the acreage under cultivation.[5] In spite of the efforts made by both sides in support of industry, production had fallen off too, especially in textiles. Even mining production had dropped in the case of iron, copper, lead, and zinc.[6] The apparent prosperity of Nationalist Spain had melted away as Franco's government had been forced to take control of the overpopulated and undernourished regions of Barcelona, Madrid, and the Levante. After the fall of Barcelona, difficulties began over food supplies: the white bread of the war years was replaced by gray.

Spain had to obtain part of her food supplies from outside. But how was this agricultural country now to live? Moreover, the Franco regime was trying to practice autarchy, like the USSR and Germany. However, what was possible, at the cost of considerable sacrifices, for the great powers, was no longer so in the twentieth century for an underdeveloped country like Spain.

In spite of the privations imposed, the maintenance of an extremely low subsistence level, and intensive propaganda about the 'Spanish fatherland' and the Iberian Empire, General Franco's government soon had a choice of only two directions: either to follow Germany and Italy and to couple Spain's fate with theirs, or to try and win the friendship of certain Western powers, Great Britain in particular. On the one hand, there was the question of gratitude for aid received during the Civil War, the community of ideology, and the eventual satisfaction of certain political ambitions; on the other hand, the need for peace and Portugal's Anglophile influence.

The commitments made by Franco at the end of the conflict seemed to prove that he had now opted for alliance with Fascism and Nazism. Membership in the Anticomintern Pact was the guarantee for it. The part played by Suñer in Spain's foreign policy seems, in spite of the reservations that the Germans may have had about him, to be proof of the highly Germanophile orientation of Nationalist policy. But, shortly after the Civil War, incidents occurred indicating the limits that the Caudillo meant to impose on his international ventures. There had been fruitless attempts to organize a meeting between Goering and Franco, and the failure of this project was the source, soon after the common victory, of initial tension between the two countries. Later on, the meeting between Franco and Hitler, after the German victory in France, came as a fresh deception to the Nazi chancellor. Clearly Suñer's opinions had not changed, and Spain remained sympathetic to a German victory, but the dispatch of the Azul Legion to the eastern front[7] was the only positive evidence of this bond. Attempts to lure Portugal away from her alliance with Great Britain proved fruitless, and Suñer's loss of influence suggested an evolution had taken place. Of course, the Spanish were able to feel that Franco had done his country a favor, soon after an exhausting civil war, by keeping her clear of the world conflict. But undoubtedly the objective in mind had merely been the stability of the regime, finally saved after the war by protection from the victorious Americans.

Spain would have been exhausted in any case, no matter who the victors were. The simpleminded may be astonished that, after a civil war fought under the banner of renovation, the fatherland and national independence, Spain was more archaic and even more dependent on others than before, in the face of the twentieth-century world. Only the Army had caught up to some extent through foreign intervention; this did not however prevent it from remaining ill-adapted to a modern war. Spain relapsed into her past through the will of the oligarchy and with the complicity of the foreign powers.

Ciano wrote in his diaries: 'Showing the atlas open at Spain, Mussolini said: "It has been open like this for three years; now, it is enough. But I already know that I must open it at another page." The dress rehearsal which was enacted on the Spanish battlefields ended just as the World War was in preparation; Hitler occupied Czechoslovakia and Mussolini was making ready to attack Albania. Shortly afterward the Hitler-Stalin pact and the attack on Poland heralded six years of world war; Mussolini's fall, the collapse of Hitler's Germany, and fresh revolutionary explosions in one country, in one continent, after another...' Twenty years later, the Caudillo was still building monuments to his glory.

Notes

1 In particular, the former premier, Largo Caballero.

2 Most of the Spanish-speaking countries in Latin America have amply benefited from the cultural and intellectual contribution of the Spanish

Republicans, who have settled down in business firms, newspapers, and universities. See on this subject the picture given by Aldo Garosci in the chapter of his work devoted to intellectual *émigrés*. (*Gli intellettuali e la guerra di Spagna* [Turin: Einandi, 1959].)

[3] Only Besteiro and Arino among the Junta's members had decided to stay in Madrid. This move can no doubt be explained both by generous feelings and by the hope that, the initial agony over, a reconciliation could occur.

[4] Corn: 1935: 41,000; 1939: 28,699. Barley: 22,320 and 14,180. Olives: 18,475 and 11,502 (in thousands of quintals: one quintal = approx. 220 lbs).

[5] For cereals, acreage fell from 8,288,000 to 6,526,000 hectares (one hectare = 2·471 acres).

[6] The only exceptions were manganese and tungsten.

[7] Under General Muñoz Grande, one of Franco's disciples.

Part 3

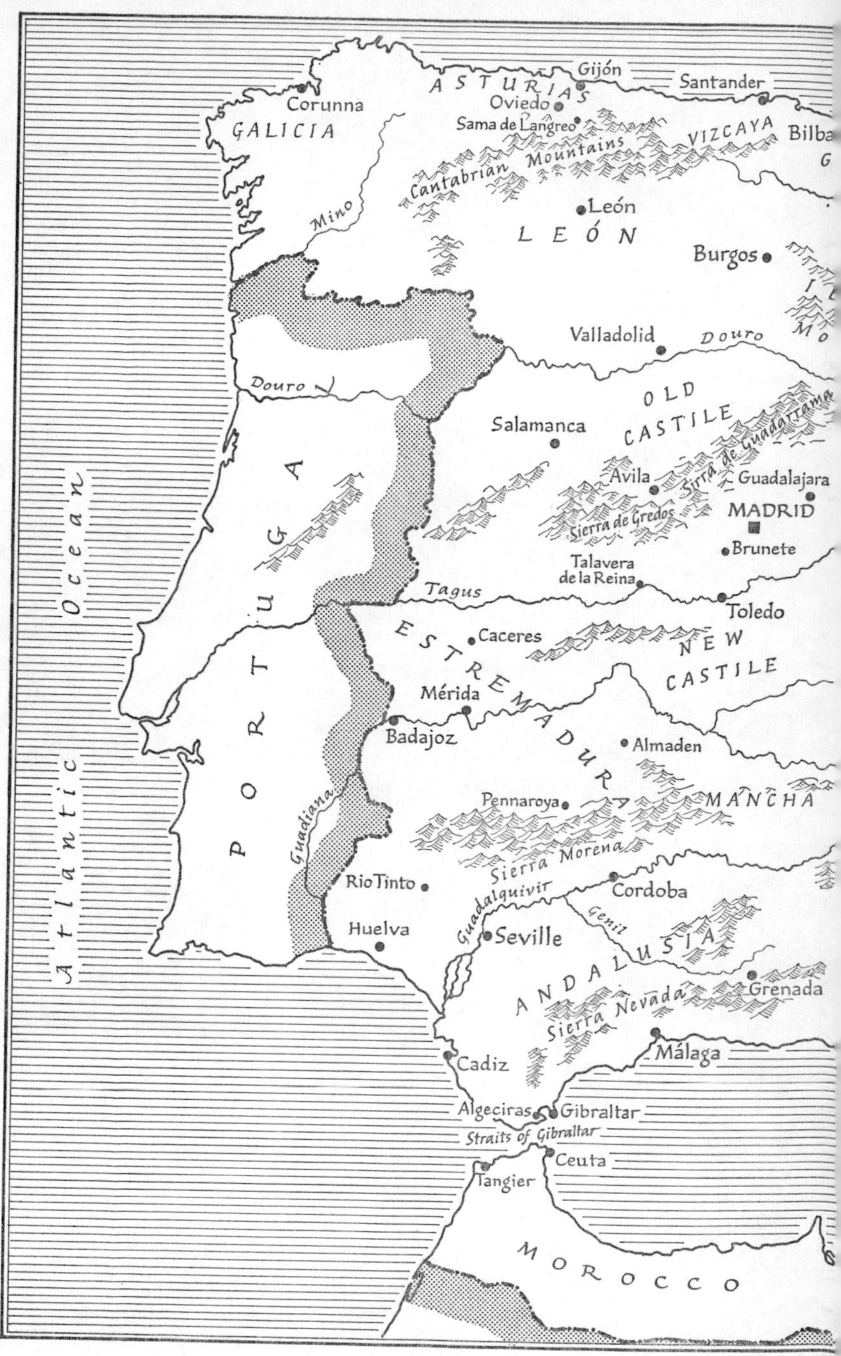

Corunna
GALICIA
ASTURIAS
Gijón
Santander
Oviedo
Sama de Langreo
VIZCAYA
Cantabrian Mountains
Mino
León
LEÓN
Burgos
Valladolid
Douro
Douro
OLD
CASTILE
Salamanca
Sierra de Guadarrama
Avila
Guadalajara
MADRID
Sierra de Gredos
Brunete
Talavera de la Reina
Tagus
Toledo
PORTUGAL
Atlantic Ocean
Caceres
ESTREMADURA
NEW
CASTILE
Mérida
Badajoz
Almaden
Pennaroya
MANCHA
Guadiana
Sierra Morena
Rio Tinto
Guadalquivir
Cordoba
Genil
Huelva
Seville
ANDALUSIA
Grenada
Sierra Nevada
Málaga
Cadiz
Algeciras
Gibraltar
Straits of Gibraltar
Ceuta
Tangier
MOROCCO

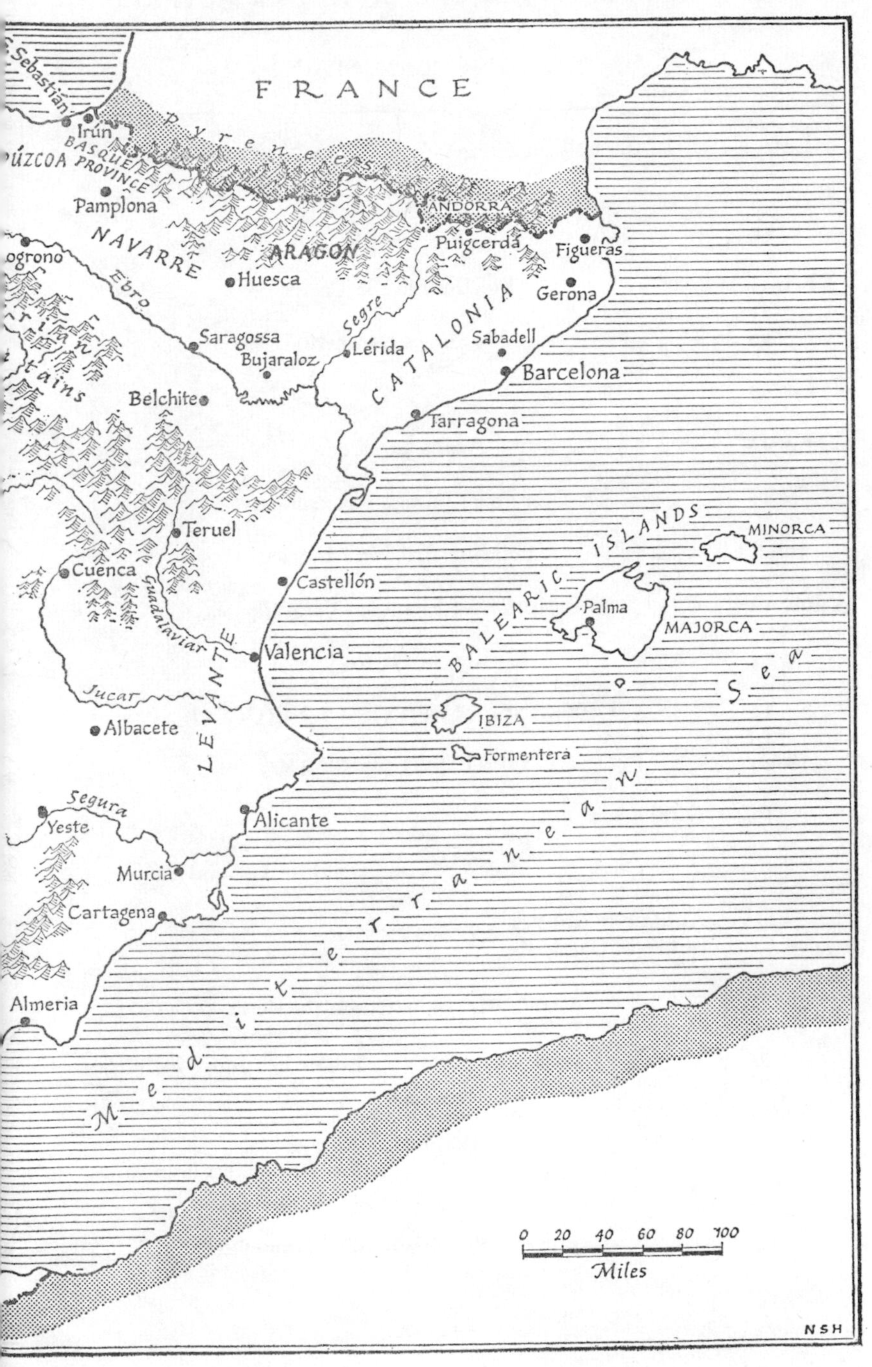

FRANCE
Pyrenees
Irún
BASQUE
PROVINCE
Pamplona
NAVARRE
Ebro
ARAGON
Huesca
Saragossa
Bujaraloz
Belchite
ANDORRA
Puigcerdá
Figueras
Gerona
Segre
CATALONIA
Lérida
Sabadell
Barcelona
Tarragona
Teruel
Cuenca
Castellón
Guadalaviar
Valencia
LEVANTE
Jucar
Albacete
Segura
Yeste
Murcia
Cartagena
Alicante
Almeria
BALEARIC ISLANDS
MINORCA
Palma
MAJORCA
IBIZA
Formentera
Mediterranean Sea
0 20 40 60 80 100
Miles
NSH

EVENTS IN SPAIN

Date	In Republican Spain	In Nationalist Spain
1936		
Feb 16	Elections to the Cortes	
20	Azaña government	
March		
May 10	Azaña president	
13	Casares Quiroga government	
June	Building strike in Madrid	
July 12	Murder of Lieutenant Castillo	
13	Murder of Calvo Sotelo	
17	UPRISING IN SPANISH MOROCCO	
18–20	UPRISING IN SPAIN	
19	Giral government	
20		Death of General Sanjurjo
21	Antifascist Militias Committee in Catalonia	
22–23	Mola's attacks halted on the sierra	
26		Cabanellas Junta in Burgos
Aug 1		
6		First Nationalist laws anticipating victory
14	Capture of Badajoz by the Nationalists	
15		

INTERNATIONAL EVENTS

Date	Connected with the Spanish Civil War	General
1936		
Feb 16		
20		
March		Reoccupation of the Rhineland by Hitler
May 10		Capture of Addis Ababa by the Italians
13		Election of the Popular Front in France
June		Blum premier
July 12		
13		Abrogation of the sanctions against Italy
17		
18–20		
19		
20		Montreux Conference on the Straits
21		
22–23		
26	Arrival of German and Italian planes in Morocco	
Aug 1	Appeal by the French government for non-intervention	
6		Metaxas seizes power in Greece
14		
15	Franco-British statement on nonintervention	

EVENTS IN SPAIN

	In Republican Spain	In Nationalist Spain
Aug 21		
Sept 4	Largo Caballero government	
5	Fall of Irún	
6		
9		
13	Fall of San Sebastián	
20	Formation of rear vigilance militias	
26	Formation of the Generalidad Council in Catalonia	
27	Fall of Toledo	
Oct 1		Franco Generalissimo
7	Decree expropriating the lands of the factionists	
10	Decree creating the Popular Army and militarizing the militias	
12	Fall of Madrid's first line of defense	
14		Statute of the JONS
15	Creation of the Commissariat-General	
22	The government approves the formation of the International Brigades	
24	Collectivization decree in Catalonia	

INTERNATIONAL EVENTS

Date	Connected with the Spanish Civil War	General
Aug 21	Italy agrees to the principle of nonintervention	
Sept 4		Execution of Zinoviev and Kamenev in the USSR
5		
6	Italian planes in Majorca.	
9	First meeting of the Non-intervention Committee	
13		
20		
26		
27		
Oct 1		
7		
10		
12	Arrival of Russian arms and cadres for the Republicans	
14		
15		
22		
24		

EVENTS IN SPAIN

Date	In Republican Spain	In Nationalist Spain
Oct 25		Decree suppressing all political and union activity
28	Largo Caballero announces Russian support and reinforcements	
Nov 2		
4	Entry of representatives of the CNT into the Caballero government	
6	Departure of the government for Valencia	
7	Franco's army in the University City	
	The International Brigades on the Madrid front	
	Formation of the Madrid Defense Junta	
Dec 5		
15	Reorganization of the security police	
21		
25		
31	Decree on municipal councils	
1937		
Jan 27	The Fifth Regiment merges with the Popular Army	
Feb 8	Fall of Málaga	
14	Demonstrations in Valencia	Demonstrations in San Sebastián

INTERNATIONAL EVENTS

Date	Connected with the Spanish Civil War	General
Oct 25		
28		
Nov 2	Russian planes in Cartagena	
4		
6		
7		
	Recognition of the Burgos Junta by Germany and Italy	
Dec 5		Proclamation of the 'Stalinist' constitution in the USSR
15		
21	Stalin's letter to Largo Caballero	
25		German-Japanese Anti-comintern-Pact
31		Italian–British gentleman's agreement
1937		
Jan 27		
Feb 8		Radek sentenced in the USSR
14		

EVENTS IN SPAIN

Date	In Republican Spain	In Nationalist Spain
Feb		Dissolution of Gil Robles's party, *Acción Popular*
28	End of the battle of the Jarama	
Mar 20–23	Italian disaster at Guadalajara	
Apr 19		Single-party decree
23	Dissolution of the Madrid Junta	
24	Bombing of Guernica	
May 2–6	Days of rioting in Barcelona	
15	Fall of Largo Caballero	
17	Negrín government	
31		
June 16	Arrest of leaders of the POUM	
19	Capture of Bilbao by the Nationalists	
23		
July 1		Collective letter from the Spanish bishops
6–28	Battle of Brunete	
		Establishment of war councils Hedilla plot and trial
10		
Aug 4		Publication of the Falange's statutes

INTERNATIONAL EVENTS

Date	Connected with the Spanish Civil War	General
Feb		
28		
Mar 20–23		Italian-Yugoslav Pact
Apr 19	Application of naval control	
23		
24		
May 2–6		
15		
17		Chamberlain succeeds Baldwin
31	Bombing of the *Deutschland*. Bombing of Almeria by the Germans	
Jun 16		Execution of Tukachevsky
19		
23	Germany and Italy abandon control	
July 1		
6–28		
10	France stops control	
Aug 4		

EVENTS IN SPAIN

Date	In Republican Spain	In Nationalist Spain
	Beginning of piracy in the Mediterranean	
Aug 11	Dissolution of the Aragon council	
15	Decree creating the SIM	
	Battle of Belchite	
26	Capture of Santander by the Nationalists	
Sept 10		
Oct 1	Split in the UGT	
7		Organization of the Social Service
		Arrival of the Apostolic Nuncio in Burgos
20	Capture of Gijón by the Nationalists	
21	Caballero kept under observation	
31	Transfer of the government to Barcelona	
Nov 6		
9		
16		
Dec 15	Beginning of the battle of Teruel	
1938		
Jan 2	Jouhaux arbitration: end of the split in the UGT	
30		Law confirming the Caudillo's powers

INTERNATIONAL EVENTS

Date	Connected with the Spanish Civil War	General
		Occupation of Peking by the Japanese
Aug 11		
15		
26		
Sept 10	Nyon Conference	
Oct 1		
7		
20		
21		
31		
Nov 6		Italy joins the Anti-comintern Pact
9		Occupation of Shanghai by the Japanese
16	Dispatch of Hodgson to Burgos	
Dec 15		
1938		
Jan 2		
30		

EVENTS IN SPAIN

Date	In Republican Spain	In Nationalist Spain
Feb 1		Formation of the first government
22	Capture of Teruel by the Nationalists	
25		
Mar 9	Offensive by the Nationalists in Aragon	
Apr 8	Prieto's departure from the Negrín government	
	The Nationalists cut Republican Spain in half	
19		Yagüe's speech in Burgos
30	Negrín's thirteen points	
June	Nationalist offensive in the Levante	
5		
19		Franco Captain-General of the Army and the Navy
25	Crossing of the Ebro by the Republicans	
Aug 16	Resignation of the ministers Ayguadé and Irujo	
Sept		
Oct		
Nov 1	End of the POUM trial	
15	Withdrawal of the Republican troops beyond the Ebro	
1939		
Jan		Law on political responsibilities

INTERNATIONAL EVENTS

Date	Connected with the Spanish Civil War	General
Feb 1		
22		
25		Halifax replaces Eden at the Foreign Office
Mar 9		Hitler completes the Anschluss Second Blum ministry
Apr 8		Execution of Bukharin and Rykov in the USSR
19		End of the second Blum ministry in France
30		
June		
July 5	Adoption of the plan for the withdrawal of volunteers by the Nonintervention Committee	
19		
25		
Aug 16		Runciman mission in Czechoslovakia
Sept		Munich agreement
Oct		Capture of Canton by the Japanese
Nov 1		Hungary receives part of Slovakia
15		
Dec		
1939		
Jan		

EVENTS IN SPAIN

Date	In Republican Spain	In Nationalist Spain
Jan 26	Surrender of Barcelona	
Feb 7	Azaña goes into exile in France	
9	End of resistance in Catalonia	
24	Azaña's resignation	
Mar 5	Appointment of Communist military leaders by Negrín	
5–6	Seizure of power by the Casado Junta	
27		
28	Entry of Nationalist troops into Madrid	
Mar 19		
20	VICTORY PARADE	
26		

INTERNATIONAL EVENTS

Date	Connected with the Spanish Civil War	General
Jan 26		
Feb 7		Proclamation by Pius XII (Cardinal Pacelli)
9		
24		
Mar 5		
5–6		Occupation of Czechoslovakia by Hitler
27	Spain joins the Anti-Comintern Pact	Lithuania cedes Memel to Germany
28		
Mar 19	End of the Nonintervention Committee	
20		German–Italian military alliance
26	Departure of the Condor Legion	

BIBLIOGRAPHY

Aguirre, José Antonio. *De Guernica a Nueva York pasando por Berlin.* Buenos Aires: Vasca Ekin, 1940. Translated into English as *Escape via Berlin.* New York: Macmillan, 1944. (The Basque president's memoirs; the early chapters deal with the Civil War.)

—— *Cinco conferencias.* Buenos Aires: Vasca Ekin, 1944.

Alba, Victor. *Histoire des républiques espagnoles.* Vincennes: Nord-Sud, 1948. (The later chapters deal with the Civil War; the author, a journalist, was close to the POUM.)

Alonso, Bruno. *La flota republicana y la guerra civil española.* Mexico City: Imprenta Grafos, 1944. (By the former Commissioner of the Fleet and Socialist deputy.)

Álvarez del Vayo, Julio. *La guerra empezó en España.* Mexico City: Séneca, 1940. Translated into English as *Freedom's Battle* (New York: Knopf, 1940). (Work on the war by the former minister, Negrín's right-hand man.)

—— *The Last Optimist.* New York: Viking Press, 1950.

Anfuso, Filippo. *Roma-Berlino-Saló.* Milan: Garzanti, 1950. (By the former Italian diplomat, Ciano's confidential agent.)

Ansaldo, Juan Antonio. *Para qué? (De Alfonso XIII a Juan III).* Buenos Aires: Vasca Ekin, 1942. (By the Spanish aviator, friend of Sanjurjo.)

Araquistain, Luis. *Mis tratos con los comunistas.* Toulouse: Ediciones de la Secretaría de Propaganda del Partido Socialista Obrero Español en Francia, 1939.

—— *El comunismo en lu guerra civil española.* Carmaux: Travailleurs Réunis, 1939. (Polemic against the Communists by Caballero's lieutenant.)

Arrarás, Joaquín. *Franco*. San Sebastián: Librería Internacional, 1937. English translation: *Francisco Franco* (London: G. Bles, 1938). (Official biography.)

Asensio Torrado, José. *El general Asensio: su lealtad a la República*. Barcelona: Artes Gráficas CNT, 1937. (*Pro domo* plea by Caballero's former adviser.)

Atholl, Katharine. *Searchlight on Spain*. Harmondsworth, Middlesex: Penguin Books, 1938. (A British view of the Civil War.)

Aznar, Manuel. *Historia militar de la guerra de España*. 1st ed. Madrid: Editora Nacional, 1940. (Official history written by a prominent figure in the Nationalist regime.)

Bahamonde, Antonio. *Un año con Queipo de Llano*. Barcelona: Ediciones Españolas, 1938. Translated into English as *Memoirs of a Spanish Nationalist* (London: United Editorial Limited, 1939). (Memoirs of an ex-Nationalist who joined the Republicans during the war.)

Bajatierra, Mauro. *Crónicas del Frente de Madrid*. Barcelona: Ediciones Tierra y Libertad, 1937. (By the correspondent of *Solidaridad Obrera*.)

Balbontín, José Antonio. *La España de mi experiencia*. Mexico City: Ediciones de la colección Aquelarre, 1952. (Memoirs of an excommunist.)

Balk, Theodor. *La Quatorzième*. Madrid: Éditions du Commissariat des Brigades Internationales, 1937. (By an officer in the International Brigades.)

Baraíbar, Carlos de. *La guerra de España en el plano internacional*. Barcelona: Ediciones Tierra y Libertad, 1937. (By Largo Caballero's former lieutenant.)

Barea, Arturo. *The Forging of a Rebel*. New York: Reynal and Hitchcock, 1946. Translated from the Spanish *La forja de un rebelde*, 3 vols. (Buenos Aires: Losada, 1951). (Autobiography; vol. 3, *La Llama*, deals with the Civil War.)

Bayo, Alberto. *Mi disembarco en Mallorca*. Guadalajara, Mexico: Imprenta Gráfica, 1944. (By the leader of the Catalan expedition to the Balearic Islands.)

Benavides, Manuel D. *La escuadra la mandan los cabos*. Mexico City: Artes Gráficas Comerciales, 1944.

—— *Guerra y revolución en Cataluña*. Mexico City: Ediciones Tenochtitlán, 1946. (The author was a member of the PSUC.)

Bernanos, Georges. *Les grands cimetières sous la lune*. Paris: Plon, 1938. (A great Catholic writer takes his stand against the Nationalists.)

Berneri, Camillo. *Mussolini alla conquista delle Baleari*. Barcelona: Oficina de Propaganda, Sección Italiana, CNT–FAI, 1937. (Study of Italian intervention at the beginning of the war.)

—— *Guerre de classes en Espagne*. Paris: Imprimerie Ouvrière, 1938. (Collection of articles appearing in *Guerra di Classe*.)

Bertrán Güell, Felipe. *Preparación y desarrollo del Alzamiente Nacional*. Valladolid: Librería Santarén, 1939. (By one of Mola's intimates.)

Beumelburg, Werner. *Kampf um Spanien*. Berlin: Gerhard Stalling Verlagsbuchhandlung, 1939. (German intervention.)

Bloch, Jean-Richard. *Espagne, Espagne!* Paris: Éditions Sociales Internationales, 1936. (Articles dealing with the beginning of the war by a Communist writer and journalist.)

Bolloten, Burnett. *The Grand Camouflage*. New York: Praeger, 1961. (The former correspondent for the United Press in Spain undertakes to show the 'camouflage' of the Revolution by the Communist party. In an appendix, a list of works on Spain deposited in American libraries.)

Borkenau, Franz. *The Spanish Cockpit*. London: Faber and Faber, 1937. (Specialist in studies on Communism; one of the most important works on the first year of the war.)

Bougoüin, E., and Lenoir, P. *La finance internationale et la guerre d'Espagne*. Paris: Centre d'Études de Paix et Démocratie, 1938. (Short pamphlet attacking the part played by high finance in the Spanish Civil War.)

Bowers, Claude. *My Mission to Spain*. New York: Simon and Schuster, 1954. (The American ambassador's memoirs.)

Brasillach, Robert, and Bardèche, Maurice. *Histoire de la guerra d'Espagne*. Paris: Plon, 1939. (By two writers of the Extreme Right.)

Brenan, Gerald. *The Spanish Labyrinth*. Cambridge: Cambridge University Press, 1943. (Essay on the social and political origins of the Civil War.)

Cacho Zabalza, Antonio. *La Unión Militar Española*. Alicante: Egasa, 1940. (Official work.)

Campoamor, Clara. *La révolution espagnole vue par une républicaine*. Paris: Plon, 1937. (The Third Force's point of view.)

Carrillo, Wenceslao. *El ultimo episodio de la guerra civil española*. Toulouse: Secretaría de Publicaciones de la JSE en Francia, 1945. (By a Socialist, a friend of Caballero and a member of the Junta.)

Casado, Colonel Segismundo. *The Last Days of Madrid*. London: Peter Davies, 1939. (A justification.)

Castro Delgado, Enrique. *La vida secreta de la Komintern*. Madrid: Ediciones y Publicaciones Españolas, 1950. (References to the war in excommunist leader's memories of the USSR.)

Cattell, David T. *Communism and the Spanish Civil War*. Berkeley: University of California Press, 1955.

—— *Soviet Diplomacy and the Spanish Civil War*. Berkeley: University of California Press, 1957. (Two documented studies by an American university professor.)

Caubín, Julián. *La Batalla del Ebro*. Mexico City, 1944. (By an officer of the Thirty-fifth International Brigade.)

Churchill, Winston. *Step by Step: 1936–1939*. London: Butterworth, 1939.

Ciano, Count Galeazzo. *Diary 1937–1938*. London: Methuen, 1942.

—— *Ciano's Diary 1939–43*. London: Heinemann, 1947.

—— *Ciano's Diplomatic Papers*. London: Odham's Press, 1948. Translation of *L'Europa verso la catastrofe*. Milan: Mondadori, 1948.

Clérisse, Henry. *Espagne 36–37*. Paris: Georges Ventillard, 1937. (The two Spains according to the special correspondent for Radio Luxembourg.)

Colodny, Robert. *The Struggle for Madrid: The Central Epic of the Spanish Conflict, 1936–1937*. New York: Paine-Whitman, 1958. (Story of the battle of Madrid by a former American combatant in Spain, in sympathy with the Communists.)

Comín Colomer, Eduardo. *Historia secreta de la segunda República*. 2 vols. Madrid: Nos, 1954. (Official history.)

Cordonié Canella, Rafael. *Madrid bajo el marxismo*. Madrid: Librería General de Victoriano Suárez, 1939.

Cot, Pierre. *The Triumph of Treason*. Chicago: Ziff-Davis, 1944. (By the Air minister in the Blum government.)

Cox, Geoffrey. *Defence of Madrid*. London: Victor Gollancz, 1937. (By an English journalist.)

Dean. *European Diplomacy in the Spanish Crisis*. (Foreign Office reports.)

Delaprée, Louis. *Mort en Espagne*. Paris: Pierre Tisné, 1937. (Articles edited by the special correspondent of *Paris-Soir*.)

Deschamps, Bernard. *La vérité sur Guadalajara*. Paris: Denoël, 1938.

Despujol, Alberto Carlos de. *La gran tragedia de España: 1931–1939*. Madrid: Cosmos, 1940. (Nationalist work.)

Díaz, José. *Lessons of the Spanish War, 1936–1939*. London, 1940.

—— *Nuestra bandera del Frente Popular*. Madrid: Ediciones Europa-America, 1936.

—— *Tres años de lucha*. Paris: Ediciones del Partido Comunista de España, 1939. (The last two books are collections of articles and speeches by the secretary-general of the Communist party.)

Díaz, Santiago. *La political social en la zona Marxista*. Bilbao: 1938. (Nationalist polemical work.)

Díaz de Villegas, José. *Guerra de liberación*. 2nd ed. Barcelona: AHR, 1958. (By a Nationalist staff officer.)

Domínguez, Edmundo. *Los vencedores de Negrín*. Mexico City: Nuestro Pueblo, 1940.

Duhalde, Pedro. *Le Nationalisme basque et la guerre civile en Espagne*. Paris, 1937. (Short commentary on the Basque problem.)

Dumas, Pierre. *Euzkadi: les Basques devant la guerre d'Espagne*. Paris: Éditions de l'Aube, 1939. (Short study by a Christian Democrat.)

Duval, General Maurice. *Les Espagnols et la guerre d'Espagne*. Paris: Plon, 1939.

—— *Les leçons de la guerre d'Espagne*. Paris: Plon, 1938. (Two technical studies of military aspects of the war.)

Dzelepy, E. N. *Britain in Spain: A Study of the National Government's Spanish Policy*. London: Hamish Hamilton, 1939.

—— *The Spanish Plot.* London: P. S. King and Son, 1937. (On the diplomatic context.)

Ehrenburg, Ilya. *¡No Pasarán!* London: Malik-Verlag, 1939. (Collection of articles.)

Ercoli, M. *The Spanish Revolution.* New York: Workers' Library, 1938. (Togliatti's pseudonym.)

Falcón, César. *Madrid.* Madrid: Nuestro Pueblo, 1938.

Farnborough, Florence. *Life and People in National Spain.* London: Sheed and Ward, 1938.

Ferrándiz Alborz, F. *La bestia contra España.* Montevideo: n.p., 1951. (The end of the Republic and the beginnings of the repression, by a supporter of Caballero.)

Fischer, Louis. *Men and Politics.* New York: Duell, Sloan and Pearce, 1941. (Several chapters deal with Spain in the autobiography of this American journalist written after his split with Stalinism.)

Franco, General Francisco. *Franco ha dicho. . . .* Madrid: n.p., 1947. (Compilation of his most important statements from 1936 to 1946.)

Galíndez, Jesús de. *Los vascos en el Madrid sitiado.* Buenos Aires: Vasca Ekin, 1945. (By a Basque Catholic.)

Galland, General Adolf. *Die Ersten und die Letzten.* Darmstadt: Franz Scheekluth, 1966. In English: *The First and the Last* (London: Methuen, 1955). (By the German air ace; part of it deals with the Condor Legion.)

Gamir Ulíbarri, General Mariano. *Guerra de España 1936–39.* Paris: Imprimerie Moderne, 1939. (By the former Republican commander of the northern front.)

García Pradas, José. *Cómo terminó la guerra de España.* Buenos Aires: Imán, 1940. (Indictment of the USSR by the former director of CNT.)

—— *Rusia y España.* Paris: Ediciones Tierra y Libertad, 1948. (Account of the final weeks.)

Garosci, Aldo. *Gli intellettuali e la guerra di Spagna.* Turin Einandi, 1959. (Analysis of works by Koestler, Malraux, Koltsov, Hemingway, and others.)

Gillain, Nick. *Le mercenaire.* Paris: Arthème Fayard, 1938. (Account by a Belgian volunteer in the brigades.)

González, Valentín (known as El Campesino). *Comunista en España y antiestalinista en la URSS.* Mexico City: Guaranía, 1952. (Series of articles, including several on the war.)

—— *Vida y muerte en la URSS.* 4th ed. Buenos Aires: Editorial Bell, 1951. In English: *Life and Death in Soviet Russia* (New York: Putnam, 1952). (By the former Communist leader, after his departure from Spain.)

Gorkin, Julián. *Caníbales políticos (Hitler y Stalin) en España.* Mexico City: Ediciones Quetzal, 1941. (On the roles of Hitler and Stalin, by the former POUM leader.)

Gutiérrez-Ravé, José. *Las Cortes errantes del Frente Popular.* Madrid: Editora Nacional, 1953.

Guzmán, Eduardo de. *Madrid rojo y negro.* Buenos Aires: Talleres Socializados del SUIPAG–CNT, 1939. (The defense of Madrid, seen from the CNT angle.)

Héricourt, Pierre. *Pourquoi Franco vaincra.* Paris: Baudinière, 1936. (Panegyric of the Spanish Nationalists by a French Nationalist.)

Hernández, Jesús. *Negro y Rojo.* Mexico City: España Contemporánea, 1946. (The role of the Anarchists during the war; written in Moscow by a Communist party leader.)

—— *Yo, ministro de Stalin en España.* 2nd ed. Madrid: NOS, 1954. (Hernández's revelations, after his split with the Communist party and his departure from the USSR.)

Hoare, Sir Samuel (Lord Templewood). *Ambassador on Special Mission.* London: Collins, 1946.

Hughes, Emmet John. *Report from Spain.* New York: Henry Holt, 1947.

Ibárruri, Dolores (La Pasionaria). *Speeches and Articles, 1936–38.* Moscow: Foreign Language Publishing House, 1938.

Iredell, Elliot Ostrehan. *Franco, valoroso caballero cristiano.* Buenos Aires: Americalee, 1945.

Iribarren, José María. *El general Mola.* Madrid, 1945. (Biograpyh.)

Irujo, Manuel de. *Inglaterra y los vascos.* Buenos Aires: Vasca Ekin, 1945.

Jacquelin, André. *Espagne et la liberté.* Paris: Kérénac, 1945. (The Republican point of view.)

Jellinek, Frank. *The Civil War in Spain.* London: Victor Gollancz, 1938.

Joubert, Vice Admiral H. *L'Espagne de Franco.* Paris: Les amis de l'Espagne nouvelle, 1938. (Sympathetic to the Nationalists.)

Jouve, Marguerite. *Vu, en Espagne, février 1936–février 1937.* Paris: Flammarion, 1937.

Kaminski, Hans Erich. *Ceux de Barcelone.* Paris: Denoël, 1937. (CNT sympathizer.)

Kindelán, General Alfredo. *Mis cuadernos de guerra.* Madrid: Plus Ultra, 1945.

Klotz, Helmut. *Les leçons militaires de la guerre civile en Espagne.* Strasbourg: Imprimerie Française, 1937.

Knickerbocker, H. R. *The Siege of the Alcazar.* Philadelphia: David, 1936. (By the famous American journalist.)

Koestler, Arthur. *Spanish Testament.* London: Victor Gollancz, 1937. (Koestler's adventures in Spain; his account of the fall of Málaga.)

Koltsov, Mikhail. *Ispanskii dnevnik* [Spanish diary]. Moscow: Sovietsky pisatel, 1957. (New edition of the *Pravda* special correspondent's diary.)

Krivitsky, General Walter. *I Was Stalin's Agent.* London: Hamish Hamilton, 1940.

Largo Caballero, Francisco. *Mis recuerdos.* Mexico City: Ediciones Alianza, 1954. (Letters of Largo Caballero about his memories at the time of his return from deportation; half the book deals with the Civil War. Caballero's real memoirs are still unpublished.)

Last, Jef. *Lettres d'Espagne.* 4th ed. Paris: Gallimard, 1938. (Letters by a Dutch writer.)

Leval, Gaston. *Né Franco, né Stalin: La collettivitá anarchica spagnola nella lotta contra Franco e la reazione staliniana.* Milan: Instituto Editoriale Italiano, 1955. (About the Anarchist collectives, by a French militant who lived through the war.)

Lizarra, A. de (Andres María de Irujo). *Los vascos y la República española.* Buenos Aires: Vasca Ekin, 1944. (Authorized account, based on Manuel de Irujo's notes, explaining the events from the Basque point of view.)

Lizarza Iribarren, Antonio. *Memorias de la conspiración: cómo se preparó en Navarra la Cruzada 1931–1936*. 3rd ed. Pamplona: Gómez, 1954. (Memoirs of the head of the *Requetés*.)

Lojendio, Luis María de. *Operaciones militares de la guerra de España 1936–1939*. Barcelona: Montaner y Simón, 1940.

Longo, Luigi. *Le brigate internazionali in Spagna*. Rome: Editori Riuniti, 1956. (The Communist point of view, by a leader in the brigades.)

López Fernández, Antonio. *Defensa de Madrid*. Mexico City: A. P. Márquez, 1945. (By one of General Miaja's colleagues.)

López Muñiz, Colonel Gregorio. *La batalla de Madrid*. Madrid: Gloria, 1943.

Madariaga, Salvador de. *España*. 4th ed. Buenos Aires: Sudamericana, 1950. English translation: *Spain* (London: Ernest Benn, 1930). (A moderate Republican's point of view.)

Marcotte, V. A. *L'Espagne Nationale-Syndicaliste*. Brussels: Imprimerie Puvrez, 1943. (By a sympathizer with Falangism.)

Martín Blázquez, José. *I Helped to Build an Army*. London: Secker and Warburg, 1939. (Memoirs of a Republican officer.)

Martínez Barrio, Diego. *Orígenes del Frente Popular*. Buenos Aires: PHAC, 1943. (Collection of articles and speeches.)

Massis, Henri, and Brasillach, Robert. *Les cadets de l'Alcazar*. Paris: Plon, 1936. English translation: *The Cadets of the Alcazar*. (New York: Paulist Press, 1937.)

Matthews, Herbert L. *The Education of a Correspondent*. New York: Harcourt, Brace, 1946.

—— *Two Wars and More to Come*. New York: Carrick & Evans, 1939.

—— *The Yoke and the Arrows*. New York: Braziller, 1957. (By the correspondent of the *New York Times*.)

Maurín, Joaquín. *Révolution et contre-révolution en Espagne*. Paris: Rieder, 1937. English translation: *Revolution and Counter-Revolution*. (New York: Pioneer Publishers, 1938.) (Work by the leader of the POUM written before the Civil War and completed with notes made by Victor Serge in 1936–1937.)

Milleron, Jacques. *Étude sur l'économie espagnole*. Rabat: Société d'Études, 1955. (Very general picture.)

Minlos, Bruno. *Paysans d'Espagne en lutte pour la terre et la liberté*

Paris: Bureau d'Éditions, 1937. (On the agrarian revolution; official Communist publication.)

Mitchell, Peter Chalmers. *My House in Málaga*. London: Faber and Faber, 1938.

Morrow, Felix. *Revolution and Counter-Revolution in Spain*. New York: Pioneer Publishers, 1938. (Trotskyist point of view by an American journalist, and not, as Cattell claims, a pseudonym for Maurín, then being held by the Nationalists.)

Munis Granadizo. *Jalones de derrota: promesa de victoria*. Mexico City: Lucha Obrera, 1948. (Full study, but short on evidence, by a Spanish Trotskyist.)

Muro Zegrí, D. *La epopeya del Alcázar*. Valladolid: Librería Santarén, 1937.

Narbona, Francisco. *Frentes del sur*. Madrid: Publicaciones Españolas, 1953. (Articles from *Temas Españoles*, of Nationalist tendency.)

Negrín, Juan. *Epistolario Prieto y Negrín*. Paris: Imprimerie Nouvelle, 1939. (Polemic on the war between the two Socialist leaders.)

—— *Lettre d'adieu aux combattants internationaux*. Paris: Comité France-Espagnol, 1940.

Nenni, Pietro. *Spagna*. Milan: Edizioni Avanti, 1958. (Short history; diary notes and articles.)

Nin, Andrés. *Les problèmes de la révolution espagnole*. Paris: Fleury, 1939. (Collection of articles and speeches. The book was destroyed as soon as it was printed. Two copies, to our knowledge, were saved: one is in the Bibliothèque Nationale, the other was kindly lent us by the man who wrote the preface, Juan Andrade.)

Orwell, George. *Homage to Catalonia*. London: Victor Gollancz, 1938. (Orwell joined the POUM militia; he gives an eyewitness account of the May days.)

Ossorio y Gallardo, Ángel. *La España de mi vida*. Buenos Aires: Losada, 1941.

—— *Vida y Sacrificio de Companys*. Buenos Aires: Losada, 1944. (By a political friend of Companys.)

Pacciardi, Randolfo. *Volontari italiani nella Spagna republicana*,

Lugano: Nuove Edizioni di Capolago, 1948. (By the Garibaldi Battalion's first commander, a Republican.)

Pamplona, Andrés. *La batalla de Teruel*. Madrid: Publicaciones Españolas, 1952. (A Nationalist; articles from *Temas Españoles*, no. 15.)

Peers, Edgar Allison. *Catalonia Infelix*. London: Methuen, 1937.

—— *The Spanish Tragedy*. 6th ed. London: Methuen, 1937.

Peirats, José. *La CNT en la Revolución española*. 3 vols. Toulouse: Ediciones CNT, 1951–1953. (Lengthy work reprinting many unpublished documents.)

Penchienati, Carlo. *Brigate internazionali in Spagna*. Milan: Echi del Secolo, 1950. (Memoirs of an Italian volunteer, hostile to Nenni and the Communists.)

Pérez Sala, Colonel Jesús. *Guerra en España: 1936–1939*. Mexico City: Grafos, 1947. (By a Catalan officer.)

Pérez Solís, Oscar. *Sitio y defensa de Oviedo*. 2nd ed. Valladolid: Afrodisio Aguado, 1937. (By one of the besieged, a former Communist who went over to the Falange.)

Perrino Rodríguez, F. *Bibliografía de la guerra civil española (1936–1939)*. Madrid: Boletín de la Dirección General de Archivos y Bibliotecas, 1954. (Incomplete bibliography, but complete for Nationalist works that appeared up to 1954.)

Prieto, Indalecio. *Cómo y por qué salí del Ministerio del Defensa Nacional*. Mexico City: Impresos y Papeles S. de R. L., 1940. (On the government crisis in April 1938.)

—— *Entresijos de la guerra de España*. Mexico City: Bases, 1953. (Various articles dealing with books: Cantalupo, Hernandez.)

—— *Palabras al viento*. Mexico City: Minerva, 1942. (Collection of articles.)

Rabasseire, Henri. *Espagne, creuset politique*. Paris: Fustier, n.d. (Well-documented study, by a German publicist, on the first part of the war.)

Rama, Carlos M. *La crisis espanola del siglo XX*. Mexico City: Fondo de Cultura Económica, 1960. (Doctoral thesis. Half of this work, which deals with the problem of the state, bears on the Civil War.)

—— *Ideología, regiones y clases sociales en la España contemporánea*. Montevideo: Ediciones Nuestro Tiempo, 1963.

Ramos Oliveira, Antonio. *Politics, Economics and Men of Modern Spain, 1808–1946*. London: Victor Gollancz, 1946. (By a supporter of Negrín; the final chapters deal with the Civil War.)

Ravines, Eudocio. *La gran estafa*. Mexico City: Libros y Revistas, 1952. (By an excommunist.)

Regler, Gustav. *The Great Crusade*. New York: Longmans, 1940.

—— *The Owl of Minerva*. London: Rupert Hart-Davies, 1959. (Autobiography by the German writer, former Communist and combatant in Spain.)

Renn, Ludwig. *Der Spanische Krieg*. Berlin: Aufbau Verlag, 1956. (The German Communist writer's account of his stay in Spain and the battles in which he took part.)

Richards, Vernon. *Lessons of the Spanish Revolution, 1936–1939*. London: Freedom Press, 1953. (Criticism of the CNT–FAI, by an Anarchist.)

Rieger, Max. *Espionage en Espagne*. Paris: Denoël, 1938. (The Communist party line on the POUM.)

Rojo, General Vicente. *¡Alerta los pueblos!* Buenos Aires: Aniceto López, 1939.

—— *¡España heroica!* Mexico City: Ediciones Era, 1961. (In these two works, the military history of the war as seen by the Republican forces' chief of staff.)

Ruiz de Alda, Julio. *Obra completa*. Barcelona: Ediciones FE, 1939. (The work of one of the founders and leaders of the Falange.)

Ruiz Vilaplana, Antonio, *Doy fe* . . . Paris: Imprimerie Coopérative Étoile, n.d. English translation: *Burgos Justice* (London: Constable, 1938.) (Confessions of a repentant Nationalist.)

Santillán, Diego Abad de. *After the Revolution*. New York: Greenberg, 1937. (Collection of articles.)

—— *Por qué perdimos la guerra*. Buenos Aires: Imán, 1940. (Study of the war and Anarchist policy by an FAI leader.)

Schultz, Wilmersdorf. *Spanien, Politiker und Generale*. Berlin: Steiner Verlag, 1939.

Sencourt, Robert. *Spain's Ordeal*. London: Longmans, Green, 1940.

Serrano Súñer, Ramón. *Entra Hendaya y Gibralter.* 3rd ed. Madrid: Ediciones y Publicaciones Españolas, 1947. (The author, Franco's brother-in-law, was also one of the men who inspired his policy.)

Sevilla Andrés, Diego. *Historia política de la zona roja.* Madrid: Editora Nacional, 1954. (The policy of the Republican camp as seen by a Nationalist.)

Sieberer, Anton. *Spanien gegen Spanien.* Vienna: Saturn-Verlag, 1937.

Solano Palacio, Fernando. *La tragedia del norte.* 2nd ed. Barcelona: Ediciones Tierra y Libertad, 1938. (By an Anarchist journalist.)

Somoza Silval, Lázaro. *El general Miaja.* Mexico City: Ediciones Tirys, 1944.

Souchy, Augustín. *Nacht über Spanien.* Darmstadt: Verlag die Freie Gesellschaft, 1957. (The history of the war, as seen by a CNT leader.)

—— *Colectivizacones: la obra constructiva de la revolución española.* Barcelona: Ediciones Tierra y Libertad, 1937.

Steer, George Lowther. *The Tree of Gernika.* London: Hodder, 1938. (On the war in the Basque provinces, by *The Times* special correspondent.)

Trotsky, Leon. *Leçon d'Espagne.* Paris: Éditions Pioniers, 1946.

Van der Esch, Patricia. *Prelude to War: The International Repercussions of the Spanish Civil War.* The Hague: Nijhoff, 1951.

Ximénez de Sandoval, Felipe. *José Antonio.* Barcelona: Juventud, 1941.

Zugazagoitia, Julián. *Historia de la guerra en España.* Buenos Aires: La Vanguardia, 1940. (By Negrín's former minister of the interior, handed over to Franco by Pétain and shot.)

ANONYMOUS AND COLLECTIVE WORKS

La causa general: la dominación roja en España. Avance de la información instruida por el Ministerio Público de España. Buenos Aires: Ediciones Españolas Unidas, 1946. English translation: *The General Cause* (Madrid: Gráficas Aragón, 1953.)

De julio a julio. Barcelona: Ediciones Tierra y Libertad, 1937. (Collection of articles that appeared in *Fragua Social*, CNT newspaper in Valencia, on the occasion of the first anniversary of the Revolution; accounts by CNT militants of the events of July 1936.)

Documents on German Foreign Policy 1918–45. Series D (1937–1945). Vol. 3, *Germany and the Spanish Civil War, 1936–1939.* Washington, D.C.: Government Printing Office, 1950.

Epopée d'Espagne. Brigades Internationales 1936–39. 2nd ed. Paris: Amicale des anciens volontiers français en Espagne républicaine, 1957. (Work carried out under the aegis of the AVER; the second edition, revised and amplified, is very different from the first.)

La persécution religieuse en Espagne. Paris: Plon 1937. (With a poem-preface by Paul Claudel.)

NOVELS

(List reduced to an absolute minimum with no pretensions to covering all the literary works touching on the Spanish Civil War.)

Hemingway, Ernest. *For Whom the Bell Tolls.* New York: Charles Scribner's Sons, 1940.

Kesten, Hermann. *Die Kinder von Guernika.* Hamburg: Rowohlt, 1955. English translation: *The Children of Guernica* (New York: Alliance Book Corporation, 1939).

Malraux, André. *L'Espoir.* Paris: Gallimard, 1962. English translation: *Days of Hope.* (London: Routledge, 1938) *Man's Hope.* (New York: Random House, 1938).

Sender, Ramon J. *Los cinco libros de Ariadne.* New York: Ediciones Ibérica, 1957.

NEWSPAPERS AND MAGAZINES

A list of the newspapers and magazines consulted in connection with this work would be too long. We shall limit ourselves to citing the complete collections, for 1936–1939, of *Le Temps*, *L'Humanité*, *Le Populaire*, *La Dépêche de Toulouse*, *Paris-Soir*, the London *Times*, the *New York Times*, and the collections, unfortunately incomplete, of *ABC* (Madrid), *Mundo Obrero*, *Claridad*, *El Socialista*, *La Batalla*, and *Solidaridad Obrera*, among others, to which we have referred in the text or the notes.

Finally, a review of our sources must mention the information kindly given us by M. K. Skrabek, who is in process of completing a study of the International Brigades.

INDEX